2/1/07

LEW —

Without you, this wouldn't have been possible.

Love always,

g.

The **SAGE** Handbook *of*
Research in
International Education

The SAGE Handbook *of*

Research in International Education

Edited by
Mary Hayden
Jack Levy
Jeff Thompson

SAGE Publications
London • Thousand Oaks • New Delhi

SAGE Publications Ltd
1 Oliver's Yard
55 City Road
London EC1Y 1SP

SAGE Publications Inc.
2455 Teller Road
Thousand Oaks, California 91320

SAGE Publications India Pvt Ltd
B-42, Panchsheel Enclave
Post Box 4109
New Delhi 110 017

British Library Cataloguing in Publication data

A catalogue record for this book is available from
the British Library

ISBN-10 1-4129-1971-1   ISBN-13 978-1-4129-1971-5

Library of Congress Control Number: 2006927994

Typeset by C&M Digitals (P) Ltd, Chennai, India
Printed in Great Britain by The Cromwell Press, Trowbridge, Wiltshire
Printed on paper from sustainable resources

Contents

Acknowledgements

A book of this size cannot be produced without support and input from a vast number of colleagues, and this particular Handbook is certainly no exception. In addition, therefore, to thanking each of the contributors who have worked long and hard to generate the individual chapters, we would also like to thank our colleagues at Sage who have been efficient, supportive and good-natured in producing this volume, as well as Jim Cambridge who – in addition to being an author himself – has generated the two indexes which we hope will help to make the contents of the Handbook accessible and user-friendly. And last, but not least, collaborating across continents on a project such as this can be challenging and fraught with potential for misunderstanding. It is good to be able to report therefore that the transatlantic collaboration of this particular group of editors has been a successful one which we have all enjoyed.

The authors and publishers are grateful for the permission for Figure 3.1 in Chapter 3, p. 44 adapted from the table by R. Richardson in D. Heater's work *World Studies: Education for International Understanding in Britain* (p. 37, 1980). R. Richardson's work was *Bulletin of Peace Proposals* Vol. 5, 1975, p. 265, London: Harrap.

We are also grateful to Taylor & Francis for Figure 3.2, in Chapter 3, p. 46, originally published in J. Lynch, C. Modgil and S. Modgil (eds) (1992) *Human Rights, Education and Global Responsibilities: Cultural Diversity and the Schools*. Vol. 4, London: The Falmer Press. The figure is from Norma Tarrow's chapter – Human Rights, p. 31.

The authors and publisher are grateful to the Copper Canyon Press for granting permission to use the poem, *The Three Goals* by David Budbill in Chapter 31, page 379 from: *Moment to Moment: Poems of a Mountain Recluse* by David Y. Budbill, September 1999, © Copper Canyon Press.

List of Contributors

Michael Allan is at the International School of Amsterdam, where he is carrying out doctoral research into cross-cultural teacher/student interaction. He has published widely in this area, presented at many international education conferences and training workshops, and has taught on the international education MA and EdD courses at the University of Bath.

Kevin Bartlett is Director of the International School of Brussels and has held prior leadership positions in Austria, Tanzania and Namibia. He has been actively engaged in the development of international education, notably through work in accreditation, leadership training and international curriculum design, in particular as initiator of the IB Primary Years Programme. Kevin is Chairman of the Board of the Council of International Schools.

Jason Beech is Director of the BA in Education at the Universidad de San Andrés in Buenos Aires, Argentina, where he also teaches Comparative Education and Education Policy. He has a PhD in Comparative Education from the Institute of Education, University of London. He has published widely; his main interests are the transfer of specialised knowledge about education in the global educational field and conditions of reception in different local contexts.

Paul Beedle is Manager of Professional Development Certification at the University of Cambridge International Examinations (CIE). An anthropologist by training, Paul has 20 years' experience of international examinations development in, for example, environmental management, vocational skills assessment and teacher education.

Angela D. Benson is Associate Professor of instructional technology at the University of Alabama and is a member of the Worldwide Universities Network (WUN) eLearning subgroup. Her current research project is a US/UK collaboration investigating the influence of course management systems on US/UK higher education institutions.

Mark Bray is Director of UNESCO's International Institute for Educational Planning, in Paris. Before taking this post he worked for two decades at the University of Hong Kong where, among other posts, he was Director of the Comparative Education Research Centre and Dean of the Faculty of Education. He has also taught in secondary schools in Kenya and Nigeria, and at the Universities of Edinburgh, Papua New Guinea and London. In 2004 he was elected President of the World Council of Comparative Education Societies (WCCES), having previously been Secretary General (since 2000) and, before that, Assistant Secretary General (since 1994).

James Cambridge is Head of Research Projects at the International Baccalaureate Research Unit, University of Bath, UK. He has worked in Britain, the Middle East and Southern Africa in a variety of educational contexts including science teaching, assessment, curriculum development, initial teacher education and continuing professional development. His current postdoctoral research interests include enquiries into organisational culture, evaluation of institutions and educational programmes, institutional mentoring partnerships, and intergenerational learning. His publications include chapters in edited books and articles in refereed journals.

Richard Caffyn is Head of Research Support and Development at the International Baccalaureate Research Unit located at the University of Bath, UK. He has worked as both a teacher and department head in a number of international schools in Norway, Azerbaijan, Romania and Austria. He is currently completing his PhD into the micropolitics of international schools.

Clive Carthew led the development of 'Internationalism in Schools – a Self Study Guide' as Chairman of the International Schools Association. He served the International Baccalaureate Organization as Curriculum and Assessment Director and as Deputy Director General. Currently he is Academic Director of an international Schools Development Corporation in the Middle East.

Nada Dabbagh is Associate Professor of Instructional Design and Technology (IDT) at George Mason University in Fairfax, Virginia. Her research explores the cognitive and pedagogical consequences of technology-mediated learning tasks, with the goal of understanding the design characteristics of distributed learning environments enabling a global and international perspective of distance education.

Perry den Brok is Associate Professor at the Institute of Education (IVLOS), Utrecht University, The Netherlands. His current research topics are teacher interpersonal behaviour in international education, cross-cultural studies on teaching and teaching in multicultural schools. He is also involved in the Bilingual and International Teacher Education Programme (BITEP) at IVLOS.

Robert DiYanni is Director of International Services at the College Board, USA. Before joining the Board in 1999, he taught English and humanities at Queens College, City University of New York; Pace University; New York University, and Harvard. He has published numerous articles and more than three dozen books on writing, literature and humanities, mostly for university students. In addition to his work at the College Board, he is Adjunct Professor of Humanities at New York University.

Tom Eason, until his recent retirement, was actively involved in the world of international education throughout most of his career with Cambridge International Examinations (CIE). Among other posts, he directed the IGCSE Office responsible for the IGCSE curriculum and examination and was, latterly, Director of International Education.

Helen Fail is course leader for the MA in Education: International Schools at Oxford Brookes University, UK. Her doctoral research was on the life histories of former international school students. She has taught French in schools in six countries and worked as a cross-cultural consultant focusing on transition and third culture kids.

William Gerritz has served as Head of School at the International School Bangkok, the American School of The Hague and the International School of Curaçao. Before entering international education, he was on the faculty of the University of California, Berkeley and worked as a policy analyst at the Far West Labs for Educational Research.

Patrick Griffin is Director of the Assessment Research Centre, Associate Dean, Innovation and Development and Deputy Dean of the Faculty of Education at the University of Melbourne. He specialises in criterion-referenced assessment frameworks and their links to instructional strategies. Through projects with the World Bank and UNESCO he has been involved in national and international measurement projects such as SACMEQ and the Vietnamese national monitoring projects, as well as numerous Australian national assessment projects.

Trevor Grimshaw is a lecturer at the Department of Education of the University of Bath, where he coordinates MA programmes in ELT and Language in Education and supervises doctoral research in these areas. He has worked as a language teacher, translator, consultant and teacher educator in various international contexts.

Konrad Gunesch is Academic Director of the English Language Centers at the Universidad Interamericana de Panamá and the Universidad Latinoamericana de Ciencia y Tecnología de Panamá. He had previous posts at the University of London's School of Oriental and African Studies (SOAS) and at the Hong Kong Polytechnic University. He completed his PhD in England, having undertaken a Masters degree in European Politics in England, Italy, Spain and France, and Law degrees and training in Germany, the Netherlands, Sweden and Canada. He has published and presented international conference papers in the fields of multilingualism, cosmopolitanism and new media.

Silvina Gvirtz is Director of the School of Education at the Universidad de San Andrés in Buenos Aires, and a Researcher of the CONICET (National Council for Scientific and Technical Research). In 2003 she was awarded the John Simon Guggenheim Fellowship, for the project: 'A comparison of models of school governance in Argentina, Brazil, and Nicaragua'. She has published books and articles in refereed journals of a number of different countries.

Mary Hayden is Director of the Centre for the study of Education in an International Context (CEIC) at the University of Bath, UK and Editor of the *Journal of Research in International Education*. Her involvement in international education began when she took up a post in 1982 with the International Baccalaureate Organization: her masters and doctoral teaching and research interests have continued to focus on international schools and international education, an area in which she has published widely.

Terry Haywood has had a long involvement with international education since he began in the profession as a physics (and occasional history) teacher. As Head of the International School of Milan he has been closely involved with ECIS, serving on the Professional Development, Accreditation and Strategic Planning Committees, while also serving on the Board of Directors, which he chaired from 1999 to 2001. His special interests lie in the development of tools for school improvement and in the promotion of international education as a learning and life experience that should be at the heart of schooling everywhere. He has been closely involved with the foundation of both the Council of International Schools and the Alliance for International Education.

Ian Hill is Deputy Director General of the International Baccalaureate Organization, based in Geneva. Prior to joining the IBO in 1993 he was director of the International School of Sophia

Antipolis, a bilingual IB Diploma school in France. From 1986 to 1989 he was senior private secretary/advisor to the Minister for Education in the state of Tasmania, Australia. His PhD thesis related to the origins and development of the IBO and its Diploma Programme.

Daphne Hobson is Executive Director of International Programmes at Lehigh University, USA and has a faculty appointment to the Department of Educational Leadership in the College of Education. She has spent her career committed to designing, developing and implementing educational programs to promote global growth and understanding between cultures and schools. She has extensive first-hand knowledge of such issues as multiculturalism, inclusion, and language diversity, having lived and worked in the international educational arena. As an academic and consultant, she has created and taught educational leadership courses infused with an international perspective.

Gerrit Jan Koopman is director of studies and teacher trainer in the Bilingual and International Teacher Education Programme (BITEP) of the Institute of Education (IVLOS) at Utrecht University, The Netherlands. His current topics of interest in education and research are training and concerns of student teachers, and interpersonal teacher behaviour in international education, as well as Content and Language Integrated Learning in international education and national programmes for bilingual education.

Hugh Lauder is Professor of Education and Political Economy at the University of Bath. He taught in London schools for six years before returning to Australasia in 1977, and came to Bath from New Zealand to take up his present position in 1996. His interests include education and the economy, globalisation and competitiveness, school performance and inequality, and research methodologies. He has published widely, both singly and with others.

Jack Levy is Professor Emeritus of International/Intercultural Education at George Mason University in Fairfax, Virginia, USA. Dr. Levy initiated GMU's Center for International Education and FAST TRAIN, a programme that provides professional development for teachers in international schools. He has coordinated educational reform projects in Indonesia and Pakistan, and directed a number of grants for teachers of English Language Learners. He has published on a variety of topics related to the influence of culture and language on education, is co-editor of the *Journal of Research in International Education*, and has taught courses and made presentations on international education, intercultural communication and second language acquisition throughout the world for more than two decades.

Harriet Marshall is a lecturer in International Education at the Centre for the study of Education in an International Context (CEIC), University of Bath, UK. She has written on a range of topics relating to global citizenship education, gender, the relationship between globalisation and the curriculum, and the movement for global education in the UK in particular.

Sarah Maughan is Head of Assessment Development and Deputy Director of the International Curriculum Division at Cambridge International Examinations (CIE). Before joining Cambridge in 1996, Sarah taught internationally for several years, in Turkey, Yemen and Sri Lanka.

John Munro is Associate Professor and Head of Studies in Gifted Education and Exceptional Learning in the Faculty of Education at the University of Melbourne. His research and teaching interests are in contemporary models of learning and knowledge enhancement, learning internationally, literacy and numeracy, gifted and professional learning. He works extensively with schools and educational providers in Australia and the UK. He has researched learning processes in the International Baccalaureate (IB) Diploma's Theory of Knowledge and Extended Essay and is an international consultant for the IB Primary Years Programme.

Tom Oden is Director of the Uruguayan American School, in Montevideo, Uruguay. Prior to that, he has been a Principal and Curriculum Coordinator at international schools in Johannesburg, South Africa; Muscat, Oman and Beirut, Lebanon. He is a doctoral candidate at the University of Minnesota, studying the organizational commitment of teachers in international schools.

José Agustín Ortiz Elías is Director of the Human Resources Management Program at the Universidad Peruana de Ciencias Aplicadas (UPC) in Lima, Peru. His Doctoral studies were in Business Management at the Universitat Politècnica de Catalunya. He is a member of the Research Committee and Regional Advisory Committee (Latin America) of the International Baccalaureate Organization (IBO), and was associate researcher at the GLOBE project, a cross-cultural research project in leadership.

Richard Pearce has worked in the UK and the USA, in national and international schools. He has written and taught on the topic of his doctoral research, identity development in international school students, including on postgraduate programmes at the University of Bath and Oxford Brookes University, UK.

David Phillips is Professor of Comparative Education and a Fellow of St Edmund Hall, University of Oxford. He has written widely on issues in comparative education, with a focus on education in Germany and on educational policy borrowing. He served as Chair of the British Association for International and Comparative Education (BAICE) from 1998 to 2000, and is an Academician of the British Social Sciences Academy and a Fellow of the Royal Historical Association. He was for twenty years editor of the *Oxford Review of Education* and serves on the editorial boards of various journals, including *Comparative Education*. He now edits the on-line journal, *Research in Comparative and International Education* and is series editor of *Oxford Studies in Comparative Education*.

William Powell has served as an international school educator for the past 30 years. He has masters degrees in education and educational administration from Manhattanville College and the College of New Jersey. Most recently he served as Headmaster of the International School of Kuala Lumpur in Malaysia. He is the author of numerous journal articles on inclusion, differentiated instruction and school leadership. He is co-author of *School Board Governance Training: a Sourcebook of Case Studies*, and has also co-authored the book *Count Me In! Developing Inclusive International Schools* with Ochan Kusuma-Powell. Bill is an Associate Trainer for the Center for Cognitive Coaching. Together, Bill and Ochan are co-directors of Education Across Frontiers, an organization dedicated to supporting international school teachers in their professional development.

Rauni Räsänen is a professor in education at the Faculty of Education, University of Oulu, Finland. Before her university career she worked as a primary and secondary school teacher and as provincial supervisor for language teaching. Since 1994 she has been responsible for the MEd International programme, a university degree programme focusing on international and intercultural education. Her main research interests include ethics of education, values and education, international education and intercultural education. She is a member of the National UNESCO Commission and academic co-ordinator of the North–South higher education project at the University of Oulu.

Fazal Rizvi is a Professor in Educational Policy Studies at the University of Illinois, having previously held a number of academic and administrative appointments in Australia, including Pro Vice Chancellor (International) at RMIT University, Melbourne, Australia. He has written extensively on theories of globalization, educational policy, student mobility and the internationalization of higher education.

Rajagopalan Sampatkumar was a senior official of the United Nations for nearly three decades and dealt with humanitarian issues. His interest in international education dates back to the 1960s when, as Lecturer at the International People's College, Elsinore, Denmark, he organised special courses on international understanding for students and teachers from North America and Europe. He served on the Governing Board of the International School of Geneva and was a Member of the Academic Advisory Committee of the International Baccalaureate Organization. As Secretary General of the International Society for Human Values, Professor Sampatkumar works closely with UNESCO in promoting human values and values-based education among children and young adults.

Martin Skelton was founding Director of the International Primary Curriculum (IPC), a curriculum that includes the development and evaluation of international-mindedness as two of its core elements. Through Fieldwork Education, Martin directs and provides consultancy and training to schools in a number of important issues, including international-mindedness, learning and the development of understanding. He has written widely on all of these themes and more.

Lesley Snowball has extensive experience worldwide, including as deputy director of the International School of Amsterdam, and, currently, as director of Putting it into Practice. She was part of the team that developed the original framework for the International Baccalaureate (IB) Primary Years Programme (PYP) and, in 2002, she initiated a system of international teacher certification, linked to her doctoral studies with the University of Bath.

Tristian Stobie has worked for 20 years as a teacher and administrator in international schools in Lesotho, Austria, The Netherlands, the United Kingdom and Monaco. He completed a masters and a doctorate degree at the University of Bath, focusing on international education, and has recently taken up the position of Head of the Diploma Programme Development with the International Baccalaureate Organization.

Wilf Stout was founding Director of five international schools in South Africa. A former biology teacher, he pioneered the IGCSE whilst at the University of Cambridge Local Examinations Syndicate. He is Director of IEI (International Education Initiatives), Treasurer of the Alliance for International Education and a doctoral student at the University of Bath. He is also currently Director of GEMS (South Africa).

Robert Sylvester has worked in international education since 1976 as a teacher and administrator, UNESCO teacher trainer in Zambia, and Principal of an international school in Botswana. He is currently Assistant Professor of Education at Bridgewater State College in Massachusetts, USA, responsible for courses related to literacy and global education.

Jeff Thompson is Emeritus Professor of Education at the University of Bath. He became involved in international education in the 1960s when working at the University of Oxford Department of Educational Studies, and has continued his involvement since that time in a number of different capacities. He held key appointments in the International Baccalaureate Organization over a period of 38 years. He teaches, lectures and researches in the field of international education, in both national and international contexts, has published widely and has received awards for his work in international education.

George Walker's career has involved him successively in British science education, school leadership and international education. In 1991 he moved to Switzerland to become Director General, first of the International School of Geneva and then of the International Baccalaureate Organization, from which he retired in 2006. He is a Visiting Professor at the University of Bath.

Lucas Walsh is a Research Fellow at Deakin University, Australia. Formerly a Research Fellow at the Monash Centre for Research in International Education and Manager of the International Baccalaureate Organization's Online Curriculum Centre, he was also a Civil Society representative at the United Nations-endorsed World Summit on the Information Society.

Theo Wubbels is Professor of Education and Vice Dean of the Faculty of Social and Behavioural Sciences at Utrecht University, The Netherlands. He teaches on interpersonal relationships and multicultural issues in education. His main research interests are interpersonal relationships in education, teacher learning and professional development.

List of Selected Abbreviations

AP	Advanced Placement
AERO	American Education Reaches Out
ATCK	adult third culture kids
CAS	Creativity, Action, Service (IB Diploma)
CERI	Centre for Educational Research and Innovation
CEWC	Council for Education in World Citizenship
CIES	Comparative and International Education Society
DfES	Department for Education and Skills (UK)
DFID	Department for International Development (UK)
DP (IB)	Diploma Programme (International Baccalaureate)
GN	global nomad
IBE	International Bureau of Education (Bureau International d'Éducation)
IBO	International Baccalaureate Organization
IBRU	International Baccalaureate Research Unit
IGCSE	International General Certificate of Secondary Education
IIE	Institute of International Education
IM	international-mindedness
IPC	International Primary Curriculum
ISA	identity structure analysis
ISA	International Schools Association
ISA	International Schools' Assessment
ISCP	International Schools Curriculum Project
K–12	Kindergarten to Grade 12 (ages 5–18)
MK	missionary kids
MNC	multinational corporation
MYP (IB)	Middle Years Programme (International Baccalaureate)
NAFSA	National Association of Foreign Student Affairs
NEA	National Education Association
NESA	Near East South Asia
NGO	non-governmental organization
OECD	Organization for Economic Co-operation and Development
OFSTED	Office for Standards in Education (England)
OU	Open University (UK)
PYP (IB)	Primary Years Programme (International Baccalaureate)
QCA	Qualifications and Curriculum Authority (England)
TCK	third culture kids

TOK	Theory of Knowledge (IB Diploma)
UBD	Understanding by Design
UNDP	United Nations Development Programme
UNESCO	United Nations Education, Scientific and Cultural Organization
UNICEF	United Nations Children's Fund
WCCES	World Council of Comparative Education Societies

Introduction

Mary Hayden, Jack Levy and
Jeff Thompson

RATIONALE

Interest in the field of international education has never been more intense than it is at present. Changes in the general world order are challenging the nature of the relationships between nations and cultures in more explicit and extensive ways than has previously been the case. Simultaneously, a rapidly increasing number of schools world-wide have been established specifically to meet the demands of those parents who, through their own global professional activities, wish to have their children educated in programmes based on international values and often in contexts other than their home country. Such schools have embraced the promotion of international education as one of their major goals and, consequently, an increasing number of organizations currently offer curricula that claim to be international in nature – the International Baccalaureate Organization (IBO) would be one example. Such global movements have generated a parallel rise in the incorporation of forms of international education within national school systems throughout the world. That, in turn, has resulted in wider forms of collaboration between schools in the public and private sectors, nationally and internationally, generating a much more substantial base of professional experience in the implementation of schemes for international education than had previously existed.

In these circumstances it is hardly surprising that research and enquiry into the nature and practice of international education has itself extended in both size and scope, particularly over the past two decades. Such research is conducted in universities, schools, government agencies, non-governmental organizations (NGOs) and other educational institutions throughout the world. Those not in schools frequently work closely with those in schools who are charged with responsibility for the design and implementation of programmes combining local requirements with international imperatives.

In addition to its widening scope, the term 'international education' has also become less easily defined as the variety of contexts increases in which that label is currently applied. Some of these applications have existed for a long time – for example, the fields of comparative and development education both have long and well-documented histories and conceptual frameworks. Quite distinct uses of the term 'international education' have appeared in the multicultural and multinational education literatures over a considerable period, and recent activity in the area of 'globalization' has only widened the various interpretations of the term 'international' as applied to a wide range of educational processes.

Such considerations underscore the need for this Handbook, which provides in part a critical overview of the origins and contributions of the various interpretations of international education, while also attempting to define more clearly than is currently the case their distinctiveness and relationship to one another. From these definitional perspectives this volume seeks to guide future interpretations of the field, as well as to identify approaches to future research that can illuminate our knowledge and understanding. In that sense, it attempts to complete, in greater detail than before, the existing map of international education and also to extend it on the basis of the research evidence presented.

Clearly, the volume cannot address all of the themes and models that the field encompasses. Nonetheless, it is an attempt to harness the knowledge and wisdom of a significant portion of international education, providing future researchers with a solid foundation. Further, the Handbook is not only a *report* on research in international education; it should also be seen as representing an international education *experience*. As such, it synthesizes research in the field, and produces new understandings for use by educators at all levels. Educational research is only as important as the policy and practice that it influences, and it is therefore intended that this volume will contribute significantly to the quality of student learning throughout the world.

COMPLEXITY OF RESEARCH IN INTERNATIONAL EDUCATION

As noted, there is to be found an ever-increasing number of forms of international education in national school systems, international schools, universities, government-approved activities and NGOs. As a consequence there are myriad orientations to

research in the field (each with its own conceptual framework), including those that focus on the following, among many others:

- historical framework, situating education within other social forces
- the purposes of schooling, including values and needs (economic and social)
- access, equity and human rights
- accountability and governance, including administrative styles
- the nature of students and educators
- economic and political development and education policy planning
- the preparation of educators
- curricular/instructional models (international-mindedness) and school organization
- identity formation (cultural, social, ethnic, etc.) of participants
- local context.

There seem to be two primary bases – one traditional and the other more recent – for the complexity of research in international education. Historically, the field has drawn on several disciplines in the humanities and social sciences, as well as on foundational aspects of education. Internationally oriented research is routinely conducted in areas including economics, political science, sociology, anthropology, language and literature, history and psychology, and applied to various aspects of education.

Globalization – the massive movement of, for example, information, technology and goods across national borders – has also altered the nature of international education research by introducing new ways of conceptualizing the field. No longer is the nation-state the sole unit of analysis, since global forces demand increased attention to factors operating beyond the national level. As a result, multilateral agencies such as the United Nations and the World Bank are increasingly becoming the source and object of research. The effect of globalization on national and local systems and culture is a frequent investigative theme that highlights the importance of context in analysis. It has brought about a fundamental change in research methodology, from large, quantitative designs to qualitative and hybrid studies that focus on micro-level effects. Globalization has also created a need for interdisciplinary teams of researchers that combine representatives from education with those from areas including the social and behavioural sciences, law, health, business and technology.

In this Handbook, we have deliberately interpreted research in international education in a broad manner. Thus we have sought to encompass research based entirely on a literary tradition together with empirical enquiry, grounded theory, and case studies in specific and more general contexts. We have encouraged from a number of authors reflection on their practice in ways that lead to enhanced understandings, through implicit and explicit theorizing, both of their own practice and that of others. It is within such a framework of complexity that the rationale for this Handbook should be understood.

AIMS

The Handbook seeks to fulfil a range of aims, with the following explicitly and comprehensively addressed:

1 to provide a historical overview of the ways in which the term 'international education' has been interpreted and to identify the antecedent conceptualizations, and relationships with other disciplines, that have contributed to current usages;
2 to provide a critical overview of contemporary research into the field and the ways in which such research output is leading to a clearer, and more coherent, theoretical understanding of the field;
3 to document research designed to explore the relationship between theory and practice in the promotion of international education in a range of formal and informal educational settings (including schools, higher education and lifelong learning), in a wide range of national and cultural contexts and;
4 to identify and explore new directions and approaches to research designed to address issues that challenge existing models and paradigms within international education.

ORGANIZATION

To achieve these ambitious aims the volume is organized in the following manner.

Part One

Part One provides a critical analysis of the theoretical basis for international education. It includes both historical and conceptual treatments of the field, and presents a variety of perspectives on which to reflect. In order that current researchers and practitioners understand its lineage, the first chapter by Robert Sylvester provides an historical perspective of research in international education. It presents both factual and conceptual treatments, through which the reader is led to appreciate the rich heritage of the field. Ian Hill then focuses on the development of the International Baccalaureate programmes, perhaps the most significant curricular undertaking in the history of international education to date, and discusses the various conceptualizations of international education that influenced the design of these programmes.

One frequently mentioned aspect of global or international education is the diverse terminology that describes it – which Harriet Marshall attempts to unravel in the third chapter. Marshall thoroughly analyses the various conceptualizations, with reference to global education traditions such as development education or world studies *and* the tradition of 'international education' in international schools and their curricula. She then asks an important question: does this big terminology debate really matter? Mark Bray's answer would be an unqualified affirmative. In his chapter Bray acknowledges the multiple meanings of the term 'international education', and then examines its applications as commonly used in international and comparative education. He notes that some bodies that were established with a focus on comparative education have broadened their compass to embrace international education. Other bodies have rejected such broadening;

but even in the settings where comparative education is not formally linked to international education, boundaries are commonly ambiguous. Bray discusses the pros and cons of this ambiguity, but sees definite advantage in its existence since such ambiguity may permit partnerships and synergies between practitioners and academics.

The next two chapters in Part One address the critical dimension of ethics and values in international education. Rauni Räsänen argues that there are issues that demand international dialogue and problem-solving such as environmental threats, energy alternatives, prevention of diseases and pollution, reduction of poverty and inequity, decreasing violence and putting an end to wars. As ethical practitioners and role models, schools and teachers need to provide students with innovative mediums of instruction and administration by which to address such concerns. Rajagopalan Sampatkumar believes that the approach to these problems requires a new understanding of global citizenship and the role of education in it. The speed and manner in which globalization is progressing leave little doubt that every one of us will have to assume global responsibility, and he stresses the importance of values-based education in response. To achieve our ideals of peace and equity we must develop the appropriate values and attitudes, and it is important that these values do not remain an intellectual residue but that they are integrated as traits of one's character.

The last two chapters in Part One – by Terry Haywood and Konrad Gunesch – focus respectively on the nature of international-mindedness (IM) and the type of individual that international education aims to promote. Haywood relates the interpretation of international-mindedness to our understanding of intelligence, and believes we must replace the notion that 'we know it when we see it' – which is how intelligence used to be perceived – with a view that allows for multiple definitions. Gunesch's central thesis is that international or global citizens should best be understood in terms of their cosmopolitanism – a personal cultural identity that facilitates transnationalism and transculturalism. Cosmopolitanism, according to Gunesch, can be thought of as 'feeling at home in the world'. It is possible to distinguish between cosmopolitanism and localism, or between people who are cosmopolitans and those who are locals. While the local may not be interested in cultural diversity, the cosmopolitan consciously values, seeks out and tries to access local cultural diversity. Clearly, in terms of global citizenship cosmopolitanism is the preferred identity.

Thus, Part One is intended to provide a solid underpinning for the rest of the volume, which addresses international education in practice.

Part Two

Moving from theory to practice, Part Two discusses learners in an international context. It includes in-depth considerations of individual students as well as discussions of cultural groupings, curricula and learning models. Helen Fail begins the section with an analysis of the life histories of three past international school students. Among other variables she examines their sense of identity, their approaches to change and relationships and various international aspects in their lives. John Munro then focuses on learning in international contexts and what this means for teaching, curriculum and teacher knowledge. According to Munro, learning is influenced by a range of cultural factors that need to be acknowledged explicitly in classroom practice and school organization. He develops one perspective on learning internationally and identifies how culture might influence knowledge enhancement by using the autonomous learner model as a starting point.

Richard Pearce returns us to the concept of culture and considers the child in an international school in terms of his/her social contexts. He suggests that these cultural environmental influences contribute to the identity of the emerging person, equipping him/her with a mosaic of cultural norms, beliefs and values which directs his/her active and reactive behaviour. Next, Tristian

Stobie provides an important complement to the Part One chapter by Hill through his use of the International Baccalaureate Diploma and Middle Years Programmes as the basis for analysing coherence, consistency and continuity in international education curricula. Robert DiYanni follows with a description of international education programmes in US secondary and higher education, including a discussion of post-secondary courses, relevant textbooks and the Advanced Placement program.

In their qualitative examination of the development of a course within the International General Certificate of Secondary Education (IGCSE) programme, Paul Beedle, Tom Eason and Sarah Maughan review the history of this most important curriculum, and provide a glimpse of the future that reflects urgency in the education of all students about their, and our, place in the world. In his discussion of standards in K–12 (kindergarden to grade 12) international education, Tom Oden presents another case study of an innovative curriculum development project that involved several schools and organizations. Globalization and learning as a social process have prompted a rethinking of distance education and created the need for a more flexible conceptual framework to address the demands of a world-wide market. The final two chapters in Part Two address this topic from past, present and future perspectives. Through examples of distributed learning delivery models, including knowledge networks, knowledge portals, telelearning and virtual classrooms and universities, Nada Dabbagh and Angela Benson describe a framework that can be used to guide the broader practice of education within and across national borders. Lucas Walsh then asks a central question: what can international educators learn from the use of information and communication technology (ICT) over the past two decades in both national and international systems? Case studies and examples are used to illustrate some key lessons, with particular emphasis on the cultural implications of ICT use for teaching and learning.

Part Three

Part Three presents ideas related to teachers and their professional development, and provides an overview of both standard and innovative approaches to teacher education around the world. Jack Levy and Mary Hayden begin, respectively, with analyses of pre- and in-service professional development curricula in international and national settings. From the variety of models they present it is clear that the preparation and continued development of international educators is a complex undertaking. Perry den Brok and Gerrit Jan Koopman then present a novel professional development vehicle in their focus on interpersonal teacher behaviour. In a report of research conducted in an international school, they describe teachers' strengths and weaknesses in relating to their students, and provide guidelines for development. Lesley Snowball follows with a notable model for an international teaching certificate in which she highlights the important competencies required by practitioners as well as a developmental route to achievement.

The fifth chapter in the section, by Patrick Griffin, describes an innovative professional development curriculum built by a partnership between commercial ICT interests, a university and a number of schools. This many-faceted programme was designed to provide educators and other practitioners with portable skills and qualifications that would permit them to work anywhere in the world. The section ends with an indictment by Theo Wubbels of the many teacher education programmes that do not address classroom management, a topic and skill that is critical to effective teaching. Wubbels also provides an excellent overview of the variety of classroom management techniques available around the world.

Part Four

Through its treatment of school improvement, governance and organizational culture, Part Four moves the analysis of international education to the institutional level. James

Cambridge and Clive Carthew address the challenge of identifying and evaluating the values espoused by international schools in their case study of the implementation of a questionnaire designed by the International Schools Association. William Gerritz and Kevin Bartlett next report on an exciting collaboration between two international schools. The institutions followed six basic improvement principles gleaned from the literature, and not only advanced their schools' goals but also produced a transferable model. Wilf Stout then shifts our focus to school governance. After an analysis of various models, he asks whether the structural nature of the governance of international schools contributes to a level of conflict that can be disruptive to long-term goal achievement.

Much has been written about organizational culture, and José Agustin Ortiz Elías adds to this literature in his chapter. He refers to 1990s research in the private sector which concludes that organizations with the ability to maintain sustained success are not those that are principally affected by market forces, resources or competitive positions, but those that are concerned with the beliefs, values, visions and satisfaction of their members. He then presents three models of organizational culture that offer the most promise for meaningful school change, and challenges us to use these frameworks to analyse our own institutions.

Richard Caffyn explores organizational culture through fragmentation. He asks us to consider whether international schools fragment into subcultures, departments and interest groups when the corporate culture is weak or imposed, or if the people involved have diverse reasons for being there. Does a school fragment further into individual interests and small-scale alliances built upon basis of needs, goals, subcultures and power structures?

The section's final chapter moves from the theoretical to the specific, as William Powell focuses on leadership and organizational culture. Research highlights the correlation between effective leadership and the cultivation of a school climate that generates reflective teaching practice and important learning relationships. Powell explores the role that school leaders play in building leadership capacity in others and reflects on how this can lead to a redefinition of the traditional three Rs: Relationships, Reflection and Renaissance.

Part Five

Part Five leads us from the present into the future as it explores the demanding challenges facing international education. These include the treatment of language, understanding cognition, upgrading curriculum, addressing global crises, the production and transfer of policy through effective research and technology use, and the omnipresent challenge of globalization.

Recognizing that language can be both a unifying and a divisive force, Trevor Grimshaw offers critical perspectives on the role of language in international education. He introduces definitions of two key terms which are essential for our understanding of how language operates in its social context, and then describes the important field of debate as an example of 'linguistic imperialism'. Grimshaw concludes by stressing the importance of a critical awareness of language in international education.

Martin Skelton returns to the definition of international-mindedness discussed by Terry Haywood in Part One. Skelton focuses on our understanding of cognition and brain behaviour to explain the difficulty in understanding the IM concept. He argues that the development of international-mindedness is more complex and messy, more personal and emotional, than many want to believe or admit. It is dependent upon a continually successful series of developments of the self that transcend and include each other, and brain research has helped to illuminate this explanation.

Fazal Rizvi's focus on curriculum brings us to another critical challenge for international education. He states that the appeal of the idea of internationalization of the curriculum appears ubiquitous and world-wide. But beyond its symbolic language and some general measures to facilitate student mobility, it is not always clear what it means. Rizvi critiques some of the ways in which the idea of internationalization of the curriculum has been operationalized, and proposes a more critical concept that seeks to develop in students a range of 'epistemic virtues' with which to interpret, reflect upon and engage the contemporary process of globalization.

George Walker next visualizes the aims and purposes of international schools in terms of the epochs they inhabit. He believes that the international school movement that began in Geneva in 1924 and greatly expanded throughout the next seven decades responded to the challenges of the twentieth century. Walker reminds us, however, that we have now passed into the third millennium and there are new crises to confront. He notes that in the past century international education was largely concerned with the relationships between groups contained within different geographical boundaries. However, as immigration between nations has increased, making the classrooms of national schools more and more culturally diverse, and as the conflicts *between* nations give way to culturally based conflicts *within* nations, national and international education are beginning to merge, making international education more of a national responsibility. Thus, working with difference and complexity should be a primary focus of international curricula.

The next three chapters address the importance of research in the advancement of international education. James Cambridge begins with a critique of the realist orientation in research methodology, and argues that its assumption of an objective reality – and the data collection schemes (such as the use of questionnaires) that it promotes – is not effective in international education. He then leads potential researchers toward a series of important questions that can improve the validity of their enquiries.

Michael Allan regrets the frequent lack of cross-cultural validity in international education research. He examines ways in which the cultural complexity of school and classroom can be penetrated by interpretive methodology, enabling crucial process factors to be identified and described within the context. Various types of ethnomethodology from within the interpretive paradigm are assessed as a means of understanding the complex nature of international schools, particularly those approaches derived from cultural studies, applied linguistics and discourse analysis.

A possible research agenda for those studying international schools and international education is presented by Hugh Lauder. The agenda is based on three emerging dimensions: the nature of the networks of which international school students are members; the formation of their views concerning key economic, social and political issues regarding globalization and their own role as global citizens; and the mechanisms of recruitment into the international school system and its relationship to the international labour market – the underlying issues of positional competition.

David Phillips then shifts the focus to the transfer of educational policy from country to country. He presents various models and cross-national examples of educational transfer and 'policy borrowing'. Phillips believes that the models need to be tested, however, in a variety of national contexts. In particular, he stresses the importance of considering the extent to which less developed countries – often the receivers of policy 'lent' by outside agencies – fit into the explanatory schemata proposed in the chapter. Moving from the theoretical to the specific, Silvina Gvirtz and Jason Beech analyse the latest reforms in Latin American educational systems. They suggest that though reform policies in the region have always been shaped by international influences, this tendency intensified in the 1980s and 1990s and official rhetoric on the topic became more similar throughout Latin America. The authors suggest, however, that these similarities do not necessarily imply that actual policies are the same in different countries, since the process of policy formulation is affected by different political and institutional culture. As already noted, globalization is one of the major threads running throughout this volume, and it takes centre stage in Daphne Hobson's final chapter on its impact on higher education. Hobson traces the rise of internationalism in post-secondary institutions and provides a number of examples of universities diversifying their student populations, services and site locations in an effort to compete.

Thus, Part Five completes the volume's chronological and theoretical sweep of issues, practices and challenges presented by the research in international education. Naturally, we hope you find the volume as intellectually stimulating and practical in its reading as did we in its editing, a privilege we have greatly enjoyed.

PART I

Historical Roots, Definitions and Current Interpretations

Historical Resources for Research in International Education (1851–1950)

Robert Sylvester

As a discipline concerned with both theory and practice, international education may be considered wide enough to embrace both education for international understanding, as it has been known for well over a century, and education for world citizenship, which many have argued in support of for centuries. Since one of the major weaknesses in the research literature for international education is the lack of a historical treatment, this chapter will focus on the most important historical resources available to the researcher for the ten decades represented in the period 1851–1950. Initial steps have been taken to link the major institutions and the chief activists in the field over the past 15 decades, but the lack of a broadly based historical research effort (Wilson 1994) has kept the field from clearly understanding a lineage with any degree of confidence. The range of activities and subject disciplines connected to international education has, in the past, included: international affairs, global education, multicultural education, peace education, exchange programmes, globalization and intercultural studies, among others (Gutek 1993; Stomfay-Stitz 1993: 86–7; Vestal 1994: 13).

Although attempts have been made to provide a guide to historical documents (Fraser and Brickman 1968; Scanlon 1959), Brickman's (1950) comprehensive encyclopedic survey stands alone in its analysis of historical documents related to international education. Brickman's bibliography indicated that there were more than 30 formal plans for some sort of international educational organization put forward between the years 1814 and 1914 from Jullien, Kemeny, Andrews and Peeters, among others. This alone could be seen to indicate evidence of a robust level of work in the field, reaching back to the middle decades of the nineteenth century.

Any historical interpretation of international education poses several challenges to the researcher. A lack of consensus on a working definition has complicated research efforts. In addition, a lack of an established literature on the history of the field has created significant hurdles to a rigorous approach to the study of international education. This chapter seeks to re-establish visibly, in the literature, the seminal contribution of Brickman (1950) to the history of the field. This chapter will also add to the range of materials that Brickman presented and provide some context to the shape of efforts in international education from the 1850s to the 1950s with the rise of institutional efforts at both the level of theory and of practice in international education.

While no single definition of the field has met with widespread approval (Spaulding et al. 1968; Butts 1969; Anderson 1981; Arum and Van de Water 1992; Vestal 1994), recent efforts have been made to find convergent lines of consideration within that research problem (Sylvester 2002a, 2003, 2005). More than five decades have passed since Brickman (1950) presented his comprehensive review of the historical resources in the field, yet no single attempt has been made during these decades to extend his groundbreaking work. This research problem has been sustained, since relatively few researchers are currently engaged in the historical aspect. This has slowed the progress of constructing a lineage, designing a methodology or establishing a content for the field (Scanlon and Shields 1968).

1851 AND THE RISE OF THE WORLD'S FAIRS

In 1851, the first of many Universal Exhibitions (World's Fairs) was held in London (Potter 1948). They were to become vital links to the many attempts to view education beyond the nation-state. An educational conference on the kindergarten and other topics was held at this first official international exposition in London with representatives from Germany, France, England and the United States (Brickman 1950; Scanlon 1960; Stoker 1933). In 1855, the Universal Exhibition was held in Paris (Potter 1948) and also included an international congress on education (Monroe, P.

1919; Stoker 1933). Harris (1898) noted that there was a portion devoted to primary education at the Paris exposition. An article in the *Journal of the Society of Arts* (Bell 1863) published in London in 1863 noted that 'The recent International Exhibition [in London] seems naturally to have led to the discussion, amongst the many distinguished men of different nations then in this country, of various plans for removing national prejudices' (p. 336). In 1873, a Universal Exhibition was held in Vienna (Potter 1948). It was reported by Stoker (1933) to include an international congress on education (citing Monroe, W.S. in Monroe, P. 1919). The International Conference on Education in Philadelphia in 1876 was attended by 13 countries and nearly every state in the American Union (Scanlon 1960) and considered by Stoker (1933, citing Monroe, P. 1919) to include an international congress on education (Gregory 1938). It was at that centennial observance in 1876 that John Eaton, the United States Commissioner of Education, presented a plan for a permanent organization to coordinate international educational conferences (Butts 1944: 19; Scanlon 1960: 5).

SPRING GROVE SCHOOL

Brickman (1962) indicated that the International College at Spring Grove, London, England, just a few kilometres east of the present Heathrow International Airport, was officially opened in 1866 and operated until 1889 (Sylvester 2002a) when the premises were sold to the Borough Road Training College. Stewart (1972) characterized the Spring Grove School as the singular success in international education in the nineteenth century. He noted that there were three proposals made between 1855 and 1862 towards the establishment of a form of international school system in Europe. Stewart reported that the school in England was not initially formed until 1863, by the formation of a provisional committee that included Richard Cobden (who died in 1865 before the school would open), Dr. W.B. Hodgson, Thomas

Twining and the scientists John Tyndall and T.H. Huxley. Brickman (1962: 230) noted that as part of this European effort, international secondary schools were also established at Chatou, near Paris, and at Bad Godesberg, near Bonn, but were discontinued after a short period in response to the Franco-Prussian War.

OPENING OF JAPAN

In 1868, the Japanese government indicated, for the first time, its desire to seek educational improvement from international sources through the Charter Oath of Five Articles. This document, which was sworn by the Emperor, stated: 'Knowledge shall be sought throughout the world, so that the welfare of the Empire may be promoted' (Brickman 1962: 221; 1964: 35). A few years later (1871–3) a delegation headed by Prince Tomoni Iwakura visited European capitals and the United States. Around the same time period, in 1870, the United States Office of Education's *Annual Report* referred to 'International Educational Relations', a term that was then common for the next several decades (Brickman 1950). Wilson (1994) suggested that Japan's Prince Tomoni Iwakura should be considered as a pioneer of international education in special respect to his leading a mission to study American and European education in 1872, a mere four years following the Meiji Restoration. Professor David Murray of Rutgers University accompanied the Japanese Vice-Minister of Education to the Philadelphia Centennial Exposition and the several international educational exhibits.

MOLKENBOER

In 1885, Herman Molkenboer, a lawyer from Holland who became a teacher, published a plan for an international education agency in a pamphlet entitled *Der Bleibende Internationale Erziehungstrat* (Scanlon 1959, 1960: 5), which

Brickman (1964) indicated was modelled upon the United States's Bureau of Education. In 1890, Molkenboer formed a Temporary Committee for the Foundation of a Permanent and International Council of Education with a supporting group known as *Pax Humanitate,* with several hundred subscribers from 17 nations. Scanlon observed that Molkenboer believed that the emphasis on international educational cooperation should be on assisting teachers to teach world understanding (Scanlon 1959: 213). In 1891, Molkenboer began the publication of a periodical entitled 'Journal of Correspondence on the Foundation of a Permanent and International Council on Education' in Westphalen. This later became a vehicle for the promotion of an international council on education and world peace (Scanlon 1960: 6). In the same year, Molkenboer presented his proposals for an international council on education in a pamphlet entitled *Die Internationale Erziehungs-Arbeit, Einstzung des Blesibenden Internationalen Erziehungs-Rates* in Flensburg, Germany (Scanlon 1960: 6).

COLUMBIAN EXPOSITION OF 1893

In 1892, the first organizational meeting of the International Kindergarten Union (later to be known as the Association for Childhood Education International – ACEI) was held at the preparatory meeting of the National Education Association for the 1893 Congress at the Baptist Church in Saratoga Springs. Wood (1903) indicated that there were 30 charter members of the Union at that time. The 1893 Universal Exhibition was held in Chicago (NEA 1894; Potter 1948) and witnessed the most historically significant international meeting of educators in the nineteenth century. The published proceedings of the Congress (NEA 1894) indicated that there were at least 58 documents presented by non-US participants in the form of addresses, papers or appendices. In total, they constituted a significant portion of the material of the congress. Compayré (1893) and Waterman (1893) highlighted the leading role of women in the Congress and listed the countries participating as: England, Russia, Germany, Austria-Hungary, Italy, Spain, Sweden, Denmark, Switzerland, France, Japan, Australia, Canada, Chile, Uruguay and the host, the United States. The scope and range of the available materials from the 1893 Congress make it fertile ground for researchers in the consideration of the roots of international education at the turn of the nineteenth century.

INTERNATIONAL BUREAU OF NEW SCHOOLS

In 1899, the International Bureau of New Schools/Bureau International des Écoles Nouvelles (Brickman 1950; Stoker 1933) was established in Geneva by Adolphe Ferrière. This was eventually to become the New Education Fellowship (Meyer 1949) and would be absorbed as a section of the Rousseau Institute in 1912 (Suchodolski et al. 1979: 43). In 1900, a coeducational school called Bedales was established with the aim that 'International goodwill … be encouraged in every possible way' (Meyer 1949: 137). In the same year, Sir Michael Sadler wrote *How Far Can We Learn Anything of Practical Value from the Study of Foreign Systems of Education?*, which Wilson (1994) considered the historical dividing line between comparative and international education and the beginning of the period of a 'scientific' consideration of comparative education. In 1920, the New Education Fellowship initiated a magazine, *Education for a New Era: An International Quarterly Journal for the Promotion of Reconstruction in Education*, edited by Beatrice Eisnor, a London school inspectress. Stewart (1972: 354) indicated that the Journal 'was international and set out to record the growth of experimental education'. In 1921, the First World Conference of New Education Fellowship was held in Calais (Gregory 1938: 184) and was formed by Europe's leading 'Progressives' into the Ligue

Internationale pour l'Éducation Nouvelle. This group was founded jointly by Adolph Ferrière and Elisabeth Rotten and was first presided over by the third founder, Eisnor. The Fellowship then sponsored two-yearly international conferences between 1923 and 1936 (Stewart 1972). The World Conference of New Education Fellowship was held in Montreux (Gregory 1938: 184) and over the next 30 years attracted between 1500 and 3000 professionals (educators, philosophers, psychologists and sociologists) from more than 50 countries world-wide (Meyer 1949: 108). The 1923 meeting requested Henri Bergson, President of the League of Nations International Commission for Intellectual Cooperation, to 'recommend the setting up in Geneva of an International Bureau of Education' (Suchodolski et al. 1979: 44).

RABINDRANATH TAGORE

In 1901, Rabindranath Tagore, the Indian Pulitzer Prize-winning poet, established Santiniketan, which would evolve in the next 20 years into an international school and world university (Kripalani 1962). In 1916, during a tour of Japan and the United States, Tagore developed the idea of creating an international school in India (Periaswamy 1976: 166) and in 1918 he announced the plan for creating that school (Visva-Bharati) near Calcutta (Periaswamy 1976: 166). The motto which he selected for the school was taken from an ancient Sanskrit verse: *Yatra visvam bhavati ika-nidam* [Where the world meets in one nest] (Kripalani 1962: 267). Gilbert Murray, the chair of the International Committee for Intellectual Cooperation, and Tagore exchanged a compelling set of correspondence in 1934. Their letters focused on the mission of education in the context of a world culture and civilization and the future needs of education in a united world. Murray spoke of a 'higher task' related to 'healing the discords of the political and material world' through the inward and spiritual life. Tagore responded by immediately invoking a 'common humanity' as the basis of their discussion and alluded to the 'inescapable moral links which hold together the fabric of human civilization' (Scanlon 1960: 106).

FRANZ KEMÉNY

In 1901, Franz Kemény published *Entwurf einer Internationalen Gesammt-Akademie: Weltakademie* in Budapest, Hungary calling for a world educational organization or *Weltakamemie* (Scott 1912; Scanlon 1960: 10–11). The pamphlet in Budapest supported six areas in which international education could be developed, including international conferences, human rights education reform of textbooks and antiracist education (Scanlon 1959: 217). In 1914, Franz Kemény (cited in Butts 1944) articulated six aspects of what he called 'international education' as part of his plan for an international institute of education which included education for peace, interracial education and world education, among others. Both of these works by Kemény are valuable to the researcher in the field in understanding the world-views of international educators at that time.

COSMOPOLITAN CLUBS

In 1903, the original Cosmopolitan Clubs were launched (Lochner 1911,1912) in the form of international clubs where representatives of each nation in the university would meet on the basis of brotherhood and equality. In 1907, the University Cosmopolitan Clubs (La Fontaine 1911 and Lochner 1911, 1912) were founded with a membership of more than two thousand, including representatives from 60 countries (Lochner 1911: 410). A Cosmopolitan Club at Oxford University formed a Central Committee for the Promotion of the Cosmopolitan Clubs, which emerged from discussions held at the First Universal Race Congress in London in 1911 (Lochner 1912).

F. FERN ANDREWS

In 1908, the American School Peace League was formed in Boston by F. Fern Andrews to promote 'the interests of international justice and fraternity' (Scanlon 1960: 8). She urged teachers' 'to build up a new people whose country is the world, whose countrymen are all mankind' (Stomfay-Stitz 1993: 45). In the same year, Andrews published an extended essay calling upon teachers to be involved in the training of world citizens (Andrews 1908). In 1910, Andrews was invited to present plans on an international council on education to the Eighteenth Peace Conference in Stockholm (Scanlon 1960: 11–12). Her plans were approved by the Conference and she sought to broaden the proposal to focus on educational relations between governments (Scanlon 1959: 217). Andrews was among the most prominent peace education activists of her time and arguably one of the most important figures in international education in the twentieth century. She was also one of the founders of the International Bureau of Education in Geneva, but her story is not well known in the literature. In 1912, Andrews persuaded the Secretary of State in the Taft administration to set in motion the elaborate diplomatic machinery needed to call an international conference on education which, over the course of the next two years, attracted widespread interest in Europe. But she ultimately faced waning interest and finally withdrawal from the political powers in the United States (Carr 1945; Scanlon 1960: 12–13). The story of F. Fern Andrews' contribution to the rise of international education deserves to be told as abundant materials are available to the researcher (Andrews 1915, 1919, 1924, 1927, 1948) in addition to her papers in collection at the Schlesinger Library, Radcliffe College in Boston.

EDWARD PEETERS

Edward Peeters (Dutch) is considered to be the first to actually create a world centre for educational information. He founded, in Ostend, a publishing firm La Nouvelle Bibliothèque Pédagogique, which published a quarterly bibliography. Unfortunately, by the onset of the First World War, that undertaking, along with some of his other efforts, failed due to lack of funding. In 1909, Peeters expanded his quarterly bibliography to a monthly publication entitled *Minerva: A Review of Information Relating to Education and the Teaching Profession* and considered the publishing of this monthly journal as the beginning of an international bureau of education (Scanlon 1960).

THE RISE OF INTERNATIONAL SCHOOLS

In 1910, Paul Geheeb established an international experimental school in Germany known as the Odenwald School, with 20 per cent of the students from international centres outside Germany. The purpose of the school was to educate cultured, social human beings. This purpose placed the school in direct conflict with the rising Nazi ideology. Geheeb later was forced to flee Germany and was directly responsible for the establishment of École d'Humanité in Switzerland in 1937 (Meyer 1949: 145). Lengyel (1951) indicated that his school in Germany, Odenwaldschule, organized the students into 'self-constituted families which treated nationality as incidental and not essential', and that 'An attempt was made to lay the basis of a new type of citizenship, *Weltburgerschaft*: citizenship of the world' (p. 603). A more recent historical treatment of Geheeb's life (Shirley 1992) provides a valuable study of the rise and struggle of an international school in the interwar period.

The year 1910 also saw the establishment of the International School of Peace in Boston (Meyer 1949) by Edwin Ginn, who was inspired by Edward Everett Hale of Boston. The purpose of the school was to educate 'the peoples of all nations to a full knowledge of the waste and destruction of

war and of preparation for war, its evil effects on present social conditions and on the well-being of future generations and to promote international justice and the brotherhood of man' (Scott 1912: 380–9). In the same year and with some degree of competition, the Carnegie Endowment for International Peace in Washington, DC was established with an endowment of 10 million dollars. It demonstrated, among other activities, support for international education for peaceful coexistence among the peoples of the world (Butler 1912, 1914; Harley 1931; Scanlon 1959, 1960).

By 1911, it became evident that there was a need for an international equivalence of diplomas. That year, discussions were held regarding the establishment of an International Pedagogical Centre (La Fontaine 1911). Hill (2001) noted that in 1926 Adolphe Ferrière, as director of the International Office of New Schools in Geneva, formally surveyed 17 leaders in educational reform regarding a proposed international curriculum effort known as *maturité internationale*, which would provide some relief to parents' concerns over university acceptance in countries other than Switzerland by students of the recently formed International School of Geneva (pp. 12–13).

In 1921, the International Folk (Peoples) High School in Elsinore, Denmark was established with the help of Danish, English and American contributions (Brickman 1950; Carr 1945; Kenworthy 1951; Stoker 1933) and modified over the next 30 years to meet the needs of a student body from more than 40 nations through both summer and winter courses (Kenworthy 1951).

OTHER IMPORTANT RESEARCH PUBLICATIONS

In 1915 John C. Faries (1915) published an important survey of the concept of 'internationalism' from an historical perspective. He included in this work the World's Fairs, international congresses and conferences and the international work of universities, societies and foundations, as well as human migration patterns. This work is an important resource for researchers interested in the nineteenth-century lineage of international education. A few years later, Paul Monroe (1919) published a *Cyclopedia of Education* and became one of the most prominent observers of international education in the next decades (Monroe 1927, 1931, 1936, 1938, 1939).

NEW INTERNATIONAL ORGANIZATIONS

In 1919, the International Confederation of Students/Confederation Internationale des Étudiants was formally established in Strasbourg by European student unions from Britain, France, Belgium, Holland, Greece, Italy, Poland, Romania, Czechoslovakia, Yugoslavia and the United States that were interested in coordinating activities and exchanging information (Altbach 1970; Brickman 1950; Harley 1931). The year 1919 also saw the creation of the Institute of International Education (IIE) in New York, which was founded to develop international understanding by means of educational and cultural activities (Brickman 1950; Duggan 1920; Harley 1931; Scanlon 1960).

LEAGUE OF NATIONS

In 1921, the League of Nations Committee on Intellectual Cooperation was created in Geneva, after the word 'Education' was removed from its name and mandate in response to nationalist sentiments among the representatives of the Allies (Brickman 1950; Harley 1931). In the same year, Dr Rudolph Laemmel of Meilen, Switzerland presented a pamphlet outlining a proposal for the foundation of an International School/*Volkerschule* to the President of the Assembly of the League of Nations (League of Nations 1922: 44; Stoker 1933: 85).

WORLD FEDERATION OF EDUCATION ASSOCIATIONS

In 1923, the National Education Association (NEA/USA) hosted a World Conference on Education in San Francisco (Gregory 1938: 202) with more than 50 national bodies present at a meeting that was organized in order to 'agree upon principles and plans for the promotion of good-will and mutual understanding … to be carried out in the schools throughout the world …' (Stoker 1933: 120). The World Federation of Education Associations (WFEA) was formed following this meeting (Brickman 1950; Harley 1931; WFEA 1926).

In 1932, in an address by the Secretary General of the World Federation of Education Associations at the Seventieth Annual Meeting of the National Educational Association in Atlantic City, Augustus Thomas (1932) suggested an undertaking by the World Federation of Education Associations to support research into a world-wide plan of education for understanding and cooperation among nations. The plan that emerged became the first broadly based attempt to develop a curriculum framework in international education. The plan became known as the Herman–Jordan plan after the donor (Mr Raphael Herman) and the prize-winning plan (by Dr David Starr Jordan of Stanford University), which included the building of a world-based curriculum through the training of teachers from a new, international point of view (Thomas 1932: 189–90). The popularity of the Herman-Jordan Plan can be measured, to some extent, by the fact that in the 1939 WFEA convention the original Herman–Jordan Plan was re-interpreted and extended by WFEA and a new committee was created to take over the work of its historical 'Herman–Jordan Section'. The new section was termed the Committee on International Education (WFEA 1939: 154–5). The association also outlined specific activities in international education, including: teaching international relations, teaching of foreign languages and cultures, establishing international speakers bureaus, promoting residence and study abroad, as well as international correspondence, review of textbooks and peace education, among others.

The School of Education at Indiana University was the site of one of the earliest and most significant educational research projects on international education. Smith and Crayton (1929) were responsible, under the auspices of the WFEA, to support the mandate of that organization which was 'that of instilling in all mankind good will toward each other' (p. 7). The purpose of the study was the development of a statement of principles towards 'education for world friendship'. Among the concepts treated in the study were: world-mindedness, internationalism, international understanding and 'a state of mind transcending national boundaries' (1929: 39–40).

INTERNATIONAL SCHOOL OF GENEVA

In 1924, the International School of Geneva/École Internationale de Genève was founded by a group of the first international organizations established under the aegis of the League of Nations, in conjunction with Adolphe Ferrière and Elisabeth Rotten of the Rousseau Institute in Geneva (École Internationale de Genève 2001; Hill 2001). From the start, the school was philosophically committed to internationalism. Wooton (1929) reported in *School and Society* that the International School of Geneva had a 'school population that is truly international in character, there being sixteen nationalities represented in the student body in grades from one to twelve, inclusive, and seven nationalities in the staff of twenty-two teachers' (p. 23). By the 1950s, Kenworthy (1951: 216) reported that the International School of Geneva had 360 students in the primary and secondary programmes under the supervision of Madame Maurette and her multinational teaching staff.

YOKOHAMA

Within weeks of the opening of the international school in Geneva in 1924, a similar school for children of foreigners was opened in Yokohama, Japan shortly after the Great Kanto earthquake (Stanworth, 1998). By 1929, Yokohama International School was linking its work with an international curriculum related to the International Fellowship for New Education. Minutes of the December 10th, 1930 meeting of the board of governors of the school indicated a serious attempt to come to grips with the points of tension between national sentiments and international aims of an international school. Stanworth (1998) related that the controversy centred on a decision whether to have a national or international focus to the curriculum.

INTERNATIONAL BUREAU OF EDUCATION

In 1925, the International Bureau of Education/Bureau International d'Éducation (IBE) was founded as a private organization by the Institut J.J. Rousseau (University Institute of Educational Services) in Geneva. Its organizing committee was chaired by Professor Edouard Claparède from Geneva (Brickman 1950: Harley 1931; Scanlon 1960: 17; Suchodolski et al. 1979) In 1929, the International Bureau of Education (BIE) was reorganized as an intergovernmental body (Brickman 1950; Carr 1944, 1945; Suchodolski et al. 1979). By 1938, the International Bureau of Education had 17 national members (Carr 1945). In Butt's (1944) translation of Rossello's (1943) landmark work, it is evident that the International Bureau of Education and those early supporters of its work represent the institutional memory of international education in the first several decades of the twentieth century. Rossello's description of that history is comprehensive and represents a vital resource for researchers (Butts 1944; Rossello 1943).

DANIEL PRESCOTT

Daniel Prescott (1930) of Rutgers University undertook a comprehensive survey of the early results of educational programmes in Europe that were concerned with international relations. With a grant from Harvard University, he travelled through European nations in 1926, including England, Switzerland, France, Austria, Czechoslovakia and Germany. Over the course of two, one-year projects (1926–7 and 1927–8), he interviewed educational leaders and teachers, visited schools and universities, examined curriculum guides and materials, surveyed professional literature and interviewed international professionals associated with the several newly formed, multilateral institutions concerned with international education. These included the International Bureau of Education and the International Institute of Intellectual Cooperation in Paris. Prescott concluded his study by outlining both the expressive definition of international education which encourages 'international understanding' and the more ideological definition which calls for the training of world citizens (p. 138) and also called for a 'scientific' grounding of international education.

In 1930, Kees Boeke's Children's Community Workshop at Bilthoven, Holland was established as an international school (Brickman 1950; Meyer 1949). Meyer noted that Kees Boeke wished, in 1949, to 'extend the work of the school on an international basis, with pupils in the Children's Community coming from many lands' (p. 586). Hill (2001) reported that decades later, Boeke persuaded UNESCO to seriously consider direct support of international schools. Boeke proposed to the assistant director-general of UNESCO a globally based network of international schools working towards world citizenship using an internationally recognized diploma.

JOHN E. HARLEY

In 1931, John E. Harley produced a 600-page encyclopedic survey of agencies 'educating for a new world' (Harley 1931). Today it represents a fundamental resource for research

in international education and catalogues a comprehensive range of organizations and schools engaged in international education in the interwar period. The publication was supported by research at the League of Nations offices in Geneva and drew from sources around the world. Another valuable research document was a study by Stewart Stoker (1933), who published a comprehensive survey of efforts to promote international understanding through formal education with a chapter devoted to international schools.

ISAAC LEON KANDEL

Isaac Leon Kandel of Columbia University may be considered the leading researcher in International Education in the twentieth century. His work during the middle five decades was matched in importance by very few other academics in the West. His views on the importance of rooting international education in the national ethic were widely demonstrated in his writings. In his seminal text on comparative education, Kandel (1933) called for the discovery of 'common elements' of international understanding, and proposed the creation of a nationalist sentiment in the context of human progress and not the narrow lens of nationalism alone (Kandel 1933: 868). This theme was to be repeated in research work throughout his lifetime. Kandel also provided a cogent and often-cited perspective on the definition of international education, or what was understood in research circles of the time as 'education for international understanding' (Kandel 1937: 36–7). His work in the field continued well beyond the Second World War (Kandel 1952, 1955, 1957; Pollock 1989).

In 1938, Collège Cévénol was founded in central France by Messieurs Trocmé and Theis as an international school that was founded upon a 'sense of idealism for world peace' and 'student exchanges as a means of facilitating intercultural understanding' (Hill 2001: 16). The same year saw Caroline Woodruff, the president of the National

Education Association (USA), preside over a remarkable Seventy-Sixth Annual Meeting of the Association in New York City in June of 1938. The theme of the meeting was 'The Responsibility of Education in Promoting World Citizenship', which was framed after a questionnaire that was widely distributed before the convention with three questions related to the teaching of world citizenship (Woodruff 1938: 44).

Shortly following the end of the Second World War, Donald Tewksbury (1945) of Teachers College in New York, wrote extensively on the 'New Directions in International Education' and reflected on the history and emergent definition of the field of international education at that time (Tewksbury 1945: 293). Tewksbury also summarized the need for international education and put forward seven 'propositions' with regard to international education given the 'world conditions' (Tewksbury 1945: 299).

UNESCO EARLY DAYS

Kenworthy (1951), in reviewing the early work of UNESCO in education for international understanding, cited an international seminar in Sèvres, France that examined the social studies programmes in various countries (Wilson 1947a, 1947b). In this report (Wilson 1947b) the aims of international education were proposed by the working group: 'In our discussions of the relationship of educational aims to international understanding, we found that four such dimensions or areas of objectives seemed to constitute the essential ingredients of international understanding or for the development of a world citizen' (pp. 27–8). Kenworthy (1947) was the lead author of a working group paper on Social Studies teaching at this UNESCO seminar. The working group report was significant in that, for the first time, a detailed description of an 'internationally minded' person, in educational terms, was developed by a widely representative group of educators.

In 1949, UNESCO convened a 'Conference of Principals of International Schools' in Paris which attracted 15 schools 'wishing to develop an international outlook' (Hill 2001: 17). Kees Boeke compiled the list of invitations based on those that he had previous contact with regarding international education. Those invited included: Kurt Hahn of Gordonstoun School in Scotland; Madame Hatinguais of the Centre International d'Études Pédagogiques in Sèvres; Madame Roquette of the International School of Geneva; Prince of Hanover from the Salem School in Germany; Quakerschool, in Eerde-Ommen in the Netherlands; the Dartington Hall and Badminton Schools in England; the Pestalozzi Children's School in Switzerland; the Odenwaldschule of Germany; the Collège Cévénol in France; Viggbyholmsskolan in Sweden; and the Riverdale Country School from the United States. It was further reported that the meeting in Paris discussed both the establishment of a worldwide network of international schools and the training of teachers for such schools (Hill 2001: 18).

WILLIAM BRICKMAN'S MILESTONE BIBLIOGRAPHY

William Brickman (1950), Distinguished Professor of Education at the University of Illinois, published the only comprehensive annotated research bibliography on the history of international education in the *Encyclopedia of Educational Research* (Monroe 1950). Brickman was considered by Scanlon and Shields (1968) to be a major historian of international education. In one of the few attempts in the twentieth century to approach the task of providing a historical framework for international education, Stewart Fraser and William Brickman (1968) published a documentary history of the field which focused on the works that were evident from the nineteenth century. They do give credit to David Scanlon, who several years earlier published a 'documentary history' of international education and they provide very detailed definitions of the field (Fraser and Brickman 1968: 1). However, Brickman's work as a historian stands alone, and also serves as an important milestone in attempts to create a credible mapping of the territory of international education through the nineteenth and twentieth centuries. At a practical level, his work is of seminal importance to an understanding of what is available to researchers.

CONCLUSION

The task of constructing a lineage for the field of international education deep into the nineteenth century now needs to be approached with confidence. The field, which emerged in a nascent form at the London Universal Exposition in 1851, within four decades would show evident interest and necessity at the Columbian Exposition in 1893. The turn of the century saw an explosion of business and professional groups operating with at least some international cooperation. The rise of international schools in London in 1866, Calcutta in 1921, in Geneva and Yokohama in 1924, eventually led to a growth that is now measured in the thousands. The interwar period witnessed the rise of both an institutional response to an emerging professional discipline (WFEA/IBE/IIE) and a significant rise in research efforts at the university level.

The century of work in international education outlined above presents abundant evidence of a clear lineage for the field deep into the Victorian Age. The challenge for researchers now is to dig deeply into the historical documents of these ten decades to find the roots of current efforts world-wide 'to build up a new people whose country is the world, whose countrymen are all mankind' (Andrews 1908: 289). The significance of these historical materials that we have yet to study is that they will, likely, inform our own understanding of the roots of our common quest.

REFERENCES

Altbach, P.G. (1970) The international student movement. *Journal of Contemporary History*, 5(1): 156–74.

Anderson, L.F. (1981) Research on Teaching Issues in International Education. A paper prepared for the National Institute of Education, National Council on Education Research, Washington, DC (ERIC document No. ED203712).

Andrews, F.F. (1908) The relation of teachers to the peace movement. *Education: A monthly magazine*, 28: 279–89.

Andrews, F.F. (1915) The education of the world for a permanent peace. In *Journal of Proceedings and Addresses of the Fifty-Third Annual Meeting of the National Education Association and International Congress on Education held at Oakland, California, August 16–27, 1915*. Ann Arbor, MI: National Education Association pp. 246–51.

Andrews, F.F. (1919) *American School Citizenship League: An Eleven Year Survey of the Activities of the American School Peace League*, Boston, MA, pp. 7–10. Cited in D.G. Scanlon (ed.) (1960) *International Education: A Documentary History*. New York: Columbia University, Bureau of Publications, Teachers College, pp. 61–4.

Andrews, F.F. (1924) International good-will day. *School and Society*, XIX (490): 576–7.

Andrews, F.F. (1927) The teacher as an agent of international good will. *School and Society*, XXVI (657): 121–30.

Andrews, F.F. (1948) *Memory Pages of My Life*. Boston, MA: Talisman Press.

Arum, S. and Van de Water, J. (1992) The need for definition of international education in U.S. universities. C.B. Klasek (ed) *Bridges to the Future: Strategies for Internationalizing Higher Education*. Carbondale, IL: Association of International Education Administrators.

Bell, G. (1863) Proposed international schools. *Journal of the Society of Arts*, XI (540): 27 March, p. 336.

Brickman, W.W. (1950) International education., W.S. Monroe (ed.) in *Encyclopedia of Educational Research*. New York: Macmillan, pp. 617–27.

Brickman, W.W. (1962) International relations in higher education, 1862–1962. In W.W. Brickman and S. Lehrer (eds) *A Century of Higher Education: Classical Citadel to Collegiate Colossus*. New York: Society for the Advancement of Education, pp. 208–39.

Brickman, W.W. (1964) Historical development of governmental interest in international higher education. In S. Fraser (ed.) *Governmental Policy and International Education*. New York: John Wiley & Sons: pp. 17–46.

Butler, N.M. (1912) Division of intercourse and education: report of the acting director. In *Carnegie Endowment for International Peace, Yearbook for 1911*. Washington, DC: Carnegie Endowment for International Peace, pp. 43–71.

Butler, N.M. (1914) The Carnegie Endowment for International Peace, *International Conciliation*, 75: 3–14.

Butts, M. (trans) (1944) *Forerunners of the International Bureau of Education: A hitherto unrecorded aspect of the history of Education and of International Institutions,* written by P. Rossello. London: Yearbook of Education, Evans Brothers.

Butts, R.F. (1969) America's role in international education: a perspective on thirty years. In Harold G. Shane (ed.), *The United States and International Education – The Sixty-Eighth Yearbook of the National Society for the Study of Education.* Chicago: University of Chicago Press.

Carr, W.G. (ed.) (1944) *International Frontiers in Education – The Annals of the American Academy of Political and Social Science.* Philadelphia: The American Academy.

Carr, W.G. (1945) *Only by Understanding* (Foreign Policy Association Headline Series), 52. New York: Foreign Policy Association.

Compayré, G. (1903) *The History of Pedagogy.* Boston, MA: D.C. Heath and Company.

Duggan, S.P. (1920) *First Annual Report of the Director: Institute of International Education.* New York: Institute of International Education.

École Internationale de Genève (2001) *1924: The Birth of the First International School.* www.ecolint.ch.

Faries, J.C. (1915) *The Rise of Internationalism.* New York: W.D. Gray.

Fraser, S.E. and Brickman, W.W. (1968) *A History of International and Comparative Education: Nineteenth-Century Documents.* Glenview, IL: Scott Foresman and Company.

Gregory, Winifred (ed.) (1938) *International Congresses and Conferences, 1840–1937: A union list of their publications available in libraries of the United States and Canada.* New York: H.W. Wilson & Co.

Gutek, G.L. (1993) *American Education in a Global Society: Internationalizing Teacher Education.* New York: Longman.

Harley, J.E. (ed.) (1931) *International Understanding: Agencies Educating for a New World.* Stanford, CA: Stanford University Press.

Harris, W.T. (1898) Our educational exhibit at the international exposition in Paris in 1900. In *National Education Association Journal of Proceedings and Addresses of the 37th Annual Meeting.* Washington, DC: National Education Association, pp. 122–31.

Hill, I. (2001) Early stirrings: the beginnings of the international education movement. *International Schools Journal,* XX (2): 11–22.

Kandel, I. L. (1933) *Comparative Education.* New York: Houghton Mifflin.

Kandel, I.L. (1937) Intelligent nationalism in the school curriculum. In I.L. Kandel and G.M. Whipple (eds) *Thirty-Sixth Yearbook of the National Society for the Study of Education, Committee on International Understanding (Part II – International Understanding Through the Public School Curriculum).* Bloomington, IN: Public School Publishing Company, pp. 35–42.

Kandel, I.L. (1952) Education, national and international. *The Educational Forum,* 16: 397–407.

Kandel, I.L. (1955) National and international aspects of education. *International Review of Education,* 1: 5–15.

Kandel, I.L. (1957) Nationalism and internationalism in education. *Harvard Educational Review,* XXVII: 75–84.

Kenworthy, L.S. (1947) Social Studies teaching and international understanding. UNESCO Seminar on Education for International Understanding (Sèvres). Paris: UNESCO Archives.

Kenworthy, L.S. (1951) The schools of the world and education for a world society. In C.O. Arndt and S. Everett (eds) *Education for a World Society.* New York: Harper and Brothers, pp. 199–230.

Kripalani, K. (1962) *Rabindranath Tagore: A Biography.* New York: Grove Press.

La Fontaine, M.H. (1911) The work done by private initiative in the organization of the world. In Gustav Spiller (ed.) *Papers on Inter-racial Problems Communicated to the First Universal Races Congress Held at the University of London, July 26–29, 1911.* London: P.S. King and Son, pp. 243–54.

League of Nations (1922) Minutes of first session of the Committee on Intellectual Cooperation. League of Nations, Geneva, 1–5 August.

Lengyel, E. (1951) Internationalism in education. In A.H. Moehlman and J .S. Roucek (eds) *Comparative Education.* New York: Dryden Press. pp. 594–620.

Lochner, L.P. (1911) The cosmopolitan club movement. In Gustav Spiller (ed.) *Papers on Inter-racial Problems Communicated to the First Universal Races Congress Held at the University of London, July 26–29, 1911.* London: P.S. King and Son, pp. 439–42.

Lochner, L.P. (1912) The cosmopolitan club movement. *International Conciliation,* 61: 3–14.

Meyer, A.E. (1949) *The Development of Education in the Twentieth Century.* Westport, CT: Greenwood Press.

Monroe, P. (ed.) (1919) *A Cyclopedia of Education.* New York: Macmillan.

Monroe, P. (1927) International aspect education. In *Proceedings of the Second Biennial Conference of the World Federation of Education Associations held at Toronto, Canada, August 7–13, 1927.* Augusta, ME: World Federation of Education Associations, pp. 142–8.

Monroe, P (1931) Proceedings of the Thirty Fourth Regional Conference of the World Federation of Education Associations, *School and Society.* 34: p. 865.

Monroe, P. (1936) *Conference on Examinations (July 1935) under the Auspices of the Carnegie Corporation, the Carnegie Foundation, the International Institute of Teachers College of Columbia University.* New York: Teachers College of Columbia University.

Monroe, P. (1938) Tokyo Conference of the World Federation of Education Associations. In *Proceedings of the Seventy-Sixth Annual Meeting of the National Education Association held in New York City, July 26–30, 1938.* Washington, DC: National Education Association, pp. 648–50.

Monroe, P. (ed.) (1939) *Conference on Examinations (July 1938) under the Auspices of the Carnegie Corporation, the Carnegie Foundation, the International Institute of Teachers College of Columbia University.* New York: Teachers College of Columbia University.

Monroe, W.S. (1919) International congresses of education. In Paul Monroe (ed.) *A Cyclopedia of Education.* New York: Macmillan, pp. 477–8

Monroe, W.S. (ed.) (1950) *Encyclopedia of Educational Research.* New York: Macmillan.

NEA (National Education Association) (1894) *Proceedings of the International Congress of Education of the World's Columbian Exposition, Chicago, July 25–28, 1893.* New York: National Education Association.

Periaswamy, A. (1976) Rabindranath Tagore's philosophy of international education. Unpublished dissertation, Loyola University of Chicago, USA.

Pollack, E. (1989) Isaac Leon Kandel: a pioneer in comparative and international education. Unpublished dissertation, Loyola University of Chicago, USA.

Potter, P.B. (1948) *An Introduction to the Study of International Organization.* New York: Appleton–Century–Crofts.

Prescott, D. (1930) *Education and International Relations: A Study of the Social Forces that Determine the Influence of Education.* Cambridge, MA: Harvard University Press.

Rossello, P. (1943) *Les Précurseurs du Bureau International d'Éducation.* Geneva: International Bureau of Education.

Scanlon, D.G. (1959) Pioneers of international education: 1817–1914. *Teachers College Record,* 62: 209–19.

Scanlon, D.G. (ed.) (1960) *International Education: A Documentary History.* New York: Teachers College of Columbia University, Bureau of Publications.

Scanlon, D.G. and Shields, J. (eds) (1968) *Problems and Prospects in International Education.* New York: Teachers College Press.

Scott, W. (1912) *World Education: a discussion of the favorable conditions for a world campaign for education.* Cambridge, MA: Harvard University Press.

Shirley, D. (1992) *Politics of Progressive Education: The Odenwaldschule in Germany.* Cambridge, MA: Harvard University Press.

Smith, H.L. and Crayton, S.G. (1929) Tentative programme for teaching world friendship and understanding in teacher training institutions and in public schools for children who range in age from six to fourteen years of age. In *Bulletin of the School of Education.* Bloomington, IN: Indiana University, Bureau of Cooperative Research.

Spaulding, S., Singleton, J. and Watson, P. (1968) The context of international development education. *Review of Educational Research,* XXXII (3): 201–12.

Stanworth, D. (1998) An international education at Yokohama International School: from theory to practice. Unpublished Masters dissertation, University of Bath, UK.

Stewart, W.A.C. (1972) *Progressives and Radicals in English Education, 1750–1970.* London: Macmillan.

Stoker, S. (1933) *The Schools and International Understanding.* Chapel Hill, NC: University of North Carolina Press.

Stomfay-Stitz, A.M. (1993) *Peace Education in America 1828–1990: Sourcebook for Education and Research.* London: Scarecrow Press.

Suchodolski, B., Roller, S., Stock, R., Avanzini, G., Egger. E. and de Oliviera, R. (eds) (1979). *The International Bureau of Education in the Service of Educational Development.* Paris: UNESCO.

Sylvester, R.F. (2002a) The 'first' international school. In M.C. Hayden, J.J. Thompson and G.R. Walker (eds) *International Education in Practice: Dimensions for National and International Schools.* London: Kogan Page, pp. 3–17.

Sylvester, R.F. (2002b). Mapping international education: a historical survey 1893–1944. *Journal of Research in International Education,* 1 (1): 90–125.

Sylvester, R.F. (2003) Further mapping of the territory of international education in the 20th century (1944–1969). *Journal of Research in International Education,* 2 (2): 185–204.

Sylvester, R.F. (2005) Framing the map of international education (1969–1998). *Journal of Research in International Education,* 4 (2): 123–51.

Tewksbury, D.G. (1945) New directions in international education. *Teachers College Record,* (5): pp 293–301.

Thomas, A.O. (1932) Education and the world viewpoint. In *Proceedings of the Seventieth Annual Meeting of the National Education Association held at Atlantic City, New Jersey, June 25–July 1, 1932.* Washington, DC: National Education Association, pp. 186–90.

Vestal, T. (1994) *International Education: Its History and Promise for Today.* Westport, CT: Praeger Press.

Waterman, R. (1893) International educational congresses of 1893. *Educational Review,* VI: 158–66.

WFEA (1926) Proposed articles of incorporation of the World Federation of Education Associations. In *Proceedings of the Sixty-Fourth Annual Meeting of the National Education Association held at Philadelphia, Pennsylvania, June 27–July 2, 1926.* Washington, DC: National Education Association. pp. 998–1003.

WFEA (1939) *Proceedings of the Meetings on Board the* S.S. Rotterdam *and at the University of Puerto Rico during the Goodwill Cruise to Latin and South America, July 7–August 28, 1939.* Washington, DC: World Federation of Education Associations.

Wilson, D.N. (1994) Comparative and international education: fraternal or siamese twins? A preliminary genealogy of our twin fields. *Comparative Education Review,* 38 (4): 449–86.

Wilson, H.E. (1947a) Report on the Summer Seminar in Education for International Understanding by the Director of the Seminar. Paris: UNESCO Archives.

Wilson, H.E. (ed.) (1947b) Working Papers on the education of adolescents in international understanding and goodwill. Seminar on Education for International Understanding at Sévres. Paris: UNESCO Archives.

Wood, S.L. (1903) The International Kindergarten Union. In *Journal of Proceedings and Addresses of the Forty-Second Annual Meeting of the National Education Association held at Boston, Massachusetts, July 6–10, 1903.* Winona, MN: NEA, p. 406.

Woodruff, C.S. (1938) Into one great educational brotherhood. In *Proceedings of the Seventy-Sixth Annual Meeting of the National Education Association held in New York City, July 26–30, 1938,* pp. 40–7. Washington, DC: National Education Association.

Wooton, F. (1929) The International School of Geneva. *School and Society* (Special Correspondence) XXX (758): 23–5 (6 July).

2

International Education as Developed by the International Baccalaureate Organization

Ian Hill

This chapter traces the development of international education as conceived and practised by the International Baccalaureate Organization (IBO) since its foundation. The first section discusses the evolving nature of international education and the learning environments in which it takes place. This is followed by the idealistic, pedagogical and pragmatic reasons for the creation of the IB Diploma Programme during the 1960s as a service to international schools. The inculcation of humanitarian values was, and still is, a major objective of an IB education. International education in practice, as depicted by the IBO's Diploma Programme, Middle Years Programme (MYP) and Primary Years Programme (PYP), is outlined in the next section. Appropriate school learning environments are then discussed, including that of the increasing number of government schools adopting an IB programme.

The importance which the IBO places on values education for responsible world citizenship is then discussed with examples from IBO documents. This is followed by the knowledge, skills and attitudes which an IB international education seeks to develop. The final section offers a diagrammatical representation of the aims of an IB education and refers to the 'IB learner profile' as a significant advance in defining international mindedness – a concept at the centre of international education.

THE EVOLVING NATURE OF INTERNATIONAL EDUCATION

Sylvester (2002) has ably demonstrated that the term 'international education' was in use from the 1860s and so were international schools. However, it was not until after the First World War that international schools gained sufficiently in world-wide distribution, and in common characteristics, that the beginnings of a movement became noticeable. These were schools catering for internationally mobile families thus leading to a culturally diverse student population. It was only after the Second World War that four successive associations were formed to bring international schools together for mutually beneficial cooperation in areas such as curriculum development, administration, recruitment of staff, teacher training and annual conferences. These associations were the Conference of Principals of International Schools 1949 (which became the Conference of Internationally Minded Schools from 1951), the International Schools Association (ISA) 1951, International Schools Services 1955, and the European Council of International Schools 1965. The first of these was subsumed into the ISA in 1969; the others are still active. For more information on this earlier period and these associations see Hill (2001a, 2001b).

In the late nineteenth and early twentieth centuries international education was understood as students being educated in a school with many different nationalities (first mooted by Comenius, quoted in Sylvester 2002: 96) or moving between a network of institutions across a number of countries to learn languages and experience different cultures at first hand (Sylvester 2002: 101), as the Conference of Internationally Minded Schools wanted to do. It was thought that international education could only take place in a context where people of other cultures were present and this explains why it was, for a long time, closely associated with international schools. Desmond Cole-Baker, head of the International School of Geneva and co-founder of the IB diploma programme, saw that international education was not just the province of international schools when he said: 'In a true international school [of diverse cultures], international education is a question of environment; in a national school it is a frame of mind''' (Cole-Baker 1989). Apart from learning other languages, the contribution to international mindedness of formal curriculum transactions within a school attracted little attention until the 1930s, when world history and world geography courses began to appear, such as those developed at the International School of Geneva (Oats 1952: 26–8).

A distinction should be made between the means by which an international education is delivered, and the knowledge, skills and attitudes which comprise it. Today, research has shown that international education manifests itself through various conduits: the formal curriculum, educational philosophy and values, teachers as role models, informal contact with people of different cultures within and without the school, and governance and management practices. Thompson (1998: 288) has proposed a tripartite model in which a balanced curriculum, cultural diversity, and administrative styles interact to deliver an international education. The International Schools Association (2001) has published an instrument for self-assessment of internationalism, which focuses on four aspects through which international mindedness can be developed: the school philosophy, the cultural composition of the school and its community (internal and external), governance and administration practices, and an international curriculum perspective. These are the transmission modes of the learning environment with which the student interacts.

Other research has concentrated on unravelling the content and pedagogical nature of an international education – the knowledge, skills and attitudes which are 'transmitted'. Much attention has been given to the concept of intercultural understanding (within and between nations) as a major component of international-mindedness: see, for example, Walker (2000b), Heyward (2002), Westrick (2004) and James (2005). A commitment to humanitarian values has also attracted considerable comment: see, for example, McKenzie (1998), Pasternak (1998), Hill (2001c), Drennen (2002: 57–9, 61–2), Gellar (2002), Walker (2004) and Clemo (2005). Other components are identified elsewhere in this chapter.

The IBO was not oblivious to these important developments; indeed, it contributed to them. IB schools represent laboratories of international education practice. The IBO has attempted to refine, through practice, the nature of international education in curriculum terms and has increasingly implemented benchmarks gleaned from the research to ensure that the learning environment of IB

World Schools (as authorized IB schools are officially named) is appropriate. The evolution of international education as formal curriculum in the IB diploma programme is treated in the next section.

THE BEGINNINGS OF THE IB DIPLOMA PROGRAMME

The IB Diploma Programme was initially a curriculum service which the ISA decided, in 1962, to provide to international secondary schools, and the IB Office (as it was initially called) was established officially in 1968 in Geneva to develop and maintain it. The staff of the International School of Geneva, where the ISA office was housed at the time, started to create the syllabi and were joined by teachers and educators from a number of countries.

The nature of this 'curriculum service' was idealistic, pedagogic and pragmatic. The ISA believed that international schools should have a programme of international education as defined by a summer course in 1950 for teachers from around the world at the International School of Geneva:

> [An international education] should give the child an understanding of his [sic] past as a common heritage to which all men irrespective of nation, race, or creed have contributed and which all men should share; it should give him an understanding of his present world as a world in which peoples are interdependent and in which cooperation is a necessity.
>
> In such an education emphasis should be laid in a basic attitude of respect for all human beings as persons, understanding of those things which unite us and an appreciation of the positive values of those things which may seem to divide us, with the objective of thinking free from fear or prejudice. (Course for Teachers Interested in International Education, Final Report 1950: Section I)

This is the first definition of international education devised by a team of practising teachers from international schools and it corresponded to the post-Second World War idealism for a peaceful world. In particular, the second paragraph of the quotation addresses the attitudinal and value dimension, the culminating point of a successful international education. The acquisition of knowledge and the development of skills are, as cognitive elements only, not a complete measure of success for an IB programme. The affective domain must also be stimulated so that attitudes of responsible world citizenship are cultivated. For example, an individual can acknowledge that cooperation is necessary, and master the skills of cooperating effectively, but if the will to cooperate is not present, the knowledge and skills have been attained in vain.

Pedagogically, good teachers saw that their internationally mobile students had different perspectives on issues, events and knowledge: what seemed true in the confines of a national context was questioned by people from other countries. This first became noticeable in history teaching, which has been used by governments to build national allegiance, sometimes at the expense of embracing a range of perspectives. This led to the notion that students in an international school should be taught critical thinking skills. Leach (1969: 208–9), one of the founders of the IB Diploma Programme at the International School of Geneva, described critical enquiry as a process where students should question accepted views, should not expect reassurance for holding conventional opinions, should dissect and weigh the issues 'in whatever universal scales the teacher may find immediately useful', and should be prepared to retreat from entrenched positions in the face of compelling argument and reflection.

The education of the whole person was an equally important pedagogical consideration which draws out emotions and forms attitudes. It was spurred on by Kurt Hahn's 'Outward Bound' movement, whereby young people built up trust and friendship, particularly between different nationalities in an international school (promoting intercultural understanding), as they faced physically demanding tasks together. Engaging in community service was also encouraged by Hahn's philosophy and adopted by Atlantic College in Wales (opened in 1962) which, in turn, influenced the emerging diploma programme when its staff joined with the Geneva teachers a couple of years later. These two activities contributed to character development. Pragmatically, there was a need for a universally recognized curriculum and examination to facilitate university acceptance around the world by internationally mobile students. Early experimental IB Diploma Programme curricula and examinations were accepted by a handful of highly reputable universities, including the Sorbonne, Oxford and Harvard.

So, as it was being formed in the 1960s, IB international education wanted students to recognize that people share a common heritage, to adopt positive attitudes about other cultures, to respect all human beings, to understand that nations are interdependent, to know about history and the present on a world scale, to be able to commit themselves to a society where one could hold opinions freely and to engage in critical thinking, physical exercise and community service.

INTERNATIONAL EDUCATION IN PRACTICE

IB Diploma Programme

The first official general guide to the IB Diploma Programme appeared in 1970. Like subsequent guides, it contained the syllabus and assessment information for each of the subjects offered at the time. Students were to study one subject from each of the following categories during the last two years of secondary education: a first and second language, humanities, experimental sciences, mathematics, the arts or another subject from one of the previous categories. Three subjects were to be taken at higher level which demanded more time and higher analytical skills than the other three at subsidiary (later 'standard') level. In addition, students had to fulfill three other requirements which took shape during the 1970s: theory of knowledge (TOK), an extended essay, and creative, physical and service pursuits.

TOK was in the 1970 guide. It was a course which explored, *inter alia*, the connections between the various branches of knowledge,

differentiated between moral and aesthetic judgments, considered processes of thought, and discussed truth and logic. TOK provided a unifying, reflective and transdisciplinary subject which is today regarded as the cornerstone of the IB Diploma Programme. Creative, physical and social service activities appeared to different degrees in each of the general guides from 1970, but these were not identified as CAS (creativity, action, service) until 1989 with the publication of *CAS Activities: Guidelines for IBO Schools* (IBO 1989). The three parts of CAS were given equal weight and students who failed to participate satisfactorily were not awarded the IB Diploma, even if they passed all subjects.

'Creativity' meant creative and aesthetic experiences such as drawing, painting, sculpture, music, dance, drama, film-making or dress. 'Action' referred to physical exertion in sport, expeditions, mountain climbing, gymnastics and so on. While community service was encouraged, it was realized that in some cultures and geographical locations this was not always easy to accomplish, so the single word 'service' was used to also include service to the school itself; for example, assisting with younger children, organizing clubs and environmental awareness action. By 1978 students were required to submit an extended essay in one of the six subjects for external examination. This exercise was valuable in developing research skills and it provided a degree of specialization in a diploma profile of breadth and balance.

Bilingual diplomas were introduced from 1974 for those candidates who presented at least one of their subjects in the humanities and experimental sciences in a language other than their language A, that is, their first language (IBO 1972: 20). From the beginning, all parts of the IB Diploma were available in English and French; Spanish was officially introduced in 1983. Student evaluation procedures demonstrated a move away from encyclopedic knowledge to a more critical, personal approach to learning. 'All forms of assessment attempt to bring out not the candidate's ability to memorize, but the extent to which he has assimilated and made his own the subject in which he is being tested' (IBO 1970: 22). The 1970 guide outlined the overall objectives of the programme. The explosion of knowledge (and this was long before the Internet) had given rise to:

- the need to educate the whole person
- a bewildering variety of choice; the need for skills and values to choose wisely
- the need to learn how to learn, 'the prime function of school education' (IBO 1970: 24).

The profile of the diploma offered breadth (students being required to study subjects from each of the major traditional disciplines), and a degree of specialization via the higher level subjects and the extended essay.

Awareness of a common humanity and social responsibility (the science courses, for example, included the ethical use of advances in the field), together with interdisciplinary learning skills, were high priorities. Students should also become 'internationally minded' – defined as gaining an awareness of cultures other than their own where the compulsory acquisition of at least one additional language would assist. In this regard, it was suggested that students from 'multinational schools' (that is, international schools) would have the advantage of personal contact with students and teachers from many lands. It was hoped that the IB programme could eventually be extended to students 'in other schools', meaning national state or private institutions. Subsequent general guides remained virtually unchanged until the 1985 version introduced for the first time the term 'critical reflection' for the TOK course and for diploma courses generally. This skill was specifically extended 'to the larger issue of international awareness': appreciating cultures and attitudes other than one's own, and being tolerant and able to communicate with others on a range of topics about which students have already formed considered opinions (IBO 1985: 2–3).

So, the IBO conception of international education focused on developing international-mindedness and it comprised the following:

- educating the whole person with academic breadth and CAS
- citizenship education via service, preferably in the community external to the school
- critical reflection, dialogue and research skills
- intercultural understanding
- learning more than one language
- lifelong education: learning how to learn
- values to enable wise choices for the good of mankind.

Middle and Primary Years Programmes of the IBO

Two important IBO events occurred during the 1990s: the adoption and development of new education programmes for the remainder of school ages. The IBO offered the Middle Years Programme (MYP) from 1994 for children from 11 to 16 years of age, and the Primary Years Programme (PYP) from 1997 for children from 3 to 11 or 12 years. Both programmes were developed at the instigation of teachers, most of whom were familiar with the Diploma Programme. They believed that international-mindedness should start earlier than the last two years of secondary school and that a continuum of international education for all school ages should be established.

The MYP was initially called the International Schools Association Curriculum (ISAC), whose profile had first been discussed at an ISA meeting in 1980 at Moshi International School, Tanzania. It is generally recognized that the major development of the ISAC occurred in a number of French-speaking state schools in Quebec, thanks to Robert Belle-Isle, director of the United National International School, New York, with cooperation from pilot schools in The Netherlands, Argentina and later elsewhere (Hill 2003: 242–3). History repeated itself. As with the Diploma Programme, the ISAC needed an infrastructure to develop further, so an agreement was reached for the IBO to take over the ISAC project in 1992. The IBO did not offer the new acquisition to schools until 1994.

The PYP evolved from a discussion amongst heads of primary schools at the ECIS administrators' conference of 1990 in Rome about a lack of coherence and inconsistency in the educational programme of international schools, urging the identification of common elements of an international primary education. The link with the MYP was not ignored but it was not the priority. By 1992 the International Schools Curriculum Project (ISCP), as it was named, was taking shape, thanks to the efforts of a loose group of dedicated teachers around the world led by Kevin Bartlett, at the time head of the primary section at the Vienna International School (Hill 2003: 245–6). Interestingly, *An International Primary School Curriculum ISA,* compiled and edited by Cole-Baker, then head of the International School of Geneva, was first published in 1966 and revised in 1970. It was not widely distributed and few copies remain today. The ISCP (International Schools Curriculum Project) group was not aware of its existence when they launched their international primary programme. As with the MYP, the ISCP lacked an infrastructure to take the project forward. So negotiations with the IBO resulted in the latter taking over full responsibility for the programme in 1997. The IBO director general remarked:

> The addition of the PYP to our menu of services to schools is both timely and historic. It means that IBO … will be able to offer a full range of options from kindergarten to pre-university, available as separate units (primary, middle, diploma) or as a coordinated continuum with an international focus. (IBO 1996: 3)

Although ISA was not involved in the ISCP initiative, it gave a historical impetus to the need for an international primary curriculum which was eventually fulfilled by the PYP.

Like the diploma programme, the MYP and PYP initially targeted the needs of international schools. In October 2006 there were 508 MYP, 296 PYP and 1,464 Diploma Programmes authorized in schools across the world. The MYP, while preserving the integrity of individual subjects, emphasizes a holistic, transdisciplinary approach. Five 'areas of interaction' are at the core: approaches to learning, community and service, health and social education, environment and *homo faber* (man the maker). These are not additional subjects; they are themes connected across the eight major subject groups which comprise a first language, a second language, humanities, technology, mathematics, sciences, the arts and physical education. The curriculum planning must be both vertical, involving teachers across the five years of the programme, and horizontal, involving teachers of the same year group. Planning is both within subject teams and in interdisciplinary teams corresponding to the areas of interaction.

The PYP places emphasis on transdisciplinary enquiry, balanced against traditional disciplines for which scope and sequence documents, corresponding to each age group, are provided. Six transdisciplinary themes establish a framework for exploring knowledge: who we are, where we are in place and time, how we express ourselves, how the world works, how we organize ourselves and sharing the planet. Teachers use unit planners to cover topics within each of these themes, drawing on two or more of the subject areas of language, social studies, mathematics, arts, science and technology, and personal, social and physical education.

The MYP and PYP eventually influenced each other, and the Diploma Programme. For example, a 'PYP student profile' was developed and then expanded for all three programmes into the 'IB learner profile' (IBO 2006: see Appendix). This is the translation of the IBO mission statement into a set of learning outcomes inherent in the IB continuum of international education where students, teachers and parents strive to be enquirers, knowers, thinkers, communicators, principled, open-minded, risk-takers, balanced, caring and reflective. As part of their internationalism, the MYP and PYP were immediately offered in English, French and Spanish; the MYP was also offered in Chinese from 1997. In consultation with the IBO, schools can teach both programmes in other languages in a bilingual context where an IBO official language is included; there are currently schools teaching the MYP and PYP in Russian, Turkish and Arabic.

Strategically the development of this suite of school-age international programmes occurred in the right order; the unsustainability of the

ISA primary years curriculum supports this view. Without the hard-earned credibility of the Diploma Programme and the IBO itself, it is unlikely that the MYP and PYP would have been so well received by schools, particularly as student success in these programmes is measured more by intrinsic value linked to the education process (although externally moderated certificates are available for the MYP), rather than by the more conventionally acceptable, because easily quantifiable, external validation of diploma programme standards by universities.

The next section considers the learning environments in which these international programmes might best occur.

IB Learning Environments

As a formal requirement, all schools applying for authorization to teach an IB programme undertake a self-study in which they respond to several questions and work towards standards relating to the practice of international education. This is an interactive process whereby the IBO also learns from schools, for example by asking them how they promote international mindedness or how they define international education (DP 2003). In particular, IBO standards for schools delineate a propitious learning environment; they are often identical and certainly similar for the three programmes, as examples to follow should demonstrate.

The concept of a cooperative learning community is an important aspect of an international education, as the following PYP required standard illustrates: 'The school has implemented a school-wide system through which teachers plan and reflect in collaborative teams.' Not only should *students* learn to achieve together, but this should be modelled by their teachers in the implementation and maintenance of the PYP (PYP 2003). Schools are also asked to indicate what the introduction of an IB programme could bring to the community within and outwith the school.

Another standard requires students to act and contribute 'to the well-being of themselves, the community and the environment' (MYP 2004).

Schools must address personal development, ecology and sustainable development through student action and reflection. Action implies the adoption of attitudes and values through knowledge and skills. Skills for resolving issues receive a particular mention in the following standard: 'In the final year of the programme in the school, students will engage in a problem-solving project culminating in the PYP exhibition' (PYP 2003).

Another question asks: 'How does your school's organizational structure support the programmes and philosophy of the IBO?' (DP 2003). Management and governance practices should facilitate the promotion of the IBO mission statement (see later) by modelling responsible 'citizenship' of the school: respecting cultural diversity, supporting action for sustainable development, promoting community service and so on.

Initially IB education was intended 'to facilitate the work of international schools and the mobility of students' as stated in one of the early development plans (IBO 1980: 1). But this was to change. Research was questioning the belief that international education belonged only in international schools and practice was showing that there were other nourishing contexts in which it could prosper. From the first half of the 1980s an increasing number of state schools adopted the IB Diploma Programme in the USA, in the Nordic countries and in The Netherlands. Piet Gathier, former director general of education in The Netherlands and outgoing president of the IBO in 1993, recognized that international education was no longer the prerogative of an exclusive group of mobile people. He said: 'Internationality has become a normal feature of our society and a condition for success in politics, economy, science and education. Today it is a must for students who want to participate fully in our changing society' (Gathier 1993).

Belle-Isle (1986) was one of the first to point out that international schools do not necessarily provide an international education. It was some time later before the idea that it could thrive in a national state or private school was more widely accepted (see, for example, Hayden and Thompson 2000: 50–1; Walker 2000a; Hayden 2002: 116). This was an important realization: international education was no longer seen as a programme only for international schools overseas, but as an experience that was an inherent part of the formal curriculum, wherever it was taught. Schools of fairly homogeneous culture gained intercultural experiences for their students via substitutes such as school trips abroad, activities and speakers in the local community, or the Internet.

There has been a gradual shift over the years towards more participation in IB programmes by government schools. For the May 2006 diploma examinations 65 per cent of the 53,540 candidates were from state institutions. By October 2006, 52 per cent of the 1,888 IB schools (including all three programmes) in 123 countries were state schools with no tuition fees. National state or private schools comprise almost 80 per cent of all IB schools; the remainder are international schools – that is, with a high degree of cultural diversity and usually a majority of internationally mobile students.

This significant trend means that IB programmes and an IB-style education are having an increasing impact on state systems of education as they seek to internationalize their curriculum. It also furnishes a different learning environment from the traditional international school. As a consequence, international education via the formal curriculum becomes more important, particularly as in one study (which did not survey national schools) this aspect was seen to be less pertinent to obtaining an international education than exposure within school to students from different cultures (Thompson 1998: 285). Does this shift mean changes to IB curricula to accommodate state schools? No. The IBO has always concentrated on the diffusion of international education by way of the formal curriculum without, however, ignoring the learning environment that is addressed at the stages of initial authorization, at subsequent programme evaluations and in teacher training workshops.

The values that an IB learning environment should emulate are outlined in the next section.

An Emphasis on Values

Hayden and Thompson (1995: 340) made this important remark: 'Clearly in the perceptions of a number of key protagonists of international education there is more to the concept than … a curriculum based in the cognitive domain'. The aims of the IBO that appeared in a 1992 strategic planning document were to educate young people to act responsibly in a complex global society, to be inquisitive and open to new ideas, and to better understand themselves and others through a heightened capacity for tolerance and respect for different points of view (IBO 1992: 1). The emphasis on attitudes and what the document describes as 'idealistic vision' highlights the affective qualities of the individual. In the same year the IBO president, Thomas Hagoort (1992: 22), stated:

> Our mission [is] the shaping, through education, of individuals in every area of the world who are better able than others to function effectively, constructively and peacefully amidst a diversity of nationalities, cultures, languages and religions – individuals who will be good citizens not only of their communities and their nations, but also of the world.

This is in tune with another comment, just the year before, which reinforced that international education is driven by an ethical base:

> A sense of values is needed to inform [the students'] studies and their life purposes as well. Without it, they may be clever, knowledgeable, even wondrously creative, but they will never become citizens of the world nor give it their gifts as should those who have known a true international education. (Mattern 1991: 216)

From 2003, the IBO subject curriculum committees of practising teachers and outside experts from different parts of the world were asked to emphasize how teachers can make their subjects more international. The internal handbook for Diploma Programme curriculum review (IBO 2005a) urges that the global importance of subjects be reflected and promoted in their aims, objectives, curriculum, assessment and teacher support materials. It also asks that international differences of perspective, economic circumstances, social and cultural diversity be recognized in the subject content. For example, the latest economics guide (IBO 2003: 5) section on internationalism states:

> Teachers ... must aim to promote ... an awareness of how the impact of economics can both improve cooperation and understanding between countries and, unfortunately, cause extensive damage. If all participants in the global economy are to achieve a better quality of life for their populations ... it means sharing concepts across cultures, against a background of economic awareness. ... students must be taught to consider economic theories, ideas and happenings from the points of view of different individuals, nations and cultures in the world economy.

Similar sections on internationalism, adjusted to suit the subject matter, are to be found in all syllabus documents from 2003. In the context of a multicultural approach to curriculum development, Diploma Programme reviewers are asked to consider how different subjects are assessed in different cultures, how this could influence the curriculum and assessment design, and how to exchange ideas and extract good practice from different cultural approaches (IBO 2005a).

The first official IBO mission statement of 1996 was entitled 'education for life' and reads as follows:

> Beyond intellectual rigour and high academic standards, strong emphasis is placed on the ideals of international understanding and responsible citizenship, to the end that IB students may become critical and compassionate thinkers, lifelong learners and informed participants in local and world affairs, conscious of the shared humanity that binds all people together while respecting the variety of cultures and attitudes that makes for the richness of life.

This was revised into a leaner version in 2002 which stated that:

> The International Baccalaureate Organization aims to develop inquiring, knowledgeable and caring young people who help to create a better

and more peaceful world through intercultural understanding and respect. ... These programmes encourage students across the world to become active, compassionate and lifelong learners who understand that other people, with their differences, can also be right.

The new 'IB learner profile' (IBO 2006: see Appendix) for the three programmes contains the following opening statement which clearly shows the values an IB education promotes: 'IB programmes aim to develop internationally minded people who, recognizing our common humanity and shared guardianship of the planet, help to create a better, more peaceful world'.

The nature of the knowledge, skills and attitudes which IB programmes seek to develop are outlined in the next section.

Knowledge, skills and attitudes

The knowledge, skills and attitudes of IB programmes correspond very closely with those identified in the literature on international education. IB students in internationally-minded schools should acquire, from a global perspective, *knowledge* about:

- world issues
- social justice and equity
- interdependence
- sustainable development
- cultural diversity
- peace and conflict
- languages.

Population concerns (migration, ethnicity, refugee issues), fresh water, terrorism and economic injustice are examples of priority global issues. Sustainable development considers a balance between economic growth, protection of the environment, a fairer distribution of material wealth and protection of the earth's finite resources. It is ecologically sensitive and influenced by population growth and movement. In the knowledge dimension students will be able to identify reciprocal influences between countries and peoples and thus realize the importance of the notion of interdependence. Awareness of the human condition leads to knowledge

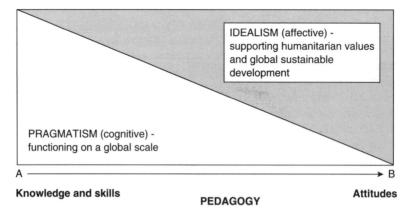

Figure 2.1 International education: pragmatism to idealism

about human rights, ethics, justice, peace and conflict. Once the panoply of cultural behaviour is tapped, the need to acknowledge a range of perspectives becomes evident, the importance of knowing one's own culture as a reference point emerges, and the way language directs thought and behaviour is learned. In sum, knowledge in these areas is indispensable in arriving at responsible world citizenship.

This knowledge is the 'stuff' with which students will work. There is nothing ideological about this content per se; it is rather utilitarian – useful to know, almost factual. Students then need *skills* with which to approach this material. They need skills to explore, for example, why cultural behaviour is different, why there can be opposing accounts of the same historical event, to what extent nations are interdependent, which areas of sustainable development need most attention, how language is inextricably intertwined with culture, the ingredients of peace and conflict, and learning how to live together (Delors 1998). They are skills of:

- critical reflection
- problem-solving
- inquiry
- working collaboratively
- language learning
- cultural literacy
- lifelong learning
- conflict resolution
- transdisciplinary and holistic learning.

Attitude*s* are the 'affective' part of the whole person. This is the ideology in international education. It is the culmination of using the knowledge and skills to fashion individual values. IB programmes seek to promote attitudes of:

- commitment to peace, social justice and equity on a world scale
- compassion and empathy for the feelings, needs and lives of others in different countries
- respect for cultural diversity and human rights
- a belief that people can make a difference
- caring for the environment
- commitment to sustainable development
- friendship and solidarity amongst peoples.

CONCLUSION

The aim of international education as conceived by the IBO is, in the words of Cambridge and Thompson (2004: 173), 'an ideology of international understanding and peace, responsible world citizenship and service'. Figure 2.1 attempts to demonstrate that students use the above knowledge and skills in the cognitive domain to develop informed attitudes in the affective and ideological domain.

Figure 2.1 is not meant to represent a linear progression over time where attitudes are formed at the end; IB students are involved in value-formation throughout their education, and values will change as more information, together with skills to analyse the information, are acquired. It is a never-ending process of accumulation of cognitive attributes which leads to value positions. Figure 2.1 is a snapshot of one of a multitude of such transactions which students will undertake and review throughout their education. The arrow on the base line is to indicate that the cognitive importance of the pedagogy decreases as we move towards point B and the attainment of international education values increases. It is at the level of values – at the attitudinal level – that the aims of international education are realized.

The 'IB learner profile' (IBO 2006) is included as an Appendix to this chapter. It is the embodiment of what the IBO means when it speaks of 'international-mindedness' and represents an important advance in the field of international education. It captures the knowledge, skills and attitudes outlined in the last section. The IBO's common programme standards and practices, to which reference has been made, are used by schools to undertake a preliminary self-study as an essential part of the authorization and subsequent programme evaluation (IBO 2005b) processes. The implementation of the 'IB learner profile' is specified in these standards, which address the nature of the school's philosophy, organization, formal curriculum, informal curriculum and interaction with the school's external community. IB World Schools work towards the attainment of these standards in order to provide a learning environment in which international-mindedness can be nurtured.

REFERENCES

Belle-Isle, R. (1986) Learning for a new humanism. *International Schools Journal*, 11: 27–30.

Cole-Baker, D. (1989) Letter to Ian Hill, 16 April, Paraparaumu Beach, New Zealand.

Cambridge, J. and Thompson, J. (2004) Internationalism and globalization as contexts for international education. *Compare*, 34(2): 161–75.

Clemo, J. (2005) Human rights, education and international-mindedness. *International Schools Journal*, XXIV(2): 24–31.

Course for Teachers Interested in International Education, Final Report (1950) International School of Geneva, 23 July–19 August. Paris: UNESCO Archives.

Delors, J. (1998) *Learning: The Treasure Within*, 2nd edition. Paris: UNESCO.

Drennen, H. (2002) Criteria for curriculum continuity in international education. In M. Hayden, J. Thompson and G. Walker (eds) *International Education in Practice*. London: Kogan Page, pp. 55–65.

DP (2003) Diploma Programme Application Form. Application for authorization. IBO document available on www.ibo.org.

Gathier, P. (1993) Open letter to the members of the IBO Council of Foundation, 22 November. Geneva: IBO archives.

Gellar, C. (2002) International education: a commitment to universal values. In M. Hayden, J. Thompson and G. Walker (eds) *International Education in Practice*. London: Kogan Page, pp. 30–5.

Hagoort, T. (1992) The IB in the twenty-first century. In *Papers from the 1992 Annual North American Regional Conference*, Breckenridge, Colorado. New York: IB North America.

Hayden, M. (2002) International education: pragmatism and professionalism in supporting teachers. In M. Hayden, J. Thompson and G. Walker (eds) *International Education in Practice*. London: Kogan Page, pp. 112–25.

Hayden, M. and Thompson, J. (1995) International schools and international education: a relationship reviewed. *Oxford Review of Education*, 21(3): 327–45.

Hayden, M. and Thompson, J. (2000) International education: flying flags or raising standards? *International Schools Journal*, XIX(2): 48–56.

Heyward, M. (2002) From international to intercultural: redefining the international school for a globalized world. *Journal of Research in International Education*, 1(1): 9–32.

Hill, I. (2001a) Early stirrings: the beginnings of the international education movement. *International Schools Journal*, XX(2): 11–22.

Hill, I. (2001b) The beginnings of the international education movement Part II. *International Schools Journal*, XXI(1): 35–48.

Hill, I. (2001c) Curriculum development and ethics in international education. *Disarmament Forum* no. 3. Geneva: UNIDR (United Nations Institute for Disarmament Research), pp. 49–58. Available from www.unidir.org.bdd (accessed June 2006).

Hill, I. (2003) Phenomenal growth of the IB. In A.D.C. Peterson (ed.) *Schools Across Frontiers*, 2nd edition. La Salle, IL: Open Court, pp. 239–80.

IBO (1970) *General Guide to the International Baccalaureate*. Geneva: IBO.

IBO (1972) *General Guide to the International Baccalaureate.* Geneva: IBO.

IBO (1980) *A Ten Year Plan for the Development of the International Baccalaureate Office.* Geneva: IBO Archives.

IBO (1985) *General Guide,* fifth edition. Geneva: IBO.

IBO (1989) *CAS Activities: Guidelines for IBO Schools.* Geneva: IBO.

IBO (1992) *Charting the Course.* Internal IBO document, Geneva.

IBO (1996) Report of the director general to the IBO Executive Committee. January, IBO archives, Geneva.

IBO (2003) *Diploma Programme: Economics.* Geneva: IBO.

IBO (2005a) Curriculum Review – a guide for Diploma Programme staff leading a curriculum review. In *Diploma Programme Procedures Handbook 2005.* IBO internal document, Cardiff.

IBO (2005b) Programme standards and practices. IBO internal document: Cardiff.

IBO (2006) *IB Learner Profile.* Geneva: IBO.

International Schools Association (2001) *Self-assessing Internationalism: an Instrument for Schools.* Geneva: ISA.

James, K. (2005) International education: the concept, and its relationship to intercultural education. *Journal of Research in International Education,* 4(3): 313–32.

Leach, R. (1969) *International Schools and Their Role in the Field of International Education.* New York: Pergamon Press.

Mattern, G. (1991) Random ruminations on the curriculum of the international school. In P. Jonietz and D. Harris (eds) *World Yearbook of Education 1991: International Schools and International Education.* London: Kogan Page, pp. 209–16.

McKenzie, M. (1998) Going, going, gone … global! In M. Hayden and J. Thompson (eds) *International Education: Principles and Practice.* London: Kogan Page, pp. 242–52.

MYP (2004) Middle Years Programme Application Form Part B. Application for authorization. IBO document available on www.ibo.org.

Oats, W. (1952) *The International School of Geneva: an Experiment in International and Intercultural Education.* Report for BEd, University of Melbourne, Australia.

Pasternak, M. (1998) Is international education a pipe dream? A question of values. In M. Hayden and J. Thompson (eds) *International Education: Principles and Practice.* London: Kogan Page, pp. 253–75.

PYP (2003) Primary Years Programme Application Form Part B. Application for authorization. IBO document available on www.ibo.org.

Sylvester, R. (2002) Mapping international education: an historical survey, 1893–1944. *Journal of Research in International Education* 1(1): 91–125.

Thompson, J. (1998) Towards a model for international education. In M. Hayden and J. Thompson (eds) *International Education: Principles and Practice.* London: Kogan Page, pp. 276–90.

Walker, G. (2000a) International education: connecting the national to the global. In M. Hayden and J. Thompson (eds) *International Schools and International Education: Improving Teaching, Management and Quality.* London: Kogan Page, pp. 93–204.

Walker, G. (2000b) One-way streets of our culture *International Schools Journal,* XIX(2): 11–19.

Walker, G. (2004) Values in education: some thoughts for Ruth. In *To Educate the Nations: Reflections on an International Education,* second edition. Great Glemham, UK: Peridot Press, pp. 83–6.

Westrick, J. (2004) The influence of service learning on intercultural sensitivity: a quantitative study. *Journal of Research in International Education,* 3(3): 277–99.

APPENDIX: IB LEARNER PROFILE 2006

IB programmes aim to develop internationally-minded people who, recognizing our common humanity and shared guardianship of the planet, help to create a better, more peaceful world. IB learners strive to be:

Inquirers
They develop their natural curiosity. They acquire the skills necessary to conduct inquiry and research and show independence in learning. They actively enjoy learning and this love of learning will be sustained throughout their lives.

Knowledgeable
They explore concepts, ideas and issues that have local and global significance. In so doing, they acquire in-depth knowledge and develop understanding across a broad and balanced range of disciplines.

Thinkers
They exercise initiative in applying thinking skills critically and creatively to pose and approach complex problems, and make reasoned, ethical decisions.

Communicators
They understand and express ideas and information confidently and creatively in more than one language and in a variety of modes of communication. They work effectively and willingly in collaboration with others.

Principled
They act with integrity and honesty, with a strong sense of fairness, justice and respect for the dignity of the individual, groups and communities. They take responsibility for their own actions and the consequences that accompany them.

Open-minded
They understand and appreciate their own cultures and personal histories, and are open to the perspectives, values and traditions of other individuals and communities. They are accustomed to seeking and evaluating a range of points of view, and are willing to grow from the experience.

Risk-takers
They approach unfamiliar situations and uncertainty with courage and forethought, and have the independence of spirit to explore new roles, ideas and strategies. They are brave and articulate in defending their beliefs.

Balanced
They understand the importance of intellectual, physical and emotional balance to achieve personal well-being for themselves and others.

Caring
They show empathy, compassion and respect towards the needs and feelings of others. They have a personal commitment to service and act to make a positive difference to the lives of others and to the environment.

Reflective
They give thoughtful consideration to their own learning and experience. They are able to assess and understand their strengths and limitations in order to support their learning and personal development.

3

The Global Education Terminology Debate: Exploring Some of the Issues

Harriet Marshall

Teachers and global educationalists are currently drowning in a sea of seemingly similar terms. Global citizenship education, international education, education with a global or international dimension, development education, world studies, education for an international understanding – and the list goes on. Debates surrounding the distinctness and relationships between such terms within the broad field of global education (used here as an umbrella term) have been around for decades – let us call this 'the big terminology debate'. In the UK this debate has been recently rejuvenated if not launched into an entirely different terrain with explicit government endorsement and advocacy of an international dimension in schools. In a rapidly changing global context this is an exciting time for teachers, activists and educationalists advocating the inclusion of an identifiable global dimension in all aspects of school life (collectively here called global educators).

There is a growing body of literature on the theme of global education, but rarely have discussions hitherto included both references to traditions such as development education or world studies (relating to the work of organizations and individuals advocating the inclusion of a global dimension in mainstream school teaching and curriculum) *and* the tradition of international education (often defined in relation to the international schools and curricula models such as the International Baccalaureate, IB). This chapter intends to acknowledge *all* such traditions, and in doing so invites readers to explore to what extent the big terminology debate continues to matter. Much of the discussion refers to the situation in the UK, but readers will no doubt be able to draw links and comparisons to situations in other international contexts. The chapter begins by outlining the key global education influences on schools and builds upon this analysis by identifying the related but often historically and theoretically distinct traditions and voices working to influence the curriculum and pedagogy of schools. Some of the discussion will relate more to secondary schools (specifically ages 11–16) than primary schools (ages 5–11), but usually global education aims to influence all stages of mainstream schooling.

THE FIELD OF GLOBAL EDUCATION IN THE UK

Throughout this chapter 'global education' is used as an umbrella term. The European Strategy Framework for Improving and Increasing Global Education in Europe to the Year 2015, also known as the Maastricht Global Education Declaration, was the end-product of the Europe-wide Global Education Congress attended by educationalists and governmental representatives from over 50 countries. The following extract from the Congress's welcome address encapsulates the underlying understanding of this chapter (one could add international education to other global education types):

> For some years now, the concept of global education – that is, education for greater justice, democracy and human rights, with a global perspective – has been gaining credence and momentum. However, the ideas and actions behind the concept are certainly not new. Many in Europe and elsewhere have been engaged in those constituent types of education that go together to make up global education – development education, human rights education, intercultural learning, education for peace and conflict resolution, environmental education and education for sustainability … What is relatively new, however, is the notion that these types of education might be brought together internationally through the umbrella term of global education. (Rugus 2002: 1)

Although global education itself can be rather woolly and has particular connotations, for example in the US it can denote a particular social studies curriculum, it is an all-encompassing term that suggests an adjectival educational model with holistic, affective, cognitive and participatory dimensions. In the field of global education in the UK different traditions exist with different levels of

'radicalism' when placed in relation to mainstream educational practice and political discourse – the term 'field' is therefore used to highlight the heterogeneous characteristics of global education.

Numerous global education-related sub-fields can be identified in the UK. Pike (1990) argues that it is possible to trace the roots of these various traditions. Interesting descriptions and analyses of the history of the field of global education exist, although often these are tightly connected to one particular tradition. For example, Hicks (2003) has considered the past 30 years of global education, Holden (2000) the history of the past 35 years of the world studies movement, Heater (1980, 1984) the history of world citizenship education since the work of UNESCO–UK and the Council for Education in World Citizenship (1939 onwards), Starkey (1994) the history of development education since the formation of the Development Education Centres (1960s onwards), and Hill (2002; also Sylvester 2002) the history of international education in relation to international schools (from the 1950s onwards) and the International Baccalaureate (from the early 1960s). Furthermore, over the years global education has become entangled with the respective histories of the intercultural, anti-racist, human rights, environmental and sustainable education agendas (as described in Dufour 1990).

To make some historical sense of the field in the UK I have distinguished between two phases: the first spans from the 1940s to the 1980s and is what I call 'the emergence of the field'; the second begins in the late 1980s/ early 1990s and could be labelled 'the field in changing times'.

Phase I

Global educational developments grew out of the nineteenth-century peace movements in the USA, Britain and continental Europe, culminating in the creation of the School Peace Leagues in the USA, Britain and the Netherlands at the first Hague Peace

Conference in 1899 (Heater 2002). In the UK the terms 'education for world citizenship', 'education for international understanding' and 'global education' were increasingly used in the second half of the twentieth century, especially in the work of the Council for Education in World Citizenship (CEWC) and the UNESCO–UK. From its birth in 1939 CEWC was a non-governmental organization (NGO) that worked with teachers and schools to incorporate global education and, like UNESCO, its objectives were 'to ameliorate the world's troubles by cultivating in the younger generation an international understanding … taken to mean both comprehension and empathy' (Heater 1984: 163). Its history is described with significant periods of 'frustrated ambition' (p. 187) because of a failure to acquire government support (financial or otherwise), as would later be the case in this phase for most other global education organizations. Nevertheless by the early 1980s the pedagogic influence of CEWC upon schools was visible and predominantly took the form of resource support for teachers and schools about how to run 'CEWC School Societies' such as special weeks, meetings, practical projects and simulation games such as MUNGAs ('Model' United Nations General Assemblies).

The 1960s and 1970s proved to be a more active period for global education as various NGOs and policies (such as the UNESCO 1974 *Recommendation on Education for International Understanding*) emerged. In Europe an international curriculum model (the IB) materialized out of the international education field (also strongly influenced by the work and agenda of UNESCO). Meanwhile in the UK regional Development Education Centres (DECs), that is regional NGOs working to promote an awareness of development issues in schools, were set up by interested individuals from the late 1960s onwards. These organizations signified the growing interest in the movement for global education. Funded by aid agencies, these centres were (and still are)

basic resource services in the form of resource shops, catalogues and small libraries; introductory in-service work and in-service work targeted at

particular areas of the curriculum; team teaching, involving co-planning …; curriculum development projects … the production of a wide range of teaching material. (Sinclair 1994: 50–1)

This form of global education maintained strong links from the outset with the development studies discourse featuring in academia from the 1960s onwards (organizations emerged in a similar way in other European countries). Development education in schools was also underpinned by the educational activities of Oxfam and the then Voluntary Committee on Overseas Aid and Development (later the Centre for World Development Education). Other national aid agencies such as ActionAid also emerged at this time. Meanwhile groups such as Friends of the Earth enhanced the movement for environmental studies, and human rights groups such as Amnesty International assisted the movement for human rights education fostered by both UNESCO and the Council of Europe.

Different traditions, discourses and ideologies were also espoused by those such as international educationalists and African and Southern development groups in this period. For example, the international or 'internationalist' education movement, tightly connected with the international or 'internationally-minded' schools, advocated a different model of global education than development education – drawing on 'internationalist' as opposed to 'development' theory. Cambridge (2001, 2002) refers to the work of Leach in 1969 and Hahn in the 1980s, who both promoted international education in mainstream state schools (although their focus was international schools). International educationalists have, like others in the broader global education field, been keen to emphasize the long history of international education theory and practice that it is not simply a 'direct outcome of the horrors of two world wars or a by-product of the second age of globalization' (Sylvester 2002: 91). In this period, international education took the epistemology and curriculum of the IB as its organizing principle with the aim to 'increase the awareness of students and promote reflection and research on global issues' (p. 92). It has been argued that international education, despite its differences to other traditions (including the fact that it worked predominantly in privately funded schools), was still critical to the movement for world citizenship and global education in this period (Sylvester 2002).

African and Southern development groups also began to foster relations with schools in order to promote global, intercultural and interracial awareness in this first phase. Most importantly, groups of black/African descent called for the critical study of colonialism as an essential part of greater understanding of development, and North–South interdependence issues (Osler 1994). Osler states that multicultural and antiracist education discourse shared the explicit 'human rights' values base with development education and other traditions in the field. Indeed, the development education agenda contributed extensively to the debate about re-examining relations with the South in a post-colonial period, and throughout the 1970s and 1980s particularly, NGOs published alternative teaching materials encapsulating new ways of thinking about the South. Some black voices were also heard via the movement for multicultural education in the 1980s – however the relationship between the extensive field of multicultural education and global education is beyond the scope of this chapter, partly because the former is the promotion of intercultural understanding within a national context whereas global education is very much the promotion of global understanding and knowledge within a global context.

Also born in this first phase was the *world studies* tradition, which constituted an example of a movement that actively sought to include a world studies 'curriculum' in schools. The world studies movement, a broad term embodying primary (ages 5–11), secondary (11–16) and teacher training projects, brought together the two strands of *world understanding* and *active learning*. The movement recognized that various global education discourses were in use, as Hicks and Townley reveal in their description of the different names given

to educational responses to global issues ('during the course of the 1970s and early 80s', 1982: 7):

> Amongst the more common phrases relating to this broad field are education for international understanding, global education or global studies, World Studies, development education and peace education. A global perspective may also be present in multicultural education, environmental studies and political education. (1982: 7)

Hicks and Townley (1982) implied that the world studies movement had the potential to unify the above strands of global education particularly because they all aimed to promote a form of 'global literacy' – although acknowledging that each strand contained its own conservative–liberal–radical spectrum (discussed further below), which explained the tensions between each strand.

In the 1960s and 1970s especially, global education traditions reflected critical pedagogic models. For example, reference has been made to the pedagogy of Paulo Freire, Julius Nyerere and Ivan Illich particularly in development education discourse, and there was an emphasis on 'people deciding for themselves', deepening people's 'understanding of their commitment and active responses to development' and 'changing attitudes and encouraging involvement' (Starkey 1994: 16). Different strands of global education, including international education (Walker 2004), also show the pedagogic influence of Jerome Bruner, who believed that 'anything can be taught honestly at any age if the concepts are appropriately framed for the particular age' (Holden 2000: 75). Indeed, the development studies, world studies, human rights and world citizenship traditions were all committed to experiential and participatory learning and

> this thinking was manifested in a methodology that encouraged small group discussion and investigation, with an emphasis on the experiential and cooperative learning and projects that celebrated diversity and challenged stereotypes. (Holden 2000: 75)

This methodology encouraged teachers to look 'anew at decision-making processes and teacher–pupil relationships' (p. 75, a methodology also encapsulated in the important publication *Global Teacher, Global Learner* (Pike and Selby 1998)). Global education in this period was therefore very much about the recognition and change of consciousness, and reflected a student-centred, competence-based pedagogy (Pike 1990), although it was working in schools that were adopting an increasingly performance, and examination-based pedagogy.

Therefore from the mid-twentieth century to the late 1980s the field of global education in the UK became more defined as networks and partnerships formed across different traditions and levels of political radicalism. However, as the Conservative government intensified its control and centralization of education, coupled with a policy emphasis on New Right marketization and economic competition, some global educators were concerned that they were not being listened to and were prepared to make changes in an attempt to change the marginality of the movement for global education in mainstream education.

Phase II (in relation to Phase I)

The second phase has been so distinguished because of key developments in the UK since the end of the 1980s/early 1990s. The core internal and contextual themes affecting the processes of change and development within the field in this period can be summarized as:

- the coordination of global education NGOs and consolidation of global education traditions;
- the increased interest of the government through the 'development awareness' work of the Department for International Development, the Citizenship Curriculum and the Department of Education's international education strategy;
- media coverage of key international agreements and policies placing the global agenda in the public eye;
- growing interest and concern about the phenomena of 'globalization', its meaning and its effects upon society and education;
- new world threats such as terrorism, space weapons and computer viruses provoking new calls for global education and global understanding.

All of these themes have recently affected the structure and content of global education curriculum and pedagogy.

In the UK global education organizations and traditions had to adapt to the changing educational climate with the official adoption of the National Curriculum in 1988 (in which cross-curricular themes such as citizenship and environmental education were recognized but attributed a fairly marginal status). By the early 1990s, the world studies project came to an end while new groups and projects emerged. Many global education-focused organizations had to find new spaces in which to operate. Meanwhile those frustrated by the limitations of traditional curricula began to look at alternative international curriculum models such as those offered by the international educationalists.

Much has been said and written about the characteristics and effects of the political climate from the end of the 1980s to the early 1990s – for example, Ball talked about this as a time in which a conservative agenda, initially sponsored by the New Right, was set up to gradually displace liberal progressive educational ideology (1990, 1994) – needless to say its effects upon empowering educational reform movements were complex. At first the field of global education became increasingly marginalized because the Conservative government failed to endorse its cause and was often suspicious of its underlying ideology (Kirby 1994). Obstacles to global education were rife, on the one hand societal and community groups faced general political criticism (Dufour 1990) and fiscal cut-backs, on the other the Department of Education continued to emphasize the distinct and independent nature of curriculum subject disciplines (a major obstacle for any subject with an interdisciplinary knowledge base).

More recently, however, the Department for Education and Skills (DfES), under the New Labour government (since 1997), endorsed the 'global dimension' (DEA 2001) of the National Curriculum subject Citizenship (DfEE/QCA 1999, 2000) and also launched its own official website on the international dimension to education in 2004 with an accompanying strategy document. The global gateway website (www.globalgateway.org), run by the British Council for the DfES, advocates UK global education strategy documents, the international school award (an accredited scheme for curriculum-based international work in schools) and has a focus on international schools linking. The DfES has also approved NGO global education publications such as *Developing a Global Dimension in the Classroom* (DEA/DfES/DFID 2000, 2005) and *Get Global!* (Price 2003). This latter Freirian-influenced project for 11–16-year-olds related to global education teaching methodology by promoting active citizenship and is a good example of how the global educators in the NGO sector and the government (in this case the Department for International Development, DFID) have been working more together. Of great significance to this relationship was the fact that the DFID also made funding available to NGOs providing support for schools teaching global education through its Development Awareness Fund. However the very different agendas of the two relevant government bodies should be recognized here, as this difference gives voice to two sometimes opposing discourses in global education – the social justice and anti-poverty agenda of the Department for International Development (DFID), and the skills, raising standards and techno-instrumentalist goals of the Education Department (DfES).

Without wishing to downplay the significance of these developments, readers should be aware that much frustration persists about the examination-focused and tightly bounded mainstream national curriculum. It must not be forgotten that, as a movement for social change, the field of global education has a strong history of grassroots activism and a cautious relationship with the state and the government department for education. Where it has existed, external policy on global education has traditionally originated from European or International sources (such as the European Global Education Commission or UNESCO). However, in recent years the Citizenship Curriculum (DfEE/QCA

1999, 2000), the Education for Sustainable Development (ESD) cross-curricular theme, the Race Relations Act (1976, 2000), the Enabling Effective Support strategy (DFID 2002) and the DfES strategy document *Put the World in Your Classroom* (DfES 2004) have had a growing, top-down policy influence at the national level. NGO policy-making in the past few years has also become more consolidated and centralized (such as the widespread endorsement of the *Curriculum for Global Citizenship*, Oxfam 1997, 2002) and this has helped strengthen the field. Meanwhile, international educationalists have recognized an increased interest in alternative curriculum models such as the IB and strategic frameworks for dealing with issues such as the increased mobility and international mixing of pupils (frameworks well established in international schools).

It can therefore be seen that the issue of ideology has continued to play an important role throughout the history of global education. In 1980 Heater included a table (adapted from Richardson 1974, in Heater 1980: 37), which summarized the differing political and ideological assumptions behind the varying world studies programmes in existence in the 1970s in the UK. An abridged version of this is included here (Figure 3.1) because it may be useful for readers to consider to what extent this ideological spectrum permeates global education traditions today in different international contexts. The ideologies of different global education groups should also be understood in the context of the ideology of the government in power.

GLOBAL EDUCATION IN CONTEXT

There are limitations with using the term global education as an umbrella term – as there would be with any of the alternatives. First, educationalists from traditions such as international education have articulated their concerns about the term (such as Walker 2004: 143) and these concerns regularly relate

'Focus'	'Conservative'	'Liberal'	'Radical'
AIMS: the educational task	To evoke loyalty to the nation	To evoke loyalty to the world community as a whole	To create justice both within and between countries
AIMS: Curriculum content	Own national history, culture, achievements, victories	World history, other cultures, East–West conflict, UN	Relevant concepts – 'structural violence', North–South conflict, systems, bias
CLASSROOM: Resources for learning	Textbooks, chalk-and-talk	Worksheets, hand-outs, 'evidence', news cuttings	Experimental – games simulations, and involvement in real issues
CLASSROOM: Teaching style	Class as basic unit, and teacher as instructor	Individuals or small groups as basic unit – teacher as guide	Variety as groupings and roles according to varying tasks
BACKGROUND: School organization	Clear boundaries – e.g. in hierarchy, distinct subjects, seclusion, segregation	Blurring of boundaries – participation, integrated studies, interaction	Variety of boundaries, according to varying tasks

Figure 3.1 Political and ideological assumptions behind the varying world studies programmes in the 1970s (adapted from Heater 1980; reproduced with permission)

to a perceived dilemma with the term 'global' as opposed to alternative terms such as 'international' (or 'world' or 'cosmopolitan'). While 'international' recognizes the existence of nation-states and, more specifically, the boundaries between them (as well as the commonalities), there is an implication that the term 'global' supersedes and sometimes deliberately ignores these barriers. For those promoting international education, an understanding of the nation-state is seen to be a necessary element of 'inter'-'national' mindedness (Skelton 2002), whereas some other global educators might be deliberately concerned about replacing nation-state-focused curricula. Secondly, there is confusion surrounding global citizenship education. Education for world or cosmopolitan citizenship (as advocated by Heater 2002 and Noddings 2005 to name but a few) has clearly identifiable philosophical roots dating back to the ideas of Socrates and the Stoics (as explored by Nussbaum 1997 and Papastephanou 2002). However, these cosmopolitan citizenry ideals

often accompanied by a philosophical defence of 'reform in liberal education' and the replacement of the more dominant communitarian notion of citizenship (Nussbaum 1997; Heater 2002) have yet to permeate mainstream global education practice where the more generic and less well-articulated notion of 'global citizenship' is preferred. However, global education does not necessarily equate with global citizenship education and a recent research project revealed how some global educators in the UK prefer not to use this term (Marshall 2005a, 2005b). Finally, it has been said that global education has become 'in vogue', in the way that international education was in the 1970s, but complications arise when both global education and international education can also be viewed as 'applied comparative education in elementary and secondary schools' (Zachariah 1992: 274). Cambridge and Thompson (2004) also articulate this dilemma in their recognition of the contrasting usages of 'international education' in educational studies:

International education is an ambiguous term ... When coupled in the string 'international and comparative education', it refers to an academic discipline involved with making international comparisons between educational systems. More recently, the term has been used to denote an ideology of education oriented towards 'internationalism' and 'international-mindedness' and the education offered by international schools. (2004: 161)

Many of these antagonisms and debates pale when the field of global education as a whole faces larger common obstacles. The contradictions of a global or internationalized curriculum in education, where education is 'almost by definition a national affair, a cultural affair as well as a competitive economic affair' (Walker 2004: 143), have led those such as Holden (2000) to talk about the 'two agendas' in operation within schools incorporating global education:

one where teachers are pressured to focus on raising standards through prescriptive teaching and another where teachers are told they must encourage debate and discussion and prepare children for active citizenship in a democratic and increasingly global society. (2000: 78)

Taking this statement further, it can be argued that the performance- and examination-based pedagogy of the National Curriculum in England and Wales, for example, is at odds with a generally competence-based, pupil-centred pedagogy advocated by global educationalists. It is widely known that where curriculum subjects (at least those that are more dominant in the school curriculum) are forms of selected knowledge, tightly bounded and intimately aligned to an examination form of assessment, alternative interdisciplinary curriculum forms that emphasize horizontal learning come up against fundamental obstacles. Some of the obstacles to global education relate to teachers' limited global knowledge (explored in Walkington and Wilkins 2000), lack of teacher training in this area, lack of coordination and agreement within the field of global education, and the low status of this cross-curricular dimension within mainstream schooling (as compared with traditional, examinable core subjects) to name but a few.

My own research of the field has suggested that the very loosely defined knowledge base of global education (also considered by Tarrow 1992), entangled with the strength of its affective and participatory dimensions, means that global education experiences a marginal status whether it seeks extracurricular, intercurricular or its very own curriculum space.

A range of responses to these dilemmas has been offered by the different traditions. Two of the better articulated have come from the human rights tradition and the International Schools/IB tradition. Unlike some of the other global education traditions, Tarrow has argued that human rights education has a clearly identifiable 'organising framework for global studies which otherwise can lack substance and focus' (1992: 27) because human rights 'are not an amorphous set of principles ... they are law' (1992: 26). Human rights education advocates an innovative, active and interdisciplinary approach to learning, but is not necessarily associated with a pedagogy that contrasts with mainstream classroom pedagogies. In other words, human rights education relates more to the ethos and climate of a school, with a clearly identifiable conceptual framework for curricula content. Like other authors (Heater 1980; Hicks and Townley 1982), Tarrow recognizes that human rights education, global education, moral education and social and civic education are all competing for attention in schools and all aiming to 'improve our capacities for living humanely and justly with one another' (1992: 29), but that

a focus on the process and content of human rights education would assure attention to the critical aspects of each ... serving as a 'unifying' factor ... Human rights content is not a curriculum add-on, but a means of unifying and integrating existing frameworks. (pp. 30–2)

Figure 3.2 illustrates an alternative way of understanding these sentiments. This model might be applied to the work of UNICEF–UK for example, where its education department strives to encourage teachers to appreciate the underlying importance of human rights

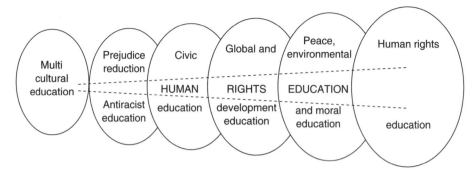

Figure 3.2   Human rights education (adapted from Tarrow 1992: 31)

principles in any global education curriculum. However, Tarrow rightly acknowledges that human rights education varies in different countries, reflecting different childhood socialization practices – and Tarrow herself was actually working within a US context although she also draws upon a range of international contexts. In the light of the UNESCO (1974, 1995) and Council of Europe (1985) resolutions on human rights education, however, it is possible to imagine that human rights curricula are becoming increasingly homogeneous, albeit with a Western-dominated ideology that needs regular critique.

A second response to the obstacles faced by global educationalists has come from the IBO and its notion of an International School with a curriculum explicitly based on international values. To create a sense of 'international-mindedness' there exists a comprehensive body of literature, a non-governmental central organization (and associated but independent International Baccalaureate Research Unit) and network of schools all of which advocate a core, 'international' curriculum. Whilst Primary Years and Middle Years programmes exist, by far the most popular curriculum model around the world originating from this organization is the International Baccalaureate Diploma for 16–19-year-olds. In the UK 52 secondary schools (excluding 16–19 only providers, of which there are an additional 19) have opted to include the IB either instead of or in addition to the mainstream Advanced

Level examinations, and whilst half of these are privately funded institutions, an increasing number of institutions in the state sector are including, or at least investigating, the IB alternative. It has of course been observed that the inclusion of the IB does not necessarily equate with a recognizably 'international' or 'global' school ethos (Gellar 2002), and that the IB curriculum alone does not an international school make. However, nearly half of those state secondary schools which teach the National Curriculum 11–16 in addition to the IB Diploma (16–18) have either been awarded the British Council's International School Award or are in the process of applying for it. Furthermore, the growing interest within the international school field in internationalizing mainstream (non-IB) schooling, transferring conceptual frameworks and incorporating notions of global or cosmopolitan citizenship suggests that this global education tradition is becoming a more prominent one in the UK today.

Having recognized the different forms of global education, I have identified four key global education influences upon UK schools today (Figure 3.3). Some of these are better conceived and more clearly bounded than others. The British Council/schools linking element is the least well defined as it has tight links with the UK government's international education strategy (receiving funding from the DFID and the DfES for its global education work) – although theoretically the British Council is a registered charity and an executive

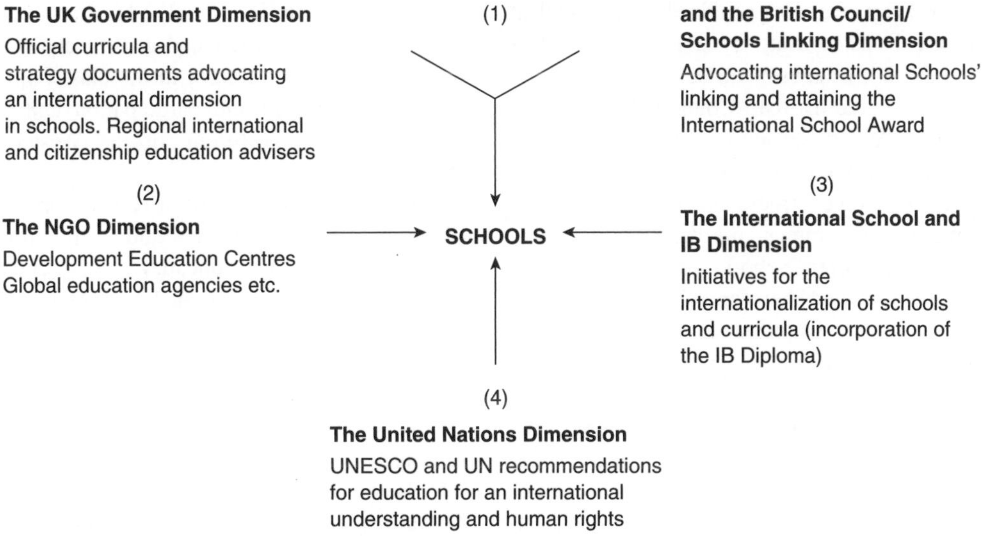

The UK Government Dimension (1)

Official curricula and
strategy documents advocating
an international dimension
in schools. Regional international
and citizenship education advisers

(2)

The NGO Dimension

Development Education Centres
Global education agencies etc.

**and the British Council/
Schools Linking Dimension**

Advocating international Schools'
linking and attaining the
International School Award

(3)

**The International School and
IB Dimension**

Initiatives for the
internationalization of schools
and curricula (incorporation of
the IB Diploma)

SCHOOLS

(4)

The United Nations Dimension

UNESCO and UN recommendations
for education for an international
understanding and human rights

Figure 3.3   Four global education influences upon UK schools today

non-departmental public body. Furthermore, the UN/human rights dimension is often linked to the work of local, national and international NGOs such as UNICEF–UK and some Development Education Centres. However, it is argued that the NGO dimension is a collection of more disparate individuals and organizations, many of whom have their roots firmly within a development education tradition. There is not room in the confines of this chapter to explore the differences and relationships between these influences, but needless to say most are interlinked, with the exception perhaps of the International School and IB Dimension which is only identifiable in a small (and often private) sector of schools (although this is changing).

Rarely has the international school and UK government dimension been so explicitly recognized in relation to the work of global education NGOs. However, in view of the fact that all such dimensions regularly use the same terminology, whether it be global education, global citizenship education, international education or human rights education, I argue that all such dimensions must now be taken seriously – in so doing we can learn to appreciate their respective histories, the similarities and the differences.

DOES GLOBAL EDUCATION NECESSARILY MEAN PUPIL EMPOWERMENT AND CURRICULUM CHANGE?

That this question is even posed will cause great distress to some global educationalists, particularly those located within the more radical spectrum of the field. For example, key global education publications and organizations explicitly advocate *Education for Change* (Kirby/DEA 1994) or *Learning for Change in a World Society* (World Studies Project 1979). However, in a political climate where terms such as global or international education and global citizenship are featuring more regularly within the discourse of official bodies, this might be a timely debate. This debate is more complicated than it might first appear and at the time of writing will involve offering more questions than answers.

The critical pedagogy and powerful affective dimension of many global education initiatives would suggest that global education necessarily requires curriculum change – indeed, it is its *raison d'être*. However, with curricula models such as the IB (even with its student-led Creativity, Action, Service programme and interdisciplinary Theory of

Knowledge course) a certain degree of student choice is taken away by a prescribed (albeit loosely) and examined curriculum. Furthermore, much of the British Council International School Award recognizes the inclusion of global education within mainstream curricula and pedagogic structures, and its schools-linking programmes are designed to work alongside current school structures. It could be hypothesized therefore, that whilst global educators' ideals of student empowerment, Freirian-inspired emancipatory pedagogy and curriculum change inspire their work, in reality the interdisciplinary nature of global education is 'disciplined' by the pedagogical realities of schools (a finding of a recent research project, Marshall 2005a).

A thought-provoking thesis on this topic has been posited by Blaney, who argues that

> Global education is supposed to empower. However ... global education is often premised on an idea about the inexorability of 'globalization' that acts to depoliticize global life and disempower students ... we also should work to disempower our students in certain respects, challenging their sense of interpretive privilege and cultural superiority. (Blaney 2002: 268)

Working within a US context, Blaney therefore suggests 'disempowerment' as a pedagogic strategy, encouraging students to foster humility and self-restraint and a better understanding of 'the self as other'. Significant to this article is the recognition that 'mutual recognition and understanding are impossible where the views and expertise of a narrow band of humanity are privileged' and where 'the line between the racists, the entrepreneurs, and the do-gooders is not so clear as we might hope' (2002: 274). He invites teachers to encourage students to question the process of constructing global problems and issues and recognize the privilege of the West when articulating understanding of the non-West. Global education therefore should include a deliberate refusal of 'the impulse to dismiss alternative values and visions simply as partisan or parochial or backward or unfashionable' (p. 277). Arguably, some global educators (such as the development educationalists) have recognized this need for

critical reflection in global education, but this has yet to be articulated as the need for tighter pedagogical control in the classroom, less student choice and participation and a deliberate 'disempowering' of the Western student.

Cambridge and Thompson (2004) further illustrate the progressive and pragmatic dimensions of global education, where calls for an internationally minded education are both a response to calls for active global citizenship ('interpreted as a response to the existence of poverty and political oppression in the world', 2004: 167) but also as a response to 'emerging affluence and entry into the global consumer economy' (p. 167). The affective dimension of global education therefore – the attitudes, ambitions, values and perceptions – may suggest the need for an empowering and critical pedagogy, but the technical-instrumental role of global education may simultaneously advocate a counter-active top-down pedagogical and curricula model that aims to best serve the needs of future, economically active global citizens. These two dimensions need not be mutually exclusive, but it is possible to argue that they could prove to be highly antagonistic. Another concerning paradox highlighted by these authors refers to the issue that whilst international education aims to foster world peace and understanding between nations, it is also 'part of the process of economic globalisation' where international schools are 'free market response[s] to a global need', and 'the presence in a country of a school offering international education may introduce competition with the national education system' (2004: 168–9).

Many of the above concerns relate to the problematic lack of a shared understanding about the definition, characteristics and role of globalization within the field of global education. Whilst some global education resources about globalization focus upon its negative and economic dimensions other understandings of globalization are identifiable. Certainly there appears to be a consensus about the need to critically engage with the meaning and effects of globalization, but whether this necessitates a student-empowering pedagogy and curriculum is yet to be agreed upon.

CONCLUDING REMARKS

The umbrella term 'global education' might be too non-specific for some within the field but its strength is that it does not exclude or discount the important contributions made by *all* of the traditions contained within it. Global education is therefore a term that has significant homogeneous and heterogeneous facets, which invites observers to recognize both the diversity of its make-up and its common underlying themes. We have an interesting situation in the UK. Global education has been rejuvenated, it is receiving unprecedented media and governmental attention, but this is happening alongside complex and often contradictory agendas. Many obstacles lie in the face of the field of global education, and I argue that these dilemmas invite us to return to debates about the purpose of education in this globalizing world.

This chapter has shown that global educators should be aware of the history and different dimensions of the big terminology debate, but it deliberately avoids answering the question about whether or not this debate really matters. This is because the question requires further research within the field, and it is essential that we listen to all dimensions of the global education field, including the international educationalists, civil servants (voices not always hitherto consulted) and the students. Although a range of literature has been recognized, this chapter ends by pointing to an absence of research into meaning-making in this increasingly debated interdisciplinary curriculum area. Research in this area also needs to take place in other educational contexts world-wide.

REFERENCES

Ball, S. (1990) *Policy and Policy Making in Education: Explorations in Policy Sociology.* London: Routledge.

Ball, S. (1994) *Education Reform: A Critical and Poststructural Approach.* Buckingham: Open University Press.

Blaney, D. (2002) Global education, disempowerment, and curricula for a world politics. *Journal of Studies in International Education,* 6 (3): 268–82.

Cambridge, J. (2001) A Big Mac and a Coke?: internationalism and globalisation as contexts for international education. Unpublished, University of Bath, available online www.staff.bath.ac.uk/edsjcc/.

Cambridge, J. (2002) Identifying the globalist and internationalist missions of international schools. Unpublished, University of Bath, available online www.staff.bath.ac.uk/edsjcc.

Cambridge, J. and Thompson, J. (2004) Internationalism and globalisation as contexts for international education. *Compare,* 34 (2): 161–75.

Council of Europe (1985) *Recommendation on Teaching and Learning about Human Rights in Schools.* Vienna: Council of Europe, Committee of Ministers.

DEA (2001) *Citizenship Education: Global Dimension.* London: Development Education Association.

DEA/DfES/DFID (2000, 2005 updated) *Developing a Global Dimension in the School Curriculum.* London: Department for Education and Skills; Department for International Development; Development Education Association; Qualifications and Curriculum Authority et al.

DfEE/QCA (1999) *Citizenship: The National Curriculum for England, Key Stages 3–4.* Suffolk: Qualifications and Curriculum Authority Publications/Department for Education and Employment.

DfEE/QCA (2000) *Citizenship at Key Stages 3–4: Initial Guidance for Schools.* Suffolk: Qualifications and Curriculum Authority Publications/Department for Education and Employment (DfEE).

DfES (2004) *Putting the World into World Class Education.* London: Department for Education and Skills.

DFID (2002) *Enabling Effective Support: Development Education in Schools* (consultation leaflet). London: Department for International Development.

Dufour, B. (ed.) (1990) *The New Social Curriculum: A Guide to Cross-Curricular Issues.* Cambridge: Cambridge University Press.

Gellar, C. (2002) International education: a commitment to universal values. In M. Hayden, J. Thompson and G. Walker (eds) *International Education in Practice: Dimensions for National and International Schools.* London: Kogan Page.

Heater, D. (1980) *World Studies: Education for International Understanding in Britain.* London: Harrap.

Heater, D. (1984) *Peace through Education: The Contribution of the Council for Education in World Citizenship.* London: Falmer.

Heater, D. (2002) *World Citizenship: Cosmopolitan Thinking and Its Opponents*. London: Continuum.

Hicks, D. (2003) Thirty years of global education: a reminder of key principles and precedents. *Educational Review*, 55: 265–75.

Hicks, D. and Townley, C. (1982) *Teaching World Studies: An Introduction to Global Perspectives in the Curriculum*. London: Longman.

Hill, I. (2002) The history of international education: an International Baccalaureate perspective. In M. Hayden, J. Thompson and G. Walker (eds) *International Education in Practice: Dimensions for National and International Schools*. London: Kogan Page.

Holden, C. (2000) Learning from democracy; from World Studies to Global Citizenship. *Theory into Practice*, 39 (2): 74–81.

Kirby, B./DEA (1994) *Education for Change: Grassroots Development Education in Europe*. London: Development Education Association.

Marshall, H. (2005a) *The Sociology of Global Education: Power, Pedagogy and Practice*. Unpublished doctoral thesis, Cambridge University.

Marshall, H. (2005b) Developing the global gaze in citizenship education. Exploring the perspectives of global education NGO workers in England. *International Journal of Citizenship and Teacher Education*, 1: 2.

Noddings, N. (ed.) (2005) *Educating Citizens for Global Awareness*. New York: Teachers College Press.

Nussbaum, M. (1997) *Cultivating Humanity: A Classical Defence of Reform in Liberal Education*. London/ Cambridge, MA: Harvard University Press.

Osler, A. (1994) Education for development: redefining citizenship in a pluralist society. In A. Osler (ed.) *Development Education: Global Perspectives in the Curriculum*. London: Cassell.

Oxfam (1997, 2002) *A Curriculum for Global Citizenship*. Oxford: Oxfam Development Education Programme.

Papastephanou, M. (2002) Arrows not yet fired: cultivating cosmopolitanism through education. *Journal of Philosophy of Education*, 36 (1): 69–86.

Pike, G. (1990) Global education. In B. Dufour (ed.) *The New Social Curriculum: A Guide to Cross-Curricular Issues*. Cambridge: Cambridge University Press, pp. 133–149.

Pike, G. and Selby, D. (1988) *Global Teacher, Global Learner*. London: Hodder and Stoughton.

Price, J. (2003) *Get Global! A Skills-Based Approach to Active Global Citizenship for Key stages Three and Four*. London: ActionAid.

Rugus, B. (2002) Maastricht Congress on Global Education: Welcome Address. Available online at www.globaleducationeurope.net.

Sinclair, S. (1994) Introducing development education to schools: the role of non-governmental organisations in the United Kingdom. In A. Osler (ed.) *Development Education: Global Perspectives in the Curriculum*. London: Cassell.

Skelton, M. (2002) Defining 'international' in an international curriculum. In M. Hayden, J. Thompson and G. Walker (eds) *International Education in Practice: Dimensions for National and International Schools*. London: Kogan Page.

Starkey, H. (1994) Development education and human rights education. In A. Osler (ed.) *Development Education: Global Perspectives in the Curriculum*. London: Cassell.

Sylvester, R. (2002) Mapping international education: a historical survey 1893–1944. *Journal of Research in International Education*, 1: 90–125.

Tarrow, N. (1992) Human rights education: alternative conceptions. In J. Lynch, C. Modgil and S. Modgil (eds) *Human Rights, Education and Global Responsibilities: Cultural Diversity and the Schools, Volume 4*. London: The Falmer Press.

UNESCO (1974). *Recommendation Concerning Education for International Understanding, Co-operation and Peace and Education Relating to Human Rights and Fundamental Freedoms*. Paris: UNESCO.

UNESCO (1995) *Declaration and Integrated Framework for Action: Education for Peace, Human Rights and Democracy*. Paris: UNESCO.

Walker, G. (2004) *To Educate the Nations 2: Reflections on an International Education*. Saxmundham, Suffolk: Peridot Press.

Walkington, H. and Wilkins, C. (2000) Education for critical citizenship: the impact of teachers' worldview on classroom practice in the teaching of values. *The School Field (International Journal of Theory and Research in Education)*, 11 (1/2): 59–78.

World Studies Project (1979) *Learning for Change in World Society: Reflections, Activities and Resources*. London: World Studies Project/One World Trust.

Zachariah, M. (1992) Linking multicultural and development education to promote respect for persons and cultures: a Canadian perspective. In J. Lynch, C. Modgil, and S. Modgil (eds) *Human Rights, Education and Global Responsibilities: Cultural Diversity and the Schools Volume 4*. London: The Falmer Press.

4

International and Comparative Education: Boundaries, Ambiguities and Synergies

Mark Bray

As noted by other authors in this book, the term international education has multiple meanings in a range of contexts. This chapter examines meanings of the term as commonly used in the domain of international and comparative education. The chapter begins with commentary on the meanings and boundaries of the pair of fields as perceived by a range of authors and organizations. It notes that some bodies that were established with a focus on comparative education have broadened to embrace international education. Other bodies have rejected such broadening; but even in the settings where comparative education is not formally linked to international education, boundaries are commonly ambiguous.

The question then arises whether this feature is problematic. It can be argued that ambiguities obstruct the development of identities, and that academics in particular have a responsibility to conceptualize fields more clearly than they commonly do in this arena. Yet it can also be argued that the ambiguities

provide valuable flexibility in conceptual space, and permit partnerships and synergies. The alliance between international and comparative education can also bring together practitioners and academics.

TERMS AND MEANINGS

A useful geographical location for commencing analysis of the meanings of international and comparative education is the USA. In that country, relationships between the pair of fields have evoked extensive commentary. In 1968, a seminal book was published with the title *Problems and Prospects in International Education*. The editors noted (Scanlon and Shields 1968: x) that few international educators had addressed the problem of definition, but asserted that substantial agreement could be found among those who had considered the matter. International education, the editors stated, was generally defined as 'the various types of educational and cultural relations among nations'. This definition was said to have come from a 1959 report of the House Committee of Government Operations of the US Congress. The definition, the editors pointed out, blurred the important distinction between practitioner and theorist. Scanlon and Shields asserted that the theoretical side was growing in importance, and their book was arguably a manifestation of that statement. However, diversity remained strongly evident in both conceptualization and practice.

In the year that this book was published, the US-based Comparative Education Society (CES), which had been established in 1956, was engaged in vigorous debate about whether its name should be enlarged to become the Comparative and International Education Society (CIES). Erwin H. Epstein was among the opponents of the change. In a Letter to the Editor of the Society's journal, *Comparative Education Review*, Epstein (1968: 376) quoted Scanlon's definition of international education which, as elaborated in the quotation presented by Epstein, stated that while originally the term applied to formal education, 'the concept has now broadened to include government cultural relations programs, the promotion of mutual understanding among nations, educational assistance to underdeveloped regions, cross-cultural education, and international communications'. Epstein argued that international education was less scientific than comparative education, and asserted that while inclusion of international education alongside comparative education would help to broaden the Society's membership base, it risked alienating key members and lessening the Society's academic prestige.

Despite the arguments presented by Epstein and others, the Society's name did change. However, the name of the journal did not: at the Society's 1968 annual business meeting, the proposal to change the name of the journal to *Comparative and International Education Review* had been rejected. The reason given, according to Epstein (1968: 376), was that such a change would have raised havoc with the printer. 'Can it be that a printer's labor is worth more than the desires of the Society's membership?', Epstein protested. 'Or, perhaps, the explanation mirrors the feeling that to link the journal's name with international education, a nonscientific area, would lessen its prestige.'

Epstein returned to this theme two decades later. He had by this time become editor of the *Comparative Education Review*, and felt a need to confront ambiguities in both the nature of the field and the function of the journal. Epstein (1992: 409) defined comparative education as 'a field of study that applies social scientific theories and methods to international issues of education'. Its equivalents, Epstein suggested, were fields dedicated to cross-societal study of other social institutions, such as comparative government, comparative economics and comparative religion (see also Epstein 1994: 918). International education, by contrast, was defined as 'organized efforts to bring together students, teachers, and scholars from different nations to interact and learn about and from each other'. Comparativists were seen, first and foremost, as scholars who were interested in explaining how and why education relates to the social factors and forces that form its context, rather than in merely knowing about other people's cultures and their education. Epstein asserted (1992: 409) that despite the change in the name of the society, 'the substance of the journal is comparative education, and, only incidentally and occasionally, international education'.

Epstein invited readers to respond to his view of the differences between the two fields, and Wilson (1994) was among those who did so. Wilson challenged the implication that international educators necessarily had rather passive, system-descriptive roles, arguing (p. 452) that 'international educators originated – and continue to practice – the melioristic trend more prominently associated with comparative education; that is, the improvement of national education systems by the addition of models, practices, innovations, and the like borrowed or transferred from other national educational systems'. Wilson proceeded to assert the value of the products from linkages between the pair of fields, describing them as twins and suggesting that they appeared more like Siamese than fraternal twins.

Related remarks had been made a few years earlier by Postlethwaite (1988: xvii), who had added a further gloss on the nature of the CIES discussions:

Strictly speaking, to 'compare' means to examine two or more entities by putting them side by side and looking for similarities and differences between or among them. In the field of education, this can apply both to comparisons between and comparisons within education systems. In addition, however, there are many studies that are not comparative in the strict sense of the word which have traditionally been classified under the heading of comparative education. Such studies do not compare, but rather describe, analyse or make proposals for a particular aspect of education in one country other than the author's own country. The Comparative and International Education Society introduced the word 'international' in their title in order to cover these sorts of studies.

Thus, the definition of international education presented here was rather different from that presented by Scanlon and Shields (1968) or by Epstein (1992, 1994). However, this definition also had wide currency and was endorsed, for example, by Crossley and Watson (2003: 18). Those authors indicated that when the British Comparative Education Society (BCES) changed its name in 1983 to become the British Comparative and International Education Society (BCIES), it did so with similar motives to those in the CIES 14 years earlier (Sutherland et al. 2007). Among the major forces for the change was financial stringency, which encouraged universities to seek resources from external projects and consultancies, and which strengthened the focus on practical dimensions in other countries as a complement to, and perhaps even a substitute for, academic conceptualization (Watson and King 1991). In the UK, a further change came in 1997, when the BCIES merged with the British Association of Teachers and Researchers in Overseas Education (BATROE) to become the British Association for International and Comparative Education (BAICE). Again, the change was

partly driven by a desire to widen the constituency and bring together practitioners as well as academics (Watson 1998).

OTHER PROFESSIONAL SOCIETIES AND THEIR JOURNALS

The CIES and BAICE are two members of the World Council of Comparative Education Societies (WCCES). This umbrella body, established in 1970, brings together national, subnational, regional and language-based societies in the field of comparative education (Bray 2003). In 2006 it had 33 member societies, of which five linked comparative and international education in their titles. In addition to the CIES and BAICE, they were the Comparative and International Education Society of Canada (CIESC), the Australian and New Zealand Comparative and International Education Society (ANZCIES), and the Nordic Comparative and International Education Society (NOCIES). The CIESC, which was established in 1967, was the first society to present the words as a pair, and did so from its inception. Joseph Katz, who was a key figure in the establishment of the CIESC, was also a strong advocate of the subsequent renaming of the US body to become the CIES (Majhanovich and Zhang 2007). The other two bodies were established after the change of name of the US body, and were influenced by that change. ANZCIES was established in 1972 (Fox 2006) and NOCIES in 1992 (Tjeldvoll 1998).

However, the names of almost all the other 28 WCCES member societies focused exclusively on comparative education. The only exceptions were the Southern African Comparative and History of Education Society (SACHES) and the Association Française pour le Développement de l'Éducation Comparée et des Échanges (AFDECE). Thus, in this collection of bodies the strength of comparative education seemed much greater than that of international education; and it had never been suggested that the title of the WCCES itself be changed to include the word International.

Further, in some countries the fields have been kept quite separate. In Spain, for example, the Sociedad Española de Pedagogía Comparada (Spanish Society for Comparative Pedagogy) (SEPC) was established in 1980. Four years later, a proposal was made to add International to this body and to make it the Sociedad Española de Educación Internacional y Comparada (SEEIC). However, this proposal was not approved (Garmendia and Ferrer 2007). When change did come, in 1994, it was just to change Pedagogy into Education so that the body became the Sociedad Española de Educación Comparada (SEEC). Similarly, in Japan a proposal during the mid-1990s to merge the Japan Comparative Education Society (JCES) with the parallel Japan International Education Society (JIES) was rejected, largely for methodological reasons concerned with the identity of the respective fields (Ninomiya 2004).

Nevertheless, several societies still face considerable confusion, which in some cases is reflected in the titles of their journals. Thus, in counterpoint to the fact that the official journal of the CIES remains the *Comparative Education Review*, the official journal of the Greek Comparative Education Society (GCES), which does not have International in its name, is the *Comparative and International Education Review*. The mission of this journal, as stated in the first issue (No.1, 2003) is to publish: 'original papers ... which present and analyze critically and comparatively contemporary educational issues, policies and trends in Europe and the world'. This statement emphasizes comparative rather than international education; and the follow-up statement that the journal 'welcomes papers which contribute to the understanding and interpretation of educational phenomena and their relationships with the social, economic, political and cultural context' does not greatly change this orientation.

Alongside this publication, the official journal of the CIESC is *Canadian and International Education*, with no mention of Comparative. The journal does state (e.g. Vol. 30, No. 1, 2001) that it is 'devoted to publishing articles dealing with education in a comparative and international perspective', but readers might justifiably wonder about the reason for including Canadian in the title and excluding Comparative. The title again reflects loose definitions of fields among particular groups and at particular points in time.

FURTHER EXAMPLES OF AMBIGUITY

Another source to which people from the field of comparative education might turn to learn about the twin field of international education is the *Dictionary of Comparative Education* edited by Groux et al. (2002). However, the entry on international education (Dhanatya 2002: 245) is arguably confusing more than it is illuminating. It begins by noting that international education is 'somewhat problematic to define' and suggests that the term 'has been interchanged with such concepts and terms as international programs, intercultural programs, multiculturalism, foreign area studies, non-Western studies, international studies, global studies, global education, and international relations'. The major goals of international education are said to be (p. 246):

1   the dissemination of new ideas and fostering of international cooperative efforts
2   development of a system of education that is more equitable and accessible to all nations and peoples
3   national and local development, including economic, political, educational and social development
4   fostering a better understanding of diversity and multiculturalism through educational exchange and new international and interpersonal relationships
5   the development of political power by gaining insights and better knowledge into various nations of the world
6   the development of global studies in academic curricula.

This set of goals would indeed be rather different from those espoused by most people who identify with the field of comparative education, and might be different from that espoused by counterparts in international education. Perhaps most surprising, though, was that although Dhanatya's article appeared in a *Dictionary of Comparative Education*, it made no mention of that field and thus attempted no explanation of how international education did or did not relate to comparative education.

The book edited by Bresler and Ardichvili (2002), which appeared in the same year, was no more satisfactory. Despite its title, *Research in International Education*, the book did contain a chapter that linked international with comparative education research (Ardichvili 2002). However, this chapter failed to define either term, and instead elided both with cross-cultural research. The result for most readers would be greater confusion rather than greater clarification about the nature and boundaries of different fields.

CONCLUSIONS

Some commentators feel that the pairing of comparative and international education is undesirable. Those commentators from the comparative education side argue that the field of comparative education already has undesirably loose boundaries, and they do not welcome further loosening through combination with another field which is defined even less distinctly. Such people commonly argue that comparative education needs tighter conceptualization in order to make a stronger academic and intellectual contribution. On the other side, many people who identify with the field of international education assert that liaison with the field of comparative education brings excessive theorizing which is divorced from practical realities. They assert the value of a practitioner-oriented field which is diverse in focus and loose in internal linkages.

Other commentators, however, are much more positive about the synergies between the pair of fields. Wilson (1994) is in this category, and has extolled the virtues of the 'academic practitioner' who fits in both worlds. Recalling the disputes in the USA during the 1960s which had ultimately led to the 'marriage' of international and comparative education in the CIES, Wilson (1994: 450)

argued that the marriage had produced a hybrid offspring whose orientation and activities had significantly changed the parent fields. The offspring, Wilson suggested, was a group of people who had been equipped with a viable academic understanding of comparative education and who had used that orientation to further the meliorative function common to both international and comparative education in their subsequent international activities.

This chapter has also noted, however, that in the context of the twin fields of international and comparative education, concepts and definitions of international education may vary widely. When taken to other arenas, concepts vary more widely still (see e.g. Vestal 1994; Sylvester 2002; Cambridge and Thompson 2004). While wide-open gates and blurred boundaries can have advantages, rarely is loose conceptualization to be recommended. Thus, it is arguable that particularly scholars and perhaps also practitioners in the fields of comparative and international education should be encouraged to think more about their own and their twin neighbours' identities. It would also be desirable for such people to go further and consider how some other domains of international education may be completely different from those that are allied to the field of comparative education.

REFERENCES

Ardichvili, A. (2002) Dealing with theoretical and methodological paradoxes in international and comparative research: what can we learn from related disciplines? In L. Bresler and A. Ardichvili (eds) *Research in International Education: Experience, Theory, and Practice.* New York: Peter Lang, pp. 1–15.

Bray, M. (2003) Tradition, change, and the role of the World Council of Comparative Education Societies. *International Review of Education*, 49 (1–2): 1–13.

Bresler, L. and Ardichvili, A. (eds) (2002) *Research in International Education: Experience, Theory, and Practice.* New York: Peter Lang.

Cambridge, J.C. and Thompson, J.J. (2004) Internationalism and globalization as contexts for international education. *Compare: A Journal of Comparative Education*, 34 (2): 161–75.

Crossley, M. and Watson, K. (2003) *Comparative and International Research in Education: Globalisation, Context and Difference*. London: RoutledgeFalmer.

Dhanatya, C. (2002) Education internationale [International Education]. In D.Groux, S. Perez, L.Porcher, V.D. Rust and N.Tasaki (eds) *Dictionnaire d'Éducation Comparée*. Paris: L'Harmattan, pp. 245–7.

Epstein, E.H. (1968) Letter to the Editor. *Comparative Education Review*, 12 (3): 376–8.

Epstein, E.H. (1992) Editorial. *Comparative Education Review*, 36 (4): 409–16.

Epstein, E.H. (1994) Comparative and international education: overview and historical development. In T. Husén and T.N. Postlethwaite (eds) *The International Encyclopedia of Education*, 2nd edition. Oxford: Pergamon Press, pp. 918–23.

Fox, C. (2006) The Australian and New Zealand Comparative and International Education Society (ANZCIES). Wollongong: University of Wollongong.

Garmendia, L.M. and Ferrer, F. (2007) The Spanish Comparative Education Society (SEEC). In V. Masemann, M. Bray and M. Manzon (eds) *Common Interests, Uncommon Goals: The Histories of the World Council of Comparative Education Societies and Its Members*. Hong Kong: Comparative Education Research Centre, The University of Hong Kong, and Dordrecht: Springer.

Groux, D., Perez, S., Porcher, L., Rust, V.D. and Tasaki, N. (eds) (2002) *Dictionnaire d'Éducation Comparée*. Paris: L'Harmattan.

Majhanovich, S. and Zhang, L. (2007) The Comparative and International Society of Canada (CIESC). In V. Masemann, M.Bray and M.Manzon (eds) *Common Interests, Uncommon Goals: The Histories of the World Council of Comparative Education Societies and Its Members*. Hong Kong: Comparative Education Research Centre, The University of Hong Kong, and Dordrecht: Springer.

Ninomiya, A. (2004) History of Japan Comparative Education Society. Presentation at the 12th Congress of the World Council of Comparative Education Societies, Havana, Cuba.

Postlethwaite, T.N. (1988) Preface. In T.N. Postlethwaite (ed.) *The Encyclopedia of Comparative Education and National Systems of Education*. Oxford: Pergamon Press, pp. xvii–xxvii.

Scanlon, D.G. and Shields, J.J. (1968) Introduction: Scope and Purposes of International Education. In D.G. Scanlon and J.J. Shields (eds) *Problems and Prospects in International Education*. New York: Teachers College Press, pp. ix–xxii.

Sutherland, M., Watson, K. and Crossley, M. (2007): The British Association for International and Comparative Education (BAICE). In V.Masemann, M.Bray and M. Manzon (eds) *Common Interests, Uncommon Goals: The Histories of the World Council of Comparative Education Societies and Its Members*. Hong Kong: Comparative Education Research Centre, The University of Hong Kong, and Dordrecht: Springer.

Sylvester, R. (2002) Mapping international education: a historical survey, 1893–1944. *Journal of Research in International Education*, 1 (1): 91–125.

Tjeldvoll, A. (1998) The NICE Initiative. In Arild Tjeldvoll, and Anne Smehaugen (eds) *Scandinavian Comparative Education: Research in Progress*. Oslo: Nordic Network of International and Comparative Education, pp. 1–7.

Vestal, T.M. (1994) *International Education: Its History and Promise for Today*. Westport, CT: Praeger.

Watson, K. (1998) Memories, models and mapping: the impact of geopolitical changes on comparative studies in education. *Compare: A Journal of Comparative Education*, 28 (1): 5–31.

Watson, K. and King, K. (1991) From comparative to international studies in education: towards the co-ordination of a British resource of expertise. *International Journal of Educational Development*, 11 (3): 245–53.

Wilson, D.N. (1994) Comparative and international education: fraternal or Siamese twins? A preliminary genealogy of our twin fields. *Comparative Education Review*, 38 (4): 449–86.

5

International Education as an Ethical Issue

Rauni Räsänen

International education is a widely used concept in the globalized world. Although it is old as an idea and concept (James 2005: 314), it had not been widely discussed until about a century ago. Intercultural education became a well-established field of practice particularly after the United Nations documents about the basic rights and UNESCO´s two publications: (1) Recommendations Concerning Education for International Understanding, Cooperation and Peace and Education Relating to Human Rights and Fundamental Freedoms (1974) and (2) Declaration and Integrated Framework of Action on Education for Peace, Human Rights and Democracy (1995). These documents were born out of the aftermath of the World Wars and were based on joint will and determination to avoid similar disasters in the future. They are reflections of the UN search for means and values to safeguard non-violence and peaceful cooperation between nations. Education was regarded as a central ingredient in that process together with other cultural, social, economic and political agendas.

The human rights tradition has not, however, been the only basis for defining international education. Definitions have varied according to the institutions, cultures, organizations and historical events generating them. In some schools more attention is given to Europe and neighbouring nations, in others global citizenship or intra-state multiculturalism gets more emphasis. In some approaches individual development and intercultural competences are the focus of education, in others societal problems and structural inequities are the starting point for action in order to change things for the better (James 2005: 313–17).

On the level of individual institutions the picture is even more diverse. Schools with a focus on international education can justify their nature by the international student body, language studies, exchange programmes, English-medium teaching, or a holistic approach to the whole curriculum and in-school ethos. The terms have also varied according to the emphasis being given; some of the most often used concepts are global education, multicultural education and intercultural education, together with the terms cross-cultural and pluralistic education.

Historical phases and events have also had an effect on the terms and the meanings attached to them. There is no doubt that human rights have had a powerful effect on the definitions, as well as the Millennium Goals and the Education for All project at present. However, unintentional changes in the sociopolitical situation, like the events of September 11th, 2001, can form people's views as well. In addition, due to multiethnic and multicultural societies, people have many pragmatic considerations concerning the competences they need in such societies and professional tasks. With reference to these orientations, Hayden and Thompson (1995) distinguish between ideological and pragmatic use of the terms. In most cases elements from both orientations are included in an individual's or institution's definitions.

Although there are slightly differing views about the meanings of international education, people agree on the need to be prepared for an increasingly multicultural and globalized world. Some also argue that states never were as monocultural and homogeneous as we were made to believe; this myth was convenient at the time when nation-states were the main organizing principles for citizenship, belonging, loyalty and identity (Hernes 2004: 20). They still are in many respects, but globalization has a dominant demographic aspect: people are more on the move than ever before in human history, and there is a dramatic increase in public and private transactions between nation-states and between various non-state actors as well (Turkovich 1997). The European Union has also challenged the unique role of nation-states as the source for identification or as the decision-making body for citizens.

At the same time, the development of new media with a global reach has changed the world for all, but particularly for the young. On the one hand, an international youth culture with common elements cuts across the boundaries, on the other hand new media technologies enable different ethnic and cultural groups to stay in touch with their country of origin or cultural subgroup. That also means that identity is increasingly mediated and conditioned by mass-communications technology. Yet migrants also live in the communities and bring with them new cultural elements that may differ from what is usually observed among the majority of inhabitants (Hernes 2004, 21–2). One additional reason for multiculturalism becoming more visible is the fact that many cultural groups that were not earlier recognized have now had their voices heard. Besides, the concept of culture has become more diverse and multilayered, including such dimensions as ethnicity, religion, language, social class, gender and profession. It is also understood that these dimensions can play different roles in various individuals' identities and at different phases of people's life histories.

The expansion of the realm of activities and consciousness means expansion of civic responsibilities. There are issues that demand international dialogue and problem-solving such as environmental threats, energy alternatives, prevention of diseases and pollution, reduction of poverty and inequity, decreasing violence and putting an end to wars. There is a need for citizenship training for expanded rights and duties as well as for forums of international dialogue and decisions. Global citizenship requires innovative mediums of administration and creative professionals. One essential condition for global citizenship is to understand the interdependence of the various parts of the world and the fact that decisions made at a local level have an effect on the global context. International and intercultural issues concern everyone in one way or another. They are not the sole province of those who migrate or work in international jobs, although they must be particularly trained for special contexts. In multicultural societies international education is about all and for all. Nieto (1996) considers multicultural literacy as important as reading, writing and arithmetic. She points out that monocultural education deprives all students of the diversity that is a part of our world.

Multicultural societies present challenges for educational planners and teachers as schools reflect the changed context. Variety of cultures, global interrelationships, intercultural communication and expansion of participation require knowledge, new skills and above all re-evaluation of earlier perspectives, attitudes and paradigms. Teachers are working at the crossroads of cultures and construct bridges between the past and future. They are supposed to provide students with competences for the present, but also for creating the future. They prepare the next generations to encounter difference, to cherish it and to learn from it. As educators they should also challenge the students to evaluate the changes. Globalization and internationalization are a part of our reality, but people give them meanings, contents and direction. They decide whether the phenomena become sources of creativity and learning or harsh competition and inequity. They decide whether these phenomena offer hope and have human faces. The substance of education is development, learning and human growth. There is a vision of becoming better, learning something valuable: that is why education can never be value-free. It takes a stand on what is meant by development or what is considered valuable for future generations.

TEACHING AS AN ETHICAL PROFESSION

The teacher's job has been understood slightly differently at different times. It has been described, for instance, as a combination of skills, a form of art, an applied science and an ethical profession. Partly due to this, teacher education has also been organized differently (Liston and Zeichner 1991; Niemi 1998; Tom 1987). It has been asked whether it should be teacher training that concentrates purely on necessary didactic skills or teacher education with the aim of creating autonomous, reflective professionals who evaluate and develop themselves and their work (Beyer 1986: 37–41; Case et al. 1986: 39). It has been questioned whether a teacher (or an educator) is merely a transmitter or maintainer of the prevailing culture or also its interpreter and evaluator. Is the teacher only a

civil servant realizing what books, curricula and authorities state or should he/she have a more active role in selecting and evaluating the aims and contents? In both cases values are transmitted. One can only ask whose values they are; are they discussed and evaluated? In multicultural societies this question becomes even more relevant than before. Whose vision of the future is dominant in the curricula as well as in the aims, contents and methods of education?

As stated before, education is never value-free. Consequently, the task of a teacher can be considered as an essentially ethical profession by its nature for many reasons:

1   Teaching and education are inevitably value-laden activities, because they deal with such issues as civilization, growth, development – the idea is to make or support someone or something to become better. The interconnectedness between values, education and school is transparent from general aims to single details such as how much attention is given to various school subjects or content areas in the curricula. The role of basic education is particularly important in the area of value education, because it includes all future citizens and lasts for a relatively long period of time.
2   Another factor that makes teaching a particularly sensitive task is the fact that the partner/client is often a child who is easy to influence and not necessarily competent to evaluate the contents or defend his/her rights in the same way as adults. Teachers have a lot of power over their pupils, e.g. through the grades they give. In this way they directly or indirectly influence children's attitudes, self-image and future opportunities. Through knowledge and skills teachers (and the whole school for that matter) affect the world-view, attitudes and competences, and understanding of cultures. Educators should be aware of their special position, children's vulnerability and the responsibility that this relationship puts on their shoulders. This position can be used to cause harm or it can bring benefit to the child and to future generations. Educators' positive effects on children can be decisive: they can encourage, inspire and open new perspectives and act as role models. They can be caring adults who consider children's individual needs as well as the well-being of societies.
3   The teacher is always a model of an adult to children whether he or she wants it or not. Pupils

observe teachers daily making decisions and solving problems, and they make conclusions about how logical or sincere teachers are in their actions. What also makes a teacher's profession ethically complex is the fact that decisions are made in the middle of diverse expectations. There are a large number of stakeholders who have the right to negotiate the direction of the work, and every teacher has many colleagues, clients and employers. Teachers must not forget their responsibilities for children, parents and colleagues, but remain faithful to the basic values of their work. Sometimes it is hard to decide what is best for individual children and future generations in the middle of the many choices and requirements.

4   The fourth criterion for considering teaching a moral profession is its wide influence on individuals, society and the future of humankind. There are no other professionals who work with all (the majority) of the people for such a long time. Considering the time, the opportunities to influence are incomparable. In this way, education is crucial for individuals and for society as well. Teachers educate citizens whose citizenship is increasingly multilayered: they need to be provided with competences to function on local, national and global levels. In addition, the European Union citizenship requires its own competences and governmental bodies.

Whilst the above mostly discusses the ethical role of teachers, what is said may be applied to all education and all educators. The role is, however, slightly different when you educate a group of children who are not your own. Children's needs and well-being are always of primary concern in all education, but professional educators consider also the group and its role as social educator. They are concerned about individual needs, but they have to reflect more on the common elements of teaching and the knowledge and value basis that is necessary for everyone and for the future of humankind. Although this may be more difficult in multicultural societies it is still an essential issue.

Researches on professional ethics have analysed the value bases of the traditional professions. Most often lawyers and medical doctors are mentioned as professionals with their own distinctive value basis and task to take care of in society. The essence of the profession can

be understood through these values. The professional ethics of doctors is based on the oath of Hippokrates and their responsibility is to take care of the health and well-being of citizens. The basic value that is common for the profession of lawyers is justice and their position in society is determined by the tasks derived from that. It has been debated whether a teacher's job is in the same sense a profession with its own academic status and autonomous role. In most cases it has been given the similar position, and it has been pointed out that professional educators are responsible for the development of individuals as well as the mental growth and civilization of humankind (Airaksinen 1998: 5–13).

APPROACHES TO MORAL EDUCATION

Teachers are supposed to educate responsible citizens for increasingly globalized societies. That is why moral education has been considered one of the central areas of education, but the approaches and methods to be used in it have changed and still vary. The approaches have been divided into different categories: (1) value transmission (2) value clarification; (3) moral development theories; (4) ethics of caring; and (5) ideals of a community of ethical enquiry. There are also theorists and practitioners who argue that teachers should only take care of the cognitive aspects of education and leave values and attitudes to parents and families. That is, however, a simplistic idea of education, because education cannot be separated from values, as has been pointed out earlier. It is realistic to acknowledge the inevitable interrelationship, be sensitive to it and reflect critically what approaches to use (Chazan 1985; Hersh et al. 1980; Kay 1975; Lipman et al. 1980; Pring 1987; Raths et al. 1978; Scharf 1978; Straughan 1988).

Direct and efficient value transmission has been used particularly with young children, and it has been defended by the existence of some universal ethical principles or at least values and norms that responsible people agree on. The golden rule of ethics (treat others as you would like to be treated yourself) or values presented in the human rights documents has been mentioned as an example of such principles. Others argue that even if such principles did not exist, it is important for the next generation to learn about the values of the society they were born into.

The school of value clarification emerged as a protest against pure value transmission; the protestors were concerned about possible brainwashing and lack of critical evaluation of different alternatives. In the value clarification approach students are not taught specific values, but they are presented with tasks and problems, which they have to solve and evaluate. The defenders of this approach argue that values that are transmitted but not understood lead to double-morality, not necessarily to morally sensitive and responsible action. They also justify their approach by pointing out that the world changes, and even many of the values we consider permanent must sometimes be reconsidered. What is vital is to lead students on the road of constant value reflection and to make them sensitive to value questions.

Psychologists like Lawrence Kohlberg (Power et al. 1989) have investigated the moral development of people in making moral judgements. He and his followers have come to the conclusion that people go through different moral stages in their lives depending on how their moral thinking is challenged. The child is concrete and instrumental in his or her thinking: prizes, punishments and consequences decide the morality of the deed. At the next stage, the opinions of peers, the members of a reference group and laws are central in the decision-making. The last stage is characterized by autonomous ethical deliberation. The person understands that laws and principles are changeable and decided by people. That is why it must be discussed whether they really safeguard a good life for everyone. Kohlberg states that people need challenge, discussion and reasoning to be able to develop in their moral thinking. As the final stage of moral development, Kohlberg describes the phase where people's actions are guided by a few principles such as equity and justice.

The representatives of the value clarification school have been accused of relativism and simplification of the relationship between an individual and society. The approach is said to have underestimated the influence of the environment: people do not live in a vacuum or make value-decisions outside of their social context. Some of this criticism has been targeted at Kohlberg as well, but the main accusation against him has been his over-emphasis on the cognitive aspects of morality and ethical education. People's ethical sensitivity or competence is not dependent on purely rational skills but on their commitment to do right and on such tendencies as empathy, perspective-taking and commitment to ethical actions.

The individual-centred approaches have been expanded to the ones, which, in addition to individual processes, emphasize community, joint discussion and solid knowledge in ethics. The supporters of these approaches argue that morally sensitive individuals and personal deliberation of ethical issues are essential, but as we live in human communities, joint decision-making based on dialogue must be practised from the very beginning. In multicultural societies, practice in observing different voices is vital, and still, on the basis of the discussions, conclusions must be drawn for the principles that protect different individuals, groups and cultures.

Well-known examples of community-based approaches are, for instance, Matthew Lipman's and Nel Noddings's schools and methods. Lipman et al. (1980) emphasize joint moral reasoning based on stories of children's lives and the relevant skills in society. The key concept in Noddings's theories (1987, 1988) is caring. She suggests a school curriculum to teach children to care for themselves, other people (close and remote ones), living creatures, natural and constructed environments, and the ideal and dreams they cherish. She argues that a micro-society like school where caring is both studied and practised is the best preparation for responsible citizenship.

Few teachers follow just one of the above approaches but combine elements from many according to children's age, context and their own basic assumptions. It is evident that pure value transmission without justification or discussion is problematic in a multicultural and rapidly changing world. To a certain extent different values should also be understood and even cherished. However, we also need agreement on some common principles, otherwise even discussion about the principles becomes impossible. Communication where others are not respected or heard does not lead to equality or fruitful cooperation. Oppression, domination and hegemony of the strong will lead to outbursts of bitterness and violence if they continue. Thus individualistic approaches in value education are needed, but they are insufficient if they do not consider the contexts and the interconnectedness of people, states and different parts of the world (Räsänen 2000a, 2000b).

THE NEED FOR COMMON ETHICAL PRINCIPLES

The ethical principles that bind cultures and societies together have been discussed a great deal, as can be seen from the human rights process, which emerged out of the tragic experiences of the World Wars. The need for such principles is widely acknowledged in an interdependent world. One of the crucial dilemmas in the discussion seems to be the question of how to combine specific cultural values and general ethical principles in order to safeguard the human rights process and peaceful cooperation in the world. It has been debated whether representatives of all cultures could agree on at least a few common principles, or whether values and norms will remain fundamentally different because of the differences between cultures. Another ethical question concerns the need and possibilities to expand the scope of caring and duties outside people's immediate contexts (cf. Noddings 1988). In the globalized world, education should respond to this need as well, and construct the curriculum and the teaching and learning methods so that they develop empathy and responsibilities towards fellow creatures whether they live far away or nearby.

The idea of universal values or global ethics is not new. The search for these values has been central in the United Nations's human rights process and among many researchers of ethics (e.g. Boulding 1988; Gerle 1995; Sihvola 2004). It has been suggested that the so-called golden rule of ethics (treating others as you would like to be treated yourself) could form a basis for universal ethics, because it exists in some form in all major religions and philosophies (Räsänen 1993: 22–3). The fact that we are all members of the same species should also evoke in us a sense of unity and oneness. Categories defining people and divisions between groups are man-made, changing and changeable, and thus somewhat artificial. Our concern should not stop at the borders; as human beings we have moral responsibilities towards each other notwithstanding state borders, culture, ethnicity, religion, gender, intelligence, skills, social class or sexual orientation. In the human rights documents, special attention is paid to minorities, the marginalized and those who, for various reasons, are not capable of taking care of their own rights. Defending the strong and powerful does not demand high moral standards; ethical orientation and courage are manifested in how individuals and society defend the human dignity and rights of those who are marginalized or discriminated.

In her book *Mikä meitä yhdistää – ihmisyys ja perusarvot* [What binds us together – humanity and basic values], Hilkka Pietilä argues that human dignity is the key concept to ethical orientation in an international world (Pietilä 2003: 45–51). The same principle is emphasized by Juha Sihvola in his book *Maailmankansalaisen etiikka* [Ethics of the global citizen] when he, referring to Immanuel Kant, states that the basis for global ethics is respect for humanity, which presupposes treating everyone as a subject and as an aim instead of suppressing people to the position of an object or a means for gaining something. Sihvola points out that respecting human dignity means more than guaranteeing formal democracy or the equality of clients and businessmen in the business world. Genuine global citizenship requires the appreciation of the many dimensions of humanity: the perception of human beings as thinking, feeling, acting and purposeful creatures. Global citizenship means commitment to a world order in which it is possible to construct humanity in all its dimensions in spite of state or cultural borders or ethnic, religious, gender, social class or other background factors (Sihvola 2004: 12). According to the basic moral teachings of the great traditions, the notion of the basic moral equality of all human beings, and the profoundly human urge to avoid unnecessary suffering form one essential point of reference when searching for global ethics (World Commission, 1995: 36).

The report of the World Commission, published under the title *Our Creative Diversity*, discusses global ethics as one of its main themes (1995: 36, 38). It emphasizes the Golden Rule, human vulnerability, attending to the human impulse to alleviate suffering and the equality of all human beings as central sources and inspiration for the core of global ethics. These derive from old philosophical and spiritual traditions of many cultures. At the same time, the report suggests that the gradual development of international human rights standards, which are based on these common cultural conceptions, has given rise to more concrete normative elements in the emerging global civic culture. It states that the demand for human rights and the consciousness of a shared ecosystem are constantly shaping people's moral ideas throughout the world. The report divides the core of global ethics into five main elements: human rights and responsibilities, democracy and civil society, the protection of minorities, the commitment to peaceful conflict resolution and fair negotiation, and equity within and between generations.

Our Creative Diversity argues that human rights are, at present, widely regarded as the standard of international conduct. It states that protecting individual physical and emotional integrity against intrusion from society; providing the minimal social and economic conditions for a decent life; fair treatment; and equal access to remedying injustices are key concerns in global ethics (World Commission, 1995: 40). It adds that fundamental threats in the eco-system make it essential for certain

new human rights, such as the right to a healthy environment, to be included in the existing codes. The report emphasizes that the rights must be combined with duties: 'options with bonds, choices with allegiances, liberties with ligatures' (p. 41). The aim, according to the report, is a society where liberty is not libertine, authority is not authoritarian, choices are more than 'actes gratuits' and bonds are more than painful restrictions. It is admitted in the report that critics dispute the universality of human rights because of their Western origin and apparently individualistic denotations. However, it is argued that the basic moral concern – to protect the integrity and to respect the vulnerability of human beings – is universal in its appeal and is part of all major traditions of moral teaching.

According to the report, democracy embodies the ideas of political autonomy and human empowerment. The report states that democracy is linked with several other values, most importantly human rights. Democracy is said to provide a basis for securing the fundamental rights of citizens, because governments and other governing bodies are forced to take actions under the pressure of public opinion. A link can be seen between development and democracy, as people are likely to be motivated to make a contribution if they can truly influence the direction their country will move towards. Democracy can also be a stabilizing factor, and thus can maintain peace if people can express their views and affect their lives and living conditions (pp. 42–4). The report also pays special attention to the protection of minorities in its concern for the effect of globalization on small cultural groups. It reminds us that the members of minorities must enjoy the same rights and freedoms as citizens in general, and the human rights of members of both minorities and majorities must be guaranteed. The report emphasizes that tolerance should be promoted and the appreciation of cultural diversity must be encouraged (pp. 44–5).

As mentioned above, the United Nations's human rights process was started after the tragedies of the World Wars, and was based on the determination of people to prevent such madness in the future. Thus, the principles and values of global ethics must be seen as a moral minimum observed by all to prevent violence and violations of human rights. However, other forms of violence and new sources of injustice are arising. New threats to the environment are emerging, and international trade presents increasing challenges for human communication, rights and justice. New situations create new tensions and conflicts. Therefore, what is now (and has always been) needed is commitment to peaceful conflict resolution and fair negotiation in which all affected parties must be represented, heard and taken seriously. In addition to this commitment, the report pays special attention to preventive measures that should be taken when building a 'culture of peace'. In this context, education is mentioned as one of the main means for promoting non-violence and tolerance in individuals who create societies where human rights and equity should be central concerns (pp. 45–6).

The last element of global ethics mentioned in *Our Creative Diversity* is equity within and between generations. It states that the ethos of universal human rights proclaims that all human beings are (or at least should be) born equal, and are entitled to enjoy the same basic rights. Thus, the basic necessities for a decent life must be the most important concern of humanity. This universality requires that we do not neglect the pressing claims of those who are poor today. Furthermore, intergenerational equity requires that present generations must take care of and use environmental and cultural resources for the benefit of future generations. The report reminds us that each generation is a user and potential enhancer of humankind's common heritage, which should be protected to ensure future generations, at the very least, the same possibilities for living on earth. It has been pointed out that modern civilizations have a lesson to learn from indigenous cultures and local cultures (p. 46), which view people as members in a chain of familial generations (Räsänen 2005: 21–4).

ETHICAL PRINCIPLES AS A PROCESS

The Declaration of Human Rights, accepted by the United Nations in 1948, is considered to be the first international human rights document. However, it has also been criticized. The main tensions in the early discussions about these rights at the United Nations's meetings were felt, on one hand, between the so-called industrialized, capitalistic states and the so-called socialistic countries, and on the other hand, between the industrialized and so-called developing countries. The industrialized countries based their rationale on the idea that human rights are inborn, which justifies the right of individuals to decide about their own matters. The emphasis in the argumentation was on freedoms and rights. According to this line of thought, individual people are subjects of rights and liberties, and norms are primarily intended to protect individuals against violations of other people or the state.

The basic understanding of human rights was considered too individualistic by both so-called developing countries and socialistic countries. Disagreement arose on the roles of the state or community and the individual, and on the balance between rights and duties. In the so-called socialistic countries, it was not considered an inborn right that a state would guarantee everyone's individual liberties. Instead, it was thought that it was the state's duty to ensure the provision of basic economic conditions of living for everyone; the citizens on their part had responsibilities to work for the common good. Both the state and individual people were considered as subjects and objects of the rights and norms (Sunnari and Räsänen 1994: 150–1). There has also been continuous discussion and debate about what the most basic rights are. The accepted version of the Human Rights Declaration emphasizes, in particular, the individual's right to life, freedom and personal safety. However, from the very beginning, special attention has been paid to minimum economic and social standards as conditions for human dignity as well.

The Declaration of Human Rights is a unique document in the process of ethical principles, in spite of the disagreements it brought about during its construction. It was a strong expression of the will among many nations to find a common moral core in order to avoid the mistreatment of people. Although the process has not been easy, it has been a starting point for further developments, such as a series of documents concerning new areas of agreements, and the further recognition of groups needing special protection (e.g. declarations or conventions concerning children, women, immigrants, indigenous people and minorities). Human rights documents differ as to their legal binding and scope. Some of them are merely morally binding recommendations or declarations, but, nevertheless, they can have a very powerful effect on the ways of thinking, and on the moral sensitivity of people. Others have been ratified by member states and, thus, have become legally binding as well.

As for the scope of human rights documents, the development has been divided into different stages. Helminen and Lång (1987) have divided the process as follows:

1 The stage of civic and political rights (from the foundation of United Nations to the end of the 1950s).
2 The stage when human rights were extended to economic, social, cultural and educational rights (the beginning of the 1960s until the end of the 1970s).
3 The stage when human rights were extended to include collective human rights.

Helminen suggests that the second stage, which also includes economic and social rights, started in the beginning of the 1960s when former colonized countries started to join the United Nations. Helminen considers the year 1974 as a dividing line after which the transition towards the third stage characterized by collective human rights began, as it was also the year when the basic ideas of a new international economic order were agreed on.

Drzewick (1986) has studied the development of human rights documents as well, and he has named the stages slightly differently: the stages of classical, social and solidarity rights. Classical rights protect basic human rights, while social rights also include social, economical, cultural and educational rights. Drzewick's discussion about solidarity rights is particularly interesting in the context of this article. According to Drzewick, these rights express the consciousness of a new type of national and international unity and of a joint responsibility of the human community. The realization of these rights presupposes joint endeavours that ignore national borders among the actors of different fields (Sunnari and Räsänen 1994: 155–7).

The present human rights discussion has also been analysed from the perspective of the above-mentioned stages. It has been pointed out that the focus has mostly been on the civic and political rights and responsibilities of human beings in the new, globalized context. On the other hand, it must be observed that all the different stages have been recognized in the discussions, although the emphasis has varied depending on the document and situation. For instance, the Millennium Goals (which by many are considered equal to the Declaration of Human Rights as to their importance) include several aspects of the social, economic, and ecological rights. The Goals draw special attention to basic education, gender equity, health, the fight against diseases and child mortality, environmental protection and efforts for sustainable development. It is important to recognize that the first goal concerns poverty reduction: the aim is to reduce utmost poverty by half by the year 2015. Poverty is understood as a multilayered and complex phenomenon that severely violates human rights and is the source of many other problems. Poverty is also a clear example of violations that cannot be abolished by concentrating on the well-being of individuals alone, but requires the reconsideration of structures including trade, treaties and the relations between the North and South. It is worth observing that the last goal is global partnership. This goal recognizes that the aims apply to all countries and require global responsibility to be shared by both rich and poor countries in a joint process.

Some have criticized the human rights process by saying that, in spite of discussions, declarations and conventions, human rights violations continue and new forms of it constantly emerge. This is true, but it does not make the process and its value basis worthless. Although there are disappointments, and practice does not always follow the announced principles, the process is worth continuing. Even in its present form, the process has had a huge effect on people's sensitivity towards human rights questions. It has given the oppressed and violated hope and some means to try to defend themselves. It has also provided international actors with a common ground and initiative for their dialogue. It is a process that cannot be neglected when teaching about the interconnected world and the conditions for making cooperation peaceful and fruitful (Räsänen 2005: 25–9).

THE VALUE BASIS OF INTERNATIONAL EDUCATION AND GLOBAL CITIZENSHIP

Discussion about global ethics and common ethical guidelines has given birth to other related concepts. For instance, global citizenship is a concept that has created discussion among social scientists, philosophers and educators (e.g. Boulding 1988; Gerle 1995; Godwin 1993; Sihvola 2004). It has also been discussed in the context of international or global education, which traditionally has included, at least, areas such as human rights education, equality education, peace education, culture education, development education and environmental education. Nora Godwin (1993), one of the developers of the idea of global citizenship, has suggested its division into the following content areas:

1 understanding the interdependence of different areas of the world, people and parts of the ecosystem
2 acknowledging the relativity of perceptions, images, views and knowledge
3 understanding the interconnectedness of the past, present and future
4 learning from conflicts and from conflict resolution
5 understanding the need for social justice.

Godwin speaks on behalf of understanding the interconnectedness of cultures, states, peoples, the past and the future, and mankind and the environment. She emphasizes the processes and the balance in the ecosystem, and 'the vision for a sustainable future and development. She also points out that realizing the narrowness and limits of one's own perceptions, beliefs and knowledge is the key to understanding the relativity and diversity of world-views. This would also lead to a consciousness of one's ethnocentrism and tendency to create stereotypes and uphold prejudices, and would hopefully lead to transformative learning processes. The last two content areas presented by Godwin can be understood as lessons from reality, from what has been learnt about the tragedies of wars and from the consequences of inequity and injustice. However, they are closely associated to value commitments, too.

On the basis of the discussion above, I will now gather together the ethical guidelines for fruitful international education and global citizenship education (Räsänen 2005: 30). First of all, cooperation must be regarded as valuable and important; people must be *willing and motivated to cooperate*. In an interrelated world with common interests and resources, there is a desperate need to cooperate, at least, about the most essential principles that affect us all. The cooperation, as any cooperation or human contact, should be based on the Kantian idea of *treating others as subjects and as goals* instead of as a means for something. This implies respect, listening and appreciating other people: *the commitment to equity* between people, groups and cultural areas. Fruitful intercultural cooperation also requires *the commitment to mutual learning and dialogue*. Equal intercultural dialogue challenges us to evaluate things from new perspectives and to widen our horizons and scope of caring. As stated before, it can thus become a powerful means for learning and being creative.

There are two more commitments to be added as ethical conditions for international cooperation. These are *the commitment to peace, and the commitment to seek sustainable development*. In this context, peace and non-violence must be understood in the broader sense, implying that peace presupposes societal structures and processes, which support equity, justice and non-violence. Societies suffering from severe poverty and hunger cannot be considered as non-violent or peaceful. The same can be stated about a world order that maintains or produces poverty and discrimination. Sustainable development is often discussed in the context of environmental issues, but it is essential to include economic, social and cultural aspects in its evaluation as well. The vision about a sustainable future is not easy to depict, but it is our duty to try to protect the environment for future generations. It is essential to continue the discussion about the content and nature of development and ask what kind of a world we would like to leave to our children and grandchildren.

CONCLUSION

This chapter started with discussion about the ethical nature of education and the teacher's profession. It came to the conclusion that education and values are closely interconnected. Education is always based on some notion of development and on what is valuable and what is not allowed. Education has always influenced people, and its function is both to socialize and to act as a change agent. Education is a value-laden activity, which means conveying in an acceptable manner something that is seen as valuable and worthwhile. These approaches were discussed in section 3 analysing the balance between individuals, groups and societies in the process of learning about values. It was emphasized that teachers must observe the multicultural aspects of modern societies, but also the common core of ethics to guarantee a safe learning environment and the human dignity of all individuals in the classroom and outside the school context. In the globalized world, the consciousness of, and responsibility for, people and other creatures living in other parts of the world need to be expanded.

Education plays the key role in global citizenship training. It can influence students through its curricula: aims, contents, methods, teaching material, attitudes and general atmosphere of the school. The hidden curriculum is as powerful as the official one. The role model given by adults, the methods used at school and the attitudes of the staff are as important as the content. It is essential that the school practises what it preaches, otherwise the whole curriculum will lose its credibility. The best results are gained through a comprehensive approach, where the school ethos and activities are consistent with the value basis of the school.

There are many activities that can support intercultural sensitivity: knowledge about cultures and societies – studies of one's own history and background, language studies, multicultural groups, excursions, guests from other cultures and intercultural projects. Amongst the core competences are the sensitivity and ability to view things from another perspective, a willingness to listen, to give voice and to respect. In other words, to treat others as subjects and as aims. Another important aspect in international education, in addition to interpersonal relations, is to study the societal and power structures and analyse what is their contribution to the order of matters in the world, and what can be done to improve them. In order to change the conditions, future generations need to study matters on individual, cultural and societal levels, and they need the knowledge, sensitivity and courage to make ethically sustainable decisions.

Internationalization as such, without the word education, is a neutral term describing the present-day phenomenon and connections between nations. This phenomenon has taken different forms and includes different activities. It infuses international communication, business, increasing mobility, cultural encounters and new possibilities. It also includes problems to be solved together. It holds promises, but the unknown also frightens. However, the phenomenon has no predetermined content or direction beyond people's actions. The content and direction of internationalization depend on us; we are all responsible for it. The term international education, because it is a value-laden term involving education, forces us to evaluate the past and various alternatives for future generations. The world of transition empties itself from many dominant modes of thinking and judgement, of acquired, unquestioned ideas and norms. It invites the exploration of new paths, leaving something behind and looking at things from a fresh viewpoint. However, particularly when changes are rapid and decisions about the unknown have to be made, we need a clear vision about what is essential in the new paths of life as well. Values give consistency and direction for education, they are the compass for navigation in changing contexts.

REFERENCES

Airaksinen, T. (1998). Opettaja, arvot ja muuttuva ammatti [Teacher, values and changing professions]. In R. Sarras (ed.) *Puheenvuoroja opettajan etiikasta.* Helsinki: OAJ, pp. 5–13.

Beyer, L. (1986) Beyond eliticism and technicism: teacher education as practical philosophy. *Journal of Teacher Education,* 37 (2): 37–41.

Boulding, E. (1988) *Building a Global Civic Culture.* New York: Teachers College Press.

Case, C.W., Lanier J.E. and Miskel C.G. (1986) The Holmes Report: impetus for gaining professional status for teachers. *Journal of Teacher Education,* 37 (4): 36–43.

Chazan, B. (1985) *Contemporary Approaches to Moral Education.* New York: Teachers College Press.

Drzewick, K. (1986) Solidaarisuusoikeudet: Ihmisoikeuksien kolmas kumous [Solidarity rights: the third revolution of human rights]. *Ihmisoikeudet,* 8 (14): 23–45.

Gerle, E. (1995) *In Search of Global Ethics.* Lund: University Press.

Godwin, N. (1993) Miten kasvaa maailmankansalaiseksi [How to become a world citizen]? *YK-tiedote,* 3: 5–7.

Hayden, M. and Thompson, J. (1995) International schools and international education: a relationship re-visited. *Oxford Review of Education,* 21 (3): 327–45.

Helminen, M. and Lång, K.J. (eds) (1987) *Kansainväliset ihmisoikeudet* [International human rights]. Tampere: Mäntän kirjapaino.

Hersh, R., Miller, J.P. and Fielding, G.D. (1980) *Models of Moral Education.* New York: Longman.

Hernes, G. (2004) Introduction. In *Planning for Diversity: Education in Multi-Ethnic and Multicultural Societies.* Policy Forum No. 17. Paris: UNESCO, pp. 17–27.

James, K. (2005) International education: the concept, and its relationship to intercultural education. *Journal of Research in International Education,* 4 (3): 313–32.

Kay, W. (1975) *Moral Education.* London: Allen & Unwin.

Lipman, M., Sharp, A.M. and Oscanyan, F. (1980) *Philosophy in the Classroom.* Philadelphia: Temple University Press.

Liston, D. and Zeichner, K. (1991) *Teacher Education and the Social Conditions of Schooling.* New York: Routledge.

Niemi, H. (1998) Tulevaisuus, nykyisyys ja menneisyys opettajan ammatissa [The past, present and future of the teacher's profession]. In R. Sarras (ed.) *Puheenvuoroja opettajan etiikasta.* Helsinki: OAJ, pp. 62–73.

Nieto, S. (1996) *Affirming Diversity: The Socio-Political Context of Multicultural Education.* New York: Longman.

Noddings, N. (1987) Do we really want to produce good people? *Journal of Moral Education,* 16 (3): 177–88.

Noddings, N. (1988) An ethic of caring and its implications for instructional arrangements. *American Journal of Education,* 96 (2): 215–30.

Pietilä, H. (2003) *Mikä meitä yhdistää: Ihmisyys ja perusarvot* [What do we have in Common: Humanity and Basic Rights]. Jyväskylä: PS-kustannu.

Power, C., Higgins, A. and Kohlberg, L. (1989) *Lawrence Kohlberg's Approach to Moral Education.* New York: Columbia University Press.

Pring, R. (1987) *Personal and Social Education in the Curriculum.* London: Hodder and Stoughton.

Raths, L.E., Harmin, M. and Simon, S.B. (1978) *Values and Teaching.* Columbus, OH: Charles E. Merrill.

Räsänen, R. (1993) In Search of Teachers' Ethics. *Acta Universitatis Ouluensis,* E12.

Räsänen, R. (2000a) Ethics, education and teacher education. In K. Kumpulainen, (ed.) In Search of Powerful Learning Environments for Teacher Education in the 21st Century. *Acta Universitatis Ouluensis,* E39: 127–36.

Räsänen, R. (2000b) Teachers' ethics, teacher education and changing horizons. In V. Sunnari and R. Räsänen, (eds) Ethical Challenges in Teacher Education and Teaching. *Acta Universitatis Ouluensis,* E45: 168–78.

Räsänen, R. (2005) Intercultural co-operation as an ethical issue. In R. Räsänen & J. San (eds) *Conditions for Intercultural Learning and Co-operation.* Turku: Finnish Educational Research Association, No. 23, pp. 15–34.

Scharf, P. (1978) *Readings in Moral Education.* Minneapolis: Winston.

Sihvola, J. (2004) *Maailmankansalaisen etiikka* [Ethics of a global citizen]. Helsinki: Otava.

Straughan, R. (1988) *Can We Teach Children to be Good*? Milton Keynes: Open University Press.

Sunnari, V. and Räsänen, R. (1994) YK: n ihmisoikeusasiakirjat monikulttuuristuvan koulun ja opettajankoulutuksen arvopohjana [UN human rights documents as the value basis of globalising school and teacher education] In. R. Räsänen, S. Anttonen, J. Peltonen and P. Toukomaa (eds) *Irti arvotyhjiön harhasta? Oulun yliopiston kasvatustieteiden tiedekunnan opetusmonisteita ja selosteita*, No. 59, pp. 149–63.

Tom, A. (1987) Replacing pedagogical knowledge with pedagogical questions. In J. Smyth (ed.) *Educating Teachers – Changing the Nature of Pedagogical Knowledge*. London: Falmer, pp. 9–17.

Turkovich, M. (1997) Educating for a changing world: challenging the curriculum. Paper given to the Second International Congress on Multicultural Education, Jyväskylä, Autumn 1997.

UNESCO (1974) Recommendations Concerning Education for International Understanding, Cooperation and Peace and Education Relating to Human Rights and Fundamental Freedoms. Paris: UNESCO.

UNESCO (1995) Declaration and Integrated Framework of Action on Education for Peace, Human Rights and Democracy. Paris: UNESCO.

World Commission (1995) Our Creative Diversity. UNESCO Report of the World Commission on Culture and Development. Paris: EGOPRIM.

6

Global Citizenship and the Role of Human Values

Rajagopalan Sampatkumar

THE DEVELOPMENT OF HUMAN SOCIETIES

Primitive human beings were gregarious and enterprising. They formed groups and dispersed in different directions to establish themselves as distinct, separate communities. With the passage of time and with the urge to discover the world around and the space beyond, contacts between the continents and communities were created gradually through adventurous travel, trade and wars. People moved, voluntarily or through compulsion, to other communities, carrying with them their wares, ideas and ideologies different from those of the communities they entered. This initially led to confrontation resulting in constant friction between communities. The 'invaders' in possession of superior skills and power subjugated and ruled the local population for their own benefit and enrichment. On the other hand, those newly arrived who were weak accepted the dire conditions in their new surroundings but were reluctant to be fully assimilated for fear of losing their cultural traits and identity, and of being relegated

to second-class citizenship. The struggle between the communities has continued for decades and centuries, leading, in some instances, to protracted armed conflict claiming a large number of innocent lives. Today, there is hardly a country that can claim to have a homogeneous, unified population in terms of ethnicity, religion, values, traditions, moral beliefs, and social structure and practices. In many, if not most countries, minorities and immigrants form part of the population. In effect, these countries are only a replica of the mosaic of ethnicities and cultures that make up our world at large.

Human evolution is propelled by discoveries and inventions that contribute to the understanding of the mysteries of nature, strengthening our survival instincts and providing tools to steadily improve the quality of life on this planet. The twentieth century saw an unparalleled advance in science and technology, transport and communication that opened up new opportunities, *inter alia*, to annihilate physical distances, communicate with one another freely and rapidly, understand and appreciate religious and cultural differences, gradually rub off national borders, and construct a global community. The two World Wars of the last century not only taught us to acknowledge the inviolability of the dignity and sanctity of the individual but also enabled the states to evolve international institutions, legal instruments and procedures to ensure the well-being of all. The fall of the Berlin Wall in 1989 and the collapse of the Soviet Union in 1991 ended the competition between the two major political ideologies, and transformed the post-Second World War bi-polar world into accepting freedom of the individual and democracy as basic instruments for achieving the greater good for the greatest number of people. During the Cold War years the so-called 'Third World' poor countries of Africa, Asia and Latin America were pawns in the rivalry between the two superpowers trying to exploit the rich natural resources of the poor countries by establishing their hegemony and carving out areas of influence. Most of the Third World countries who were in their infancy of nationhood and ruled by unscrupulous, corrupt politicians and despots, naïvely submitted themselves to free, unfettered exploitation. With the sudden demise of communism and break-up of the Soviet Union their usefulness in the power-play faded, obliging them to redefine their new role in order to regain their dignity and take their rightful place among the world community. At the same time the benign neglect of the developed world to the appalling conditions of poverty and hopelessness gave way to genuine concern for creating and sustaining appropriate political, economic and social infrastructures that could ensure the well-being of people in the developing countries. The attention of the world was directed to instituting processes leading to full democracy, safeguarding fundamental human freedoms, establishing the rule of law, empowering vulnerable groups including women, and promoting good governance in those countries that lacked it. There is now a growing awareness that human survival and future development can be achieved not through isolation and division but by building a cohesive,

interdependent world where no one single community's well-being takes precedence over that of others.

GLOBALIZATION

Today, the most compelling phenomenon that touches every country and every individual is 'globalization'. There has been much wrangling in academic circles that what we loosely call globalization is in fact confused with internationalization. For the purists, true globalization is characterized by the elimination of nation-states and the erasing of national borders. But, these drastic changes are not likely to happen even in the distant future. The term globalization has come into common usage since the 1980s to signify integration of economies around the world, particularly through trade and financial flows (Crafts 2000).

Globalization *per se* is not anything new, nor is it mysterious. Globalization could be detected whenever there had been contacts between peoples through trade, culture or immigration, though countries could choose to isolate themselves and remain impervious to outside contacts and influences. It is useful to distinguish economic, political and cultural aspects of globalization, although all three aspects are inextricably intertwined. In a globalized economy goods and capital move freely across the borders but not without impact on culture. Establishment by multinational corporations of manufacturing units in textile and other industries with imported capital has given rise to new employment opportunities for unskilled and semi-skilled women in developing countries who are traditionally confined to performing household chores. These women acquire the capacity to earn salaries, thereby reducing their economic dependence on male members who have been the sole breadwinners of the family. The relative economic independence of women will likely have repercussions on traditional male–female relationships, family structure and hierarchy, eventually bringing about changes in social norms and practices with respect to gender, family, marriage, number of children etc. The import of clothes, food and other products can likewise significantly impact traditional customs and values. The popularity of jeans among young women in societies that prescribe a different dress code is indicative of the challenge to the authority of the older generation and traditions. International food chains such as McDonald's and Kentucky Fried Chicken introduced new items of food that influenced and changed local eating habits. They have also provoked a wider discussion on food and health, especially of children and adolescents.

It is a generally held view that globalization has its origins in the West, which uses it as a vehicle to spread Western values and ideologies to the rest of the world. In practice, however, wholesale export and imposition of Western ideas and values has not been as straightforward as one might imagine. The target population is usually suspicious of anything coming from external sources and, therefore, reluctant to readily accept and assimilate imported goods and ideas radically different from their own. For instance, the attempts of the West to universalize the concepts of capitalism, free trade, human rights and democracy initially met with flat refusal from many countries in the rest of the world, including the Soviet Union and its satellite states. It took several decades and a certain number of adjustments in response to local cultural sensitivities before non-Western countries were inclined to accept them. On the other hand, it is not uncommon that non-Western religions, medicine, goods, art, literature and food habits have found their way to the West where they are accepted and admired, thanks to globalization. The strong influence of African, Latino and Caribbean music on Western non-classical, modern music is widely acknowledged. Westerners who are constantly subjected to stress and suffer from stress-related ailments resort to meditation and yoga imported from the East. Western Christians who are unable to find answers to their spiritual quest convert to Islam or Buddhism. Acupuncture is recognized as a credible treatment for certain ailments among allopathic doctors and patients in Western countries. Globalization has made choices more meaningful because of their ready availability.

Since 1945, globalization has become identified with a number of trends, including greater interstate movement of commodities, money, information and people; and the development of technology, organizations, legal systems and infrastructures to allow this movement. Free market economy and liberalized international trade received a boost in the 1980s from new technological innovations that helped completion of easier and quicker trade and financial transactions. Likewise, the formation of non-military regional groupings like the European Economic Community (EEC), resulting from the 1957 Treaty of Rome, and the Association of South East Asian Nations (ASEAN), formed as a result of the Bangkok Declaration of 1967, paved the way for increased cooperation among their member countries. Economic cooperation meant harmonization of trade, monetary and fiscal policies of individual member-countries. The merger of the three European institutions – the European Coal and Steel Community (ECSC), the European Atomic Energy Community (EURATOM) and the European Economic Community (EEC) – in 1967 into the European Union with a single Commission, Parliament and Council of Ministers is a commendable example of 'globalization' in a regional context. Cooperation among member-states of the European Union extends beyond sheer economic issues into judicial, social and cultural aspects. Free movement of people to other countries within the European Union for residence, education or employment, harmonization of trade, monetary and fiscal policies, and retracing a common cultural heritage and ethos have contributed towards establishing a common identity for all citizens of the European Union. Similar experiments in other parts of the world have not borne comparable results.

Many antiglobalization activists perceive economic globalization as an instrument in the hands of multinational corporations whose sole motive is to increase profits to the detriment of freedom of the individual. Flooding newly emerging markets with a wide range of material goods at affordable prices encourages uncontrolled consumerism. Interests of powerful multinational corporations are promoted at the expense of the well-being of the vast majority of people and the natural environment. These corporations infiltrate political life and exert undue influence on policymakers of nation-states. Globalized economic activities have scant regard for local religious, cultural and social sensitivities. National culture and traditional values come under severe strain to fall in line with a monolithic global ethos dictated by giant multinational corporations. Supporters of globalization counter these criticisms by pointing out that when promoted with circumspection globalization can lead to higher, efficient output, lower prices and increased employment in all the countries involved. Wide disparities between developed and developing countries, and uneven distribution of wealth among various sections of population within a country can be progressively redressed by added opportunities for entrepreneurship and employment through globalization.

Despite its shortcomings, globalization in the broadest sense, encompassing economic, social, political and cultural aspects, is inevitable and unstoppable. It is almost a necessity to live and work within the contours of globalization if human beings wish not to repeat the grave mistakes of the past but build an integrated society where differences in race, colour, gender, religion, culture or nationality will not deny to anyone the opportunity to progress and succeed. Care should be taken, however, to ensure that globalization does not obliterate individuality or unwittingly allow national culture to be subsumed by a global culture. The success of globalization may in the future be judged by our ability to maintain our cultural distinctions while creating a new understanding of the global community.

CHALLENGES FOR THE NEW MILLENNIUM

As we cruise forward in to the new millennium we realize the stark contrasts between laudable achievements and dismal failures. We have made impressive progress in science and technology, transport and communication, connecting more and more people and places around the world in ways that were previously unimaginable, exploring space, lifting more people above the poverty line and bringing timely succour and comfort to those in need. In spite of this, the world is riddled with serious problems, many of them human-made. The richest 50 million people in Europe and North America have the same income as 2.7 billion poor people in developing counties, and 20 per cent of the people in the developed countries consume 86 per cent of the world's goods (UNDP 1998). The gross domestic product (GDP) of the poorest 48 nations, representing a quarter of the world's population, is less than the combined wealth of the world's three richest people. The poorer the country the more likely it is that debt repayments are extracted directly from people who neither contracted the loans nor benefited from them. According to the World Bank, the developing world now spends US$13 on debt repayment for every US dollar it receives in grants (World Bank 1999).

Nearly nine million children die of preventable diseases each year in Sub-Saharan Africa and South Asia, and 500,000 mothers die during pregnancy or at childbirth. In Africa, one child dies of malaria every 29 seconds and one person is infected with HIV/AIDS every 6.4 seconds. The proportion of the world's population living in countries where per capita food supplies are below 2,200 calories per day decreased from 56 per cent in the mid-1960s to below 10 per cent by the 1990s. At the same time, half of the children in South Asia are undernourished and half of the world's population lacks access to adequate sanitation. Though the percentage of people in developing countries living on less than a dollar a day has halved in the past

20 years, millions of people continue to die each year because they are too poor to stay alive. Between 1950 and 1999, global literacy increased from 52 per cent to 81 per cent of the world's population, though nearly a billion people entered the twenty-first century unable to read a book or sign their name (UNICEF 2004). Presently, one-third of children in the developing world do not complete the first four years of school.

Material progress and large-scale stock-piling of sophisticated weapons for use by well-trained armed forces have not made our world any safer. While billions of dollars are invested in procuring guns and weapons, funds for healthcare, primary education and social security are drastically reduced. More than 800,000 people, mostly civilians, die each year as a result of armed conflicts (Commission on Human Security 2003). In 2000 world military expenditures reached one trillion US dollars – a per capita average of US$162. According to UNICEF, with only 10 per cent of that amount all basic needs of every single needy person on earth could have been met (UNICEF 2000). Scores of armed conflicts have continued for decades in different parts of the world in spite of the international community's efforts to resolve them. In addition, a new wave of terrorism that began in 2001 in the USA has spread to other countries, threatening the safety and security of people around the world. Response to these acts of violence has been impulsive and brutal, without any serious attempt to identify and address the root causes.

Problems of poverty, ignorance, disease, deprivation and underdevelopment are compounded by environmental degradation. Unbridled expansion of industrialization, overutilization of natural resources, wanton destruction of flora and fauna, and pollution of air and water with hydrocarbons and toxic waste have lead to the disconnectedness of human beings from their environment. Our greatest challenge is how to meet our current needs without depleting the resources required for future needs. Specialization in narrowly defined areas of knowledge and skills has resulted in limiting our ability to fully comprehend the interconnectedness between nature and human being, between cause and effect. When the facts we collect are incomplete and out of context, the decisions we make are likely to be imperfect, short-sighted and detrimental to the future of humanity.

We are at a point in human evolution when we can ill afford to be egotistical and seek well-being and happiness only for ourselves to the exclusion of others. Neither can we produce and consume material goods endlessly without inflicting negative consequences on our fellow human beings and on planet earth. Our needs and whims will have to be evaluated in relation to those of other human beings. Physical distances and cultural compartmentalization cannot any longer come in the way of connectivity and common humanity. Events affecting any single individual or group of individuals are bound to have direct or indirect repercussions on others, sooner or later. Our attitude towards religion, culture, social customs and political institutions different from our own has to be guided by humility and based on objectivity. As the world shrinks into a global village, it is imperative to review the perceptions of oneself, of the overall biodiversity and of the relationship between the two. We might end up discovering that our traditional sense of belonging and allegiance is no longer valid and needs revision.

CITIZENSHIP

In order to live in harmony in a global environment and interact with it in a positive manner we should first examine our identity and determine where our allegiance lies. Part of an individual's identity is provided by citizenship. The concept of citizenship has evolved through the ages. In Western traditions Aristotle (384–322 BC) was the first to have attempted to define citizenship as a relationship between Greek city-states and people residing in them. Not all inhabitants were citizens – only those who enjoyed rights to participate in political life and hold judicial office. Thus, citizenship represented political identity endowed with rights and obligations. With the passage of time the context in which citizenship was conferred had changed from city-state to empire to territory over which polity exercised its authority. Today, the concept of citizenship is embedded in the nation-state, which is facing new challenges from cultural diversity, international migration and from citizens handicapped by deepening economic and social inequalities. Formal citizenship rights cannot be fully enjoyed in practice, especially by the poor, those marginalized and consigned to the lower rungs of the social ladder (Turner 1994). At the same time, because of the emergence of international institutions and organizations like the United Nations, the International Criminal Court and the World Trade Organization as well as regional groupings like the European Union, the preponderance of the nation-state in controlling and directing the political, economic and social aspects of its citizens is waning (Delanty 1995). The Maastricht Treaty of 1993 extends citizenship beyond the nation-state and gives additional political and legal rights to all EU citizens not previously granted by individual nation-states to its citizens (Martiniello 2002). These developments together with the intensification of the process of globalization bring into focus the continued relevance (or irrelevance?) of modern citizenship as developed within the nation-state.

GLOBAL CITIZENSHIP

Allegiance can be either vertical or horizontal. Our loyalty can be towards the village of our birth, a state or country we reside in, or a region we belong to. Those holding dual or multiple citizenships owe allegiance to more than one country. Horizontally, one's loyalty can simultaneously be extended to a specific culture, community and state, and there is no hierarchy of allegiance. Ideally, our ultimate allegiance should be to respect human freedoms and rights, sustain biodiversity and strive for a better world to ensure the welfare of all. In order to develop global consciousness, while elevating allegiance to the global level citizenship should be extended beyond nation-state and region to global citizenship.

The idea of belonging to one human family, transcending allegiance to one's local community, was mentioned in the Holy Qu'ran and in ancient Hindu scriptures. The Stoics, too, asserted the ultimate moral equality of all human beings, thereby replacing loyalty to a particular earthly city by loyalty to the universal heavenly one. The Indian Nobel Laureate Rabindranath Tagore denounced nationalism, which, in his opinion, was 'the organized gregariousness and mechanical gluttony to protect the interests of those within it' (Tagore 1961). He pleaded for openness, implored his compatriots to embrace cosmopolitan humanism and consider themselves an integral part of humanity. During the past two centuries philosophers like Immanuel Kant and Karl Jaspers have developed values and concepts to support global or cosmopolitan citizenship (Carter 2001). There are several theories of global citizenship with varied interpretations (see, for example, Falk 1994 and Habermas 1994). Today, the term 'global citizenship' is frequently used even though there is no world state to grant political identity to global citizens or protect them. Many researchers, scholars and activists perceive global citizens as a civil society movement to step in when nation-states acting alone are not able to solve major problems confronting humanity. Global citizens see themselves not simply as citizens of a country or region but also as human beings in league with other human beings on the other side of the cultural wall, across national frontiers (Dower 2004). Awareness and genuine concern for humanity are the motive force for action by global citizens.

ATTITUDES

Right attitudes are vital to enable present and future generations to cope with the complexities of life fuelled by diversity and globalization. There is a strong tendency to create the myth that differentiation based on culture, religion, language and ethnicity, and the effects – both positive and negative – of globalization, belong only to the world outside our national borders. In reality, as mentioned elsewhere, national environment already has or increasingly takes on all the ingredients inherent in the current global context. Millennia of human migration and centuries of colonization have been the architects of creating multiethnic, multi-religious, multilingual, multicultural societies in many countries on every continent. Some countries, like the USA and India, have been reasonably successful in creating a common national identity for their respective populations after decades of internal strife, civil wars, and political and territorial readjustments. Nonetheless, there are persistent disgruntled groups, serving as a reminder that reconciliation and harmonization cannot be taken for granted and have to be nurtured for all time to come. Many African countries, like the Congo and Sudan, have a long, long way to go before diverse tribal and linguistic sections of the population are galvanized into accepting a common national identity. European countries lumbered with ethnic and religious minorities made up of immigrants and refugees frequently face social unrest claiming a toll on cherished values of human rights, secularism and tolerance. It has also generated fresh discussions regarding nationality and citizenship, and compatibility between the two. The traditional characterization of Europeans as Caucasian Christians may soon need re-examination. In spite of differences in scale, both global and national problems stem from the same incongruity between the individual and her or his environment. Hence, attitudes essential to understanding and dealing with global issues are equally relevant for resolving problems in one's own national backyard.

TROUBLE-MAKERS AND TROUBLE-SHOOTERS

Enthusiasts scrambling to form groups of global activists to wage wars on injustice, poverty, social marginalization, violations of human rights, environmental degradation etc. hurriedly place the responsibility for the world's ills at the doorsteps of various legal entities: multinational companies with an insatiable thirst for profits have exploited national resources of developing countries and have widened the gap between the rich and the poor world-wide; governments and international institutions like the World Bank and IMF have drowned Third World populations in heavy, perpetual national debts and have failed to eradicate poverty; pharmaceutical and other industries pollute the atmosphere and destroy biodiversity while governments are tongue-tied and remain passive spectators; good governance is compromised because corruption is seeping through every layer of government and society. The list is not exhaustive. A distinct impression is created that trouble-makers and trouble-shooters are born different and ordained to remain in their respective camps without any possibility for mobility. Fortunately, more often than not, many people end up in a particular situation or station in life by choice or accident. If our decisions and actions are motivated by a genuine desire to share with and care for our fellow human beings, the institutions in whose names we act will be immaterial. What becomes primordial is the way our attitudes are chiselled. In this regard educators take on a commendable responsibility to ensure that future generations will be worthy custodians of human civilization.

THE ROLE OF EDUCATION

Immanuel Kant wrote, 'out of the crooked timber of humanity no straight things can ever be made' (Kant 1784) This is a serious indictment, which extinguishes our optimism to detect anything positive in human personality and behaviour. If this will be the final verdict there is nothing but gloom for the future of humanity. Luckily, a couple of centuries earlier William Shakespeare called man 'the paragon of animals' (*Hamlet*, 1601). No one does wrong willingly, as Socrates contended. If everyone is morally good, this moral goodness should be reflected in unselfish compassion for others. The German philosopher Arthur Schopenhauer, inspired by Plato, Kant and the Upanishads, believed that a good person is one who, not making the usual distinction between himself and others, is filled with universal compassion. Thus he acts on the principle 'injure no one; on the contrary, help everyone as much as you can' (Sprigge 1999). Perhaps, all of them were right, as the modern geneticists would opine. For, it is human nature to respond to nurture not withstanding our genetic make-up at birth. 'It is not nature *or* nurture, it is nature *and* nurture' that shape human personality (Hamer and Copeland 1999). Therefore, the role of education in discovering and shaping positive attitudes in children and adolescents during school years is extremely important. It should be emphasized that right attitudes are *sine qua non* for building a future where diversity will be an asset not an impediment, and interdependence will be the social architecture cemented by globalization, both within national borders and without. Our ability to overcome differences without resorting to violence and to promote harmony and peace among individuals and communities would depend on how parsimonious we wish to be in pampering our ego and how sincere we are in conceding 'other people can also be right' (IBO 2005). Here education can play a vital role. Both national and international curricula will have to incorporate subjects or courses that will enable students to successfully cope with the complexities of the real world.

VALUES-BASED EDUCATION

As individuals we wish to be cared for, and be able to enjoy tranquility and recognize our surroundings as they are with the help of our faculties. These are the things that were available to us at the time of our entry into the world. Translated into values, they are Love, Peace and Freedom. These basic human values are annotated and expanded as time passes and our contact with the surroundings widens. Soon we realize that our neighbours too have the same cravings. Tolerance and Concern become corollaries to Love, Nonviolence to Peace, and Respect to Freedom. These values are fundamental and common to all human beings whatever may be their cultural or religious orientation. 'Running like a fine thread through the fabric of our existence, values weave through every form and action' (Parekh 2000). Values enable us to choose when presented with options. Since the choices we make are likely to affect other people and the environment it is important that our values help us make judicious choices. Basic values that are inherent in all human beings have been reinforced by the teachings of major world religions. These values are nurtured, enhanced and modified by exposure to and education in family, school and community surroundings.

The importance of values-based education cannot be over-emphasized. The speed and manner in which globalization is progressing leave little doubt that every one of us will have to assume global responsibility. Disparities among world civilizations should be acknowledged and ways and means have to be found to overcome differences peacefully. Damage inflicted on the environment by man-made disasters needs to be repaired ensuring that similar damage can be avoided in the future. Human solidarity based on mutual respect, tolerance and concern will enhance our capacity to meet challenges to our security, welfare and progress. Building a common humanity reflecting the mosaic of all cultures and religions will be a tribute to our wisdom and maturity. To achieve these ideals we must rely on the appropriateness of our decisions that can be ensured only by our attitudes formed by values. Values can be introduced in imparting knowledge through education in different ways. What is relevant is that these values do not remain an intellectual residue but are integrated as traits of one's character. This will require practical training and individual and group assignments in which values are identified, reinforced and developed.

REFERENCES

Carter, A. (2001) *The Political Theory of Global Citizenship*. London: Routledge.

Commission on Human Security (2003) *Report of the Commission*. New York: United Nations.

Compte-Sponville, A. (1996) A *Small Treatise on the Great Virtues*. New York: Metropolitan Books, Henry Hold and Company.

Crafts, N. (2000) *Globalization and Growth in the Twentieth Century*. IMF Working Paper No. 00/44, Washington, DC.

Delanty, G. (1995) *Inventing Europe: Idea, Identity, Reality*. London: Macmillan.

Dower, N. (2004) *Introduction to Global Citizenship*. Edinburgh: Edinburgh University Press.

Falk, R. (1994) The making of global citizenship. In Bart van Steenbergen (ed.) *The Condition of Citizenship*. London: Sage.

Habermas, J. (1994) Citizenship and national identity. In Bart van Steenbergen (ed.) *The Condition of Citizenship*. London: Sage.

Hamer, D. and Copeland, P. (1999) *Living with Our Genes*. London: Macmillan.

IBO (2005) *Mission Statement*. International Baccalaureate Organization (IBO), Geneva.

Kant, I. (1784) *Idee zu einer allgemeinen Geschichte in weltbürgerlicher Absicht* [Idea for a universal history from a cosmopolitan point of view].

Levine, M. (2002) *A Mind at a Time*. New York: Simon & Schuster.

Martiniello, M. (2002) Citizenship. In David Goldberg and John Solomon, (eds) *A Companion to Racial and Ethnic Studies*. Oxford: Blackwell.

Parekh, B. (2000) *Rethinking Multiculturalism*. Basingstoke: Macmillan.

Sprigge, T.L.S. (1999) Arthur Schopenhauer. In Ted Honderich (ed.) *The Philosophers*. Oxford: Oxford University Press.

Tagore, R. (1961) *The Religion of Man*. London: Unwin Books.

Turner, B.D. (1994) Postmodern culture/modern citizens. In Bart van Steenbergen (ed.) *The Condition of Citizenship*. London: Sage.

UNDP (1998) *1998 Human Development Report*. New York: United Nations Development Programme.

UNICEF (1999, 2000, 2003, 2004). *The State of the World's Children*. New York: UNICEF.

World Bank (1999). *Global Development Finance*. Washington, DC: World Bank.

7

A Simple Typology of International-Mindedness and Its Implications for Education

Terry Haywood

The search for a commonly agreed definition of international education has a substantial history that is well documented. Although there appears to be wide recognition of the value and importance of this form of education, be it for the individual, the national society or the global community, it has been particularly hard to pin down precisely what is involved. Fundamentally, the word 'international', whose literal significance refers to interaction between nations, may not be adequate to describe what many educators have really intended when using it as an adjective in the educational context, where they would like it to imply a combination of political astuteness, communication skills across languages, elements of multicultural understanding, global awareness and responsibilities involved with national and global citizenship. A complicating factor can be identified in its relationship with the international schools movement and its promotion in national schools, where it takes on distinct and different meanings that are not always compatible and do not always share a common literature of research or terminology. It has become so apparent that we cannot settle on a commonly agreed definition that there are now widely held views which suggest that the term *international education* might simply be too vague to be really useful. It has, for example, been suggested that we should consider adopting a different term altogether, a recent contender in this respect being '*education for cosmopolitanism*' (Gunesch 2004). Edna Murphy (2000) has gone so far as to ponder whether 'it is time to stop quibbling over definitions, to stop trying to organize the unorganizable … We might want to accept that, finally, we do not in this community speak with one voice'. Meanwhile, Ian Hill (2000), in an article that has become seminal by the simple fact that its recommendation has been widely adopted, argues the case for using 'education for international-mindedness' as a term that is easier to understand and which can more effectively drive the educational process.

Hill's advocacy of *international-mindedness* has a number of important implications. Not least, it shifts the focus of attention towards outcomes of education rather than on the process itself. Instead of defining a particular kind of education, which may restrict the type of school or student population to which it can apply, this approach moves towards identifying some key learning objectives that are attainable in a wide range of contexts. However, it also introduces (or re-introduces, since it is not altogether a novelty) a term that itself begs for definition in terms of specific criteria. Newcomers to the field will be forgiven for imagining that experienced colleagues can categorize international-mindedness with respect to knowledge and skills around which the educational process can be structured, but it remains a disheartening fact that Hill's invitation to explore the meaning of this term has still not led to any agreed understanding on what is really involved. The literature is scanty as regards research to identify hard learning outcomes and this extends even to authorities that have a stated commitment to these outcomes. The International Baccalaureate Organization's Primary Years Programme, for instance, stresses the importance of its student profile (now termed the 'learner profile'), which it describes as follows:

> The student profile describes a list of attributes that promote academic rigour and the establishing of a personal value system leading to international-mindedness. It is expected that PYP teachers will assess and report on individual student development regarding each of these attributes. (IBO 2006)

The IBO has gone some way towards defining international-mindedness through the ten attributes of the learner profile and international educators have become familiar with their generic aspirations. Even so, there is scant guidance on assessment and reporting and little formal basis for understanding precisely what outcomes each attribute will lead to or how the profile might be reflected in students at different stages of development through the programme. Consequently, the treatment of international learning, even in schools that adopt the PYP, is in stark contrast to the way that learning is structured and assessed in mathematics, sciences, the humanities and the arts.

Regarding international-mindedness, there seems to be a prevailing perception that 'we know what we mean even if the definition is still under construction'. This chapter sets out to challenge this perception by arguing that work on the definition is not under construction in any profound way and that we cannot simply assume that 'we know what we mean'. Indeed, I will try to demonstrate that there are diverse and sometimes incompatible perspectives in the way that educators infer international-mindedness. It is, I suggest, time that we face these issues and move towards identification of what our educational objectives should really be since the absence of a more articulate position is not helpful to schools or to students. What follows is a conjectural outline of how we might go about this in a way that opens the potential of international learning goals to a wide range of schools working in any social or cultural context.

REFLECTIONS ON THE NATURE AND EXPRESSION OF INTERNATIONAL-MINDEDNESS

I would begin by making an analogy between the interpretation of international-mindedness and the way that our understanding of *intelligence* has evolved in the past couple of decades. Educators seem to discuss international-mindedness as if it were a distinct entity and that 'we know it when we see it'. This used to be the case with intelligence, which could even be expressed quantitatively as IQ or as a g factor. But just as many educators and psychologists have moved away from thinking about intelligence as a single entity and find it more helpful and relevant to identify a multiplicity of forms (Gardner 1996, 1999), I suggest that we need to evolve beyond our current thinking and its generic references to a sort of international-mindedness (IM) factor to think instead about the multiple and distinct forms in which IM might reveal itself. Indeed, central to my thesis is the proposition that international-mindedness is actually a multi-faceted entity that can be represented in a wide variety of practical forms. I will actively make use of the IM acronym in the following pages as I attempt to identify some of its forms before moving on to break down the concept into component elements in order to propose a number of specific learning and universal outcomes from the educational experience.

Gardner's platform of multiple intelligences has come under scrutiny as a scientific proposition but his work has in any case been pivotal in opening the way for new approaches that look at how education can be structured for learning that is meaningful for the student and is also related to the real world of human interaction. By bringing our definition of IM into sharper focus and drawing out some of its different manifestations, my hope is that we can empower schools in more countries and contexts to reconsider how they cater for and recognize international learning while helping students towards their own interpretations at the same time. However, before moving on to the educator's perspective and to the development of concepts and attitudes in young learners, it is useful to start from the 'big picture' and I will do this by developing a tentative typology that describes briefly a number of the practical forms in which IM can be recognized.

Diplomatic IM

The professional training of the diplomatic corps and the mindset of many lifetime diplomats incorporate explicit use of numerous core skills and abilities that are fundamental to IM. Diplomacy is traditionally based on respect for the nation and culture with which the diplomat is interacting. It almost always involves the learning of a new language, including nuances of verbal and non-verbal expression, and it rarely intrudes on or invades the cultural mores of the other country. Personal histories show how diplomats have to draw on these skills in their working lives,

being expected to spend relatively short postings in very different cultural environments and always being expected to forge constructive ties with the host country. There are, however, some special features of the diplomat's role that derive from the basic objective of diplomacy, which is ultimately to work for the interests of their own nation. It might be argued that the ideal goal is to seek objectives that are mutually beneficial for both nations, the host and the hosted, but this can be a moot point. It can also be problematic to find the right partners for diplomatic reference in societies that are undergoing significant social or political change. Almost by definition, diplomatic IM tends to involve relations with dominant social groups as the representatives of power and influence but this might restrict understanding of society and culture on a wider level. Especially during times of rapid social change, or in nations where there are significant regional, social or cultural divisions with different values and attitudes, the diplomat also needs to have a keen sense of political and social trends.

Political IM

Although it is a valuable component of the diplomat's toolbox, political awareness predisposes to a very different form of IM. For one thing, it does not imply a particular national perspective and the political analyst can genuinely believe in promoting the best interests of all in global terms. On a practical and personal level, moreover, it consists of a very different set of skills, leaning toward the theoretical and sometimes not involving any of the refined communication and interpersonal abilities that a diplomat is called upon to display. One form of political IM is exemplified by commitment to the ideals of the United Nations Organization and the belief in systems for reaching negotiated solutions to global concerns and international conflict. There are, however, more radical forms of political internationalism and there is a substantial history of academic and practical activists who use the study of social, economic or environmental trends to justify the promotion of universal solutions which are perceived to be in the best interests of all. Examples range from the classic Marxist tradition, based on global unity of the working classes to bring about the end of capitalism, to thinkers inspired by Fukuyama's (1992) contention that we have come to the 'end of history' and who argue that it is time for all nations to adopt democratic capitalism as the only proven model of a free society that works effectively in the interests of its population over time. The conclusions of political IM can lead to such contrasting positions which are all international in origin, nature and impact. For the most part they share a similar claim that their proposals for action are not only beneficial to national and global societies but are also in some way 'inevitable' or 'intrinsically right', emerging as the product of serious academic considerations or research rather than as negotiated settlements or compromises.

Economic and commercial IM

Since the earliest days of human history, trade and commerce have been major contributors to international-mindedness, powered by curiosity, need and the demand for products not available in the local environment. Long-distance trade encourages the acquisition of language and practical skills for interpersonal interaction analogous to diplomatic IM. Today, the business world continues to generate a strong international mindset based on an understanding of languages, cultures and ways of thinking and with a profound interest in social and global trends and markets. Interestingly, some of the most influential research into IM, such as the work of Hofstede (1997), and Hampden-Turner and Trompenaars (1997), has its roots in business organizations and communities and finds these enterprises to be among its most avid clients in terms of professional training for the acquisition of international and intercultural skills. Commercial forces also played a massive part in the development of international education,

from the pioneering days in the 1950s with the appearance of a transnational business class, to the emergence of international education as an attractive proposition for local entrepreneurial thinkers in many countries, reflected (most recently) in the expansion of international schooling in China. It is easy to imagine that there is a relationship between economic thought and political ideology, but although there are strong links at the conceptual level, commercial interests probably drive the need for a particular form of IM irrespective of political allegiances or outlook.

Spiritual IM

If commerce promoted a practical form of IM from early in human history, some of the first theoretical and ethical bases for internationalism were developed through religious propositions and belief systems. Some observers are prone to see in religion a potential to divide rather than unite. Not only do the unequivocal positions of some established religions assert that it is not possible to adhere to two faiths at the same time or even to seek a compromise or diplomatic 'middle way', they also encourage the notion that adherence to an alternative belief system will impact seriously on the individual's long-term prospects (in the afterlife) and thereby pose issues such as proselytism or even the elimination of rival faiths. As Sartori (2002) has pointed out, the acceptance of the principle of tolerance in this context is a major achievement and it is one that European culture embraced only after decades of strife during the Reformation. But it might equally be argued that over many centuries the great religious movements were also the only powerful motivators of a mindset that genuinely envisaged the unity of mankind irrespective of nationality or race. They did this in different ways: Christianity and Islam, for instance, expounded a belief in the equality of all men and women before God, while Hinduism placed the human condition in a complex cosmological framework that included all living beings. To deny the powerful influence of this spiritual form of IM is to ignore one of the most profound and influential forms of internationalism, yet secular activists are often wary of devotional movements and it can be difficult for them to debate issues on this level as opposed to using rational or scientific analysis. We must, though, learn to recognize the contributions that have been made by these movements and by their religious leaders to a genuine international-mindedness based upon spiritual values that can engender a common sense of the destiny of humanity as a whole and the place of mankind in the universal order. All the great religions have developed theologies of coexistence and share concern about values and the human condition that enables a productive dialogue to take place. An active group of spiritual thinkers continues to promote peaceful collaboration through interfaith dialogue (Runzo et al. 2003). Given the value of religion for many people across the world and its importance in global affairs, this component of IM cannot be ignored.

Multicultural IM

Multiculturalism is characterized by the celebration of coexistence. There have been a number of significant historical moments (such as Abassid Baghdad or medieval Cordoba and Sicily) where cross-fertilization between cultures led to extremely productive intellectual and economic innovation, but the recent incentive for multicultural ideologies has almost certainly been the emergence of societies in the developed world that have been led to question their 'national' cultures as a result of mass immigration. The impact of multiculturalism is predominantly seen in the context of national education systems, where its exponents have developed sophisticated approaches to teaching concepts, skills and attitudes for intercultural competence, such as those derived from Bennett's (1993) 'stages of cultural sensitivity'. If multiculturalism in the local environment often has the goal of producing integrated and thriving mixed communities, the extension of this mindset to the world stage would appear to be a natural

evolution and one from which international educators can draw productively.

Human rights IM

The signing of the UN Charter of Human Rights in 1948 appeared to signal a common vision of human values embraced by nations across the world. Of course, this was not the case. For reasons that range from deliberate avoidance to diverse interpretation, there is still a wide variety in the rights accorded to individuals in different societies. Groups such as Amnesty International, which have come to the fore in promoting the universal application of human rights, allow for little or no negotiation based on cultural differences when what they see as 'core' human values are at stake. Sometimes the values involved might be seen to be typical of Western democracies but even within these societies they are not uniformly applied or understood. Recent issues in this respect range from capital punishment to the treatment of prisoners of war or the wearing of headscarves and religious symbols in schools. From an internationalist perspective the human rights form of IM can sometimes be problematic, raising questions about the extent to which we are willing to recognize other cultures and the role of the individual and institutions in society. However, both the desire to see a common system of rights applied in all nations and the search to identify those rights are often recognized as hallmarks of the internationalist mindset (Clemo 2005).

Pacifist IM

Throughout the long and violent history of humanity, a high value has been placed on peace and it is a condition that has rarely, if ever, been taken for granted. Pacifism as an ideology, however, is a relatively recent movement, which promotes the resolution of all conflicts without any recourse to force. Consequently, it tends to be open to tolerance and negotiation and it can sometimes seem to adopt a relativistic stance as regards cultures and political order. However, this is not always the case and some movements founded on principles of non-violence might still have strongly held beliefs as regards human rights or spiritual values.

Humanitarian IM

The tragedy of the human condition is no better expressed than through the gross inequalities of life offered to children at birth. Poverty is the most aggressive curse of mankind and the struggle to combat its horrors is probably the most pressing immediate concern in terms of the suffering and death caused on a daily basis. Humanitarian IM is the mindset that poses this as the prime challenge facing us today. There are some highly visible exponents in the public eye, such as the Live 8 movement, and many people are drawn to commit their personal lives and careers in this area, from voluntary or professional workers with aid agencies to economists and politicians trying to identify short- and long-range strategies to boost economies, provide sustainable agriculture and offer better prospects for future generations. The motivation behind this form of IM is almost always an instinctive human response to help those in need, but the elaboration of this mindset into a practical response can operate at a number of levels and these include political and economic considerations that are not always mutually compatible. Routes to development can be proposed from opposing political stances, yet there is no reason to think that they do not originate from a common underlying international-mindedness.

Environmentalist IM

The recognition that environmental issues can be a question of global relevance as opposed to merely local problems is a recent phenomenon. It derives from growing scientific awareness that there seems to be a delicate and insecure equilibrium of conditions in the thin region where life exists just above the earth's crust. Concern that human intervention is disturbing this balance has resulted in the growth of an environmentalist IM which identifies

this as the major issue facing humanity in the emergent future. Numerous other global concerns also reflect this type of IM, such as the depletion of energy sources and the need to find long-term sustainable options, the impact of pollution and the elimination of waste in local as well as global environments. In some ways, Environmental IM may be part of a wider *Scientific IM*, which includes numerous other concerns such as the emergence of new diseases and the impact of biotechnology on agriculture and medicine.

Globalization and IM

The impact of globalization has generated a novel way of viewing world affairs. This complex interaction of technological, social, political and economic processes gives rise to a dynamic and powerful set of aspirations that we can characterize as a distinct form of IM which focuses on coming to terms with these changes and trying to envisage what the long-term implications of globalization will be. Although it is possible to express this form of IM as an academic fascination with the evolution of peoples and societies, the notion of globalization is not usually regarded as value-free. Some see the phenomenon as a threat to traditional cultural expressions or to already stretched resources that will only lead to an increase in world poverty: others are concerned that, to date, it has been closely identified with Westernization, a form of cultural imperialism; others suggest that it actually offers all nations increased access to the world market which, if exploited appropriately, will enable a redistribution of wealth in favour of the development of nations that are currently oppressed by poverty.

ESSENTIAL AND SUPPORTING COMPONENTS OF INTERNATIONAL-MINDEDNESS

This simple typology of international-mindedness is open to substantial analysis and critical appraisal. In the way I have presented it, however, it is not intended to be either a scientific undertaking or a Gardnerian classification of mindsets so much as an illustration of the diverse ways in which international-mindedness can be articulated in practice. None of my IM forms will be unfamiliar territory to international educators and, given the profound commitment that some internationalists demonstrate towards particular aspects of world affairs, the conjectural summaries might well appear to be rather trite or shallow. However, if we move to assess these expressions of IM from the perspective of the international educator then a number of issues emerge which I believe are far from being trite or shallow.

First of all, we need to recognize that these adult expressions of international-mindedness are not in themselves objectives we should in any way identify as learning outcomes in their own right. The educator's role is not to direct students towards a particular style of IM, but is instead to encourage a predisposition towards international-mindedness in general that will allow students to develop their own responses and channels of expression. A corollary of this is that we have to respect and value the variety of personal responses which our students display in terms of the actions prompted by their developing IM. We have to recognize that there may well be disparate responses not only in terms of the specific thinking that individuals prioritize, for instance whether they lean towards spiritual or environmentalism expressions, but also as to the specific stances taken within each position. There is no monopoly on the right way to think and act internationally and the educator ought to avoid any form of indoctrination even if well intended. This generic appreciation of IM only takes us back to our position at the outset, however, and I believe that we can and should be able to refer to much more specific criteria (and associated assessment rubrics) that are far from being generic in nature. This is something to which I will return shortly.

It is not difficult to imagine that differences of opinion will be central to any debate on internationalism. Indeed, there may even be degrees of implicit incompatibility between different types of IM – in other words, some forms of IM may be mutually exclusive rather than complementary. It is not too difficult to think of situations where the action determined by one form of IM contrasts *in toto* with the action prescribed by another form. For instance, can we always reconcile the Human Rights IM with more culturally sensitive approaches inherent in the Diplomatic, Multicultural or Pacifist forms? To take an extreme but realistic example, when we are dealing with a well-established culture that has strong popular allegiance but perceives equality of the sexes or individual rights in a different way from our own, questions of prioritization in our attitudes are inevitable. This consideration does not just apply to fundamentalist religious cultures. An equally challenging perspective is the assertion by Nisbett (2003) that intrinsic thinking processes around the world differ to the extent that there is a recognizable diversity in the concept of justice between the USA and Asia as regards a simple statement such as 'the law is equal for all'.

Pearce's (2002, 2003) account of the futility of searching for absolute universal values is highly relevant in this respect. As he points out, the vast majority of cultures adheres to similar general values and these include apparently similar notions of justice, human rights and responsibilities, loyalty to the community, the importance of truth, and so on. However, misunderstanding (and mistrust) can develop out of the way that these values are prioritized in different cultural expressions. For example, when people are faced with having to prioritize between loyalty to their friends and family as opposed to telling the truth to a teacher about a suspected case of plagiarism or copying, we might not get identical responses from people who claim to adhere to similar value systems. This is not just a test of personal character, but also of cultural allegiance and the way that the values to which individuals adhere are prioritized in their own thought processes. Similarly, there can be variations in the ways that adults demonstrate international-mindedness and in the priorities they allocate to different forms even when they appear to have a commonality of commitment.

Where does this leave us on the question that I posed at the outset, and how has it helped to move us towards the identification of a specific set of learning outcomes related to international-mindedness? It may seem that the discussion so far has complicated this question rather than having resolved it. By representing IM in such a multitude of forms, however, we can also begin to identify some of the common or '*essential*' elements of which it is composed and separate out some of the '*supporting*' attributes.

In the literature and practice of international education we can identify two distinct approaches to the organization of teaching and learning. The traditional one, exhibited in Mattern (1990), tended to focus on *subject-specific* curriculum content based around the identification of knowledge, understanding and skills which are seen to contribute to an international mindset. The more recent approach, perhaps best represented by the IBO Primary Years Programme, stresses the creation of a school-wide learning environment in which subject content is absorbed into the holistic learning experience, which also emphasizes the development of attitudes as well as knowledge, concepts and skills. Both approaches reflect a typically Western tradition in education: indeed, they embody features of research, debate and educational thinking that are often not only Western but also distinctly Anglo-American in origin. It would probably be most revealing to investigate just how indebted the current expressions of international curricula are to a relatively small number of sources, especially Dewey and Gardner. The exponents of these approaches might claim that they have universal value, based as they are on theories of mind and on a psychology and pedagogy of learning that are potentially universal in application. But others, such as Cambridge (2003), have warned of globalizing tendencies and the failure of these approaches to recognize non-Western expressions of education and cultural mindsets. Dewey would have understood this position clearly: 'the conception of education as a social process and function has no definite meaning until we define the kind of society

we have in mind' (Dewey 1916). Indeed, no matter how appropriate and successful Western educational models are in their own contexts, we cannot expect them to be accepted uncritically as models for the organization of teaching and learning in other cultural settings. On the contrary, the internationalist argument would probably contend that each culture (and maybe even each school) has to develop its own educational model that combines an emphasis on IM with roots in its own circumstances, in the culture and make-up of the students it serves, and (in Dewey's terms) in its own perception of social organization.

Although this is an explicit encouragement to proliferate diversity in education, I believe that it also leads to a genuine basis for common ground as regards the promotion of IM. Indeed, if we can begin to think about international learning in terms of specific criteria with age-appropriate outcomes, then we can move away from the generic into treating IM as a hard learning area, as we do for other components of the curriculum. This is a major challenge but if progress can be made in this direction then the core features of IM can acquire the status of common ground by providing a uniform terminology and basis for ongoing enquiry and development by international educators from diverse cultural traditions. One approach to finding this commonality can be through the identification of 'essential' and 'supporting' components of IM. Essential components are the minimum a school must provide to enable the potential of IM to develop in young people in any of its forms. They may be universal in nature, while 'supporting' features can contribute to IM but are fundamentally located in the local culture of the school. Drawing on the typology introduced previously, I suggest that the following components are essential to any educational process for international-mindedness:

- curiosity and interest in the world around us, based on knowledge of the earth and on its human and physical geography
- open attitudes towards other ways of life and a predisposition to tolerance as regards other cultures and their belief systems

- knowledge and understanding of the scientific basis that identifies the earth's environment as a common entity of value to everyone
- recognition of the interconnectedness of human affairs (in place and time) as part of the holistic experience of life
- human values that combine respect for other ways of life with care and concern for the welfare and well-being of people in general.

Any school that holds international-mindedness as one of its professed outcomes must ensure that strategies are firmly in place to ensure that the learning experience provides for all these areas. None of them can be taken for granted as part of a student's natural development nor as features that can be learned by osmosis from the scholastic environment without an explicit statement of aims, objectives and expectations for what this learning will imply for students of different ages. The list includes specific content and knowledge in areas such as geography and science. It calls on the need to address the concept of interrelatedness in direct terms. And although the approaches to learning in each of the above areas can be culturally determined, there is no need for the outcomes to be locally distinct. Indeed, it may even be possible to draw up content, skills and attitudes that are genuinely universal in these five areas, and there is no reason why the objective of such a common benchmark should not be a unifying feature to which all 'internationally-minded' schools can adhere. Conjectural as it is at this stage, work towards the cross-cultural definition of this common ground would make a fascinating project for further research.

The list of five *essential* components comprises the core international learning experience of students but it by no means determines the entire curriculum they encounter in school. Everything else that is included in their learning programme can be modeled on local cultural forces determined within the school's own context with no expectation of common ground or common outcomes. These features, which can all contribute to learning for IM but which are not essential components, include:

- the way that curriculum is designed and constructed
- pedagogy and educational philosophy
- the role of teachers and school organization
- approaches and expectations for learning in specific areas not included in the five essential components (including mathematics, the arts and languages)
- every other aspect of school.

Supporting components are not any less important than essential components in the holistic education of the learner but, whereas the former can aspire to universality, the latter allow for different cultural priorities and norms to express themselves. I have singled out *languages* from the above list because it is a good example of how these 'supporting' components can be structured in different ways. Is it, for instance, essential to be bilingual or multilingual in order to be internationally-minded? Or can we accept that our learning outcomes for language skills will be best determined by local educators who tailor their objectives to their own cultural environment and to the overall school philosophy? A bilingual (Anglo-Chinese) school in Shanghai will approach this in one way, an international school in Vienna will take a different route, a multicultural school in London will adopt another, while a monolingual school community in any part of the world will choose yet another. We cannot set standards, benchmarks, expectations (or even the inclusion of foreign language) as an essential criterion for international-mindedness. What we can do is expect each school to develop a strategy for its community, to make it explicit how this strategy supports international learning, and to identify outcomes and assessment approaches for students at different ages.

I am less concerned with supporting components because they have an indeterminate potential for diversity. This variety is exciting and celebratory, just as one would hope from international encounters in which cultural traditions and norms are respected and valued. What really interests me is the focus on essential components, which ought to be the common denominator for internationally-minded schools … wherever they operate.

A SUMMARY AND AN APPEAL

This short chapter has tackled perhaps the most ambitious theme of international education, and its scope has inevitably led to condensation of ideas and supporting research. Whether or not its conclusions will be of value to international educators, I hope at least that it will provoke reflection on a number of levels.

The first of these is concerned with going beyond Murphy's (2000: p. 8) contention that '*we do not in this community speak with one voice*' and with seeking to '*organize the unorganizable*'. There can still be many voices – but it is at least possible for them to share a common language. Another concern at this level is to encourage deeper thinking about what we really mean by international-mindedness. The term is often used generically in a way that diminishes meaning, but I still believe that it can become the central concept in helping us to determine what we really want international education to be about.

The second level relates to the recognition that there can be many distinct ways of educating for IM. We must not be limited by our current cultural conditions but neither must we promote any single model for international learning as universal in relevance or as superior to other forms. It might be entirely appropriate for us to believe that the model we have constructed or adopted for our own school is the most suitable one for our own environment, but it is frankly imperialist, globalist and anti-internationalist to presuppose that this same model will also be the most appropriate one for other schools, or that it is the only one that determines international learning outcomes.

The third level, however, suggests that although there are many different ways of educating for international-mindedness, this does not mean that there is no common ground. On the contrary, there ought to be very clear commonality and much greater interaction across cultures, languages and school systems based on the recognition of components that are essential to any form of international education.

On the fourth and final level, I reiterate that international learning outcomes must be identified just as precisely as those we set for mathematics, science, humanities or other components of the traditional curriculum. This is all too rarely the case, sometimes on account of the 'real' prioritization of interests that arises in managing a successful institution in a competitive market place, but also because some teachers have difficulty in structuring learning in an area for which they have probably received little formal training or preparation. But if international education is really going to come of age, then we really need to include it as a 'formal' learning area to be charted within any international school with clearly indicated outcomes for students at each age level, accompanied by assessment strategies and approaches to teaching and learning.

None of the above can be realized in isolation and there is an underlying need for those interested in extending the provision of international education to develop a forum for exchange and cooperation. At the risk of introducing a cultural paradigm for the second time, the words of Dewey (1916: p. 16) make a fitting call to action: 'things gain meaning by being used in a shared experience or joint action'.

REFERENCES

Bennett, M.J. (1993) Towards ethnorelativism: a developmental model of intercultural sensitivity. In *Education for the Intercultural Experience*, 2nd edition. Yarmouth: Intercultural Press.

Cambridge, J. (2003) Identifying the globalist and internationalist missions of international schools. *International Schools Journal*, XXII (2): 54–8.

Clemo, J. (2005) Human rights, education and international-mindedness. *International Schools Journal*, XXIV (2): 24–31.

Dewey, J. (1916) *Democracy and Education*. New York: MacMillan.

Fukuyama, F. (1992) *The End of History and the Last Man*. Glencoe, IL: Free Press.

Gardner, H. (1996) Multiple intelligences: myths and messages. *International Schools Journal*, XV (2): 8–22.

Gardner, H. (1999) *Intelligence Reframed*. New York: Basic Books.

Gunesch, K. (2004) Education for cosmopolitanism? Cosmopolitanism as a personal cultural identity model for and within international education. *Journal of Research in International Education,* 3 (3): 251–75.

Hampden-Turner, C. and Trompenaars, F. (1997) *Riding the Waves of Culture: Understanding Cultural Diversity in Business,* 2nd edition. London: Nicholas Brealey.

Hill, I. (2000) Internationally minded schools. *International Schools Journal,* XX (1): 24–37.

Hofstede, G. (1997) *Cultures and Organizations: Software of the Mind.* New York, McGraw–Hill.

IBO (2006) www.ibo.org/pyp/curriculum/profile/

Mattern, G. (1990) The best of times, the worst of times, and what to do about it on Monday morning. *International Schools Journal,* 19: 35–47.

Murphy, E. (2000) Questions for the new millennium. *International Schools Journal,* XIX (2): 5–10.

Nisbett, R.E. (2003) *The Geography of Thought.* New York: Free Press (Simon and Schuster).

Pearce, R. (2002) The creation and promotion of values in international education. Presentation at the conference on Interpreting International Education, Geneva, 2002 (summarized on http://www.bath.ac.uk/ceic/geneva2002/) with extended personal correspondence).

Pearce, R. (2003) Cultural values for international schools. *International Schools Journal,* XXII (2): 59–65.

Runzo, J., Martin, N. and Sharma, A. (2003) *Human Rights and Responsibilities in the World Religions.* Oxford: Oneworld Publications.

Sartori, G. (2002) *Pluralismo, multiculturalism e estranei.* Milan: RCS.

8

International Education's Internationalism: Inspirations from Cosmopolitanism

Konrad Gunesch

It may come as a surprise that within the literature on international education, there is no single coherent picture of the 'internationalism' or 'international-mindedness' within the individual that, presumably, international education aims to develop. Indeed, current concerns over international education appear to centre on definitions of the field and of international schools, the nature of an international curriculum and the organization and management of international schools. This can, for instance, be observed in most of the contributions within the leading textbooks on international education in recent years (see Blandford and Shaw 2001, and the edited books by Hayden and Thompson 1998 and 2000, as well as by Hayden, Thompson and Walker 2002). Even those contributions that imply aims and outcomes of international education in terms of desirable developments and transformations in the individual learner contain remarkably little in terms of clarification and theorization of their nature. Undoubtedly,

the aims and outcomes of international education in terms of desirable developments and transformations in the individual learner are implicit in much of this writing, but remarkably little is directed at clarifying and theorizing their nature. For instance, writings on the key concept of students' identities in international schools (Pearce 1998) and on the issue of the meaning of 'home' for 'disoriented children' (Walker 1998) both appear centrally in the analysis of cosmopolitanism presented here, while the so-called 'third culture kids', a particular and relatively tiny group that are atypical in relation to the majority of the world's young people, are identified partly as a 'problem' for international education and partly as an 'ideal model' of desirable individual outcomes (Langford 1998), but are discussed in empirical and pragmatic rather than conceptual or theoretical terms.

I would argue, therefore, that there is a need for a clearer account of the nature of the 'international' individual that international schools – and international education in national schools – may be aiming to promote. This chapter attempts to provide a model for a potentially desirable individual outcome of an international education, but rooted in the concept of cosmopolitanism, rather than internationalism, for reasons that are discussed below. The chapter introduces and proposes 'cosmopolitanism' as a *personal* cultural identity form for and within the rather *institutionalized* setting of 'international education'. It specifically proposes a complementary model to the notion of 'internationalism' within 'international education'. The conceptualization of cosmopolitanism is taken from the author's study of 'The relationship between multilingualism and cosmopolitanism' (Gunesch 2002). This study developed working definitions of cosmopolitanism and multilingualism, both hitherto not existing in that form, by means of a critical analysis of literature. This analysis led to the development of a 'cosmopolitan matrix', representing the key components of cosmopolitanism. The empirical part of the study analysed how a group of 11 students, selected for their multilinguality, revealed themselves in terms of cosmopolitan cultural identity according to the developed matrix of cosmopolitanism. In this chapter, the cosmopolitan aspect of that research, that is, that matrix, will be presented and related to 'international education' and specifically 'internationalism'. This chapter has taken a theoretical approach in that the conceptual framework of cosmopolitanism is based on a comprehensive literature synthesis.

The implications of this conceptualization are, however, also practical, since the model of cosmopolitanism was itself consequently tested for its robustness and real-world applicability with the group of multilingual students. First, the 11 students confirmed each of the categories of the literature matrix presented below as relevant to their personal cultural identity. Secondly, since the students did so to a varying extent and degree within each category, it produced a pattern of 'cosmopolitan responsiveness' for each student and for subgroups among the 11 students. In the end, this enabled a synthesis to be made of three 'cosmopolitan ideal types' across the student group. These three ideal types were later labelled 'Advanced Tourist', 'Transitional Cosmopolitan' and 'Interactive Cosmopolitan'. With these ideal types previously not existing in the literature, and with 'individual multilinguality' as the decisive selection criterion for the student group in the first place, this allowed the study to relate multilingualism and cosmopolitanism by adding to and refining the existing literature categories of cosmopolitanism. It must, however, be stressed that due to the exploratory character of this research it was not possible to go on to establish any kinds of 'causality' implications. For these reasons, it is claimed that the model of 'cosmopolitanism' can also hold its own in the world of international education, as set out below.

Cosmopolitanism as an inspiration for internationalism

The motivation for wishing to breathe some fresh life into international education's internationalism, and especially for seeking inspiration from cosmopolitanism, has several reasons: for once, there is an ongoing discussion of what constitutes 'internationalism' or the element of 'international' in the context of international education. Unsurprisingly, the literature that tries to come to grips with the definition of the element 'international' in the concept of 'international education' is vast (see for example Allan 2003: 83; Gellar 2002: 30; Hayden et al. 2000: 107–21; Mackenzie 2000: 42, 48–50; McKenzie 1998: 243–4; Skelton 2002: 44; Thompson 1998: 278). Instead of discussing the novelty or essentiality of yet another element of 'international' or 'internationalism', the proposed model will involve cosmopolitanism as an alternative or complementary element. Cosmopolitanism seems to be especially fit for this purpose, as there are writers in its literature who regard internationalism, although a component of cosmopolitanism with a specific meaning discussed below, as being no longer sufficient and wish to transcend the idea of internationalism as being based on nation-states (Rée 1998: 88; Sarup 1996: 142).

From a practical viewpoint, cosmopolitanism as an individual identity form does not (yet) have any comparable significant, widespread or traditional institutional attachments, like schools or associations. This removes the need to put the proposed model of cosmopolitanism in an institutional setting such as international schools or organizations, whereas 'internationalism', 'being international', 'international-mindedness' or 'international attitude' seem to belong to a much more institution-bound area of investigation within such frameworks as 'international schools' (see Allan 2003: 83; Hayden et al. 2000: 107–12), 'international education' (see Hayden and Thompson 1995: 394) or 'international curriculum' (see Mackenzie 2000: 42, 48–50; McKenzie 1998: 243–4; Skelton 2002: 44–53; Thompson 1998: 278–81).

Having said that, the proposed model of cosmopolitanism as a personal cultural identity form *can*, and as it will be argued, *should* be applied and used, theoretically and also practically, by international educators, globally mobile people as well as anyone else who believes that he or she could benefit from its theoretical and practical implications of cosmopolitanism. As Gellar puts it: 'The fact that the world is small, fragile, and its inhabitants increasingly dependent on one another … has also made it imperative that international educators … focus on issues and problems that are transnational and transcultural' (2002: 32). Cosmopolitanism will be presented as a model for such transnationalism and transculturalism, being an original model not least because, as mentioned, it wishes in parts to *transcend* the idea of internationalism as well as that of nation-states. Therefore, a special focus will be on the relationship between cosmopolitanism and internationalism, as well as on the relationship between cosmopolitanism and the nation-state.

CONCEPTUAL FRAMEWORK

The matrix of cosmopolitanism

The literature openly admits cosmopolitanism to be lacking a sharp and detailed definition, and to be an identity form *sui generis* (see Anderson 1998: 267; Brennan 2001: 76; Clifford 1998: 365; Eagleton 2000: 63; Mehta 2000: 621; Pollock et al. 2002: 1; Robbins 1998b: 12; Waldron 1995: 110, 112), a 'term with a complex history' (Mehta 2000: 620), and a 'subject of interdisciplinary debate' (Dharwadker 2001: 1). Therefore, the definition of cosmopolitanism below is a literature matrix of cosmopolitan cultural identity with writings from several disciplines. It is not merely a literature review, but a literature synthesis, that has been, in turn, subjected to substantial critical thinking. Cosmopolitanism can usefully be pre-defined by the catchword phrase reoccurring in the literature of 'feeling at home in the world' (see for instance the title of Brennan's 1997 book *At Home in the World: Cosmopolitanism Now*). This 'feeling at home in the world' could be specified as interest in, or engagement with, cultural diversity by straddling the global and the local spheres in terms of personal identity. Straddling in this sense means having one foot in each sphere, and finding a balance in which the global is decisive without necessarily dominating all the time.

The cosmopolitan straddling the global and the local

In terms of a simplifying model, one can distinguish between cosmopolitanism and localism, or between people who are cosmopolitans and locals. While the local may not be interested in cultural diversity, the cosmopolitan consciously values, seeks out and tries to access local cultural diversity. Since that cultural diversity always comprises the respective local(s), cosmopolitanism logically presupposes localism (Friedman 1994: 204–5; 1995: 78–9; Hannerz 1990: 237, 249–50; 1996: 102, 111; Pollock 2002: 17). Other literature amends the global and local existences with a notion such as 'living in between' or a 'balancing act' (Anderson 1998: 276; Clifford 1992: 108; 1997: 36; Rabinow 1986: 258). These existences, then, do not have to be exclusive opposites, but can be seen as the extreme ends of a continuum, with a possible development process for the individual from local to cosmopolitan. This continuum idea is relevant also to other aspects of the cosmopolitan model.

Cosmopolitan competence or mastery

The cosmopolitan's access to local cultural diversity leads to a competence or mastery in the respective local culture(s). Depending on the degree of that competence or mastery, one can speak of 'connaissance', rather than (mere) 'dilettantism' (Hannerz 1990: 239–40; 1992: 252–3; 1996: 103). These two can again be seen as extreme ends of a continuum along which the cosmopolitan can advance, and which serves to distinguish between different cosmopolitans with respect to their local competence, as well as between different degrees of competence (from one local culture to another) within the same cosmopolitan person.

The cosmopolitan metacultural position

While the previous competence aspect of cosmopolitanism could be described as knowledge, or an objective characteristic of a cosmopolitan person, an attitude, or a subjective characteristic of cosmopolitanism is phrased by Hannerz as 'a willingness to engage with the Other, an intellectual and ethic stance of openness toward divergent cultural experiences' (1992: 252; similarly 1990: 239; 1996: 103; similarly Abbas 2002: 211; Fullinwider 2001: 341; Papastephanou 2002: 69–70), it can refer to the ways in which access to, as well as competence within, the respective local culture is thought. It also allows for individual dislike of what is

open-mindedly engaged with. That is, the individual cosmopolitan, while able to engage with a local culture, is not necessarily committed through that engagement positively to endorse that culture, either in its entirety or with respect to components of it.

The question of mobility or travelling

On the one hand, travelling is indispensable for cosmopolitan experiences (Appadurai and Breckenridge 1998: 5; Beck 2000: 96; Clifford 1992: 103). On the other hand, it is not sufficient unless done with the background and the attitude of connaissance and cultural engagement, lest it be mere tourism (Hannerz 1990: 240–2; 1992: 246–8; 1996: 105; Robbins 1998a: 254; Tomlinson 1999: 186). Hence while the so-called 'third culture kids' (TCKs) or 'global nomads' have (by definition, already during their developmental years) fulfilled the travelling aspect (Langford 1998: 30; Pollock and Van Reken 2001: 19; Tokuhama-Espinosa 2003: 165), which might give them a head start with respect to the formation of a cosmopolitan cultural identity, the mere fact of being a third culture kid does not yet make them cosmopolitan.

The relationship between cosmopolitanism and tourism

The mobility aspect also evokes a comparison with the image of the typical tourist. As the adjective 'typical' suggests, the tourist lacks both the objective requirement of competence or mastery as well as the subjective requirement of pursuit of open-minded, deep and meaningful engagement with cultural diversity. The tourist prefers to hang on to holiday stereotypes and cultural clichés with respect to the target culture (Baumann 1996: 29; Bruckner 1996: 247–9; Carter 2001: 77; Curtis and Pajaczkowska 1994: 201; Featherstone 1993: 182; 1995: 98; Fischer 1996: 73–6). Taking out the 'typical' does, however, mean that even a cosmopolitan can engage in tourism (Appiah 1998: 91). As with the cosmopolitan–local image, one could see this either as a clear dichotomy, or as a continuum that makes it possible for an individual to develop from tourist to cosmopolitan. Indeed, the investigated multilingual individuals defined an intermediate category of 'advanced' tourist on such a continuum.

Home for the cosmopolitan

Even with a shorthand definition such as 'at home in the world' (Brennan 1997), the question of where 'home' is for the cosmopolitan individual is perplexing or paradoxical (Beck 2002: 36; Eagleton 2000: 63; Iyer 2000: 136; Mathews 2000: 151, 194; Turner 2002: 60). With a variety of accessed and accessible cultures, home might not be the 'home culture' any more, due to acquired multicultural perspectives or identifications. For that reason, the 'classical home' as locals know it might have ceased to exist. Or, it might indeed be the classical home, albeit seen from the new cosmopolitan perspective, which would then alter its original meaning. Home could also take on an entirely new meaning formed from the multicultural perspective of the cosmopolitan individual (Hannerz 1990: 240, 248; 1992: 253–4; 1996: 110). Another possibility is a multiplicity of homes, combining several or all of the previous alternatives, while logically and logistically home cannot be everywhere. In the end, the question of home remains literally wide open.

The relationship between cosmopolitanism and the nation-state

A very important and extensive discussion point recurring in the literature is the relationship between cosmopolitanism and the nation-state or national identity. It is included in our matrix of cosmopolitan cultural identity in the sense that the nation-state deeply permeates the daily life of contemporary persons in a variety of ways, culturally as well as politically. While the borders between cultural or political permeation

are often impossible to delineate clearly, the general salience of the nation-state for identity issues is reflected in literature that does not treat cosmopolitanism, but describes national identity and the nation(-state) as still the globally most prevalent single identity frame or reference point, compared to other possible identity frames or reference points (see just Greenfeld 1996: 10; Guibernau 1996: 73; 2001: 257; Moore 2001: 56; Opello and Rosow 1999: 253–4; Parmenter 1999: 454; Smith 1991: 170; Wallerstein 1991: 92).

Cosmopolitan models opposing the nation-state

If one keeps in mind the etymological meaning of 'cosmopolitan' from classical Greek *kosmou politês* as a 'citizen of the world', of which the literature is aware (Carter 2001: 2 and 2005: 21; Cheah 1998: 22; Derrida 1997: 11; Edwards 2001: 34; Heater 2000: 179 and 2002: 7, 27; Münch 2001: 69; Pollock 2002: 25; Robbins 1992: 184; Tomlinson 1999: 184; Wollen 1994: 189), some authors can be seen as stating the logical consequence of this:

> Cosmopolitans are, almost by definition, people who regret the privileging of national identities in political life, and who reject the principle that political arrangements should be ordered in such a way as to reflect and protect national identities. (Kymlicka 2001: 204; similarly Buzan, Held and McGrew 1998: 388–9; Friedman 1994: 204–5; 1995: 78–9)

Sarup and Rée both go considerably further in their personal involvement and attempt to construct a new model of cosmopolitanism or world citizenship:

> I think we should be thinking in terms beyond the nation-state. Internationalism is inadequate because it assumes the existence of the nation-state. I suggest that we try and discover a new form of world citizenship. Is it too idealistic to hope that, wherever you are, you are a citizen of that place? ... A cosmopolitan is ... one 'who has no fixed abode' or one 'who is nowhere a foreigner'. (Sarup 1996: 142–3)

> Is it possible to hope for a new cosmopolitanism, after internationality? ... Perhaps we may look forward to a future in which people could interpret themselves without any reference to the idea that

their nation is their self, in fact without any essential reference to nationality at all ... A new cosmopolitan world, which could put the illusions of internationality behind it, for good. (Rée 1998: 88)

Strongest of all, in her essay 'Patriotism and cosmopolitanism', Martha Nussbaum (described by Heater 2002: 11 as 'one of the most influential scholars in the field of cosmopolitan writing'), holds an 'emphasis on patriotic pride' to be 'morally dangerous' (1996: 4), and 'nationalism and ethnocentrism' as a 'morally irrelevant characteristic' (p. 5). She explicitly puts forward a model of cosmopolitan identity as 'world citizenship' based on the Greek Stoics after Diogenes the Cynic (pp. 6–9) but filled with contemporary meaning. It reiterates several aspects of the cosmopolitan matrix developed by this author, while others are taken up by critical literature discussed below:

> The Stoics stress that to be a citizen of the world one does not need to give up local identification, which can be a source of great richness in life. They suggest that we think of ourselves not as devoid of local affiliations, but as surrounded by a series of concentric circles. The first one encircles the self, the next takes in the immediate family, then follows the extended family, then, in order, neighbours or local groups, fellow city-dwellers and fellow countrymen – and we can easily add to this list groupings based on ethnic, linguistic, historical, professional, gender, or sexual identities. Outside all these circles is the largest one, humanity as a whole. Our task as citizens of the world will be to 'draw the circles somehow toward the centre' (Stoic philosopher Hierocles, 1st – 2nd century CE), making all human beings more like our fellow city-dwellers, and so on. We need not give up our special affections and identifications ... But we should ... give the circle that defines our humanity special attention and respect (Nussbaum 1996: 9).

Models reconciling cosmopolitanism and the nation-state

In decisive opposition to Nussbaum's model, a number of authors explicitly embrace the nation-state attachment. As a result, the model of a 'rooted cosmopolitanism, or if you like, a cosmopolitan patriotism' (Appiah 1998: 91) is put forward, which stresses the feasibility and necessity of having loyalties to nation-states as well as to larger and smaller entities at the same time:

> The cosmopolitan patriot can entertain the possibility of a world in which *everyone* is a rooted cosmopolitan, attached to a home of his or her own, with its own cultural particularities, but taking pleasure from the presence of other, different, places that are home to other, different, people ... We cosmopolitans *can* be patriots ... It is because humans live best on a small scale that we should defend not just the state, but the county, the town, the street, the business, the craft, the profession, the family, *as* communities, as circles among the many circles narrower than the human horizon, that are appropriate spheres of human concern. We should, in short, as cosmopolitans, defend the right to live in democratic states, with rich possibilities of association within and across their borders. (Appiah 1998: 91, 95, 96, 97, original emphases; similarly Bhabha 1996: 202; Cohen 1992: 483; Hollinger 1995: 5; Malcomson 1998: 234–5, 242–3; Robbins 1998b: 1)

To sum up the relationship between cosmopolitanism and the nation-state: while models opposing nation-states seek forms of attachment and identity only beyond the nation-state, models that reconcile cosmopolitanism and the nation-state argue for forms of attachment and identity within, as well as beyond, the nation-state. The decisive point is that for both strands of cosmopolitanism, identity and attachment, forms *beyond* the nation-state are a matter of course. The whole discussion hinges on the desirability of forms of attachment and identity *within* the nation-state. This means that while larger dimensions than the nation-state are taken for granted, the nation-state is not (not even by those supporting it). Useful as an overall summary of the theoretical implications of this complex issue is Robbins's suggestion that 'there is no simple relation between cosmopolitanism and the state' (1998b: 8). In sum, this is one of the most interesting aspects of the cosmopolitan matrix with respect to 'international education' and its discussion about 'internationalism', since 'cosmopolitanism' offers quite a different take on this notion.

Literature summary

The following are the main areas of personal concern or engagement for a cosmopolitan person according to the synthesized literature:

- *a straddling of the 'global' and the 'local' spheres,* with a decisive impact of the global ('world citizen')
- *a 'connaissance' with respect to (local) cultural diversity wherever possible,* otherwise an interested 'dilettantism'
- *a general willingness and openness towards engagement with cultural diversity,* which yet allows for 'dislike'
- *the mobility to travel,* with a discussion about whether this is sufficient
- *an attitude not of the 'typical tourist',* while the 'occasional tourist' accommodates fewer concerns
- *a notion of 'home' that can be extremely varied,* while it is no longer undisputedly the 'home culture', it also is not 'everywhere'
- *a critical attitude towards the (native) nation-state,* which can range between 'rooted' and 'unrooted' identity expressions.

The differentiation between cosmopolitanism and globalization

Globalization is associated with cultural uniformity (Jameson 2000: 51; Sifakis and Sougari 2003: 60; Watson 2000: 68–71) rather than with cultural diversity (Scholte 2000: 23). Cosmopolitanism, however, is only concerned with cultural diversity.

For that reason, globalization defined as going 'global and local at the same moment' (Hall 1991: 27; similarly Featherstone 1993: 169; Held et al. 1999: 28) is not the same as the cosmopolitan straddling of the global and the local. Historically, the globalization debate originated in the twentieth century (Nicholson 1999: 24; Scholte 2000: 16), while the idea of cosmopolitanism goes back to the Greek Stoics of the first and second centuries BC, and has thereafter been strongly debated, especially in the seventeenth/eighteenth century, and recently, as of the early 1990s (see Carter 2001: 1; Derrida 1997: 47–8, Edwards 2001: 34; Fougeret de Monbron 1970; Heater 2000: 179–80; 2002: 11, 26, 40; Malcomson 1998: 233).

The differentiation between cosmopolitanism and internationalism

The differentiation between 'cosmopolitanism' and 'internationalism' as *independent*

concepts is a complex one, further complicated due to internationalism being, as mentioned above, a *component* of the synthesized cosmopolitan matrix. However, with the above in mind, especially considering the relationship between cosmopolitanism and the nation-state, the following points seem crucial:

- Inter-*nationalism* by definition centres around *national* (meaning *nation-state*) categories, which triggers several logical geographical, political and cultural limitations from the viewpoint of cosmopolitanism.
- Internationalism cannot question, or transcend, or even try to ignore as a category, the nation-state as such, which are strongly discussed features of cosmopolitanism.
- Internationalism cannot explain why a person's 'home' might actually be outside his or her own nation-state, or in several parts of the world, as symbolized in the cosmopolitan shorthand definition of 'feeling at home in the world'.
- 'Being international' is defined as having 'attitudes which place the cultures and views of others on a par with one's own' or as 'showing respect for others' (Hayden et al. 2000: 120). The possibility of viewing other cultures and views actually *above* one's own or showing *more* than just respect for others (for example, a strong emotional involvement or an emulation of local knowledge or habits) is thus better conceivable in cosmopolitanism.
- Cultural issues that are below or above the nation-state remit (for instance interest in small-scale local cultural diversity, like regions or cities, or an overarching identity dimension covering the whole world) are easier to capture with cosmopolitanism, defined above as 'straddling the global and the local'.

CONCLUSION

The identity model of cosmopolitanism presented here is a personal and individual choice with which individuals, be it educator, pupil, parent or private person, can enrich their professional as well as their private lives, in theory as well as in practice. Its definitions are related to the individual learner rather than 'international education' or 'international schools'. As such, an international education inspired by cosmopolitanism would be based on a clear conceptualization of the outcomes, in terms of 'cosmopolitanism' or 'the cosmopolitan individual', rather than on an educational context, such as a particular type of school, or on a purpose arising from particular views of the 'needs' of contemporary global society.

So which shape does this inspiration take practically? Cosmopolitanism might not need to replace internationalism, but it can challenge or at least question the nation-state and all identity and cultural attachments that are connected with it *if and where* that proves to be advantageous to the philosophy of 'international education' in the sense of 'international understanding'. It can provide a cultural depth of engagement with other cultures, loci and locals which internationalism, for reasons of its inherent traditional geographical, geopolitical and political definition and scope, even within the educational context of international education, cannot provide. Above all, it can provide a personal and individual identity notion of knowledge of and engagement with local cultural diversity, which in the end is part and parcel of the notion of 'international understanding' that lies at the core of international education. As such, cosmopolitanism can be an agenda of international education for the individual in terms of the development (along the continua and criteria suggested) of the characteristics of a cosmopolitan person. The notion of continua of development would allow for multiple agendas to suit the wide range of 'clients' found in a wide range of international schools (which includes locals and various degrees of 'tourists' as defined above).

While the above characteristics of cosmopolitanism and the cosmopolitan individual do suggest a possible model for the individual outcomes of an international education (and, hence, in turn serve as a source of definition of such an education), it should be noted that this model is not narrowly prescriptive with respect to educational experience or curriculum. There are certain educational objectives implicit in the model – summarized, for both the model and its overarching educational purpose, in one catchword phrase as 'world citizenship in terms of individual engagement with cultural diversity' – but the model itself

is not predicated on any specific educational programme. It is for this combination of freedom of programmatic constraints, motivation by specific feasible aims and substantiation by specific workable criteria, that cosmopolitanism can soundly and emphatically inspire international education's internationalism, now and in the future.

REFERENCES

Abbas, A. (2002) Cosmopolitan de-scriptions: Shanghai and Hong Kong. In C.A. Breckenridge, S. Pollock, H.K. Bhabha and D. Chakrabarty (eds) *Cosmopolitanism.* Durham, NC and London: Duke University Press. pp. 209–28.

Allan, M. (2003) Frontier crossings: cultural dissonance, intercultural learning and the multicultural personality. *Journal of Research in International Education,* 2 (1): 83–110.

Anderson, A. (1998) Cosmopolitanism, universalism, and the divided legacies of modernity. In P. Cheah and B. Robbins (eds) *Cosmopolitics: Thinking and Feeling Beyond the Nation.* Minneapolis and London: University of Minnesota Press, pp. 265–89.

Appadurai, A. and Breckenridge, C. (1998) Why public culture? *Public Culture Bulletin,* 1 (1): 5–9.

Appiah, K.A. (1998) Cosmopolitan patriots. In P. Cheah and B. Robbins (eds) *Cosmopolitics: Thinking and Feeling Beyond the Nation.* Minneapolis and London: University of Minnesota Press, pp. 91–114.

Baumann, Z. (1996) From pilgrim to tourist – or a short history of identity. In S. Hall and P. Du Gay (eds) *Questions of Cultural Identity.* London: Sage, pp. 18–36.

Beck, U. (2000) The cosmopolitan perspective: sociology of the second age of modernity. *British Journal of Sociology,* 51 (1): 79–105.

Beck, U. (2002) The cosmopolitan society and its enemies. *Theory, Culture and Society,* 19 (1–2): 17–44.

Bhabha, H.K. (1996) Unsatisfied: notes on vernacular cosmopolitanism. In L. García-Moreno and P.C. Pfeiffer (eds) *Text and Nation: Cross-Disciplinary Essays on Cultural and National Identities.* Columbia, OH: Camden House. pp. 191–207.

Blandford, S. and Shaw, M. (eds) (2001) *Managing International Schools.* London: Routledge.

Brennan, T. (1997) *At Home in the World: Cosmopolitanism Now.* Cambridge, MA: Harvard University Press.

Brennan, T. (2001) Cosmopolitanism and internationalism. *New Left Review,* 2 (7): 75–84.

Bruckner, P. (1996) The edge of Babel. *Partisan Review,* 63 (2): 242–54.

Buzan, B., Held, D. and McGrew, A. (1998) Realism versus cosmopolitanism: a debate between Barry Buzan and David Held, conducted by Anthony McGrew. *Review of International Studies,* 24 (3): 387–98.

Carter, A. (2001) *The Political Theory of Global Citizenship.* London and New York: Routledge.

Carter, A. (2005) Migration and cultural diversity: implications for national and global citizenship. In S.H. Tan (ed.) *Challenging Citizenship: Group Membership and Cultural Identity in a Global Age.* Aldershot: Ashgate, pp. 15–30.

Cheah, P. (1998) Introduction part II: the cosmopolitical – today. In P. Cheah and B. Robbins (eds) *Cosmopolitics: Thinking and Feeling Beyond the Nation.* Minneapolis and London: University of Minnesota Press, pp. 20–41.

Clifford, J. (1992) Traveling cultures. In L. Grossberg, C. Nelson and P.A. Treichler (eds) *Cultural Studies.* New York and London: Routledge, pp. 96–116.

Clifford, J. (1997) *Routes: Travel and Translation in the Late Twentieth Century.* Cambridge, MA and London: Harvard University Press.

Clifford, J. (1998) Mixed feelings. In P. Cheah and B. Robbins (eds) *Cosmopolitics: Thinking and Feeling Beyond the Nation.* Minneapolis and London: University of Minnesota Press, pp. 362–70.

Cohen, M. (1992) Rooted cosmopolitanism: thoughts on the left, nationalism, and multiculturalism. *Dissent,* 39 (4): 478–83.

Curtis, B. and Pajaczkowska, C. (1994) 'Getting there': travel, time and narrative. In G. Robertson, M. Mash, L. Tickner, J. Bird, B. Curtis and T. Putnam (eds) *Travellers' Tales: Narratives of Home and Displacement.* London and New York: Routledge, pp. 199–215.

Derrida, J. (1997) *Cosmopolites de tous les pays, encore un effort!* Paris: Éditions Galilée.

Dharwadker, V. (2001) Introduction: cosmopolitanism in its time and place. In V. Dharwadker (ed.) *Cosmopolitan Geographies: New Locations in Literature and Culture,* New York and London: Routledge, pp. 1–13.

Eagleton, T. (2000) *The Idea of Culture.* Oxford: Blackwell.

Edwards, R.R. (2001) 'The metropol and the maystertoun': cosmopolitanism and late medieval literature. In V. Dharwadker (ed.) *Cosmopolitan Geographies: New Locations in Literature and Culture.* New York and London: Routledge, pp. 33–62.

Featherstone, M. (1993) Global and local cultures. In J. Bird, B. Curtis, T. Putnam, G. Robertson and L. Tickner (eds) *Mapping the Futures: Local Cultures, Global Change.* London: Routledge, pp. 169–87.

Featherstone, M. (1995) *Undoing Culture: Globalization, Postmodernism and Identity.* London: Sage.

Fischer, G. (1996) Tourist or explorer? Reflection in the foreign language classroom. *Foreign Language Annals,* 29 (1): 73–81.

Fougeret de Monbron, L. (1970) *Le cosmopolite, ou le citoyen du monde.* Bordeaux: Ducros (written in 1750).

Friedman, J. (1994) *Cultural Identity and Global Process.* London: Sage.

Friedman, J. (1995) Global systems, globalization and the parameters of modernity. In M. Featherstone, S. Lash and R. Robertson (eds) *Global Modernities.* London: Sage, pp. 69–91.

Fullinwider, R. (2001) Multicultural education and cosmopolitan citizenship. *International Journal of Educational Research,* 35 (3): 331–43.

Gellar, C.A. (2002) International education: a commitment to universal values. In M. Hayden, J. Thompson and G. Walker (eds) *International Education in Practice: Dimensions for National and International Schools.* London: Kogan Page, pp. 30–5.

Greenfeld, L. (1996) Nationalism and modernity. *Social Research,* 63 (1): 3–40.

Guibernau, M. (1996) *Nationalisms: The Nation-State and Nationalism in the Twentieth Century.* Cambridge: Polity Press.

Guibernau, M. (2001) Globalization and the nation-state. In M. Guibernau and J. Hutchinson (eds) *Understanding Nationalism.* Cambridge: Polity Press, pp. 242–68.

Gunesch, K. (2002) The relationship between multilingualism and cosmopolitanism. Unpublished PhD thesis, University of Bath, UK.

Hall, S. (1991) The local and the global: globalization and ethnicity. In A.D. King (ed.) *Culture, Globalization and the World-System: Contemporary Conditions for the Representation of Identity.* London: Macmillan, pp. 19–39.

Hannerz, U. (1990) Cosmopolitans and locals in world culture. In M. Featherstone (ed.) *Global Culture: Nationalism, Globalization and Modernity.* London: Sage, pp. 237–51.

Hannerz, U. (1992) *Cultural Complexity: Studies in the Social Organization of Meaning.* New York: Columbia University Press.

Hannerz, U. (1996) *Transnational Connections: Culture, People, Places.* London and New York: Routledge.

Hayden, M.C. and Thompson, J.J. (1995) Perceptions of international education: a preliminary study. *International Review of Education,* 41 (5): 389–404.

Hayden, M. and Thompson, J. (eds) (1998) *International Education: Principles and Practice.* London: Kogan Page.

Hayden, M. and Thompson, J. (eds) (2000) *International Schools and International Education: Improving*

Teaching, Management and Quality. London: Kogan Page.

Hayden, M., Thompson, J. and Walker, G. (eds) (2002) *International Education in Practice: Dimensions for National and International Schools.* London: Kogan Page.

Hayden, M.C., Rancic, B.A. and Thompson, J.J. (2000) Being international: student and teacher perceptions from international schools. *Oxford Review of Education,* 26 (1): 107–23.

Heater, D. (2000) Does cosmopolitan thinking have a future? *Review of International Studies,* 26 (5): 179–97.

Heater, D. (2002) *World Citizenship: Cosmopolitan Thinking and Its Opponents.* London and New York: Continuum.

Held, D., McGrew, A., Goldblatt, D. and Perraton, J. (1999) *Global Transformations: Politics, Economics and Culture.* Cambridge: Polity Press.

Hollinger, D.A. (1995) *Postethnic America: Beyond Multiculturalism.* New York: Basic Books.

Iyer, P. (2000) *The Global Soul: Jet Lag, Shopping Malls, and the Search for Home.* New York: Vintage Books.

Jameson, F. (2000) Globalization and political strategy. *New Left Review,* 2 (4): 49–68.

Kymlicka, W. (2001) *Politics in the Vernacular: Nationalism, Multiculturalism, and Citizenship.* Oxford: Oxford University Press.

Langford, M. (1998) Global nomads, third culture kids and international schools, in M. Hayden and J. Thompson (eds) *International Education: Principles and Practice.* London: Kogan Page, pp. 28–43.

Mackenzie, J. (2000) Curricular interstices and the theory of knowledge. In M. Hayden and J. Thompson (eds) *International Schools and International Education: Improving Teaching, Management and Quality.* London: Kogan Page, pp. 42–50.

Malcomson, S.L. (1998) The varieties of cosmopolitan experience. In P. Cheah and B. Robbins (eds) *Cosmopolitics: Thinking and Feeling Beyond the Nation.* Minneapolis and London: University of Minnesota Press, pp. 233–45.

Mathews, G. (2000) *Global Culture/Individual Identity: Searching for Home in the Cultural Supermarket.* London and New York: Routledge.

McKenzie, M. (1998) 'Going, going, gone ... global!' In M. Hayden and J. Thompson (eds) *International Education: Principles and Practice.* London: Kogan Page, pp. 242–52.

Mehta, P.B. (2000) Cosmopolitanism and the circle of reason. *Political Theory,* 28 (5): 619–39.

Moore, M. (2001) Globalization, cosmopolitanism, and minority nationalism. In M. Keating and J. McGarry (eds) *Minority Nationalism and the Changing International Order.* Oxford: Oxford University Press, pp. 44–60.

Münch, R. (2001) *Nation and Citizenship in the Global Age: From National to Transnational Ties and Identities.* Basingstoke and New York: Palgrave.

Nicholson, M. (1999) How novel is globalization?. In M. Shaw (ed.) *Politics and Globalization: Knowledge, Ethics and Agency.* London and New York: Routledge, pp. 23–34.

Nussbaum, M.C. (1996) Patriotism and cosmopolitanism. In J. Cohen (ed.) *For Love of Country: Debating the Limits of Patriotism.* Boston, MA: Beacon Press, pp. 2–17.

Opello, W.C. and Rosow, S.J. (1999) *The Nation-State and Global Order: A Historical Introduction to Contemporary Problems.* Boulder, CO and London: Lynne Rienner.

Papastephanou, M. (2002) Arrows not yet fired: cultivating cosmopolitanism through education. *Journal of Philosophy of Education,* 36 (1): 69–86.

Parmenter, L. (1999) Constructing national identity in a changing world: perspectives in Japanese education. *British Journal of Sociology of Education,* 20 (4): 453–63.

Pearce, R. (1998) Developing cultural identity in an international school environment. In M. Hayden and J. Thompson (eds) *International Education: Principles and Practice.* London: Kogan Page, pp. 44–62.

Pollock, D.C. and Van Reken, R.E. (2001) *The Third Culture Kid Experience: Growing Up among Worlds,* 2nd edition. London: Nicholas Brealey.

Pollock, S. (2002) Cosmopolitan and vernacular in history. In C. Breckenridge (eds) *Cosmopolitanism.* Durham, NC and London: Duke University Press, pp. 15–53.

Pollock, S., Bhabha, H.K. Breckenridge, C.A. and Chakrabarty, D. (2002) Cosmopolitanisms. In C.A. Breckenridge, S. Pollock, H.K. Bhabha and D. Chakrabarty (eds) *Cosmopolitanism.* Durham, NC and London: Duke University Press, pp. 1–14.

Rabinow, P. (1986) Representations are social facts: modernity and post-modernity in anthropology. In J. Clifford and G.E. Marcus (eds) *Writing Culture: The Poetics and Politics of Ethnography.* Berkeley and Los Angeles: University of California Press, pp. 234–61.

Rée, J. (1998) Cosmopolitanism and the experience of nationality. In P. Cheah and B. Robbins (eds) *Cosmopolitics: Thinking and Feeling Beyond the Nation.* Minneapolis and London: University of Minnesota Press, pp. 77–90.

Robbins, B. (1992) Comparative cosmopolitanism. *Social Text,* 31/32: 169–86.

Robbins, B. (1998a) Comparative cosmopolitanisms. In P. Cheah and B. Robbins (eds) *Cosmopolitics:*

Thinking and Feeling Beyond the Nation. Minneapolis and London: University of Minnesota Press, pp. 246–64.

Robbins, B. (1998b) Introduction part I: actually existing cosmopolitanism. In P. Cheah and B. Robbins (eds) *Cosmopolitics: Thinking and Feeling Beyond the Nation.* Minneapolis and London: University of Minnesota Press, pp. 1–19.

Sarup, M. (1996) *Identity, Culture and the Postmodern World.* Edinburgh: Edinburgh University Press.

Scholte, J.A. (2000) *Globalization: A Critical Introduction.* London: Macmillan.

Sifakis, N. and Sougari, A.M. (2003) Facing the globalization challenge in the realm of English language teaching. *Language and Education,* 17 (1): 59–71.

Skelton, M. (2002) Defining 'international' in an international curriculum. In M. Hayden, J. Thompson and G. Walker (eds) *International Education in Practice: Dimensions for National and International Schools.* London: Kogan Page, pp. 39–54.

Smith, A.D. (1991) *National Identity.* London: Penguin.

Thompson, J. (1998) Towards a model for international education. In M. Hayden and J. Thompson (eds) *International Education: Principles and Practice.* London: Kogan Page, pp. 276–90.

Tokuhama-Espinosa, T. (2003) Third Culture Kids: a special case for foreign language learning. In T. Tokuhama-Espinosa (ed.) *The Multilingual Mind: Issues Discussed by, for and about People Living with Many Languages.* Westport, CT and London: Praeger, pp. 165–9.

Tomlinson, J. (1999) *Globalization and Culture.* Cambridge: Polity Press.

Turner, B.S. (2002) Cosmopolitan virtue, globalization and patriotism. *Theory, Culture and Society,* 19 (1–2): 45–63.

Waldron, J. (1995) Minority cultures and the cosmopolitan alternative. In W. Kymlicka (ed.) *The Rights of Minority Cultures.* Oxford: Oxford University Press, pp. 93–119.

Walker, George (1998) Home sweet home: a study, through fictional literature, of disoriented children and the significance of home. In M. Hayden and J. Thompson (eds) *International Education: Principles and Practice.* London: Kogan Page, pp. 11–27.

Wallerstein, I. (1991) The national and the universal: can there be such a thing as world culture? In A.D. King (ed.) *Culture, Globalization and the World-System: Contemporary Conditions for the Representation of Identity.* London: Macmillan, pp. 91–105.

Watson, C.W. (2000) *Multiculturalism.* Buckingham and Philadelphia: Open University Press.

Wollen, P. (1994) The cosmopolitan ideal in the arts. In G. Robertson, M. Mash, L. Tickner, J. Bird, B. Curtis and T. Putnam (eds) *Travellers' Tales: Narratives of Home and Displacement.* London and New York: Routledge, pp. 187–96.

PART II

Students and their Learning

9

The Potential of the Past in Practice: Life Histories of Former International School Students

Helen Fail

As the number of international schools has grown significantly in the past 50 years, so has the interest in the effects of these schools on the young people who attend them. This chapter summarizes the findings from a study which examined the life histories of a group of former international school students.

TERMINOLOGY

The term 'Third culture kid' or 'TCK' was originally coined by the Useems to describe the children of expatriates working in India (Useem, Donoghue and Useem 1963). Pollock and Van Reken's (1999) book has popularized the term, although the definition may not accurately describe the international school student:

> An individual who, having spent a significant part of the developmental years in a culture other than the parents' culture, develops a sense of relationship to all of the cultures while not having full ownership in any. Elements from each culture are incorporated into the life experience, but the sense of belonging is in relationship to others of similar experience. (Pollock and Van Reken 1999)

The Useems' original definition of 'third culture', as an 'interstitial culture' created as people from different societies relate to each other, does more accurately describe the typical international school culture (Useem et al. 1963). It could be argued that students educated in a 'third culture' become TCKs even if they do not fit the definition. Adults with such a background are referred to as 'adult third culture kids' or 'ATCKs'.

McCaig's (1992) definition of 'global nomad' is simpler and more encompassing but has not gained such wide acceptance:

> A global nomad is a person of any age or nationality who has lived outside of his/her passport country because of a parent's career. (McCaig 1992)

Leaving aside the inadequacy of the descriptors and adopting the term TCK for convenience's sake, what have been some of the findings in the research regarding the characteristics of children who have lived outside of their passport country?

FINDINGS FROM THE LITERATURE

Identity and belonging

With regard to identity formation, there is discussion of marginality (Downie 1976; Bennett 1993, Schaetti 1996) which can have positive or negative outcomes. Fluidity and change in self-perception are said to be inevitable (Adler 1975; Weinreich 1983; Pearce 1998). A critical period is the return to the passport country with possible identity crisis and readjustment problems (Krajewski 1969; Gleason 1970; Cassady 1971; Downie 1976; Dormer 1979; Schulz 1986; Uehara 1986; Ridley 1986; Pollock and Van Reken 1999). Regarding a sense of belonging, there are conflicting findings. TCKs are said to be rootless (Bushong 1988; Loewen 1993; Pollock and Van Reken 1999; Jordan 2002), with no sense of home or belonging (Wertsch 1991). On the other hand, they are at home everywhere and anywhere (Useem 1984; Pollock and Van Reken 1999). Fail (1995) found respondents rated their sense of belonging to relationships much higher than to geographical places.

International aspects to their lives

Students at international schools are claimed to be more interested in following an international lifestyle in the future (Gerner et al. 1992). Research amongst ATCKs seems to confirm this prediction (Cottrell and Useem 1994; Schaetti 1996; Bell 1997; Powell 1998; Pollock and Van Reken 1999; Cottrell 2002). This might manifest itself in terms of an expanded world-view (Gleason 1970). An interest in, and an acceptance of, other cultures, is seen as evidence of an internationally-minded person (Krajewski 1969; Gleason 1970; Beimler 1972; Gerner et al. 1992; Langford

1997; Pollock and Van Reken 1999). Gerner et al. *(1992)* found international school students were more interested in travel than their monocultural counterparts and they have an interest in and a desire to learn new languages (Rainey 1971; Useem 1984; Langford 1997; Pollock and Van Reken 1999). There is plenty of evidence to suggest that TCKs are bilingual or multilingual (Willis et al. 1994; Fail 1995; Ender 1996; Langford 1997).

Approach to relationships

It is suggested that TCKs share common traits in their approach to relationships (Langford 1997; Pollock and Van Reken 1999). They only develop superficial relationships, as a protective measure against the pain of parting (Darnauer 1969; Werkman 1979; Wertsch 1991), which places limits on the level of intimacy in relationships (Van Reken 1995). ATCKs have difficulty in making long-term commitments to people (Wertsch 1991; Fail 1995; Pollock and Van Reken 1999). However, they invest in relationships with people of different nationalities, particularly as a life partner (Lykins 1986; Cottrell 1993; Khatib-Chahidi et al. 1998; Jordan 2002). They are said to be adaptable and flexible (Useem 1984; Langford 1997; Pollock and Van Reken 1999; Knell 2001) but there seems to be a discrepancy between their ability to make friends easily and adjustment difficulty when going away to college (Krajewski 1969; Gleason 1970; Cassady 1971; Schulz 1986; Ridley 1986). Reverse culture shock (Austin 1986) has been documented with reference to children (Werkman 1986; Guither and Thompson 1986).

Higher education

Useem (1993b) reported that 81 per cent of ATCKs had earned at least a Bachelor's degree (compared with 21 per cent of the American population). Other research details the percentage of those going on to higher education: 94 per cent (Wickstrom 1993), 91 per cent (Willis et al. 1994), 97 per cent (Fail 1995) and 96 per cent (Ender 1996).

Conclusions

Findings oscillate between positive outcomes emphasizing the benefits of being a TCK (Downie 1976; Lykins 1986; Useem 1993a, 1993b; Cottrell and Useem 1993; 1994; Cottrell 1993) and negative reports focusing on associated psychological problems (Werkman 1979; Wickstrom 1989; Wrobbel and Plueddemann 1990; Wertsch 1991). Psychological studies (Werkman 1979; Wickstrom 1989; Wrobbel and Plueddemann 1990; Wertsch 1991) found those with emotional problems. Themes that emerge from the literature are: issues of belonging and rootlessness, level of education, travel, linguistic ability, cross-cultural relationships and friendships, international aspects to one's life, adaptability and flexibility, mobility and long-term commitment.

NATURE OF RESEARCH ON TCKs

Research findings on TCKs tend to be based on case studies from psychiatry for people presenting with problems (Werkman 1979; Wickstrom 1989; Wrobbel and Plueddemann 1990; Wertsch 1991) or larger-scale studies based on postal questionnaires (Sharp 1987; Gerner et al. 1992; Useem 1993a; Langford 1997). Some surveys have been based on small samples (Fleming 1947; Fail 1995), focusing on people of a particular nationality (Cottrell 1993; Useem 1993a; Cottrell and Useem 1993, 1994) or a particular parental sponsorship group (Andrews 1995). The majority of ATCKs studied have been Americans (Useem 1993a; Cottrell 1993; Cottrell and Useem; 1993, 1994; Andrews 1995; Ender 1996), who experienced an American-style education. Several schools have surveyed their alumni (Parker 1936; Fleming 1947; Harper 1969; Miller 1981; Michell 1988; Willis et al. 1994; Lehman 1997).

Other sources of information

Published anecdotal evidence (Pollock and Van Reken 1999; Knell 2001) has tended to reinforce research findings based on limited or specific samples. Many of the assertions about TCKs – for example, being good at making friends quickly, being adaptable and flexible, having a sense of belonging to others of similar experience (Pollock and Van Reken 1999) – cannot easily be tested in a postal questionnaire. There were 166 dissertations and theses related to TCKs produced during the 1970s and 1980s, and 18 in the 1990s (Useem 1998, 1999). However, there have been an increasing number of journal and magazine articles with anecdotal evidence as the years have progressed (Useem 1998). The combination of research evidence and anecdotal evidence has led to a growing acceptance of the concepts and characteristics of TCKs (Pollock and Van Reken 1999).

RATIONALE FOR LIFE HISTORIES

The challenge, in the light of divergent findings, was to design an approach combining the postal survey and an intensive multiple case study. The postal survey was used to identify potential participants who would be willing to reflect in greater depth on the development of their lives. With life histories one is seeking to understand how past experience has affected the present. A multiple case study examining the lives of several alumni would provide explanation, detail, thoughts, remembered feelings, 'thick description' (Geertz 1993) and would be a lens through which to view other research findings. Case studies focus on particular individuals, not in order to generalize but in order to understand the particular case (Stake 1995). Previous data from surveys (Cottrell 1993; Useem 1993a, 1993b; Cottrell and Useem 1993, 1994; Andrews 1995; Fail 1995; Ender 1996) seemed to indicate certain tendencies in the lives of ATCKs such as living out of their passport country as adults (Fail 1995), having international aspects to their lives (Fail 1995) and marrying cross-culturally (Cottrell and Useem 1994). The statistical results from the postal questionnaire would provide comparative data with other studies (Wrobbel 1990; Cottrell 1993, 1994; Useem 1993, 1994; Andrews 1995; Fail 1995; Ender 1996). Individual cases would create triangulation, an opportunity to explore 'how' and 'why' questions (Yin 1994), as well as increasing reliability and validity (Robson 2002).

A total of 329 questionnaires were sent to alumni from an international school and 104 completed questionnaires were returned. Twelve individuals were chosen for in-depth interviews, of whom one was an airline pilot. The interviewees were selected to be as different from each other as possible based on their responses to the questionnaire. A more detailed explanation of the data analysis of the questionnaire and interview transcripts is available elsewhere (Fail 2002).

PURPOSE OF THE RESEARCH

The overarching research aim was to examine the impact of an international school education on individual lives. It included such questions as:

1 Do former international school students have a sense of belonging to a particular place or country or is it in terms of relationship to others of similar experience? (Pollock and Van Reken 1999)
2 Is there evidence that they are internationally-minded? (Gleason 1970; Beimler 1972; Langford 1997)
3 Is there evidence that they are interested in travel? (Gerner et al. 1992)
4 Is there evidence that they are interested in languages? (Gerner et al. 1992, Langford 1997)
5 Is there evidence that they are following an international lifestyle? (Gerner et al. 1992)
6 What is significant in their approach to relationships and whom do they befriend? (Langford 1997; Pollock and Van Reken 1999)
7 What evidence of adaptability and flexibility is there in their lives? (Langford 1997; Pollock and Van Reken 1999)
8 What evidence of long-term commitment is there in their lives? (Werkman 1979; Wertsch 1991)
9 To what level have they pursued higher education? (Willis et al. 1994; Fail 1995)
10 What partner has the person chosen and why? (Cottrell 1970; Khatib-Chahidi et al. 1998)
11 How do they define themselves in terms of their identity? (Herrmann 1997; Pearce 1998; Munayer 2000)
12 How has the person coped with loss and separation? (Wickstrom 1989; Van Reken 1995; Knell 2001)

DISCUSSION OF THE FINDINGS

The findings were analysed by combining data from the questionnaires alongside data from the interviews (Fail 2002). These evolved into four main themes.

1 Identity and belonging

The results showed a broad continuum, with Richard being an example, on one end, of someone who has always lived in his passport country as an adult but with no sense of belonging or national identity. On the other end of the spectrum were people such as Bilal and Christina, with a multiple sense of belonging and strong sense of national identity even though they have never lived in their passport countries as adults. Virtually all the respondents claimed a sense of belonging amongst fellow internationalists, Mathias being the most articulate about it (Fail et al. 2004).

2 Attitude towards change

Since most of the respondents had massive changes forced upon them as children these have affected several areas of their lives. Change covered adaptability and flexibility and loss and separation. Pollock and Van Reken (1999) and Wertsch (1991) speak of the legacies of unresolved grief and its effect. Considered as a continuum, there were different responses. Anna represents someone who coped poorly with change and who needed psychiatric treatment, while Pierre coped extremely well with it. There are those who actively embrace change as adults, such as Mathias, and those who actively avoid it, such as Miriam. It does not necessarily follow that those who coped poorly as children with change, such as Lara, avoid it as adults. Lara and Anna, for example, learned how to deal with change as children and have gone on to actively embrace it as adults. Heidi's inability to form close friendships may be the result of the unresolved grief from her own childhood. Those who embrace change and actively pursue it often need a lifestyle with variety and change built into it, such as Michel, otherwise they can become bored and stifled, such as André.

3 Approach to relationships

The section on friendships, partners and long-term commitment was relevant in considering the alumni's approach to relationships. In most cases there was evidence of long-term commitment to a life partner as well as the maintenance of long-distance and long-term friendships. The questionnaire revealed a tendency to find a partner either from a different culture or with an international background (73 per cent); 99 per cent of the respondents currently had friends of different nationalities and with an international background. This is in keeping with Pollock and Van Reken's (1999) claim that TCKs relate well to other people like themselves.

4 International aspects to their lives in the future

Eleven aspects were chosen as being evidence of an international lifestyle. These were based on assertions, predictions or findings from other researchers as follows:

1 Living in a country that is not one's passport country. (Pollock and Van Reken 1999)
2 Being in a cross-cultural partnership. (Cottrell and Useem 1994)
3 Having friends from other nationalities or with an international background. (Pollock and Van Reken 1999)
4 Using more than one language on a regular basis. (Rainey 1971)
5 Travelling internationally for work on a regular basis. (Gerner et al. 1992)

6 Travelling internationally for work or pleasure. (Gerner et al. 1992)
7 Having a career that has international aspects. (Gerner et al. 1992)
8 Having family members living in other countries. (Pollock and Van Reken 1999)
9 Having passports from more than one country. (Pollock and Van Reken 1999)
10 Raising bilingual children. (Fail 2002)
11 Sending one's children to an international school. (Fail 2002)

Of these 11 characteristics, only one of the 11 interviewees exhibited less than half of them. Seven of the respondents exhibited 8 or more of the characteristics, with 3 people, Mathias, Lara and Christina, exhibiting 10 of the 11 characteristics.

Conclusions

A sense of belonging or identity, an approach to relationships and attitudes towards change are internal but will inevitably affect the behaviour associated with an international lifestyle. The questionnaire data revealed international features of the respondents' lives in terms of how multilingual, well-travelled and cross-culturally experienced they were but did not necessarily expose how they felt. The interview data revealed some surprising feelings.

DISCUSSION OF INDIVIDUAL LIFE HISTORIES

The following three vignettes reveal three different responses to an international childhood.

Richard: limited international lifestyle

Richard is British (both parents are British). He attended an international school in Switzerland from the age of 7 until he returned to university in his home country. He dropped out of university after suffering from severe culture shock. He did attend another university, graduated and has lived in the same city ever since. He is single. He takes vacations abroad and has stayed in touch with a few school friends. His sister has lived and worked in some African countries since her training as a teacher and takes exotic holidays all over the world.

Richard suffered from severe reverse culture shock when he discovered he was not the British person he thought he was. He had problems integrating with British people and felt very different from them. He was articulate about the profound impact the experience had on him and yet blamed his personality for the fact that he does not like change. He says he does not feel English even though he has lived in Britain since he was 18 (he is now over 50). What is strange is that although evidence of an international lifestyle is limited (he has friends from other nationalities with an international background and he travels internationally for pleasure), when one considers identity, change and relationships there are some striking features. He has struggled with his identity as he does not feel English. The identity crisis he experienced at 18 has not really changed, he has just learned to live with the fact that he feels like a hidden immigrant (Pollock and Van Reken 1999).

Richard admits that he is resistant to change and avoids it. He attributes that to the combined shock of moving back to Britain and his personality. Although Richard does not exhibit many features of an international lifestyle, the experience of living in another country has had an impact. As he says:

> It's coloured my perception of everything and made me think about everything in a way different, the way I perceive things, way differently from the way I would have perceived things if I hadn't gone there, so it's not just one thing it's EVERY-THING. (Richard)

Although there is little evidence of an international lifestyle on the surface, Richard, internally, feels different from other people, but that difference is not immediately apparent to those around him.

Heidi: a moderately international lifestyle

Heidi's father was French and her mother was Scandinavian. Her parents met in the United

States and her early years were spent there and in Scandinavia following her parents' divorce. When Heidi was 8 years old her mother died and she went to her father. He took her to France and left her with his family. She spoke English and Norwegian but was sent to a French school. At 13 she went to live with her father in Switzerland. She attended an international school. She trained as a medical doctor and married a Swiss accountant. She had three children. She has always worked. After 24 years of marriage, her husband left her and she has moved with her youngest child to a new apartment. Her eldest daughter is married to a European from a different nationality. Her children attended local Swiss schools but her youngest son is now attending a Scandinavian school in addition to the local school so that he can learn the language. In the two years since her husband left, Heidi has started attending a Scandinavian church and has made friends with many Scandinavian expatriates.

The international aspects to Heidi's life include: living outside of her passport country, using more than one language on a regular basis, having two passports, having members of her family living in other countries, having friends from another nationality and with an international background and travelling internationally for pleasure. She had 6 out of the 11 characteristics. It is clear from Heidi's life history that she has had an unusual and very traumatic background. In her early years she was exposed to divorce, cross-cultural moves, two languages, death of her primary caregiver and was then, at the age of 8, left with strangers in a new country and language. Heidi has no sense of belonging or identity in Switzerland even though she has lived there for 35 years. She calls herself a '100 per cent imported product'. She has changed jobs frequently and yet was married and lived in the same home for 24 years. She is currently in a stage of transition, making new friends and building a new life in the two years since her husband left. She has a rather stoical attitude to change:

> There is a saying in French, 'Marche ou grève' – just walk on or you die in the place, that was something I've done ever since. (Heidi)

She has coped with change when it has been thrust upon her because she has had no choice. She has not actively sought it and yet she has coped with the major traumas in her life. With regard to relationships, she comments that she has always been a loner and relied upon herself. She does not have a close relationship with her father and she does not see her elder son very often. Heidi said her ex-husband was not interested in her background. She has now made changes in her life since her marriage ended. She has left behind the Swiss friends and started making connections with the expatriate world in Switzerland. Although she has lived in Switzerland for so long and French is her strongest language, she does not have a sense of belonging or identity there. Like Richard, the internal feelings are not necessarily consistent with the outward reality. Unlike Richard, Heidi is in the process of reinventing herself and giving expression to her Scandinavian side which has been hidden for so long.

Christina: a very international lifestyle

Christina was born in Chile, although both her parents were Bolivian. They returned to Bolivia until she was 3. The family then moved to Switzerland where she attended an international school in English. When she was 10, the family moved to Mexico for a year where she attended a French school. She spoke Spanish, English and French. The family then returned to Switzerland. She subsequently trained in Switzerland as a simultaneous translator, which included a year in Europe where she met the Iranian man who was to become her husband. She married and moved to Europe and lived there for two years in two different countries. They then moved to Iran, where she had a son. As the situation changed in Iran, Christina left with her son and went back to Switzerland. Her husband eventually joined her. Her daughter was born in Switzerland. Her son attended a Swiss school and her daughter has attended an international school and has gone to the United States for college. Christina has always worked as a freelance simultaneous translator in Spanish, French and English.

According to the characteristics of an international lifestyle, Christina has all of them except two passports: she lives in a country that is not her passport country; she travels internationally for work and pleasure; she uses more than one language on a regular basis; her career has international aspects to it; she is married cross-culturally; not all her family lives in the same country; her children are bilingual and one of them attended an international school; and she has friends from other nationalities and with an international background. As regards belonging and identity, Christina has a sense of belonging in Switzerland and Bolivia and feels at home in both those places. She has never wanted to give up her Bolivian passport but feels it may be practical to take Swiss identity to ease travel. She is comfortable and at ease with herself and has tried to give her children a sense of pride in their unique identity of being half Bolivian, half Iranian and raised in Switzerland. She thrives on change, loves travelling, enjoys her job, which demands flexibility, working at a moment's notice and is both pressured and stimulating. She enjoys the freedom it gives her, the opportunity to travel and all the different people she meets while doing it. She and her husband are part of the international community and also have many Iranian friends in Switzerland. As a child, Christina always saw moving as a big adventure which she enjoyed. She enjoyed the years she spent living in Iran, where she made friends and gave birth alone in a hospital shortly after arriving. She was vivacious, enthusiastic, positive and totally at ease with herself and in her environment. Christina is someone who lives out her international background in an international lifestyle and is clearly happy and contented with her life and situation. There is no discrepancy between her background and her present day situation.

What conclusions can be drawn?

The three life histories presented above represent current day lifestyles which, according to the data given on the questionnaire, could be described as 'not international', 'moderately international' and 'very international'. However, the facts often hide the emotional experience of the respondents, who revealed more in the interview. Richard has not found a way of integrating his past into his present. His past comes as a surprise to people because it is hidden. He does not appear to have satisfactorily resolved the identity crisis which was his greatest challenge when he moved back to England. According to Marcia (1966), he is still in a state of identity diffusion. He does not have a strong sense of identity. Heidi, on the other hand, is in a state of moratorium (Marcia 1966). She is starting to reinvent herself and give expression to her international identity in the wake of her divorce. She is currently in a state of change and flux. Christina has reached a state of identity achievement (Marcia 1966) as she is totally at ease and comfortable with her international identity and lifestyle.

The three respondents who were chosen represent three different nationalities and three different responses to their background. Their experience at an international school was a part of their background and may have been overshadowed by more dramatic life experiences.

IMPLICATIONS OF FINDINGS

The effects have been wide-ranging on all the students who attended the international school regardless of the other international influences on them. For some it was their entire international experience (Michel and André) and for others it was part of a much broader international experience (Christina, Pierre, Mathias). It has raised issues that may be pertinent to those currently studying in international schools. Although the case study presented here is not generalizable since the data come from one school and one that may not be 'typical' of international schools (Pearce 1998), the test of a case study is whether the data presented resonate with the reader (Yin 1994). To what extent would current international school students relate to the comments on identity,

change, relationships and international aspects to their lives? It remains to be seen.

REFERENCES

Adler, P.S. (1975) The transitional experience: an alternative view of culture shock. *Journal of Humanistic Psychology*, 15: 13–23.

Andrews, L. (1995) Measurement of adult MKs' well-being. *Evangelical Missions Quarterly*, October, pp. 418–26.

Austin, C.N. (ed.) (1986) *Cross-Cultural Re-entry: A Book of Readings*. Abilene, TX: Abilene Christian University Press.

Beimler, R.R. (1972) An exploratory study of the relationship between cross-cultural interaction and the social values of 'concerned worldmindedness' held by multi-national student groups at the American High School in Mexico City. PhD thesis, Michigan State University, USA.

Bell, L. (1997) *Hidden Immigrants: Legacies of Growing Up Abroad*. Notre Dame, IN: Cross Cultural Publications.

Bennett, J.M. (1993) Cultural marginality: identity issues in intercultural training. In R.M. Paige (ed.) *Education for the Intercultural Experience*. Yarmouth, ME: Intercultural Press.

Bushong, B. (1988) Where do I sleep tonight? MKs and mobility. *Evangelical Missions Quarterly*, October, pp. 352–6.

Cassady, M.S. (1971) Overseas missionary children's college adjustment. MS thesis, University of Tennessee, USA.

Cottrell, A.B. (1970) Interpersonal dimensions of cross-cultural relations: Indian–Western marriages. PhD thesis, Michigan State University, USA.

Cottrell, A.B. (1993) ATCKs have problems relating to own ethnic groups. (Article 4) *Newslinks*, xiii: 2 (Princeton, NJ).

Cottrell, A.B. (2002) Educational and occupational choices of American adult third culture kids. In M.G. Ender, (ed.) *Military Brats and Other Global Nomads: Growing Up in Organization Families*. Westport T: Praeger, pp. 229–53.

Cottrell, A.B. and Useem, R.H. (1993) TCKs experience prolonged adolescence. (Article 3) *Newslinks*, xiii: 1 (Princeton, NJ).

Cottrell, A.B. and Useem, R.H. (1994) ATCKs maintain global dimensions throughout their lives. (Article 5) *Newslinks*, xiii: 4 (Princeton, NJ).

Darnauer, P.F. (1969) Army brats – Growing up in an army family. In H.I. McCubbin, B.B. Dahl and E.J. Hunter (eds) (1976) *Families in the Military System*. London: Sage.

Dormer, R. (1979) We are the rootless ones. *Ecolint Newsletter* no. 13, Spring.

Downie, R.D. (1976) Re-entry experiences and identity formation of third culture experienced dependent American youth: an exploratory study. PhD thesis, Michigan State University, USA.

Ender, M.G. (1996) Growing up in the military. In C. Smith (ed.) *Strangers at Home: Essays on the Effect of Living Overseas and Coming 'Home' to a Strange Land.* New York: Aletheia.

Ender, M.G. (ed.) (2002) *Military Brats and Other Global Nomads: Growing Up in Organization Families.* Westport, CT: Praeger.

Fail, H. (1995) Some of the outcomes of international schooling. MA dissertation. Oxford Brookes University, UK.

Fail, H. (2002) An examination of the life histories of a group of former international school students. Unpublished PhD thesis: University of Bath, UK.

Fail, H., Thompson, J. and Walker, G. (2004) Belonging, identity and third culture kids. *Journal of Research in International Education* 3: 319–38.

Fleming, R.L. (1947) Adjustment of Indian missionaries children in America. PhD thesis, University of Chicago, USA.

Geertz, C. (1993) *The Interpretation of Cultures.* London: Fontana Press.

Gerner, M., Perry, F., Moselle, M.A. and Archibold, M. (1992) Characteristics of internationally mobile adolescents. *Journal of School Psychology,* 30: 197–214.

Gleason, T.P. (1970) Social adjustment patterns and manifestations of worldmindedness of overseas-experienced American youth. PhD thesis, Michigan State University, USA.

Guither, H.D. and Thompson, W.N. (1986) Return, readjustment, and reminiscence. In C.N. Austin (ed.) *Cross-Cultural Re-entry: A Book of Readings.* Abilene, TX: Christian University Press, pp. 207–18.

Harper, E.S. (1969) *Post-School Adjustment of Woodstock School Graduates: A Guidance Survey, Classes of 1965–68.* India: Woodstock School Mussoorie.

Herrmann, C.B. (1977) Foundational factors of trust and autonomy influencing the identity formation of the multicultural lifestyled MK: a dissertation. PhD thesis, Northwestern University, Evanston, IL, USA.

Jordan, K.F. (2002) Identity formation and the adult third culture kid. In M.G. Ender (ed.) *Military Brats and Other Global Nomads: Growing Up in Organization Families.* Westport, CT: Praeger, pp. 211–28.

Khatib-Chahidi, J., Hill, R. and Paton, R. (1998) Chance, choice and circumstance: a study of women in cross-cultural marriages. In R. Breger and R. Hill (eds) *Cross-Cultural Marriage: Identity and Choice.* Oxford: Berg. pp. 49–66.

Knell, M. (2001), *Families on the Move: Growing Up Overseas – and Loving It!* London: Monarch.

Krajewski, F.R. (1969) *A study of the relationship of an overseas-experienced population based on sponsorship of parent and subsequent academic adjustment to college in the United States.* PhD thesis, Michigan State University, USA.

Langford, M.E. (1997) Internationally mobile pupils in transition: the role of the international school. MA Education dissertation, University of Bath, UK.

Lehman, L.L.J. (1997) Woodstock – its effectiveness in fulfilling states goals and objectives as a Christian international residential school: a survey of the graduates 1976–1995. Doctoral dissertation, Columbia Pacific University, USA.

Loewen, B. (1993) Where's home? closing the MK's identity gap. *Evangelical Missions Quarterly,* January 93, p. 52–5.

Lykins, R. (1986) Children of the third culture. *Kappa Delta Record,* Winter, pp. 39–43.

Marcia, J.E. (1966) Development and validation of ego identity status. *Journal of Personality and Social Psychology,* 3: 551–8.

McCaig, N.M. (1992) Birth of a notion. *The Global Nomad Quarterly,* 1 (1): 1.

Michell, D.J. (1988) *A Boy's War.* Singapore: OMF.

Miller, S. (1981) *Pigtails, Petticoats and the Old School Tie.* Sevenoaks: OMF.

Munayer, S. (2000) The ethnic identity of Palestinian Arab Christian adolescents in Israel. PhD thesis, University of Wales, Cardiff.

Parker, A.E. (1936) An analysis of the factors in the personality development of children of missionaries. MA dissertation, University of Chicago, USA.

Pearce, R. (1994) International Schools: the Multinational Enterprises' Best Friends. *Relocation News.* 33, October: 8.

Pearce, R. (1998) *Developing cultural identity.* In M. Hayden and J. Thompson (eds) *International Education: Principles and Practice.* London: Kogan Page.

Pollock, D.C. and Van Reken, R.E. (1999) *The Third Culture Kid Experience: Growing Up among Worlds.* Yarmouth, ME: Intercultural Press.

Powell, J. (1998) MK research: some notes and observations. In J. Bowers (ed.) *Raising Resilient MKs.* Colorado Springs, CO: ACSI.

Rainey, M.C. (1971) Language learnings of overseas-experienced American teenagers. PhD thesis, Michigan State University, USA.

Ridley, S.M. (1986) *A study of the identity achievement of overseas experienced missionary children.* MA Thesis, Wheaton College, IL, USA.

Robson, C. (2002) *Real World Research, 2nd edition.* Oxford: Blackwell.

Schaetti, B. (1996) Phoenix rising: a question of cultural identity. In C. Smith (ed.) *Strangers at Home: Essays on the Effects of Living Overseas and Coming 'Home' to a Strange Land.* New York: Aletheia.

Schulz, D.M. (1986) A study of third-culture experience in relation to the psycho-social adjustment of returned Church of Christ missionary families. PhD thesis, University of Nebraska, USA.

Sharp, L.W. (1987) Patterns of religiosity, worldmindedness and commitment to justice issues for Brazil-experienced missionary children. PhD Thesis, Calgary, Alberta, Canada.

Stake, R.E. (1995) *The Art of Case Study Research.* Thousand Oaks, CA: Sage.

Uehara, A. (1986) comparison of reentry adjustments between Japanese and American students: an inter-actionist perspective. PhD thesis, University of Minnesota, USA.

Useem, R.H. (1984) *Third culture children.* Notes on a lecture given at the US Information Services in Lusaka in March 1984. Wheaton, IL.

Useem, R.H. (1993a) Third culture kids: focus of major study. (Article 1) *Newslinks,* xii, 3 (Princeton, NJ).

Useem, R.H. (1993b) TCKs four times more likely to earn Bachelor's degrees. (Article 2) *Newslinks,* xii, 5 (Princeton, NJ).

Useem, R. H. (1998) *A Third Culture Kid Bibliography.* East Lansing, MI: USEEM.

Useem, R.H. (1999) *Addendum 1 to A Third Culture Kid Bibliography.* East Lansing, MI: USEEM.

Useem, J., Donoghue, J.D. and Useem, R.H. (1963) Men in the middle of the third culture. *Human Organization,* 22 (3): 169–79.

Van Reken, R.E. (1995) Possible long-term implications of repetitive cycles of separation and loss during childhood on adult missionary kids (AMKs). Paper originally presented at Christian Association for Psychological Studies (CAPS) Convention, Lancaster, PA 1987, updated January 1995.

Weinreich, P. (1983) Emerging from threatened identities. In G. Breakwell (ed.) *Threatened Identities.* Chichester: John Wiley.

Werkman, S.L. (1979) The effect of geographic mobility on adolescents. In S.C. Feinstein and P.L. Giovacchini (eds) *Adolescent Psychiatry Vol. VII: Developmental and Clinical Studies.* Chicago: University Chicago Press, pp. 175–90.

Werkman, S.L. (1986) Coming home: adjustment of Americans to the United States after living abroad. In C. Austin (ed.) *Cross-Cultural Re-Entry: A Book of Readings.* Abilene, TX: ACU Press.

Wertsch, M.E. (1991) *Military Brats.* New York: Harmony Books.

Wickstrom, D. (1989) Emotional and behavioural patterns of adult MKs. In J. Bowers (ed.) (1998) *Raising Resilient MKs.* Colorado Springs, CO: ACSI.

Wickstrom, D. (1993) Educational experiences of adult MKs. Paper presented to 7th Annual Meeting of MK CART/CORE 29–30 April, Colorado Springs, CO.

Willis, D.B., Enloe, W.M. and Minoura, Y. (1994) Transculturals, transnationals: the new diaspora. *International Schools Journal,* XIV (1): 29–42.

Wrobbel, K.A. (1990) Adult MKs: how different are they? *Evangelical Missions Quarterly,* April, pp. 164–70.

Wrobbel, K.A. and Plueddemann, J.E. (1990) Psychosocial development in adult missionary kids. *Journal of Psychology and Theology,* 18 (4): 363–74.

Yin, R.K. (1994) *Case Study Research: Design and Methods.* Thousand Oaks, CA: Sage.

10

Learning Internationally in a Future Context

John Munro

Ms Zuango teaches History in an international school. In her class are students from 21 nationalities. One of the topics she teaches is Revolutions. One example of a twentieth-century revolution is that led by Castro in Cuba. The students in her class learn about the topic by reading commentaries written by English-speaking historians.

Throughout the topic Ms Zuango encourages her students to reflect on their existing knowledge and to think about the teaching information using higher-order thinking skills; to analyse, evaluate, integrate and synthesize their knowledge at any time and to form a more general understanding of the Cuban revolution and of revolutions more generally.

Like many of her colleagues teaching at the school, Ms Zuango has become aware of a range of learning issues. Students differ in their entry knowledge of the topic being taught. Differences in language and conceptual knowledge are often not as influential on learning as differences in the attitudinal dispositions linked with the concepts and how the students prioritize key ideas. Some students need to make greater 'adjustments' in their knowledge

to acquire the 'preferred interpretation' of the topic than others.

The students also differ in their approach to learning. They differ as to how they transform their knowledge and the conditions under which they are motivated to learn. They differ in the beliefs they have about how to learn; some, for example, are less likely to question, analyse or evaluate the teaching information and prefer to internalize the ideas presented. They differ also in their perceptions of acceptable learning outcomes and their knowledge of how to display learning outcomes. Some find it harder to 'play the assessment game' than peers.

Ms Zuango and her colleagues are keen to foster an educational provision that could be called 'international'. They believe that they have some of the necessary ingredients: a student cohort that represents several cultures and a curriculum that is taught in many schools that call themselves 'international'. They are not as sure whether their teaching fosters an 'international' understanding of the key concepts or topics, or even what this might 'look like'. Nor are they sure that their teaching effectively takes account of multicultural ways of learning the key ideas.

The teachers in Ms Zuango's school are not alone. Interest in the questions they raise was shared by participants at the 2004 conference of the Alliance for International Education held in Dusseldorf, Germany. The focus of this biennial conference was 'Education for International Mindedness' (www.intedalliance.org/browse). One of its seven strands was *Learning internationally and its implications for pedagogy and curriculum.* The focus of this strand was learning in international contexts and how this contributes to a development of international-mindedness. Issues included:

1   models for understanding learning internationally
2   the influence of culture on knowledge and learning
3   teaching, pedagogy and curriculum that enhance international-mindedness
4   learning internationally in the future, emerging types of knowledge and ways of thinking
5   lifelong learning and links with vocational education for international/global work contexts
6   relevant teacher professional knowledge
7   school-level processes likely to foster international learning.

The outcomes generated by the strand can be read on the website (www.intedalliance.org/browse).

The strand examined in depth what learning and teaching internationally might 'look like'. One aspect of the recommended approach involved building an awareness of the assumptions about learning and teaching that students and teachers from different cultures bring to an international school community. A second aspect examined how to capitalize on this multiplicity of interpretations and perspectives for the good of all. It was noted that in many international schools Western thought and culture were prevalent in both the teaching practice and in the assumptions made about learning. It was recommended that for the future it might be necessary to broaden the traditional Western 'models' of education and learning. Understanding about international education has evolved to a point where cultural dissonance is seen as an important influence in many international schools.

Learning is a complex process. There is a plethora of issues that one could examine under the umbrella of 'learning internationally'. This chapter examines two of them: (1) international perspectives on what is learnt, that is, the learning outcomes; and (2) international perspectives on how it is learnt, that is, the activity that leads to the learning outcomes.

HOW INTERNATIONAL ARE THE OUTCOMES OF LEARNING?

What does the adjective 'international' mean in terms of learning outcomes, that is, the knowledge gained as a result of learning? We can contrast it with 'national' knowledge outcomes. One might speculate that a topic learnt by a group of students is more likely to be called 'international' if:

1   It is learnt as having a range of multicultural aspects, that is, students learn that the topic is constructed or understood in multiple ways, each representing a national or cultural perspective. Consider a class learning about gravity. Instead of learning about gravity only from a Western European perspective, the class can be encouraged to ask: 'Who was the first Chinese to discover gravity?' and to research the knowledge of gravity that Australian aboriginals have that allows them to hit a distant kangaroo with a boomerang. A quick review of the commonly used textbooks on physics indicates no reference to the development of gravity other than through Newton.
2   Students learn that the various cultural or 'national' understandings for the topic did develop in order to assist a culture or nation to deal with particular aspects of it. They learn that each aspect has value within that culture for solving problems or for enhancing understanding. This may lead students to become aware that:

   • All knowledge is 'our most appropriate interpretation at this point in time' rather than being set in concrete and absolute.
   • Cultures differ in how they define concepts and each interpretation may be unique and have value.

- Understanding concepts or a topic from multiple cultural perspectives can lead to a richer and more useful understanding of the topic. Students can learn to explore, compare and link or combine multiple cultural interpretations of a topic, without loss of uniqueness.

3 Students gradually become aware of what constitutes an international understanding of a concept or a topic. A focus on international understanding may optimize the extent to which students see the value of a broader multicultural knowledge lens. This lens helps them to look for and see topics in terms of their cultural links. It is particularly important when individuals from different cultures communicate and when individuals access information sources from other cultures.
4 Students, through learning and valuing the multiple understandings of individual concepts and topics, gradually develop attitudes of tolerance, respect and international valuing.

What is being proposed here is that a positive disposition to international-mindedness may be developed in part through conceptual teaching that encourages students to understand key ideas from a range of cultural perspectives. These aspects of curriculum modi fication may be investigated empirically in the future, both through action research paradigms in classrooms and in more quantitative studies. One might speculate that the teaching more likely to foster this approach to concept learning would:

1 encourage students to think about concepts and topics from a range of cultural perspectives, attempting to discover how particular cultures define the concepts and to ask themselves such questions as: 'What is the cultural foundation for these ideas? Why did the culture develop them? How do they fit within the broader knowledge of the culture?'
2 encourage students to develop a valuing of different cultural understandings of a topic.
3 help students to recognize what is common and shared about a topic at an international level and what is unique to each culture. They can explore how uniqueness to a culture at one time can enrich the international perspective later.
4 help students reflect on, and identify, the thinking that led to the particular cultural embodiments

and to see how these can be integrated into enhanced, broader ways of thinking.
5 foster values such as tolerance rather than prejudice, by having students learn the values first in relation to specific 'concrete' concepts and topics and then gradually abstract and generalize them.

INTERNATIONAL PERSPECTIVES ON HOW KNOWLEDGE IS LEARNT

A second dimension focuses on how knowledge is acquired, that is, how learning occurs. We know intuitively that cultures differ in how they learn. We noted earlier that Ms Zuango and her colleagues were aware that students in their classes differed in their approach to learning in a range of ways. They were keen to implement educational provision that took account of multiple ways of learning, some of which reflected international influences.

In order for them to investigate this process systematically, they need to use an explicit and robust model of learning. The research on learning is voluminous, with a plethora of learning theories. These theories differ in how teaching-friendly they are and how easily contextualized they are in the world of twenty-first-century classrooms (or even twentieth-century classrooms).

AUTONOMOUS LEARNERS ENGAGED IN KNOWLEDGE ENHANCEMENT

One model of learning that has emerged in Western education and guided research over the past two decades is that of the autonomous learner, who is self-managing and self-directing in her or his learning activity (Ablard and Lipschultz 1998; Boekarets 1997; Pintrich 1995). Versions of this model have been used to examine a range of aspects related to learning.

In this chapter, self-directed learning activity is seen to be in balance with externally-directed learning in any context. Terms such as 'self-directed' and 'autonomous' are used to indicate the extent of the balance. The nature of the balance, it is proposed, varies culturally.

Cultures differ, for example, in how they conceive autonomous, self-directed learning. This was shown starkly in the recent Australian film *Rabbit Proof Fence*. This film told part of the life story of three indigenous girls who had been moved to a Western community school approximately 2,500 miles from their home in Western Australia. While the girls showed a low level of self-managed learning in the school, they were able to navigate their way back to their home by drawing on a range of knowledge and ways of thinking that would be the envy of most people. Their capacity to understand and 'read' totally unfamiliar environments and contexts, to make effective decisions and to solve problems allowed them to survive and to avoid capture by the police and skilled indigenous trackers. Their level of self-directed autonomous learning in the latter context was spectacular.

Cultures also differ in how they interpret the adjective 'autonomous' when used to describe thinking and learning. Autonomy in these activities is modelled and encouraged in a range of ways. Cultures differ in the areas of knowledge in which they permit, teach or foster autonomy of thinking. The opportunities students have to learn to be autonomous thinkers and learners vary.

A particular classroom context may offer a restricted range of opportunities for students to be autonomous. Ms Zuango and her colleagues need to be aware that the students in their classes differ in their preparedness to engage in autonomous learning and what they understand by it. Students may differ in their earlier experiences of learning and thinking in self-directed versus externally-directed ways. Those who achieve autonomy in ways not fostered by the classroom climate may display higher dependence, less initiative and disengagement from learning. Teachers need to understand and to account for this variation in their teaching.

The balance between self-directed versus externally-directed learning has a matching distinction in theories of knowledge construction (that is, constructivism). One view is that knowledge represents the real world and exists independently of the knower (Jonassen 1991)

and that learning involves constructing this representation, that is, empirical constructivism. A second view is that reality does not exist, knowledge cannot be objective or absolute (Von Glasersfeld 1995) and that individuals construct their own interpretations of it (radical constructivism). This has been modified into a third view that individuals agree to construct a consensus interpretation, that is, social constructivism (Heylighen 1993). Cultures differ in their composite position on these interpretations of knowledge construction and on the learning activities they encourage for each.

There is another issue that Ms Zuango and her colleagues need to consider. The international curriculum they teach has its origins in Western thinking and models of education. They are aware that any teaching makes assumptions (usually implicitly) about how learning occurs. They are also aware that the greater the mismatch between these assumptions and the ways in which particular students learn, the less likely the students are to achieve successful outcomes.

As a first step in understanding the range of ways in which students from different cultures learn, the present discussion uses the model of the autonomous learner. Just as learning in a self-managing and directed way depends on the content or subject being learnt, so it is proposed that: (1) learners may show culturally specific ways of learning autonomously; and (2) an awareness of the multiple ways in which students do this can enhance the education and understanding of all students.

A KNOWLEDGE ENHANCEMENT MODEL OF LEARNING: LEARNING ACTIONS

Learning activity can be described from the perspective of knowledge enhancement. This perspective defines learning in terms of the processes involved in increasing or modifying what one knows, does, believes and thinks. It explores the question: What do individuals need to do to construct further their knowledge of a topic? This chapter examines cultural influences on learning using the autonomous learner framework as a reference point.

The model for identifying how learners enhance their knowledge was developed as follows (Munro 2003a, 2003b, 2004, 2005). A range of largely Western public domain theories of learning was analysed to identify the learning activities that each validated to describe how students change what they know. These were synthesized into a generic framework. In this context the term 'knowledge' refers to the totality of what one knows and includes one's: propositional and conceptual knowledge and the associated procedural knowledge; attitudinal beliefs; beliefs about learning and how to learn and how to apply one's knowledge; and world beliefs.

The key learning actions include the following. Learners:

1 frame up a challenge or reason for learning an idea
2 develop an awareness of the outcome or goal of the learning
3 make links with and use what they already know about the topic
4 develop a learning pathway to their goal
5 learn the new ideas in limited, supported, 'scaffolded' ways in specific contexts
6 deepen and abstract what they have learnt
7 invest positive emotion in the new knowledge
8 identify the learning actions or strategies they used to learn
9 monitor their learning, see themselves making progress
10 store what they have learnt in memory and practise remembering it
11 automatize what they have learnt
12 apply, transfer and generalize the new knowledge and use it creatively and innovatively
13 organize what they have learnt for assessment purposes.

Each learning action is a thinking strategy that individuals or groups can use to modify or enhance their knowledge. Together they provide an explicit, systematic framework for transforming or enhancing knowledge. Learners use them as 'self scripts' to guide their thinking and to manage, direct and regulate their learning activity. The self scripts can catalyse or 'trigger' each action.

The learning actions are used in clusters

The learning actions are not used in a linear one-directional sequence. Instead, they can be categorized into three clusters. Those to do with:

1 orienting one's knowledge (that is, 'getting it ready') for learning
2 changing one's knowledge
3 consolidating and transferring the knowledge change.

Within each cluster, two or more actions may share a reciprocal relationship at any time. As well, in line with parallel information processing theories, learners can potentially use more than one at once.

During the early phase of learning, learners use actions 1–4, to orient their existing knowledge to the problem or focus of the learning. They switch between their purpose for learning, likely outcomes and what they know. They may revise what they think the outcome will be, re-shape the challenge and modify their proposed learning pathway.

During the knowledge change phase, learners switch mainly between interactions 5–8. They learn new experiential, conceptual, attitudinal and thinking aspects of the ideas. In many situations they learn new ideas in specific contexts in 'scaffolded' ways first and then generalize these, even when new ideas are introduced in abstract ways. Once they have begun to abstract an idea, they switch to particular contexts to test their comprehension.

They link emotion in the new knowledge across this phase. They can also reflect on and review the actions they use to learn across this phase.

The third phase of knowledge change is when the learners consolidate what they have learnt. They review explicitly the new ideas, link them with what they knew, build memory 'icons' for them and practise recalling them. They see their learning progress and may automatize aspects of what they have learnt so it can be used more easily to build further learning. Cultures differ in how they encourage learners to prioritize and link ideas, the memory icons they use and the extent to which they value automatizing the new knowledge.

They can now generalize the new understanding more widely and think more creatively about it. They explore and analyse it from a range of perspectives, see how far they can transfer it (near and far transfer) and use the knowledge in open-ended creative problem-solving. As well, they can organize it for assessment purposes. They reflect on the contexts in which they need to display the knowledge and how they can align it with various assessment criteria.

How learners manage and direct their learning

Even though several actions are potentially available at any time during learning, some dominate. Learners differ in how they direct or manage how they use these actions (their metacognitive knowledge, Schraw and Moshman 1995). This depends on several factors, including their beliefs about the topic they are learning, whether they can learn it successfully (Pajares 1996), or how particular learning contexts will allow them to learn (Zimmerman and Schunk 1998).

Learners' beliefs are linked with learning actions. The belief that a goal is to discover a new way of solving a problem triggers different learning and thinking actions from the belief that the goal is to learn an established solution procedure (Biggs 1987). As well, the amount of control learners believe they have in the learning context influences the actions they use. Time constraints, needing to meet external criteria and a need to learn and memorize the ideas in an unquestioning way for later reproduction, lead to restricted knowledge enhancement.

Learners can use the actions spontaneously or be cued to use them. Those who use them mainly when instructed or cued are more dependent and externally managed. Learners who use them autonomously and spontaneously in a strategic, selective way are the more self-managing and directing learners. Their use in a self-directed way depends on

the content or subject being learnt. Learners may be more self-managing in some areas of knowledge than in others.

The set of actions is learnt through meaningful interactions with one's culture

Cultures differ in how they construct and value each action. The work of Au and Entwistle (1999), Chan (1999), Walker and Dimmock (2000) and Drake (2004) assists in elucidating potential sources of variation. The following differences illustrate these. While they are presented as dichotomous, it is recognized that each 'dichotomy' represents a continuum, with a difference in degree or extent.

1 Cultures differ in their assumptions about what constitutes knowledge and the areas of knowledge available for change. They vary in the extent to which (a) culturally valued knowledge is available for change during learning and (b) the focus is on learning as enquiry versus learning as inculcation and transmission. Some value increased knowledge generally, a knowledge of how to learn and a positive disposition to 'lifelong learning'.
2 Cultures differ in the nature of the creative outcomes they value. Some cultures prefer bounded creative activity that does not question deep cultural values. Others tolerate or encourage this level of questioning. Believing that a culture's knowledge of a topic is its best impression at one point in time has different implications for creativity and innovation than believing that knowledge is absolute and 'fixed'.
3 Cultures differ in the perceived locus of knowledge, whether it is referenced within the individual or within the group or culture. This difference influences beliefs about the source and ownership of knowledge and the preparedness to question or change what is known.
4 Cultures differ in the extent of focus on learning as an individual versus a group activity. Rather than a focus on self-talk by individuals during learning, the culture may foster group dialogue. Teaching strategies for stimulating existing knowledge may vary from individually focused provocative questions to small group activities to telling students the areas of existing knowledge that will be required or assumed by the teaching.
5 Cultures differ in the opportunities they give learners to show what they know. This influences

how knowledge is assessed and the pedagogy used. They differ in the extent to which they encourage students to question what they know during learning, identify explicitly what they don't know, take risks with what they do know, tolerate uncertainty and learn through modelling and imitation.

6 Cultures make characteristic assumptions about what constitutes effective learning–teaching inter-actions. These are usually coded implicitly in their metaphors and beliefs about educational provision. They are rarely made explicit in Western approaches to formal education.

CULTURAL INFLUENCES ON THE LEARNING ACTIONS

Each action has both generic and culturally specific aspects. The set of learning actions provides a valuable tool for analysing learning internationally. We can examine how students from different cultures go about using each action.

(1) A purpose for learning

The first learning action relates to learners framing up a purpose or reason for learning a topic. The 'challenge to learn' can be concep-tualized as lying on a dimension ranging from an interest in knowing more about a topic and reducing uncertainty to achieving outcomes unrelated to the topic, such as being accepted by others or course entry criteria.

Cultures differ in how they encourage students to frame up purposes for learning. Some encourage students to question their existing knowledge in terms of its relevance or appropriateness. Individual curiosity leads to challenges and goals for learning. Other cultures encourage students to internalize the existing knowledge of the culture. The goals of learning are framed in terms of what is known by others (Chan 1999). Questioning key concepts is not valued and may be per-ceived as threatening.

Cultures also differ in the extent to which students are encouraged to frame up purposes independently, for example, to develop a per-sonal curiosity about areas of knowledge versus leading all students to frame up shared purposes for learning. Students from different cultures may differ in the extent to which they learn to develop their own reasons for learning and the contexts under which they frame up challenges or problems.

Western theories of learning use the con-cept of the state of 'cognitive conflict' (Lowenstein 1994). It is the mechanism for catalysing or stimulating learning in both the Piagetian and Vygotskian frameworks, in which it is developed as 'sociocognitive con-flict' (Tudge 1990). It can range from an emotional drive to satisfy one's curiosity to an explicit challenge or question to be answered. Western approaches to pedagogy frequently focus on stimulating this state.

The above discussion suggests that this state, at least in the sense described by Piaget and Vygotsky, may be inappropriate for learning from some cultural perspectives (Chan 1999). Some students in an international school may not feel motivated to learn by being encouraged to question what they know about a topic.

(2) Possible outcomes of the learning

Learners form an impression of the possible desired outcome of the learning. For example, they visualize where they will end up, what they will know, be able to do or what they may believe or feel. They 'see' the goals as per-sonal experiences (Locke and Latham 1990; Pintrich and Garcia 1991). This gives them a direction or focus for their learning.

Cultures differ in how they foster this. A key dimension here is the focus on individ-ual versus group learning. Location on this dimension influences how students learn to visualize the possible outcomes of learning. Some cultures encourage learning through the individual pursuit of knowledge, for example, through personal enquiry and problem-solving. Students may visualize the outcome of the learning as a report of an investigation in which they display their changed knowledge of the topic.

Others focus more on collaborative or group learning, with information presented didactically and with limited opportunity for learning through personal pursuit. Students may visualize the learning outcome as completion of a set of tasks that will be administered to the group as a whole and in which they will show their awareness and mastery of the knowledge taught to the group.

(3) What learners know about the topic

Learners make links with what they know about the topic. Knowledge change begins here. This action involves several aspects.

One aspect is *what they know about the topic.* Students' existing knowledge of a topic can be represented and stored in a number of ways: in imagery, as experiences in particular contexts (their 'episodic knowledge'); in more abstract, decontextualized ways; and in action ways. These multiple forms of knowledge have been described in terms of dual coding theory (Paivio 1991) and multiple intelligences (Gardner 1995). These descriptions have been simplified into learning styles (for example, Riding and Cheema 1991) and cognitive styles (for example, Munro and Howes 1998).

Cultures differ in the problems they need to solve, the tools they use and the valuing they place on different types of knowledge. Episodic knowledge is more culturally specific than abstract knowledge. Students from different cultures differ in how they use their knowledge to make decisions and to solve problems and to meet the range of needs of the culture.

The Australian film *Rabbit Proof Fence* mentioned earlier illustrates this. One can only marvel at the knowledge displayed by the three young girls as they made their trip home. They showed a spatio-temporal and environmental knowledge of their world, a spiritual knowledge, focus and determination that differed significantly from that of the conventional Western Australian adolescent. Their capacity to use this knowledge and their relationship or affinity with the country is difficult for non-indigenous Australians to understand.

Cultures differ in the symbolism they use to represent complex ideas. Western cultures use discrete, atomistic and depersonalized linguistic concepts and abstract symbolism while other cultures may use icons, actions, linguistic narrative, song and poetry. The more analytic, decontextualized, detailoriented ways of thinking that characterize Western thinking are less likely to accommodate the links between ideas shown in indigenous Australian knowledge and thinking.

A second aspect relates to *what they know about how to transform their knowledge* or how to learn (for example, Biggs 1987; Davidson and Sternberg 1998; Jausovec 1994). Students from different cultures differ in what they know about how to learn (Au and Entwistle 1999; Chan 1999).

A third aspect relates to *what they believe about themselves as learners of the ideas,* how they value the ideas, and whether they believe they can learn the topic successfully (their self-efficacy, for example, Nichols and Utesch 1998; Pajares 1996). Learners' self-efficacy judgements affect how they learn and the effort they invest. They make these judgements quickly and unconsciously, and independently of their actual level of ability.

A fourth aspect relates to *students' beliefs and metaphors about the accepted roles of learners and teachers* (Pintrich et al. 1993). Student roles can vary from the belief that students learn by being programmed to the belief that students learn by questioning, analysing and building ideas.

Cultures differ in the beliefs they foster about the role of formal education. Those that see it as 'enculturation' foster metaphors that value the internalization of existing cultural knowledge. Those that see it as a route to a cultural transformation foster the questioning and challenge of existing cultural knowledge.

A fifth aspect relates to *self-initiated enquiry-based learning.* A catalyst for autonomous learning involves students identifying what they don't know about a topic, or 'holes' in their existing knowledge. They frame these up as unanswered questions about it. These are the challenge for learning mentioned earlier. They provide the basis for self-initiated learning and for learning in enquiry and problem-based curricula.

Identifying what one doesn't know about a topic assumes both that the learner takes an active role in the learning and that learners are encouraged to see their knowledge of a topic as being incomplete or 'our best interpretation at this time', rather than being absolute and 'set in concrete', not to be questioned. Cultures differ in the extent to which they see subjects or topics open to interpretation and available to be questioned. Some students may be reluctant to question topics that other students are comfortable questioning.

A sixth aspect relates to *cultural beliefs about when to display knowledge*. The display of knowledge is frequently critical in formal Western educational contexts. Students are identified as having learnt a topic when they can display knowledge of it. Some cultures encourage students to display knowledge spontaneously and to make opportunities for showing what they know. Some encourage students to show what they know only when the students are invited to do so. Other cultures do not encourage the display of knowledge except when there is a particular problem to be solved or dealt with.

(4) A pathway to the goal

Learners build or 'see' a possible pathway to their goal. This is a critical aspect of successful learning. Students who can see a possible pathway are more likely to maintain engagement and perseverance. While the pathway that learners will follow may change direction during the learning activity, at any time it assists in orienting the learning.

Cultures differ in how they conceive the learning pathway and the opportunities they provide students to do this. The autonomous learner model assumes the ability to develop and implement personal learning pathways. To achieve this, students need to learn to plan their pathways through a topic, decide the range of learning resources they may need to use and indicators of progress to their goal, for example, what they might expect to have achieved at various points on the pathways.

Cultures in which student learning is more directed externally require students to perceive the learning pathway in terms of group or collaborative issues. Their learning pathways specify the learning outcomes and progress points the group will be intended to meet.

(5) Learn in specific contexts

Learners learn the new ideas in specific contexts in limited, supported, 'scaffolded' ways by linking what they know into new ideas. They make new links between ideas they already know. They differ in how they do this. These differences are to some extent learnt from one's culture. We can describe the various ways in which learners do this on a number of dimensions that indicate how they 'balance' their learning activity:

- Some cultures encourage individuals to make small, sequential links between ideas, with a focus on detail, while others encourage making larger, holistic links between ideas. Some cultures think in more linear, serial ways while some think in more circular ways.
- Some cultures link ideas more in specific contexts in time and space and may link ideas in action sequences; they form images, episodes or experiences of new ideas. Others value more linking ideas in verbal, abstract, less contextualized ways. Some cultures may value imagery thinking over abstract thinking. Individuals in these cultures may have difficulty expressing creative ideas, for example, in abstract ways such as in sentences and may prefer to make models or represent the novel ideas pictorially.
- Some cultures encourage individuals to think intuitively about the ideas, explore and trial particular components and then use context-evaluative thinking, while others prefer to learn deductively by identifying rules and procedures and place greater value on 'objective logic'.
- Some cultures encourage individuals to question what they know and to challenge conventional knowledge and beliefs in adversarial ways and to use this to bridge from existing to new ideas. Others prefer individuals to learn not by questioning what is known but to learn by accepting and internalizing more complex relevant knowledge and by building collaboratively on this.

Chan (1999), for example, notes that Chinese students are taught to respect knowledge and the expertise of their teachers and parents and to avoid challenging either the knowledge they are being taught or its teachers. Students inculcated in these values may be expected to learn differently from those who have learnt in a culture in which questioning the existing knowledge and the teacher is valued.

Pedagogic practice in classes that include students from a range of cultures needs to respond to the challenge of balancing the use of different ways of questioning. Some students may prefer to question overtly a topic and seek a dissonance in it. They may prefer to learn by asking questions and then to pursue the knowledge to answer the questions. Other students may prefer to learn and internalize the topic, inherently trusting it and their teachers, and then to explore and extend within the topic, maintaining a 'harmony' within it.

These different ways of learning a new set of ideas, informed in part by one's earlier cultural experiences, influence how students approach learning at any time and need to be taken into account by the teaching that is provided.

(6) Abstract or deepen the new understanding

Western approaches to education frequently require students to 'deepen their new understanding' or to generalize their knowledge through abstraction. The Western focus assumes that students have access to particular types of symbolic system and ways of thinking. These include analysing aspects of ideas taken out of specific contexts (or 'decontextualizing'), selecting and reorganizing the main and subordinate ideas, summarizing and re-prioritizing the ideas and generalizing from specific instances.

Other cultures place less value on abstraction and differ in the ways in which they encourage it. Chinese approaches, for example, tend to value the functional and practical aspects of knowledge and focus on the concrete rather than abstract forms of ideas (Chan 1999). The Western focus on scientific objectivity and inductivism is not the preferred way

of thinking for all cultures. This focus may conflict with alternative value systems.

It may not be unreasonable that international curricula require this level of understanding. They need to recognize, however, that learners from different cultures may differ in their disposition to thinking that leads to this form of knowledge and their valuing of it.

(7) Invest positive emotion in the new knowledge

When students invest positive emotion in their new knowledge, they will be more motivated to learn about the topic and use that learning on future occasions (Zimmerman et al. 1992). To make this investment, they need to see that: (a) the new ideas have a value or use for them; and (b) it was their mental activity that learned the ideas.

Most of the research on this aspect has been from a Western perspective. Western cultures tend to neglect the emotional aspects of learning. Perhaps as a consequence, reduced motivation to learn culturally valued ideas is a characteristic of many Western cultures. Particularly in the adolescent years, student disengagement and alienation is a commonly reported problem.

Cultures differ in the types of learning outcomes they value and the values they want students to link with them. The teaching conditions for motivating students from one culture may not work as effectively for students from other cultures. Teachers in international contexts may need to examine the conditions under which their students are both prepared to make an emotional commitment in the ideas they are learning and motivated to be self-directing learners of the ideas. It may be inappropriate to assume that all students will be motivated in identical ways to learn the same topic or subject.

(8) Store what they have learnt in memory

Storing what has been learnt in memory and recalling it is a critical aspect of knowledge enhancement (Baddeley 1990). Students do this by 'compressing it' into its key ideas, linking it with what they know, building memory 'icons' and practising recalling it. Teaching can 'take for granted' this aspect of learning and assume that all students can use memory processes with equal efficiency.

Cultural influences on memory have several sources. Students differ in their dominant forms of existing knowledge and earlier experience adding to it. Some cultures value storing knowledge in imagery forms while others value more abstract forms (Chan 1999). Cultures also differ in how the processes of memorization and understanding of new ideas are integrated (Kember 1996; Marton et al. 1997).

(9) Identify how they learnt

This is a key action for teaching students to be autonomous, self-directing learners (Ablard and Lipschultz 1998; Boekarets 1997; Pintrich 1995). To achieve this, they reflect on their learning activity and identify what helped them to learn. This includes both the learning strategies and the metacognitive control they use. They may build an explicit knowledge of how they learnt and the learning strategies they used.

The little research available suggests that cultures differ in both the goals or purposes, contents and processes of the reflective thinking activity. Western approaches focus on verbal descriptions of thinking. Students learn the language for talking about how they learn. Ms Zuango and her colleagues, however, may not be justified in assuming that all of their students think, or think about thinking, in verbal ways. Such beliefs neglect non-verbal aspects of thinking. The cultures of their students may differ in the extent to which they value or encourage the dominance of verbal thinking.

The Western relationship between language, culture and thinking comes from the sociocultural framework proposed initially by Vygotsky (1978). A key aspect of this is that students learn the ways of thinking and conceptualizations used in their culture through their social interactions with significant others (Wertsch 1985). Language is seen as the most complex way in which ideas are shared.

Obviously, cultures may differ in how they think about the same ideas, how they construct thinking and learning and in their attitudes or dispositions to them. They may differ in their use of verbal versus non-verbal reasoning and in the distinctions they make between various forms of reasoning. The same learning outcomes may be generated by different cognitive strategies in different cultures.

Teaching practice needs to resist the Western assumption that ways of thinking employed by all students can be described most effectively in verbal propositions, that students' thinking can be differentiated and that aspects can operate independently. Teaching that assumes largely verbal descriptions of thinking may limit the extent to which alternative ways of thinking emerge or are valued. Some students may begin to doubt the 'inherent' ways of thinking they had learnt in earlier cultural interactions.

The focus here recommends that students in international contexts learn to increase their knowledge of how to learn and think in a range of ways. International educators intending to enhance their students' knowledge in this area may need to give consideration to this issue and to examine the ways in which different cultures think about learning and thinking. This will influence both what is taught and the pathway and means of teaching it.

(10) Making progress as a learner

We noted earlier that a key influence on learning is students' self-efficacy, or belief that they can learn a topic successfully. These beliefs are acquired when students perceive they can learn particular topics. Teaching and cultural variables influence how students do this.

Individuals develop these beliefs by reviewing and reflecting on their learning progress. They are determined in part by the criteria or indicators of progress students use, such as the apparent ease of learning the topic, the level of interest it elicited from them, the value of the learning outcome for them; and partly by the feedback they receive from significant others in the learning context, such as their teachers and peers. The indicators that students use to gauge their progress can either be learnt from the learning context or be largely self-generated.

Cultures differ in what they teach students about the criteria for success or progress in learning. Chan (1999), for example, compares the attributes of learning valued by Confucian and Western-based cultures. Learning in the former context is more likely to seen as successful if the student achieves various social and collaborative achievement criteria; the indicators for learning success are determined by the group. Thus, while students across cultures are likely to monitor their learning progress, they differ in the criteria and the types of feedback information they use to do this.

(11) Automatize what they have learnt

Learners automatize aspects of what they have learnt so it can be used for further learning. They do this by automatizing links between ideas and organizing what they know into larger 'chunks'. This action has frequently been confused with 'learning by rote'. The distinction between the two is based on students' access to meaning during learning. Learning by rote usually refers to situations in which this access is not available. Automatizing what has been learnt, on the other hand, involves learning ideas initially in attention-demanding, meaning-based ways. Repeated use leads to links between ideas becoming 'better programmed' and less demanding of thinking space or attention.

Cultural influences on this action have frequently been misinterpreted (Biggs 1994). Chinese students, for example, use repetitive learning strategies which have often been incorrectly described as rote to assist them to recall knowledge (Au and Entwistle 1999). Once they understand the new ideas, these strategies help them to link them with other ideas in increasingly sophisticated ways.

(12) Transfer and generalize the knowledge

This action, increasingly fostered in Western education in recent decades, involves thinking about the new knowledge in creative ways, exploring its transferability and generalizability using a range of 'higher order' thinking strategies. Students analyse, evaluate and synthesize aspects of the new knowledge from a range of perspectives and develop an enhanced understanding of it.

Cultures differ in how they foster these 'open-ended' ways of thinking about the ideas. Chan (1999), for example, comments that Chinese classrooms are less likely to foster creative thinking or active and critical enquiry. She reports Biggs's (1994) observation that while there is a valuing of the one 'right way' convergent learning outcomes, teachers encourage higher-level thinking rather than the simple rote learning strategies. It is important that international education examines the ways in which different cultures elaborate and extend their knowledge, in both creative and critical ways.

(13) Organize what they have learnt for assessment

Being able to show what one knows is a key aspect of successful learning. The autonomous learner model focuses students' attention on 'reading' assessment contexts and tasks and on aligning what they know with the 'window of opportunity' provided by these contexts. They need to organize what they have learnt for display purposes and to reflect on how they will apply their knowledge in particular assessment contexts.

This action is the 'flip-side' of assessment. Rather than focusing on procedures for evaluating what students know, it examines what students learn and how to show best what they know. Students need to learn the different purposes for which their knowledge is assessed and what the feedback they receive during assessment means for what they know and for themselves as learners. They benefit, for example, by knowing how to use the feedback they receive during formative assessment activities to reflect on and modify, if necessary, what they know.

Cultures differ in the ways in which they encourage and teach the display of knowledge. Increasing students' knowledge of the conventional ways in which this is done in a range of cultures increases students' capacity to learn and to think internationally. A curriculum is more internationally equitable if all students share a common knowledge about how to show what they know.

THE LEARNING ACTIONS MODEL AS A TOOL FOR RESEARCHING LEARNING INTERNATIONALLY

The set of learning actions provides a useful tool for analysing learning internationally in a range of ways. It has been used above to summarize and collate what it known about particular aspects of cross-cultural learning and to speculate about particular influences that may elicit research interest in the future.

The set of actions can be used to speculate about the conditions under which students from different cultural perspectives may most effectively be assisted to achieve their potential. The above review shows that each aspect of the model can be framed in multiple ways.

The speculations and possibilities about learning internationally can be investigated using applied classroom research practices, for example, action research, to identify the conditions under which particular teaching procedures are most useful in international classrooms. Options for teaching procedures associated with each of the learning actions provided by Munro (2003b, 2004) can be used as a starting point for this professional learning.

CONCLUSION : A FRAMEWORK FOR LOOKING AT LEARNING INTERNATIONALLY

This chapter assumes that international education needs to be informed by an explicit consideration of international learning. Without this it is proposed that international education will be like a ship without a rudder. We live in an increasingly 'internationalizing' world. The need to understand international learning is not restricted to teachers in 'international schools'. Our students and our cultures experience information that is increasingly international in its sources and dispositions.

This chapter focuses on learning in international contexts and what this means for teaching, curriculum and teacher knowledge. Learning is influenced by a range of cultural factors that need to be acknowledged explicitly in classroom practice and school organization. It has developed one perspective on learning internationally and identified how culture might influence knowledge enhancement by using the autonomous learner model as a starting point.

Learning in international contexts is a complex process. Teachers and schools need a tool for unpacking its components. The explicit learning framework can be used to explore learning from a range of cultural perspectives and to encourage reflective learning and thinking from multinational perspectives. It can assist in the internationalization of tasks, in professional development and teacher training through its explicit focus on learning and thinking internationally.

It assumes that an international education approach would capitalize on the multiple cultural embodiments of topics and ways of learning. These can be used to enrich and maximize the learning processes and outcomes of all students. It could foster both (1) positive international values by encouraging positive attitudes to and a valuing of specific concepts from a multinational perspective and (2) a high level of cultural awareness, sensitivity and acceptance. In short, it provides the positive values and beliefs that characterize an international educational perspective for twenty-first-century thinking and living.

REFERENCES

Ablard, K. and Lipschultz, R.E. (1998) Self-regulated learning in high-achieving students: relations to advanced reasoning, achievement goals, and gender. *Journal of Educational Psychology*, 90 (1): 94–101.

Au, C. and Entwistle, N. (1999) 'Memorisation with understanding' in approaches to studying: cultural variant or response to assessment demands? Paper presented at the European Association for Research on Learning and Instruction Conference (Gothenburg, August).

Baddeley, A. (1990) *Human Memory*. Hillsdale, NJ: Lawrence Erlbaum.

Biggs, J. (1987) Learning Process Questionnaire. Hawthorn, V: Australian Council for Educational Research.

Biggs, J. (1994) Asian learners through Western eyes: an astigmatic paradox. *Australian and New Zealand Journal of Vocational Educational Research*, 2(2): 40–63.

Boekarets, M. (1997) Self-regulated learning: a new concept embraced by researchers, policy makers, educators, teachers and students. *Learning and Instruction*, 7 (2): 161–86.

Chan, S. (1999) The Chinese learner: a question of style. *Education and Training*, 41(6–7): 294–306.

Davidson, J.E. and Sternberg, R.J. (1998) Smart problem solving: how metacognition helps. In D.J. Hacker, J. Dunlosky and A.C. Graeser (eds) *Metacognition in Educational Theory and Practice*. The Educational Psychology Series. Mahwah, NJ: Lawrence Erlbaum, pp. 47–68.

Drake, B. (2004). International education and IB Programmes: worldwide expansion and potential cultural dissonance. *Journal of Research in International Education*, 3: 189–205.

Gardner, H. (1995) Reflections on multiple intelligences. *Phi Delta Kappan*, 77(3): 200–7.

Heylighen, F. (1993) Epistemology introduction. Principia Cybernetica Available at http://pespmc1.vub.ac.be/EPISTEMI.html, accessed on 14 December 2005.

Jausovec, N. (1994) Metacognition in creative problem solving. In M.A. Runco (ed.) *Problem Finding, Problem Solving, and Creativity*. Norwood, NJ: Ablex.

Jonassen, D. (1991) Objectivism vs. constructivism. *Educational Technology Research and Development*, 39(3): 5–14.

Kember, D. (1996) The intention to both memorise and understand: another approach to learning. *Higher Education*, 31: 341–54.

Locke, E.A. and Latham, G.P. (1990). *A Theory of Goal Setting and Task Performance*. Englewood Cliffs, NJ: Prentice Hall.

Lowenstein, G. (1994) The psychology of curiosity: a review and reinterpretation. *Psychological Bulletin*, 116: 75–98.

Marton, F., Watkins, D. and Tang, C. (1997) Discontinuities and continuities in the experience of learning: an interview study of high-school students in Hong Kong. *Learning and Instruction*, 7: 21–48.

Munro, J. (2003a) Facilitating effective learning and teaching: snapshots. *The Specialist Schools Trust Journal of Innovation in Education*, 1(1): 29–32.

Munro, J. (2003b). 'How people learn'. Keynote presentation at the Biennial Curriculum Corporation Conference *How to Teach Better*, 12 and 13 June 2003, Perth. www.curriculum.edu.au.

Munro, J. (2004) Application of an explicit model of learning to the enhancement of pedagogy. Professional learning through networks. Specialist Schools' Trust Seminar held in London, 7–8 October 2004.

Munro, J. (2005) Learning to learn for knowledge enhancement. Invited keynote paper as part of *Learning to Learn*, the 3rd iNet Online Conference of The Specialist Schools Trust (United Kingdom) and iNet (www.sst-inet.net/olc/papers.aspx?id=3) on 7–13 March 2005. The paper was allocated its own 24-hour online discussion.

Munro, J. and Howes, D. (1996) The effect of cognitive style on learning to write a letter of complaint. *British Journal of Educational Psychology*, 68(2): 243–54.

Nichols, J.D. and Utesch, W.E. (1998) An alternative learning program: effects on student motivation and self-esteem. *Journal of Educational Research*, 91: 272–7.

Paivio, A. (1991) *Images in Mind*. Hertfordshire: Harvester Wheatsheaf.

Pajares, F. (1996) Self-efficacy beliefs in academic settings. *Review of Educational Research*, 66(4): 543–78.

Pintrich, P.R. (1995) Current issues in research on self-regulated learning: a discussion with commentaries. *Educational Psychologist*, 30: 171–2.

Pintrich, P.R. and Garcia, T. (1991) Student goal orientation and self-regulation in the college classroom. In M. Maehr and P.R. Pintrich (eds) *Advances in Motivation and Achievement: Goals and Self-regulatory Processes*, Vol. 7. Greenwich, CT: JAI Press, pp. 371–402.

Pintrich, P.R., Marx, R.W. and Boyle, R.A. (1993) Beyond cold conceptual change: the role of motivational beliefs and classroom contextual factors in the process of conceptual change. *Review of Educational Research*, 68 (2): 167–99.

Riding, R.J. and Cheema, I. (1991) Cognitive styles: an overview and integration. *Educational Psychology*, 11: 193–215.

Schraw, G. and Moshman, D. (1995) Metacognitive theories. *Educational Psychology Review*, 7(4): 351–71.

Tudge, J. (1990) Vygotsky, the zone of proximal development, and peer collaboration: Implications for classroom practice. In L.C. Moll (ed.) *Vygotsky and Education: Instructional Implications of Sociohistorical Psychology.* Cambridge: Cambridge University Press, pp. 155–72.

Vygotsky, L.S. (1978) *Mind in Society.* Cambridge, MA: Harvard University Press.

Walker. A. and Dimmock, C. (2000) One size fits all? Teacher appraisal in a Chinese culture. *Journal of Personnel Evaluation in Education*, 14(2): 155–69.

Wertsch, J.V. (1985) *Culture, Communication, and Cognition: Vygotskian Perspectives.* Cambridge: Cambridge University Press.

Zimmerman, B.L. and Schunk, D.H. (1998) *Self-Regulated Learning: From Teaching to Reflective Practice.* New York: The Guilford Press.

Zimmerman, B.J., Bandura, A. and Martinez-Pons, M. (1992) Self-motivation for academic attainment: the role of self-efficacy beliefs and personal goal setting. *American Educational Research Journal*, 29: 663–76.

11

Culture and Identity: Exploring Individuals within Groups

Richard Pearce

Montaigne noted in his 'Essay on the Education of Children':

> When, according to our common practice, a teacher undertakes to school several minds of very different structure and capacity with the same lessons and the same measure of guidance, it is no wonder that, among a whole multitude of children, he scarcely finds two or three who derive any proper profit from their teaching. (Montaigne 1579/1958: 55)

Given the great variety of children in the average international school, the concerns Montaigne expressed are multiplied beyond his imagining. In the more than 2000 such schools now in existence (Brummitt 2003) a systemic problem is the adjustment of new students to the local norms when they arrive. Since the modal length of stay is frequently two to three years (Skelton 2002: 41), and adjustment to a new academic language takes up to seven years (Carder 1991), it is a matter of surprise that international school students ever 'derive any proper profit from their teaching'.

It is vitally important that they adjust as quickly and effectively as possible to the receiving school, so that learning can proceed.

Compounding the issue is the sudden deprivation of important social contacts (Furukawa et al. 1998), and the possibility of 'culture shock' (Oberg 1960; Furnham and Bochner 1986), both of which may impair the capacity for adaptation to their new school and country (Schaetti 1993). It is therefore important to monitor the progress and process of adjustment of the individual student, and to consider how this may be supported despite the great diversity of cases.

Education can be seen in social terms as a society's way of transmitting to its young the necessary knowledge and skills for its historically accumulated way of life. Hannerz (1992: 83) has described education from an anthropological point of view as 'institutionally specialized transmission of knowledge and development of cultural competence'. In the definition of Goodenough (1957), a society's culture is 'whatever one has to know or believe in order to operate in a manner acceptable to its members'. Small wonder, then, that when families move to live among other societies they have anxieties about the education of their children, and this anxiety is focused upon the institutional education provided by schools.

The case will be made that the child in an international school develops by normal processes but within a unique sequence of social contexts (Pearce 1998). It is suggested that these cultural environmental influences contribute to the identity of the emerging person, equipping them with a mosaic of cultural norms, beliefs and values which directs their active and reactive behaviour. These three cultural elements are seen in this analysis as variants of a single neurological phenomenon, though they are usefully distinguished in most studies of human behaviour. As Harré remarks: 'the task of psychology is to lay bare our system of norms of representation and to compare and contrast the enormous variety of systems; the rest is physiology' (1989). International education operates in an environment in which a growing child moves through an 'enormous variety of systems', and conventional norms of representation from one culture may not apply in others. Accordingly, the study described here uses a model of human action constructed as close as possible to the universal level of physiological process which underlies the myriad processes of human behaviour and of social development.

Walker (2000) describes international schools as generally being characterized by 'a Western liberal, humanist culture'. Nevertheless, Matthews (1989) has observed a dichotomy between 'ideology-driven' and 'market-driven' schools, distinguished by the philosophies of their foundation. They can be described in economic terms as respectively framed by the 'supply-side' influence of idealistic staff and 'demand-side' forces of the market. Research is normally demand-led in response to perceptions of problems held by the sponsoring bodies (Spector and Kitsuse 1977), which in the case of education means national governments. A case will also be made that most research has therefore been done within specific local 'system(s) of norms of representation', and that care is needed in transferring the findings of national research to international schools. Governments raise national funds by taxation in order to fulfil politically agreed national aims. The schools that serve the internationally mobile have no governmental base to fund or organize research, let alone national aim. There is therefore a tendency for practitioners and researchers to look to the relevant home system for research and models of practice, where 'home' is defined by the national affiliations of the institution or its employees. In some countries there are indeed national policies which have been generated in response to cultural diversity.

NATIONAL RESPONSES TO CULTURAL DIVERSITY

Cultural difference between the subject and his or her social environment, a core characteristic of international education, has been viewed and researched in national settings in several ways (e.g. Keats 1993). In this context two useful terms are 'enculturation', the reaction of an individual developing cultural competence in an initial cultural register, and 'acculturation', if developing a new register when already maturely competent in one. Berry (1980) has classified acculturation in terms of two dimensions: relations within the culture and contact with the dominant community (Figure 11.1).

Weinreich (2002) follows Erikson in viewing enculturation as a lifelong activity, a view that prompts the question of whether enculturation may be a more appropriate parallel than acculturation to the personal trajectory of the child growing up in a series of countries. In countries welcoming immigration, such as the USA, cultural diversity is an immanent problem which is to be overcome by acculturation, in which schools play a central role in the assimilation of diverse newcomers (Stewart and Bennett 1991). The acceptance of assimilation as a national goal in the USA has provided a model for many American-system international schools, giving them a useful facility for inducting new

	Own culture valued	Own culture not valued
Host culture valued	Integration	Assimilation
Host culture not valued	Isolation	Marginalization

Figure 11.1   Acculturation as classified by Berry (1980)

students rapidly. Where diversity is pre-existent in the nation, as in Canada or New Zealand, integration of coherent communities has been preferred to assimilation, generating a strong national commitment to 'multiculturalism'. However, a 'multicultural' alternative policy which contravened the requirement to assimilate has been widely denigrated in the USA, since any significant division is unacceptable in an assimilationist society. Marginalization is also perceived as a danger in societies in which assimilation is expected, while it is less of a threat where multiculturalism makes divisions acceptable. As Harré (1998: 179) has observed:

> It is curious that at this time when life in the United States displays more cultural uniformity than it has done since the war between the states there has appeared a stream of writings about the predicaments of those who have to adapt to a variety of cultural roles. Writings such as these must make strange reading for polyglot Europeans or Indians, moving freely about their respective complex social worlds.

For the domestically mobile community 'transition' paradigms have focused attention on the needs of students arriving in a new district, and this concept has been transferred into international school practice in American-system schools around the world (Schaetti 1993; Pollock and Van Reken 1999). However, there is a risk that the local norms and practices will be imposed by universalist practitioners on other people and situations as an 'imposed etic' (Berry 1969); cross-cultural criteria need to be applied before transplanting domestic practices (Gerner and Perry 2002). Berry et al. (1992: 260) offer the useful proposition that 'We shall consider a concept ... to be a universal when on

theoretical grounds there is reason to accept it as invariant across all cultures, when there is empirical evidence to support this claim and when there is no empirical evidence to refute it'.

Where culturally separate communities are in contact within a country, as in many developing countries, there is a perception of state education as the blender of the subordinate with the dominant, sometimes referred to as 'modernization' (Inkeles and Smith 1974). This is generally fostered by the state. On the other hand, cultural distinctiveness may be promoted by new nations seeking to distinguish themselves from previous colonial models, or countries seeking to protect their cultural identity from 'globalist' influences. National solidarity, often in the absence of long-standing traditions, has been reinforced by the deliberate adoption of 'Asian values' in Thailand, Malaysia or Singapore, or of 'Pancasila' (the five national principles enunciated by President Sukarno) in Indonesia (Thomas 1997, 2000). At the same time there has been a noticeable trend for local elites to use international schools as an alternative to the national system which is Anglophone and thus gives privileged access to Western economies. There may be an underlying sense that the Western model, redolent of colonial elitism, is of intrinsically higher status (Lowe 2001).

The third culture kid (TCK) paradigm (Useem and Downie 1976) – and its synonym 'global nomad' (GN) (McCaig 1999) – have been advanced as an account of the life experience of the mobile child, and descriptive accounts are in common use among counsellors. Their accumulated experience has built this into a fruitful typology productively used in many studies (Useem and Cottrell 1996;

Schaetti 2000) and as a basis for curriculum design and therapeutic intervention. However, it remains tuned to US American norms of social structure and expectation (Pearce 2002) so that for other nationalities it is less reliable as an account, and therefore as a basis for interventions, as Harré (1998) has observed (see above).

'Culture shock' (Oberg 1960; Furnham and Bochner 1986) is often cited as a disturbing experience associated with international relocation. It offers a further typology of phenomena and reactions, but from an early date (Adler 1975; Furnham and Bochner 1986) accounts have noted that the experience is not universally shared. Some protection seems to be available through possession of a 'complex self' (Linville 1985), and the author has proposed several sets of 'good movers' (Pearce 1996) whose background has given them an enhanced tolerance of alterity which protects against culture shock.

Professional practice must depend largely upon national typologies as a first approximation to understanding the mobile child, but the abundance of exceptions makes it clear that the full range of life-trajectories displayed by the internationally mobile families requires case-based research. The following model is devised as an aid to the analysis of individual cases in terms of the variables specific to the subject's life history.

THE MODEL

While doubt is sometimes cast upon the capacity of empirical evidence to represent accurately any mental function, Hannerz (1992: 18) has responded to similar expositions of the impossibility of demonstrating classical realism with the pragmatic argument that 'Nature, of the non-humanmade kind, is really out there, and some of the ideas people have about it serve them better than others in dealing with it.' In accordance with Harré's (1989) claim that 'The task of psychology is to lay bare our system of norms of representation …; the rest is physiology', this model takes the level of physiology to be existent, and offers a

set of parsimonious representations of the operation of the nervous system.

In this conceptualization many of the familiar taxa and sub-units of psychology are omitted. While locally of great and proven value there can be serious doubts at several levels concerning their identity of meaning in other societies. Wierzbicka (1991: 333) points out that core cultural values are often represented by key words of the communal language, which are intrinsically untranslatable. For example, a Western-derived parameter such as self-esteem may give consistently repeatable results when applied in a non-Western setting, but its validity still needs demonstration since the connotations of the results may be different. In practice, an everyday example of this in international schools is the new parent who says at interview 'we are only looking for a *good* school', as though this conveyed universal meaning.

In essence, the model draws upon conceptualizations from neurobiology, cognitive science, psychological and cultural anthropology, developmental and cross-cultural psychology, which are currently converging to build a picture of the acquisition and operation of the socially transmitted values used in human judgement. An appropriate starting point is the collaborative effort to unify the human sciences by a number of distinguished American academics in the late 1940s which was summarized by Parsons and Shils (1951) in *Toward a General Theory of Action*. This synthesis was notably reiterated by the psychological anthropologists (D'Andrade and Strauss 1992; Strauss and Quinn 1997). Their conceptualization of human behaviour is extended here. In the present account the value system is seen not as a modifier but as the director, of supreme importance in evaluating observed (and self-observed) behaviour, and directing the selection of 'right' actions. As in human DNA, the vast majority of nervous connections will provide identical actions in all individuals, as Schwartz and Bilsky's (1987) account proposes (see below) and as survival demands. The work of Edelman (1987), LeDoux (2002) and many others has established plausible mechanisms for the development of these immense neurological patterns. It is conventional to apply the term 'culture' only at the level at which difference is consciously perceptible. To the extent that distinctive patterns of values evolve locally and provide a local repertoire for social acquisition by individuals, they constitute the local culture; to the extent that an acquired set of values (broadly speaking) forms an individual's personal pattern, they constitute the identity.

At an empirical level this conception of values can be explored in Personal Construct Psychology (PCP) (Kelly 1955) as the favoured settings on those scales which Kelly described as personal constructs, characteristic of the individual. Hofstede (1991: 8) wrote, 'values are broad tendencies to prefer certain states of affairs over others'; for present purposes the perceived set of more and less desirable states of affairs constitutes a construct. The quality of 'preference' attached to a value is viewed as isomorphic with what has been described by Damasio (1994) as a 'Somatic Marker', a positive or negative stimulus from a somato-visceral nerve circuit in association with the value, which becomes linked with it through experience. These 'gut feelings' give a subjective perception of a positive or negative emotion.

In addition to single circuits, any frequently used neurological units are seen as open to recognition and somatic marking. Thus a hierarchy of sub-units of behaviour exists, open to comparison and selection at a range of levels: we could learn to value a single phoneme of 'correct' pronunciation as 'good', or a complete schema of local identity in which that phoneme is part of the characteristic accent. There is such a nexus of associations attached to a local identity, each with its emotional loading, that once we identify with the self-image, any aspect resonates as 'ours'.

THE NATURE OF VALUES

The present account extends the concept of 'values' to include criteria that are commonly distinguished as 'norms' or 'beliefs'. This needs some exploration. Schwartz and Bilsky (1987: 550) offer a similar general view of values as 'conceptions of the desirable that influence the ways people select action and evaluate events', a treatment that is broadly adopted here. They attempt to define values in terms of their contribution to human survival, as 'cognitive representations of three types of human requirements:

- biologically based needs of the organism
- social interactional requirements for interpersonal communication
- social and institutional demands for group welfare and survival'.

They refer to terminal values (chosen objectives) and instrumental values (chosen processes). It should be noted that some instrumental values affect the way we take on new values, and also that some instrumental values become cognitively promoted to iconic roles as though they were terminal (as in the expression 'cleanliness is next to godliness').

Referring to the conventional distinction between moral and normative values, one can suggest that certain rules for operation of the system emerge, either ontogenetically or phylogenetically, as essential for functioning. They are expressible in discourse between individuals at a conscious level. They are reinforced by supplementary neural adjustment to occupy a pre-eminent position, as 'moral values'. Examples are truth-telling (reliable use of verbal representations) or loyalty (reliable emotional social relationships). In many societies these vital values are reinforced by association with a transcendental authority through whom emotional loading is added to the motivational power of the value. Where this authority is divine or numinous, such as ancestors or an inherited attachment to Land or People, it is resistant to challenge. However, even when endowed with transcendental authority, these moral values have a definition arising from the individual's experience, and locally specific priorities (Sen 1999: 235). Rehearsing the calculation of these priorities is the matter of literature, and this heuristic role perhaps explains the universal occurrence of myths and stories. Weinreich (Weinreich and Saunderson 2003) refers to the 'informal ideologies' by which we live everyday life. More formally, international schools often aspire in their mission statements to build specific values of 'internationalism' into the student's growing value system. It is salutary to bear the mechanism and developmental process in mind while planning to teach such lessons to Montaigne's 'minds of very different structure'.

Connectionist Theory (McClelland et al. 1986) postulates that many separate regions of the brain operate in similar ways but that their simultaneous activities are linked as modules of a larger system (Dehaene and Naccache 2001). The interplay between modules in an experienced brain is integrated at various levels in the neurological hierarchy (LeDoux 2002). At conscious levels these are variously perceived and described as constructs (Kelly 1955), schemata (Strauss and Quinn 1997) or as scripts (Schank 1982). The huge complexity of human decision-making is simplified by subconscious identification of an experience or event with a recognized category; it only remains to apply the relevant construct scale and decide whether the value on the scale is the 'right' one or a 'wrong' one. It is proposed that fundamentally the same process occurs at both subconscious and conscious levels, building a programme of reactions to external stimuli, some unconscious and some conscious. Though this account may sound reductionist, the astronomical complexity of interactions, including interpersonal discourse and the individuality of the experiences from which the system is built, ensures that behaviour is infinitely unpredictable. Adjustment is a burst of activity in the programme-building process.

BUILDING THE VALUE SYSTEM

Development of the value system is seen as an epigenetic interplay (Erikson 1968) between the existing values and the social environment which delivers new experiences. In this the social framework has great importance, beginning with the parents and progressing to include all major social engagements. Vygotsky's concept of the framework in which new experiences are met is adduced by Bruner

(1986) as being necessary for mental development. The necessary emotional weighting is derived from emotionally loaded experiences, most commonly within emotionally salient social relationships. Turiel et al. (1987: 191) summarize the proposition of Shweder that 'Moral evaluations and judgements are transmitted to children by those referred to as "local guardians of the moral order" (especially parents) in the context of routine practices (especially within daily life)'. Garbarino and Bronfenbrenner (1976: 73) say of attachment that 'Without this development of affective and cognitive orientation to other people, the motivation to incorporate a system of morality defined and directed by social agents may well not arise'. Bronfenbrenner's systems approach (Bronfenbrenner 1986) has much to recommend it where the environment, rather than the subject, is the topic of research. Weinreich (Weinreich and Saunderson 2003) points out that negative affect may also enforce value change, just as both the beginning and ending of a romantic relationship can bring sudden changes of norms and predilections. Some analyses focus on the agency of significant others; this conceptualization allows not only for the influence of the familiar and trusted teacher but also for a traumatic encounter with strangers in a new school.

Strauss and Quinn (1997) offer the best account of the internal dynamics of the value system. They propose that there are centripetal tendencies inclining the value system towards internal consistency and stability over time. With support from connectionist theory, they note that new elements which are consonant with the existing system may readily be fitted within it. At the same time, Strauss and Quinn note centrifugal tendencies that permit interactions with new stimuli from the external environment to generate new elements and arrangements of the internal system. Such openness is a necessary property of young children as they assemble a value system, but at some stage must cede priority to the certainty which is required for autonomous adult life.

In accepting a new or changed value into the system many established links are being challenged. A metaphor could be the building of a bird's nest: the tree branch imposes physical givens, and successive additions from the locally available repertoire of materials are added according to the skills of the operator and the opportunities and constraints of the existing structure. The resulting structure, the individual's identity, is a work in progress, constantly subject to development and repair during enculturation, but required to function adequately at all times. Some modes of value change were reviewed by Rescher (1969). Change can mean the adoption of a new construct, the modification of a preferred point, the modification of salience, the reclassification of an item into a favoured or disfavoured category, or even the development of a new, locally valid, facet of situated identity. Teachers are well aware, as Montaigne commented above, that work on so complex a structure demands the best possible combination of generalizations with particular knowledge of their students' state and understanding (Cushner 1990, Thomas 2000). The outcome of this lifelong internal adjustment at any time is that it is the best possible – but inevitably incomplete – approximation to equilibrium. The quest for dynamic equilibrium within the value system is also performed by individuals, including the present writer and other researchers. This quest is here referred to as 'cognitive homeostasis' (Pearce 2003), and includes the reactions to cognitive dissonance described by Festinger (1957): 'the existence of dissonance, being psychologically uncomfortable, will motivate the person to try to reduce the dissonance and achieve consonance. When dissonance is present, in addition to trying to reduce it, the person will actively avoid situations and information which would likely increase the dissonance'.

Thus far the account has predominantly expressed educational and psychological concepts in the terms of neurobiology and cognitive science. In order to investigate at the level of behaviour the present account turns to the descriptions provided by constructivism and personal construct psychology. These are considered to give a representation of human development in terms sufficiently fundamental to satisfy the cross-cultural criteria, and to be appropriate to the study and treatment of internationally mobile children in their varied cultural contexts over a period of time.

INVESTIGATING DEVELOPMENT

Personal Construct Psychology (PCP) (Kelly 1955; Bannister and Fransella 1986) traces the changes in the importance and application of personal constructs, the scales on which an individual evaluates the world. Weinreich's Identity Structure Analysis (ISA) (Weinreich 1980/1986; Weinreich and Saunderson 2003) is a development of this approach which can be used at a nomothetic or an idiographic level. It has been used to follow the evolution of the social environment and of the value system of students over their first year in a new international school and has potential for use in monitoring problematic cases.

ISA gives an account of the identity as a dynamic and historic description of the person. In Weinreich's words (Weinreich and Saunderson 2003):

> ISA refers to the structural representation of the individual's existential experience, in which the relationships between self and other agents are organised in relatively stable structures over time, but which become further elaborated and changed on account of new experiences.

The list of significant members of their social environment, and also some of the major constructs by which they evaluate the world, is evoked from the participant's own world-picture by means of semi-structured interviews. The set of constructs comprises some standard items relevant to all school systems as well as some specific to that person and their social world, selected from a compendium generated for the project. An individualized appraisal instrument is built of these entities and constructs, which the participant can complete in the first week in the new school, at the end of the first term and at the end of the year. In completing this the participant proposes how those entities, including several facets of the participant's self, would apply those constructs, on a 5- or

7-point bipolar scale. The entities include a mandatory set that permit cross-comparisons internal and external to the system. For example, evaluations attributed to 'me as I would like to be' are taken to depict a sample of the participant's own idealistic value system. A computer program using Boolean algebra relates other appraisals to this one, and to one another. In this way changes in an individual over time and individual differences in the process of adjustment may be observed.

The program can, for example, demonstrate transparently the degrees of similarity of views and closeness of relationship between the participant and the other entities. Appraisals at intervals can show progressive changes. It is important to note that the ISA parameters are not crude 'imposed etic' measurements by which distant individuals are invalidly compared, but express essential relationships between elements of identity using data that have been derived from that person's own emic constructs (Pike 1954/1966).

ISA PARAMETERS

The ISA appraisal is a set of declared and attributed evaluations using a bipolar scale between two neutrally expressed extremes, showing the direction and magnitude of the entity's evaluations. The following are among the ISA parameters which may be derived from it.

'Ego involvement' summates the strength of all the views attributed to one entity, giving a measure of the clarity with which that entity's views may be called to mind. This is taken to reflect the salience of that entity in the perceived social world of the participant, a parameter close to the salience of an individual as role model.

'Evaluation' is an indication of the similarity between the participant's aspirational self and another entity, reflecting the extent to which that entity is evaluated as possessing 'good' characteristics and 'bad' characteristics. Even aspects of the self can be evaluated, as we normally perceive ourselves as less than perfect, particularly in situations in which we feel we are making compromises.

'Identification' is a term frequently applied to comparisons of self and another. It is used in ISA, but unlike Evaluation, Identification is the sum of only those appraised positive attributes that coincide with those of the self. 'Empathetic Identification' is the similarity of current self and the other, 'Aspirational Identification' the similarity of positive attributes of aspirational self and other, and 'Contra-identification' is the sum of differences between aspirational self and other.

'Structural Pressure' (SP) is a complex measure. It is an indication of the tendency to apply a particular construct in the same way as the overall evaluation of 'good' and 'bad'. A construct with high Structural Pressure always contributes to the judgement of another, and is known as a core evaluative construct. In the course of value change there is a time when a value is used in dissonant ways in different circumstances so that the net SP falls before rising again as the new application comes into general usage.

'Situated Identities' are self-perceived images located in a specific setting of time or place. By comparing the evaluations made in the persona of the 'current self' with those attributed to aspects of self in the past, in other locations, or in ideal imagination, one can show self-perceived trends over time or the differential use of values in different situations. Thus the appraisals are always made at the present moment, but some show that at the moment of appraisal there was a sense that at another time or place they were or would be different.

'Conflicts in Identification' are measures of the conflict that can arise from an overall perception of similarity between self and another person which is nevertheless in conflict with a number of perceptions of undesirable qualities in the other. The two quantities are multiplied, since the overall effect is dependent upon both identification and repulsion. To resolve the conflict would require either the complete acceptance of such qualities within oneself or rejection of the other. Such tensions are seen as needing active resolution in the process of negotiating identity development. This kind of situation is to be expected where students attempt to join new peers in their different way of life. It may pass through the situation of 'cognitive dissonance' between evaluation of self and action by self described by Festinger (1957).

DISTINCTIVE OUTCOMES OF THE ISA ANALYSIS OF IDENTITY

A pioneer study by Keats, Keats, Biddle, Bank, Hauge, Wan-Rafaei and Valantin (1983) explored the relative frequency with which four types of referent others – parents, siblings, peers and other adults – were used as sources of help by children in seven communities around the world. They showed that the various communities turned to these sources with different priorities, and that the source consulted varied according to the question. The latter observation distinguishes between the situated identities the student has available to operate in different parts of their lives. Keats has reviewed the work which she and her collaborators in South-East Asia have carried out in multicultural societies (Keats 1993), and has noted the opportunity that ISA offers (1993: 16).

In international schools ISA has only been used in one completed study, applied to three cohorts of secondary and primary level children in several schools in the Netherlands (Pearce 2005). Initially proposed as a low-definition nomothetic study, this became a high-definition idiographic longitudinal study covering the first year after the students' arrival, and including some 'control' cases who had been in attendance for at least one year. The outcome suggests that there is considerable potential for monitoring the adjustment of students, as well as fine-resolution observations on individual cases.

The approach proposed here offers some insights that are not available through other analyses, which normally compare the student's progress with a preconceived set of stages. Some parameters are so obvious as to offer checks of validity. On arrival a student shows through 'ego-involvement' a clear vision of the values of former entities, but little knowledge of new ones. This reverses over time, and

participants come to show a sense that 'current self' has clearer awareness of such views than did 'self-in-the-past'. In one case a spoiled appraisal was identified by this check.

In some cases ISA results challenge or resolve pre-existing uncertainties. For example, it is commonly found that before returning home a student may 'cut off' from friends in the expatriate community. This is represented in TCK and GN literature as a reduction in the intensity of engagement (Pollock and Van Reken 1999: 63), but in a case analysed through ISA (Pearce 2005: 253) it has been shown that a returning French teenage boy achieved this outcome, not by being less ego-involved, but by returning to the values of his home country rather than those used in expatriate life. This is the attitude portrayed by the fox with the grapes in Aesop's fable: in the revised evaluation the grapes are not less important, simply less desirable. The significant conclusion is that there is no single 'authentic' set of values; alternative sets of values persist within an available repertoire, and may be evoked when appropriate to the needs of the whole system.

Cognitive dissonance as described by Festinger (1957) is that stage in the change of value use at which one or the other of evaluation and action has changed, but not yet both. The subject either believes a new thing to be good but still performs the old, or vice versa. Adjustment cannot be simply measured by the performance of new routines. Results of ISA show that some students will watch and learn what, in Goodenough's words, 'is acceptable to [a society's] members', or will perform what they still believe is wrong but gradually become reconciled to it. A Korean girl adopted the former course, and an Armenian boy the latter. A French boy with many years' overseas experience had achieved highly by host school standards, but aligned himself against the new teachers who accepted inferior work from his peers, since his original values were still applied rather than local ones accepted. Interestingly, this student reorientated himself on the news that he was to return to France. Instead of valuing students above teachers he came to value all things French over all things connected with his host school and country. This demonstrates the increased salience of one situated identity over another in the new situation.

In an intermediate situation the Structural Pressure on a construct is seen to pass through zero as some situated identities accept the new value before others. The phase of contingency is often a time of uneasy compromise between the old and new self, until either 'right' and 'wrong' become reversed, or there is a mature acceptance of relativism. It is not surprising that, just as early bilingualism gives a metalinguistic appreciation of the relativity of language (Leopold 1953/1971), the experience of cultural diversity gives a metacultural view of culture. In the study a Korean girl with previous overseas experience found adjustment difficult and was isolated although her English was faultless, while an Armenian boy in the same class was relaxed and sociable though very weak in English. The Korean girl identified with her English teacher at home, and aspired to academic fluency; in contrast, the Armenian boy had ample identifications with Armenian relatives, including his diasporic host family, and needed English only for conventional social contact with his peers, for whom he actually had little respect.

CONCLUSION

It has been proposed that the adjustment being carried out most of the time by most students in international schools uses the same means as the development of identity in static children. Analysis of identity at the level of process reveals a wide range of content, and a wider range of interactions. It is apparent that the development of identity is not Newtonian and predictable, but is an interactive and self-regulating complex of processes, only uniform at the level of process. Changes in the value system can to some extent be explicated retrospectively, and this can suggest ways in which that particular child may be open to influences, desired or undesired, which are the professional concern of the school. At the same time it may be possible to monitor the

progress of a child undergoing adjustments, whether normal or potentially pathological, and to watch for extremes of dissonance or conflict, especially where emotionally salient individuals are involved. TCK and GN paradigms are valuable pointers to possible threats to psychological health, but in each case assume a predictable set of stages. These measures, like 'Transition Programmes', need to take account of the evident diversity of reactions to the hazards of relocation. Although more time-consuming and harder to explain, an individualized monitoring process will yield better results than simple stage accounts. Monitoring with ISA also claims the merit of greater emic validity than typologies derived in one community and applied world-wide. It is to be hoped that ISA and other approaches will in due course be tested more widely so that this promise can be authenticated or falsified.

REFERENCES

Adler, P.S. (1975) The transitional experience: an alternative view of culture shock. *Journal of Humanistic Psychology,* 15 (4): 13–23.

Bannister, D. and Fransella, F. (1986) *Inquiring Man: the Psychology of Personal Constructs.* Harmondsworth: Penguin Books.

Berry, J.W. (1969) On cross-cultural comparability. *International Journal of Psychology,* 4: 119–28.

Berry, J.W. (1980) 'Introduction', in H.C. Triandis and J.W. Berry (eds) *Handbook of Cross-Cultural Psychology,* vol. 2. Boston, MA: Allyn and Bacon.

Berry, J.W., Poortinga, Y.H., Segall, M.H. and Dasen, P.R. (1992) *Cross Cultural Psychology: Research and Applications.* Cambridge: Cambridge University Press.

Bronfenbrenner, U. (1986) Ecology of the family as a context for human development: research perspectives. *Developmental Psychology,* 22 (6): 723–42.

Brummitt, N. (2003) ISD database. In E. Jabal (2006) Learning from Hong Kong Alumni: lessons for school leadership, *International Journal of Leadership in Education,* 9 (1): 21–44.

Bruner, J. (1986) *Actual Minds, Possible Worlds.* Cambridge, MA: Harvard University Press.

Carder, M.W. (1991) The role and development of ESL programmes in International Schools. In P.L. Jonietz and D. Harris (eds) *World Yearbook of Education:*

International Schools and International Education. London: Kogan Page.

Cushner, K. (1990) The formal classroom. In R. Brislin (ed.) *Applied Cross-Cultural Psychology.* Newbury Park, CA: Sage.

Damasio, A.R. (1994) *Descartes' Error: Emotion, Reason and the Human Brain.* New York: Putnam.

D'Andrade, R. and Strauss, C. (eds) (1992) *Human Motives and Cultural Models.* Cambridge: Cambridge University Press.

Dehaene, S. and Naccache, L. (2001) Towards a cognitive neuroscience of consciousness. In S. Dehaene (ed.) *The Cognitive Neuroscience of Consciousness.* Cambridge, MA: MIT Press.

Edelman, G. (1987) *Neural Darwinism: The Theory of Neuronal Group Selection.* New York: Basic Books.

Erikson, E. (1968) Identity and identity diffusion. In C. Gordon and K.J. Gergen (eds) *The Self in Social Interaction.* New York: Wiley.

Festinger, L. (1957) *A Theory of Cognitive Dissonance.* London: Tavistock, pp. 1–31.

Furnham, A. and Bochner, S. (1986) *Culture Shock.* London: Methuen.

Furukawa, T., Sarason, I.G. and Sarason, B.R. (1998) Social support and adjustment to a novel social environment: experiences of adolescents on an international exchange programme. *International Journal of Social Psychiatry,* 44 (1): 56–70.

Garbarino, J. and Bronfenbrenner, U. (1976). The socialization of moral judgement and behaviour in cross-cultural perspective. In T. Lickona (ed.) *Moral Development and Behaviour: Theory, Research and Social Issues.* New York: Holt Rinehart Winston, pp. 70–83.

Gerner, M. and Perry, F. (2002) Gender difference in cultural acceptance and career orientation among internationally mobile and non-internationally mobile adolescents. In M.G. Ender (ed.) *Military Brats: Growing Up among Organizations.* Westport, CT: Praeger. pp. 165–92.

Goodenough, W.H. (1957) Cultural anthropology and linguistics. In P. Garvin (ed.) Report of the Seventh Annual Round Table Meeting on Linguistics and Language Study. Georgetown University Monograph Series, *Language and Linguistics, 9.* Washington, DC: Georgetown University.

Hannerz, U. (1992) *Cultural Complexity: Studies in the Social Organization of Meaning.* New York: Columbia University Press.

Harré, R. (1989) Language games and texts of identity. In J. Shotter and K.J. Gergen (eds) *Texts of Identity.* London: Sage.

Harré, R. (1998) *The Singular Self: An Introduction to the Psychology of Personhood.* London: Sage.

Hofstede, G. (1991) *Cultures and Organizations: Software of the Mind.* London: HarperCollins.

Inkeles, A. and Smith, D.H. (1974) *Becoming Modern: Individual Change in Six Developing Countries.* Cambridge, MA: Harvard University Press.

Keats, D. (1993) Cross-cultural contributions to schooling processes in multicultural environments. In Symposium on International Perspectives on Culture and Schooling, Institute of Education, Department of International and Comparative Education, 11–13 May.

Keats, J.A., Keats, D.M., Biddle, B.J., Bank, B.J., Hauge, R., Wan-Rafaei and Valantin, S. (1983) Parents, friends, siblings, and adults: unfolding referent other importance data for adolescents. *International Journal of Psychology,* 18: 239–62.

Kelly, G.A. (1955) *The Psychology of Personal Constructs,* vols I and II. New York: Norton.

LeDoux, J. (2002) *Synaptic Self: How Our Brains Become Who We Are.* New York: Viking Penguin.

Leopold, W.F. (1953/1971) Patterning in children's language learning. In A. Bar-Adon and W.F. Leopold (eds) *Child Language: A Book of Readings.* Englewood Cliffs, NJ: Prentice-Hall.

Linville, P. (1985) Self-complexity and affective extremity: don't put all of your eggs in one cognitive basket. *Journal of Social Cognition,* 3 (1): 94–120.

Lowe, J. (2001) International examinations: the new credentialism and reproduction of advantage in a globalising world. In M.C. Hayden and J.J. Thompson (eds) *Managing International Education.* London: Kogan Page.

Matthews, M. (1989) The scale of international education, Pt I. *International Schools Journal,* 17: 7–17.

McCaig, N.M. (1999) Foreword. In D. Pollock and R. Van Reken (1999) *The Third Culture Kid Experience: Growing Up Among Worlds.* Yarmouth, ME: Intercultural Press, pp. ix–xvi.

McClelland, J.L., Rumelhart, D.E. and the PDP Research Group (1986) *Parallel Distributed Processing: Explorations of the Microstructure of Cognition,* Vol. 2: *Psychological and Biological Models.* Cambridge, MA: MIT Press.

Montaigne, M. de (1579/1958) On the education of children. In *Essays.* London: Penguin.

Oberg, K. (1960) Cultural shock: adjustment to new cultural environments. *Practical Anthropology,* 7: 177–82.

Parsons, T. and Shils, E.A. (1951) *Toward a General Theory of Action.* Boston, MA: Harvard University Press.

Pearce, R. (1996) Kipling's cat: learning from the new student. *International Schools Journal,* XV (2): 23–30.

Pearce, R. (1998) Developing cultural identity in an international school environment. In M. Hayden and J. Thompson (eds) *International Education: Principles and Practice.* London: Kogan Page.

Pearce, R. (2002) Children's international relocation and the developmental process. In M.G. Ender (ed.) *Military Brats and Other Global Nomads.* Westport, CT: Praeger.

Pearce, R. (2003) Cultural values for international schools. *International Schools Journal*, 22 (2): 56–65.

Pearce, R. (2005) Developing a model of identity as a means of monitoring newly relocated students in International Schools. Doctoral thesis, Department of Education, University of Bath, UK.

Pike, K.L. (1954/1966) *Language in Relation to a Unified Theory of the Structure of Human Behaviour.* Glendale, CA: Summer Institute of Linguistics, 1954, and The Hague, Netherlands: Mouton, 1966.

Pollock, D.C. and Van Reken, R.E. (1999) *The Third Culture Kid Experience: Growing Up Among Worlds.* Yarmouth, ME: Intercultural Press.

Rescher, N. (1969) What is value change? A framework for research. In K. Baier and N. Rescher (eds) *Values and the Future.* New York: The Free Press. pp. 68–95.

Schaetti, B. (1993) The life-long impacts of an internationally mobile childhood. In European Council of International Schools Conference, The Hague, November.

Schaetti, B.F. (2000) *Global Nomad Identity: Hypothesizing a Developmental Model.* (vol. 9992721.) Ann Arbor, MI: ProQuest.

Schank, R.C. (1982) *Dynamic Memory.* Cambridge: Cambridge University Press.

Schwartz, S.H. and Bilsky, W. (1987) Toward a universal psychological structure of human values. *Journal of Personality and Social Psychology*, 53(3): 550–62.

Sen, A. (1999) *Development as Freedom.* New York: Alfred Knopf.

Skelton, M. (2002) Defining 'International' in an international curriculum. In M. Hayden, J.J. Thompson and G. Walker (eds) *International Education in Practice: Dimensions for National and International Schools.* London: Kogan Page.

Spector, M. and Kitsuse, J.I. (1977) *Constructing Social Problems.* Hawthorne, NY: Longman.

Stewart, E.C. and Bennett, M.J. (1991) *American Cultural Patterns: A Cross-cultural Perspective,* rev. edition. Yarmouth, ME: Intercultural Press.

Strauss, C. and Quinn, N. (1997) *A Cognitive Theory of Cultural Meaning.* Cambridge: Cambridge University Press.

Thomas, E. (1997) *Researching Values in Cross-Cultural Contexts.* In Values Education and the Curriculum Conference, Institute of Education, 10–11 April.

Thomas, E. (2000) *Culture and Schooling: Building Bridges between Research, Praxis and Professionalism.* Chichester: John Wiley.

Turiel, E., Killen, M. and Helwig, C.C. (1987) Morality: its structure, functions, and vagaries. In J. Kagan and S. Lamb (eds) *The Emergence of Morality in Young Children.* Chicago: University of Chicago Press, pp. 155–244.

Useem, R.H. and Cottrell, A.B. (1996) Adult third culture kids. In C. Smith (ed.) *Strangers at Home: Essays on the Effects of Living Overseas and Coming 'Home' to a Strange Land.* Bayside, NY: Aletheia Publications.

Useem, R.H. and Downie, R.D. (1976) Third-culture kids. *Today's Education*, Sept./Oct.: 103–5.

Walker, G. (2000) One-way streets of our culture. *International Schools Journal*, 19 (2): 11–19.

Weinreich, P. (1980/1986) *A Manual for Identity Exploration using Personal Constructs.* University of Warwick: Centre for Research in Ethnic Relations.

Weinreich, P. (2002) Personal communication.

Weinreich, P. and Saunderson, W. (2003) *Analysing Identity: Cross-cultural, Societal and Clinical Contexts.* London: Routledge.

Wierzbicka, A. (1991) Japanese key words and cultural values. *Language in Society*, 20(3): 333–85.

12

Coherence and Consistency in International Curricula: a Study of the International Baccalaureate Diploma and Middle Years Programmes

Tristian Stobie

This chapter raises questions and explores concepts that may be helpful in judging coherence, consistency and continuity in the curriculum in international schools. It is based on a doctoral enquiry that specifically considered the coherence and consistency of the International Baccalaureate Middle Years and Diploma Programmes (Stobie 2005a). The intention here is not so much to summarize this research (as this has already been reported in Stobie 2005b), but rather to reflect on some of the broader questions raised.

A good deal has been written about different perspectives on curriculum and international curriculum, and, where relevant, some of these concepts are briefly reviewed below. The focus here, however, is different and may be encapsulated in the question: What characterizes a coherent and consistent international curriculum?

This is an important question to consider not just for academic, but for practical, reasons. Many schools that consider themselves 'international', because of their composition, location and/or curricula offer a variety of different curricula experiences to students. Some follow a recognized curriculum continuum, for example the Primary Years Programme (PYP), Middle Years Programme (MYP) and Diploma Programme (DP) of the International Baccalaureate Organization (IBO). Other schools design their own curricula and/or mix national curricular requirements with their own curricula or with those of organizations like the IBO or the English International General Certificate of Secondary Education (IGCSE).

The first part of this chapter reviews very briefly some relevant concepts from the curriculum studies literature. The second part reports on some of the relevant findings of the research enquiry into the coherence and continuum of the International Baccalaureate Middle Years and Diploma programmes and explores their implications for those not only involved in the teaching of IB programmes, but more generally.

CONCEPTS OF CURRICULUM

Lawton (1983: 1–3) points out that conceptions of curriculum could be placed on a continuum. At one extreme would be a narrow definition in terms of specific taught content and on the other, the broadest interpretation, would be the whole of educational studies. This includes not only what is taught but how and why and in what cultural and ideological contexts. In the United States the concept of curriculum, according to Moon (2002: 191), is holistic. It encompasses subjects, the connections between subjects, teaching methods and all aspects of schooling. Typically, countries in mainland Europe have no word that translates well to curriculum. Instead, a number of different parts are separately identified that contribute to the learning process.

The issue of breadth is, therefore, central to any consideration of curriculum. The term curriculum can be used (narrowly) to focus on the planned academic programme or to refer to broader objectives that include individual, personal and social development and affective education. The term is sometimes used to refer to the 'formal' curriculum (Kelly 1989: 13), all activities allocated on the school timetable or the 'informal' curriculum, recognizing the many activities that go on after school or during breaks. The term 'hidden' curriculum is sometimes used to describe the environment in which the curriculum is delivered and the unintended, unconscious or unplanned outcomes of its delivery. According to Vallance (1991: 40): 'The hidden curriculum refers to those practices and outcomes of schooling which, while not explicit in curriculum guides or school policy, nevertheless seem to be a regular and effective part of the school experience.'

The existence of a hidden curriculum raises the issue of intention in curriculum, of planned and unplanned outcomes. Stenhouse highlights this, saying (1975: 2–6) that curriculum can refer to a 'written prescription of what it is intended should happen in schools' (the intended curriculum) or alternatively 'what actually happens to children in school' (the experienced curriculum).

Curriculum must be profoundly influenced by school culture. Deal and Nolan (1982: 11–17) argue that schools are defined by ideologies. Ideologies 'provide patterns of thinking that influence instructional approaches, student–teacher interactions and curriculum content. There are interlacing educational ideologies so schools may contain individuals operating from different ideological perspectives.'

Lawton further points out (1983: 4) that:

Teachers and educational administrators as well as politicians all operate with some kind of social theory in the sense of a set of assumptions, value positions, and ideas about the purpose of society. These views may, however, lack coherence and some assumptions may contradict others. One important function of curriculum studies then is to clarify issues and questions, to relate points of view to more general ideologies.

As it is impossible for any curriculum to be value-free, one attribute of coherence implied by Lawton is that the intended and experienced curriculum should share a consistent set of values. Lawton, many years later, returns to this point in identifying a main failing of the National Curriculum in England (1996: 8), arguing that curriculum planners have mixed different curricular models, based on differing ideologies, with insufficient attention being paid to problems of compatibility.

Ross (2000) uses metaphor, in this instance of different gardens, to highlight different ideological approaches to curriculum. A 'Baroque garden' illustrates the construction of curriculum around the transmission of content through clearly defined and separated subjects or disciplines (Ross 2000: 97). Ross argues that this academic and classical humanist approach has been the dominant paradigm in English schools and is the most common form of curriculum construction. Other types identified by Ross (2000) are the 'Victorian garden', representing utilitarian/vocational curricula which are objectives-led and focus on the training and the development of competences, and the 'cottage garden', which refers to child-centred, developmental, progressive curricula focusing on individual growth rather than examination performance.

From a different starting point Kelly (1986: 6) argues that one way of viewing different educational ideologies is through different theories of knowledge. The rationalist perspective emphasizes reason and accepts the existence of a priori knowledge independent of the senses. The empiricist perspective, on the other hand, emphasizes that knowledge is constructed by humans and is evolutionary. The implications of this distinction are important to Kelly since the rationalist perspective accepts the intrinsic superiority of certain kinds of knowledge. Kelly points out that one ideological tradition, the classical humanist, is based on a rational perspective and has its origins in classical education and the Platonic ideal of transmitting the high culture from one generation to the next (1986: 168). Another is based on an empirical perspective that emphasizes knowledge gained through the senses as an evolutionary process.

All curricula, national or international, require selection to be made. The selection process is bound to be based on values about what is considered to be important. Lawton (1983: 28) emphasizes the importance of cultural transmission, making available to the next generation the most valued aspects of culture. Hirst and Peters (1970: 63) justified curriculum selection around fundamental forms of thought that they considered central to understanding and structuring the world, while Phenix (1964) argues that the primary goal of education is to analyse the nature of meaning.

COHERENCE, CONSISTENCY AND CONTINUITY

Literature explicitly considering curriculum coherence and consistency is very thin. Many of the concepts briefly considered in the previous section such as breadth, depth, balance and ideology are important when considering curriculum coherence and consistency but, by themselves, they are inadequate. For an intended curriculum continuum to be considered 'coherent and consistent' it must have an identifiable philosophy as well as clearly specified aims and objectives. These should indicate the values base, involving the assumptions about the nature of knowledge and learning, against which the prescribed programme syllabuses and broader planned activities can be compared for consistency and coherence.

According to Barrett, Jamison and Weston (1992: 3), 'A coherent curriculum, like a poem, has a distinctive form and adds up to a satisfying whole that in some way makes sense to those who experience it.' Barrett et al. (1992) raise a number of questions to consider when judging whether a curriculum is coherent. Is the curriculum design internally coherent? How well does what is learned, the methods of learning and assessment fit together? Is the implementation process coherent? Is there a coherent structure within which the curriculum can be managed? To whom is the curriculum coherent?

The term 'continuity' suggests coherence and consistency between different age-specific levels of the programme. Agreements about curriculum continuity are one indicator of consistency. According to Derricott (1985: 16), 'Continuity necessitates the presence of an agreed curriculum plan ... continuity implies agreement at the levels of aims and objectives, selection and organization of content, skills and methods of assessment.'

For a programme to be consistent, the implication is that there must be a clear understanding of, and agreement with, a common curriculum philosophy and curriculum aims and objectives that transcend different age groups encompassed by the curriculum framework. Agreement and understanding imply consultation and professional development. When considering the experienced curriculum, rather than the intended curriculum, the implication is that individuals and school communities 'buy into' and share this common understanding and live it.

One question stands out. Does effective continuity imply sameness? Derricott believes it does not and recognizes the place of planned discontinuity in a curriculum continuum, believing compatibility to be a more important concept (1985: 156):

> Planned discontinuity as opposed to unplanned discontinuity would seem to have a clear purpose ... planned discontinuity is a deliberate change in practice with the intention of stimulating growth and development ... it could be manifest in a deliberate and abrupt change of teaching or content as a symbol of the process of maturity or growing older. The disequilibrium caused by such an experience challenges children to accommodate to it and to develop new ways of learning.

CURRICULUM IN AN INTERNATIONAL CONTEXT

International schools, and the curricula they use, are subject to political and economic forces in the same way as are national curricula. Matthews (1989) argues that international schools are subject to two driving forces, ideology and the market, and that most international schools are predominantly market-driven since their continued existence depends on satisfying the demands of their customers who expect effective and easy transfer back to national and other international schools and on to universities. These schools expect that the curricula used in their schools will lead to high status employment for their children. The International Baccalaureate programmes or the IGCSE, from the perspective of market-driven schools, might be seen as a mechanism for attaining positional advantage in a globally competitive market place for graduating students (Stobie 2001).

Arguably, the decision about what to include in international curricula is an even greater issue than in national curricula, because the possibilities transcend national and cultural boundaries. Lawton's universals (1983) might provide one framework for considering what to select in an international context. Hayden and Thompson (1996), based on a survey of more than 3,000 students and approximately 300 teachers in international schools, suggested a parallel with Lawton's work, arguing that there are a number of universals which characterize any institution claiming to promote an experience of international education. These are: exposure to students of different cultures within the school, teachers as exemplars of international-mindedness, a balanced formal curriculum, informal aspects of the school and exposure to others of different cultures outside the school. They argue that 'the essence of international education lies not so much in its association with a particular location, but rather in association with the crossing of frontiers, be they physical or intellectual' (Hayden and Thompson 1995).

Thompson (1998) goes on to stress that, to be committed to effective international education, schools must concentrate on much more than the formal academic curriculum. Internationalism must permeate the ethos of the school and is essentially experiential. This includes administrative styles as well as a broad and balanced curriculum and a cultural diversity of students and staff, at least in outlook if not national and cultural composition. Thompson describes the importance of 'interstitial' learning as the mortar that binds academic subjects (the bricks of the curriculum) together. It is in the interstitial mortar that the development of most international understanding takes place.

Thompson (1998) warns that if credentialism is the priority, and if this requires external examinations as evidence of objective attainment, there may be some conflict of interest between the market-driven and the ideological/pedagogical forces. Specifically there is a danger that fundamental principles that cannot be easily assessed through an external examination can be neglected:

> International examination systems hold particular responsibilities in such cases, where it is often extremely difficult to reward individual learning

Table 12.1   Descriptive summary of the International Baccalaureate Diploma Programme and Middle Years Programme

	Diploma Programme	Middle Years Programme
Age range	A two-year course for the 16–19 age range. University Preparatory	Five-year programme for the middle years of schooling, 11–16 age range
Historical origins	International Baccalaureate Organization was established in 1968 to administer the Diploma which had been conceived and initially developed by the International Schools Association	Developed in the late 1980s as the International Schools Association Curriculum. Taken over by the International Baccalaureate Organization in 1994
Subject requirements	Students study six subjects (Two Languages, Mathematics, a Science, a Social Study and one Art or another subject taken from Science, Language or Social Studies)	Students study eight disciplines (Two Languages, Humanities, Technology, Science, Mathematics, Arts, Physical Education)
Other distinguishing requirements	Students study Theory of Knowledge, complete an Extended Essay and a CAS (Creativity, Action, Service) programme	Teachers teach their discipline through five cross-curricular themes (Areas of Interaction): Approaches to Learning, Environmental Education, Health and Social Education, Community Service, Homo Faber. Students complete a personal project
Assessment	Predominantly through external examination. Also moderated coursework	Schools who want certification submit coursework for moderation. No examinations

Source: Adapted from IBO 2003

gains in some of the important curricular objectives relating to the international nature of the programme. In turn, the lack of visibility of such objectives in the testing arrangements leads easily to a lack of acknowledgement of their significance in the full education received by the students, with a corresponding decrease of the importance attached to them by parents, administrators, board members, sometimes teachers in planning programmes and, most importantly, often by the students themselves, who may well devalue such aspects of their international education.

THE COHERENCE AND CONSISTENCY OF THE INTERNATIONAL BACCALAUREATE MIDDLE YEARS AND DIPLOMA PROGRAMMES

This section briefly reviews some of the findings of a research enquiry conducted as part of a doctoral programme at the University of Bath (Stobie 2005a, 2005b) with a view to considering some of the broader issues raised by the study. The enquiry focused on the Middle Years Programme (MYP) and

Diploma Programme (DP) of the International Baccalaureate Organization (IBO). Table 12.1 gives an introductory overview of the programmes. The research enquiry was divided into two parts. The first part considered the intended curriculum progression and the second part focused on the experience with the continuum in two case study schools.

The historical origins of the Diploma and MYP give a good insight into the ideological basis of the intended curricula. In considering factors that shaped the Diploma in the 1960s and 1970s, Hill's description (2001) of three forces is illuminating. These are utilitarian (a school leaving programme facilitating university entrance), ideological (development of international perspectives to promote understanding and peace) and pedagogical (the promotion of critical thinking and problem-solving and a balanced and broad-based curriculum educating the whole person).

The Middle Years Programme, formerly named the International Schools Association Curriculum (ISAC) until the IBO took over its management in 1994, was inspired by similar ideological and pedagogical principles to the

Diploma. The fact that the MYP was not conceived as a school leaving certificate was viewed by Gerard Renaud (1989), one of the most influential thinkers behind its development, as an opportunity to make the ISAC more progressive, visionary and internationally focused than the Diploma. The significance of this distinction is important in understanding the orientation, structure and development of the two programmes. The need for acceptance by universities of the Diploma required external examinations and the prescription of a good deal of content. It forced subjects to be essentially treated as 'discrete' and constrained the development of holistic learning. By contrast, the MYP expected teachers and schools to take a more active role in school-based curriculum development, through school development of cross-curricula themes that were infused in subject teaching called 'Areas of Interaction': Approaches to Learning, Community Awareness and Service, Homo Faber (the creative genius of humans), Environmental Education and Health and Social Education.

The Diploma and MYP are different in some notable ways. But are they coherent and consistent? The MYP provides more of a framework, requiring teachers and schools to flesh out content, although assessment criteria for the end of the programme are defined. The examinations orientation of the Diploma results in a more tightly defined curriculum, although teachers still exercise considerable choice and the study of international and local texts and perspectives is expected. The fact that the MYP requires the study of eight disciplines (art, technology and PE being compulsory) and the Diploma six also suggests the MYP is broader and more balanced. Despite differences, the research study suggested that there is considerable coherence and consistency between the programmes, at least in the intended curricula and on the level of philosophy, aims and objectives. A paper published by the IBO, Monograph 4 (IBO 2002), summarizes an IBO review of the philosophy and overarching framework of all of its programmes. Table 12.2 shows evidence found in IBO curriculum documents in

relation to IBO claims for common characteristics of the two programmes.

Table 12.3 summarizes aims, objectives and content found in IBO curriculum guides that support the IBO assertion made in Monograph 4 that 'the MYP and Diploma promote International Understanding and World Citizenship'.

CASE STUDY OF THE EXPERIENCE OF THE IB CURRICULUM CONTINUUM IN TWO SCHOOLS

As the brief review of selected literature at the start of this chapter suggested, it is not possible to assume that an 'intended' curriculum progression will be the same as that 'experienced' in schools. Each school, indeed each teacher, will have their own ideology and values that will impact on the experienced curriculum. In order to see what the experience of schools was with the IB Diploma/MYP curriculum continuum a case study of two schools was completed in the second part of the enquiry. This section reviews some of the findings from the case studies that inform the question raised at the start of the chapter: what characterizes a coherent and consistent international curriculum?

The study was conducted in two experienced IB schools (referred to as school 'A' and 'B') and was based on interviews with teachers and students who were involved with both programmes. It was anticipated that an examination of what was similar and different about the experience with the curriculum continuum in very different schools would be more illuminating than studying two very similar schools. Similarities between the schools were that they were both very international in student composition and had extensive experience with the MYP and Diploma programmes. Differences were that school A was independent of state ties. The majority of the teachers in school A were recruited from overseas, predominantly the USA and the UK. School A also had much higher fees than school B as it was not state-subsidized. School B, which operated a bilingual stream for host

Table 12.2   Summary of evidence found in IBO curriculum documents (produced between 1997 and 2004) in support of assertions made in monograph 4 concerning diploma and MYP shared features

IBO claim (adapted from shared features identified in monograph 4)	MYP	Diploma
Study across broad and balanced range of knowledge. Drawing on content from educational cultures across the world	Requirement to study eight subjects including Technology, the Arts and PE	Requirement to study six subjects. At least two languages required
	Content drawn from different world cultures (examples: large degree of freedom, and encouragement to select local case studies in social studies, flexibility to select world literature)	No PE, Arts or Technology requirement. Arts can be studied, but as an option, not a requirement
		Content drawn from different world cultures (examples: world literature in English, international case study in Geography and Economics)
Special emphasis on language acquisition and development	MYP may be taught in any language	Two languages required. Three can be studied concurrently in full DP
	Two languages required. Must be studied every year of the MYP	Framework of A1, A2, B and *ab initio* (beginner) languages allows for study at a wide range of levels
	Students encouraged to study their best/native language but option to define the language of instruction in the school as language A	Very large number of language A courses supported
Opportunities for engaging in transdisciplinary learning as well as the study of individual subjects	Common areas of interaction and the fundamental concepts require teachers to make interdisciplinary connections	Theory of Knowledge provides a separate course that links the academic subjects
	and to plan curriculum around transdisciplinary themes	New transdisciplinary courses piloted
		Little required interdisciplinary work. Curriculum organized through the academic disciplines
Developing learning to learn skills	Approaches to Learning as a required interdisciplinary component	Metacognition developed through the reflective Theory of Knowledge course
	The personal project requiring a demonstration of research skills	The extended essay requires development of research skills
		Implicit rather than explicit in the programme
Provides students with opportunities for individual and collaborative planning and research	Considerable opportunities because of the flexibility of the framework	Courses require collaborative activities and individual work. Opportunities for collaborative inquiry-based work (Group 4 Science project, Geography). Extended essay requires individual research
	Horizontal curriculum planning is required	
Community service requiring action and reflection	The development of community awareness and community service required as an area of interaction	Community service required through the CAS Programme

country nationals alongside an international stream, had a large student population from the host country. A substantial number of teachers in school B were host country nationals, trained in the host country. There were many more part-time teachers in school B than in school A. Students in school B who were in the bilingual stream also had

Table 12.3   Examples of aims, objectives and content found in the curriculum guides (produced by the IBO between 1997 and 2004) that support the assertion 'the MYP and Diploma promote International Understanding and World Citizenship'

	MYP	Diploma
Language A	*Aim:* Comprehend more clearly aspects of their own culture and those of other cultures by exploring the interdependence of human beings through a number of works	*Content:* Study of world literature
	Content: Developing schemes of work that develop intercultural awareness (and other concepts and areas of interaction)	*Aim:* Broaden the students' perspective through the study of works from other cultures and languages
Language B	*Content:* Developing schemes of work that develop intercultural awareness (and other concepts and areas of interaction)	*Aim:* Develop students' awareness of the relationship between the languages and cultures with which they are familiar
		Obj: Show an awareness of, and sensitivity to, the cultures related to the language studied
Social Studies/individuals and Society	*Aim (Geog):* Analyse, according to a variety of subjective viewpoints, the ways in which societies live in, locate, organize, compete for and perceive space	*Aim:* Develop an awareness in the student that human attitudes and beliefs are widely diverse and that the study of society requires an appreciation of such diversity
	Aim (History): Develop an understanding of history from a local to a global perspective	*Aim (Economics):* Promote an awareness and understanding of internationalism in Economics
	Content: Write a programme of study that develops intercultural awareness (and other concepts and areas of interaction)	*Content (Economics):* emphasis on development and international economics *Content (Historyl):* regional options
Sciences	*Aim:* Become confident and responsible citizens in a rapidly changing world, able to take or develop an informed interest in matters of Scientific import	*Aim:* Raise awareness of the moral, ethical, social, economic and environmental implications of using science and technology
	Aim: Develop an awareness of Science as an increasingly international activity involving cooperation at all levels	*Obj:* Demonstrate the personal skills of cooperation, perseverance and responsibility appropriate for effective scientific investigation
	Content: Write a programme of study (within the prescribed framework) that develops intercultural awareness (and other concepts and areas of interaction)	*Content:* Group 4 project: allows students to appreciate the environmental, social and ethical implications of Science
Mathematics	*Aim:* Appreciate the international dimensions of Mathematics and its varied cultural and historical perspectives	*Aim:* Appreciate the international dimensions of mathematics and the multiplicity of its cultural and historical perspectives
Arts	*Aim:* Develop receptiveness to visual and performing art forms across time, place and cultures, and perceive the significance of these art forms as an integral part of life	*Aim:* Promote visual and contextual knowledge of art from various cultures

(Continued)

Table 12.3   (Continued)

	MYP	Diploma
	Obj: Show sensitivity to their own and different cultures	*Aim:* Enable students to learn about themselves and others through individual and collaborative engagement with the visual arts
	Content: Developing schemes of work that develop intercultural awareness (and other concepts and areas of interaction)	*Obj:* Show some awareness of the cultural, historical and social dimensions of themes in more than one cultural context (Research workbook)
Technology	*Aim:* Develop an appreciation of the international and intercultural aspects of technology	*Content:* Group 4 project (as Science above)
	Content: Developing schemes of work (as above)	
PE	*Aim:* Demonstrate the ability to critically reflect upon physical activity in both a local and intercultural context	N/A
	Content: Developing schemes of work (as above)	

significant additional national requirements to meet, while school A did not have this constraint and could focus solely on the IB programmes.

The study suggested that the MYP and Diploma are perceived to be philosophically coherent and consistent by the majority of teachers and administrators in both schools. The ways in which they are seen to be consistent match those stated by the International Baccalaureate Organization in the 'Articulation of the Programmes Monograph' (IBO 2002, see Table 12.2). Both programmes were perceived to be: broad-based, holistic, to emphasize and support language development, provide international perspectives, focus on learning how to learn, develop critical thinking skills, encourage independent enquiry and emphasize community awareness and service.

Teachers, administrators and students recognized that the Diploma and MYP programmes develop these attributes differently. The MYP was considered to be much more holistic and flexible, a consequence of a less rigid syllabus and no external examinations. The Diploma was seen to be much more rigid, prescriptive and academically demanding, a consequence of external examinations based in part on prescriptive university expectations.

The consequence of these differences was identified as important by all and had a profound influence on how they approached the programmes.

Most teachers and administrators in both schools (but more so in school B than A) felt that the shared philosophy did not, however, mean a common pedagogy. In the Diploma the overriding priority identified by administrators and teachers was preparing students for the demanding IB external examinations, which was clearly perceived to require a more traditional focus and preparation than that encouraged by the MYP's looser framework. This fact of a shift in approach, brought on by the existence of examinations in the Diploma, was widely reported. For many teachers and students this was seen as a natural progression. For others it was viewed as too much of a leap.

The comments of two teachers illustrate this, as follows:

On paper, yes they have a common philosophy. I only know that for Mathematics they talk about the usefulness and beauty of Mathematics, the cultural background to Mathematics, all of these in both sets of documents. In practice I feel that there is so little time to complete the Mathematics programme for the Diploma and we don't have time to bring out these things as much as we would like to. It is more just learning the skills needed to pass the examination. (Mathematics teacher school B)

In the Diploma there is a get down to business, we have got to get this done by this deadline kind of grocery store list of things to do that begins immediately at the beginning of the 11th grade. The time element is looser in the MYP in terms of production; everything can be explored. (English teacher school A)

The way in which teachers tended to describe the continuum suggested an implicit assumption that the Diploma was essentially fixed. Only one teacher interviewed questioned whether the Diploma should be adapted to the MYP, rather than the MYP to the Diploma; specifically, whether the Diploma should rely less on examinations and more on 'authentic' forms of assessment and have less prescribed content.

The perception emerged that important learning objectives clearly identified in the Diploma Programme are considered less important (or not even recognized) by a number of teachers in practice because of the pressure they are under to get students through a tough and traditional academic examination. Many teachers and administrators felt that the 'holistic' elements of the Diploma were only bolted onto the programme through courses like the Theory of Knowledge and CAS and were not their responsibility.

Most teachers did not report being influenced in the approach they adopted to teaching of the Diploma by their MYP experience. There were a few exceptions to this, however, where teachers understood the fundamental concepts of the MYP as IB continuum concepts rather than just being specific to the MYP. Almost all teachers, however, reported that teaching the Diploma was significantly impacting on how they taught the last two years of the MYP as they used it to prepare students for the demands of the Diploma programme.

Teachers in school B were stressed by having to teach additional subjects as part of national education requirements at both MYP and Diploma level. Partly as a consequence they found it very difficult to find the time and resources to spend on curriculum and

assessment preparation needed to fully develop the MYP. The fact that school B had a large number of transient part-time teachers and a high teacher and administrator turnover rate compounded the difficulty. School B is, however, not unique in terms of the many schools teaching the MYP who try to match state requirements (or the requirements of other curricula like the IGCSE) with IBO expectations.

LESSONS SUGGESTED BY THIS RESEARCH RELATING TO CURRICULUM COHERENCE AND CONSISTENCY

It is possible to make some tentative propositions based on the findings of this research enquiry, as follows:

- Teachers who are held to account for examination results are likely to teach to the test and undervalue non-examined curricula components. A balance needs to be struck where earlier curricula experiences recognize the importance of examination performance, providing directed preparation. Assessment in non-examined learning objectives needs to be given significance in all years.
- Where possible, terminology between curricula and different age groups should be consistent. In the case of the IBO, a common student profile, the learner profile, has been recently introduced that applies to the PYP, MYP and Diploma that has helped with the coherence of IB curricula terminology.
- The expectations placed on teachers and students in schools that run different curricula together at the same time can be enormous. Sometimes these curricula are based on different ideologies and are more dissimilar than similar.
- Some curricula, like the IBO programmes in general (and particularly the PYP and MYP) require considerable teacher creative professionalism. Since effective creative professionalism requires teachers to understand fully and to support the principles of the programmes, and have time to develop these in practice, professional development is critical. Schools must provide a supportive environment, which allows teachers time to plan and develop the curriculum individually and collectively.

- Having stable school leadership and not too high teacher turnover helps ensure continuity and retain experience.
- Teaching across divides can help teachers smooth out the transition for students between different programmes.

CONCLUSIONS

An image comes to mind. When John Fines was asked about the problem of content coverage in the teaching of History he is quoted as saying:

> It is just like trying to stuff a barrage balloon into a Gladstone bag with the train already prepared to leave the station. The too muchness of it all is perhaps the most impressive sensation, the smallness of the space allocated a close second, but possibly it is the haste of the operation that we all recognize, racing like demented jockeys for 1945 or wherever the syllabus ends feeling like there might be a winning post after all. (Portal 1987)

This analogy applies beyond History instruction to the curriculum as a whole. The solution to a multitude of demands and expectations can be to add requirements with insufficient consideration given to issues of coherence and meaningful continuity. The problems can become even more acute when curricula are linked together which are based on different ideological models like those suggested by Ross (2000), referred to earlier. An example of this is the experience some schools have had in trying to combine the IGCSE and the IB MYP in the middle years. Even when a school adopts a recognized curriculum continuum that, in terms of the intended curriculum, is coherent it cannot assume that the experienced curriculum will work as intended.

At the start of this chapter the question 'What characterizes a coherent and consistent international curriculum?' was posed. Some tentative answers are considered below.

1 There is an identifiable and agreed philosophy with clearly specified aims and objectives. These should indicate the values base, the assumptions about the nature of knowledge and learning, against which the prescribed programme syllabuses and broader planned activities can be compared for consistency and coherence.

2 Administrators, teachers, students and parents must buy into and live the internationalist philosophy to help ensure the experienced curriculum is the same as the intended curriculum.

3 Internationalism must permeate the ethos of the school, as well as the intended curricula, and be essentially experiential.

4 Any curriculum discontinuity should be planned rather than accidental or unintended. For example, if a programme for younger students is more enquiry-based and becomes more content and objectives-led as they grow older, with culminating examinations, the school must recognize a potential tension between these different models and work on ensuring continuity. Is the discontinuity actually working as planned or does it just happen?

5 Assessment should include meaningful ways to record and measure non-tested components of the curriculum.

The experienced as well as the intended curriculum should be regularly evaluated to ensure, amongst other things, that important unexamined learning objectives are given due weight.

REFERENCES

Barrett, E., Jamison, J. and Weston, P. (1992) *The Quest for Coherence: Managing the Whole Curriculum 5–16.* Slough: National Foundation for Educational Research.

Deal, E. and Nolan, R. (1982) Alternative schools: a conceptual map. In V. Lee and D. Zeldin (eds) *Planning the Curriculum.* London: Hodder and Stoughton, pp. 11–17.

Derricott, R. (1985) *Primary to Secondary: Curriculum Continuity.* Windsor: Nelson.

Hayden, M.C. and Thompson, J.J. (1995) International education: the crossing of frontiers. *International Schools Journal,* 15 (1): 13–20.

Hayden, M.C. and Thompson, J.J. (1996) Potential difference: the driving force for international education. *International Schools Journal,* 16 (1): 46–57.

Hill, I. (2001) Early stirrings: the beginnings of the international education movement. *International Schools Journal,* 20 (2): 11–21.

Hirst, P.H. and Peters, R.S. (1970) *The Logic of Education.* London: Routledge.

International Baccalaureate Organization (2002) Mongraph 4: Articulation of the Primary Years Programme, the Middle Years Programme and the Diploma Programme. IBO Grand-Saconnex/Geneva, Switzerland.

International Baccalaureate Organization (2003) Today's Students for Tomorrow's World: An International Education. IBO Grand-Saconnex/ Geneva, Switzerland.

Kelly, A.V. (1986) *Knowledge and Curriculum Planning.* London: Harper and Row.

Kelly, A.V. (1989) *Curriculum Theory and Practice.* London: Paul Chapman.

Lawton, D. (1983) *Curriculum Studies and Educational Planning.* London: Hodder and Stoughton.

Lawton, D. (1996) *Beyond the National Curriculum: Teacher Professionalism and Empowerment.* London: Hodder and Stoughton.

Matthews, M. (1989) The Scale of International Education, Part One. *International Schools Journal,* 17 (Spring): 7–17.

Moon, B. (2002) Understanding the context of curriculum. In B. Moon, A.S. Mayes and S. Hutchinson (eds) *Teaching, Learning and the Curriculum in Secondary Schools.* London: Routledge.

Phenix, P.H. (1964) *Realms of Meaning.* New York: McGraw-Hill.

Portal, C. (ed.) (1987) *The History Curriculum.* London: Falmer Press.

Renaud, G. (1989) Approaches to Learning. Unpublished paper presented to the International Schools Association Conference.

Ross, A. (2000) *Curriculum Construction and Critique.* London: Falmer Press.

Stenhouse, L. (1975) *An Introduction to Curriculum Research and Development.* Oxford: Heinemann.

Stobie, T. (2001) The International Baccalaureate and positional competition in a global marketplace. Unpublished essay in partial completion of Doctor of Education Degree, University of Bath, UK.

Stobie, T. (2005a) Do the Middle Years and Diploma Programmes of the International Baccalaureate provide a coherent and consistent international curriculum? Thesis for Doctor of Education degree, University of Bath, UK.

Stobie, T. (2005b) To what extent do the Middle Years Programme and Diploma Programme of the International Baccalaureate Organization provide a coherent and consistent educational continuum? *International Schools Journal,* 25 (1): 30–40.

Thompson J.J. (1998) Towards a model for international education. In M. Hayden and J.J. Thompson (eds) *International Education, Principles and Practice.* London: Kogan Page.

Vallance, E. (1991) Hidden curriculum. In A. Lewy (ed.) *The International Encyclopedia of Curriculum.* Oxford: Pergamon Press.

13

Internationalizing the US Secondary and University Curriculum

Robert DiYanni

One could argue that the seeds for the globalized study of literature in US colleges and universities were sown in the early decades of the twentieth century, with Ezra Pound, whose study of Chinese and Japanese literature and culture extended his expertise in Romance languages and literatures, and among whose many books was a small gem of a literature anthology, *Confucius to Cummings*. Since the late 1980s and early 1990s, however, there has been a significant movement in US secondary schools and universities towards globalizing the curriculum. Three trends testify to and illustrate how a more internationalized curriculum has taken shape in schools, colleges and universities. The first is the development of college and university courses in world literature, world history and cultural geography; and an ancillary further development of courses, programmes, core curricula and departments of area studies. The second is the creation by major publishers of textbooks for introductory courses in these subjects and study areas. And the third is the development of Advanced Placement Program® (AP®) courses and examinations in Comparative Government and Politics World History, Human Geography and a new initiative in World Languages and Cultures, including AP Chinese, Japanese, and Italian. This chapter considers each of these strands, along with related issues involved in globalizing, what had been for many decades, a course of study with a distinctly Western focus and a highly Eurocentric curriculum.

US COLLEGE AND UNIVERSITY LITERATURE CURRICULA

As a university professor of English for most of my career, I taught, for many years, courses in British, American and European Literature. Such courses were common in practically every US college and university curriculum. The focus of many of those courses was the literary works in and of themselves, without offering significant attention to their social, historical and cultural contexts. The first thing to change with this curricular model was that the works, whether British, American, or continental European, began to be viewed less as verbal icons, self-sufficient and complete in themselves, and more as reflections and embodiments of social mores, historical issues and cultural values. Context became much more important.

This is not the place for a discussion of the transformation of the English curriculum from one that emphasized literary and linguistic aspects of literary masterworks to one that considered various cultural, social, political and other values reflected in them. Interested readers are referred to Robert Scholes (1999), *The Rise and Fall of English*.

As the first step in globalizing the US university curriculum, such a trend took the emphasis off traditional formal literary elements, such as plot, character, structure and theme, and placed it on social and cultural approaches to literary study, including feminist, Marxist, new historicist, and other external contextual considerations. Various minority groups, especially African Americans, Latino (Hispanic) Americans and Asian Americans, brought many social, political, economic, cultural and historical questions to the study of literature. These groups demanded and received a place in the curriculum. They also brought new ways of reading into the literature classroom.

And while they did not bring at first a fully fledged global perspective to the study of literature, the varied minority groups did call attention to a wide range of class, ethnic, and racial issues – as women had done in raising and highlighting issues of gender and power before them. This new emphasis on issues of class and power among women and ethnic and racial minorities in the study of literature was an important step toward opening up the literary canon to include not merely works by hyphenated American minority writers, such as Toni Morrison, Sandra Cisneros and Chang-rae Lee, but also works by authors from other countries writing in English. There had always been, of course, a place for writers from other countries in literary anthologies used in college courses, but those writers

tended almost exclusively to be white males, often of European ancestry. What changed in the last decades of the twentieth century is that a broader notion of what constituted international authors became entrenched in literary circles. Tolstoy and Chekhov, Ibsen and Strindberg, Borges and Garcia Marquez remained in the textbooks and the course syllabi, but they found themselves in the company of many previously canonically excluded writers from a wider variety of ethnic and racial backgrounds.

EUROPEAN LITERATURE AND WORLD LITERATURE

At Pace University, where I taught literature for twenty years beginning in 1981, students had the option of taking a course in American Literature, British Literature, or World Literature. But this last course, in World Literature, listed as the writers to be studied only white European males – all the usual suspects, some of which I have just mentioned, and others which included Kafka, Mann, Pasternak, Pirandello and other literary luminaries. Around 1990, a number of us teaching the World Literature sections began to open the course beyond such writers. A number of factors contributed to this decision. The most prominent was the fallout from the debates of the 1970s and 1980s when the avant-garde in literature departments began crusading for curricular change. By the late 1980s and early 1990s the changes that had taken place on a small scale in a small number of universities had grown to encompass a much larger constituency. Many more professors and a much larger number of universities had become persuaded that the university literature curriculum needed to be expanded.

Part of the reason for the delay among these larger numbers was that they needed time to broaden their own intellectual horizons. Many of those teaching literature in the universities, particularly those tenured and teaching literature rather than writing courses, had been trained decades earlier before the debates about the literary canon occurred. Many of the younger faculty entering teaching during the years of those debates, and who in fact contributed to those debates, were often relegated to teaching composition and the most introductory of literature courses. In those courses, these new members of college and university faculty often introduced texts and materials that had not been previously seen in writing courses. Instead of having students read imaginative literature as the basis and stimulus for writing assignments, these new instructors ranged farther afield to include political discourse, social analysis, film and video, popular songs, even densely written literary theory. And when they did include literature, it was often to introduce previously marginalized writers who represented something other than the mainstream Anglo-European or American literary traditions.

Yet another reason a larger number of college instructors began internationalizing their teaching repertoire was that publishers began producing world literature textbooks. The first was Harper Collins, which published *The World Reader* in 1994. A few years later, Norton published its first real world literature textbook, one that included Asian and African literature along with the European and Latin American works that had been featured in earlier editions of its previously titled *World Literary Masterpieces*. Other publishers were slow to follow, as these mini-libraries of world literature were expensive to produce, requiring the coordinated work of many specialists across a broad spectrum of languages, literatures and cultures. Nonetheless, in 2004 Longman published *The Longman Anthology of World Literature*, the third major textbook contribution to the field.

With the availability of these world literature textbooks, which included important historical and contextual information about the works as well as the works themselves, teachers had a source from which to draw, and they had a mini-library in which to read and educate themselves. Also important were a number of reliable resources that provided expert scholarly support for college instructors for whom a number of world literary traditions were

unfamiliar, and yet ones they were willing to begin learning and teaching. Columbia University published a pair of volumes that included historical and critical guidance in teaching Asian texts. And a then new website, 'Voice of the Shuttle', became increasingly important as a support resource for college faculty teaching all kinds of literature, including world literature.

Of course, one should not neglect to mention the work of comparative literature scholars, as well as that of translators, both of which broadened the scope of literary study. Their work provided the foundation upon which the edifice of world literature could be built. And whatever limits and focuses literary translators and scholars of comparative literature set themselves (focusing on Germanic or on Romance languages, for example), their work remains an important part of the globalization of literary study.

Interested readers can plunge further into the topic of what constitutes world literature by looking into a recent collection of articles gathered in *Debating World Literature*, edited by Christopher Prendergast (2003), especially the lead article, 'The World Republic of Letters'. A number of contributors in that volume take up the definition of 'world literature' with reference to Goethe's *Weltliteratur*, considering its various legacies and variable understandings, interrogating Goethe's term for ways in which it remains as vital today as it did in his own time. Also noteworthy is David Damrosch's *What is World Literature?* (2003), in which Damrosch riffs on Goethe's definition and himself defines world literature as the corpus of works that circulate beyond the borders of the countries in which they were written.

FROM WESTERN CIVILIZATION TO WORLD HISTORY

In the same way that US college and university literature courses have become more globalized, so too have college courses in history. For many years, the required history survey in US colleges and universities was either a course in American History or one in

Western Civilization. After the debates of the 1970s and 1980s, history departments began offering courses in World History to complement those in American and European history. And by the end of the 1990s, World History eclipsed Western Civilization at the university level, especially at public universities (Lindvedt 2003). Analogously, World History is frequently taken by students in US public high schools, with most states requiring it for graduation, including California, New York and Texas, which together include nearly half the school-age population in the country (Lintvedt 2003). Further, by the end of the millennium, two-thirds of students attending US public high schools had taken a course in World History. And as we advance further into the first decades of the new century, this trend for US high schools, colleges and universities is accelerating.

As with the globalization of the US college literature curriculum, the expansion of history from an emphasis on national and European political history to include study of non-Western civilizations has come with the development of World History textbooks for both the secondary and university markets and with instructors willing to undertake self-study in the newly emerging discipline. Along with these trends, a number of programmes in World History have emerged, including doctoral programmes, such as those at Columbia, Northeastern and Washington State universities (Lindvedt 2003).

Ancillary developments to support the emergence of *World History Connected* as a discipline include the establishment of the *Journal of World History* in 1990 and the holding of an annual World History Conference sponsored by the World History Association, now in its seventeenth year. In addition, the World History Association has published since 2003 an online journal, *World History Connected*, which includes articles, research, databases and teaching resources for secondary and university teachers of World History.

An important article published in the inaugural issue of *World History Connected* is Patrick Manning's 'Navigating World History', a synopsis of his book of that title

(2003). Manning cites William H. McNeill's *Rise of the West* (1963) as opening up the professional study of world history. Manning does not neglect the importance of national histories among world historians, but notes that 'it has now become almost automatic for world historians to view "the nation" as only one of numerous social perspectives, and in viewing the nation, to consider it from any of several disciplinary perspectives' (*World History Connected*, 1 (1): 4). Among the supranational perspectives are not merely the regional or the continental, but perspectives that span the entire globe and that include not only human and early pre-human history, and not merely the history of the earth, but the history of the universe going back to the 'Big Bang'. Manning mentions the work of David Christian as a stellar example, particularly his recent book *Maps of Time* (2003).

In a pattern similar to that for the emergence of an increasingly globalized literature curriculum in US higher educational institutions, some programmes of study in world history emerged out of those devoted to area studies. Manning argues, however, that 'the approach to world history that came out of area studies treated world history as Third World history' and that it treated world history 'as the comparison of continental regions' rather than treating continental interactions or global patterns (2003: 4).

With global studies, historical study was pushed further toward world history, according to Manning, in its 'conceptualization of the earth as a unit of social and economic analysis' (p. 4). Further, he accords the recent trend in economic globalization some influence in conceiving of the earth 'as a historical unit'. However, as Manning points out, the global studies approach emphasizes economic and environmental issues, along with aspects of international relations, and that these issues tend to reflect current issues and problems, with little historical emphasis.

World History, in Manning's summary description, differs from both area studies and from global studies in addressing a wider range of topics, identifying connections, 'tracing broad patterns', and 'clarifying relationships among different scales of the world's events and processes'. Many would agree with him when he notes that World History is 'one of the most exciting areas in scholarship and teaching today' (p. 4).

INTERNATIONALIZING THE US UNIVERSITY CORE CURRICULUM

Along with these new courses in World History, US colleges and universities internationalized their curricula another way: by creating core curricula that required students to take Humanities courses (mostly History, Literature, Philosophy and Art history) in non-Western areas. Such courses were typically 'area studies' courses offered either by area studies programmes, which in some institutions existed within traditional disciplinary departments, and in others occupied their own departments. There has been considerable debate about whether area studies or world history is the better way to globalize the university history curriculum. And though both types of courses and programmes can peacefully coexist in university course bulletins, it is the type of course that becomes mandated or required that achieves dominance, at least in numbers of students who take the courses and faculty who teach them.

Many universities have taken another path by establishing special global courses as part of their core curriculum. These global courses have been created specifically for general education programmes. Fairleigh Dickinson University in New Jersey, for example, provides a first Core course requirement entitled 'The Global Challenge', which is offered online, and then, later, as a face-to-face course, 'Cross-cultural Perspectives', the third in a four-course sequence of globally focused core courses (www.fdu.edu). Drury University in Springfield, Missouri, begins its core curriculum with a course entitled 'Global Awareness and Cultural Diversity', which blends the two strands that sometimes compete with one another in core curricula (www.drury.edu). In addition to special global courses, some universities, such as St Lawrence University and the University of Tennessee, have developed programmes with a strong global basis. St Lawrence's Cultural Encounters Programme provides an academic context for students to experience studying, working and living among people from different cultures. Many of the courses in the programme are interdisciplinary and all include opportunities for students to connect their experience of study abroad with their academic studies (www.stlawu.edu). The University of Tennessee offers a major and minor in Global Studies, which includes an interdisciplinary component and an emphasis on global change as it occurs socially, politically and economically (http://utk.edu).

Many other universities, however, have not adopted special global courses to launch a university core curriculum or to serve as its capstone. Rather, they have taken an areas-of-knowledge approach, using a set of existing courses in various departments from which students choose a certain number (often two) to satisfy a general global requirement. Pace University, in New York, for example, lists 60 courses spanning more than a dozen departments and programmes, from which students can satisfy the 'World Traditions and Cultures' requirement (http://pace.edu).

And, in a surprise swerve from its current core curriculum, which is really a set of distribution requirements that focus on modes of enquiry across the curriculum, a Harvard University review group has proposed to replace a suite of required courses with a few foundational courses in the sciences, which will allow for a more open and varied set of general education course options for Harvard's undergraduates. What's interesting is that even while promoting greater curricular choice for students, the proposing committee acknowledges the importance of a global perspective, and 'recommends that all Harvard College students pursue a significant international experience'. For just over half of Harvard's undergraduates this 'significant international experience' involves a semester of study abroad. The proposal goes on to recommend a swift expansion in 'opportunities and assistance for international study' to improve students' 'education in the broader world' (http://harvard.edu).

Regardless, however, of differences among the universities and the ways they introduce international perspectives into the curriculum, the fact that so many US colleges and universities have moved beyond a provincial curriculum is noteworthy. Establishing global knowledge and understanding as central concerns of the US university core curriculum is cause for celebration.

ADDITIONAL GLOBAL CURRICULAR DEVELOPMENTS

A number of other curricular developments in US colleges and universities echo and support the globalizing of the curricula in literature and history. One is the introduction, mostly in the last decade or so, of introductory humanities courses and programmes, always interdisciplinary and sometimes also global. Global interdisciplinary humanities courses provide an alternative to the area studies approach in literature and history as a way to expose US university students to cultures and civilizations beyond the Western tradition.

Along with such courses and programmes have come textbooks that include a global approach to the teaching of interdisciplinary humanities. One of the first to introduce a global perspective among textbooks for humanities courses is Gloria Fiero's *The Humanistic Tradition*, now in its fifth edition (2005). This book provides for the comparative study of Eastern and Western traditions, as in her chapter that includes Christianity and Buddhism, and in her comparative discussion of the Roman Empire and the Han dynasty. Although most of the books published for use in the introductory humanities course have a strong Western focus, a few of them, like Fiero's, move beyond the West. The most extensive coverage of the non-Western world is found in Benton and DiYanni's (2007) *Arts and Culture*, which includes the broadest coverage of Africa, China, India, Japan, and Meso- and Latin America to be found in such texts. In addition, a number of these books,

The Humanistic Tradition, and *Arts and Culture* among them, include special highlighted features and spreads that invite cross-cultural consideration and aim to promote cross-cultural understanding.

Among recent curriculum-extending developments is a grant-supported project on General Education and Global Learning sponsored by the Luce Foundation and organized by the Association of American Colleges and Universities (AAC&U). The Global Learning initiative is designed to establish global knowledge and understanding as core concerns of the curriculum among US colleges and universities. Sixteen colleges have been selected to participate in developing a curriculum that uses global issues to reform general education. Participating faculty will receive training to provide them with the tools needed to teach globalized general education courses (AAC&U press release, 11 July, 2005).

The Global Learning initiative, which is being directed by AAC&U's director of global initiatives, is part of AAC&U's 'Shared Futures: Global Learning and Social Responsibility', begun in 2001. Goals of the larger project, which include an initiative on Liberal Education and Global Citizenship as well as the new Global Learning initiative, include 'assisting campuses in educating students to become responsible citizens of the nation and the world' and developing curricula that 'deepen student knowledge of the world, challenge unexamined assumptions about American identity and global citizenship, and test our commitments and ideals for a world lived in common' (www.aacu-edu.org).

The goals of the initiatives are to help students to do the following:

* gain a deep, comparative knowledge of the world's peoples and problems
* explore the historical legacies that have created the dynamics and tensions of their world
* develop intercultural competencies … and see the world from multiple perspectives
* sustain difficult conversations in the face of highly emotional and perhaps uncongenial differences
* understand – and perhaps – redefine democratic principles and practices within a global context

- gain opportunities to engage in practical work with fundamental issues that affect communities not yet well served by their societies
- believe that their actions and ideas will influence the world in which they live (www.aacu-edu.org).

On the schools front, it is worth noting that a number of educational organizations and associations have developed global initiatives with curricular implications, some of which are limited to their members, whereas others have no such limitation. One such group is the National Association of Independent Schools (NAIS), whose Global Initiatives Objective is to assist independent schools in their efforts 'to nurture the skills and perspectives that help students become global citizens and global leaders, and to assist their students in making contributions across borders' (http://nais.org). One of the latest NAIS global initiatives is Challenge 20/20, which brings together pairs of schools, one in the USA and the other in another country, to work together to solve a global problem. Among the benefits for participating schools are promoting experiential learning, developing globally based curricula, building educational partnerships world-wide, enhancing cross-cultural learning and understanding, and educating students to be global citizens (http://nais.org/go/challenge2020).

AP AND THE INTERNATIONALIZATION OF THE SECONDARY SCHOOL CURRICULUM

The AP Program of the College Board has often been seen as an American programme, one that developed in the USA to meet the needs of students in their final years in US secondary schools. But there is more to the story, for as the AP Programme developed, it began to be adopted by international schools around the world. In addition, the AP Programme is becoming recognized, on an increasing basis, by numerous universities outside the USA. The story of the development and the internationalization of the AP Programme by means of professional development for international teachers, recognition of AP by international

universities, and the development of close working relationships between the College Board and regional educational associations world-wide, has been told in a pair of articles published in the *International Schools Journal* (DiYanni 2002, 2003). The focus here is on how the development of individual global courses, the emergence of an AP world language initiative and the globalizing of an international AP diploma, collectively have internationalized the AP Programme, which is offered in secondary schools throughout the world, though predominantly in North America.

In keeping with developments in US colleges and universities, the development committee of AP Art History has broadened the scope of the AP Art History Exam to include non-Western art and architecture. Also in keeping with developments in university curricula, the AP Spanish Literature development committee has modified the required texts for study to include works written by authors in countries other than Spain.

The AP Exam in Art History, for example, since 1998 has addressed approximately 20 per cent of its content to artistic traditions beyond the European. The AP Course Description for Art History specifies that these other traditions can comprise Africa, the Americas, Asia, Oceania, the Near East, and global Islamic traditions (*AP Art History Course Description*, May 2006, May 2007, p. 7). Moreover, the AP Exam in Art History assesses students' knowledge of cultural artistic traditions beyond the European by means of both multiple-choice and essay questions.

The AP Spanish Literature Exam, which has recently been modified, is now based on a course of study that includes a reading list designed to expose students to 'the diverse literature written in Spanish' to help them 'reflect on the many voices and cultures' included in that literature (*AP Spanish Course Description*, May 2005, May 2006, p. 28). The works to be studied reflect ethnic, gender and geographical diversity, and include writers spanning seven centuries from Spain, Mexico, the Caribbean, the Southern Cone, Central America, Puerto Rico and the USA, as well as Afro-Cuban writers.

Beyond the globalization of individual courses, such as Art History and Spanish Literature, the College Board's AP Programme has introduced into its portfolio of AP courses and exams three courses that are distinctive in their global reach and their international inclusiveness. The first of these, AP Comparative Government and Politics, was introduced in the academic year 1986–87. The purpose of the course is to introduce students to key concepts in political science as they are used to study political processes and outcomes in various countries. Among its aims is to highlight 'the importance of global political and economic changes' (*AP Government and Politics Course Description* May 2006, May 2007, p. 23). Six countries and their governments provide the basis of course study: China, Great Britain, Iran, Mexico, Nigeria and Russia. These varied countries and governments offer a spectrum of political processes and practices, which are studied via comparative analysis.

Since we live in an interdependent world, since globalization has such important political consequences, and since it has become an increasingly important concept in recent decades, the AP Comparative Government course gives the subject considerable attention. Aspects of globalization studied include the relationship of participating states to the World Trade Organization and the EU; the relationship between domestic and global economic and political forces, demands, and contexts; the development of world-wide consumer culture; the cultural aspects of globalization; and various forms of disaffection with and backlashes against globalization (pp. 29–30).

As with Comparative Government, so with the AP course and examination in AP Human Geography, which was first offered in the academic year 2000–01. The purpose of the course is to introduce students to the study of 'patterns and processes that have shaped human understanding, use, and alterations of Earth's surface' (*AP Human Geography Course Description* May, 2006, May 2007, p. 3). Students analyse social organization and its environmental consequences, and learn to apply the methods and tools geographers employ. Among the topics considered in the course and tested on the AP Human Geography Exam are Population, Cultural Patterns and Processes, Industrialization and Economic Development, Cities and Urban Land Use, and the Political Organization of Space, each of which has a global dimension. In studying human population, for example, students 'analyse the distribution of the human population at different scales: global, continental, national, state or province, and local community' (p. 6). The study of population touches on other matters of global concern, including environmental degradation, regional industrial differences, population growth and fertility rates in different parts of the world, as well as varied political sentiments accorded to immigrants and foreigners (p. 7).

Analogously, the topic of Cultural Patterns and Processes is steeped in a deeply global perspective, beginning with definitions of culture that assess cultural differences in language, ethnicity, gender, race and religion, past and present. A persistent emphasis for this topic is analysing the ways culture shapes human–environmental relationships. And so too with the other topics taught in the AP Human Geography course and tested on the AP Human Geography Exam. Indeed, 'globalization' is listed along with 'regionalization' as a core concept considered in the course.

The most recent of the AP globally based courses is AP World History, which was first offered in the academic year 2001–02, and which has had the biggest following. In May of 2002, more than 20,000 students, mostly in the USA, took the first AP World History Exam. Since then more than 140,000 students have taken the exam, with the 2006 cohort at approximately 85,000.

The purpose of the AP World History course is to develop a solid understanding of 'the evolution of global processes and contacts, in interaction with different types of societies' (*AP World History Course Description,* May 2006, May 2007, p. 3). The course emphasizes 'the nature of changes in international frameworks and their causes and consequences, as well as comparisons among major societies' (pp. 3–4). The course offers global coverage, with representation from Africa, Asia, Europe and the Americas. Because college and university courses in World History vary considerably in approach, framework, content and themes, the AP World History development committee decided to create a course that focuses on points of contact among civilizations and on the theme of continuity and change.

The chronological boundaries of the AP World History course – from pre-history to the present – are in major periods with recommended content percentages and time allocated to each period:

Foundations: c.8000 BCE – 600 CE	19–20%	7 weeks
600 CE – 1450	22%	8 weeks
1450 – 1750	19–20%	7 weeks
1750 – 1914	19–20%	7 weeks
1914 – the present (p. 5)	19–20%	7 weeks

The course focuses on six overarching themes:

1 the dynamics of continuity and change across world history, including causes and consequences
2 patterns and effects of interaction among societies and regions
3 the effects of technology, economics and demography on people and the environment
4 systems of social structure and gender structure
5 cultural, intellectual and religious developments, including interactions among and within societies
6 changes in functions and structures of states, including the emergence of the nation state. (p. 6)

The course emphasizes ways that major developments illustrating the six thematic areas link the history of the world's major regions. Coverage of European history is limited to 30 per cent of the total course, and emphasizes topics 'important to Europe in the world and not just to Europe itself' (p. 7). The USA is included in the course 'in relation to its interaction with other societies' and is 'limited to appropriate comparative questions and to US involvement in global processes' (p.7).

A final distinctive characteristic of the course is its attention to three habits of mind particularly important in developing an understanding of world history:

• seeing global patterns and processes over time and space while also connecting local developments to global ones and moving through levels of generalizations from the global to the particular
• comparing within and among societies including comparing societies' reactions to global processes
• being aware of human commonalities and differences while assessing claims of universal standards, and understanding culturally diverse ideas and values in historical context. (p. 8)

Complementing and extending the globalizing impulse of AP social science courses, the AP World Languages Initiative has extended the internationalization of AP courses and examinations in another direction. The languages of this initiative are Italian, Chinese and Japanese. Before discussing the first of the new World Languages Initiative AP offerings, AP Italian Language and Culture, we should touch on an explanation for the reasons behind this recent College Board AP initiative.

In June 2003, the Trustees of the College Board approved a plan for new AP courses and exams in world languages and cultures: Chinese, Italian and Japanese. These would be the first new language offerings to be added to the AP Program portfolio since its inception in 1955. The introduction of these new exams was seen as an important step in a commitment by the College Board to 'further multiculturalism and multilingualism in secondary education' (http://apcentral. collegeboard.com). And, as College Board President Gaston Caperton has noted (see website), 'world events make it ever more obvious that a broad knowledge and understanding of other languages and cultures is essential for young people'.

The first of the new language and culture offerings to be introduced was AP Italian Language and Culture, the course for which was launched in the autumn of 2005, with the first examinations administered in spring 2006. Like the other new language courses soon to follow, the AP Italian Language and Culture course is designed to be 'comparable to college/university courses in the language that serve as a transition between language courses and linguistics or content-based courses, which are typically taught in the fourth semester, or the equivalent, of university language study' (*AP Italian Language and Culture Course Description*, (draft) p. 4; available on the AP Central website).

Each of the new AP language course offerings includes a cultural component. The committee that developed the AP Italian Language and Culture course thus lists among the course goals and objectives in the *Course Description* that students 'write compositions in Italian on cultural topics' and that they demonstrate 'knowledge of aspects of Italian geography, contemporary life in Italy, the arts and sciences, social customs and traditions, and contributions of Italians and Italian Americans to the world' (p. 4). Similarly, the AP Japanese Development Committee writes in its *AP Japanese Language and Culture Course Description* that students be introduced to 'a broad spectrum of Japanese culture', and that 'students gain an appreciation of contemporary social, political, or educational issues; to the place of religion within Japanese society; or to traditional versus modern male and female gender roles' (*AP Japanese Language and Culture Course Description* (draft), p. 2; available on apcentral. collegeboard.com).

In addition to reading and writing about aspects of Japanese culture, students taking the AP Japanese Language and Culture Exam are expected to respond to speaking and writing prompts 'in a culturally appropriate manner' (p. 4), whatever the level and specific content and context of the question. Students are required in both the speaking and writing portions of the exam to describe and express 'an opinion about a Japanese cultural practice or product' (p. 9–10). Cultural knowledge is, thus, addressed in the exam in a variety of ways.

Very much in the mode of the AP Japanese Development Committee, the committee responsible for developing the AP Chinese Language and Culture Examination writes in its corresponding course description that the aim of the course is to enable students to develop their Chinese language proficiency 'across the full range of language skills within a cultural frame of reference reflective of the richness of Chinese language and culture' (*AP Chinese Language and Culture Course Description* (draft) p. 1; available on apcentral. collegeboard.com). They also note that though the course focuses on language proficiency, it interweaves 'level- and age-appropriate cultural context throughout' and that 'authentic sources … support the linguistic and cultural goals of the course' (p. 1).

Of all the new AP world language course descriptions, the AP Chinese Language and Culture Course Description places the greatest emphasis on cultural aspects. In describing course content, for example, the authors of the course description note that 'students' awareness and appreciation of the elements of Chinese culture is a pervasive theme', and that the course 'engages students in an exploration of both contemporary and historical Chinese culture' (p. 2). Chinese cultural topics include 'geography and population, ethnic and regional diversity, travel and transportation, climate and weather, holidays and food, sports and games, and current affairs' (p. 2).

Additional course elements include 'significant persons, products, and themes in Chinese history', including 'Chinese contributions to philosophical thought, government institutions, and artistic pursuits', such as calligraphy, painting, literature, music and folk arts (p. 2). Not to be overlooked is that the course also views Chinese culture 'in an international context', with students learning how 'Chinese culture and society have influenced and been influenced by the global community'.

THE ADVANCED PLACEMENT INTERNATIONAL DIPLOMA (APID)

One additional way in which the AP Programme and the AP curriculum have become more internationally oriented is with the introduction and revision of the Advanced Placement International Diploma, or APID. First introduced in 1995, the APID is a globally recognized certificate for students with an international outlook. Available to students attending secondary schools outside the USA and to US resident students applying to universities outside the country, the APID is not a substitute for a high school diploma, but rather an indicator of outstanding academic excellence.

To earn an APID, a student must earn grades of 3 or higher on at least five AP Exams in the following content areas:

1 two different AP Exams from the English and World Languages areas
2 one AP Exam designated as offering a global perspective: AP World History, AP Human Geography, or AP Comparative Government and Politics
3 one AP Exam from the Sciences or Mathematics content areas
4 one additional AP Exam from among any content areas except English and World Languages.

CONCLUSION

The past two decades have seen dramatic changes in the internationalization of curricula in secondary schools, colleges and universities in the USA. The movement from relatively static and fixed canons of literature to a more fluid and varied set of writers and works studied in literature courses represents one instance of this change. The gradual supplanting of courses in Western Civilization with those in World History represents another. Greater attention to world literature and history and to world language study at both the school and university level, often institutionalized in state mandates for schools and in core curricula or distribution requirements in universities, adds a third dimension to the globalization of US secondary and university curricula.

In addition, the College Board's expansion of its AP Programme with a suite of new offerings in World Languages, including its first offerings in Asian language and culture courses and examinations, along with the development of new global courses in history, geography and comparative government and politics, reflects a dramatic increase in the numbers of students in secondary schools and universities taking courses grounded in multiple global perspectives. The newly revised AP International Diploma brings these developments to a culmination in a kind of evolutionary convergence. Much progress, clearly, has been made toward developing a more global curriculum in US educational institutions. But much remains to be done, not only to sustain and expand these developments, but also to reap the educational, social and cultural benefits they promise.

REFERENCES AND FURTHER READING

Advanced Placement Program Course Descriptions: Art History; Government and Politics; Human Geography; Spanish; and World History (2006) New York: The College Board.

Benton, Janetta and DiYanni, Robert (2007) *Arts and Culture: An Introduction to the Humanities*, 3rd edition. Englewood Cliffs, NJ: Prentice Hall.

Christian, David (2003) *Maps of Time: Big History*. Berkley, CA: University of California Press.

Cunningham, L. and Reich, J. J. (2005) *Culture and Values: A Survey of the Humanities*, 5th edition. Boston, MA: Thomson/Wadsworth.

Damrosch, David (2003) *What is World Literature?* Princeton, NJ: Princeton University Press.

DiYanni, Robert (ed.) (1994) *The Reader's Advisor, Volume 2: The Best in World Literature*, 14th edition. New Providence, NJ: Bowker.

DiYanni, Robert (2003) The Internationalization of the Advanced Placement Programme *International Schools Journal*, XXII (2): 25–33.

DiYanni, Robert (2002) The origins and development of the Advanced Placement Programme. *International Schools Journal*, XXII (1): 31–42.

Fiero, Gloria (2005) *The Humanistic Tradition*, 5th edition. New York: McGraw-Hill.

Lawall, Sarah, Maynard, Mack et al. (2002) *The Norton Anthology of World Literature*, 2nd edition. New York: W.W. Norton.

Lindvedt, Ane (2003) The demography of World History in the United States. *World History Connected*, 1 (1). worldhistoryconnected.press.uiuc.edu (accessed 2006).

Manning, Patrick (2003) Navigating World History. *World History Connected*, 1(1). worldhistoryconnected. press.uiuc.edu (accessed 2006).

Manning, Patrick (2003) *Navigating World History*. London: Palgrave-Macmillan.

McNeil, J.R. and McNeil, William H. (2003) *The Human Web*. New York: W.W. Norton.

McNeil, William H. (2003) An emerging consensus about World History? *World History Connected,* 1 (1). worldhistoryconnected.press.uiuc.edu (accessed 2006).

McNeil, W.H. (1963) The *Rise of the West.*

Prendergast, Christospher (2003) *Debating World Literature*. London: Verso.

Scholes, Robert (1999) *The Rise and Fall of English.* New Haven, CT: Yale University Press.

14

A Case Study of the Development of an International Curriculum Leading to IGCSE Certification

Paul Beedle, Tom Eason and
Sarah Maughan

It opens your eyes wide to the outside and inside
world.

This student, from the Edron Academy, Mexico City, is describing her experience of the Cambridge IGCSE course, Natural Economy, recently renamed Environmental Management. That any course of study should prompt such a response is a cause for celebration. That the comment should so eloquently reflect the ambitions of the course designers, makes it doubly gratifying. Environmental Management is concerned with education for sustainable development. It embodies the 'International' in IGCSE – the International General Certificate of Secondary Education. This chapter explores the development of the course, which can be thought of as being at the international heart of IGCSE. It is a story of aspiration, endeavour and reflection. The case study provides valuable insights into the process of creating and establishing a learning programme concerned with international-mindedness for students in international

secondary education. Towards the end of the chapter there is a glimpse of the future, reflecting a new urgency in the education of all students about their, and our, place in the human and natural environment.

THE ORIGINS OF IGCSE

UK beginnings and international interest

Since its inception 20 years ago, IGCSE has developed into the most popular international programme for students aged 14–16 (Cambridge International Examinations 2006a). It has found a comfortable place in many educational contexts. It thrives in what might be termed archetypal international schools with nomadic student bodies and teaching faculties, independent English-medium and bilingual schools, and schools working in a predominantly or entirely national context. IGCSE, or its variants, has also been used to form the basis of national examination systems by governments in Africa and the West Indies or as an alternative to local systems in public (state) schools in a growing number of countries, including the United States and New Zealand.

IGCSE's current reach results from what was initially a series of British, or more accurately English initiatives, which reflected the spirit of educational change during the final decades of the twentieth century. IGCSE's roots can be traced back to the early 1970s, when Cambridge Assessment (then the University of Cambridge Local Examinations Syndicate – UCLES) and the East Anglian Examinations Board (EAEB) joined forces to develop a new 16+ examination to replace the existing Ordinary (O) Level and Certificate of Secondary Education (CSE). Until then there had been significant examination segregation between O Level, traditionally managed by examination boards with a university base and targeted at more able students, and CSE, aimed at those of lower academic ability. This reflected the national pattern of academically selective grammar schools and secondary modern schools.

With the development of comprehensive schools during the 1960s and 1970s and the abolition of secondary selection examinations within most local education authorities, the continued segregation of students into O Level and CSE seemed increasingly anachronistic. The development of a joint 16+ examination reflected a general desire for a more inclusive assessment system. The 16+ was targeted at the top 60 per cent of the school population and enabled one examination to lead, as appropriate, to either O Level or CSE certification. It soon became very popular and the collaboration between Cambridge and EAEB was mirrored by other university and regional boards. Where the 16+ was not in use, there was a growing and expensive trend to enter students for both O level and CSE. In 1978 the Waddell Committee, established by the then Secretary of State for Education Shirley Williams, considered the possibility of a unified examination system and reported strongly in its favour. These

developments set the background for national change in the mid-1980s – the abolition in the UK of separate O Level and CSE examinations, and their replacement by the General Certificate of Secondary Education (GCSE) (Roy 1986).

The reforms were closely observed by Cambridge's international constituencies – Ministries of Education with which Cambridge had long-standing and continuing partnerships, and also international schools, especially in Europe. In many cases these schools employed O Level as a precursor to Advanced (A) Level examinations or to the International Baccalaureate Diploma. A series of discussions took place around and within the 1985 European Council of International Schools (ECIS) conferences in Vienna and The Hague, and as time passed it became clear that international schools were rather more keen on the reform than were the Ministries. It was also clear that they would prefer an internationalized rather than UK-only version of the GCSE examination.

In 1985 the decision was taken to proceed:

[We are] aware of the need, as expressed by teachers and educationalists in many parts of the world, for an extended form of certification. This need is twofold. First, there is the desire to maintain a system of assessment which parallels developments in the UK. By tying [IGCSE] as closely as possible to the standards and aims of GCSE, [we] will maintain our long-standing role as a provider of examinations which have world-wide acceptance. Secondly, the opportunities for secondary education in many countries are being broadened and, in designing the [IGCSE] examinations, [we are] committed to providing syllabuses appropriate to the wider range while maintaining the standards of the present O Level examination for the more able candidates. (Cambridge Council for Examination Development 1985)

Cambridge clearly wished to adhere as closely as possible to the General Criteria for GCSE, for example, enabling differentiation, skills development ('can do') and positive achievement. But at the same time the content and style of each syllabus had fully to meet the needs of an international student and teacher audience.

Initial activities

Development of the IGCSE was undertaken on a number of fronts:

- Individual subject syllabuses and specimen materials were developed in consultation with teachers in international schools. A key objective was to ensure ease of progression into A Level and International Baccalaureate programmes. Thirty syllabuses were in place for the first examination in June 1988.
- A coherent IGCSE curriculum was developed in which, for example, cognate subjects shared (as far as possible) the same assessment domains. This objective was fully realized in the International Certificate of Education (ICE), a group award based on students' IGCSE exam success across a wide range of subjects.
- There was close collaboration with a number of other international education organizations, especially ECIS, the International Schools Association (ISA) and the International Baccalaureate Organization (IBO). In due course, this collaboration included teacher training and promotional activities.
- Work was done on UK, US and wider international recognition of IGCSE, to ensure it had the same currency as O Level and UK GCSE examinations.
- The experience of developing the 16+ assessment was used to ensure a continuity of standards from O Level/CSE to GCSE, and between GCSE and IGCSE.

Consultation with international schools led to some pragmatic decisions to ensure the new examination was appropriate to those schools. Probably the most significant divergence from the UK GCSE was that coursework was made an option (rather than being compulsory) in nearly all IGCSE subjects. At the same time, Cambridge was determined to ensure that those teachers who did opt for coursework were effectively trained. In a series of events in 1986 over 600 teachers were trained in coursework assessment. The last of those events was held after the ECIS Annual Conference in Montreux. This event was significant for other reasons, as it was at this Conference that the idea of the Natural Economy syllabus was first put forward, by Prince Philip, Duke of Edinburgh, following his address to the conference.

DESIGN: THE INTENDED CURRICULUM

From Natural Economy to Environmental Management

As can be seen in Figure 14.1, IGCSE Natural Economy was first examined in 1991, and was renamed Environmental Management in 2004.

Since IGCSE is subject-based, the syllabus was designed as an interdisciplinary subject, in which learning objectives, curriculum content and assessment had to be made explicit, exact and workable. Cambridge had to pin down the 'international' in 'international education'. As Martin Skelton has observed, this not only involves a balanced approach to intercultural similarities and differences, but also a rigorous definition of relevant knowledge, skills and understanding appropriate for the age and stage of learners, and a formal curriculum structure which is properly supported by assessment and curriculum and teacher support (Skelton 2002).

This has been an innovative curriculum development. It was not intended to be an experiment or research project. However, as with IGCSE itself, evaluation has been an ongoing and integral strand in the management of the subject, both to quality assure the assessment of candidates and to identify how, over time, to improve the syllabus, examination and curriculum, and teacher support materials. This case study is based on such evaluation, and draws upon the testimonies of students, teachers and examiners.

Purpose

A course in Environmental Management calls upon young people to be participants in defining the future of their world. (Cambridge International Examinations 2006b)

This curriculum development was stimulated by a number of factors. First, it was a response to growing awareness within the international community that current patterns of development were damaging the environment, and that this was not sustainable in the long term. For

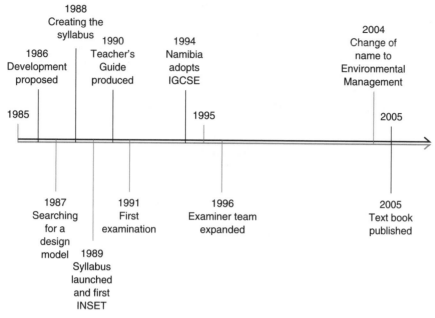

Figure 14.1 Timeline of events in the life of IGCSE Natural Economy/Environmental Management

example, the 1980 Report of the Independent Commission on International Development Issues (the Brandt Report) stated:

schools all over the world should pay more attention to international problems so that young people will see more clearly the dangers they are facing, their own responsibilities and the opportunities for cooperation – globally and regionally as well as within their own neighbourhood. (1980: 11)

The first Natural Economy syllabus was a direct response to the 1987 (Brundtland) Report of the UN World Commission on Environment and Development (*Our Common Future*), which articulated the concept of sustainable development. The syllabus has kept pace with subsequent international events for example, the launch of UNESCO's Decade of Education for Sustainable Development in January 2005. As a result, IGCSE Environmental Management is increasingly relevant to education authorities and institutions in countries where sustainable education has become a matter of policy and practice, such as India.

Secondly, in developing the syllabus Cambridge was responding to direct requests from international agencies and organizations. At the 1986 ECIS Conference, Prince Phillip spoke not only as Chancellor of the University of Cambridge but also as the President of the World Wildlife Fund (WWF) (HRH Prince Philip 1988). From the first stages of development, Cambridge consulted with WWF and other agencies such as Worldaware, and their officials were directly involved in syllabus design and implementation.

Thirdly, although 'environmental awareness' was becoming more accepted as an additional flavour in existing subjects, and learning resources concerned with environment and development were becoming more available, many international educators were keen to develop a forward-looking programme to provide a more purposeful and systematic framework for environmental education.

Last but not least, Cambridge recognized that the development of an environmental syllabus would be worthwhile, not only to develop ideas and ideals, but also to encourage interest and take-up of IGCSE itself as a new international curriculum. Many of the schools represented in Montreux, for example, expressed a strong interest in such a syllabus as a cornerstone of the IGCSE curriculum.

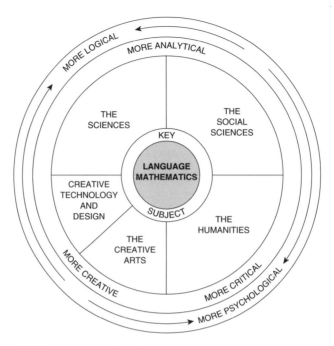

Figure 14.2   The IGCSE 'curriculum wheel'

Definition

According to Paul Hirst, each discipline in the curriculum has its own central set of concepts, distinct logical structure, statements that relate knowledge to real experience, and techniques for testing these statements. Subjects also interrelate, and the overlaps and connections between subjects are fertile ground for learning (Hirst 1974). The new subject certainly had a clear ideological basis, as expressed in the aims of the syllabus. But it also needed a sufficient epistemological rationale, the essential core of knowledge and enquiry to define the subject and to explain and justify its role within the curriculum as a whole.

The title of Natural Economy was adopted for a number of reasons, including, it was argued, the fact that it would denote the subject's distinct nature. Natural Economy was not to be Geography, or Biology, under another name. It was to be a coherent, inter-disciplinary subject, drawing upon fields such as Biology, Geography, Economics and Anthropology.

So what should be at the heart of Natural Economy? One viewpoint was that it should be the science of the natural system, another

that it should be the science of environmental management. There was much debate, but the latter view prevailed, on the basis that the interests of students, teachers and international agencies were better served by a subject that focused knowledge and enquiry on real-life behaviours rather than on intellectual constructs.

Ironically, in practice one of the (few) barriers to establishing the subject proved to be its name. For many teachers, students and parents, the name Natural Economy often seemed to denote something peculiar, obscure and of minority interest. The change of name to Environmental Management responded to this feedback, and has been universally welcomed. Above all, it clearly communicates the purpose and essence of the subject.

Initially, it was seen as likely and desirable that Natural Economy would be a compulsory subject within the IGCSE curriculum, as it represented the principal aims and values of an international education. The IGCSE curriculum was originally conceived in terms of a wheel in which individual subjects exerted particular forces, given their essential characteristics (Figure 14.2). The subject groupings in the optional group award, the International Certificate of Education (ICE), correspond to these. Given its rationale, it is not surprising that Natural Economy was initially placed in its own group, signifying its intended special, central function at the hub of the curriculum wheel.

By 1991 however, the subject groupings were rationalized, and Natural Economy was placed in both Sciences and Humanities, giving candidates and schools flexibility in their subject combinations within ICE. Natural Economy was now regarded as an optional subject. This was consistent with the Cambridge tradition, which successfully provides for international education by openness and encouragement rather than prescription. But for a subject breaking new ground, it was feared that this ambiguous place in the ICE classification system might signify lower value and lead to marginalization.

At the time, there was insufficient confidence to insist that this new subject should play a central role in the curriculum. There was significant competition, at times even jealousy, between subjects and their champions, within the examination board and within schools, and strong forces of conservatism were also influential. Stratification and competition between subjects are characteristics of the curriculum (Young 1999). Natural Economy would have to survive and grow strong on the basis of pioneers choosing, rather than being told, to take on the new. This is often the way with innovation.

Development

To specify curriculum content effectively for an interdisciplinary subject, it is probably better not to be a polymath! There can be a temptation to try to map every corner of 'international-mindedness' in great detail. Early definitions of possible subject scope (produced by a university consultant) were breathtakingly encyclopaedic. Their content was unworkable and unrealistic.

The challenge of developing an IGCSE subject syllabus and examination was then taken up by a small team composed of experienced international teachers, involved in work with WWF and Worldaware. In terms of subject background, the team comprised two geographers and a biologist, supported by a subject officer whose background was social anthropology.

Although the team of examiners has changed and grown over the years, this balance has been a constant feature, and corresponds with the balance of the subject itself. Environmental Management examiners need to have specialist technical knowledge, and to enjoy working together in a team with specialists from other areas. They need to be able to think and to learn outside of the comfort of their own specialist subjects, to be imaginative and creative in their approach to setting assessments, and to be enthusiastic and realistic about the learning opportunities which this subject offers for teachers and students. In other words, their approach to the subject should model the approach they expect from teachers and students.

In the context of a brand new subject the design team faced age-old questions:

- What shall we teach?
- How shall we teach it?
- How can we organize it?
- How can we evaluate it?

The solution came in the form of the curriculum matrix – the unique organizing principle of this syllabus. For each of the four spheres of the environment (e.g. the biosphere), students first learn about how the natural system works, then how humans have used the natural resource, the impact of such use and finally how this aspect of the environment may be managed sustainably for the future.

The matrix (see the Appendix to this chapter) gives teachers and learners a clear framework for learning. It indicates the breadth of the subject, the depth to which each learning objective should be taken, and the interconnections within the subject. Understanding the science of the natural system is not an end in itself. Students need to apply scientific knowledge in order to understand environmental impact, and make informed judgements about environmental management. The matrix is particularly useful in helping teachers to see the links and synergies between environmental and development issues that cut across traditional subject boundaries. This was especially important in the beginning, when the new subject had to be taught by teachers trained in more traditional subjects.

The design model of the matrix has helped to future-proof the syllabus – it has needed only minor updates over the years. It is a syllabus which is robust and flexible in a rapidly changing world. In the examination itself, new examples are brought in gradually – questions contain sufficient information to enable candidates to work with the data presented. These questions then become teaching and learning resources for the future (Cambridge International Examinations 2006a).

Over time, the examiners have refined the assessment scheme for the subject. There are two written papers, involving structured questions in which candidates apply their knowledge in response to a range of sources, using case studies they have studied. Candidates can then either carry out a coursework project, involving the investigation of local environmental issues or take an alternative to coursework paper, which provides a real-life scenario for which a microcosm of real(istic) data is provided, and assesses skills of planning, analysis and making judgements.

The examiners need to design questions that are sufficiently and equally accessible to candidates who live and learn in a very wide range of local contexts, providing the opportunity for candidates to apply their knowledge and skills in addressing real problems and issues. The expectations of candidates need to be appropriate for this stage of education – questions should be sufficiently structured and guided.

To establish confidence in, and a shared understanding of, such a new subject, curriculum and teacher support has been crucial. Cambridge has held many training events for teachers, focusing on the design of learning activities and resources. For example, an integral part of training is a field trip, in which the teachers themselves, in the role of learners, explore an environment in order to identify and review opportunities for viable projects.

Teachers learn how best to advise and prepare their own students for this kind of investigation, including the layout and content of the project. In addition, a Teacher's Guide was produced, which was written by one of the first teachers involved with the subject, and offered practical advice to the growing community of Natural Economy teachers.

PRACTICE: THE CURRICULUM IN ACTION

The designers of curriculum and assessment in Cambridge have been determined to create and communicate a framework which is as clear and as supportive to teachers and learners as possible. They want to ensure that the intended curriculum corresponds as closely as possible to the curriculum that is taught and learned – wherever this may be.

Only 12 candidates were entered for the very first examination, in June 1991. Now IGCSE Environmental Management attracts thousands of candidates each year. What is their experience of the subject, and that of their teachers? How does this compare with the intentions of the curriculum designers? The following issues have been highlighted in feedback from teachers and students.

Relevance

The ethos of the subject matches the commitment of individual international schools in many different parts of the world. There is a consensus that the subject leads to 'international-mindedness', which is positive, realistic, open-minded and well-informed. Environmental Management is not a vehicle for environmental propaganda or an environmentalist's charter. Students are encouraged to examine options and recognize that respect for the environment (and for local people) is more likely to be achieved in association with economic development.

For example Clayton Lewis, Director of the International School of Luxembourg, has recently commented that if students are to engage with global issues, then the kind of paradigm offered by Environmental Management is exactly what is needed, because students can examine contemporary issues, drawing upon a range of disciplines, and are required to think systematically as they consider solutions for the future (Lewis 2006).

We can compare this with comments from students themselves:

> You become part of a group which wants and finds it necessary to develop a new relationship between mankind and nature.
>
> It's interesting because you learn about the whole earth nowadays and not about one village area from years ago.

There is also a consensus that this IGCSE, as for other IGCSE subjects, enables students to develop skills of enquiry, presentation and analysis, evaluation, judgement and decision-making. It encourages teachers to develop their own knowledge and skills as educators. For example, here are comments from teachers in the American British Academy (ABA) in Oman:

> The course has been very popular with both teachers and students, mainly because it covers material which is so relevant and current, with the topics that we are studying frequently appearing in the media. As a result of this, our students do a lot of independent research. Teachers enjoy teaching the course as the curriculum is not prescriptive and is truly international. The course enables us to use different teaching strategies, and the teachers never feel under pressure to cover a specific amount of content in preparation for the exam. Frequently our students (we have over 50 different nationalities at ABA) are our best resource.

And from the English School, Los Olivos, in Valencia, Spain:

> My students find the course enjoyable: it improves their thinking skills, provides topics for debate and improves environmental awareness. At the same time, the course encourages the application of learning from many areas of the curriculum, especially maths and science, as well as from personal experience and local and world affairs.

In Namibia, where some 25 per cent of the secondary student cohort enters for Environmental Management, the Minister of Education has described the subject as fitting the circumstances of Namibia 'like a glove'. Not only does it provide for an understanding of the main resource underpinning Namibia's economy, but it also requires an understanding of the environmental issues arising from the impact of development and exploitation.

The subject matter and the hands-on approach to learning, encouraged by the assessment model, have also meant that the syllabus is linked to employment creation and higher education. For example, the Polytechnic of Namibia has linked the syllabus to their career path qualifications in Nature Conservation, geared to employment in major tourist spots in National Parks and on private game farms. Southern Cross High School in Ecuador comments:

> lots of former students tell me that when they have had to deal with contents and abilities in this field in College and Universities in different countries such as Mexico, USA and Italy, they have found themselves more capable than students without this IGCSE experience.

Choice

Schools that choose Environmental Management do so because it motivates teachers and students through its focus. Although freedom of subject choice characterizes IGCSE, space in the curriculum and timetable is always finite and as a result many IGCSE schools do not run an Environmental Management course. This may be because they feel that their IGCSE subjects already provide sufficiently for international-mindedness and environmental education. It may also be because school, student and parent priorities lie elsewhere.

Cambridge does not exclude candidates for other subjects, such as Geography or Biology, from entering Environmental Management. Some schools decide to make this a core subject, while for others it is optional. One of the pressures on subject choice is the perception by parents and students of direct relevance to a future career. When IT, medicine and engineering are seen as leading to a guaranteed profession, it is often challenging for teachers and careers advisers to explain the relevance of Environmental Management to employability, even though there are plenty of opportunities directly in the environmental sector, and sustainability is rising up the agenda for many professions, such as architecture.

Since Environmental Management is not a compulsory subject in IGCSE either at the system level (regulated by Cambridge), or the institutional level (specified by the school), there is a question of consistency and comparability. Put bluntly, how do the environmental knowledge, understanding, skills and awareness of an IGCSE student who has studied Environmental Management compare with those of another student who has not? This should be a topic for future research.

Local and global

Teachers of Environmental Management need to help their students engage with problems that can at first sight seem global, gigantic and impossible to tackle. One answer is to set up local activities, such as home energy efficiency projects and school-based recycling campaigns, which companies and not-for-profit organizations can be invited to sponsor.

The Arab Unity School (AUS) in Dubai provides an example:

> We have always believed in taking care of the environment for a safe and better tomorrow. This is why the school has given priority to this subject in our curriculum. Students' interest and enthusiasm regarding a better environment have resulted in the setting up of our 'AUS Environmental Club', and the Club members actively participate in the regular clean up campaign in Dubai. The school is also a member of the Emirates Environmental Group. Our students enthusiastically participate in all its activities. Regular workshops are held for students and teachers to generate awareness of the pressing environmental issues. The Club members frequently visit all the classes to motivate students to take care of the environment in school and at home.

Whether or not candidates are entered for the coursework component, local, national and regional case studies are essential ingredients in all Environmental Management courses. Each school has its particular setting. Students can develop the skills of identifying and analysing a local scale environmental problem and contextualizing impact and management aspects. They are taught how to collect and analyse data and how to apply investigative techniques, before attempting to reach any meaningful conclusions.

There can be difficulties in local investigations, although these are general and not particular to Environmental Management. For example, companies and others may not be keen to provide information or to answer questions. It may be physically difficult or dangerous to travel in a specific locality. Some expatriate teachers are not prepared themselves to draw upon the local context for case studies, but fall back on familiar material drawn from their place of origin, such as the UK. A typical comment made by schools taking Environmental Management is that the syllabus effectively guards against a bias towards content from the UK and the developed world, unlike more traditional subjects.

The global information explosion over the past 20 years, not only through the Internet but also satellite broadcasting, means that far more learning resources are available to teachers and students than when the syllabus was introduced. The difficulty now is how to make the most appropriate selection – but this applies across all subjects, not just Environmental Management.

Teacher and curriculum support

Practice varies concerning staffing. In some schools, particular teachers with sufficient experience, interest and enthusiasm take the lead and become the Environmental Management teacher, while in others a team-teaching approach is adopted. The subject seems to attract those teachers prepared to innovate, to search out resources, to design learning activities for themselves and to form local teacher groups, such as those in Argentina, Namibia and the UAE.

We have always encouraged teachers to be opportunistic and to draw on a wide range of sources, and such opportunism has characterized teaching of this subject. But a new subject needs a new, shared language of terminology and discourse. The syllabus, question papers, examiner reports, distance training manuals and other information from Cambridge all help this, but with hindsight it is clear that there was a real need for a suitable text book from the out-set. Publishers typically (and not surprisingly) look for volume sales, which subjects in their infancy cannot guarantee. It is only relatively recently that a text book has been published which brings together, in a central resource, a bank of material that covers the breadth of the syllabus and indicates the recommended teaching approaches (Pallister 2005).

LESSONS LEARNED

Reflecting on the experience of IGCSE Environmental Management, a number of significant issues emerge which throw light on the development of such a new, interdisciplinary subject for international-mindedness:

- *Clarity of purpose*: The development should not be speculative – it should respond to matters of global concern.
- *Definition of ideas and knowledge*: There needs to be precision especially about the core knowledge, concepts etc. which define the heart of the subject.
- *Choice*: A decision has to be made about whether it should be a compulsory or optional subject, weighing up the plus and minus points of either path.
- *Presentation as a framework for learning*: Teachers and students need a clear and coherent programme such as the curriculum matrix.
- *Balance of the design/examiner team*: The designers need to be as interdisciplinary as the subject, working as a team that sees the subject from both the teachers' and students' point of view.
- *Assessment that supports learning*: The assessment scheme needs to enable and demonstrate active learning.
- *Teacher support on a continuing basis*: Training, guidance and other support are vital, and have to be provided over a considerable time to ensure quality and consistency.
- *Curriculum support as an integral part of the provision*: This support, including materials for students as well as teachers, needs to be available from the start (e.g. a text book and Web-based resources).

Developing a new curriculum

How is the IGCSE curriculum developing to meet the changing needs of our rapidly changing world? Currently, a set of new syllabuses is in preparation, designed to run in parallel with existing syllabuses. These new syllabuses will meet the requirements of the new global environment, and will take advantage of developments in both teaching and learning theory, and in the skills and content needed in different subject areas. They will also take advantage of the new technologies now available for delivering information and collecting evidence. A set of curriculum guidelines has been produced which defines the principles for the new IGCSEs in individual subjects.

These principles attempt to define the personal attributes that students must have in the twenty-first century. They must be:

- versatile and adaptable, able to deal with uncertainty and to solve problems resourcefully by applying what they have learned, and through enthusiastic lifelong learning
- literate and numerate and able to communicate confidently and creatively
- respectful of cultural diversity, and able to understand, share and cooperate with people of different cultures.

As a result, the new IGCSEs aim to:

- be learner-centred: with opportunities for students to select topics and options that reflect their own contexts and interests
- be skills-focused: to develop students with transferable skills that can be applied in a changing world
- be varied in assessment so that students with different learning styles can respond in ways that best reflect their strengths
- integrate new technologies to reflect the ways in which the students learn and communicate, and to reflect the requirements of future careers
- encourage learners to investigate knowledge from different cultural perspectives and explore how local practices can have global consequences.

AN IGCSE FOR THE TWENTY-FIRST CENTURY

One of the new IGCSEs will be an interdisciplinary subject concerning global issues and citizenship, which builds very strongly on lessons learned from the Environmental Management syllabus. A new curriculum area is being created, and we must again clearly define a set of core concepts and principles. Another similarity is that a key strand of this new area will include analysis of global issues and the positive impact of the individual upon these issues.

The new syllabus considers key questions or topics relating to global issues and citizenship from philosophical, spiritual, moral and ethical perspectives, and as a result teams of experts with different perspectives will again need to work together to agree a syllabus content and structure. The aims of the syllabus will be achieved as follows:

- Teachers and students will be able to select topics that have an impact on their local context, and consider these from a local as well as a global perspective.
- A focus on skills – a key aspect of this syllabus as there will be little prescribed content. Students will be encouraged to question, to analyse and to think critically about the topics being considered, to communicate their ideas effectively, to research supporting evidence, and to work effectively as part of a team to reach a consensus (where appropriate).
- Teaching by cross-curricular teams or by a single innovative teacher, as suits the needs of the school.

The assessment models are currently being considered, but it is hoped that students will be able to build 'portfolios' of responses over the duration of a course in the way that best suits them. These could include video, auditory material (music or spoken work), artwork, physical objects, written responses, computer-generated animations or games. Reflections on their own development and on the development of the work during the course will be required in support of the evidence.

Many of the questions being asked during the current development echo those asked during the creation of the original Natural Economy IGCSE. For example, what should the syllabus be called? The name will shape the perceptions of students, teachers, parents and other interested parties, such as universities and employers. Position in the curriculum is also, again, being considered – should this syllabus be part of a compulsory core, to be studied by all students undertaking a group

award, or should it be optional? Remembering the experience of Natural Economy, how can we be sure to establish this new interdisciplinary subject at the heart and soul of the 'new IGCSE'? Finally, the best form of teacher support and development is again being discussed. Experience has shown that resources should be available from the outset.

The syllabus is currently in the early stages of development, but as with Environmental Management, an extensive programme of consultation and piloting will be followed prior to it being made available as part of the 14–16 curriculum.

CONCLUSION

This chapter has looked at IGCSE past, present and future. The focus on IGCSE Environmental Management as a case study shows that the subject-based approach to curriculum development has many strengths, especially where curriculum developers do all they can to ensure that the curriculum in practice corresponds to intentions. The case study also reveals some of the limitations of the subject-based approach – for example, how difficult it is to establish a new subject's credentials in the academic curriculum when it is presented as an option. Even subject name is a critical factor.

The lessons learned from these experiences are now being applied by Cambridge in developing IGCSE for the future. As a curriculum for international education, IGCSE is thus based clearly on research, development and reflective practice, ensuring that the experiences and needs of teachers and learners remain paramount.

ACKNOWLEDGEMENTS

The authors would like to acknowledge the help of Hamish Aitchison (WWF), Stephen Tomkins (Homerton College, Cambridge), John Pallister (CIE Chief Examiner), Ray Howarth (CIE Representative, Southern Africa) and the teachers and students at Arab Unity School, Dubai; American-British Academy, Oman; Southern Cross High School, Ecuador; Instituto Bilingue Victoria, Mexico; Edron

Academy, Mexico; English School Los Olivos, Spain; Colegio Hispano Britanico, Spain.

REFERENCES

Cambridge Council for Examination Development (1985) Internal proposal, 7 November 1985.

Cambridge International Examinations (CIE) (2006a) www.cie.org.uk.

Cambridge International Examinations (CIE) (2006b) Introduction to the 2007 IGCSE Environmental Management syllabus. www.cie.org.uk.

Hirst, P. (1974) *Knowledge and the Curriculum*. London: Routledge and Kegan Paul.

HRH Prince Philip, Duke of Edinburgh (1988) *Down to Earth*. London: Collins.

Lewis, C. (2006) International but not global: how international school curricula fail to address global issues and how this must change. *International Schools Journal*, XXV: 2.

Pallister, J. (2005) *Environmental Management*. Oxford: Oxford University Press.

Report of the Independent Commission on International Development Issues (1980) *North–South: A Programme for Survival* (The Brandt Report). London: Pan Books.

Roy, W. (1986) *The New Examination System – GCSE*. Beckenham: Croom Helm.

Skelton, M. (2002) Defining 'international' in an international curriculum. In M. Hayden, J. Thompson and G. Walker (eds) *International Education in Practice*. London: Kogan Page, pp. 39–54.

United Nations World Commission on Environment and Development (1987) *Our Common Future* (The Brundtland Report). Oxford: Oxford University Press.

Young, M. (1999) The curriculum as socially organized knowledge. In R. McCormick and C. Paechter (eds) *Learning and Knowledge*. London: Sage, pp. 56–70.

APPENDIX

RESOURCES	→ DEVELOPMENT →	IMPACT	→ MANAGEMENT
HOW DOES THE NATURAL SYSTEM WORK?	HOW DO PEOPLE USE NATURAL RESOURCES?	HOW DOES DEVELOPMENT CHANGE THE ENVIRONMENT?	HOW CAN THE ENVIRONMENT BE DEVELOPED SUSTAINABLY?
All students should have knowledge and understanding of:	*All students should have knowledge and understanding of:*	*All students should be able to analyse and discuss:*	*All students should be able to analyse and discuss:*
↓	↓	↓	↓
The water cycle	**Human intervention in the water cycle**	**Water hazards**	**Clean, safe water strategies**
How the water cycle operates	Collection and control of water for a variety of uses:	The causes and consequences of water pollution:	Ways of improving water quantity, quality and access:
	water supply (storage, transfer, dams, reservoirs); industry and domestic use; waste disposal; power; agriculture (irrigation)	impact on natural ecosystem, the physical environment, human activity and health	pollution control, improved sanitation, distribution for more efficient water use, desalination
↓	↓	↓	↓

15

The Role of Standards in K–12 International Education

Tom Oden

This chapter discusses the role of standards in international education, and especially K–12 (kindergarten to grade 12) international schools. The first section provides an overview of how standards are used in a sample of national systems, followed by a more specific review of their recent history in the USA. It then analyses the introduction and current status of standards in international schools, and focuses on an innovative curriculum development project that involved several schools and organizations. Finally, the chapter concludes with some thoughts on the future directions of the use of standards in schools around the world.

OVERVIEW – NATIONAL STANDARDS

The idea of using a set of standards and benchmarks to guide education is not new. Throughout the world most countries have a centralized, national curriculum that is based upon a set of common learning goals. In fact, the USA is something of an abnormality, with its decentralized education system that is predicated on local control of schools. However, even though there is no formal national system in the USA, many authors feel that there is significant convergence in terms of ideas and expectations and thus the curricula used in school districts across the country are, in practice, highly normed (Powell et al. 1985; Sizer 1985 and others).

The term standard refers to a statement of what learners should know, or be able to do, as the result of their educational experience in a school system. These concepts of 'knowing' and 'doing' are often differentiated into standards that address content and skills. Standards typically address large concepts and procedures that underlie various fields of study. In most standards systems, the standards themselves are subsequently broken down into smaller statements, or benchmarks, that describe what the developmentally appropriate level of attainment would be for a particular standard at a given age or year of schooling. The following Grade 5 example from the Virginia Standards of Learning for English (Revised) demonstrates this convention:

5.4 **The student will read fiction and nonfiction with fluency and accuracy.**
      (a)   **Use context to clarify meaning of unfamiliar words.**
      (b)   **Use knowledge of root words, prefixes, and suffixes.**
      (c)   **Use dictionary, glossary, thesaurus, and other word-reference materials.**

UNDERSTANDING THE STANDARD (Teacher Notes)	ESSENTIAL UNDERSTANDINGS	ESSENTIAL, KNOWLEDGE, SKILLS AND PROCESSES
• The intent of this standard is that students will continue to build vocabulary by applying their knowledge of word structure and context clues to determine the meanings of unfamiliar words. • Students should read about 120 words per minute in grade level material. • Students will continue to build their knowledge of word origins by learning about Greek and Latin affixes. • Students will also use word-reference materials to learn new words.	**All students should:** • apply knowledge of word structure and context clues to determine the meanings of unfamiliar words • read with fluency and accuracy.	**To be successful with this standard, students are expected to:** • use context to infer the correct meanings of unfamiliar words • apply knowledge of root words, prefixes, and sufsfixes • continue to learn about Greek and Latin affixes • use word references and context clues to determine which meaning is appropriate in a given situation • identify the word-reference materials, such as a dictionary, glossary, or thesaurus, that is most likely to contain the information needed • understand that often a word can be divided into root word, prefix, and suffix in order to determine its pronunciation • understand how a prefix changes the meaning of a root word • read familiar text with fluency, accuracy, and expression.

(www.pen.k12.va.us/VDOE/Instruction/English/englishCF.html)

Reviewing different curricular designs in countries around the world shows that the most common areas for standards to be written are in the traditional content areas such as Language Arts, Social Studies, Mathematics and Science. In terms of sophistication, a simple system would include the standards, an intermediate system would include standards and appropriate benchmarks and an advanced system would include standards, benchmarks and exemplars of attainment. In terms of differences, some countries contain specific standards in the area of Religious Education, Vocational Education, World Languages and Literacy. The presence, or absence, of these types of standards suggests certain developmental or societal preferences in terms of those countries. Table 15.1 provides a review of the types of standards employed in a sample of countries around the world.

Further analysis of the use of standards and benchmarks suggests that there are two broad phases in terms of their use. The first would be developing and publishing these learning targets. Once they are in place, a subsequent process becomes possible, where they can be used to guide improvement efforts. In the UK, for example, the use of standards and benchmarks is a prominent part of two types of educational reform. One is measured against external entities, while the other is focused on internal targets. With respect to external comparisons, the advent of international comparisons, such as the TIMMS study, has enabled governments to view their own educational systems in increasingly analytical comparison

Table 15.1   Types of standards in selected countries

Country	Language Arts, SS, Math, Science	Religious Education	Vocational Standards	World Lang.	Key resources
UK	x	x	x	x	Qualifications and Curriculum Authority www.qca.org.uk National Curriculum in Action www.ncaction.org.uk
France	x		x	x	Qualifications and Curriculum Authority www.inca.org.uk/france-system-special.html
Japan					Ministry of Education, Culture, Sports, Science and Technology www.mext.go.jp/english/index.htm
China					Ministry of Education of the People's Republic of China www.moe.edu.cn/english/index.htm
South Korea	x	x[a]	x	x	Qualifications and Curriculum Authority www.inca.org.uk/korea-curricula-mainstream.html
Singapore	x	x[b]	x	x	Ministry of Education www.moe.gov.sg
India	x		x	x	National Curricular Framework: www.ncert.nic.in/sites/publication/schoolcurriculum/NCFR%202005/contents2.htm Syllabus for Primary, Upper Primary, Secondary single and Higher Secondary Classes www.ncert.nic.in/Syllabus/Syllabus_contents.htm
Chile	x		x	x	Ministerio de Educación www.mineduc.cl/index0.php?id_portal=1#
South Africa	x		x	x	Department of Education www.education.gov.za Revised National Curriculum Statement www.polity.org.za/html/govdocs/policy/2002/curriculum/part2.pdf
USA	x			x	Professional Associations and State Depts of Education

[a] Referred to as 'Moral Education'.
[b] Referred to as 'Civics and Moral Education' (CME).

to others. Responding to the results of an Organisation for Economic Cooperation and Development (OECD) survey in 2000, British Secretary of State for Education, Estelle Morris, used the results of the survey and Britain's relative success to justify her party's political position:

> The survey was carried out in 2000, and 265,000 15-year-olds from 32 countries were interviewed and tested on their abilities in reading, mathematics and science. In all three categories, Britain was well above average. In reading, Britain came fifth, in mathematics eighth and in science fourth. ... The survey gives ammunition to those who think that after a decade of controversial educational reforms, Britain is finally heading in the right direction. Estelle Morris, the secretary of state for education, described the results as 'a vindication of the reform of the last few years'. (*Economist*, 12/8/2001)

In that light, the results of the UK students when measured against the other nations suggests a positive outcome. However, the same survey also showed, despite the successes, that

Britain had 'one of the widest gaps in attainment in reading between pupils from the wealthiest and poorest quartiles. South Korea and Finland, by contrast, have the smallest differences' (*Economist*, 12/8/2001).

Depending on political orientation, the use of standards and benchmarks can mean different things, as well as identify conflicting priorities, for different audiences.

THE STANDARDS MOVEMENT IN THE USA

A movement to identify strict national standards of learning began in the USA in the 1950s, fuelled by the Soviet achievements in aerospace. More recently, in the 1980s, against a backdrop of concerns about diminishing economic advantage, especially when compared to Japan, and sizeable demographic shifts in the population, renewed attention was paid to the idea of creating common standards in the traditional academic areas. The anxious mood of the times is captured by the title of the National Commission on Excellence in Education's seminal prescription, *A Nation at Risk* (1983), which offered a strong plea for standards based on two core principles:

1. **Excellence:** There was a widely held belief that the USA was losing its competitive edge economically and that the overall rigour and quality of the US educational system needed to be enhanced.
2. **Equity:** Wholesale demographic changes were taking place in the USA, particularly with respect to non-native English speakers entering school and larger numbers of minority and economically disadvantaged students. The desire was to ensure that this broad population would also receive a quality education.

The two, often competing, principles of excellence and egalitarianism have long been a feature of public discourse in American life. In the 1980s, while many voices called for a unified set of national standards, political pressure (and the desire to remain loyal to the principles of the US Constitution) prevented that level of consolidation. Instead, their

development and implementation were scaled up in both public and private education, and were led by state governments and national discipline-based professional associations. By the early 1990s, 49 of the 50 states and the leading professional associations such as the National Council of Teachers of English (NCTE) and the National Council of Teachers of Mathematics (NCTM) all had published their own standards. While there is significant debate about their effectiveness in facilitating school improvement (O'Day 2002; Ogawa et al. 2003), by the end of the twentieth century the presence of curricular standards became an accepted feature of US public schools.

STANDARDS IN INTERNATIONAL EDUCATION

Until very recently, the development of standards for K-12 international education has paralleled, although occasionally lagged behind, the national school process. Today, however, there are emerging issues that make the international context unique. These include continuing debates about the nature of the terms *international* school and *international-mindedness*. As described by Haywood (2005: 9), 'It is now recognized that the process of encouraging *international-mindedness* calls for a *consciously structured educational experience* [emphasis added]: it is not just the natural consequence of putting children of different nationalities together in the same playground'. The change in outlook toward a global perspective has had a corresponding effect on standards. Lewis (2005: 21) notes that if schools are to promote this sort of global awareness, then they 'should develop standards and benchmarks that reflect an international, multicultural perspective. Students should be able to demonstrate their understanding that there are valid perspectives other than their own and that there is a relationship between our dispositions and behaviour. The benchmarks must also ensure that students acquire the knowledge and skills that are necessary to be informed citizens and contributors to society'.

Table 15.2   Benchmarks for OXFAM Knowledge Strand, Social Justice and Equity

Pre KS1 Pre stages P1–P3 Under 5s	What is fair/unfair What is right and wrong
KS1 Stages P1–P3 Ages 5–7	Awareness of rich and poor
KS2 Stages P4–P6 Ages 7–11	Fairness between groups Causes and effects of inequality
KS3 Stages P7–S2 Ages 11–14	Inequalities within and between societies Basic rights and responsibilities
KS4 S3 Standard grade Ages 14–16	Causes of poverty Different views on the eradication of poverty Role as Global Citizen
Ages 16–19	Understanding of global debates

The set of standards that Lewis describes is quite different from those arising from the traditional focus on content areas. Perhaps the most fully developed curriculum in this area is offered by Oxfam on its 'Cool Planet for Teachers' site (www.oxfam.org.uk/cooplanet/ teachers/globciti/curric/curric.htm). Using the Key Stages of the National Curriculum in England and Wales as its organizing principle, the curriculum lays out a course of study in the following areas:

- **Knowledge and Understanding:** Social Justice and Equity, Diversity, Globalization and Interdependence, Sustainable Development, Peace and Conflict.
- **Skills:** Critical Thinking, Ability to Argue Effectively, Ability to Challenge Injustice and Inequity, Respect for People and Things, Co-operation and Conflict Resolution
- **Values and Attitudes:** Sense of Identity and Self-Esteem, Empathy and Sense of Common Humanity, Commitment to Social Justice and Equity, Concern for the Environment and Sustainable Development, Belief that People Can Make a Difference.

The Oxfam framework is relatively simplistic, with one or two benchmarks typically defining the developmentally appropriate knowledge and behaviour. For example, the knowledge strand for *Social Justice and Equity*

lists the sequence of benchmarks shown in Table 15.2.

At face value, the benchmarks leave much room for development; however, the potential impact of their specification should also not be overlooked. There is a large body of research, from the Effective Schools movement in the 1980s (Lezotte 1991) to the recent work of Schmoker (1999), which points to the centrality of measurable goals and clear targets in matters of school improvement. Oxfam guidelines also emphasize geography, which is often marginalized in American curricula, but which plays a much more central role in European schools. While only a single example, it is interesting to consider how the work of an NGO such as Oxfam has transformed the curriculum of public education to create materials that challenge traditional academic disciplines.

STANDARDS, GLOBALIZATION AND THE CHALLENGES OF POSTMODERNISM

The development of K–12 curriculum (national and international) and standards is influenced by educational, political, economic and cultural considerations. There appears to be a growing consensus that the post-industrial world requires a different sort of educational system than that which created it. Suarez-Orozco (2005: 209) claims that socializing the youth of today means 'preparing them to engage with a world of ever growing diversity and complexity'. In a similar vein, Howard Gardner notes that:

> The skills and competencies needed for identifying, analyzing, and mobilizing to solve problems from multiple perspectives will require individuals who are intellectually curious and cognitively flexible, tolerant of ambiguity, able to synthesize knowledge within and across disciplines, culturally sophisticated, and able to work collaboratively in groups made up of individuals from diverse backgrounds. (Gardner, in Suarez-Orozco 2005: 212)

The convergence of these two lines of thinking, that the evolving challenges of the world require a different set of skills of its inhabitants, provides one focus for the development of standards in international education. According to Betts (2004), many international schools commonly claim in their mission statements that they are preparing 'global citizens' and there is, allowing for semantics, a 'surprising degree of unanimity' about what that term means. What are less developed, and less understood, are the skills that teachers need to deliver this curriculum to students and the tools available to assess their progress. Betts suggests that the skills and understandings that are sought for students must be practised and internalized by the adults and therefore given 'higher priority in our staff development schemes' (p. 5). She also argues that the type of sophisticated performance assessments that are being developed in traditional content areas must also be developed in the area of global citizenship. What is interesting to note is how important the idea of grappling with values and value premises is becoming to the educational context. As Betts points out, 'there still seems to be a level of discomfort in our schools with regard to assessing attitudes. Global citizenship is at least as much about attitudes and resultant behaviours than it is about content

knowledge. And we continue to resist holding our students to the same high ethical and values-related standards as we do for academics (even though our mission statements make equal claims for both)' (p. 5).

At its core, the development of these types of standards for international schools is part of a debate about the role that schools should fill in society that traces back to at least the story of Socrates in Western civilization. It is beyond the scope of this chapter to review the sociological history of educational institutions, but it is worth noting that a growing number of practitioners and scholars feel that the context of schools is dramatically changing and the technical development of standards and curriculums in areas such as global citizenship is the surface manifestation of deep questions about politics, identity and purpose.

One place where the standards movement in schools intersects with external political realities is in early childhood education. Increasingly today, the political and social costs of uneducated or poorly educated youth, at a macro level, appear to trump purely national educational planning. For example, Sperling and Herz (2004) summarize a series of NGO reports that confirm the high returns that derive from educating girls. They include:

- economic benefits, including higher wages
- greater agricultural productivity
- health benefits and HIV prevention.

While their call for special initiatives that target girls' education is not new, they make a concurrent claim that is striking: 'These endeavours will work only in the context of a broader focus on *universal* basic education for all children' (p. 215).

Whether politicians have the will ultimately to deliver this universal basic education is debatable; however, what is clear is that there is a growing consensus about what this early educational experience should look like. Kagan, Britto and Engle (2005) describe the work of the Going Global project, a six-nation initiative involving early childhood educators from Brazil, Ghana, Jordan, Paraguay, the Philippines and South Africa to develop, test and implement a set of learning standards. According to the authors, the cross-cultural dimension of the project created a richer set of standards. For instance, they reviewed the standards and benchmarks for early childhood education that exist in 46 US states and found that they predominantly emphasize cognition and language development, even though the incidence of childhood obesity is at epidemic levels. Kagan et al. found it instructive that all six sets of standards developed by the countries in the Going Global Project covered multiple domains of childhood development, including health/nutrition/safety and motor development (p. 206). The creation of sets of standards that concurrently identify commonalities and allow for individual application can be a vital tool for developing nations around the world. Levine (2005: 196) quotes statistics from UNESCO that show by 2015 the world's four most populous nations – China, India, Brazil and Indonesia – will educate 10 times the number of children than will be educated in the USA. Obviously, the nature and the quality of that education will have a huge impact on the future of the world.

PROJECT AERO: A CASE STUDY IN INTERNATIONAL COLLABORATION ON STANDARDS

AERO: the development of the standards

The introduction of standards into K–12 international schools has followed much the same pattern as that which occurred in the USA. While, as noted above, there are some disagreements over the definition of the term 'international school', there are basically two types. The first tends to offer a replica of a national curriculum in an expatriate setting, such as the British School of Muscat, the Deutsche Schule of Beirut or any number of French Lycées. The second type of school offers an American or a hybrid international curriculum to its students (a hybrid programme is a combination of an American programme

and an international curriculum, such as the International Baccalaureate or the International Primary Curriculum). It is this latter group of schools that this section addresses because standards are already present, de facto, in national schools.

These international schools are not formally linked nor organized into a single system, but they do share various modes of affiliation and utilize similar structures and pedagogies. The introduction of standards into their context is a recent phenomenon. Anecdotal evidence suggests that a number of schools began to individually adopt sets of standards from the USA in the mid-1990s. According to Dr Beatrice Cameron, of the Office of Overseas Schools of the US State Department:

> When I arrived at A/OS in 1992, the Standards Movement was underway in the States. When I was assigned to the Near East South Asia region in 1997, David Chojnacki, the Executive Director, and I began to talk with schools in the region that were looking for ways to approach standards. Some were using North Carolina, some Montana, some California, some the disciplinary sets, such as NCTM or NCTE. Discussions began about which states were best for different content areas, and one software company even offered all the state standards and benchmarks so you could pick and choose … but it was a bit overwhelming and schools were confused about how to proceed or reticent to start. At that point, we started to explore the idea of creating a consolidated set of standards for international schools that would be more user-friendly and build on the work that had already been done in the States. (Personal communication, 5 December 2005)

These conversations and experiences were the beginning of a joint effort between the Office of Overseas Schools (A/OS) of the US State Department and the Near East South Asia (NESA) Council of Overseas Schools, which became known as Project AERO, the acronym for *American Education Reaches Out*. In the autumn of 1998 a group of administrators from international schools met to discuss the idea of creating a set of academic standards for international schools and to devise a work plan to achieve that goal. From the outset, the AERO work had two main goals:

- to create standards that international schools could adopt in four academic disciplines – Language Arts, Social Studies, Mathematics and Science
- to create a framework for curriculum consistency in a transient workplace (www.nesacenter. org/aero).

As a starting point, the group used a document created by the Council of Basic Education (CBE), a prominent American NGO, that consolidated the standards and benchmarks that had been written by the various states and professional associations into a single set. It identified the ideas that were common to all, after allowances for semantics. The resulting list of standards and benchmarks became known as the *Standards for Excellence in Education* or the SEE Standards. They served as the basis of the work by the AERO task force, which included representatives from 12 schools around the world:

- American Community School, Amman
- American Cooperative School, Tunis
- American International School, Dhaka
- American International School, Johannesburg
- American International School, Riyadh
- American International School, Tel Aviv
- American School Foundation, Monterrey, Mexico
- International School of Islamabad
- International School of Luxembourg
- International Schools Group, Dhahran
- Nido de Aguilas International School (Santiago)
- Singapore American School

These schools were selected to create a working group with geographic balance, differing perspectives and varying stages of curriculum complexity. By 2004, the group created the AERO standards that are available in the public domain at www.nesacenter.org/aero.

These AERO Standards are notable for at least two reasons. First, their concise format is a response to the common criticism against large and expansive sets of standards and benchmarks. Often, these lists contain so many ideas and targets that they become unmanageable. In contrast, the AERO set is extremely economical and trenchant. For instance, it lists the following number of vertical, K–12 standards:

- English/Language Arts: 9
- Mathematics: 11
- Science: 24
- Social Studies: 8

In addition, due to time limitations the group only designed benchmarks for four developmental levels – Grade 2 (or 3), Grade 5, Grade 8 and Grade 12 – which correspond to the divisional exit grades typical to most American-style schools. Instead of a voluminous document that further complicates the complex process of curricular revision, the AERO standards and benchmarks have proved to be more of a guideline for the schools that have chosen to use it. According to Kevin Schafer, Director of The American International School of Muscat (TAISM), which began using AERO in the spring of 2001, the ideas have become an important framework for his school:

We didn't want to re-invent the wheel and have yet another discussion about what the standards should be. AERO synthesized all of that work and allowed us to start very far down the road in terms of standards and benchmarks. In the space of 6 months, we went from having nothing in terms of standards to have a guiding framework. Within another year, we'd used that template to create our own standards in benchmarks in the other curricular areas – Health & Physical Education, World Languages and Fine Arts. Since then, we have filled in the benchmarks for other grade levels that are not present in the original AERO set, as well as for the other content areas. We thought that was going to be a difficult process, but it actually went very smoothly and simply. In some ways, the fact that we had to add to the framework forced us into some institutional ownership for the standards and benchmarks. The AERO people talk about 'adapting and adopting' the ideas and that has proved to be a very important concept for us. Without it, I think the AERO work would have been yet another external, or 'outside', idea that never really took hold in the day-to-day reality of school. Because our own people grappled with the ideas, it has a much higher degree of salience for us ... Of course, since then, we have fine-tuned the ideas and gone on to do significant work in terms of aligning our assessment system(s) to the standards and benchmarks, but I am amazed at how much of the original work has held. (Personal communication, February 2006)

The concise nature of the AERO standards, while laudable in terms of focus, does require a trade-off in terms of the information provided for teachers. Earlier in the chapter, an example from the Virginia standards of learning was presented. The following is the analogous item from the AERO set:

Standard 1: Students will read fluently using the skills and strategies of the reading process.

By the end of grade 4:
a. Apply knowledge of word relationships, root words, derivations, suffixes, and affixes to determine the meaning of words.
b. Apply knowledge of synonyms, antonyms, and idioms to determine the meaning of phrases.
c. Use appropriate strategies (e.g., previews text, pictorial clues, contextual clues, predictions) when reading for different purposes (e.g., full comprehension, locating information, following multiple-step instructions, and personal enjoyment).
d. Use a dictionary and a thesaurus to determine the meaning of words.

While the focus of each is the same, the Virginia example is more robust in terms of the level of specification of the learning to be achieved.

Another significant aspect of the AERO standards is that they do attempt to address the specific context of international schools. In terms of the actual benchmarks themselves, they tend to be set at higher levels of attainment than those of US schools as a result of the fairly privileged demographics of most international schools. They also engage the multicultural aspects of international schools. In some cases, that was a fairly straightforward process; for instance, the inclusion of different measurement systems – miles and kilometres, pounds and kilograms – in Mathematics. In other cases, this engagement proved to be quite complex. The discussions surrounding the development of the Social Studies standards and benchmarks were particularly contentious, reflecting the conflicted nature of this academic discipline to begin with, as well as the challenges and opportunities implicit in teaching the subject in an inherently cross-cultural environment. According to one of the participants, Mark Baker, who was the Curriculum Coordinator at the American International School of Johannesburg:

Within the group, we could never reconcile the competing frameworks with respect to the content. It was too loaded a topic, with individuals advocating for a vast array of topics and ideas. Every time we started down that road, two things happened. One, we had huge arguments about opinions that could never be 'solved'. We also started to generate the excessive numbers of benchmarks and targets that we had pledged to avoid. (Personal communication, January 2006)

Eventually, the group decided to develop a dualistic framework that laid out general standards and benchmarks that any school could address, with an accompanying topic grid that provided possible content options to address the various standards. This development, and the dilemma it was designed to circumvent, are explained by the following statement from the project website (www. nesacenter.org/aero/SocialStudies/Social StudiesQs.html):

Overview of Standards

In recognition of the widely varying environments of American/international schools, the AERO social studies standards and benchmarks have been written to give schools a high level of flexibility in developing curriculum. They focus on key ideas and principles in social studies without specifying the content that should be learned by students so they can gain understanding of the key ideas. At the same time, the AERO team also recognized the value of providing content suggestions to guide teachers and curriculum coordinators as they develop units that will bring students to accomplishment of the standards and benchmarks. To that end, a set of suggested social studies topics to accompany the benchmarks has been developed and distributed on a CD-ROM. For questions about this, please contact AERO project manager Stephanie Soper at stephaniesoper @yahoo.com.

AERO: the challenges of implementation

As the work of the AERO Project unfolded in schools around the world it encountered a number of issues. The conflict over content within the Social Studies discipline elicited a well-known challenge for educators seeking to collaborate across cultural and national boundaries. While the AERO standards are not meant to advance a particular political agenda, they are also not value-free. Rebecca New (2005: 203) argues that today's 'multinational endeavors challenge the simple notion of "knowledge transfer" and suggest, rather, a process of exchange, critique, and collaboration that is politically complex and culturally situated'. For some schools, the mere presence of the word *American* in the term AERO was enough to disqualify it from attention, based on a predisposition to view American education as excessively sheltered and solipsistic. Furthermore, one of the axioms of change management is that true changes require the development of new organizational capacities (Evans 1996; Garmston and Wellman 1999). With respect to the introduction of standards and benchmarks, one of the things that became obvious to the practitioners involved with the work is that there were huge differences between devising the standards, what the AERO group referred to as *Design and Development*, and actually using them in schools to inform instruction, or *Implementation*. As schools around the world began to experiment with the AERO standards, their efforts created an almost immediate need for additional professional development. One of the findings of the schools that began using AERO was that its effective implementation required a higher degree of planning and assessment literacy in the organization than was typically present. With respect to planning, two popular approaches, Understanding by Design (Wiggins and McTighe 1998) and Curricular Mapping (Jacobs 1997) began to play an important role in the discussion of standards. While critics of educational change efforts often note that many innovations tend to be faddish and additive, as opposed to integrated within the existing framework, in this instance, both of these ideas were present in many international schools, but not necessarily utilized in an intentional manner. Schools began to use curricular mapping to surface and share what they were doing with curriculum. They followed the basic premise of Understanding by Design (UBD) – that of 'backward design' – to organize instructional planning, with the initial step of UBD – 'Identify the Desired

Result' – essentially equated with specific benchmarks. Another focus area became assessment, because assessing in a standards-based system is quite different from assessing in a criterion-referenced system. Finally, since the AERO Project was envisioned from the outset to be voluntary, as opposed to externally mandated, the schools that began to use it were moving at different speeds and generated different organizational needs.

To support these burgeoning and highly differentiated needs, the Office of Overseas Schools (A/OS) created a series of professional development opportunities for AERO, including seminars at the various regional teacher and administrator conferences (ECIS, NESA, EARCOS, etc.), as well as an intensive, week-long curriculum writing workshop for international school teams that meets each summer at the Potomac School in McLean, VA. There is also evidence that individual schools began to band together to form learning communities devoted to curriculum development and standards design. An example of this form of partnership is the arrangement developed between the American School of Doha and The American International School of Muscat. Their common curricular platform enabled them to share resources such as the cost of a visiting consultant, and to co-examine their assessment and professional development practices. In this manner, they are reflective of a general trend toward networking and information exchange that Friedman (2005) and others have noted is characteristic of the emerging global economy, as well as the shift in international educational exchange that New (2005: 202) characterizes as moving 'from a process of *knowledge transfer* to a process of *appropriation* characterized by debate and collective inquiry'.

Another challenge that emerged in the work of Project AERO was its potential conflict with curricular designs in place at other schools. In the international school context, one of the most widely used curriculum frameworks is that of the International Baccalaureate (IB). As mentioned earlier, there is a perception on the part of some educators that American-style education tends to subsume, or marginalize, other visions of education that are more internationally oriented. Given the growth in the number of schools using the AERO standards since 2000, it is worth looking at whether its expansion does truly create this type of conflict. Upon close examination, however, the IB Primary Years Programme (PYP), IB Middle Years Programme (MYP) and to a great extent, the IB Diploma Programme are essentially content-free. They focus on an integrated design and stipulate themes and avenues of enquiry, but rarely specify precise content. Therefore, instead of being in opposition, it is possible to view the combination of AERO and IB as having a certain synergy, with the standards and benchmarks providing more specific learning targets for the avenues of thematic enquiry and content exploration stipulated by the IB Organization (IBO).

While the AERO standards and benchmarks were never intended to be a required facet of American international schools, they are now being used in over 100 schools around the world. While much work remains to be done in terms of developing the capacities of international school teachers to teach in a standards-based framework and scaling up and sharing the organizational learning and successes of the individual schools involved, there is a general sense that Project AERO has achieved its original goals of becoming a viable and voluntary framework that could help enhance curricular continuity. This sentiment was captured by one of the original members of the AERO Task Force, Wendy Macarthur (2006), who is the Lower School Principal/Curriculum Specialist at the International School of Belgrade:

> As a practitioner I would say ... the best thing about standards in international education is that they are eliminating the 'suitcase' curriculum. When teachers walk into a school, they are increasingly provided with curriculum documents and unit plans and the expectations are clear as to what should be taught and what students should know. They are also fabulous for communicating with parents. I find that expatriate and international parents are understandably concerned about the academic standard of the school and they are often reassured once they see the

standards documents. (Personal communication, 8 February 2006)

CONCLUSIONS AND RECOMMENDATIONS

This chapter has provided an overview of the standards movement in international education, with specific reference to international schools. It is intended to be a starting point for future investigation, and not a comprehensive review of the topic. As such, it has certain limitations. The first is that most of the research on national systems was done via the Internet and utilized documents that are in English, or English-translations of other languages. In addition, the subject matter is relatively recent and not the subject of extensive scholarly investigation. Finally, the case study is based on accounts of current practitioners, as opposed to the findings of researchers, and those closer to action research than traditional quantitative or qualitative analysis.

However, even with these limitations in mind, the topic of standards and benchmarks in international schools does appear to be a fertile area for future study and investigation. Recalling New's (2005) distinction between 'knowledge transfer and appropriation characterized by debate and collective inquiry', the gradual expansion and democratic evolution of the AERO work is very similar to the characteristics desired in learning organizations and professional communities. Educators interested in working with standards in international schools can benefit from the experience of the pioneering schools and address the capacity issues in areas such as planning and assessment that the early schools struggled with. They can also draw from a growing pool of work that uses standards and benchmarks to frame discussions of external comparison and internal improvement. Perhaps most importantly, they can understand that addressing the issue of standards not only focuses on traditional content areas and processes, but also fundamental questions about the roles and responsibilities of schools.

While certainly speculative, it is tempting to view the use of standards in international schools as an indicator of a new direction for international education. Traditionally, schools codified and clarified learning targets in traditional academic areas. The review of the AERO Project is a good example of this trend, with its initial focus on Language Arts, Social Studies, Mathematics and Science, and its current exploration of World Languages, Visual Arts and Music. This work is important and valuable, yet the broad, conventional strokes to some extent obscure the coming urgency of another set of global imperatives.

Even within the early AERO discussions, issues of globalism and internationalism manifested themselves. At the outset of the AERO work in 1999, these were relatively new concerns. Today, there are stand-alone sets of dispositional standards and benchmarks that describe what it means to be a 'global citizen.' Similarly, in areas such as early childhood education, sets of standards are part of a broader, multinational effort to eradicate poverty and encourage sustainable development. In these new, emergent cases, the role of standards is not so much to look inward, but to see outward. In very real ways, they are facilitating the description of our complex, challenging and changing world.

REFERENCES

Betts, B. (2004) The challenge of global citizenship in our schools. *Journal of Innovative Teaching,* (Brussels, Belgium, CESSIB) 2: 4–5.

Evans, R. (1996) *The Human Side of School Change.* San Francisco, CA: Jossey-Bass.

Friedman, T. (2005) *The World is Flat: A Brief History of the Twenty-first Century.* New York: Farrar, Straus and Giroux.

Garmston, R. and Wellman, B. (1999) *The Adaptive School: A Sourcebook for Developing Collaborative Groups.* Norwood, MA: Christopher-Gordon.

Haywood, T. (2005) The Alliance for International Education – making possible the age of influence. *International Schools Journal,* XXIV: 2.

Jacobs, H.H. (1997) *Mapping the Big Picture: Integrating Curriculum and Assessment K–12.* Alexandria, VA: ASCD.

Kagan, S.L., Britto, P.R. and Engle, P. (2005) Early learning standards: what can America learn? What can America teach? *Phi Delta Kappan,* 87: 205–8.

Levine, M. (2005) Take a giant step: investing in pre-school education in emerging nations. *Phi Delta Kappan,* 87: 196–200.

Lewis, C. (2005) 'What must a school do to be globally responsible.' *International Schools Journal,* XXIV: 2.

Lezotte, L.W. (1991) *Correlates of Effective Schools: The First and Second Generations.* Okemos, MI: Effective Schools Products.

National Commission on Excellence in Education (1983) *A Nation at Risk: the Imperative for Educational Reform.* A Report to the Nation and the Secretary of Education, US Department of Education. Available at www.ed.gov/pubs/NatAtRisk/index.html (accessed 2006).

New, R. (2005) Learning about early childhood education from and with Western European nations. *Phi Delta Kappan,* 87: 201–5.

O'Day, J.A. (2002) Complexity, accountability, and school improvement. *Harvard Educational Review,* 72: 3.

Ogawa, R.T., Sandholtz, J.H., Martinez-Flores, M. and Scribner, S.P. (2003) The Substantive and Symbolic Consequences of a District's Standards-Based Curriculum. *American Educational Research Journal,* 147.

Powell, A.G., Farrar, E. and Cohen, D.K. (1985) *The Shopping Mall High School: Winners and Losers in the Educational Marketplace.* Boston, MA: Houghton Mifflin.

Schmoker, M. (1999) *Results: The Key to Continuous School Improvement,* 2nd edition. Alexandria, VA: ASCD.

Sizer, T. (1985) *Horace's Compromise: The Dilemma of the American High School.* Boston, MA: Houghton Mifflin.

Sperling, G. and Herz, B. (2004) *What Works in Girls' Education: Evidence and Policies from the Developing World.* Washington, DC: Council on Foreign Relations.

Suarez-Orozco, M. (2005) Rethinking education in the global era. *Phi Delta Kappan,* 87: 209–12.

Wiggins, G. and McTighe, J. (1998) *Understanding by Design.* Alexandria, VA: ACSD.

16

Technology, Globalization and Distance Education: Pedagogical Models and Constructs

Nada Dabbagh and Angela D. Benson

Telecommunications technology has radically changed the way we learn. Internet connectivity and the World Wide Web's universal browser protocol have paved the way to widespread collaborative activities and information-sharing capabilities that until only a few years ago were not perceived possible (Dabbagh and Bannan-Ritland 2005). How have these new technologies impacted distance education? More specifically, how have they influenced the implementation of distance education programmes and initiatives that combine local requirements and international imperatives? This chapter describes the general characteristics and pedagogical trends that permeate traditional distance education and introduces distributed learning as an overarching conceptual framework that enables a global and international perspective of distance education. Examples of K–12 and higher education distributed learning delivery models that emerged due to advancements in Internet- and Web-based technologies are also described.

TRADITIONAL DISTANCE EDUCATION

Correspondence study

Traditional distance education began with print-based correspondence courses over one hundred years ago (Galusha 1997; Picciano 2001; Schrum 1999). The practice was known as 'correspondence study' or 'extension courses' and was established initially in Europe, crossing the Atlantic in 1873 (Schlosser and Simonson 2003): 'The original target groups of distance education efforts were adults with occupational, social and family commitments', and the focus was on 'individuality of learning and flexibility in both time and place of study' (Hanson et al. 1997: 4). Guided readings, frequent tests and free pacing of progress through the programme by the student were key elements of traditional or classic settings of distance education.

Correspondence study courses were delivered primarily through print media with the content segmented into manageable units providing a lot of structure to ensure success. Correspondence study courses benefited from the planning, guidance and pedagogical practices of an educational organization without being under the continuous and immediate supervision of tutors present with their students in lecture rooms or on the premises. Moore (1994) refers to this type of correspondence study as non-autonomous or teacher-determined, and gauges the degree of learner autonomy by determining how much guidance a learner needs in formulating objectives, identifying sources of information and measuring objectives. Moore notes that in most conventional educational programmes, resident or distance, the learner is very dependent on the teacher for guidance, and the teacher is active while the student is passive.

Independent study

Independent study is another pedagogical model of traditional distance education in which the curriculum is more responsive to students' needs and goals, and the student 'accepts a high degree of responsibility for the conduct of the learning program' (Hanson et al. 1997: 9). Moore (1994) and Wedemeyer (1981) emphasized the very important characteristic of independent study, and that is the *independence* of the student. The concept of student independence and autonomy continues to be a distinguishing feature between conventional and more innovative educational settings and a critical factor in designing effective distance education environments.

The nature of interaction

Another distinguishing feature of traditional distance education is the absence of face-to-face interaction with teachers and peers. Although several telecommunications technologies such as audio and videoconferencing have enabled a *simulated* human interaction learning context, the absence of face-to-face

interaction in classic distance education settings has been identified as one of the main causes for loss of student motivation, leading to attrition, particularly in Internet-based courses (Galusha 1997). Additionally, there are some educators who view the introduction of educational telecommunications systems as 'an imposition that diminishes human interaction in instruction and learning undermining an essential element in the quality of the educational experience' (Duning 1993: 19). A similar perspective on interaction is echoed by distance education students who report feelings of alienation and isolation and feel that 'the *distance* aspect of distance learning takes away much of the social interactions that would be present in traditional learning environments' (Galusha 1997: 9).

However, recent pedagogical and technological innovations in distance education have increased the potential for interaction and collaborative work (Riel and Harasim 1994). Interaction took on a new meaning extending beyond learner–teacher, learner–content and learner–programme modes to learner–learner and learner–group modes. The concept of *distance* became relatively unimportant or blurred (i.e. not limited to the physical separation of the learner and the instructor), challenging traditional models of distance education. Pedagogical models or constructs such as open or flexible learning, distributed learning and learning communities began emerging, prompting the reconceptualization of distance learning. Two underlying principles or concepts played an important role in this development: *globalization* and *learning as a social process*. We elaborate on these two principles below.

GLOBALIZATION AND ITS IMPACT ON DISTANCE EDUCATION

While there are numerous definitions of the term, globalization can be described as a psychological phenomenon that can be applied to many contexts to imply that most people are connected simultaneously with distant events, directly or indirectly, intentionally or unintentionally, promoting a perception or an awareness of the globe as a single environment (Evans 1995). Terms such as the 'information revolution' and the 'end of geography' underlie this somewhat ambiguous concept and give rise to two discrete dimensions of the concept: (1) increasing or stretching the scope of an activity; and (2) deepening the interconnectedness of an activity (Walker and Fox 1996). In multinational corporations for example, economic activities are stretched across the world as geographical constraints recede and economic relationships intensify, in the sense of increased interconnectedness making the distinction between domestic and worldwide economic activity difficult to sustain, and creating a new global capitalist order which exercises decisive influence over the organization (Held and McGrew 2002). In brief, globalization can be thought of as 'the widening, intensifying, speeding up and growing impact of world-wide interconnectedness' (Held and McGrew, n.d.).

The cultural and technological preconditions for globalization were not in place until the late 1970s and early 1980s. Evans (1995: 258) argued that 'globalization is not a technical outcome of the development and implementation of communications and transport technologies; rather it is a social, economic, political and cultural outcome', which has radically changed the way people view, understand and engage the world in which they live. Therefore, both the technological and sociocultural structures and practices of our society had to evolve in order for globalization to take on its new meaning in the information age. With these preconditions now firmly in place, the modern meaning of globalization implies a global perspective of the particular area of study, a perspective that arises from the increased interdependence of technological advances and sociocultural changes (Dabbagh and Bannan-Ritland 2005).

Telecommunications technology has played a significant role in realizing this modern meaning of the concept, particularly with regard to distance education. Recent advances in telecommunications technology have redefined the boundaries and interactional pedagogies of a traditional or classic distance education environment by stretching its scope and deepening its interconnectedness. New learning interactions that were not perceived possible before can now be facilitated, such as the coupling of experts from around the world with novices, accessibility of global resources, the opportunity to publish to a world audience, the opportunity to take virtual field trips, the opportunity to communicate with a wider range of people, and the ability to share and compare information, negotiate meaning and co-construct knowledge (Dabbagh and Bannan-Ritland 2005). These activities emphasize learning as a function of interactions with others and with the shared tools of the community, which brings us to the second principle or concept prompting the reconceptualization of distance education: learning as a social process.

LEARNING AS A SOCIAL PROCESS AND ITS IMPACT ON DISTANCE EDUCATION

Learning can be viewed as a social process in which social interaction plays an integral part and the emphasis is on acquiring useful knowledge through enculturation (understanding how knowledge is used by a group of practitioners or members of a community). The socialization of knowledge is based on the idea that knowledge is always under construction (fluid, dynamic), taking on new meanings relative to the activity and situations in which it is being explored (Brown et al. 1989). In other words, there is a social framework or culture surrounding a learning context and its constituents are the learners, the interactions that those learners engage in, and the tools that enable those interactions. This social framework forms a learning community or a community of practice in which knowledge is shared and distributed amongst its constituents.

The concept of the social framework within which knowledge is constructed is rooted in the epistemological perspective of social constructivism. Social constructivism is largely attributed to Vygotsky's approach to developmental psychology in which he argues that children develop in social or group settings, and therefore learning is a socially mediated activity (Maddux et al. 2001). Vygotsky emphasized the critical importance of interaction with people in cognitive development, and the importance of cognitive tools that a culture gives a child to further his/her growth, such as language, cultural history and social context. Knowledge in this context is perceived as belonging to, and distributed in, communities of practice or 'environments of participation' in which the learner practices the patterns of inquiry and learning, and the use of shared resources is part of the preparation for membership in a particular community (Firdyiwek 1999). This view of knowledge is known as *distributed or situated cognition*. It is also known as cultural knowledge, social knowledge and social cognition. Rather than thinking of cognition as an isolated event that takes place inside one's head, cognition is looked at as a distributed phenomenon – one that goes beyond the boundaries of a person to include environment, artifacts, social interactions and culture (Rogers 1997; Hutchins and Hollan 1999).

In educational settings, distributed cognition is manifested in learner–instructor, learner–learner, learner–content and learner–media interactions (Moore and Kearsley 1995). These types of interaction are perceived as tools or activities that promote higher-order thinking and sustain motivation in distance education settings (Navarro and Shoemaker 2000). In Internet or Web-based enabled learning environments, distributed forms of interaction can take place in knowledge networks, virtual classrooms, telelearning and other online and e-learning contexts where groups of learners or professionals with a common goal congregate to share information and resources, ask questions, solve problems and achieve goals, and in doing so, collectively build new knowledge

and evolve the practices of their community (Dabbagh and Bannan-Ritland 2005). These learning environments are made possible by telecommunications technology which, as described earlier, is fundamentally responsible for increasing the interconnectedness and scope of interactions and activities providing a global perspective on a particular area of study.

To summarize, learning as a social process emphasizes meaningful activity through social interaction. Telecommunications technology has increased the interconnectedness of activity and interaction and stretched their scope, leading to the evolution of technological and sociocultural structures and practices of our society and the emergence of a psychological phenomenon known as globalization. Learning as a social process and globalization are inextricably linked, providing a viable thesis with which to rethink or reconceptualize distance education. In essence, the principles of learning as a social process and globalization have redefined the boundaries of distance education and possible interactional pedagogies, paving the way to a new pedagogical construct known as distributed learning.

DISTRIBUTED LEARNING

Distributed learning can be described as the deliberate organization and coordination of distributed forms of interaction and learning activities to achieve a shared goal (Dabbagh and Bannan-Ritland 2005). The following attributes apply to this pedagogical construct:

1　Globalization and learning as a social process are inherent and enabled through telecommunications technology.
2　The concept of a learning group is fundamental in achieving and sustaining learning.
3　The concept of distance is relatively unimportant or blurred, and does not necessarily imply the 'long distance' physical separation of the learner and the instructor.
4　Teaching and learning events are distributed over time and place, occurring synchronously and asynchronously using different media.
5　Learners are engaged in multiple forms of interaction, including learner–instructor, learner–learner, learner–group, learner–content and learner–media.

Distributed learning provides a new and broader perspective for approaching the implementation of distance education programmes, which are facing new trends and challenges. For example, globally, it is estimated that the number of students seeking access to higher education will grow to 97 million in 2010 and 159 million by 2025 (West 1997). This is certainly a complex challenge that higher education institutions are facing. In addition, there is a growing need for more diversified and flexible types of higher education such as lifelong learning, certification training and just-in-time learning due to new trends in student demographics and profiles, especially in countries that are changing from post-industrial to knowledge economies (Wende 2002). Distributed learning can help address these issues because it is education delivered anytime, anywhere, using a variety of media.

Distributed learning also provides the potential for a myriad of new alliances between educational institutions, businesses, foreign governments and international organizations, which can offer and use it in new and innovative ways within and across national borders (Potashnik and Capper 1998). Examples of such alliances include initiatives by the International Baccalaureate Organization, the Global Teaching and Learning Project, European SchoolNet, International Environmental Education, Institute of International Education, World Universities Network, and the World Bank's Education for the Knowledge Economy (EKE) and Education For All (EFA), to name a few. These alliances are redefining distance and international education and creating a new global market for higher and K–12 education, resulting in new pedagogical trends sometimes described as transnational education, borderless education or global e-learning (Wende 2002). This growing international clientele requires a technological infrastructure and delivery models that support the characteristics of distributed learning described above. We describe these delivery models below and provide examples in K–12 and higher education contexts.

DELIVERY MODELS AND APPLICATIONS OF DISTRIBUTED LEARNING

When Internet- or Web-based technologies such as hypermedia, multimedia, asynchronous and synchronous communication and collaboration tools, video and web conferencing tools, and course management systems, are used to support or enable distributed learning, specific delivery models or technology-driven applications result. Examples include knowledge networks, knowledge portals, tele-learning and virtual universities and classrooms. These delivery models constitute the technological infrastructure for distributed learning and span the continuum from informal learning environments that allow learners and communities to address their own self-defined need for information and knowledge, to more formal and well-defined learning environments in which the learning objectives, content and activities are explicitly defined and guided by teachers and scholars. Table 16.1 presents these delivery models and examples of implementation in K-12 (Kindergarten to Grade 12) and higher education contexts. The examples are divided into informal and formal learning environments and across and within border alliances, to provide a broad perspective of how distance education combines local requirements and international imperatives. It is important to note that these examples were researched in December 2005 and January–February 2006, and as is characteristic of the globalizing nature of the Internet, some of these examples may have evolved, moved to new locations, or become inactive by the time this chapter is published or read.

Knowledge Networks

Knowledge networks are telecommunication networks the purpose of which is to collect and disseminate information and support the production and utilization of knowledge through collaborative action. Initially formed by geographically separated higher education institutions that

Table 16.1 How schools and universities engage in distributed learning

Distributed learning delivery models	Informal learning environments		Formal learning environments	
	Knowledge networks	Knowledge portals	Telelearning	Virtual school
Across borders				
K–12	World Wise Schools	Global School Net	Epals.com Classroom Exchange	NESA (Near East South Asia Council of Overseas Schools) Virtual School project (NVS)
Higher Ed.	MERLOT: Multimedia Educational Resource for Learning and Online Teaching	Globalization and Education Portal	Horizons Virtual Seminar Series	Public Policy and Management (PPM) Masters Programme at University of York (UK)
Within borders				
K–12	Hong Kong International School's DragonNet	The Online Learning Centre (New Zealand)	Tele-Learning for Imprisoned Peoples (Austria)	The Virtual High School (VHS)
Higher Ed.	The Open University Knowledge Network (OUKN)	@Campus Mexico	TeleLearning Network of Centres of Excellence	African Virtual University (Kenya)

needed to share information, knowledge networks have evolved to include business networks, school networks and profession-oriented networks where relationships and information needs are always shifting and changing (Allee 2000). Knowledge networks are considered loose and informal learning environments because information-sharing goals are constantly evolving to meet the needs of participants. In education contexts, several *within and across borders* knowledge networks have been formed to support the learning needs of faculty, students, parents and administrators among others.

Examples – across borders

MERLOT, or Multimedia Educational Resource for Learning and Online Teaching (www.merlot.org), is an example of an across-borders knowledge network that serves an international audience and a broad knowledge area – education. MERLOT is a collection or repository of peer-reviewed online learning resources designed primarily for faculty and students of higher education and organized by specific education discipline communities (e.g., Physics, Arts, Biology, World Languages,

etc.). MERLOT's vision is to be a premiere online community where faculty, staff and students from around the world share their learning materials and pedagogy.

World Wise Schools (www.peacecorps. gov/wws/) is an example of an across-borders knowledge network for K-12 teachers and students. The network provides global access to learning materials and lesson plans, to promote cross-cultural understanding and awareness of the rich heritage and broad representations of peoples within their own communities through the experiences of Peace Corps volunteers based across the globe.

Examples – within borders

The Hong Kong International School's DragonNet (http://dragonnet.hkis.edu.hk/) is an example of a within borders K–12 knowledge network. The DragonNet community consists of the Hong Kong International School's faculty, students, parents and alumni who both access and publish information to the network. The network features newsletters, events calendar, lesson plans and online discussions. DragonNet began in 1998 and has since accumulated over 70 publishers including parents, faculty and students. These publishers are supported by a group of 11th and 12th Grade high school students called Sysops (System Operators) who administer the DragonNet.

The Open University Knowledge Network (OUKN) (kn.open.ac.uk/public/) is an example of a higher education within borders knowledge network. It is a private network where OU staff explore and share knowledge related to teaching and learning. OU staff and project teams may publish to the network and access any of the more than 1,500 web pages and thousands of documents. OUKN was developed by the Institute of Educational Technology (IET) at the UK's Open University, which provides advice on the use of modern technologies to support effective learning, particularly distance learning and e-learning in higher education.

Knowledge Portals

A knowledge portal is an information service metaphor adopted by the Internet commerce environment, public service education and media organizations to imply the legitimate aggregation of others' content into a single and simplified local entry point providing a 'safe harbor' for users in a virtual world (Vedro 1999). The concept of a knowledge portal began with search engines and web interfaces like Yahoo! Excite and Netscape, with the goal of providing information on a broad array of subjects and services and the capability to personalize the interface by users (Eisler 2000). Other descriptions of knowledge portals include a destination and launching point, a place for self-service and non-stop learning, a knowledge depot, and a gateway for access, information and learning communities.

Knowledge portals are considered informal distributed learning environments because users can access a variety of learning resources, services and communities, and can customize the portal to suit their individual information needs. Most colleges and universities are transforming their home pages to knowledge portals (also known as campus portals)

where students, faculty and administrators can accomplish a variety of tasks from a single gateway or entry point. Students can, for example, search for academic programmes, apply online, download documents and forms, register for courses, check grades, news and weather, and much more.

Examples – across borders

The Global SchoolNet (www.globalschool net.org/) portal provides access to learning materials and communities supporting and facilitating global collaboration of member schools, communities and businesses. It also provides shared access to learning materials resulting from these member collaborations. More than a million students from 45,000 schools across 194 countries have participated in Global SchoolNet since its inception.

The Globalization and Education portal (globalizationandeducation.ed.uiuc.edu/)at the University of Illinois at Urbana– Champaign is an ongoing project of multinational students enrolled in the Global Studies in Education graduate programme. In addition to serving as a gateway to resources on international education, both in the USA and abroad, the portal facilitates discussion and dialogue around issues of globalization by providing forums where site visitors can submit essays and papers and links to blogs where discussion of these topics is ongoing.

Examples – within borders

The Online Learning Centre (www.tki.org.nz/e/tki/), an initiative of the New Zealand Ministry of Education, is the country's bilingual education portal. The portal provides access to educational and curricular materials for teachers and school administrators in both English-speaking and Maori-speaking New Zealand school communities. In addition, the portal provides an online discussion forum for teachers.

@Campus Mexico (www.campusmexico.gob.mx/) is another example of a within borders portal, developed by the Mexican government. It provides information related to capacity-building, training and certification for all public service employees in Mexico. The portal supports the government's goal of moving from a hiring and promotion system based on political influence and connections, to one based on individual merit. The portal provides access to educational resources that enable all employees to further their knowledge and skills.

Telelearning

'Telelearning is making connections among persons and resources through telecommunications technologies for learning-related purposes' (Collis 1996: 9). Telelearning can include the following instructional activities: tele-access (use of online resources); virtual publishing (making class materials available for public distribution via telecommunication networks); tele-presence (the ability to use telecommunications technologies for exploratory purposes at a remote site); tele-mentoring; tele-sharing (supporting the exchange of all forms of information resources between users through telecommunications technologies); and tele-collaboration (the use of telecommunications technologies for distributed problem-solving, collaborative design and cross-classroom collaborative enquiry) (Schrum and Berenfeld 1997). Telelearning is a more formal distributed learning environment as it is usually initiated by an educational institution, school, or professional development organization and associated with credit courses, degree programmes and certification.

Examples – across borders

The Horizons Virtual Seminar Series (www.wun.ac.uk/view.php?id=1320), sponsored by the World Universities Network (WUN), is an example of across-borders telelearning. The goal of the virtual seminar series is to promote dialogue among faculty, students and postgraduates in WUN member institutions across the globe, specifically those in the USA, UK, Norway and the Netherlands. Currently, seminar series address the subject areas of Human Geography, Bioinformatics, Earth Systems Science, and Social Policy and Social Work.

Each series typically follows the academic calendar with approximately 10–12 virtual seminars held each semester. Each series is supported with a dedicated website that provides access to related educational resources and a link to the archived videostream of the event.

ePals Classroom Exchange (www.epals.com/), an Internet community of collaborative classrooms engaged in cross-cultural exchanges, project sharing and language learning, is a K–12 example of across-borders telelearning. There are over 100,000 classrooms, six million students and almost 200 countries participating in this initiative. ePals students and teachers have access to a number of collaborative technologies to support their learning activities and projects, including messaging tools, discussion boards and an instant language translator.

Examples – within borders

An example of within-borders telelearning is the TeleLearning Network of Centres of Excellence (www.telelearn.ca). In this network, an interdisciplinary research team of more than 60 faculty from the areas of education, the social sciences, computer science and engineering representing 28 Canadian universities are working with client communities to achieve the Tele Learning•NCE mission, which is to enhance and expand lifelong learning opportunities.

The Tele-Learning for Imprisoned People Development Partnership (Telfi) (www.esf.at/html-englisch/projekte/sonstiges/projektetelfi.htm) is another example of within-borders telelearning. It provides a variety of e-learning opportunities to prepare inmates in Austrian penal institutions for life on the outside after release. Key to the success of the programme was the installation of a central prison education server and server platform that comply with the security requirements of the individual prisons.

Virtual classroom

A virtual classroom is a formal distributed learning environment. It resembles a classroom environment with the absence of face-to-face interaction. 'Students in the virtual classroom share their thoughts with professors and classmates, using computers and software that enables them to send and receive messages, interact with professors and classmates, read and comment on lecture material, take tests, and receive feedback without having to attend scheduled classes' (Hiltz 1990: 133).

Examples – across borders

The NESA (Near East South Asia Council of Overseas Schools) Virtual School project (NVS) (http://nesacenter.org) is a collaborative effort between NESA and the US state Department's Office of Overseas Schools (A/OS). The goal of this project is to provide a powerful vehicle for students and teachers to learn about and benefit from an online academic environment. Currently there are 12 NESA member schools participating and other NESA member schools are being invited to join the consortium. NVS utilizes the Blackboard learning management system, which allows each participating school to create its own informational portal page that provides access to online courses, learning resources, virtual science fairs and other synchronous and asynchronous educational events.

The Public Policy and Management (PPM) Masters programme at York University in the UK (www.york.ac.uk/depts/spsw/ gsp/ mappm.html) is an example of a higher education virtual classroom delivery model. To achieve its goal of providing a global, international and comparative perspective in the programme, PPM courses were developed by a multinational team, consisting of five US scholars and two UK scholars. This international perspective is also reflected in the programme enrolment, which includes more than 100 students from 25 countries. The programme is delivered online and asynchronously using the Moodle (moodle.org) open source course management system.

Examples – within borders

The Virtual High School (VHS) (www.govhs. org) is an example of a K–12 virtual classroom delivery model. VHS is a collaborative effort where high schools from all over the United States participate and offer courses online. VHS was made possible in part by the US Department of Education, and in the 2000–2001 school year more than 150 schools and 3,000 students participated. A VHS course, known as a NetCourse, is a course in which all learning activities occur online primarily asynchronously using computer conferencing or bulletin board systems (Riel and Harasim 1994). Up to 20 students can enrol in a VHS NetCourse and the participants can be from all over the country, creating a learning environment that is content-rich, diverse and collaborative.

The African Virtual University (AVU) (www.avu.org/default.asp) is an example of a higher education virtual classroom delivery model deployed within the borders of the African continent. AVU, which began as a project of the World Bank, seeks to build capacity and support economic development in Africa by providing world-class quality education and training programmes to students and professionals in Africa. Based in Kenya, AVU has 47 learning centres in 27 African countries. AVU partners with universities across the world to develop courses for delivery to African students, professionals and civil servants through the AVU network and the WebCT learning management system. Teaching methods include a blend of online and in-class learning and flexible delivery systems, combining e-learning, discussions with onsite facilitators, web seminars and video broadcasts.

CONCLUSION

Distance education has significantly changed over the years from a social, pedagogical and technological perspective (Dabbagh 2004). Advances in telecommunications technology coupled with the growing, diversifying and worldwide demand for higher education have challenged traditional teaching practices and pedagogies and created an international market for education. Globalization and learning as a social process have prompted a rethinking of distance education and instantiated the need for a broader and more flexible conceptual framework to address the demands of this global market. This chapter described a pedagogical model or framework, distributed learning, which can be used to guide the broader practice of education within and across national borders. Distributed learning is transforming K–12 and higher education to learning communities that act as academic and social support structures for multicultural and multinational education. The chapter also provided examples of distributed learning delivery models including knowledge networks, knowledge portals, telelearning and virtual classrooms and universities. The authors acknowledge that these examples are but a snapshot in time of the myriad of across- and within-borders applications of distributed learning. A more comprehensive review would consult multilingual resources and would be ongoing. The global market for education is leading to new educational trends sometimes described as transnational education, border-less education, global e-learning, flexible learning, open learning and others. As these trends continue to emerge, their practical implications will need to be examined and new learning theories and models will be needed to capture these developments.

ACKNOWLEDGEMENT

Parts of this chapter appeared in Dabbagh, N. and Bannan-Ritland, B. (2005) *Online Learning: Concepts, Strategies, and Application*. Upper Saddle River, NJ: Merrill/Prentice Hall.

REFERENCES

Allee, V. (2000) Knowledge networks and communities of practice. *OD Practitioner,* 32(4): 4–13.

Brown, J.S., Collins, A. and Duguid, P. (1989) Situated cognition and the culture of learning. *Educational Researcher,* 18(1): 32–42.

Collis, B. (1996). *Tele-learning in a Digital World.* Boston, MA: International Thompson Computer Press.

Dabbagh, N. (2004) Distance learning: emerging pedagogical issues and learning designs. *Quarterly Review of Distance Education,* 5(1): 37–49.

Dabbagh, N. and Bannan-Ritland, B. (2005) *Online Learning: Concepts, Strategies, and Application.* Upper Saddle River, NJ: Pearson Prentice-Hall.

Duning, B., Van Kekerix, M. and Zabrowski, L. (1993) *Reaching Learners through Telecommunications.* San Francisco, CA: Jossey–Bass.

Eisler, D.L. (2000) The portal's progress: a gateway for access, information, and learning communities. *Syllabus,* 14(2): 12–18.

Evans, T. (1995) Globalisation, post-Fordism and open and distance education. *Distance Education,* 16(2): 256–69.

Firdyiwek, Y. (1999) Web-based courseware tools: where is the pedagogy? *Educational Technology,* 39(1): 29–34.

Galusha, J.M. (1997) Barriers to learning in distance education. *Interpersonal Computing and Technology Journal,* 5(3–4): 6–14.

Hanson, D., Maushak, N.J., Schlosser, C.A., Anderson, M.L., Sorensen, C. and Simonson, M. (1997) *Distance Education: Review of the Literature,* 2nd edition. Bloomington, IN: Association for Educational Communications and Technology.

Held, D. and McGrew, A. (n.d.) Globalization: Entry for Oxford companion to politics. In D. Held, A. McGrew, D. Goldblatt and J. Perraton (eds) *Global Transformations.* Retrieved from www.polity.co.uk/global/globocp.htm (23 January 2004).

Held, D. and McGrew, A. (2002) *Globalization/Anti-globalization.* Cambridge: Polity Press.

Hiltz, S.R. (1990) Evaluating the virtual classroom. In L. Harasim (ed.) *Online Education: Perspectives on a New Environment.* New York: Praeger, pp. 133–83.

Hutchins, E. and Hollan, J. (1999) *COGSCI: Distributed Cognition Syllabus.* Retrieved from http://hci.ucsd.edu/131/syllabus/index.html (14 November 1999).

Maddux, C.D., Johnson, D. and Willis, J.W. (2001) *Educational computing: Learning with Tomorrow's Technologies,* 3rd edition. Needham Heights, MA: Allyn and Bacon.

Moore, M.G. (1994) Autonomy and interdependence. *American Journal of Distance Education,* 8(2): 1–5.

Moore, M.G. and Kearsley, G. (1995) *Distance Education: A Systems View.* Belmont, CA: Wadsworth.

Navarro, P. and Shoemaker, J. (2000) In M.G. Moore and G.T. Cozine (eds) *Web-based Communications, the Internet and Distance Education.* University Park, PA: The American Center for the Study of Distance Education, The Pennsylvania State University, pp. 1–15.

Picciano, A.G. (2001) *Distance Learning: Making Connections across Virtual Space and Time.* Upper Saddle River, NJ: Merrill/Prentice Hall.

Potashnik, M. and Capper, J. (1998) Distance education: growth and diversity. *Finance & Development,* 35(1): 42–5.

Riel, M. and Harasim, L. (1994) Research perspectives on network learning. *Journal of Machine-Mediated Learning,* 4(2–3): 91–114.

Rogers, Y. (1997) A brief introduction to distributed cognition. Retrieved from www.cogs.susx.ac.uk/users/yvonner/dcog.html (8 November 1999).

Schlosser, L.A. and Simonson, M. (2003) Distance education: *Towards a Definition and Glossary of Terms.* Retrieved from www.aect.org/Intranet/ Publications/ Disted/Disted.asp.

Schrum, L. (1999) Trends in distance learning: lessons to inform practice. *Educational Media & Technology Yearbook,* 24: 11–16.

Schrum, L. and Berenfeld, B. (1997) *Teaching and Learning in the Information Age.* Boston, MA: Allyn and Bacon.

Vedro, S.R. (1999) Toward the knowledge portal: public broadcasting and university continuing education in the Internet age. *Technos,* 8 (4): 1–5.

Walker, G.R. and Fox, M.A. (1996). *Globalization: An Analytical Framework.* Indiana Journal of Global Legal Studies, 3 (2): 375–412.

Wedemeyer, C.A. (1981) *Learning at the Back Door: Reflections on Nontraditional Learning in the Lifespan.* Madison, WI: University of Wisconsin Press.

Wende, M.C. van der (2002) The role of US higher education in the global e-learning market. *Center for Studies in Higher Education, University of California, Berkeley, eScholarship Repository.* Retrieved from http://repositories.cdlib.org/cshe/CSHE1-02 (16 July 2006).

West, R. (1997) Review of higher education financing and policy. *Report of the West Review.* Canberra: Department of Education, Training and Youth Affairs.

17

The Future of E-learning in International Education: Issues, Challenges and Lessons from the Past Two Decades

Lucas Walsh

From developments in mass transportation through to the use of the World Wide Web for distance education, technology continues to play a significant role in shaping international education by extending the possibility for teaching and learning and the exchange of people and ideas across geographic and cultural borders. The rate of technological development and diffusion has been so intense during the past 30 years that it is difficult to forecast the future impact of information and communication technologies (ICTs) on international education.

In the so-called 'age of the BlackBerry', there are numerous innovative uses of current technologies, such as mobile cellphones, Personal Digital Assistants, Text-Messaging, blogging, podcasting and other modes of communicating to extend teaching and learning. However, there is no systematic or extensive use of these recent technologies specifically to further international education so it is difficult to suggest that any one of these will assume greater significance during the next few

decades. It is simply too soon to tell and the temptation to place too much significance on current trends in the technical development of ICTs must be resisted at this point.

Notwithstanding the point just made, there are some lessons from the recent use of ICTs in education that provide considerable insight into the major challenges to the progress of international education over the next 20–30 years. In international education, the impact of globalization is most visibly manifest in the flows of students and knowledge across territories. Political and economic interdependence facilitated by globalized media have on the one hand enabled greater intercultural awareness and mobility of students; on the other hand, the uneven and market-driven development of ICTs in education during the past two decades highlights how these media can also facilitate cultural homogeneity and compromise the quality of teaching and learning in international education.

This chapter reflects on some of the key issues that are likely to arise from the use of

ICTs in international education in the future. Rather than focus on the impact of technological innovation, this chapter explores how, based on recent developments, the use of ICTs in international education will continue to be shaped by economic globalization. The central question for this chapter is: what can international educators learn from the use of ICTs in both national and international education from the past two decades? Case studies and examples from the period are used to illustrate some key lessons that will continue to have relevance for the future use of technology to facilitate international education, with particular emphasis on the cultural implications of ICT-use for teaching and learning. The final part of the discussion explores some broader issues arising from the digital divide and the importance of developing technological literacies in both teachers and students.

ICTs, GLOBALIZATION AND E-LEARNING

During the past 15 years, use of the Internet for 'electronically mediated learning' – or e-learning – has developed dramatically. Characterized by the use of electronic media, such as the Internet, CD-ROM, e-mail, interactive television, satellite, video and other delivery methods, there is no agreed definition of 'e-learning'. The term is widely used to describe any learning undertaken through electronic delivery. The following discussion will focus on the development and use of the Internet.

At the outset it will be important to clarify the distinction between a number of commonly used terms. *Distance education* involves 'the provision of programs of study which provide both content and support services to students who rarely, if ever, attend for face-to-face teaching or for on-campus access to educational facilities' (Cunningham et al. 1998: 23). Students have typically chosen distance education because on-campus education is impractical for them due to geography, work and family commitments (Ryan 1998: 17). This form of e-learning is delivered through electronic media, such as the Internet, radio and television. *Flexible learning* 'implies the same concept of student choice of modes of delivery of instructional material ... with a higher emphasis on the use of multimedia/communications technologies. It is operationalised as a mixture of face-to-face teaching (often in "block" or intensive periods) and independent learning, typically utilising computer-based supplementary teaching materials'. Flexible learning 'implies a focus on the core activity of education, the learning process in the individual student, and student choice regarding the methods employed in that process' (Cunningham et al. 1998: 24). *Open learning* is conventionally applied to 'an organisational approach which ... permits students, irrespective of previous credentials, to enrol in programs of study characterised by an element of student choice in relation to time, place and pace of study, and ideally in relation to mode of learning (i.e. by print, audiovisual, etc.); it may thus incorporate a mixture of face-to-face and electronically-mediated learning experiences'. Open learning has tended to take place in the form of off-campus delivery of learning modules, often to the workplace (Cunningham et al. 1998: 23).

THE DEVELOPMENT OF E-LEARNING IN HIGHER EDUCATION DURING THE 1990s

Growth in e-learning has been largely driven by the higher education, vocational training and professional development sectors in the English-speaking 'West'. E-learning is often promoted to overcome practical limitations of time and space. The Internet, for example, allows for the overcoming of spatial restrictions on educational delivery to enable courses to be studied by any student, at any time, from anywhere in the world. It has created opportunities and challenges for international education providers as means for enabling distance education and other modes of flexible and open learning online.

A number of virtual universities emerged during the 1990s that delivered courses online without a conventional home campus. Institutions such as the University of Phoenix and the Western Governors University saw the Internet as a way of facilitating a less regulated higher education market. The Western Governors University sought to 'expand the marketplace for instructional materials, courseware, and programs utilizing advanced technology', as well as 'identify and remove barriers to the free functioning of these markets, particularly barriers posed by statutes, policies, and administrative rules and regulations' (Noble 1998: 361). Similarly, in other parts of the world, such as Australia, there was a growth in various Web-based tertiary courses servicing a global educational market (West 1998). Given that education in Australia had by 2004 become the eighth largest export industry (Reid and Loxton 2004), the incentive to develop and market transnational courses for distance, open and flexible delivery is significant. Australia is by no means an isolated example.

Much of the early software for e-learning was developed through collaborations between university and software developers and then sold to other universities. There continues to be a huge market for these products, particularly in response to the growth of online courses in North America. Learning management software enable students to access materials; teaching tools and learning objects online via browsers, such as WebCT (www.webct.com) and Blackboard (www.blackboard.com), are examples of these kinds of products, all of which seek to standardize online course development and simplify ICT support and training at the deliverer's end.

The adoption of ICTs to facilitate the transnational delivery of international education is fundamentally tied to broader processes of globalization. The intensive rate of adoption is integrally linked to internationalization as a necessary adjustment to 'new realities' brought about by the globalization of the world economy, a growing interdependence of nations enmeshed by new information and communications technologies in interconnected 'knowledge industries' and 'world best practice' in the global market place. In countries such as Australia, internationalization has often been in response to the 'communications revolution' and knowledge-intensive information economy (Australia TAFE International 1996).

The main motivation for distance, flexible and open learning during the 1990s was not student demand but interest from educational providers, who believed that new technologies would allow them to reach distant students and introduce greater economies of scale to the 'production' of education. By the late 1990s, more than 50 per cent of American universities offered online courses. One US Department of Education project anticipated over one million online courses in 1999; however, enrolment rates for these online courses did not match expectations (Shrivastava 1999). Nevertheless, the expansion of online courses internationally has been tremendous. There is scarcely a university that is not seeking to make its courses available to fee-paying students as part of a revenue-raising strategy. Financial motivations continue to drive the development of ICTs in international education and impact on the nature and quality of teaching and learning in significant ways.

ICTs, LEARNING AND PEDAGOGY: THE CHALLENGES OF CULTURAL DIFFERENCE

Online courses use a combination of Web pages, video and audio files, e-mail, asynchronous and synchronous chat. The communicative capacity of online education has enabled geographically dispersed students to have more social interaction with their 'virtual' classmates than older forms of distance education, facilitating (in theory) the creation of online communities of independent learners. Notions of independent learning underpinning the use of ICTs in education are significant to this discussion.

In 1999, a colleague and I interviewed lecturers and senior administrators throughout South East Asia on the cultural impact of ICTs on higher education, such as the Internet, in a new area of e-learning: the virtual university, in which the vast majority of learning took place via the Internet and CD-ROM (Ziguras 2000). A senior manager of one such virtual university provided insight into how students with different learning styles were expected to adapt to the model of independent learning required when studying off-campus and online. When asked if it would be safe to say that many students prior to entering this university are accustomed to more teacher-centred, didactic pedagogies from their earlier schooling, the director concurred. When it was suggested that given the Western model of independent learning adopted by this virtual university, many of these students may face difficulty adjusting to the self-guided learning required in this e-learning environment, he responded (without hesitation) that this was not a problem because the first CD-ROM the students received 'taught' them how to learn independently. The assumptions behind this highly problematic approach to online learning and reliance on technology raise serious questions about the pedagogical and learning assumptions underlying this use of e-learning across different cultural settings.

Just as European models of classroom education were used across various cultures during the colonial era, Western models of e-learning are often applied to different societies with little thought of the cultural compatibility of their pedagogical frameworks or content. This globalization of educational delivery has involved a process whereby the cultural specificity of educational content has been removed in order to make a course universally applicable and marketable. Many online courses have been offered internationally but not modified to suit the local sites of delivery. Educational providers have instead aimed to make their courses less reliant on local conditions and more attractive to international students. Cultural diversity is often unacknowledged and treated unproblematically in e-learning design and content. Most e-learning frameworks and software packages tend to be developed in the English language (often originating in North America). Implicit in many of these 'globalized' courses are Western models of learning. The success of global distance

education in the 1990s relied on 'developing curriculum that is relevant to learners wherever they happen to reside' and which 'transcend[s] local cultural and language barriers' (Bates and de los Santos 1997: 49). The cultural impact of this approach to distance learning has a number of significant features.

The University of the South Pacific (USP) is an example of an explicitly multicultural institution that adopted a model of distance education in which cultural differences were treated superficially. During the 1990s, USP developed a large distance education programme, with more than 5,000 students spread across numerous countries, islands, languages, cultures, population sizes, economies and educational systems. Courses were delivered in English to students, a high portion of whom were public servants (whose studies were rewarded with promotions), female domestic workers and some school leavers (Thaman 1997). The head of USP's School of Humanities at the time, Konai Helu Thaman, observed that 'in the context of USP, the cultural backgrounds of learners are seldom taken into consideration either in course design or in the actual teaching or learning process' (Thaman 1997: 29). Attention to local cultures and values was 'confined to special customs and traditions manifested in song and dance; they may be useful for tourism purposes but are bad for education and business development'. Thaman further argued that education providers failed to understand that 'the mode of teaching and learning associated with distance education, like schooling in the 19th century, is, by and large, alien to most Pacific cultures. Pacific people traditionally learned from one another, through their interaction. The teacher–learner relationship was an intimate one where observation and imitation were basic means of learning' (p. 30). In classroom teaching, students had little concept of independent learning. This pedagogical clash of cultures was exacerbated by a taboo in Pacific cultures of questioning elders (Wah 1997). The lack of attention to local cultures, she argued, was evident in the educational content as well as the pedagogic model implicit in the framework:

In relation to the content of most distant education courses at our university, few are written with Pacific cultures in mind and fewer still incorporate elements of Pacific cultures – knowledge, skills and values – of the students' home cultures ... There is an urgent need for those responsible for preparing and delivering distance education courses for students in Pacific island countries to recognise the value of Pacific cultures to the people of the region. In the current euphoria to globalise educational opportunities and sell education, using whatever means possible, to more people in different parts of the globe, distance educators have often fallen into improvisation which, besides doing irreparable damage to the target population, may also make future educational innovations more difficult. (Thaman 1997: 31–4).

ICTs, cultural difference and independent learning

Another example is the development of distance learning in Indonesian higher education. During the 1980s, the Universitas Terbuka attempted to import a Western model of distance education based on the UK's Open University. This model assumed that its learners were autonomous, self-directed students experienced in independent, text-based learning, despite the fact that Indonesian culture is strongly orally based and 'heteronomous', in the sense that individual difference is frowned upon while learning by emulation and conformity is rewarded. In educational terms, this means that students unquestioningly absorb the information provided to them by teachers (Dunbar 1991). Traditionally, examination was largely conducted by multiple-choice questionnaires and students were not expected to do independent research or critically evaluate course materials. As an oral culture, Indonesian society emphasizes face-to-face interaction in groups whereas reading and writing are not widely practised, despite improving rates of literacy. These cultural factors meant that students experienced difficulty learning within the Western distance model underpinning this mode of distance education, which used text-based materials within an independent learning framework. In its first decade, distance learning at Universitas

Terbuka was seen to be a failure. The model had little appeal to either students or lecturers, who were themselves educated in a very different cultural milieu (Dunbar 1991).

ICTs, cultural difference and the Confucian Heritage Model

Kelly and Ha (1998) contrast the Western model of independent learning underlying these distance modes to another approach to teaching and learning in Asia: the Chinese 'Confucian Heritage Cultures'. This approach to education in Hong Kong is a step-by-step approach in which the initial stages of learning strongly draw upon memorization through repetition (Ziguras 1999). The teacher, under this Confucian model, decides how much information to give to the students for further exploration and analysis, which differs from the Western model in which students are encouraged to experiment and explore first, then develop a deeper understanding of the subject at hand (Kelly and Ha 1998; Ziguras 1999). Kelly and Ha contrast the role of the Asian teacher with the conventional Western approach:

We can see clear differences between the Chinese and Western teachers in their interpretation of how educational goals are achieved and the attributes of effective teachers, as well as a marked conflict between the academic goals of most teachers and the more vocationally oriented goals of students. Clearly though the style of teaching adopted by Chinese teachers of working step-by-step through the subject, paying individual attention to students and personalizing the relationship with students was more consistent with students' evaluation of effective teachers than the 'professional' but more distant approach of the Western teachers ... The esteem in which teachers are held and the uniquely close relationship between Chinese teachers and students ... can influence the attitudes of potential students and employers towards distance education as a valid mode of study per se. (Kelly and Ha 1998: 29–30)

Consequently, this mode of e-learning has been implemented differently in Hong Kong, maintaining a central role for the teacher. The Web has been used deliberately as a way of disseminating printed course material, while e-mail has been used to facilitate teacher–student communication.

It is important that the future use of ICTs to facilitate international education not only uses cultural diversity as a resource, but also deliberately considers its implications for any teaching and learning that take place online (Salmon 2000). During the past several years a more informed awareness of different methods of learning via the Internet has emerged, along with the development of educational strategies encouraging students to reflect on how they learn, what their particular learning skills are and how to adapt their preferred learning style to the Web (Collis 1999; Collis and Moonen 2001). For international education providers, the relationship between students' uses of ICT and cultural differences needs to be reconsidered in a more dynamic way. This includes an understanding of how difference works relationally through the structural operations of e-learning in, for example, the design of websites and software, time allocation, practices of assessment and pedagogy, which ascribe privilege to certain values while marginalizing others. The problem in a global environment is not that students are different, but that educators sometimes find it difficult to 'read' difference (Rizvi and Walsh 1998). As a result, some differences are sometimes overlooked when they should not be and, on other occasions, they are seen to make more of a difference than they should. In order to avoid devaluation and potential erosion of local cultures, the use of ICTs in international education must have scope to incorporate local cultures into the curriculum, as well as the teaching and learning frameworks implicit in its use.

Developing appropriate models of teaching and learning for online delivery will continue to be one of the great challenges to international educators. In the case of distance learning it is important to remember that the actual study experience is relatively isolated. Students must be self-motivated, self-directed learners (Cunningham et al. 1998). This model of independent learning has not been successful for many students. For example, some distance students at Franklin University in the US found that they were really not independent learners, and that they needed the social interaction of the classroom to be able to physically engage people (e.g. to observe body language). Distance education research has shown that students prefer to study on campus (McVay 1998). The point here is that where international education providers seek to make available opportunities for study and access to resources via ICTs, it is important that the full utility of the media is exploited based on the needs of the learners rather than using a given medium for its own sake.

The benefits of mixed modes of e-learning

The best uses of e-learning at present employ a blend of online teaching and learning resources with other media, such as printed hard copy, and with face-to-face classroom activities – and this combination of modalities will continue to be important in the future development of international education. ICTs will be best used to extend existing teaching and learning environments, to add value to that which teachers already do well. As Ziguras and Rizvi (2001: 162) point out:

> Transnational education providers need to remember that the habitual ways of teaching and learning are resilient not because they are the most effective means of 'delivering information' but because of the richness of the learning relationships that are developed through ongoing face-to-face interaction. The future of international online education will be determined by the extent to which the Internet is able to enrich and internationalize these face-to-face relationships.

As with any face-to-face learning, much of the educational value of e-learning lies in the cognitive and adaptable approaches to learning underpinning the use of the technology. It has been rightly pointed out that 'the greatest impact ... on the quality of the students' learning resides in the way a technology is used and not in the characteristics of the medium itself' (Inglis et al. 2000). Nevertheless, to extend the now clichéd observation of Marshall McLuhan, the medium will continue to shape the message, and what remains significant for international education is the question of how the medium shapes the learner. There is a cautionary example of how a group of learners in northern Brazil, whose classes were broadcast via television, was convinced that a triangle had curved sides because they were viewing it through a malfunctioning TV. The one student who initially disagreed (using the very principles of geometry they were studying) eventually relented to social pressure to agree with fellow students (Tiffin and Rajasingham 1995: 95).

ICTs AND THE PRIVATIZATION OF EDUCATION

Another area of significance to international education concerns the role of private corporate interests in the development and provision of ICT architecture, infrastructure and e-learning tools. During the past three decades, problems of space, storage, time and teacher–learner ratios have provided the impetus for educationalists to seek new technological solutions to these problems of scarcity. The use of ICTs to facilitate distance learning is promoted as a viable technological alternative (Tiffin and Rajasingham 1995: 74–88). It is argued that distance learning 'liberates' public education from the limitations of time and space because students are no longer dependent on institutions being open at fixed times and there are no physical restrictions on the size and number of students (Tiffin and Rajasingham 1995: 15–16). Arguing that millions of fee-paying students would finance the best research and facilities, Tiffin and Rajasingham ask:

> Is this to do to learning what McDonald's did to eating? Are we talking about 'hamburgerising' how we teach and franchising the facilitation of education? Where skills and knowledge are not embedded in a cultural matrix, as for example in mathematics and science, why not develop

instruction as a product that is easy to deliver and digest and appeals to the taste of learners around the world? (1995: 166–7)

The socioeconomic effects of commercialization on education are an an ongoing concern for educators in general (Kozol 1993; Cope and Kalantzis 1997), and the provision of technological resources in particular – from school PCs to search engines – will continue to be an issue while educational institutions are exposed to market pressures. In the USA, for example, commercial interests have taken advantage of this gap in technological access and expertise, which has been exacerbated by cuts to government funding of public schooling. A disturbing example from within the US national education system is the 'Burger King Academy'. By 1993, 'Burger King Academies' were established in at least 14 US cities. These fully accredited, quasi-private high schools were provided with extensive technological resources, such as television satellite dishes, but at a price: every day, over 90 per cent of the 8 million students (and their teachers) had to sit through at least 90 per cent of a news programme provided by an advertising company, Whittle Communications, which included advertising by such corporate giants as Snickers and Burger King (Kozol 1993: 9; Berman 1992: 10–11). This advertising was by contract required viewing for those schools' students. At the time, Whittle Communications invested over $300 million in 40 per cent of the American Education System. 'It's open season on marketing', said the corporation's president (Cole-Adams 1993: 52). By the mid-1990s, Whittle Communications had collapsed; however, the company's attempt to use technology to exploit a marketing opportunity serves as an interesting cautionary tale of the dangers of multinational corporate intervention in education – particularly at a time when education funding is increasingly scarce, and when basic ICT resources, such as Internet search engines, basic software and operating systems, are increasingly dominated by a relatively few commercial developers (e.g. Google and Microsoft).

BRIDGING THE DIGITAL DIVIDE: DEVELOPING TECHNOLOGICAL LITERACY

An ongoing issue for ICT use in international education is the so-called 'digital divide'. The digital divide is characterized by a lack of digital skills, inadequate access to computers and networks, insufficient user-friendliness and lack of opportunities for the use of media by people across the developing and developed world (Hacker and van Dijk 2000: 9). While there has recently been a push to move away from the notion of a digital divide towards a more inclusive discourse (Muir 2004; Annan 2005), the challenge for providing digital skills and resources continues to be significant – with important implications to students, teachers, curriculum development and research in international education.

Developing digital literacy in students, teachers and the curriculum

The first area concerns the development of digital literacies amongst students, to enable them to navigate and use the vast resources created by computer networks. In a poem written in 1934, T.S. Eliot asks 'Where is the wisdom we have lost in knowledge? Where is the knowledge we have lost in information?' (Eliot 1963: 161). Though written decades before the Internet, it is a question that has heightened significance in the information age. The challenge for international educators is to develop in their students (and teachers) the technological literacies to be able to access, navigate and reflect critically on the ways in which electronic media, such as television and the Internet, are used in classrooms, homes and other spheres of life. As a cluster of processes, values and strategies, internationalization has became firmly enmeshed in technological change. In the context of this development, educators rightly ask: how will students acquire the internationalized skills and knowledge contemporary life requires (Whalley 1997)? For example, the

materials available on the Internet are not subject to the same type of selection as materials in libraries, so rather than simply accessing this information, students need critical skills which enable them to situate the information within a broader intellectual, social and moral field. These skills are necessary not only to navigate the Web, but also e-learning software in general. For example, Sherry Turkle highlights the need to make students more critically aware of the values underlying both technology and e-learning materials (Turkle 1997).

The role of the teacher, the second area, is significant here. In e-learning, there is a danger in underestimating and devaluing the role of the teacher in providing, facilitating and guiding students through strategies in which information is converted to knowledge. The key to this process of conversion is making connections between ideas, places, cultures and people. The mass media today are so ubiquitous that the need to provide young people with the critical skills to evaluate and navigate the sensory assault of information is crucial in both e-learning environments and everyday life. Nevertheless, as today's 'media savvy' students become tomorrow's educators, teachers will reclaim a degree of control of learning environments in which ICT plays an important role.

The third area of relevance to international educators concerns the international curriculum. At the 2005 World Summit on the Information Society, UN Secretary-General Kofi Annan asked: 'What do we mean by an "information society"? We mean one in which human capacity is expanded, built up, nourished and liberated, by giving people access to the tools and technologies they need, with the education and training to use them effectively' (Annan 2005). It is argued that 'In the Information Age … [t]here is no longer any "canon", and universities should therefore concentrate on simply teaching students how to learn, and how to access this information-rich environment rather than focussing on content' (West et al. 1998: 46). Fazal Rizvi and I have suggested that universities, for example, need to develop new literacies and learning spaces that are relevant to the emerging challenges of globalisation. As universities increasingly adapt to competitive corporate environments in which cost-effectiveness is an integral aspect of on-going development, they have realised that a careful re-examination of the goals of curriculum development is required if higher education is to prepare students, teachers and citizens for the global environments of the approaching millennium. (Rizvi and Walsh 1998: 7)

Following from the discussion earlier, ICTs will continue to facilitate engagements by students with culture difference both within and beyond conventional spaces of learning (e.g. student exchange programmes). It must become more than just a response to emergent global conditions; the development of e-learning tools needs to incorporate a framework of values and practices that raise awareness and appreciation of cultural differences as the basis for developing the necessary skills and literacies for a changing world.

The ongoing challenge of access

There are other broader related issues that will be of significance to international educators, particularly to researchers. Access to information is of particular significance to international education research. Recent initiatives such as *CopyLeft*, the Budapest Open Access Initiative, the Berlin Declaration, Creative Commons and the Open Courseware Initiative highlight the importance of ensuring that there is open access of knowledge and the preservation of intellectual freedom with respect to intellectual property and cultural diversity in all media. Following on from the discussion of corporate domination of ICT development above, the danger of multinational corporate domination and/or monopolization of software and hardware markets is particularly significant. (Efforts by Web search giant Google to censor its China site in collaboration with government efforts to control the Internet is another useful warning in this regard.) As information and communication technologies continue to intensify transnational flows of cultural commodities, texts, images and artefacts, as well as ideas, ideologies and values

(Cunningham et al. 1998; International Monetary Fund 1997), there will be an ongoing technical challenge to develop digital infrastructure and services that are interoperable and as widely accessible as possible.

CONCLUSION

Characterized by twin forces of mass migration and electronic mediation, globalization will continue to intensify the fluid experience of 'global life' (Appadurai 1996). For international education providers, it is important to understand the central role that economic globalization will continue to play in enframing the flexible delivery, distance and other forms of e-learning.

One of the main drivers of e-learning in international education will continue to be revenue. So much of its development during the past two decades has been motivated by economic imperatives. Online study in tertiary education is still regarded as highly profitable. Regrettably, teaching and learning have often appeared to be after-thoughts in this market-driven and technology-led paradigm. For example, concern has been expressed that encouraging virtual mobility might become a 'cost-cutting substitute' for actual mobility. The Higher Education Information System of Germany (1995) has argued that physical and virtual mobility should ideally exist in a reciprocal relationship as two approaches to internationalization. Other current issues will continue to pose significant challenges to the transnational delivery of online courses, such as accreditation, certification and quality assurance.

But of central importance to this discussion is the engagement of cultural differences through international education. Exposure to new ideas, new cultures and new markets through international education and mass media will continue to expand awareness of diversity and cultural differences. On the other hand, driving much of the development of ICTs in international education is the very real propensity of globalization to promote cultural homogeneity. The main risk is that flexible learning technologies will facilitate further the removal of cultural specificity in order to make a transnational study more universally marketable and available on a global scale. A challenge faced by international educators will be to ensure that the quality of teaching and learning is not compromised by technological development that is either purely driven by the technology or financial interests or, worst of all, both, as the case of the Burger King Academy described above illustrates. Relevant here is an often-cited quote posted on the Internet over a decade ago:

> In 1884 Samuel F.B. Morse sent a message [the first by electric telegraph] from Washington to Baltimore asking: 'What hath God wrought?' The question remains unanswered … (Gehl and Douglas 1994)

REFERENCES

Annan, K. (2005) Statement by H.E. Mr Kofi Annan, Secretary-General of the United Nations, World Summit on the Information Society, Tunis, 16 November 2005 at www.itu.int/wsis/tunis/statements/docs/io-un-opening/1.html (accessed 10 February 2006).

Appadurai, A. (1996) *Modernity at Large: Dimensions of Cultural Globalisation.* Minneapolis: University of Minnesota Press.

Australia TAFE International (ATI) (1996) *Guidelines for Australian TAFE Institutions: A National Framework for the Internationalisation of Australian TAFE.* Queensland: Australia TAFE International and the Australian National Training Authority.

Bates, A.W. and de los Santos, J.G.E. (1997) Crossing boundaries: making global distance education a reality. *Journal of Distance Education,* 12(1–2): 49–66.

Berman, E.H. (1992) The political economy of education reform in the 1990s. *Education and Society,* 10(2): 3–14.

Cole-Adams, K. (1993) Soft sell goes to school. *Time Magazine (Australia),* 15 November 46: 2–5.

Collis, B. (1999) Designing for differences: cultural issues in the design of WWW-based course-support sites. *British Journal of Educational Technology,* 30(3): 201–15.

Collis, B. and Moonen, J. (2001) *Flexible Learning in a Digital World.* London: Kogan Page.

Cope, B. and Kalantzis, M. (1997) Facing our educational futures. *Education Australia Magazine,* Issue 37, July.

Cunningham, S., Tapsall, S., Ryan, Y. Stedman, L., Bagdon, K. and Flew, T. (1998) *New Media and Borderless Education: A Review of the Convergence between Global Media Networks and Higher Education Provision.* Canberra: Australian Government Publishing Service.

Dunbar, R. (1991) Adapting distance education for Indonesians: problems with learner heteronomy and a strong oral tradition. *Distance Education* 12(2): 163–74.

Eliot, T.S. (1963) The Eagle Soars in the Summit of Heaven, in *Choruses from 'The Rock'* (1934). In *Collected Poems, 1909–1962.* London: Faber and Faber.

Gehl, J. and Douglas S. (1994) *Edupage,* at www.ee.surrey.ac.uk/Contrib/Edupage/1994/06/14-06-1994.html (accessed 17 September 2004).

Hacker, K.L. and van Dijk, J. (eds) (2000) *Digital Democracy: Issues of Theory and Practice.* London: Sage.

Higher education Information System (Germany) 1995. *Gearing Up for Europe via Student Mobility and the Internationalisation of Study.* September 1995, at http://www.eaie.nl.

Inglis, A., Ling, P. and Joosten, V. (2000) *Delivering Digitally.* London: Kogan Page.

International Monetary Fund (1997) *World Economic Outlook, 1998.* Washington, DC: International Monetary Fund.

Kelly, M.E. and Ha, T.S. (1998) Borderless education and teaching and learning cultures: the case of Hong Kong. *Australian Universities' Review,* 1: 26–33.

Kozol, J. (1993) The sharks move in. *New Internationalist,* No. 248 (October): 8–10.

McVay, M. (1998) *How to be a Successful Distance Student.* Posting to DEOS-L – The Distance Education Online Symposium, <DEOS-L@LISTS.PSU.EDU>.

Muir, K. (2004) *Connecting Communities with CTLCs: From the Digital Divide to Social Inclusion.* Report by the Smith Family (June). Sydney, Australia.

Noble, D.F. (1998) Digital diploma mills: the automation of higher education. *Science as Culture,* 7(3): 355–68.

Reid, A. and Loxton, J. (2004) Internationalisation as a way of thinking about curriculum development and quality. In Rob Carmichael (ed.) *Proceedings of the Australian Universities Quality Forum 2004,* AUQA Occasional Publication, Adelaide, Australia, 7–9 July 2004.

Rizvi, F. and Walsh, L. (1998) Difference, globalisation and the internationalisation of curriculum. *Australian Universities' Review* 41(2): 7–11.

Ryan, Y. (1998) Time and Tide: Teaching and Learning Online. *Australian Universities' Review*, 1: 14–19.

Salmon, G. (2000) *E-Moderating: The Key to Teaching and Learning Online*. London: Kogan Page.

Shrivastava, P. (1999) Online learning trends and the online learning paradox. *The Technology Source Archive*, retrieved from http://technologysource. org/article/online_learning_trends_and_the_online_learning_paradox (13 July 2006).

Thaman, K.H. (1997) Considerations of culture in distance education in the Pacific Islands. In L. Rowan, L. Bartlett and T. Evans. (eds) *Shifting Borders: Globalisation, Localisation and Open and Distance Education*. Geelong: Deakin University Press, pp. 23–36.

Tiffin, J. and Rajasingham, L. (1995) *In Search of the Virtual Class: Education in an Information Society*. London: Routledge.

Turkle, S. (1997) Seeing through computers: education in a culture of simulation. *The American Prospect*, 31: 76–82.

Wah, R. (1997) Distance education in the South Pacific: issues and contradictions. In L. Rowan, L. Bartlett and T. Evans. *Shifting Borders: Globalisation, Localisation and Open and Distance Education*. Geelong: Deakin University Press, pp. 69–82.

Walsh, L. (2005) *Globalisation, internationalisation and the recognition of cultural diversity in Australian education during the 1990s*. Proceedings of the Politics of Recognition: Identity, Justice, Respect Conference, Deakin University, 30–31 July 2005, Deakin University Australia.

West, R., Banks, G., Baume, P., Chipman, L., Clark, D., Doherty, C. and Lee Dow, K. (1998). *Learning for Life: Review of Higher Education Financing and Policy*. AGPS Canberra, Department of Employment, Education, Training and Youth Affairs.

Whalley, T. (1997) *Best Practice Guidelines for Internationalising the Curriculum: British Columbia*. Douglas College for the Province of British Columbia, Ministry of Education, Skills and Training and the Centre for Curriculum, Transfer and Technology.

Ziguras, C. (1999) Cultural diversity and transnational flexible delivery. In J. Winn (ed.) ASCILITE99 – *Responding to Diversity*. Proceedings from the 16th Annual Conference of the Australasian Society for Computers in Learning in Tertiary Education. Brisbane: Queensland University of Technology.

Ziguras, C. (2000) *New Frontiers, New Technologies, New Pedagogies: Educational Technology and the Internationalisation of Tertiary Education in South East Asia*. Research Report for Telstra Australia prepared by Monash Centre for Research in International Education, Monash University, Australia.

Ziguras, C. and Rizvi, F. (2001) Future directions in international online education. In Dorothy Davis and Denis Meares (eds) *Transnational Education: Australia Online*. Sydney: IDP Education Australia, pp.151–64.

PART III

Teachers and their Development

18

Pre-service Teacher Preparation for International Settings

Jack Levy

Given the amount of globalization and mobility transforming the world, it is reasonable to expect a plethora of teacher preparation programmes for international settings (where the term 'international settings' refers to classes and schools that enroll students from different countries, or have various national origins and home languages, including international schools that cater to the ex-patriot student, as well as domestic schools that feature second language learners of diverse heritage). While this is not exactly the case, their numbers are on the rise and there are clear efforts to develop the instructional knowledge and skills that apply to both domestic and international kindergarten to grade 12 (K–12) students. This chapter will present three approaches to the topic of international teacher education. The first section will generally describe pre- and in-service programmes that prepare faculty to teach abroad, or who are already serving overseas. This will be followed by an examination of domestic global teacher education programmes, which situate national multicultural concerns within an international context. The third major section will focus on programmes that develop teaching skills for domestic primary and secondary students of diverse backgrounds, some of which are international. While this last group of programmes and practices is oriented toward national settings, the skills and knowledge that are hopefully developed in graduates can easily transfer abroad.

TEACHER EDUCATION FOR NON-DOMESTIC SETTINGS

This section describes programmes and practices for faculty who are preparing to teach or who are already serving outside of their home countries. Most of the programmes cited cater for staff members at international schools overseas. These schools, referred to often in this Handbook, enroll both ex-patriot students from international families and/or affluent local students who have frequently travelled or lived abroad.

A number of universities in the UK, Canada and the USA offer pre- and in-service programmes to international school educators. At the pre-service level teacher candidates work toward a licence or certificate that is awarded by a government or university. They generally receive a qualification in primary education, a secondary subject area, or K–12 English as a Second Language (ESL) or English to Speakers of Other Languages (ESOL). Coursework is either offered on the home campus or at university centres throughout the world.

Most university-based in-service professional development leads to a masters degree, though there are a few doctoral programmes available for international school educators. The masters coursework is frequently offered on-site at the international school and is designed as much as possible around the needs and interests of the faculty. Curricula range from hybrid models in which the university combines a required core sequence of classes with others selected from a broad menu, to straightforward coursework in which individual class titles do not change but the content is adaptable to the local context. These types of programmes have existed for more than 40 years, and have expanded in number and design with increasing globalization.

There is also a wide range of professional development available to international school educators through national governments, international associations and NGOs. The US State Department's Office of Overseas Schools supports a number of activities at American international schools. In addition, there are regional associations of international schools that also facilitate the professional growth of teachers and administrators. Finally, a number of NGOs and individual consultants also assist international schools to meet their professional development needs. For further analysis of professional development in international education the reader is referred to Chapter 19 of this Handbook by Mary Hayden.

As might be expected, the conceptual framework for most of these programmes is constructivist. Instructional strategies generally emphasize enquiry, student-centred approaches and reflective practice. Occasionally, coursework is also presented from a postmodern, social action perspective.

PRE-SERVICE GLOBAL TEACHER EDUCATION FOR DOMESTIC AND NON-DOMESTIC SETTINGS

Because national teacher education systems are concerned with preparing faculty for the home country, pre-service teachers do not normally study comparative systems nor do they often travel abroad. Nonetheless, some national education systems are increasingly recognizing the importance of globalization and are reforming teacher preparation curricula accordingly. The literature reviewed for this chapter (which is limited) has been derived mostly from the USA and UK, though there are undoubtedly global teacher education efforts under way in other countries.

In the UK, a focus on global citizenship through education (then known as World Studies) began in the 1930s. In the 1970s Oxfam organized a global teacher education project around this principle. The notion of global citizenship gained in popularity until it was placed on the official agenda for education (called *Education for Citizenship*) by the government in the 1990s. During this period, the themes of international understanding, justice and human rights, sustainable development and cultural pluralism were emphasized in a number of teacher education programmes (Steiner 1996). These orientations continue up to the present day. A similar effort took place in the USA, spurred on by scholars such as Merry Merryfield (1994, 1995, 1997; Merryfield et al. 1997).

Conceptualization and content

Merryfield (1995) sets forth the primary features of sound global education programmes and activities in the USA. First, teachers need *global knowledge* about the world in general as well as the subjects they teach. An effective programme includes *cross-cultural experiences*, both at home and abroad. The global content should be *infused throughout the teacher education* programme, including field experiences, internships and sites for school/university collaboration. Global teacher educators and their pre-service teacher students should be ready to *deal with controversy*, since international education involves a variety of perspectives on occasionally problematic topics. Finally, sound programmes feature *interdisciplinary, curricular connections* between multicultural and global education as well as other related fields (peace education, conflict resolution, etc.) (Merryfield 1995: 2–4). In a later publication (Merryfield et al. 1997: 1–25) the authors present some essential questions that designers of global teacher education programmes need to address:

1 *Conceptualization:* How is global education conceptualized within the programme or university? There are, of course, a number of perspectives to consider, including a focus on values held by self and others, multiple realities, cross-cultural awareness and comparisons between local and global issues. British global teacher education tends to centre on inequities, social justice and development (Steiner 1996) and there are a variety of programmes in the USA (e.g. Teachers College, Columbia) that also share this perspective.
2 *Global content:* How will teacher candidates acquire the knowledge of the world and its peoples? There is a variety of disciplines within the social, behavioural and physical sciences that can be consulted for content.
3 *Intercultural Learning:* How will future teachers experience, participate in and learn to live with cultures different from their own? What types of experiences will provide the knowledge and skills to successfully communicate across cultures?
4 *Pedagogy for a global perspective:* What instructional methods will teachers learn that are appropriate for a global perspective and how will they learn them? Who will model them and how will teachers be able to apply these strategies to individual students? (Merryfield et al. 1997: 1–14).

While there is a clear overlap between the British and American conceptions of global teacher education, an edited volume by Steiner (1996) that reviews global teacher education in the UK characterizes the field as more oriented toward social justice, educational development and inclusion, as opposed to an exclusionary comparative approach. As stated, the UK global education movement was originally known as 'World Studies' when

it began in the 1930s. It has since evolved into a version of global education that includes concepts from various fields and movements: peace education, the green movement, antiracist and multicultural education; the women's movement, human rights education, futures education and development education (Richardson, in Steiner 1996: 3–5).

As noted above, the focal point of British global education and global teacher education continues to be world citizenship – that is, a planetary awareness of both diversity and commonalities, with a clear goal of inclusion. Richardson (1996: 5) lists four aspects of global citizenship that are both structural as well as personal:

1 status, rights and obligations
2 social inclusion and active participation
3 sentiment and sense of identity
4 political literacy and skill.

In her characterization of a global teacher, Steiner (1996) emphasizes the postmodernist, social justice aspect of the field. She states that a global teacher:

- Is interested in and concerned about events and movements in the local, national and global community;
- Actively seeks to keep informed while also maintaining a skeptical stance towards her sources of information;
- Takes up a principled stand, and supports others who do so, against injustice and inequalities relating to race, gender, class, physical or mental attributes, and to international systems of trade, finance and production;
- Informs herself about environmental issues as they impact upon her community and on other communities and ecological systems globally; Values democratic processes as the best means of bringing about positive change and engages in some form of social action to support her beliefs. (p. 21)

In practice

While there are a number of global teacher education efforts, they are not without weaknesses. In an extensive study of the international components of undergraduate secondary teacher preparation programmes in the USA, Schneider (2001) provided some recommendations for improvement. After collecting data from more than 100 university educators and 65 teachers in more than ten states, she reported that the single greatest need is in academic and career *advising*. Future secondary teachers in the areas that she surveyed felt that they were not advised sufficiently about international opportunities and perspectives. In addition, undergraduates were not aware of the services provided by the *Office of International Programmes*. Further, they stated that their *curricula* did not include enough globally oriented content – a majority of the respondents suggested that more international courses or content needed to be integrated to the existing curriculum and presented through a variety of forums and learning experiences. Of particular attention was the need for increased *study of world languages*. Nearly all of the respondents felt that teachers should attain a practical proficiency level in a second language. There was also universal support for increased *study abroad* experiences for both pre-service candidates and faculty. The participants agreed that *professional development* be provided for university faculty in international education, and that candidates for professorships should demonstrate both international and foreign language competence. Other recommendations included the strengthening of *teacher licensing* requirements to include global considerations (Schneider 2001: 1–10).

In two separate studies Merryfield outlined the most salient characteristics of successful global teacher education programmes and the staff members who implement them. In research conducted on six exemplary global programmes, she found that all pursued similar goals, featured content that was based on global interconnectedness, and offered a delivery mechanism that emphasized active, experiential learning and reflective practice. Teacher participants isolated three particular aspects of the programmes that were memorable: the relationship between multicultural and global education, the emphasis on global and local linkages in terms of economic interdependence, and the use of the environment as

a springboard for discussion of multiple perspectives (Merryfield 1994: 4–9).

Merryfield (2000) then conducted a study of 80 effective global teacher educators to discern the qualities and experiences that facilitated their success. The most meaningful occurrences were those in which participants interacted with different cultures and had to adjust to varying norms, values and practices. In most of these cases the participants were in the minority and their learning grew out of feelings of awkwardness, confusion and sustained reflection. Notably, there was a significant difference in the responses of people of colour (outsiders in their own country who were discriminated against) and whites who travelled abroad. Nonetheless, this speaks to the importance of experiential learning in the preparation of teachers for international settings.

There are many examples of teacher education programmes that use international content to prepare teachers for both domestic and overseas settings. For example, an increasing number of teacher candidates in Europe, the USA, Australia and Canada choose to complete an internship outside of their home countries. At Bilkent University in Ankara, Turkey, student teachers serve in five different schools, only three of which are local. They also teach in a school in either Istanbul or Izmir, and one in the USA. One of the Ankara settings is an international school (Sands and Stevens 2004: 278). In addition to an overseas internship, there are a variety of other global teacher education efforts, including professional development schools' networks in global education, cross-cultural experiential education with international students, overseas study tours, student and teacher exchanges, and semesters abroad (Merryfield et al. 1997: 10–11; Steiner 1996).

PRE-SERVICE MULTICULTURAL TEACHER EDUCATION FOR DOMESTIC SETTINGS

In general, however, the international-oriented teacher education programmes, policies and practices referred to above are exceptions to the rule (Merryfield 2000). Despite the influence of globalization, teachers who are prepared for multicultural settings normally focus on diverse domestic student populations, which also include some students who have recently immigrated or speak a second language at home. While it is not clear how the knowledge and skills used with diverse national students would apply in an international context, there is a definite overlap.

Relevant factors

There is a number of variables that influence how well teachers prepared through a national system can work with international student populations. These include the diversity, location and political status of the country in which the teacher is educated and its national policies toward multiculturalism.

1 Diversity of country

In an international analysis of ethnic diversity, van den Berghe (1989, in Craft 1996: 1) concluded that, by the criterion of 90 per cent or more of the population speaking the same language, only 10 per cent of the 150 countries in the United Nations in 1989 could be called culturally homogeneous. Clearly, multilingualism is typical in most societies. It seems logical, therefore, that the greater the ethnic and linguistic diversity in a country the greater the chance that the teacher has been educated to work with students from various language and cultural backgrounds. Unfortunately, this is not always the case, as noted in The Bahamas, where 'primary school teachers are not being exposed to the content and methodology courses in their training that would prepare them to teach Standard English to Bahamian Creole speakers as well as to an increasing number of non-native speakers of English (largely of Haitian origin) who are entering the school system' (National Task Force on Education in the Bahamas 1994, in Jennings 2001: 114).

(a) Governance: One important consideration in terms of the approach to pluralism in teacher education is governance. In a system

where control devolves to the state or region – such as in the USA, Germany, Australia and Canada – concern for preparing teachers for plural school environments very much depends upon the context within various locales. Even in more centralized countries such as China, France, Greece, Japan, Sweden and Thailand, where the national government decides on the content of teacher education, there is a variety of approaches (Watson 1996: 166).

Many countries, however, do include policy statements acknowledging the importance of diversity in education and teacher preparation. Often teacher education governing bodies include standards and competencies that broadly address the importance of diversity and respect for different cultures, such as this statement from the Norwegian Ministry of Education:

> At the same time, education should pave the way for a society based on individual freedom and self-determination, where individuals show responsibility for their own and other people's lives and well-being. Education should promote respect and tolerance for different cultures and life styles, and thereby combat discriminatory attitudes. It should also foster moral responsibility for the society and the world that we live in. (KUF 1999: 10, in Stephens et al. 2004: 123)

In an analysis of education policy across 25 European countries, the OECD (2005) noted that high quality teachers can create effective learning environments for different types of students. Specifically, they can 'deal effectively with different languages and student backgrounds, … be sensitive to culture and gender issues, … promote tolerance and social cohesion, … respond effectively to disadvantaged students and students with learning or behavioral problems' (OECD 2005: 2). This recognition has placed greater responsibility on teacher education institutions to prepare practitioners with relevant knowledge and skills.

In the USA most pre-service teacher education programmes emphasize diversity and multicultural education for domestic student groups. Indeed, one of the unit standards of the National Council for the Accreditation of Teacher Education (NCATE) is directed toward diversity:

The unit designs, implements, and evaluates curriculum and experiences for candidates to acquire and apply the knowledge, skills, and dispositions necessary to help all students learn. These experiences include working with diverse higher education and school faculty, diverse candidates, and diverse students in P–12 schools. (NCATE 2002:10)

(b) Status of cultural groups:

The nature of a country's diversity is another aspect tied to international teacher education. The recognition given to pluralism depends on how different groups are perceived by governments in terms of their economic, political or numerical status. Many governments state that they value diversity yet practice assimilation. In the mid-1990s, Japan and Thailand were countries in which little accommodation of minorities was found in teacher education. As stated by Watson:

in societies that are multiethnic or multilingual as a result of war, colonialism, conquest and history – such as Belgium, Cameroon, China, India, Malaysia, Nigeria, Singapore, Switzerland, the former USSR, to name but a few – emphasis in teacher education is inevitably concerned with linguistic and cultural differences. Teachers are expected to be at least bilingual, and where relevant, to be aware of ethnic and cultural differences. This is particularly true in India, Malaysia and Singapore. Trainee teachers are recruited from the different ethnic groups and are expected to understand and be sympathetic towards other groups; but in all cases, the national language (Hindi or Bahasa Malaysia) has to be promoted above the other languages. (1996: 167)

(c) Immigration:

Countries that have experienced large-scale immigration, such as the USA, Canada and Western Europe, have experimented with a variety of policies regarding assimilation and acculturation. These have resulted in different emphases in teacher education – for example, from bilingual education to English as a Second Language, and/or from antiracist education to a concentration on basic literacy. In Sweden teachers could be prepared to teach in any of more than 50 languages. France, like the USA, has also allowed for the different language mediums of instruction, but was mostly concerned with the preservation of French as the national language. Germany, in contrast,

recruited Turkish and Croatian teachers, and provided courses in multicultural education in teacher preparation curricula (Watson 1996).

While, as expected, there is no single pattern of teacher preparation in pluralist societies, many countries recognize the importance of educating teachers to work effectively with immigrant students. As stated in a 2002 EURYDICE publication:

Immigration has altered the working conditions of teachers in many European countries, and had a direct impact on the composition of classes. Teachers may be confronted with different cultures, religions, and languages in a single learning environment. Not all pupils necessarily relate to this environment in the same way and many often have insufficient knowledge of the language of instruction. Attention is therefore increasingly devoted to the acquisition of methods involving cross-cultural approaches to teaching, as well as the psychological and sociological aspects of handling situations that arise in a multicultural context. (EURYDICE 2002: 48)

(d) Internal cohesion:

Naturally, those countries whose citizens are divided by social and political cleavages will have greater difficulty in addressing international/multicultural content in teacher education. Israel's Ministry of Education has not been able to develop a comprehensive policy on pluralism in education, and as a result, multiculturalism in teacher education is practised on a voluntary basis (Yogev 1996: 57). Morrow (1996: 95) cites a similar situation in post-apartheid South Africa.

2 Geographic location

Another significant factor is the geographic location of the country, and the nature of its interactions with its neighbors. Discussions within the European Union continue regarding a teacher qualification that would be accepted throughout the region. Similarly, the South East Asia Ministers of Education Organization (SEAMEO) frequently discusses educational issues of importance to the area. One example with relevance to international education and pluralism is the efforts of Vietnam to prepare teachers for multigrade teaching with minority groups in rural areas. Since this is a characteristic of many of the SEAMEO countries, the results of the effort (funded by UNICEF) will have an impact beyond Vietnam (Thomas 1996: 123). Similarly, members of the Caribbean Community Secretariat (CARICOM) emphasize the need for teachers to be prepared for 'inclusive' education. 'Inclusive' in this case refers to youngsters who hitherto have been excluded from final examinations and boys in the Caribbean school systems who are underachieving (Jennings 2001: 128).

3 National policy toward multiculturalism

A third factor is the importance placed on multiculturalism and multilingualism by the national government. In The Netherlands, for example, Dutch students often learn three or more languages (Dutch plus English, German, French or Spanish) because citizens frequently travel outside the country for business, education or pleasure. As a result, a Dutch teacher might be more capable of working with students from different countries than a teacher from a largely monolingual society.

Countries that value multiculturalism will prioritize diversity in the recruitment and employment of teachers and teacher educators. This has been the case for the past decade in the UK (Basit and McNamara 2004) and the USA. A society that seeks to identify and prepare representatives of various ethnic, class and gender groups for the classroom will quite possibly produce teachers who are globally minded. A society that focuses on gender-equality will probably graduate teachers who are sensitive to differences.

4 Curricular frameworks

Domestic multicultural teacher education programmes combine two broad models in their approach to preparing teachers for pluralist settings, one called 'inside-out' and the other 'outside-in'. The 'outside-in' model is generally more prevalent since it consists of culture-specific and culture-general content that relates to students from cultures with whom the teachers will most likely work. For example, in The Netherlands multicultural teacher education might include content on the

societies in former Dutch colonies, such as Surinam, The Antilles and Indonesia, as well as countries that send workers to The Netherlands such as Morocco and Turkey (Campbell 1993). The multicultural education component of US teacher preparation programmes often includes content about African Americans, Hispanics, Asian Americans and Native Americans. A culture-general focus is designed to enable teachers to develop skills and knowledge that are applicable with diverse student groups. Thus, pre-service candidates might study the work of researchers who analyse culture from a variety of perspectives, such as Hofstede, Hall and Kluckholn. Unfortunately, unless they spend a great deal of time in fieldwork and internship in diverse settings, the preparation is not very effective.

In the 'inside-out' approach the teacher reflects on his or her own cultural development. It is thought that once this is understood, he or she is better able to work with children who are experiencing their own identity development. Most domestic multicultural programmes include both approaches in varying degrees.

Multicultural teacher education emphasizes the importance of constructivism and multiple perspectives. As noted by James Banks in his five dimensions of multicultural education, the importance of multiple perspectives is based on the idea of knowledge construction:

> Teachers need to help students understand, investigate, and determine how the implicit cultural assumptions, frames of references, perspectives and biases within a discipline influence the ways that knowledge is constructed. (Banks and Banks 2003: 23)

While written policies and anecdotal records of multicultural practices are well conceived, it is not clear how effective they are. In the USA racial and class differences continue to be a significant predictor of the academic achievement gap. Further, a not uncommon characteristic of pre-service teacher education is the occasional disconnect between the methodology taught at the tertiary institution and that practised in schools. Often, pre-service teachers learn student-centred, constructivist strategies that are favoured by teacher educators in universities and government centres. When they arrive in schools however, they often encounter traditional, teacher-centred contexts that require them to unlearn their progressive orientation. A typical case is Guyana, where 'teachers find that much of the knowledge and skills they gained in training cannot be implemented in the classroom on account of the "strong examination orientation"' (Jennings 2001: 108). As a result, while pre-service teachers might learn to respect the importance of multiple perspectives, this might not transfer into their actual classroom practice. Further, teacher education programmes in developing countries tend to focus on subject matter knowledge and teaching strategy, rather than coursework to reduce prejudice and provide for social justice (Watson 1996).

Even if teacher preparation programmes emphasize constructivism and multiple perspectives, there is limited evidence that they favour multiple *international* perspectives. The variety of views on a particular topic might reflect different political, social, or cultural positions taken with a country rather than between countries. Once again, however, in societies with large immigrant populations a constructivist orientation might present the perspectives from these different communities. In addition, those who have been trained to work with diverse domestic student groups would hopefully be able to transfer their skills to international contexts.

SUMMARY AND RECOMMENDATIONS FOR FUTURE RESEARCH

In recognition of the multiple definitions of the terms 'international settings' and 'international teacher education', this chapter approached the topic broadly. It examined pre-service teacher preparation from three perspectives – programmes oriented toward teachers who serve abroad, those that include global content in their national programmes, and those that focus on domestic multicultural concerns. In each category the professional development provided was constructivist in nature and emphasized multiple perspectives and reflective practice. While it is not clear how effective any of these orientations are towards producing internationally-minded teachers or students, all three perspectives highlight the knowledge and skills to facilitate global awareness.

As noted, the chapter was intended as an overview of the field rather than an extensive analysis. As a result, its coverage is limited in two main ways. First, the discussion targeted the preparation of pre-service teachers in global education. This does not deny the importance of the continuing professional development of in-service teachers in international issues. As noted, this topic is addressed elsewhere in this Handbook by Mary Hayden (Chapter 19).

Second, the research reviewed was accessed through Internet searches conducted on the websites of libraries, bookstores, publishers and popular search engines. While this yielded a number of print and electronic sources, not all the literature uncovered through this process was accessible practically, and this limited the coverage. The majority of research reviewed took place in English-speaking Western countries. It was written in English and largely produced by Western publishers. There are probably accounts of global teacher education efforts that are written for non-English audiences. These might include descriptions of programmes in Europe that attempt to prepare teachers for service throughout the Union, or similar attempts in Asia or Latin America.

To offset these limitations, future reviews of international teacher education should be conducted by a team of researchers with multilingual ability and access to a wider variety of literature. Such research might be part of a broader initiative to highlight various perspectives on the field and develop pilot partnerships across countries. The effort might be jointly sponsored by a cross-national group of education organizations such as UNESCO/

UNICEF, the Association for Teacher Education in Europe (ATEE), the American Association of Colleges of Teacher Education (AACTE) and/or the newly formed Alliance for International Education (AIE).

In closing, it can be said that the dynamic and crucial outgrowths of globalization have not been lost on teacher education. From a variety of perspectives and mechanisms, organizations and individuals are slowly responding to the challenge of building international awareness and teaching skill. Hopefully, these efforts will both increase and improve with time.

REFERENCES

Banks, J. and Banks, C. (2003) *Multicultural Education: Issues and Perspectives,* 4th edition. Boston, MA: Allyn and Bacon.

Basit, T.N. and McNamara, O. (2004) Equal opportunities or affirmative action? The induction of minority ethnic teachers. *Journal of Education for Teaching,* 30(2): 97–116.

Campbell, H.W. (1993) Interculturalism and Dutch teacher education. In G. Verma (ed.) *Inequality and Teacher Education.* London: Falmer Press, pp. 133–43.

Craft, M. (ed.) (1996) *Teacher Education in Plural Societies.* London: Falmer Press.

EURYDICE (The Information Network on Education in Europe) (2002) *The Teaching Profession in Europe,* vol. 3: *Profile, Trends and Concerns. Report I: Initial Training and Transition to Working Life. General Lower Secondary Education.* Brussels: EURYDICE (ISBN 2-87116-341-3, 1-101).

Jennings, V. (2001) Teacher education in selected countries in the Commonwealth Caribbean: the ideal of policy versus the reality of practice. *Comparative Education,* 37(1): 107–34.

KUF (Kirke, Utdannings-Og Forskningsdepartementet) [Norwegian Ministry of Education] (1999) *Praktish-pedagogisk utdanning* [Practical teacher education]. Oslo: Norgesnettradet. In P. Stephens, F. E. Tonnessen and C. Kyriacou (2004) Teacher *training* and teacher *education* in England and Norway: a comparative study of policy goals. *Comparative Education,* 40(1): 109–30, 123.

Matua, M. and Sunal, C.S. (eds) (2004) *Research on Education in Africa, the Caribbean, and the Middle East.* Greenwich, CN: Information Age Publishing.

Merryfield, M. (1994) *From teacher education to the classroom: reflections of teachers on their teacher education experience in global education.* ERIC Document ED392 724, reproduced by the Education Research Service, pp. 1–25.

Merryfield, M. (1995) *Teacher Education in Global and International Education.* ERIC Digest, ED384601, pp. 1–6.

Merryfield, M. (2000) Why aren't teachers being prepared to teach for diversity, equity, and global interconnectedness? A study of lived experiences in the making of multicultural and global educators. *Teaching and Teacher Education,* 16 (4): 429–43.

Merryfield, M., Jarchow, E. and Pickert, S. (eds) (1997) *Preparing Teachers to Teach Global Perspective: A Handbook for Teacher Educators.* Thousand Oaks, CA: Corwin Press.

Morrow, W. (1996) Teacher education and pluralism in South Africa. In M. Craft (ed.) *Teacher Education in Plural Societies.* London: Falmer Press, pp. 95–107.

National Task Force on Education in the Bahamas (1994) *Education: A Preparation for Life, Final Report (January).* Nassau, The Bahamas: National Task Force on Education. In V. Jennings (2001) Teacher education in selected countries in the Commonwealth Caribbean: the ideal of policy versus the reality of practice. *Comparative Education,* 37 (1): 107–34, 114.

NCATE (National Council for the Accreditation of Teacher Education) (2002) *Professional Standards for the Accreditation of Schools, Colleges and Departments of Education,* 2002 Edition. Washington, DC: NCATE, pp. 1–61.

OECD (Organization of Economic Cooperation and Development) (2005) *Teachers Matter: Attracting, Developing and Retaining Effective Teachers.* Paris: OECD Education and Skills Series, 2005, 6: 1–240.

Richardson, R. (1996) The terrestrial teacher. In M. Steiner (ed.) *Developing the Global Teacher.* Oakhill, UK: Trentham Publishers, pp. 3–10.

Sands, M. and Stevens, D. (2004) Teacher education in Turkey: issues and trends. In M. Mutua and C.S. Sunal (eds) *Research on Education in Africa, the Caribbean, and the Middle East.* Greenwich, CN: Information Age Publishing, pp. 267–82.

Schneider, A. (2001) Internationalizing teacher education: what can be done? A research report on the undergraduate training of secondary school teachers. Washington, DC: US Department of Education, ERIC: ED480869.

Steiner, M. (Ed.) (1996) *Developing the Global Teacher.* Oakhill, UK: Trentham Publishers.

Stephens, P.I, Tonnessen, F.E. and Kyriacou, C. (2004) Teacher *training* and teacher *education* in England and Norway: a comparative study of policy goals. *Comparative Education,* 40(1): 109–30.

Thomas, E. (1996) Teacher education in South East Asia: prospects for a North–South dialogue with a difference. In C. Brock (ed.) *Global Perspectives on Teacher Education*. Wallingford, UK: Triangle Books, pp. 123–51.

van den Berghe, P. (1989) Plural society. In A. Kuper and J. Kuper (eds) *The Social Science Encyclopaedia*. London: Routledge. In M. Craft (ed.) (1996) *Teacher Education in Plural Societies*. London: Falmer Press, p. 1.

Verma, G. (ed.) (1993) *Inequality and Teacher Education*. London: Falmer Press.

Watson, K. (1996) Comparative perspectives and paradigms. In M. Craft (ed.) *Teacher Education in Plural Societies*. London: Falmer Press, pp. 159–71.

Yogev, A. (1996) Practice without policy: pluralist teacher education in Israel. In M. Craft (ed.) *Teacher Education in Plural Societies*. London: Falmer Press, pp. 57–71.

19

Professional Development of Educators: the International Education Context

Mary Hayden

ESTABLISHING THE CONTEXT

Writing about international education is fraught with potential pitfalls, arising not least from the differences in terminology adopted in different parts of the world – even among those who are native speakers of the language in which this chapter is written. The chapter will thus begin by defining the context in which it is set and the terminology to be used. It has been established earlier in this volume that the very concept of international education from which the Handbook derives its title is open to interpretation: in describing what she refers to as the 'big terminology debate', for instance, Harriet Marshall refers to terms including development education, comparative education, education for international understanding, world studies, global education and global citizenship education all being related and used to mean similar things in different contexts (see Chapter 3).

Another context in which the term international education is often used is that of the growing number of international schools around the world; developing rapidly since the Second World War in particular, these schools – which may have little in common overall – describe themselves as international schools for a variety of reasons including the nature of the student population, the nature of the curriculum offered, marketing and competition with other schools in the area, and the school's overall ethos or mission (Hayden 2006). For the most part private and fee-paying, many international schools 'serve the children of those international organizations and multinational companies whose parents are called upon to work in many different countries and to change their assignment at frequent intervals' (Murphy 1991: 1). The staff 'also represent a mixture of nationalities, usually with no particular nationality predominating. Such schools normally teach an international programme of study or one or more national programmes (but not generally of the country in which they are to be found) or a combination of both' (Chesworth and Dawe

2000: x). In this chapter the focus will be on the development of educators involved in some way in international education, with that term being used in a loose, inclusive sense to embrace educational provision in international schools as well as in more nationally based schools that might also be considered to have a link to international education.

If the concept of international education is difficult to define, so too is the term 'educator' as used in the title of this chapter. Sometimes taken as synonymous with the term 'teacher', it will be used here more broadly to include those from different stakeholder groups involved in the education of young people. Teachers, managers (a term most frequently encountered in British-influenced contexts to describe, for instance, Heads of Department, Deputy Heads, Heads of School), administrators (more often encountered in American-influenced contexts, and commonplace in international schools when referring to Principals and Heads of School) and Board members will all be considered, for the purposes of this chapter, as included within the term 'educator'.

And crucially, it is important that we define what is meant here by professional development in a context where, again, different terminology is used to mean similar things. Professional development will be interpreted here in the sense proposed by Day (1999), to consist of 'all natural learning experiences and those conscious and planned activities which are intended to be of direct or indirect benefit to the individual, group or school and which contribute, through these, to the quality of education in the classroom. It is the process by which, alone and with others, teachers review, renew and extend their commitment as change agents to the moral purposes of teaching; and by which they acquire and develop critically the knowledge, skills and emotional intelligence essential to good professional thinking, planning and practice with children, young people and colleagues through each phase of their teaching lives' (p. 4). Similarly, Dean argues that professional development is 'career long, starting with initial training and continuing until retirement. It is an active process. The

teacher must actually work to develop. Development does not happen merely as a result of years of teaching' (1991: 7).

The focus of this chapter will be on the 'second stage' of professional development referred to by Dean; not what he described as initial training, or what might be described elsewhere as pre-service education or initial teacher education, but those aspects of development relating to educators who are already in post. (For a discussion of pre-service education, see Chapter 18 by Levy in this Handbook.)

THE ADULT AS LEARNER

One characteristic common to all forms of professional development is that they apply to adults, rather than children, as learners. Knowles described 'the art and science of helping adults learn' as andragogy, as opposed to pedagogy, or 'the art and science of teaching children' (1984). To be effective, Knowles argues, learning designed for adults needs to take account of the following key principles.

All adults:
- are autonomous and self-directed, and need to be given freedom to direct themselves
- have accumulated a foundation of life experiences and knowledge, to which they will need to connect any new learning
- are goal-oriented and tend to have a problem-centred orientation to learning: they will want to know how new learning will help them to achieve goals and deal with problems
- are relevancy-oriented and will want to see a reason for learning something
- are practical, focusing on those aspects of new learning that will be most useful to them
- have established values, beliefs and opinions; teaching strategies will need to demonstrate respect for these
- tend to show increasing divergence in individual differences with age; teaching strategies will need to take account of this.

This last principle links to the other crucial point to be borne in mind here: the individuality of all learners in terms of preferred styles of learning. Kolb's 'learning cycle', including preferences for active, reflective, theoretical and pragmatic approaches to learning (1999), is perhaps the most frequently cited, though not the only, model which highlights the fact that a 'one size fits all' approach to learning is unlikely to be successful for all. Differences in individual responses to the provision of information need also to be acknowledged: Joyce and Showers (1980), for instance, stress that 'ownership' of the content of any training provided (which is necessary for learning to occur and to impact on practice) is only likely to occur when concepts covered and awareness of them are synthesized in practical application to a new situation.

Working with adults as learners thus requires a different, though related, set of skills to those required when working with children, placing the individual who is in the 'teacher' position in the role of 'facilitator', creating an environment conducive to self-directed learning. Principally, therefore, the 'teacher' or 'andragogue' has the role of designer and manager of processes and procedures that will facilitate the acquisition of content by the learners and, secondarily, has the role of content resource – in essence linking learners to various resources upon which they may draw (e.g. peers, those with particular expertise, written materials or media resources) (Knowles 1984). Clearly the relationship between skills required for working with adults and those required for working with children do not fit neatly into two discrete boxes that are drawn upon depending upon the age of the student group. Indeed, there are critics of Knowles who contend that the distinction between andragogy and pedagogy is an artificial one, and that all teachers in all situations should be familiar with both approaches. It is certainly the case that, at times, the andragogue may need to draw upon the skills of the pedagogue, having judged in a particular context for a certain individual that a pedagogical strategy would be appropriate (where for instance an adult is, perhaps at the very outset of the learning experience, a dependent learner before being helped to take increasing responsibility for their own learning). Equally,

the skills of the andragogue may be called upon when working with school-age students, particularly perhaps with older students approaching the stage of moving on to university-level study or employment, where any preparation for a more self-directed approach to learning is likely to be advantageous. Part of the skill of the teacher lies in judging which approach is appropriate in each situation encountered. 'Teachers should … know how to select, evaluate, improve and create or recreate strategies for effective intervention' said Braslavsky (2003: 180–1). Where the learners are professional educators, it is clear that any form of professional development, if it is to be successful, will need to be led by an individual or individuals with skills as a facilitator rather than purely as an imparter of content knowledge, even though that skill may also, on occasion, be required.

To be successful, too, given the self-directed nature of adult learning and its tendency to be goal-oriented, practical and relevancy-oriented, those participating need to be motivated to learn. Motivation may be extrinsic: the promise of a 'reward' in the form of a salary increase, perhaps, on successful completion of a course, or the award of a Masters or Doctoral degree which is likely to enhance promotion prospects. Alternatively, motivation may be intrinsic in terms of interest in learning for its own sake, increased self-esteem or greater self-confidence (Herzberg 1966; Maslow 1970). A combination of intrinsic and extrinsic motivators is not uncommon; indeed it would be hoped that, however strong the extrinsic motivator(s), at least an element of intrinsic motivation would always be present. The nature of that motivation is likely to vary between individuals, depending on a range of factors including age, status, personal ambition and aspirations, responsibilities and perceived expectations of others. The form of professional development likely to be most appropriate to them will vary according to a similar set of factors, and a number of different possibilities offered within the context of international education will be discussed in the remainder of this chapter. Before doing so, one other issue must be addressed: if the educators for the purpose of this chapter are taken to be the teachers, administrators and members of the Board, then who are the 'andragogues' or facilitators who might support them in the learning process?

WHO EDUCATES THE EDUCATORS?

The pros and cons of professional development organized internally within schools and that brought in from outside are oft debated. This section will consider a number of issues under the headings of internal provision, external provision (non-award-bearing) and external provision (award-bearing).

Internal provision

Writing in the context of international schools, Powell argues strongly for what he refers to as a broad vision of professional development which has as its objective the building of 'a culture of reflective teaching practice, so enhancing the quality of education provided within the school. Reflective practice … is not something that happens by imposition on teachers, but rather it represents the professional growth that teachers increasingly provide for themselves through collaborative reflection on teaching and learning' (2000: 98). Warning of the professional dangers of following the example of many teachers who 'continue to teach behind closed doors in isolation from their colleagues', Powell argues that '[p]rofessional isolation perpetuates professional ignorance' (2000: 98) and goes on to highlight the importance of linking professional development to school improvement so that its success is judged by 'whether it alters instructional behaviour in a way that benefits students' (2000: 99). Five common characteristics of effective professional development that can be directly linked to school improvement are, he suggests:

- a team approach
- strong leadership and active administrative support

- sustained focus
- modelling what is to be achieved
- keeping current.

(Powell 2000: 99–100)

Such characteristics are also to be found where action research approaches are adopted by teachers and others as a means of better understanding and thus improving their own practice. Indeed it is clear that some forms of professional development are most logically internally organized and provided. The induction (or orientation) of new teachers and administrators into the ways of working within a particular school, for instance, which 'makes them feel welcome and familiarizes them with the people they will work with, their surroundings and the organization's routines, thus reducing initial confusion and encouraging them to become productive' (Stirzaker 2004: 33) is best organized by those already experienced in the ways of that school, most likely with an emphasis on the involvement of relatively new employees who will be better able to empathize with the newcomer's concerns than may colleagues of longer standing (Fowler 1996: 29). In-school professional development opportunities could also be taken to include coaching and mentoring, appraisal programmes for both teachers and administrators (including the Head) as well as training for new Board members, and appraisal (often referred to in this context as 'evaluation') of the school Head and Board members including Board Chair, as recommended by, *inter alia*, Bowley (2001) and Hodgson (2005).

The 'ownership' of school developments that can arise from shared participation in ongoing professional development activities among colleagues, as alluded to by Powell above, should clearly not be underestimated. 'Professional development must be woven into the fabric of strategic planning,' says Richards, 'since the teachers are the instruments through which successful cultural change can be accomplished. No matter how well constructed are the administrative structures, or well articulated the rationale for change, the ownership of development must be shared with the teaching staff as a whole' (2002: 102).

The strengths of professional development organized internally within schools notwithstanding, a good deal of externally-offered professional development also takes place within both national and international schools, and it could be argued that each has its own valuable contribution to make in this context. Squire, for instance, emphasizes the importance of achieving a good balance between internally- and externally-organized professional development opportunities in schools (2001: 13). Externally-organized professional development opportunities are many and varied, and will be considered here under two main headings: non-award-bearing and award-bearing.

External provision (non-award-bearing)

Under this heading are included those externally-organized professional development activities that do not lead to qualifications, or awards, such as Masters or Doctoral degrees. Such activities can themselves be subdivided into those aspects of professional development externally organized through conferences, workshops and courses in an off-site location – often to participants from a number of different schools – and those offered by an external organization on-site for one school in particular.

Off-site external provision

For a school that offers an externally devised curriculum, participation of teaching staff in such externally-offered professional development activities may be non-negotiable. Before a school can be authorized to offer the International Baccalaureate (IB) Primary Years Programme, for instance, those staff intending to be involved in its implementation must have undergone appropriate training, as determined by the IB Organization (IBO 2006). Indeed, for those schools offering any of the externally developed programmes familiar within international schools, such as the IB Diploma, Middle Years and Primary Years programmes,

International GCSE and International Primary Curriculum (IPC), participation by teaching staff in workshops relating to those programmes can be a regular occurrence. Teaching staff from international schools are often also regular participants in conferences organized by international organizations such as the European Council of International Schools (ECIS 2006) or regional associations such as the Federation of British International Schools in South and East Asia (FOBISSEA 2006) or the Association of International Schools in Africa (AISA 2006). Conferences and workshops organized by representatives of national systems may also be attractive to teachers from international schools, as they might to administrators. Administrator-specific conferences and workshops are also offered within the international schools context by organizations such as ECIS, the Academy for International School Heads (AISH 2006), the Principals Training Center (PTC 2006) and the International Leadership and Management Programme (ECIS 2006). And for those other educators to whom reference has been made, the Board members, there are professional development opportunities available in the way of 'Board training institutes' offered by organizations such as the Council of International Schools (CIS 2006), which also offers 'Partnership Development Program Workshops' designed for Head of School and Board Chair to participate in together (CIS 2006). National conferences, too, such as that of the American Educational Research Association, frequently offer international education components.

In such situations the professional development offered tends to be generic in content, based on an expectation that the various participants will take from it what they find relevant to their own context and apply it as appropriate to their own practice. The extent to which such an expectation is actually borne out in reality is at the root perhaps of the scepticism shown by Richards (2002) in suggesting that:

There are courses to suit every school's pocket and needs, as well as courses to cure every malaise known to education, including a number not yet identified by the researchers. Most do not carry health warnings, yet the request to 'post this in the faculty room' is as insidious as a virus, and in the frontier territory of international education, purveyors of snake oil abound. (2002: 99)

Certainly, experience would suggest that the expectation underpinning the 'cascade'-type model, where one representative of a school attends a conference and then feeds back what he or she has learned to school colleagues for the benefit of all, is somewhat optimistic unless systems are in place within school to ensure the effective dissemination of what has been learned. And even then, Powell argues (citing Sparks and Hirsh 1997), there is little evidence that such newly acquired knowledge and skills are translated into improving instruction within the classroom (2000: 97).

On-site external provision

Professional development activities offered by someone external to the school but within school premises, and for teaching and/or administrative staff of that school specifically, might in general be expected to be more effective than off-site provision, given the likelihood of such activities being more 'customized' to the needs of the particular school than other types of activity can be. And indeed some such activities clearly are very effective. Powell, for instance, though favouring in general internally-organized, ongoing forms of professional development, admits that 'there are times when short-term, external consultants can be useful' (2000: 97). Powell is among those who have concern more broadly, however, that such input does not necessarily impact upon the practice of participating faculty: 'the influence of outside experts in terms of effecting lasting school improvement', he says, 'often disappears as soon as they do' (2000: 97). Particularly, perhaps, where no provision is made within school for systematic follow-up after such input, it may well be difficult to see any resulting improvement in practice across the school – even though individuals may have benefited professionally from the experience.

External provision (award-bearing)

It is undoubtedly the case that, within the international school context, those who aspire to promotion to an administrator post (such as Principal or Head of School) need to be in possession of a Masters degree. Indeed, as increasing numbers hold Masters degrees the numbers of administrators embarking on part-time Doctoral programmes has also increased (Hayden 2006). Similar trends can be observed among teachers and administrators in some, though not all, national systems. Evidence to suggest that holding a Masters or Doctorate leads to improvement in a teacher's or administrator's practice tends to be anecdotal, and undoubtedly what is learned during the course of study – what is learned from research, as well as learned from other colleagues – does have such an effect for many individuals. It would seem unlikely, however, that all of those enrolling on such programmes are motivated to engage in further study for the intrinsic rewards (such as personal satisfaction, interest and increased self-confidence) it might bring. A more likely underlying cause is a phenomenon closely related to that described by Lowe (2000a, 2000b) as having been identified by, *inter alia,* Dore and Collins as 'credentialism', whereby students are motivated to gather increasing numbers of educational qualifications as a means of improving their employment prospects. One interpretation of the increased demand for Masters and Doctoral programmes among teachers and administrators could thus be that individuals are using such qualifications as a means of establishing a competitive edge, whether in the international school market or in that of international education promoted in national schools.

Indeed similar trends are developing within some national systems, and universities in a number of countries are responding accordingly. With increased availability of technological support to facilitate travel and communication, a number of different models have developed for the provision of courses designed to be studied on a part-time basis by those who might be described as mid-career professionals. Linked no doubt to the increasing prominence of English as a global language, many of these universities are in English-speaking countries and offer their programmes through the medium of English to both native and non-native English speakers. Maxwell et al. (2004) for instance, writing in the context of Australia and citing Moses (2002), refer to the USA, the UK and Australia as being the three major tertiary education providers worldwide. Maxwell et al. go on to describe an EdD programme developed by the University of New England, New South Wales, for Taiwanese students which incorporates a mixture of on-campus study and off-campus study in Taiwan. Also in the context of Australia, Pyvis and Chapman (2005) discuss a number of issues arising within the context of a programme described as 'offshore' in the sense of being offered by an Australian university in another country (in this case Singapore, the programme being jointly developed with a Singaporean provider). Within the UK context, the University of Bath offers both Masters- and Doctoral-level courses through models that allow participants to participate in courses based on campus over intensive one-week periods and/or to complete courses entirely at a distance through electronic contact with Bath-based tutors. The Masters programme also offers the facility of courses being taught in what are described as Study Centres in a number of locations world-wide, with follow-up support being provided electronically (Hayden and Thompson 1996; Wikeley and Muschamp 2004). In the USA, George Mason University has established a centre in the United Arab Emirates to provide graduate coursework and programmes for international as well as national educators.

A number of issues clearly arise in the development of such programmes, some of which are discussed by the authors referred to above. Issues relating to protecting standards, provision of tutorial and pastoral support, and ensuring appropriate levels of English are common to all such programmes. A more thorny issue perhaps is that of the nature of the programme being offered. The universities named here are all sensitive to the potential for

charges of educational imperialism to be brought as they offer Western-style courses that promote particular views on what it means to be educated. Maxwell et al., in raising this issue, refer to their programme as being 'contextually respectful' in the sense that it is respectful of the students' home contexts: 'the program does not presume that answers to questions of interest to Taiwanese are to be found solely in the Australian context or setting. Nor does it presume that questions of interest to Australian academics are of interest to the Taiwanese, or relevant to their context' (2004: 79). It also has to be recognized that, no doubt connected to increasing globalization trends in education as in other contexts, and unpalatable as this may be in some respects, such Western, English-medium programmes have a certain international currency. A question to be asked, perhaps, is what alternatives might be offered to the current choice between national programmes available either within or beyond their own boundaries?

In this respect it is interesting to consider the situation within secondary (rather than tertiary) level education, where many developments have taken place within the past 50 years leading to the present-day situation where a number of international programmes are offered for study within both national and international schools world-wide. Brief reference has been made above to just some of them – the three IB programmes, IGCSE and IPC – and there are others: a K–12 global education movement has been growing over the past 20 years in the USA, for instance.

Thompson (1998) developed a four-way categorization of curricula designed for use internationally, which can be summarized as follows:

- *Exportation:* the marketing abroad of existing national curricula and examinations, with little if any adjustment to take account of the different context and a value system 'unapologetically that of the country from which it is exported'.
- *Adaptation:* where existing national curricula and examinations are adapted for the national context, with the 'inherent value system' not likely to change at all and the risk of, as Thompson puts it, an 'unwitting process of educational imperialism'.

- *Integration:* where 'best practices' from a range of 'successful' curricula are brought together into one curriculum for operation across a number of systems or countries (with attendant challenges potentially to be faced from the different values and ideological positions in question).
- *Creation:* the development of a programme 'from first principles'.

(1998: 278–80)

Among the curricula offered at secondary level world-wide, principally in international schools, are examples of each of these four categories. Among the programmes offered at tertiary level, however, and in particular at postgraduate level (the level under discussion here within the context of professional development), it is arguably the case that examples currently exist of the first two categories only. Such programmes may be exported, in the sense that the same programme as is offered to 'home' students in the national context is offered to others, with little if any change in model. Alternatively, they may be adapted, in order to make the model flexible enough to be followed by those not based in the 'home' context and, in some cases, by being 'respectful' (as Maxwell et al. (2004) describe it) of the context of the participants. It may also be the case, as with the programmes offered by the University of Bath, for instance, or the aforementioned George Mason University center in the UAE (which has the stated purpose of offering as many bilingual, English-Arabic courses and programmes as possible), that specific courses are developed and offered within the programme which have a focus on the international context.

At secondary level, programmes have been developed that are described by Thompson (1998) as 'integrated' or 'created', but no such programmes appear to exist within the postgraduate education context. Is this because there is no demand for them? Or because the notion of developing such a programme is not a meaningful one? An immediate response might be that no international university exists to take responsibility for the development of such a programme, and that without the existence of an internationally recognized or accredited university no programme offered could have any credibility. In national systems, postgraduate qualifications only have as much credibility as the university that awards them, and the credibility of the university is established within its own national context through the award of a Charter (or equivalent) that bestows upon it degree-awarding powers. But it could be argued that when, for instance, the first International Baccalaureate programme (the Diploma) was developed and first awarded in 1970, there was no existing school-level examining body to give the new programme its credibility: this was hard won over many years. Could an equivalent process be developed at postgraduate level? Another response might be to ask who would want an internationally offered Masters programme rather than one offered from a national context; equally, that question could have been (and no doubt was) asked about the IB Diploma Programme when it was set up as an alternative to the English A Level, French Baccalauréat, American Advanced Placement and other national qualifications – but the IB Diploma has gone on to establish a niche for itself among those who now find it preferable to any of the more nationally focused programmes.

Perhaps the analogy is not a good one, in that at least part of the rationale for development of the IB Diploma was to assist international schools in catering for the needs of globally mobile students with different aspirations in terms of the country in which they anticipated pursuing university-level study. Such a situation does not arise within the context of postgraduate study. Careful consideration would also need to be given, if such a programme were to be developed at postgraduate level, to its content: would its focus be on knowledge, understanding, skills, comparative aspects of pedagogy, or …? Whether or not the notion of developing such a qualification is realistic, there is, nevertheless, an issue to be raised with respect to the relevance to those educators who have made their career in international education of postgraduate award-bearing courses that are all essentially grounded in national contexts.

CONCLUSION

This chapter has raised a number of issues relating to professional development for educators working within international schools and other international education contexts, some of which may well have wider applicability. It is clear that the various models of professional development have different strengths and it would seem that there is room for all of them at different times and in various contexts. Perhaps it is unrealistic to expect that a major new development will lead to postgraduate qualifications being offered by a non-nationally based university. What could be envisaged, however, is a greater degree of collaboration across national boundaries (and not just within the 'Western' world) between universities working together to internationalize the content and style of the programmes offered to professional educators. In discussing on-site professional development by external providers, Powell describes a relationship established between his own international school (the International School of Tanganyika, IST, in Tanzania) and the State University of New York College at Buffalo (Buffalo State) whereby Buffalo State would send a professor to IST to teach a graduate level course and IST would provide a teacher volunteer to co-plan and co-teach it (2000: 107). Collaboration could also be envisaged with organizations such as ECIS, currently developing certification recognizing experience of international school educators (EUS 2006), and the IBO, now developing a teacher award for teachers of IB programmes. Indeed the newly developing Alliance for International Education (2006) would seem to offer opportunities for collaboration between various combinations of organizations with an interest in international education. Such collaboration, whether between external organizations as a means of internationalizing their input, or between external providers and school to ensure the relevance and subsequent application of the input, would seem to offer a way forward which would help to ensure that international school educators, to return to the words of Day (1999), 'acquire and develop critically the knowledge, skills and emotional intelligence essential to good professional thinking, planning and practice ... through each phase of their teaching lives'.

REFERENCES

AISH (Academy for International School Heads) (2006) www.academyish.org (Accessed 18 January 2006).

Alliance for International Education (2006) www.intedalliance.org (accessed 15 April 2006).

AISA (Association of International Schools in Africa) (2006) www.aisa.or.ke (accessed 18 March 2006).

Bowley, N. (2001) *Evaluating the Head and the Board.* In W. Powell, N. Bowley and G. Schoppert (eds) *School Board Governance Training: a Sourcebook of Case Studies.* Great Glemham, Suffolk: John Catt Educational Ltd, pp. 128–42.

Braslavsky, C. (2003) Teacher education for living together in the 21st century. *Journal of Research in International Education,* 2 (2): 167–83.

Chesworth, N. and Dawe, A. (2000) *The Executive's Guide to International Schools.* London: Kogan Page.

CIS (Council of International Schools) (2006) www.cois.org (accessed 17 April 2006).

Day, C. (1999) *Developing Teachers: the Challenges of Lifelong Learning.* London: Falmer Press.

Dean, J. (1991) *Professional Development in School.* Buckingham: Open University Press.

ECIS (European Council of International Schools) (2006) www.ecis.org (accessed 17 April 2006).

FOBISSEA (Federation of British International Schools in South and East Asia) (2006) www.fobissea.org (accessed 18 March 2006).

Fowler, A. (1996) *Employee Induction,* 3rd edition. London: Institute of Personnel and Development.

Hayden, M.C. (2006) *Introduction to International Education.* London: Sage.

Hayden, M. and Thompson, J. (1996) An investigation of the effectiveness of an evaluation instrument designed for use with modular Masters courses in a range of international contexts. *Assessment and Evaluation in Higher Education,* 21(1): 55–68.

Herzberg, F. (1966) *Work and the Nature of Man.* London: Staples Press.

Hodgson, A. (2005) *Introduction to the World of Governance.* In A. Hodgson and M. Chuck (eds) *Governance in International Schools.* Great Glemham, Suffolk: Peridot Press, pp. 7–11.

IBO (International Baccalaureate Organization) (2006) www.ibo.org (accessed 17 April 2006).

Joyce, B. and Showers, B. (1980) Improving inservice training: the messages of research. *Educational Leadership*, 37 (5): 379–85.

Knowles, M. (1984) *Andragogy in Action*. San Francisco, CA: Jossey-Bass.

Kolb, D. (1999) *Learning Style Inventory*. Boston, MA: McBer and Co.

Lowe, J. (2000a) International examinations: the new credentialism and reproduction of advantage in a globalizing world. *Assessment in Education*, 7 (3): 363–77.

Lowe, J. (2000b) Assessment and educational quality: implications for international schools. In M.C. Hayden and J.J. Thompson (eds) *International Schools and International Education: Improving Teaching, Management and Quality*. London: Kogan Page, pp. 15–28.

Maslow, A.H. (1970) *Motivation and Personality*. London: Harper and Row.

Maxwell, T.W., McConaghy, C. and Ninnes, P. (2004) Offering a Doctoral program internationally: tensions and congruities. *Journal of Research in International Education*, 3 (1): 71–86.

Moses, I. (2002) Teaching and Learning: 2A Internationalisation, presentation, Australia-Taiwan Conference on Higher Education. Adelaide, 8–9 April.

Murphy, E. (ed.) (1991) *ESL: A Handbook for Teachers and Administrators in International Schools*. Clevedon, UK: Multilingual Matters Ltd.

Powell, W. (2000) Professional development and reflective practice. In M.C. Hayden and J.J. Thompson (eds) *International Schools and International Education: Improving Teaching, Management and Quality*. London: Kogan Page, pp. 96–111.

PTC (Principals Training Center for International School Leadership) (2006) www.theptc.org (accessed 30 March 2006).

Pyvis, D. and Chapman, A. (2005) Culture shock and the international student 'offshore'. *Journal of Research in International Education*, 4 (1): 23–42.

Richards, N. (2002) Professional development: an international schools' perspective. In M.C. Hayden, J.J. Thompson and G.R. Walker (eds) *International Education in Practice: Dimensions for National and International Schools*. London: Kogan Page, pp. 99–111.

Sparks, D. and Hirsh, S. (1997) *A New Vision for Staff Development*. Alexandria, VA: Association for Supervision and Curriculum Development.

Squire, L. (2001) School improvement and professional development in international schools. In S. Blandford and M. Shaw (eds) *Managing International Schools*. London: Routledge Falmer, pp. 105–22.

Stirzaker, R. (2004) Staff induction: issues surrounding induction into international schools. *Journal of Research in International Education*, 3 (1): 31–49.

Thompson, J.J. (1998) Towards a model for international education. In M.C. Hayden and J.J. Thompson (eds) *International Education: Principles and Practice*. London: Kogan Page, pp. 276–90.

Wikeley, F. and Muschamp, Y. (2004) Pedagogical implications of working with Doctoral students at a distance. *Distance Education*, 25 (1): 125–42.

20

Interpersonal Teacher Behaviour in International Education

Perry den Brok and Gerrit Jan Koopman

The study of teacher–student relationships is crucial to the improvement of all education, whether international or national. Such a focus can have an immediate positive impact on classroom instruction and student learning, as well as on teacher education and research. This chapter presents a model for understanding such relationships in terms of the perceptions that students (and occasionally teachers) have of teachers' interpersonal behaviour. It focuses on corresponding research on teachers' interactions with students in both multicultural domestic and international contexts. The chapter will analyse teacher–student interaction from an interpersonal viewpoint, the importance of student perceptions and the effects that culture may have on these perceptions and the resulting classroom climate. Since research with the model presented is scarce in the international context, most attention will be directed to studies of domestic classes. However, given the multiethnic nature of both multicultural and international classes, the investigations reviewed provide valuable knowledge for international education.

Rationale

There are several reasons to focus on teacher interpersonal behaviour. Of particular interest is the influence of culture (and/or national origin) on teacher–student relationships in the international classroom. In addition, the nature of the communication between teachers and students affects class management, student achievement and motivation, instructional effectiveness and teacher job satisfaction.

Naturally, both students and teachers in international settings must exhibit sound intercultural communication skills (Ting-Toomey 1999). Further, an understanding of these abilities is basic to education because teacher–student communication 'is such an archetypical human phenomenon, so deeply rooted in the culture of society, that cross-cultural learning situations are fundamentally problematic for both parties' (Hofstede 1986: 303).

Analysing and enhancing teachers' intercultural competence can be approached from various perspectives, but there is a strong argument for a focus on teacher–student interpersonal behaviour. Teaching and learning require perception and communication, both of which are culturally influenced (e.g. Au and Kawakami 1994; Grossman 1995; Nieto 1996; Samovar and Porter 1995; Stefani 1997). Cultures differ in the type of information perceived, stored and used (Cole and Scribner 1974; Segall et al. 1990). As a result, an extensive literature on cultural differences in cognition, conceptualization and knowledge construction has accumulated (for a review, see Hofstede and Hofstede 2004).

When communicating, people simultaneously send both content and relational messages and the nature of the relationship often determines how the communication is interpreted (e.g. Watzlawick et al. 1967). Further, communication occurs in a *systemic* manner – messages sent by person A affect the response of person B, which then affects the response of person A, and so on. Thus, an analysis of the effects of teacher–student communication yields insights into the factors that influence students' behaviour and learning processes (e.g. Watzlawick et al. 1967; Shuell, 1996). This heightens the importance for teachers to understand the interpersonal relationship preferences and perceptions of students.

A focus on interpersonal behaviour is also justified for other reasons. The nature of teacher–student communication is a major component of classroom management (e.g. Doyle 1986), an area of concern for both experienced and inexperienced teachers (Veenman 1984). Research has shown that students' perceptions of teacher behaviour are strongly related to student achievement and motivation in all subject areas (Brok et al. 2004; Wubbels and Brekelmans 1998) and that healthy teacher–student relationships are a prerequisite for engaging students in learning activities (Brekelmans et al. 2000; Wubbels and Levy 1993). Moreover, when teachers and students enjoy positive communications, teachers exhibit greater job satisfaction and experience less burnout (e.g. Ben-Chaim and Zoller 2001; Wubbels and Levy 1993).

The importance of student perceptions

Including students as a source of information in teacher assessment has several advantages. Usually, students have participated in many lessons, both those of the teachers being assessed as well as of their colleagues. As a result, they have more experience observing a particular teacher than external, expert observers and their observations are therefore usually very stable. Further, using average student perceptions (for example, aggregations of the opinions of all the students in a class) in assessments enables many assessors to participate, rather than one. This also limits bias caused by the personal beliefs and characteristics of a single assessor. Composite judgements by students also display high validity and reliability. This is particularly true for secondary education students' perceptions (e.g. Fraser 1998), such as those reported on in the present chapter. Third, research has shown that students' perceptions are usually closer to those of external observers than the self perceptions of teachers (Wubbels, Brekelmans et al. 2006). Apparently, teachers incorporate their own ideas about good teaching and expectations in their self-perceptions, while these have less influence on students' observations. A fourth reason for using student perceptions is that these affect to a large degree what students learn and how they achieve (Shuell 1996). In other words, students largely react to what they observe and interpret from their teachers' behaviour. Last, involving students in the assessment of their teachers acknowledges them as the primary consumers of education, and their opinions must be taken seriously. Research has shown that this can be done successfully with secondary education students' judgements – more so than with primary education students – and with respect to topics that are linked to general educational aspects (e.g. Fraser 2002).

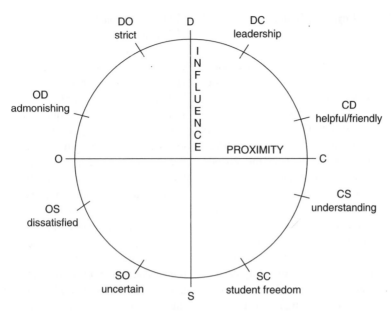

Figure 20.1   The Model for Interpersonal Teacher Behaviour (MITB)

THE MODEL FOR INTERPERSONAL TEACHER BEHAVIOUR

In order to analyse teacher–student interpersonal behaviour in the international context, it is important to provide a theoretical framework to describe and analyse teacher behaviour. The Model for Interpersonal Teacher Behaviour (MITB), which was extrapolated from the work of Leary (1957) by Wubbels, Créton and Hooymayers (1985), provides such a foundation. The Leary model and related circumplex frameworks have been used to investigate interpersonal behaviour in many settings and cultures (Lonner 1980). The two communication dimensions formulated by Leary, and reconceptualized by Wubbels, Créton and Hooymayers (1985) – Influence and Proximity – are universally accepted to interpret interpersonal behaviour (Adamopoulos 1988; Lonner 1980; Triandis 1994). This makes the concept particularly suitable for international education settings.

As noted, the Model for Interpersonal Teacher Behaviour (see Figure 20.1) describes teacher behaviour according to two dimensions: *Influence* (the degree to which the teacher is in control in the teacher–student relationship) and *Proximity* (the degree of cooperation between teacher and students). The influence dimension is characterized by teacher dominance (D) on one end of the spectrum and teacher submission (S) on the other end. Similarly, the proximity dimension is characterized by teacher cooperation (C) on one end and by teacher opposition (O) on the other. The two dimensions can be depicted in a two-dimensional plane, that can be further subdivided into eight categories or sectors of behaviour: leadership (DC), helpful/friendly (CD), understanding (CS), student freedom (SC), uncertain (SO), dissatisfied (OS), admonishing (OD) and strict (DO). Each sector can be described in terms of the two dimensions: leadership, for example (DC), contains a high degree of influence with some level of cooperation; helpful/friendly (CD) behaviour some dominance with high levels of cooperation, etc.

THE MITB and intercultural communication

The two dimensions of Influence and Proximity are particularly relevant because of their strong connection to aspects of intercultural communication. In previous research (e.g. Brok et al. 2002) Influence and Proximity were significantly related to three dimensions that describe culturally influenced behaviour and cognition: immediacy, collectivism and power distance. (Although such cultural dimensions can be used to explain perceptual differences between groups of students within classes, they should never be used to label or value individual students' views and background, since this may easily lead to stereotyping.) The *immediacy or approach–avoidance* dimension is anchored on one extreme by actions that simultaneously communicate closeness, approach and accessibility, and on the other by behaviours expressing avoidance and distance (Andersen 1985). Highly immediate cultures are often found in South America, the Middle East and Southern and Eastern Europe, whereas North America and Northern Europe are societies of comparably low immediacy (Collier and Powell, 1990). In class, strong immediacy is reflected in teacher behaviour that is supportive, friendly and occasionally emotional, and students who form close bonds with their teachers (e.g. Hofstede 1986). Students from highly immediate cultures might expect their teachers to display higher amounts of Proximity than students from less immediate cultures. The degree of *collectivism* in a culture determines the extent to which people emphasize community, shared interests, harmony, tradition, the public good and maintaining face (Kim et al. 1994). A collectivist class is characterized by students who prefer small group work and who do not speak in the whole group unless called upon. There is an emphasis on grades, the retention of 'face' or honour. Occasionally, teachers might be expected to give preferential treatment to some students, such as group leaders (Hofstede 1986). Students from collectivist cultures might be more sensitive to preserving face.

Power distance (PD) is defined by Hofstede (1991) as the degree to which power, prestige and wealth are unequally distributed in a culture. Cultures with high PD scores on Hofstede's index believe that control and influence are concentrated in the hands of a few rather than more equally distributed. In classes marked by high power distance, teachers are greatly respected by students because of their age and profession, classes tend to be teacher-centred and students are rarely critical or challenging (Hofstede 1986).

As can be seen, culture – in terms of the three dimensions above – affects students' and teachers' perceptions of the teacher's interpersonal behaviour in a number of ways: through their values and norms, through their interpretations of observed teacher behaviours and through differential treatment of students by the teacher (e.g. Brok 2001). Using the MITB to explain teachers' interactions with students can thereby illuminate potential aspects of culture that contribute to the learning environment.

TEACHER INTERPERSONAL BEHAVIOUR IN MULTICULTURAL AND CROSS-NATIONAL CONTEXTS: A REVIEW OF RESEARCH ON PERCEPTIONS AND BEHAVIOUR

This section briefly reviews the outcomes of research from domestic *multicultural* classes in The Netherlands, the United States, Australia, Singapore and Brunei, as well as from comparisons of interpersonal styles across countries. The analysis provides support for several elements of the MITB. First, there appears to be evidence that teachers treat students from different nationality backgrounds differently. Difference in teacher treatment is likely to result in varying student perceptions – for example, students may perceive more or less teacher proximity or dominance. It has been found that US teachers, for example, treat students of colour (particularly African-Americans) less positively than Caucasians: they are criticized and disciplined more often, and receive less attention and praise (Irvine 1986; Simpson and Erickson 1983). Additionally, research reports that Asian-American students are an often overseen (or unnoticed) group in the classroom, because they tend to take a low profile (Marcus et al. 1991). In European (for example, Dutch) classrooms, it appears that minority students are cited more often for discipline problems than their mainstream counterparts (Wubbels, Brok et al. 2006).

There is also evidence that students' perceptions of their teachers are related both to national origin as well as cognitive and affective outcomes. In a study of 952 university students, Sanders and Wiseman (1990) found that the attitudes toward various subjects of Hispanic-American origin were significantly more positively affected by their perceptions of teacher cooperation than the attitudes of students of other ethnic backgrounds. The correlations between Proximity and school test scores were lower for African-American students than other ethnic groups. As such, teachers had less (positive) effects on these students' test scores through their interpersonal behaviour than they had on other students' scores, although cooperative behaviour by the teacher has a systematic positive effect on the test scores of all students. For the Moroccan and Turkish students in a study by Brok, Veldman, Wubbels and van Tartwijk (2004), a stronger effect was found between Influence and Proximity and student subject-related attitudes than for Dutch students and students from other countries. Thus, not only did these students report higher amounts of Influence and Proximity by their teachers, they were also more motivated toward the subjects. In addition, there are indications that Western students have different perceptions of their teachers' interpersonal behaviour than their non-Western peers. In general, in multicultural classes in the Netherlands, Australia and the USA, students from non-Western cultures perceived more teacher Influence and Proximity than did students from Western cultures (Brok et al. 2002; Evans and Fisher 2000; Levy et al. 2003). These findings have been consistent when using a variety of ethnic indicators, such as self-defined ethnic membership, country of

birth of the student or his/her parents, language spoken at home or the number of years respondents have lived in the country of study. In a similar fashion, studies show that non-Western teachers (for example, Asian or Latin American teachers) are perceived as both more dominant and cooperative than Western teachers (Brok et al. 2002; Brok et al. 2003; Khine and Fisher, 2002; McCroskey et al. 1995). No clear evidence was found for the expectation that teachers' and students' perceptions were closer to each other when they shared the same ethnicity than when they came from different groups. For example, Brok et al. (2002) found no differences between student and teacher perceptions on both interpersonal dimensions for same or other ethnic background of student and teacher. According to the research reviewed, neither teachers nor students have a more favourable perception of someone from their own ethnic background than they have of an outsider. This result disagrees with the conventional wisdom reported in much of the literature, which assumes that people from the same in-group interpret behaviour similarly and treat their cultural colleagues more positively.

While the research above describes the perceptions of individual students, similar findings have been reported for classes in which there are a variety of cultures represented. The more non-Western students or different cultural groups in class, the more teacher dominance and proximity are perceived (Brok and Levy 2005). Because teachers often recognize the relationship between teacher Influence and Proximity and student achievement, they try to exhibit leadership, helpful/ friendly and understanding behaviours in class. Some research has begun to investigate strategies that evoke perceptions of high Influence and Proximity, and Table 20.1 lists the methods employed by veteran teachers of multicultural classes. (e.g. Wubbels, Brok et al. 2006).

While the strategies listed in Table 20.1 were observed in domestic multicultural classes, they clearly apply to international settings. These techniques are quite similar to those mentioned in the literature on multicultural education (e.g. Evertson and Harris 1999; Scarcella 1990; Zeichner 1996)

Table 20.1   Strategies found in multicultural classes of experienced teachers to realize high amounts of perceived Influence and Proximity

Interpersonal dimension	Situations/themes	Suggested strategies by teachers
Influence	Coping with relative intense student emotional responses	• keeping corrections small and of low intensity • indicating with-it-ness ('I see you are ...') • signaling that disruptions are observed and considered a violation of rules • sending non-verbal messages of rest and control (small gestures, eye contact, etc.) • repeating earlier agreements with students • repeating and reminding students of important tasks and instructions • showing to students possible consequences of their behaviour • showing own feelings and emotions
	Negotiating without giving in and at the same time honouring student perspectives and needs	• providing sound reasons for judgements • listening to arguments of students (without directly giving in) • implying that a decision is a given and is outside oneself or the student • indicating own feelings about a decision • relating judgement to observations made • partially rewarding students and showing how the remainder of the reward can be obtained
	Providing and strictly enforcing clear procedures and sound rules	
	Preventing escalation of conflicts	
	Showing self to be in control	• taking a central position in class • indicating non-verbally the beginning of the lesson (raising head and voice)
	Helping students to focus on rational arguments instead of power arguments	
	Frequent and varied testing	
	Providing structured variety	• providing clear lesson structure • preparing lessons from a content and process point of view • grading/correcting tasks/tests with great care and very accurately • writing a lesson plan on the blackboard • telling the students what will happen during the lesson • engaging in a variety of tasks and classroom activities • organizing frequent and repeating central, whole-class moments • providing students with deadlines or timelines • explaining goals/purposes of activities explicitly
	Making no mistakes in content or procedures	
Proximity	Focusing on cooperation of leader of the peer group	• approaching rest of peer group to signal continuation of relationship after conflict with peer leader

Table 20.1   (Continued)

Interpersonal dimension	Situations/themes	Suggested strategies by teachers
	Coping with relatively intense student emotional responses	• compensating corrections immediately with positive remarks, smiles or acknowledgement of changed behaviour • limiting own use of bans on behaviour/commands
	Using small rather than intense corrections (eyes, gestures instead of words)	
	Putting limits to students	
	Providing constructive and adequate feedback	• referring explicitly to behaviour and not the person • asking other students to join in or give assistance when answering questions or completing tasks • compensating corrections with positive remarks • giving feedback without causing humiliation, or loss of face
	Correcting students needs to be followed by making rapport	• organizing short student–teacher meetings after lesson • showing rest of the class a relationship is restored
	Showing humour	
	Building trustful relationships, e.g. through physical contact	
	Showing respect and providing frequent compliments and rewards	
	Actively engaging in probing for individual student's interests, beliefs and background	• listening to students on school-related and non-related issues • observing students during classroom activities • speaking with students after lessons or in the hallways • contacting parents of students • moving between students' seats/taking non-central position • welcoming students and greeting them

Source: Wubbels, Brok et al. 2006

and classroom management (Freiberg and Driscoll 1996; Woolfolk 2001), which suggests that they are also applicable in international contexts.

Although these studies provide a potentially useful knowledge base for teachers in international education, their findings should be interpreted with care. First, the majority of the studies have been conducted in multicultural domestic classes in a few Western (or Asian) countries. These contexts differ from those in international schools, which often attract students from different socioeconomic backgrounds and countries of origin, and whose classes may differ in the number and make-up of cultural groups. As a result, differences in perceptions between students and their teachers will differ between these classes and warrant their own line of research. Second, the majority of the studies used the Model for Interpersonal Teacher Behaviour as their theoretical rationale and operationalized this model through the *Questionnaire on Teacher Interaction* (QTI: Wubbels et al. 1985). Despite the fact that the QTI is one of the most widely used classroom instruments, has cross-national validity and appears to be highly valid and reliable (Wubbels, Brekelmans et al. 2006), other frameworks and instruments or data collection methods are possible and might be valuable in their own respect.

RESEARCH ON TEACHER INTERPERSONAL BEHAVIOUR

Research on teacher interpersonal behaviour in international schools – using a similar framework as described above – has been scarce. Nevertheless, this section discusses some results of action research conducted by international school teachers. Some of the studies involved students' and teachers' interpersonal ideals: how participants would like their best (or ideal) teachers to behave. These outcomes illustrate both students' and teachers' beliefs about the behaviours that develop strong classroom relationships, and hence positive student achievement. Van Oord and Brok (2004) found ethnicity-related differences in a study of 215 high school students' interpersonal ideals in two international schools in Norway and Wales. Students from South America preferred teachers who were less cooperative than their counterparts from other countries. In addition, Nordic students' ideal teachers were stricter and provided their classes with less responsibility.

In addition to the research on international school teachers, data were collected on pre-service teachers over a five-year period (2000–2004) at the authors' teacher training institute (Bilingual and International Teacher Education Programme, Utrecht University). More than 1,500 students at schools with international populations rated the interpersonal behaviour of 56 student teachers using the QTI. In addition, the pre-service teachers also provided self-perceptions regarding their real behaviour as well as ideal. Data were collected at the beginning and end of the training programme, and are reported in terms of *interpersonal profiles* that were established from prior research using the QTI (see Figure 20.1). The profiles, which have been shown to be relatively stable, describe teachers who are predominantly Directive, Authoritative, Tolerant/Authoritative, Tolerant, Uncertain/Tolerant, Uncertain/Aggressive, Drudging and Repressive (Brekelmans et al. 1993). The Authoritative, the Tolerant/Authoritative and the Tolerant type are patterns in which students perceive their teachers relatively high on the

Proximity Dimension, with the Tolerant type lowest on the Influence Dimension. Less cooperative than the three previous types are the Directive, the Uncertain/Tolerant and the Drudging teacher, with the Uncertain/Tolerant type lowest on the Influence Dimension. The least cooperative teachers are characterized by the Repressive and Uncertain/Aggressive patterns. Repressive teachers are the most dominant (but not necessarily the most successful in terms of student outcomes) of all eight types. The graphic representations in Table 20.2 follow the eight sectors of the Model of Interpersonal Teacher Behaviour. The shaded portion indicates teacher behaviour for that sector (see Figure 20.1). While the comparisons are rough due to differences in setting, Table 20.2 presents profiles for experienced teachers in multicultural domestic schools, student teachers in domestic training programmes and student teachers in the selected international training programme.

From the results in Table 20.2 it appears the student teachers in the international programme most often exhibited Tolerant/Authoritative, Tolerant and Authoritative behaviours, according to their students. The first two profiles are quite common, both among experienced and regular student teachers. The last profile (Authoritative), however, seems to distinguish this group from their peers in regular teacher education programmes. Another difference between the two groups can be seen in the Uncertain/Tolerant profile, which international student teachers do not exhibit as much as their mainstream peers. It should be noted that the Directive, Authoritative and Tolerant/Authoritative types usually realize higher achievement and attitudinal outcomes than the other types (e.g. Brok et al. 2004).

The same research agenda that produced the student teacher data above has also provided useful action research outcomes. The investigations were conducted by student teachers during their initial training and can only be considered tentative. Nonetheless, they have generated helpful ideas for future research in international education. For example, two cohorts of student teachers (20 student teachers from the Utrecht University Bilingual and

Table 20.2 Graphic representation of the eight patterns of interpersonal profiles and their presence (in percentage scores) in regular and international (teacher) education settings

Interpersonal type	Experienced teachers (n = 1,600) in regular schools	Student teachers (*n* = 540) in regular teacher education programmes	Student teachers (n = 56) in international teacher education programmes
Directive	19	5	8
Authoritative	23	8	17
Tolerant/ Authoritative	14	13	25
Tolerant	19	39	33
Uncertain/ Tolerant	9	26	6
Uncertain/ Aggressive	3	5	3
Repressive	5	1	3
Drudging	8	3	5

Note: Source for the experienced teachers was the study by Brekelmans, Wubbels and Brok (2002); source for the student teachers in national schools was a study by Somers, Brekelmans and Wubbels (1997)

Table 20.3   Behaviours perceived as 'strict' by students from international schools in different countries

Nationality	Behaviour regarded as strict
Venezuelan	Consistency, straightforwardness, setting clear rules, confidence, high standards, distance and not hesitant to use penalties such as extra work, contacting parents and detention
Hungarian	Demanding silence, employing strong sanctions and pupils being frightened of the teacher. However, the pupils here also link strictness to being a real leader. A real leader needs to be strict, in their opinion
Norwegian	Setting someone apart, sending someone out, detention, demanding students to answer quickly, difficult tests, making it hard to get a good grade, calling parents
Ghanese	Demanding a quick answer, strict on homework and reminding the students to do their work, doing something without a fair reason
South African	Shout often, punish, pupils have to do homework, not allowed to make unnecessary noise and have to be in time for the lesson

International Teacher Education Programme) interviewed secondary students in various international schools about the concept of 'strictness' in their respective cultures. These interviews reveal notable differences between students' countries of origin (see Table 20.3).

As seen in Table 20.3, students from some countries – such as Venezuela, Norway and Ghana – connected strictness to high demands, testing and grading, which are all evaluative teacher behaviours. Among students from other countries, however, strictness seems to evoke images of teacher control and correction of off-task students. In addition, Venezuelan and Norwegian students related strictness with teachers' contact with parents regarding problems, whereas this was not explicitly mentioned by students from other countries. Other action research revealed that Nordic students linked strictness and leadership behaviour more closely than their peers from other nations (Nieuwdorp-Tramper and Holwerda-van den Berg 2004). Such reported cultural differences are in alignment with cross-national research on the validity of the QTI, showing that in some Asian countries (Singapore, Brunei) Strictness and Leadership occupy more distant positions on the interpersonal circle (see Figure 20.1) than in Australia or the Netherlands where they display much more overlap (Brok et al. 2006). As was the case with multicultural domestic teachers, these action research projects reiterate the necessity for international school faculty to be aware that interpersonal concepts and behaviours vary in meaning across

nationality groups and lead to different culturally based perceptions of 'good' teaching and relationship-building.

TOWARD BUILDING BLOCKS FOR TEACHER EDUCATION AND PROFESSIONAL DEVELOPMENT PROGRAMMES FOR AN INTERNATIONAL CONTEXT

This final section presents an analysis of the data presented above, as well as some guidelines for teacher education and professional development. Research on interpersonal behaviour in multicultural and cross-national contexts demonstrated that teachers' approaches to students and students' perceptions of their teachers are influenced by ethnicity. Students from different cultural groups appear to rate teachers differently even if they think they are treated equally by the teachers. These differences can be interpreted along the cultural dimensions discussed earlier. In many Western countries, people are more individualistic than those in the East and South. They may be less inclined to focus on (or notice) behaviours that are associated with Approach/Immediacy or Collectivism and they may not act in a manner that will build proximity. At the same time there is a more horizontal relationship between teachers and students, and Western-born pupils may also be less inclined to focus on proximity-oriented behaviour because of the absence of or implicit nature of power struggles in the classroom. Consequently, Western teachers may demonstrate fewer Proximity behaviours, and Western-born students may also be less focused on them, resulting in lower influence ratings for their teachers. This interpretation requires further study.

In addition, the research indicates that interpersonal behaviour may vary in its effect on subject-related attitudes (or achievement) across cultures, and that a variety of behaviour strategies may be employed in the classroom to achieve high perceptions of Influence and Proximity. For the preparation of teachers for international settings, this implies that awareness-raising with respect to the complex nature of culture and teacher–student interaction is necessary. As has been noted often in the literature, teachers should familiarize themselves with the cultural backgrounds and current status of their students. They should also reflect on their actual classroom behaviour, either through video review, third-party observations and/or data collected from students via interview or questionnaire.

The limited research on interpersonal behaviour in international settings suggested that student teachers behave according to different profiles, and these can be improved with teacher education or professional development. In addition, students' (and teachers') views about good or ideal interpersonal teaching, and/or the meaning of interpersonal concepts like strictness or student freedom, may vary according to culture. This implies that collecting data from multiple views (for example, ideal perceptions, student perceptions, teacher self-perceptions) with the instrument(s) and framework described, either during teacher education and professional development programmes or as part of quality assurance and assessment procedures, can be very helpful.

How, then, can teachers or schools proceed after they have received feedback from students and other educators? Most importantly, teachers should reflect on their outcomes, especially on the relationship between their ideal, their own and their students' perceptions, and possible cultural influences. Without this self-analysis, chances are that teachers will not change their behaviour nor gain deeper insight into their own personal communication style with students. Such reflection

can take the form of a small discussion or a more elaborate trajectory involving peer-coaching or clinical supervision. Other activities may involve comparing personal outcomes with those of colleague teachers as well as analysing the results from different classes (for example, the class the teacher regards as the best and the one he or she regards as the worst). In addition, teachers can discuss the results with their classes in order to get a more accurate understanding of student perceptions. This is important, since effective teachers generally see themselves the same as their students. Finally, teachers can link their outcomes to other data sources such as observations (from video), personal logs or lesson material, and compile a portfolio of their interpersonal behaviour. It is very important that teachers move beyond the data-gathering stage toward meaningful reflection and strategies for improvement.

Finally, it is clear that teacher preparation programmes should include content on interpersonal behaviour. The pre-service teacher, as opposed to his or her more experienced colleague, is often overwhelmed by the complexity of the teaching profession and finds it difficult to distinguish between the various roles required. How can content on intercultural/interpersonal teaching be incorporated into a teacher preparation programme? The following principles for the development of interpersonal competency for international education are based on the research described above as well as current views on teacher training.

First, in order to analyse and cope with new and complex situations a strong focus on reflective skills seems beneficial (Korthagen 2001). The reflective principle is based on the assumption that reflective teachers are capable of consciously structuring situations and systematically analysing problems, and as a result develop better interpersonal relationships with students than their non-reflective colleagues (e.g. Korthagen 2001). It is helpful for the teacher candidate to have a conceptual, theoretical foundation that supports his or her reflection. For example, the theories presented in this chapter – the *systems approach to communication* (e.g. Watzlawick et al. 1967), the *Model for Interpersonal Teacher Behaviour* (e.g. Wubbels et al. 1985) and the *cultural dimensions* (e.g. Hofstede 1991) – are useful in helping future teachers to structure and analyse their experiences. The theories are helpful because they are understandable and can be applied across cultures.

A second important feature is the distinction between the various roles of the teaching profession (e.g. Brekelmans et al. 2000; Shuell 1996). By clarifying these responsibilities and skill sets and explicitly adding the role of intercultural communicator, pre-service teachers must focus on existing intercultural differences within the international classroom, including their own cultural identities and that of others. The underlying approach here is the creation of a 'sphere of interculturality' in order to make prospective teachers aware of the fact that the learning of culture is more than just the transfer of information between cultures and that national identities (including one's own) are not monolithic (McKay 2002). To achieve this, it seems straightforward to place student teachers in international classrooms abroad after they have served in a more familiar domestic setting. Further, the teacher preparation programme should generate opportunities for the pre-service teacher to exchange experiences and reflect on his or her behaviour with colleagues. In terms of the topic and framework of this chapter, several learning activities can be designed towards this end. These might include small data collection tasks, such as interviewing one or two students on certain interpersonal concepts (strictness *vs* leadership or the role of teachers in providing students with responsibility for their own behaviour. The pre-service teachers might administer the QTI in their classrooms and discuss the outcomes with their peers. Finally, they may engage in more in-depth action research projects on interpersonal topics. Such topics could involve both quantitative and qualitative designs and could address the following themes, among others:

- the link between interpersonal behaviour and student outcomes
- differences between teacher and student perceptions

- differences between perceptions of different classes
- comparisons of perceptions within and between different (types of) international classes
- variables that affect student and teacher perceptions
- strategies that seem to be effective in the classroom to achieve high amounts of influence and proximity
- improving the interpersonal climate in the international classroom.

Overall, these activities serve two important purposes: not only are they valuable learning experiences for the teachers concerned, but they can also help to expand a much-needed knowledge base on teacher interpersonal behaviour in the international context.

REFERENCES

Adamopoulos, J. (1988) Interpersonal behavior: cross-cultural and historical perspectives. In M.H. Bond (ed.) *The Cross-Cultural Challenge to Social Psychology*. Newbury Park, CA: Sage, pp. 196–207.

Andersen, P.A. (1985) Nonverbal immediacy in interpersonal communication. In A. W. Siegman and S. Feldstein (eds) *Multichannel Integrations of Nonverbal Behavior*. Hillsdale, NJ: Lawrence Erlbaum Associates.

Au, K.H. and Kawakami, A.J. (1994) Cultural congruence in instruction. In E.R. Hollins, J.E. King and W.C. Hayman (eds) *Teaching Diverse Populations: Formulating a Knowledge Base*. Albany, NY: State University of New York Press.

Ben-Chaim, D. and Zoller, U. (2001) Self-perception versus students' perceptions of teachers' personal style in college science and mathematics courses. *Research in Science Education,* 31: 437–54.

Brekelmans, M., Levy, J. and Rodriguez, R. (1993) A typology of teacher communication style. In T. Wubbels and J. Levy (eds) *Do You Know What You Look Like?* London: The Falmer Press, pp. 46–55.

Brekelmans, M., Sleegers, P. and Fraser, B. (2000) Teaching for active learning. In R.J. Simons, J. van der Linden and T. Duffy (eds) *New Learning*. Dordrecht: Kluwer Academic Publishers, pp. 227–42.

Brekelmans, M., Wubbels, Th., & Brok, P. den (2002) Teacher experience and the teacher-student relationship in the classroom environment. In S. C. Goh & M. S. Khine (eds) *Studies in educational learning environments: an international perspective*. Singapore: World Scientific, pp. 73–99.

Brok, P. den (2001) *Teaching and Student Outcomes. A Study on Teachers' Thoughts and Actions from an Interpersonal and a Learning Activities Perspective.* Utrecht: WCC.

Brok, P. den, Brekelmans, M. and Wubbels, T. (2004) Interpersonal teacher behavior and student outcomes. *School Effectiveness and School Improvement,* 15(3/4): 407–42.

Brok, P. den, Fisher, D., Brekelmans, M., Wubbels, T., & Rickards, T. (2006) Secondary teachers' interpersonal behaviour in Singapore, Brunei and Australia: a cross-national comparison. *Asia-Pacific Journal of Education, 26*(1): 79–95.

Brok, P. den, & Levy, J. (2005) Teacher-student relationships in multicultural classes: reviewing the past, preparing the future. *International Journal of Educational Research, 43*(1/2): 25–38.

Brok, P.J. den, Levy, J. Rodriguez, R. and Wubbels, T. (2002) Perceptions of Asian-American and Hispanic-American teachers and their students on interpersonal communication style. *Teaching and Teacher Education,* 18: 447–67.

Brok, P. den, Levy, J., Wubbels, T. and Rodriguez, M. (2003) Cultural influences on students' perceptions of videotaped lessons. *International Journal of Intercultural Relations,* 27(3): 355–78.

Brok, P. den, Veldman, I., Wubbels, T. and Tartwijk, J. van (2004) Teacher interpersonal behaviour in Dutch multicultural classes. Paper presented at the annual meeting of the American Educational Research Association, San Diego, April 2004.

Cole, M. and Scribner, S. (1974) *Culture and Thought: a Psychological Introduction.* New York: John Wiley & Sons.

Collier, M.J. and Powell, R.G. (1990) Ethnicity, instructional communication and classroom systems. *Communication Quarterly,* 38(4): 334–49.

Doyle, W. (1986) Classroom organization and management. In M.C. Wittrock (ed.), *Handbook of Research on Teaching.* New York: Macmillan, pp. 392–431.

Evans, H. and Fisher, D. (2000). Cultural differences in students' perceptions of science teachers' interpersonal behaviour. *Australian Science Teachers Journal,* 46: 9–18.

Evertson, C.M. and Harris, A.H. (1999) Support for managing learning-centered classrooms, the classroom organization and management pr gramme. In H.J. Freiberg (ed.) *Beyond Behaviourism: Changing the Classroom Management Paradigm.* Needham Heights, MS: Allyn and Bacon, pp. 59–74.

Fraser, B.J. (1998) Science learning environments: assessment, effects and determinants. In B.J. Fraser and K. Tobin (eds) *International Handbook of Science Education.* Dordrecht, The Netherlands: Kluwer, pp. 527–64.

Fraser, B.J. (2002) Learning environments research: yesterday, today and tomorrow. In S.C. Goh and M.S. Khine (eds) *Studies in Educational Learning Environments: an International Perspective.* Singapore: World Scientific, pp. 1–27.

Freiberg, H.J. and Driscoll, A. (1996) *Universal Teaching Strategies,* 2nd edition. Boston, MA: Allyn and Bacon.

Grossman, H. (1995) *Teaching a Diverse Society.* Boston, MA: Allyn and Bacon.

Hofstede, G. (1986) Cultural differences in teaching and learning. *International Journal of Intercultural Relations,* 10: 301–20.

Hofstede, G. (1991) *Cultures and Organizations: Software of the Mind.* London: McGraw-Hill.

Hofstede, G. and Hofstede, G.J. (2004) *Cultures and Organizations: Software of the Mind: Intercultural Cooperation and Its Importance for Survival.* New York: McGraw-Hill.

Irvine, J.J. (1986) Teacher–student interactions: effects of student race, sex and grade level. *Journal of Educational Psychology,* 78, 14–21.

Khine, M.S. and Fisher, D. (2002) *Classroom environments, student attitudes and cultural background of teachers in Brunei.* Paper presented at the conference of the American Educational Research Association, New Orleans, April 2002.

Kim, M.S. Sharkey, W. and Singelis, T. (1994) The relationship between individuals' self-construals and perceived importance of interactive constraints. *International Journal of Intercultural Relations,* 18(1): 117–40.

Korthagen, F.A.J. (2001) Evaluative research on the realistic approach and on the promotion of reflection. In F.A.J. Korthagen, J. Kessels, B. Koster, B. Lagerwerf and T. Wubbels (eds) *Linking Practice and Theory: the Pedagogy of Realistic Teacher Education.* Mahwah, NJ: Lawrence Erlbaum Associates, pp. 88–107.

Leary, T. (1957) *An Interpersonal Diagnosis of Personality.* New York: Ronald Press Company.

Levy, J., Brok, P. den, Wubbels, T. and Brekelmans, M. (2003) Students' perceptions of interpersonal aspects of the learning environment. *Learning Environments Research,* 6(1): 5–37.

Lonner, W.J. (1980) The search for psychological universals. In H.C. Triandis and W.W. Lambert (eds) *Handbook of Cross-cultural Psychology,* vol. 1. Boston, MA: Allyn and Bacon, pp.143–204.

McKay, S.L. (2002) *Teaching English as an International Language: Rethinking Goals and Perspectives.* New York: Oxford University Press.

Marcus, G., Gross, S. and Seefeldt, C. (1991) Black and white students' perceptions of teacher treatment. *Journal of Educational Research*, 84(6): 363–7.

McCroskey, J.C., Fayer, J.M., Richmond, V.P., Sallinen, A. and Barraclough, R.A. (1996) A multi-cultural examination of the relationship between nonverbal immediacy and affective learning. *Communication Quarterly*, 44(3): 297–307.

McCroskey, J.C., Richmond, V.P., Sallinen, A., Fayer, J.M., & Barraclough, R.A. (1995) A cross-cultural and multi-behavioral analysis of the relationship between nonverbal immediacy and teacher evaluation. *Communication Education*, *44*:281–91.

Nieto, S. (1996) *Affirming Diversity: The Sociopolitical Context of Multicultural Education*. New York: Longman.

Nieuwdorp-Tramper, H. and Holwerda-van den Berg, G. (2004) *The best teacher in the eyes of Norwegian students*. Unpublished Masters thesis. Utrecht: IVLOS, Bilingual and International Teacher Education Programme.

Oord, L. van and Brok, P. den (2004) The international teacher: students' and teachers' perceptions of preferred teacher–student interpersonal behaviour in two United World Colleges. *Journal of Research in International Education*, 3(2): 131–55.

Samovar, L.A. and Porter, R.E. (1995) *Communication between Cultures*, 2nd edition. Belmont, CA: Wadsworth.

Sanders, J.A., & Wiseman, R.L. (1990) The effects of verbal and nonverbal teacher immediacy on perceived cognitive, affective and behavioral learning in the multicultural classroom. *Communication Education*, *39*: 341–53.

Scarcella, R. (1990) *Teaching Language Minority Students in the Multicultural Classroom*. Englewood Cliffs: NJ: Prentice Hall.

Segall, M.H., Dasen, P.R., Berry, J.W. and Poortinga, Y.H. (eds) (1990). *Human Behaviour in Global Perspective: An Introduction to Cross-cultural Psychology*. New York: Pergamon Press.

Shuell, T.J. (1996) Teaching and learning in a classroom context. In D.C. Berliner and R.C. Calfee (eds) *Handbook of Educational Psychology*. New York: MacMillan, pp. 726–63.

Simpson, A.W. and Erickson, M.T. (1983) Teachers' verbal and nonverbal communication patterns as a function of teacher race, student gender and student race. *American Educational Research Journal*, 20: 183–98.

Somers, T., Brekelmans, M. and Wubbels, T. (1997). *Development of student teachers on the teacher–student relationship in the classroom*. Paper presented at the 7th Conference of the European Association for Research on Learning and Instruction, Athens.

Stefani, L.A. (1997) The influence of culture on classroom communication. In L.A. Samovar and R.E. Porter (eds) *Intercultural Communication: A Reader*, 8th edition. Belmont, CA: Wadsworth.

Ting-Toomey, S. (1999) *Communicating Across Cultures*. New York: The Guilford Press.

Triandis, H.C. (1994) *Culture and Social Behavior*. New York: McGraw–Hill.

Veenman, S.A.M. (1984) Perceived problems of beginning teachers. *Review of Educational Research*, 54: 143–78.

Watzlawick, P., Beavin, J.H. and Jackson, D. (1967), *The Pragmatics of Human Communication*. New York: Norton.

Woolfolk, A. (2001) *Educational Psychology*, 8th edition. Boston, MA: Allyn and Bacon.

Wubbels, T. (1992) Taking account of student teachers' preconceptions. *Teaching and Teacher Education*, 8(2): 137–49.

Wubbels, T. and Brekelmans, M. (1998) The teacher factor in the social climate of the classroom. In B.J. Fraser and K.G. Tobin (eds) *International Handbook of Science Education, Part One* London: Kluwer Academic, pp. 565–80.

Wubbels, T. and Levy, J. (1993) *Do You Know What You Look Like?* London: Falmer Press.

Wubbels, T., Brekelmans, M., Brok, P. den, and Tartwijk, J. van (2006) An interpersonal perspective on classroom management in secondary classrooms in the Netherlands. In C. Evertson and C.S. Weinstein (eds) *Handbook of Classroom Management: Research, Practice and Contemporary Issues*. New York: Lawrence Erlbaum Associates, pp. 1161–91.

Wubbels, T., Brok, P. den, Veldman, I. and Tartwijk, J. van (2006) Teacher interpersonal competence for Dutch multicultural classrooms. *Teachers and Teaching: Theory and Practice, 12* (4): 407–33.

Wubbels, T., Créton, H.A. and Hooymayers, H.P. (1985) *Discipline Problems of Beginning Teachers, Interactional Teacher Behavior Mapped Out.* Abstracted in Resources in Education, 20 (12): 153, ERIC document 260040.

Zeichner, K. (1996) Educating teachers for diversity. In K. Zeichner, S. Melnick and M. Gomez (eds) *Currents of Reform in Preservice Teacher Education*. New York: Teachers College Press.

21

Becoming More Internationally-Minded: International Teacher Certification and Professional Development

Lesley Snowball

With thousands of schools, tens of thousands of teachers and hundreds of thousands of students, international education is a rapidly growing sector, with growth stimulated by both necessity and ideology. As an increasing number of migrant workers move from country to country and an increasing number of parents purposefully choose a culturally and linguistically diverse education for their children, international education is undergoing a redefinition, from an exclusive system primarily for the children of transient professionals, into inclusive global education for both international and national systems.

As a direct result of the cultural and economic globalization and the associated mobility referred to throughout this Handbook, communities worldwide (and particularly major cities) are becoming increasingly diverse. As a typical example, in a recent census, Amsterdam's non-Dutch inhabitants became the majority when their numbers passed beyond the 50 per cent mark. Such statistics mean that international education can no longer be the domain of

an elite minority within international schools. Further, cultural and linguistic complexity make it the reality for many national schools as well. This in turn increases the need for faculty with specialized knowledge about the international context of education and skill in developing relevant curriculum and pedagogy.

However, there is little reflection of this need in teacher training programmes throughout the world. As noted in Chapter 18 in this Handbook by Levy and in previous research by this author (Snowball 1997, 2002), most teachers are only prepared for their immediate domestic context. This chapter will outline the specific knowledge and skills required of 'world-class' faculty, presented as seven standards for International Teacher Certification (ITC) (Snowball 2004).

THE CERTIFICATION PROCESS

As illustrated by the model in Figure 21.1 (Snowball, K. and L. F., 2004), to receive the

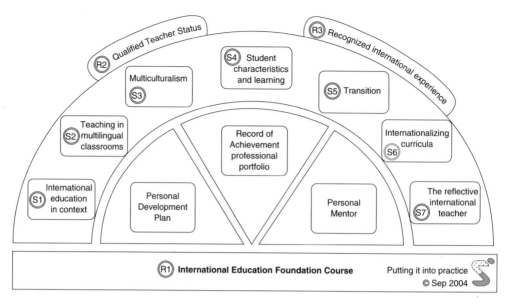

Figure 21.1 International Teacher Certification model – standards and requirements

ITC a teacher would need to submit a portfolio of evidence demonstrating achievement of each standard, and would be supported in doing so by a foundation course, an experienced mentor and a personal development plan. Such a system would recognize teachers for their specialized knowledge, skills and experience; focus and synthesize professional development from diverse sources; offer recruiters greater assurance of teacher preparation; and provide a common definition of an effective international teacher.

STANDARDS

Each standard is presented below, along with a rationale that has been drawn from the literature and extensive personal research with educators world-wide.

Standard 1: International education in context

The teacher understands the international context of education, appreciating both the unique profile of each school and the diversity amongst education systems, as well as the

roles played by major educational organizations, regionally and globally.

In practice, the international teacher:

(a) contributes to the ideal of developing globally minded students
(b) appreciates the rewards of working in culturally and linguistically diverse settings
(c) contributes positively to meet the challenges raised by cultural and linguistic diversity
(d) participates in social and educational projects within the local and global communities
(e) is knowledgeable about educational systems and practices world-wide.

Rationale

International education can be said to include schools that are international by name and schools that are international by nature (and, of course, some that are both). Hayden and Thompson (1998: 285) highlight 'teachers as exemplars of international-mindedness' as one of the core features of international education, 'whether or not that be in an institution called an international school'.

Within the broader context of education, international schools represent one element of internationalism alongside the multiculturalism and multilingualism that are typical within many national schools, and the diversity within and amongst different countries' education systems. In 'a world dominated by supranational production and trading forces, international cultural icons and common environmental problems on the one hand, and intensified and often painful expressions of local identity and regional singularity on the other' (Steiner 1996: xiv), the international teacher, aiming to develop internationally-minded students, should be aware of internationalism in this broader context. As an educator, a teacher has a unique opportunity to extend students' knowledge and understanding beyond the immediate and the familiar, and to nurture a disposition for compassion and action globally.

Standard 2: Teaching in multilingual classrooms

The teacher values students' multilingual abilities and demonstrates understanding of the processes involved in language acquisition and development in the first and subsequent languages.

In practice, the international teacher:

(a) encourages students to use their first language for personal, social and academic reasons
(b) plans and implements differentiated learning experiences and assessment strategies appropriate to students' language profiles.

Rationale

Of the areas identified, language is, arguably, the most fundamental, because it is related to cognition, self-esteem, cultural identity and general development. In addition, language diversity within and amongst students is widespread in most education systems. Linguists estimate that the world's peoples speak 5,000–6,000 languages, with English understood and spoken, to some extent, by around one-third of humanity (O'Neil 2005). Of the 162 countries or territories in UNESCO's World Culture Report 2000 (UNESCO 2000), 36 (22 per cent) have two or more official languages, while only seven (4 per cent) are listed as having only a single language in daily

use: for the majority of the world, multilingualism is a practical daily reality.

Clearly, skill in speaking more than one language may not always be a possible prerequisite for teaching multilingual students. Nonetheless, at a minimum, teachers should have a good understanding of how students acquire and develop language, and how they can best facilitate this complex process. Research on this topic abounds, and indeed many teacher training programmes do seem to make a gesture towards internationalism through the inclusion of some form of multilingual awareness component. However, most of these are offered only as electives, and relatively few teachers have an in-depth understanding of their own or other languages (especially of those outside their immediate language family), while even fewer appreciate the complex web of factors affecting multilingual learners or have adequate practical strategies to support them. The professional development of teachers world-wide would be enhanced by the theoretical knowledge of leading linguists such as Crystal (1997) and Krashen (1981, 1982), who have extended our understanding of the functions and functioning of language; by the findings of researchers such as Cummins (1994) and Collier and Thomas (2002), who have consistently advocated support for mother-tongue maintenance; and by the practical strategies suggested by educators such as Sears (1998), who shows a genuine appreciation of the challenges faced by second-language learners.

Such enhanced understandings could, to some extent, guard against outdated practices that are still found in many schools, both international and national. For example, students and their parents are encouraged to stop using the mother-tongue in the belief that language is subtractive rather than additive. Article 5 of UNESCO's Universal Declaration on Cultural Diversity (UNESCO 2001) states that, 'All persons have therefore the right to express themselves and to create and disseminate their work in the language of their choice, and particularly in their mother-tongue', and Collier and Thomas (2002) provided conclusive evidence of the importance of mother-tongue support on long-term academic achievement. Worryingly, however, they also found evidence of widespread parental misunderstanding about the benefits of such language support, and further instances of this have been encountered world-wide – for example, during this author's extensive work with bilingual teachers in Peru, parental non-cooperation was reported as a major factor in the failure of bilingual programmes. The role of teachers in convincing and reassuring parents is critical, but is clearly contingent on the teachers themselves understanding the issues and implications.

Standard 3: Multiculturalism

The teacher employs strategies that facilitate the academic achievement of students from diverse cultural groups.

In practice, the international teacher:

(a) demonstrates the use of several different approaches to integrate content about cultural groups into the curriculum

(b) helps students understand that knowledge is constructed, and is influenced by the biases, frames of reference and perspectives of individuals, groups and disciplines

(c) proactively employs strategies to develop positive attitudes and ensure equal status of different cultural groups.

Rationale

Cultural diversity is the norm for schools world-wide and can be considered a school's richest, most accessible resource. To facilitate best use of this resource, and optimize student achievement, teachers must be aware of cultural differences beyond the immediately visible surface aspects of the so-called 4Fs – fashion, festivals, flags and food. They need to be sensitive to the less visible aspects of culture, such as teaching and learning philosophies, communication styles, beliefs and values. These are illustrated clearly by Fennes and Hapgood's use of an iceberg model (1997). The iceberg analogy is well chosen, since it is through discovery of the 'subsurface' aspects that the real riches of a

culture can be understood and enjoyed. It is equally true that to be unaware of, to ignore or misinterpret them, creates the danger of potential cultural collision. Barna (1998: 173) asks why, despite good intentions and potential mutual benefit, contact with other cultures is so often frustrating and fraught with misunderstanding, and she goes on to propose 'six stumbling blocks': assumption of similarities, language differences, non-verbal misrepresentations, preconceptions and stereotypes, tendency to evaluate and high anxiety caused by uncertainty.

In a culturally diverse school, teachers will interact with several different cultures each day. It is therefore essential that they are aware of the potential barriers to effective communication, and have a generic appreciation of the fundamental nature of cultural characteristics. Of particular importance is sensitivity to significant home–school differences for individual students. The optimal situation is for each student to develop and value his or her own cultural identity while being enriched by contact with the cultures of others. Carlos Cortes (1994: 22–35) refers to this process as acculturation (an additive process of adapting to mainstream culture) as opposed to assimilation (a subtractive process of adopting another culture in place of your own).

Encountering contrasting cultures can make us more aware of our own, and students experiencing home–school differences between values and practices can become confused, especially if the transition into the new culture has been sudden, such as that caused by a move to a new country. For example, students brought up in a culture where teachers are revered are more likely to have difficulty adjusting to a school emphasis on student initiative and questioning. In addition, families whose culture encourages comparison and competition with others might be less likely to understand students working at their own pace or in cooperative groups. Further, communities that regard student difficulties in school as shameful might be more likely to refuse offers of diagnosis and extra support. Such cultural dissonance may even arise from the seemingly simple question of the student's age – while many cultures calculate age from the date of birth, others use the date of conception. Having a teacher insist that you are one year younger can be very distressing for a student, and can create potential administrative chaos with class placements!

Standard 4: Student characteristics and learning

The teacher is familiar with international student characteristics, including stage theories of development, age-level characteristics and student variability in learning.

In practice, the international teacher:

(a) provides learning opportunities that are adapted to diverse learners and align with their intellectual, social and personal development levels
(b) demonstrates sensitivity to the multiple experiences of learners and addresses different learning and performance modes
(c) makes appropriate provisions (in terms of time and circumstances for work, tasks assigned, communication and response modes) for individual students who have particular learning differences or needs.

Rationale

The need for teachers to have an in-depth understanding of student learning is fundamental. Even schools that are culturally and linguistically homogeneous will have students with a wide variety of individual characteristics, background experiences and learning styles, while in more heterogeneous schools, this diversity is amplified. Effective teachers in these settings must be able to recognize learning variability, and apply a broad, open-minded understanding of pedagogy that includes awareness of diverse theories of thinking and development. Further, they must be proactive in tailoring their teaching to optimize each student's academic and social growth.

This author's research into traits of effective teachers (Snowball 2004) showed that both parents and teachers themselves rated 'pedagogical understanding (how students learn)'

and 'differentiated teaching for diverse learning styles' amongst the most desirable traits. The proliferation of brain research over the past two decades has dramatically impacted understanding of learning, and theories such as Gardner's Multiple Intelligences (1983), and approaches such as constructivism (Brooks and Brooks 1993), Socratic enquiry (Fisher 1998) and differentiation (Tomlinson 1999) are now commonly included in teacher preparation programmes. Yet such programmes vary greatly in the relative emphasis they place on what to teach (curriculum) and how to teach (pedagogy), and teachers still emerge with a detailed understanding of their subject area/s but little real understanding of how students develop and how learning works (Snowball 2004).

Arthur Steller, president of ASCD 1994–1995, identifies a significant aspect of the problem in his foreword to *Multiple Intelligences in the Classroom* (Armstrong 1994: v):

> Many educators are acquainted with Howard Gardner's theory of multiple intelligences. They can name most if not all of his seven intelligences, and they can even give examples of how they've used them in their life. I suspect relatively few, however, have made the seven intelligences a regular part of their classroom teaching.

Translating theory into practical, accessible ideas as Armstrong does with MI, and others such as Brooks Fisher and Tomlinson do with constructivism, Socratic enquiry and differentiation, is a prerequisite for successful teacher implementation.

Standard 5: Transition

The teacher is sensitive to the difficulties transition can cause and, in addition to handling personal stresses effectively, is skilled in supporting students and parents.

In practice, the international teacher:

(a) adapts easily to new situations
(b) systematically uses strategies to facilitate new students becoming as effective as possible as soon as possible

(c) offers additional support to new parents
(d) facilitates students' onward transfer.

Rationale

There is significant evidence that world-wide mobility will increase. In the year 2000, for example, Germany reported 7 million foreign residents compared with 2.5 million in 1970, while world-wide the number of migrants (defined as persons outside their country of birth or citizenship for 12 months or more) increased from 85 million in 1975 to 154 million in 1990 and 175 million in 2000.

> Migration is a response to differences, and rising differences, in demographics and economics plus revolutions in communications, transportation and rights that facilitate movement over borders promise ever-more international migration for employment. (Martin 2003)

In addition to this international mobility, a parallel trend shows continuing decreases in job tenure, creating increasing intranational mobility within countries world-wide. The UK Office for National Statistics (Macauley 2003) reports that 'In 1996 half of all employees had been working for the same firm for five years or less. This had fallen to four years by 2001'. The trend also appears stronger in younger age groups: 'In 2001 51 per cent of those in the 18–24 age group were in the same job as 12 months ago, compared with 86 per cent for those aged 50 or over'. In countries as far apart as China and Peru, rural–urban migration is creating similar patterns (the average job tenure in Chinese rural–urban migrants was reported as 4.5 years, in contrast with 7.4 in the USA and 11.3 in Japan) (Knight and Yueh 2004).

In such a mobile world therefore, an understanding of transition and its effects is another essential aspect of being an effective teacher. Teachers must be prepared to deal with the transition issues mobility can create – for students, parents and themselves – which can range from minor settling-in adjustments to more serious problems. Transition can help students become confident in establishing relationships yet it can also prevent them from making lasting friendships; for parents it can result in a very relaxed attitude to education or in irrational anxiety directed towards the school; and for teachers themselves it can create a network of colleagues and friends around the world yet it can interfere significantly with both professional and personal life. Such negative and positive aspects of transition are poignantly illustrated by the personal accounts in Pollock and van Reken's *Third Culture Kids:* 'each move offered something to look forward to while something had to be given up ... some essential part of our lives was always someplace else ... We learned to be happy and sad at the same time' (Pollock and van Reken 2001: 60).

The importance of 'awareness' as one of the most effective means of dealing with transition stress is emphasized in Bill Powell's article, 'Orchids in the bathroom' (2001), which powerfully conveys how even internationally mobile veterans can be swamped by waves of unexpected and disorientating 'nostalgia'. An effective international teacher will deal with potential problems proactively, for example by helping to implement a transition programme that supports both students and parents, and by building aspects of transition awareness into the curriculum.

Standard 6: Internationalizing curricula

The teacher actively seeks to enrich both what and how they teach with multiple international perspectives, acting as a role model in developing internationally-minded students.

In practice, the international teacher:

(a) is familiar with existing international curricula
(b) is able to internationalize units of work
(c) demands that students seek and consider multiple perspectives
(d) critically assesses resources to avoid bias and stereotyping
(e) utilizes the experience of students and parents to present authentic perspectives and opinions.

Rationale

This chapter began by declaring that international education includes schools that are international in name and schools that are international in nature – the same can be said of curricula. There are international curricula specifically designed for an international context, and internationalized curricula modified to promote an international orientation. While the former has tended to be used more in international schools and the latter in national schools, there is an increasing blurring of the lines, with many national schools adopting international curricula such as the International Baccalaureate programmes, and many international schools using modified national curricula. An international teacher should become familiar with a range of different programmes, in particular considering what makes them international. What is taught and how it is taught must be relevant to all students, moving beyond national knowledge and boundaries to take into account both local and global issues and perspectives, cultural and linguistic diversity and the concept of global citizenship. Internationalism must be infused across all subject areas, with all resources used, and most importantly, in the mindsets of teachers. It 'is not an additional subject – it is an ethos' (Young 2000: 2).

To be most effective, international perspectives should be explicitly stated. Examples include the internationalism practices presented in the IBO programme's evaluation standards (International Baccalaureate Organization 2005) and the internationalism objectives that run parallel to subject area objectives in the International Primary Curriculum (2001). However, in practice, it is often left to the individual teacher to implement modifications, largely dependent on the extent of his or her own international-mindedness, experience and access to appropriate resources. The result is that even schools that call themselves international and use an international curriculum may demonstrate a lack of meaningful international perspective throughout the programme.

Whether or not working within an international curricula framework, the ability to internationalize units of work is therefore a key skill for international teachers. It is essential that teachers critically assess resources to avoid bias and stereotyping, while nurturing in students the disposition to recognize and question such bias – the diversity of their classrooms is a valuable resource in itself, offering opportunities to share authentic perspectives and opinions from students' own experience and expertise. Whatever ages or subjects taught, teachers must encourage students to seek and consider multiple perspectives, compare and contrast familiar with unfamiliar, and investigate global issues with a problem-solving approach and an attitude of active altruism. And finally, by identifying and assessing the concepts, knowledge, skills and attitudes that typify internationally-minded students, teachers will have some measure of their success.

Standard 7: The reflective international teacher

The teacher is a reflective practitioner who continually evaluates the effects of his or her choices and actions on others (students, parents and other professionals in the learning community) and who actively seeks out opportunities to grow professionally.

In practice, the international teacher:

(a) uses classroom observation, information about students and research as sources for evaluating the outcomes of teaching and learning and as a basis for experimenting with, reflecting on, and revising practice
(b) seeks out professional literature, colleagues and other resources to support his or her own development as a learner and a teacher
(c) draws upon colleagues within the school and other professional arenas world-wide as supports for reflection, problem-solving and new ideas, actively sharing experiences and seeking and giving feedback
(d) regularly participates in professional development activities, including action research, to improve practice.

Rationale
Reflection and continuous improvement are key characteristics of any successful teacher, but for those working in diverse international settings there are additional dimensions. Beginning with the teacher's initial decision

to work in an international school (whether in name or nature), reflection is a key element: choosing to teach in a different country or school system often involves a new process for finding the job and requires serious reflection on adaptability and compatibility. In addition, using a different curriculum and resources can make experienced teachers feel like novices again and requires resourceful reflection on previous practice. Further, working with colleagues and students from different backgrounds can bring beliefs and values into question and requires deep reflection on personal traits and professional skills.

Most international schools are independent with limited professional support systems, especially in an unfamiliar language environment. As a result, teachers have to be highly self-reliant in terms of professional development and career advancement. In this context, international teachers are often more actively reflective – for example, keeping professional portfolios, initiating action research projects, reading and writing for professional journals. It also seems that many international schools, being largely independent of overseeing authorities, do not have formalized teacher evaluation systems, which again require teachers to rely on their own reflection for assessment of their teaching.

In David Perkins's *Smart Schools* (1995: 222), teacher reflection is a major focus, with three main groups being identified:

> Group One teachers resist scrutiny and counsel from others and show little tendency to reflect on their own practice ... Group Two teachers ... rethink their own practice according to their classroom experiences. But they do not welcome the eyes, minds and mouths of outsiders, even outsiders who teach across the hall. Group Three teachers not only pursue self-examination but throw the door open to collegial interaction around their teaching.

The international teacher needs to be in Group Three – he or she must demonstrate desire to enhance his or her instructional repertoire and learn from colleagues, both locally and world-wide.

CONCLUSION

In both international and national systems around the world, schools and education authorities emphasize international ideals for their students. They use terminology such as 'contributing responsibly in a global community', 'becoming an integral part of our diverse multicultural society', and 'education for international understanding'. Yet how can schools and governments hope to fulfil such missions when many of the teachers they hire have little preparation in the key elements of internationalism?

The Conference of Internationally-Minded Schools of 1949–69 (Hill 2001) attracted support from national as well as international schools, with the aim of furthering world peace and international understanding through education, and could be regarded as the first promoter of the concept of an international education certificate for teachers. With the ongoing trend for globalization, and the increasing need for international understanding, teacher certification is now seen as essential by governments and educators. It is clear that curricula should include peace studies and conflict resolution, interdependence and intercultural communication, human rights and social responsibility, world issues and problem-solving skills, with an overall aim of developing students who are not only internationally-minded but internationally hearted. If we accept that teachers are key factors in educational effectiveness then it follows that they need the specialized knowledge, skills and characteristics to nurture this in students. It is time to initiate a systematic approach to the preparation of teachers in key elements of internationalism, both by integration of this content into existing teacher training and through the development of new tailored programmes.

REFERENCES

Armstrong, T. (1994) *Multiple Intelligences in the Classroom*. Alexandria, VA: ASCD.

Barna, LaRay M. (1998) *Stumbling Blocks in Intercultural Communication* In M.J. Bennett (ed.) *Basic Concepts of Intercultural Communication.* Yarmouth, ME: Intercultural Press, pp. 173–89.

Brooks, J.G. and Brooks, M.G. (1993) *In Search of Understanding: The Case for Constructivist Classrooms.* Alexandria, VA: ASCD.

Collier, V. and Thomas, W. (2002) *A National Study of School Effectiveness for Language Minority Students' Long-Term Academic Achievement.* Berkeley, CA: Center for Research on Education, Diversity & Excellence.

Cortes, C.E. (1994) *Multiculturation: An Educational Model for a Culturally and Linguistically Diverse Society.* In K. Spangenberg-Urbschat and R. Pritchard (eds) *Kids Come in All Languages.* Newark, NJ: International Reading Association.

Crystal, D. (1997) *Encyclopedia of Language.* Cambridge: Cambridge University Press.

Cummins, J. (1994) The acquisition of English as a second language. In K. Spangenberg-Urbschat and R. Pritchard (eds) *Kids Come in All Languages.* Newark, NJ: International Reading Association.

Fennes, H. and Hapgood, K. (1997) *Intercultural Learning in the Classroom: Crossing Borders.* London: Cassell.

Fisher, R. (1998) *Teaching Thinking.* London: Cassell.

Gardner, H. (1983) *Frames of Mind: The Theory of Multiple Intelligences.* New York: Basic Books.

Hayden, M.C. and Thompson, J.J. (1998) (eds.) *International Education Principles and Practice.* London: Kogan Page, p. 285.

Hill, I. (2001) Early stirrings: the beginnings of the international education movement. *International Schools Journal,* XX(2): 19–21.

International Baccalaureate Organization (2005) *Programme Evaluation Standards.* Cardiff: IBO.

International Primary Curriculum (2001) *International Primary Curriculum.* London: IPC.

Knight, J. and Yueh, L. (2004) Job mobility of residents and migrants in urban China. *Journal of Comparative Economics,* 32(4): 637–60.

Krashen, S. (1981) *Second Language Acquisition and Second Language Learning.* Oxford: Pergamon Press.

Krashen, S. (1982) *Principles and Practices of Second Language Acquisition.* Oxford: Pergamon Press.

Macauley, C. (2003) Job mobility and job tenure in the UK. www.statistics.gov.uk (accessed 15 January 2005).

Martin, P.L. (2003) *Managing Labor Migration: Temporary Programs for the 21st Century.* Geneva: International Labor Organization.

O'Neil, D. (2005) Ethnicity and race: world diversity patterns. Palomar College On-line tutorials http://anthro.palomar.edu/tutorials (accessed 15 January, 2005).

Perkins, D. (1995) *Smart Schools.* New York: Simon and Schuster, p. 222.

Pollock, D.C. and Van Reken, R.E. (2001) *Third Culture Kids.* Yarmouth, ME: Intercultural Press.

Powell, W. (2001) Orchids in the Bathroom. *International Schools Journal,* XXI: 1.

Sears, C. (1998) *Second Language Students in Mainstream Classrooms.* Clevedon, UK: Multilingual Matters.

Snowball, K. and L.F. (2004) *International Teacher Certification Model – Standards and Requirements.* Amsterdam: Putting it into Practice.

Snowball, L.F. (1997) Professional development strategy for international schools. Proposal to IBO Director of Academic Affairs and ECIS Executive Secretary.

Snowball, L.F. (2002) What makes an international teacher – the case for an International Teacher Certificate. Paper presented at Alliance for International Education Conference, Geneva; ECIS Annual General conference, Berlin; and proposal to ECIS Executive Secretary/ Professional Development Committee.

Snowball, L.F. (2004) An overview of the ECIS/PiiP teacher certification process. Paper presented at Alliance for International Education Conference, Düsseldorf.

Steiner, M. (ed.) (1996) *Developing the Global Teacher.* Stoke-on-Trent: Trentham Books, p. xiv.

Tomlinson, C.A. (1999) *The Differentiated Classroom: Responding to the Needs of All Learners.* Alexandria, VA: ASCD.

UNESCO (2000) *Cultural Diversity, Conflict and Pluralism.* Paris: UNESCO.

UNESCO (2001) *Universal Declaration on Cultural Diversity.* Paris: UNESCO.

Young, M. with Commins, E. (2002) *Global Citizenship: The Handbook for Primary Teaching.* Oxford: Oxfam Publishing.

22

Innovation in Learning: Global Vision or Dream?

Patrick Griffin

What are the benefits of an international curriculum to individuals, educators, commercial and government interests? Can such a curriculum be built entirely upon a set of key generic or interdisciplinary competencies, as envisaged by the OECD's Definition and Selection of Competencies (DeSeCo) Project and currently evidenced in schools in Victoria, Australia, through the development of Essential Learning Standards for all students (OECD 2005; VCAA 2005)? Or does it need to include a specific set of skills tailored to meet a niche in the employment market to ensure that students have pathways to higher education and employment opportunities? How do educators find a balance between the immediate demands of the workplace and broad-based generic skills when devising a curriculum that is truly international?

The idea of an international curriculum explored in this chapter was built on a partnership between commercial ICT interests, a university and schools, and was designed to educate people who had portable skills and qualifications that would permit them to work anywhere in the world. The project, named Digital Harbour, was an attempt to establish a school linked to a university, to the community, to industry and to the global rise of digital technology. It aimed to educate for a global future in an information world and to connect students from around the globe into a single learning community. Its curriculum was based on innovation and digital technology.

This chapter describes an idea for the development of an international curriculum that was explored by the Faculty of Education at the University of Melbourne. In 2001, the Faculty was approached by Ms Di Fleming, the principal of a girls' grammar school. Ms Fleming had a vision of an international school of the future. It was and is a bold plan. It did not evolve in the fashion outlined in the following discussion but it is described as if it had eventuated strictly according to the vision to permit the possibilities and complexities of such an idea to be fully explored. The vision was embraced enthusiastically by the Faculty and the University administration. Parts of the ideas have been realized, as organizations and individuals who perhaps are not even aware that the vision of Digital Harbour has influenced them have implemented similar plans. So much of the vision has happened that perhaps the possibility of bringing it all together might not be unrealistic. At the end of the Chapter I will explore the reality of what actually evolved from the project, and consider the implications for educators who face the challenge of developing an international curriculum.

THE CENTRE FOR INNOVATION IN LEARNING

Digital Harbour had as its centrepiece a Centre for Innovation in Learning (the Centre), through which it was planned to study how information and knowledge were developed, distributed and consumed in much the same manner as industrial products were manufactured, distributed and consumed in an industrial era. The Centre had several components. These were a college for high school students (the College), which incorporated a Youth Technology Incubator, the Faculty of Education (the Faculty), which delivered a teacher education programme, a Research Institute (the Institute), an Online Learning Centre and an Early Learning Centre. The external components were independent entities organized, staffed and financed using their own means, but focused on the same overall mission and vision and forming a Faculty collaborative learning centre. This turned out to be the Achilles' heel of the whole vision. External finance for these kinds of programmes was difficult to find. Central to each of these was a specialized planning programme that focused the direction of the curriculum and research in each of the components. This programme was in addition to the overall programme, and curriculum for the College, and influenced the teacher education, research and early learning programmes through a series of exploratory investigations called The Think Tank Programme. For the Faculty, the emphasis was to be primarily a teacher education and curriculum research-focused entity that had the goals to:

- prepare people, materials and ideas through innovative research, development, and delivery
- promote innovation and links between industry, education, commerce and technology

- maintain the leading edge in research, teaching and learning, development and delivery of education programmes and ideas; develop, adopt and promote a global perspective on curriculum, teacher education, research, hypothesis-based learning; and provide a basis for professional development of teachers and community leaders in the link between education and industry.

The Centre was located at a single site as part of a redeveloped dockland precinct, which allowed it to integrate programmes, staffing and the student body. The model was based in the structure of the hospital teaching and research system. In the medical education model researchers, teachers, students and administration work together under the one roof of a teaching hospital. In this case all the players were under the roof of the Centre and there were links established with industry and technology just as in the medical system.

In early learning programmes there was a central theme of developmental learning and research, through the Centre, in which teachers modelled teaching and learning, undergraduate teacher programmes and postgraduate research in early learning in a digital environment emphasizing an international interaction of children.

The College was a secondary level or high school education enterprise. It focused on the development of innovative projects through links with university faculties, an hypothesis-based curriculum, research and the relevance of information and communication technology and scenario planning. With several sessions per day, online and onsite learning, and flexible programming, the designed curriculum consisted of core and elective study areas, with a highly selective student group and an internationally marketed curriculum.

A central aspect of the College structure and process was the Youth Technology Incubator. This combined a unique international and e-learning hypothesis-based curriculum that was broad and innovative and linked to a formal and industrial, commercial incubator, where students worked with innovators and designers in the area of actual technological and industrial incubation of ideas and products. The curriculum, therefore, was based on and linked to hypothesis learning (Fogarty, Perkins and Barell 1992; Perkins 1995), addressing global and international issues (Armstrong 2000). It was stimulated by the outcomes of a 'think tank', and hence an integration of research, industry, school and university (Brown, Collins and Duguid 1989).

The Centre, through its component parts, was designed to provide short-, medium- and long-term solutions for a range of problems and social and technological research issues. The College was designed to showcase models for learning that brought together innovative teacher education alongside enterprise commitment to mutual futures. Training teachers occurred alongside executive and management programmes that influenced the strategic futures of international ICT companies. This model was designed to be implemented within and across participating organizations on a global basis to help in forecasting innovative thinking that could bring new products to market. The Centre worked with the College and the Research Institute and, through this, the university partnerships and other formal local, rural, national and international relationships to broker consultation where appropriate.

THE THINK TANK PROGRAMME

This programme was invitational, with each member of the Think Tank (TT) Programme team representing a different way of thinking about the world. The first programme included a conservationist, an architect, a musician, a politician, an actor, a sculptor, an economist and a small business manager. Each programme was different by the nature of its membership. Each invitee had to have earned a reputation as a leading thinker in his or her chosen field of expertise.

The Centre and the College helped to facilitate the work of groups of TT People who brought together ideas, issues, problems, scenarios and previously unconnected hypotheses which in turn influenced the College curriculum, the teacher education programme and the issues to be addressed by the multidisciplinary teams in an overarching Research Institute. The outcomes of this deliberation, research and curriculum development were expected to be the realization of commercially viable products, materials, procedures and services that would engage researchers, postgraduate students and undergraduate students with teachers and students across the Institute, the Faculty, the Centre and the College as a whole.

The Centre took responsibility, through the Think Tank Programme, for bringing together the idea leaders to provoke, argue, stimulate and ultimately create conversation leading to hypotheses, which formed the basis of a possibility- and problem-based curriculum and learning as well as identifying a series of research themes addressing global and e-learning issues (Barker and Wendel 2001; Dede 1996; Garrison 2000). This took place on a regular and frequent basis with its investigative and exploratory meetings coordinated jointly by the Centre and College through the Youth Incubator. These meetings, both real and virtual, gave each member limited tenure. The strength of the model lay in the special expertise and the contribution that each of the participants could make and the synergy and innovation that could be derived from bringing together such people. The meetings were charged with identifying international, social, environmental and technological issues that could be addressed as curriculum by the students in the College, the teacher education programme, and the Institute components of the Centre. The Think Tank sessions aimed at generating ideas and hypotheses to be addressed by all components of Digital Harbour. These included the middle school electives, research projects, global collaborative projects in teacher education and learning scenarios that reflected the environmental conditions emanating from set hypotheses. This in turn generated a curriculum that could be disseminated world-wide. An anticipated outcome of this approach was the development and nurturing of a generation of youth to act as leaders in dealing with the global issues and technological needs of society in an advanced and world leadership model (Drucker 1994). Links between the incubator and university faculties, industry research and development units were designed to form the commercial incubator components of the Digital Harbour.

The output to be generated from the Centre's Think Tank Programme was diverse:

- hypotheses-driven curriculum for the College, to be marketed on a global basis
- tangible commercial products
- opportunities for joint sponsorship of invitees through government, education and enterprise partnerships
- a curriculum and model that could be replicated worldwide.

The Faculty

The links with the University were especially important. Through the Faculties, an innovative environment was created where engineers, musicians, architects, multimedia sculptors and mathematicians could collaborate within a sympathetic, incubator environment where their ideas were strategically managed in a creative and commercial manner.

There were a number of significant driving forces behind the creation of the Centre at the University. There was a strong national and state government agenda to promote innovation and commercial success in the information and communication industries by encouraging new high technology business creation and growth (Department of Education and Training 2003). The research undertaken by the national IT&T Task Force identified the need to develop education and training programmes that met the needs of emerging industry across the nation with a global perspective.

In the field of professional learning for teachers, there had to be a seamless integration of the teacher education curriculum and postgraduate programmes linked to the research programme and curriculum of the College and the Early Learning Centre. This ensured the development of specialized, teacher education programmes for e-development and delivery with a global emphasis, a chance to lead in

teacher and other professional education programmes designed especially for internationalization and Internet and video delivery around the globe. It was intended for a multinational student group, based on the recruitment of international students at both undergraduate and postgraduate levels, and at the senior levels of secondary college.

In the Faculty, the research and teaching emphasis and direction shifted to encompass learning in a range of settings over the human lifespan and to produce teachers who excelled in all of those areas. In doing so, the teaching and learning tools were developed to include the digital media. Learning settings also included both real and virtual environments.

To achieve this, learning was linked to innovation so that technology, design and innovation were seamlessly integrated (Lynch and Fleming 2005). The innovative curriculum had to be distinguished from a curriculum based on innovation. Within the Centre, the College enabled innovation to become an elective programmes. 'Innovation 101', for example, designed as an undergraduate subject across all faculties of the University, was intended to bridge across faculties and the College. Centre components were responsible for the synthesis and integration of ideas and procedures, products that came from the work of the operational Centre components. The University appointed a Deputy Vice Chancellor for Innovation and Development and the Faculty has an Associate Dean with the same portfolio.

The College also investigated the possibility of adopting packaged curriculum solutions, where they provided underpinning skills and approaches to problem- and hypothesis-based learning solutions. This offered an additional means of ensuring that students had access to state-of-the-art course offerings. Evaluations of such branded electives became part of the programme of research, development and evaluation projects of the research and the curriculum development teams formed to accommodate the programming relationships between the University, industry and enterprise partners and the College. Relationships were established with companies who were prepared to maintain a showcase of their leading edge technologies central to the programme. These included publishers of software and learning materials as well as leading biotechnology, spectroscopy, audio and technology companies.

The Research Institute

In establishing the Centre there were plans for research into teaching and learning with a multidisciplinary approach across faculties and industries. The Centre linked with enterprises and industry, postgraduate research training programmes, schools, technology, industry and commerce, held together by an e-education research agenda leading to a global approach to research and development in curriculum, teaching, learning and assessment.

Leadership of the Centre was expected to be multifaceted. A sponsored Chair was sought for the University to be used for a range of visiting scholars on a short-term basis. The role of the Chair's occupants was to focus on leadership in innovations in learning and to provide leadership in research at University level.

The College leadership position was also expected to provide a vision for the College and the Youth Incubator and innovation education as well as leadership and direction within the Think Tank Programme's hypothesis-driven curriculum. This position was also to be occupied for short periods to ensure that the vision remained cutting edge, but overlapped with the leadership of the Centre. A long-term appointment of an administrator to organize resources and schedules and incorporate the hypothesis-based learning into the daily schedules was considered essential.

The Institute's prime responsibilities included the role of establishing global networks and partnerships with industry, enterprise, government, community and education. It was also to establish a research agenda based on innovation in learning and establish strategies that would lead to the realization of these programmes. In addition to these global alliances, it was to link with, identify, confirm and manage sponsorships and establish relationships within the strategic partners. This

now falls under the responsibilities of the Faculty's Associate Dean, International.

The Institute provided opportunities for staff from University faculties and the College to work with students in research and development projects. It acted as a launching pad for competitive research funds to establish, within the Centre and its components, a permanent core of University and industry research staff drawn from a range of faculties and industries, as well as leading researchers.

It was also a natural setting for industry research training programmes that linked the University, school and industry in collaborative projects that, given the philosophy of Digital Harbour, brought together education, training, enterprise and research. As a consequence of the Think Tank Programme, research opportunities emerged that had strategic, social, economic, scientific and educational importance, founded within a context of innovation.

Teacher education programme

The teacher education programme of the Centre was not constrained by local teacher training needs. It focused on internationalizing the teacher education curriculum. This meant that the technology of the teacher education function of the Centre was advanced on the technology of the school system. It purposely prepared teachers for an e-education future. This emphasized ICT Learning Tools and aimed to place the Faculty of Education at the forefront of a global teacher education curriculum.

The main goal of the Teacher Education Centre was the production of an elite teaching force, members of which would be able to market their skills globally wherever e-education and technology-based education occurred. They were expected to be a multinational group who could be deployed across the curriculum and within their special teaching areas.

Universitas 21 (U21) and other international links were discussed as links to an international degree in Innovation in Learning. These studies were to be based on ICT

Learning Tools and e-education. Teacher education was to take place across diverse industry/commercial and school environments, recognizing that teachers need practical experience where the learning takes place and across the lifespan rather than being restricted to schools. It represented the notion that praxis was at the heart of teacher education.

The Early Learning Centre

The Early Learning Centre (ELC) provided an exemplary education and care setting for approximately 200 children aged 0 to 8 years. It also provided a research, demonstration and teacher training facility for the University. The ELC helped to explore the implications of the digital world on children's play, communication, learning and the learning environment and teacher education that emanates from this. The primary function of the ELC was to serve as an active centre for research, innovation and teacher training that would demonstrate exemplary models for learning that meet the needs of individual children and preservice teachers.

Informed by theory and a commitment to research into teaching and learning, the ELC offered a curriculum model that acknowledged the roles of teachers, children, parents, researchers and 'industry partners' in the learning process. A combination of a developmentally appropriate curriculum, which addressed all developmental areas and was based on the setting of long-term objectives, worked alongside a responsive curriculum model, which responded to the children's individual learning styles and interests, as well as the changing needs of society. Within a framework of hypothesis-based learning, children were challenged by teaching strategies that encouraged imaginative problem-solving and critical thinking as well as the basic skills (Collins et al. 1989). The ELC also provided a mandatory service for families living within the Centre precinct as well as those people working and commuting to the precinct each day.

A community of learners was expected to evolve; a community encompassing children and their families who worked with teachers as 'co-constructors' of curriculum. Teachers incorporated knowledge of children and families with curricula content that responded to the needs of a knowledge-and technology-based economy; industry partners committed to high-level achievement and the maintenance and development of leading edge technologies. The ELC was committed to exhibitions and performances that acknowledged the significance of the thoughts, perceptions and abilities of the young child as expressed in their art. A Children's Art Gallery and Performance Space presented a new vision, one that stimulated and challenged parents and other visitors to recognize and value the personal and social comments inherent in the processes and products of the art of young children.

The College and Incubator

Through the incubator function of the College, young people were provided with an opportunity to pursue innovative projects and ideas. In addition to a normal enrolment cohort of students, the incubator provided the opportunity for youth from all parts of the community, local, urban, rural, national and international settings to work on innovative projects and link these to the proposed commercial incubator, University faculties, industry partners and commercial interests. This role of the incubator also catered for a cohort of students enrolled full time, undertaking the curriculum developed through the Centre's Think Tank Programme, research and teacher education components. The students enrolled in the College enjoyed a unique curriculum and opportunity to engage in an education experience geared particularly to the internationally oriented hypothesis-based learning programme. Students were also recruited from local, national and international communities.

Initially, the College was to cater for 14–18 year-olds with Middle, Senior Schools and Foundation Studies. These levels concentrated on the preparation of overseas students for University entrance. Students were accommodated in Digital Harbour on both short-term and long-term bases to cater for the full-time students as well as those from rural and other remote locations. In time, the College planned to establish a Junior and Junior Secondary School so that there would be continuity in student learning and the learning environment.

The College curriculum emphasized a range of capabilities for every student. While the student body was expected to have specialized skills in dealing with information communications technology, they were also offered a curriculum that would develop them holistically. By the time students began it was assumed that they were ready to explore a wide range of study choices. The core curriculum was reduced significantly to allow opportunities for in-depth learning, problem-solving and independence in learning and collaboration. The programme was based on a series of questions/hypotheses where the body of knowledge emerged from student enquiry.

The College provided a learning context where students were able to develop and apply their skills, competencies and attributes in an enterprise context. 'In situ' assessments, combined with formalized modes of assessment, were designed to meet the needs of new forms of credentialing agencies that would emerge around the globe. It was designed as a learning context where young people had the respect of the Centre's enterprise partners. Through an alliance of international partners, to be established in similar contexts throughout the world, a new globally recognized credential was envisaged, not to replace but to take a different path to the local end-of-school credential and the existing international credential. It was expected to set students of the College apart, with an intellectual and marketable advantage over those who had pursued credentials that were more traditional. It was expected to be a truly global approach to ICT education for youth leading to their involvement in research and development processes.

Recruitment was restricted in the first instance to the numbers already assured of exit places in higher education, industry and other partner arrangements which would ensure further opportunities as knowledge workers engaged with learning institutions and enterprises.

In addition to students learning at the senior years of secondary school, a mixture of pre-service and postgraduate students and staff from the University was woven into the hypothesis-based learning activities of the College. This was achieved largely through the activities of the Research Institute.

Key skills in teaching students how to learn focused on how to process information both analytically and intuitively, to understand themselves as learners and as information-knowledge manipulators. These were key skills to help students engineer their own learning contexts in order to optimize learning efficiency (for example, moving between individual and small group collaborative-learning problem-solving contexts) and how to analyse information-input situations in terms of the processing demands required. Students learned how to transform their knowledge in a range of ways according to task demands and parameters, how to think creatively and to recognize boundaries to thinking.

The College programme

Core content knowledge was elaborated in a range of forms; students developed knowledges conceptually and learned how to process and evaluate information. A significant approach within the College was an elective program for Years 9–12. While the Year 11 and 12 students were bound in part by the final year examination requirements, they also had the flexibility to enrol in a number of electives outside the boundaries of the local Year 12 examinations and credential programme. The College ran programmes 48 weeks of the year and, in doing so, catered for the wider community. The elective 'Innovation 101' provides an example of the focus on innovation across the Centre. In addition to participation in Innovation 101, which became an essential ingredient of degree courses across the University, the College also ran summer and 'Solstice Schools' to maximize student access around the globe. This especially catered for students from rural centres as well as other metropolitan schools, whose special interests in innovation and hypothesis-based learning could be accommodated within the College. A further elective on the strategic management of innovation was also designed for undergraduates in degree courses.

Enterprise, engineering and education: a collaborative learning model

The Centre assumed coordination and collaborative roles with the aim of integrating innovative ideas. While it was not necessary to integrate across all Faculties all the time, there were clear advantages of bringing a number of Faculties together. For example, because there were virtually no trained teachers in the areas of robotics, megatronics, software development, genetic engineering, multimedia and architecture, many innovative electives could be created by inviting undergraduates across Faculties at the University of Melbourne to work with school students and Education Faculty members to create a unique programme. The following elective programme was proposed to the Faculty of Engineering. It set out to create a unique relationship between the Faculties of Engineering and Education at the University of Melbourne, the College within the Digital Harbour, an enterprise (e.g., Festo) and the Institute of Engineers Australia (Victoria) to achieve the following:

- the *promotion of engineering* as a study for girls in particular
- to expand the introduction of *industry standard technologies* into the school curriculum
- to *promote teaching* as a profession for graduate engineers through the provision of a project-based elective developed on site at the school with the support of particular engineering firms
- to establish an *enterprise practice* where companies would second a number of their engineers to work in schools for a semester-length programme on a part-time basis to ensure the ongoing development of a rigorous and innovative curriculum that would in turn lead to innovation and the need for incubation and start-up funding
- to work with the Institute of Engineers to create an *Educator in Enterprise Database* online (i.e., www.educatorengineers.com); a sector of the National Engineering Awards would include the Innovation in Engineering and Education Awards, the recipients of the awards would gain a study grant to one of the tertiary institutions in the Universitas 21

- to build a *succession plan* for the continuation of existing and new robotics and systems and engineering electives for schools
- to create a group of educators committed to the *promotion and expansion of robotics*, systems and technology, materials and technology and the integration of technologies such as genetics and engineering which currently reflects a global trend and the next wave of emerging technologies.

The College was different in terms of a traditional school's instruction model of teaching and learning. Practical recognition was given to the students' need to learn in a socially constructivist environment where they could explore, construct, simulate, program, model, integrate, project, predict, analyse, diagnose, problem-solve and create. Students and their teachers had the opportunity to exhibit their understanding through digital-oriented language using digital technology-based tools.

Digital technology exerted a powerful influence on communication, integration and all aspects of learning. Teachers and students explored and revealed their understanding through the use of information technologies, as they could increasingly have a powerful influence on learning, construction of knowledge frameworks and communication. All students and staff had access to distributive, portable computer technology to ensure portability from one learning environment to the next.

This technology had a supporting role in the problem resolution process. It was assumed that students, staff and researchers went beyond the framework and restrictions of traditional schooling. Students and teachers learned to simulate, program, predict, construct, author, communicate and navigate across both real and virtual contexts, without restrictions of location, schedules, or technology.

Innovation

The College encouraged brilliant young innovators, researchers and students from the University, from the community and from other backgrounds to work with its students in an environment where innovation, problem-resolution and start-up went hand in hand.

Opportunities were available for selected youths from many backgrounds to attend and work with the technology and the specialist staff and students of the College in an incubator environment. Links with industry and commerce provided opportunities for students to meet, learn from and interact with successful role models. As a part of this, the University participated in much of the innovative education by involving staff from such faculties as Engineering, Commerce and Arts and so on. Their involvement provided a means of engaging both University staff and students with College staff and students in state-of-the-art thinking and development in a range of disciplines. The means of achieving this was through a Collaborative Research Centre.

The hypothesis-based learning was established through the Think Tank Programme teams that met together. Their task was to identify the drivers of change, trends, global issues, major needs and problems that require solutions, recommendations or lines of action. These would become the foundation of hypothesis-based learning.

Teams of students, College staff, University staff and representatives from industry and community (where available) worked together to address the concepts within the hypotheses and to learn together. The College staff established the roles and responsibilities of each of the players in collaboration with the University and industry partners.

The problem identification led the development phase by approximately six months and the process of 'think tank' and hypothesis-based learning ensured that the curriculum remained innovative. It also meant that the research agenda of the Centre remained current. Innovation itself needed to be a serious part of the underpinning skills of the students.

Scenario planning

Innovative thinking was enhanced through scenario planning. Students at all levels of education in the Centre were given the opportunity to create and explore unpredictable scenarios. Scenario planning was a tool used by many learning organizations to develop creative and future challenges (Fogarty et al., 1992). Students could create specific scenarios that were thoroughly explored (e.g., *The Alternative Future: Scenarios for Business in Australia to the Year 2015*, Australian Business Futures, 2001).

The programme enabled the students to integrate core, elective and on-location programmes. There was a study selection framework that ensured a balanced programme, but there was nevertheless a concentration on the development of information and communication skills. The core and elective programmes were consistent with the overall philosophy of whole-person development, generic skills including interpersonal skills and supported by a pastoral care programme involving students, teachers, University staff and personnel from industry and commerce.

An essential characteristic of the programme was a comprehensive strategy for ongoing development of the research, teaching and development staff. This involved regular meetings of teams to plan, monitor and to improve the quality of teaching and learning materials, their delivery presentation and dissemination and opportunities to become more expert hypothesis-based learning practitioners. Models for staff development and learning included a range of procedures that allowed the development and automatic use of effective teaching procedures, the means for allowing these to be improved, benchmarking and review procedures. Group problem-solving, an adult 'community of learners', cognitive task analysis, coaching and demonstration procedures supplemented more conventional approaches to ongoing teacher development.

Students were drawn from geographically dispersed areas and included a significant proportion of students from a range of countries in addition to catering for students from rural and other often disadvantaged areas locally. A series of support programmes was established to ensure that socioeconomic status was not a barrier to involvement in the programme. The College sought to attract, from all areas and backgrounds, students who were keen to learn in an environment that was different from the traditional school. They needed to be familiar with and comfortable in using ICT and with working in teams and independently. Above all, they needed to be motivated to learn and to respond positively to high expectations. The College sought to ensure that its student profile was broadly representative of the community at large and not drawn from a narrow sector or stratum of society. The development of specific selection procedures that addressed the qualities of a College student was a priority research project.

Relationships with accrediting agencies

The College was aware that students graduating from Year 12 needed to have a formally recognized credential. However, partnerships within the College organization required a guarantee of places for exit students. This meant that formal arrangements needed to be made with the University through foundation programmes and other alternative entry programmes such as advanced credit in first year subjects for appropriate students and study programmes within the College. They would not need to be enrolled as students in local Year 12 credentialling programmes. The curriculum emphasized the specialized skills offered by enterprise and industry partners rather than the more generalized training packages offered under the current Australian Qualification Framework. The specialized credentials emphasized the higher-level competencies that formed part of the technological and intellectual development required by those enterprise partners and that were internationally recognized. Special arrangements needed to be made for students to gain direct entry to University through an induction programme similar to that which was operated by the University's Engineering Faculty for international students. These arrangements had to operate through foundation and advanced entry programmes.

The College, in collaboration with the University, developed and evaluated packaged curriculum solutions such as those offered by such organizations as Cisco Academy and Microsoft for their relevance to problem-based learning issues. This was an additional means of ensuring that students had access to state-of-the-art course offerings. Where strategic alliances allowed, recognized enterprise-based credentials were also made available to the College students. In many instances, the strategic alliance with such large transnational corporations rendered the traditional credentialling process redundant and made a ready-made market niche for a new college type credential.

WHAT EVOLVED?

It has always been planned that the model would be implemented in other sites such as London, British Columbia, Singapore, Hong Kong, Shanghai, Toronto and Freiberg, and an international network of like colleges would emerge. This international network and the potential for the dissemination of the hypothesis-based curriculum would mean that a new international credential could be developed, based on the internationally recognized approach to learning, its credibility enhanced by the involvement of the University and other institutions, partnerships with leading global enterprises and a permanent approach to the development of a cutting-edge curriculum.

Digital Harbour never eventuated in the style described above, but so much has developed in disparate settings that it may be possible in the near future that a closer version might materialize. It failed initially only because of the lack of financial backing and a shift in industry emphasis at an important time. This is not unusual, because developed economies all face the same problem of predicting the needs of a dynamic and shifting employment marketplace. The flow on to schools means that education systems and innovators are constantly looking for that meaningful link between education and the economy that leads to a curriculum capable of equipping students for a full participation in society, as has been outlined in the DeSeCo project.

The Research Institute will be embodied in the Melbourne Education Research Institute;

the Early Learning Centre continues to educate young children in an old school building in another part of Melbourne. The Global Learning Centre has evolved as the online and professional learning Centre within the Faculty of Education. The Youth Incubator has emerged in another University (the RMIT University) under Di Fleming's leadership and has been funded under the state government's innovation strategy. The Chair in Innovation has not really eventuated but there is an Associate Dean and the Faculty has developed a strategy where world leaders are about to take up short-term appointments and develop programmes in research and teaching. The Think Tank Programme has not developed but high-level connections and futuristic planning meetings between the Business School, Medical Faculty and the Faculty of Education together with leaders in school welfare, health and education state departments have developed linking research and teaching. A great deal of the Digital Harbour vision has been realized, albeit in disparate and unconnected settings.

REFERENCES

Armstrong, T. (2000) Multiple intelligences. www. thomas armstrong.com/multiple_intelligences.htm (accessed 24 March 2006).

Australian Business Futures (2001) The Alternative Future: Scenarios for Business in Australia to the Year 2015.

Barker, K. and Wendel, T. (2001) e-Learning: Studying Canada's Virtual Secondary Schools (Research Series #8). Kelowna, BC: Society for the Advancement of Excellence in Education.

Brown, J.S., Collins, A. and Duguid, P. (1989) Situated cognition and the culture of learning. Educational Researcher, 18: 32–42.

Collins, A., Brown, J.S. and Newman, S.E. (1989) Cognitive apprenticeship: teaching the craft of reading, writing and mathematics. In L.B. Resnick (ed.), Knowing, Learning and instruction: Essays in Honor of Robert Glaser. Hillsdale, NJ: Lawrence Erlbaum Associates, pp. 453–94.

Dede, C. (1996) Emerging technologies and distributed learning. American Journal of Distance Education, 10 (2): 4–36.

Department of Education and Training (2003) National Industry Education Forum: Business, Industry, Key Competencies and Portfolios – a proposal for reporting student performance in key competencies. Melbourne: DE&T.

Drucker, P. (1994) Knowledge Work and Knowledge Society – the Social Transformations of this Century. Edwin L. Godkin Lecture, Harvard University. www. harvard.edu/~ksgpress/drucklec.htm (accessed 24 March 2006).

Fogarty, R., Perkins, D. and Barell, J. (1992) How to Teach for Transfer. Palatine, IL: Skylight Publishing.

Garrison, R. (2000) Theoretical challenges for distance education in the 21st century: a shift from structural to transactional issues. The International Review of Research in Open and Distance Learning, 1 (1). www.irrodl.org/index.php/irrodl/article/view/2/22 (accessed 20 March 2006)

Lynch, G and Fleming, D. (2005) Design, technology and innovation. Paper presented at the International Conference on Engineering Design, ICED 05, Melbourne, 15–18 August 2005.

OECD (2005) The definition and selection of key competencies: executive summary. www.pisa.oecd.org/dataoecd/47/61/35070367. pdf (accessed 30 January 2005).

Perkins, D.N. (1995) Outsmarting IQ: The Emerging Science of Learnable Intelligence. New York: The Free Press.

VCAA (Victorian Curriculum and Assessment Authority) (2005) Victorian Essential Learning Standards. http://vels.vcaa.vic.edu.au/ (accessed 30 January 2005).

23

Classroom Management Around the World

Theo Wubbels

The ability to manage a class positively is recognized as a universal prerequisite for effective teaching (Shimahara 1998a). Teachers throughout the world cite classroom management, including discipline and student misbehaviour, as one of the most important problems they face. This is especially true with beginning teachers, who consistently indicate that classroom management is their highest priority (Evertson and Weinstein 2006a). One might expect therefore that student teachers are concerned about relationships with their students and discipline problems and it is somewhat surprising that Murray-Harvey, Silins and Saebel (1999) found these concerns but also found that other concerns such as high workload and being observed were even more stressing. Their comparison between student teachers in Singapore and Australia did not show differences between these two countries.

Further, management issues are a major cause for teacher burnout and job dissatisfaction (e.g. Blase 1986; Friedman 1995; Ingersoll 2001). Lewis, Romi, Qui and Katz (2005) also point to the detrimental effects of poor classroom management: it stimulates student resistance and subsequent misbehaviour and it may produce school violence. The opposite is also

true: orderly classroom environments are consistently related to student achievement and student assumption of responsibility for learning (e.g. Creemers 1994; Fraser 1998, Lewis et al. 2005). Clearly, when students are able to plan and carry out their own learning they are better prepared for their later role in society. Teachers' effectiveness in classroom management and students' assumption of responsibility will strengthen each other mutually.

In studies in the USA, classroom management is usually defined as the actions teachers undertake to create an environment that facilitates both academic and social-emotional learning. While definitions differ slightly in other countries, in general it is clear that classroom management has two distinct purposes: it seeks to establish an orderly environment so students can engage in meaningful academic learning and it aims to enhance student social and moral growth. Most publications on classroom management also mention the need to effectively handle student misbehaviour and disruptions as a requisite for creating an orderly environment. Evertson and Weinstein (2006a) mention five teacher tasks in the domain of classroom management: developing caring supportive relationships, organizing and implementing instruction in ways that optimize students' access to learning, using group management methods, promoting students' social skills and self-regulation and using appropriate interventions for students with behaviour problems. This chapter provides an overview of the varied approaches to classroom management throughout the world. It focuses on the first purpose listed above: the actions teachers undertake to create a productive environment for meaningful academic learning.

This chapter begins with the observation that attention to classroom management issues is amazingly low in teacher education, educational research and in descriptions of teacher competence. Comparative studies alluding to classroom management are then reviewed, followed by a description of six approaches to classroom management and some examples of strategies found in particular countries. Thus, the chapter does not offer a cross-cultural comparison of classroom management between countries, but rather provides an overview of the varied approaches to classroom management available across the world.

CLASSROOM MANAGEMENT: A NEGLECTED AREA?

Given the concern of teachers with classroom discipline and difficult student behaviour it is remarkable how few teacher education programmes explicitly address the topic. Stough (2006) showed that only about 30 per cent of the teacher education programmes in the USA have a course whose title refers to classroom management issues. Courses on this topic often conceal it in euphemisms such as 'Creating community in the classroom' or 'Curriculum and management' etc. There is no indication that the situation differs in other countries. A quick glance at teacher education programme websites from Australia, Germany and the Netherlands revealed very few courses explicitly referring to discipline. Similarly, professional standards for teachers in the USA, the UK, Australia, Canada (Ontario) and the Netherlands include little about classroom

management skills. Underlying this low emphasis clearly is the idea that if teachers are able to motivate students the need for disciplinary actions is low.

Similarly the amount of research on classroom management is limited compared to other educational fields. There are few presentations made on the topic at research conferences (Evertson and Weinstein 2006a). The recent publication, however, of the *Handbook of Classroom Management: Research, Practice and Contemporary Issues* (Evertson and Weinstein 2006b), has brought together an impressive knowledge base. As a result, it is clear that a great deal of attention is paid to discipline issues, but they are frequently presented under titles as varied as 'managing group work in the heterogeneous classroom', 'building and sustaining caring communities' or 'extrinsic rewards and inner motivation'. Apparently 'classroom management' is not a term *en vogue* and authors therefore prefer to use phrases that elucidate the aims that classroom management pursues rather than its techniques.

COMPARATIVE STUDIES

Comparative studies on education show both similarities and variations between countries. It is striking that all over the world primary and secondary education is conceived of as bringing 25–45 students together (usually peers from the same age) in classrooms with one teacher. The recent video segment of the Third International Mathematics and Science Study of 8th grade mathematics teaching revealed that teachers all over the world talk much more than their students: the teachers said eight words for every word uttered by students. In 90 per cent of the lessons textbooks or worksheets were used. In general, then, classrooms are teacher-centred – the teacher instructs and students listen or answer questions. Some variation was noted in the amount of seatwork and group work (relatively high in the Netherlands, Switzerland and Australia) and the pedagogical approach to mathematics. Further, there were very few differences noted in the relationships between teacher and students (Hiebert et al. 2003).

LeTendre, Baker, Akiba, Goesling and Wiseman (2001) mention that in education world-wide many things have become globally isomorphic: the overall 'charter' of the modern school is by and large a global one, with similar curricula, textbooks and materials. Nonetheless, local cultures have influenced schooling on the micro-social level, and it is these differences that often account for variations between schools and teaching.

Searching the literature through the ERIC and Google Scholar databases with keywords such as 'international', 'cross-cultural', 'cross-national' in combination with 'classroom management' or 'misbehaviour' and 'discipline' yields relatively few citations. Not many are added from a contents review of educational and international education journals such as the *Journal of Research in International Education, Compare, Prospects (Quarterly Review of Comparative Education)*, and *Current Issues in Comparative Education*. Comparative studies of classroom management in different countries (teacher beliefs, strategies, programmes to cope with violence or discipline problems) are almost non-existent.

The available comparative research falls into two categories. The first group of studies focuses on teacher beliefs and student perceptions of classroom management. The second directly relates to teaching practices and tangentially provides insights on class management.

Classroom management studies

Lewis et al. (2005) studied students' perceptions of classroom discipline strategies in Australia, China and Israel as a follow-up to a similar study by Lewis (2001) in Australia. The issue of classroom discipline was of moderate concern for teachers, and they did not perceive much student misbehaviour. One noteworthy result was that the differences between countries were small. Naturally, perceptions of classroom management are influenced by many variables, not least of which are the nationality and culture of the observer. For example, in previous research it

appeared that Dutch teachers' view of an orderly classroom was interpreted as disorder by American teachers (Wubbels et al. 2006). This may also have been the case in the Israeli classrooms, which are often judged to be well-managed by Israelis but unruly by outsiders. Because of varying cultural norms, teachers in different countries will interpret the amount and severity of discipline issues differently than outside observers. There were several strategies in the Lewis et al. (2005) study that were measured reliably: punishment, discussion, recognition of appropriate behaviour, aggression (negate students' sense of well-being and natural rights), involvement in decision-making and hinting (providing students with awareness that all is not as it should be). Hinting, recognition and discussion appeared to be the most commonly utilized strategies in the countries studied. Despite the general similarities, small differences were observed. Punishment was used fairly often in Israel and Australia. Aggression was employed the least across the countries, while the Australian and Israeli teachers generally refrained from using involvement in decision-making. Chinese teachers were rated as less punitive and aggressive than their Australian and Israeli colleagues, and more inclusive and supportive of student voices. This result might be explained by a lower level of disruptive student behaviour in Chinese classrooms. Australian teachers allowed the least amount of discussion, and were seen as the most punitive.

Whitman and Lai (1990) compared classroom management in selected schools in Hawaii and Japan. This is one of the studies that confirms the notion (Katz 1999) that classrooms in the United States (in this case Hawaii) are less orderly than those in Japan. In addition, this research demonstrated that Hawaiian teachers' vision of effective classroom management emphasized clear structure and rules for acceptable student behaviour, an approach that was not preferred by the Japanese teachers. The authors felt that the Japanese teachers needed to better anticipate and forestall student disturbances before they occured.

Several cross-national studies on teacher-student interpersonal relationships have been conducted with implications for classroom management. These are reported in this Handbook by Perry den Brok and Gerrit Jan Koopman in Chapter 20. In addition, Mitchel (2001) demonstrated that in the United States, Chinese-American teachers tend to model submission to authority rather than assertiveness and individualism, in contrast to their non-Asian American teacher peers.

Teaching practices studies

Osborn et al. (2003) studied classrooms in Denmark, France and England. While classroom management and discipline issues were only analysed in a small part of this research, it did yield some instructive results. In general, teacher roles and classroom interaction across the three countries were similar, though there were some differences. For example, Danish teachers saw themselves primarily responsible for the entire development of students, whereas their French counterparts saw themselves more as subject specialists (the English teachers fell in between). From the classroom management perspective this implies that Danish teachers saw a greater role in building social skills with their students. French classrooms seemed to be more orderly than the English or Danish in terms of noise level, with students remaining in their seats all the time. English and Danish teachers seemed to be more flexible in allowing student talk and movement related to the learning task, whereas the French teachers more than their English and Danish colleagues controlled students all the time. This result may be due to the fact that in France less group work was observed than in the two other countries. A striking issue in England was the concern about dress (school uniforms) and the appearance and behaviour of students outside the classroom. In Britain teachers and researchers alike seemed to be bothered by students' deviations from the norms regarding the dress code in and outside school, whereas in France and Denmark such aberrations (dyed hair, wearing baseball caps, etc.) were not an issue.

There is a long tradition of comparative studies on teaching and learning by the International Association for the Evaluation of Educational Achievement (IEA). Examples of their studies are the First, Second and Third International Mathematics and Science Study. The third study (TIMSS) was later continued as the Trends in Mathematics and Science Study. It is noteworthy that an examination of this research yields hardly any mention of classroom management practices. There is some reference to the amount of time spent off-task, which varied between 5 per cent (USA, Australia and the Netherlands) and 2 per cent (Czech Republic and Japan). Interestingly, outside interruptions in classroom activities were seen rather frequently in Australia, Hong Kong, the Netherlands and the USA (about 30 per cent of the lessons had at least one outside interruption), whereas in Switzerland, the Czech Republic and Japan the figure was approximately 10 per cent. Interruptions that seemed to be under the teacher's control were also relatively frequent in the Netherlands and the USA (about 20 per cent of the lessons had at least one interruption of more than 30 seconds) whereas these were virtually absent in Japan. Finally, teachers in the Netherlands stood out in interrupting students during individual work by making public announcements (64 per cent of the lessons). Teachers in the USA did this in 28 per cent of their lessons, and in other countries this occurred in only about 10 per cent. The level of uninterested students reported by teachers was lower in Japan than in the USA (Hiebert et al. 2003).

As a follow-up of the TIMSS research several publications have studied differences between American and Japanese (and occasionally, German) primary mathematics lessons. It is striking that despite teachers' concerns about classroom management there is not much in these studies that refers either directly or indirectly to classroom management. Although the Classroom Environment Study of the IEA (Anderson et al. 1989) focused on classroom environments, this study, in terms of classroom management, also mainly refers to the amount of off-task behaviour and hardly to what teachers do about this. The study reported that the number of teacher disciplinary actions varied from about 1 per cent of the teacher acts in Thailand, Korea, and Canada (Ontario) to about 5 per cent in Australia and 8 per cent in Israel. Hungary, the Netherlands, Nigeria and Canada (Quebec) fell in between these extremes (Anderson et al. 1989: 114). Similarly the on-task behaviour varied widely from about 96 per cent of the time in Thailand to only 60 per cent in Israel. In a similar vein, students in Australia and Canada (Ontario) reported more often than in most other countries that their teachers had problems in coping with misbehaviour. Interestingly, in both Australia and Thailand students indicated that their teachers quite often raised their voices because of classroom noise.

Summary of comparative studies

Generally, lesson structures seem to converge across countries but the concern for discipline problems may differ. In South East Asia, China and Japan classrooms seem to be more orderly than in the West. This is probably related to the esteem for teachers exhibited in the various societies, from high in the East to low in the West. Fewer discipline problems naturally contribute to a more stable class atmosphere.

Differences in discipline problems may explain some of the observed differences between nations in teaching methods. In the USA teachers seem to be preoccupied with student motivation and attention, whereas Japanese teachers tend to focus on engaging students in difficult problems (Stigler and Hiebert 1999). This may explain why American teachers use transparencies (and more modern technology, such as the Internet) often as a cognitive focus whereas Japanese teachers are much more reliant on the blackboard.

The development and maintenance of student self-esteem is a greater concern in the USA than in Japan (Stigler and Hiebert 1999), and to a lesser degree in the UK compared to France (Osborn and Planel 1999). This might explain why American teachers quickly redirect incorrect responses to other students

to arrive at the right answer, whereas in Japan they are more carefully analysed to ensure full understanding. A noteworthy study by Santagata (2005) reported that Italian teachers were more like Japanese than American teachers in this respect.

Taken together, the foregoing research does not provide a clear picture of cross-national differences in classroom management practices. This is due to the aforementioned lack of effort to conduct such research, as well as the fact that comparative studies address numerous variables and vary a great deal from country to country. Nonetheless, one possible conclusion from the literature is that in Western countries classrooms seem to be less orderly than in Asia. It is interesting to note that from a Chinese perspective the Japanese are concerned more about classroom discipline than are the Chinese (Mak 1998). Whereas American observers often refer to China and Japan in a similar way, the Japanese and Chinese observers see differences between themselves. Probably the further an observer is away from what is familiar the more things seem similar.

APPROACHES TO CLASSROOM MANAGEMENT

A framework for an international analysis of the different approaches to classroom management can be found in the recent *Handbook of Classroom Management* (Evertson and Weinstein 2006b). Six distinct classroom management strategies were selected: those that focus on external control of behaviour, on internal control, on classroom ecology, on discourse, on curriculum, and on interpersonal relationships. The core beliefs of each approach are presented below. Actual classroom management programmes usually integrate elements of these different types. For example, McCaslin et al. describe a programme for self-regulation that combines principles of behaviour modification in order that students develop internal control over their own learning (McCaslin et al. 2006).

Behavioural

The behavioural approach is probably the oldest research-based strategy for classroom management (Landrum and Kauffmann 2006). The approach can be traced to five behaviourist learning principles first espoused by Skinner. The first states that positive reinforcement will strengthen behaviour by applying a stimulus (or reward) following the desired behaviour. For example, teachers following this principle will reward children with recess time or a sticker once the child behaves in the desired manner. The second principle, called negative reinforcement, removes a (usually negatively experienced) stimulus in return for the desired student behaviour. For example a teacher might not assign homework if students complete their tasks in class on time. The third principle, extinction, may occur when a reinforcer declines or disappears. With time, the disruptive student behaviour will usually also gradually decline. Teachers who ignore attention-getting student behaviour are implementing the Extinction principle. 'Response cost punishment', the fourth principle, refers to a reinforcer that is withdrawn: if, for example, students have not been given homework they may receive an additional assignment if they do complete their tasks on time (in other words, freedom from homework is withdrawn). Finally, the most controversial principle is punishment, in which teachers present aversives. In general, this principle is used as a last resort and only for severe student misbehaviour. The earliest (mid-twentieth century) empirical studies on classroom management (see Brophy 2006) compared punishment with reward, and usually concluded that praise and reward had more positive effects.

Based on these principles, several programmes for behaviour modification aimed at shaping wanted student behaviour, and translating laboratory approaches to the classroom, have been developed (often with special needs children). In general, interventions based on the five principles are not used haphazardly, but are applied after a thorough student behaviour analysis. Students are usually observed systematically first and then single variables are manipulated in interventions. After a lot of experience with interventions aimed at individual students these have also been applied to whole classes (Brophy 2006).

Contemporary behaviourists typically distinguish between procedures for increasing desired behaviour and procedures for decreasing undesired behaviour (Brophy 2006). The former techniques include token reinforcement programmes, earned points credit systems, praise and approval, modelling, programmed instruction, self-specification of contingencies, self-reinforcement, establishment of clear rules and directions, and shaping through successive approximations. The latter techniques include extinction, reinforcing incompatible behaviours, self-reprimands, time-out from reinforcement, relaxation (for fears and anxiety), response cost, medication, self-instruction and self-evaluation.

The behavioural approach is found most prominently in special education and early childhood classrooms. Because it focuses on external control of student behaviour it has become quite controversial. In contrast, there are behavioural interventions that emphasize self-regulation with little external reinforcement, so there is a clear overlap with strategies used by non-behavioural psychologists and teachers following the theories discussed below.

Internal control

The 'internal control' approach is more humanistic and emphasizes students' integration of society's values and attitudes so that prosocial behaviours are internally motivated (Elias and Schwab 2006). This is manifested by a student-centred orientation to classroom management. Weinstein (1998) observed in the United States a shift between 1970 and 1995 from emphasis on behavioural external control to classroom management practices for internal control. Two distinct approaches aim at developing internal control – the first focuses on social emotional learning (Watson and Battistich 2006) and the second on the community (Elias and Schwab 2006).

When focusing on social emotional learning, self-discipline and self-control are promoted by developing emotional competence. According to Elias and Schwab (2006), four essential steps have to be followed by teachers: teaching social emotional skills (such as knowing yourself, making responsible decisions, caring for others), building caring relationships with students, setting firm and fair boundaries and sharing responsibilities with students.

The 'caring community' movement can be traced back to Neill's creation of an alternative school community in Summerhill (1960), and to many other educational reformers in the twentieth century (Freire, Freinet, Boeke). The second and fourth steps of the social emotional approach describe the central theme of the caring community movement. One goal of this child-centred approach is to build discipline with dignity, usually in school-based intervention programmes. These programmes theoretically emanate from a variety of perspectives: humanistic, social cultural, moral development, etc. Proponents therefore believe that it is possible to follow a number of educational avenues and arrive at the conclusion that caring communities are important for socializing students. As a result, there are varying conceptions of community in these programmes, since some are constructivist, others democratic, still others caring. What they all have in common, however, is a positive developmental view of children and recognition of the social context of their lives. Coercion in this approach is seen as incompatible with respect for students' autonomy and a positive child view.

Ecological

The ecological approach originates from a biological concept referring to the study of behaviours in natural habitats. This approach to classroom management emphasizes the organization of classrooms (the natural habitat). According to Doyle (2006), classrooms are characterized by multidimensionality (the large quantity of events and tasks), simultaneity (many things happening at once), immediacy (the rapid pace of events), unpredictability

(unexpected turn of events), publicness (the teacher being witnessed by many students) and history (the accumulation of common sets of experiences and norms). Educators who adhere to this perspective define order in terms of students following a teacher-centred orientation in class (i.e. following the teacher's programme of action).

As noted, the 'natural habitat' of classrooms is multidimensional. Based on extensive observation of American classrooms several common types of activities have been noted. These include recitation, seatwork, small group and cooperative learning teams, and transitions. It is important to note that this research was conducted mostly in primary classrooms in the USA, with less representation of secondary contexts. Clearly in other cultures other classroom formats might be found. Important points of leverage for creating a productive environment are the management of transitions between lesson parts, orchestrating classroom activities, establishing classroom rules and procedures, in conjunction with developing routines in particular at the start of the school year, and the physical design of the classroom setting (Doyle 2006).

Landmark studies of the ecological perspective on classroom management were conducted by Gump (1967) and Kounin (1970), who introduced the concept of the ripple effect. This is the effect that teacher 'desists' (when the teacher calls a halt to misbehaviour) have on students other than those who were behaving inappropriately and to whom the intervention is directed. Clarity of desists appeared important for effects on both target students and the other students in the classroom. Other important teacher behaviours were 'withitness' (showing that the teacher was aware of what was going on in the classroom, and communicated this awareness to students), 'overlapping' (being able to attend to two or more events at the same time) and maintaining a smooth momentum in a lesson. In the case in which students are reluctant to participate, a teacher must stimulate student involvement through group alerting and accountability signals to indicate a warning, such as the raising of a finger, or shutting off the lights. Further, they need to enforce continuity, and to use challenges and variety. Successful managers create order by creating all kind of academic student activities, thus anticipating potential misbehaviour, and they catch misbehaviour early when it occurs. Interventions are inherently risky because they call attention to potentially disruptive behaviour and might, ironically, lead the class further away from the task at hand, while not necessarily regaining stability. Because of these risk factors, successful interventions tend to have a private and fleeting quality that does not interrupt the flow of events. In addition to occurring early, they are often quite brief and do not invite further comment from the target or audience students (see Doyle 2006). An example of this can be seen when a teacher stands next to an offending student, but does not interrupt the lesson.

Discourse-centred

Stubbs (1976) in Great Britain and Cazden (1986) in the United States were originators of studies of classroom management that focused on the discourse patterns of teachers and students. From a sociolinguistic point of view it was assumed that participants' interpretations of the social situation influenced both the speaker's choice of what could be said and the listener's interpretation. Discourse-centred classrooms place the emphasis on communication, constructivism and teacher–student relationships (Morine-Dershimer 2006). The relationships between teachers and students are asymmetrical; communicative participation affects student achievement; contexts are constructed during interactions (e.g., rules for participation are implicit; behaviour expectations are construed as part of interactions); meaning is context-specific (e.g., meaning is signalled verbally and non-verbally, communicative competence is reflected in appropriate behaviour); and inferencing is required for conversational comprehension (e.g., form and function in speech used in conversations do not always match, and frames of reference may clash).

Classroom discourse studies generally corroborate ecological teacher strategies for class

management. These include active listening, varying questioning processes, listening to conversations of students to understand the social processes being enacted, and providing students time to understand and practice patterns of interaction appropriate to each new type of learning activity. Teachers are encouraged to establish a clear set of rules and routines early in the school year (Doyle 2006). To assist students with behaviour problems, Morine-Dershimer (2006) advises teachers from the discourse perspective to provide all students with extensive opportunities to learn, to reconsider attitudes and perceptions of pupils' abilities while observing them in atypical activity settings, to use communication patterns and participation structures that promote inclusion of students who exhibit communicative differences, and to be alert to ways communicative behaviour of the teacher may constrain instructional discourse.

Curricular

In this approach the curriculum becomes the starting point for efforts to engage students in academic activities. Curricular content is created in such a way that students are motivated to participate enthusiastically, thus indirectly reducing misbehaviour (Hickey and Schafer 2006). The aim is the collective participation of students based on sincere academic interest and with as few external rewards as possible – in contrast to the behavioural approach, which engages individual students according to the principles of behaviour modification.

There is a wealth of literature about the design of intrinsically rewarding learning environments (see, for example, Jacobson and Kozma 2000). An interesting example is the problem-posing approach in science education (Klaassen 1995; Lijnse and Klaassen 2004), which demonstrates how familiarity with student thought processes can help teachers develop meaningful, motivational curricular materials. Another example of the curricular approach is the participation-centred method by Hicke and Schafer (2006). They focus on the organization of classroom activities that help students engage in domain-specific discourse. This implies a curriculum as authentic domain knowledge practice, as representations of what happens in authentic discussions associated with expertise in the domain, for example, forms of mathematical discourse. They construct materials, instructions and activities that enhance the extent to which students try out the nuances of authentic mathematical discourse.

Interpersonal

A last approach to class management originated from the seminal work of Lewin, Lippitt and White (1939) on social climate and leadership. They described three leadership styles: authoritarian (the leader assigns tasks and gives step-by-step instructions, praises or blames), democratic (group members decide about tasks in group discussion, responsibility-taking is encouraged with input from the leader as a resource person), or *laissez-faire* (group members are left on their own to determine what to do and how to do it, with the leader ostensibly participating as little as possible). The democratic leadership style outperformed the other two in terms of student responsiveness and initiative.

The interpersonal approach to classroom management focuses on creating productive relationships between teachers and students. As noted in this Handbook by den Brok and Koopman (Chapter 20), two independent characteristics of teacher behaviour can be used to map the teacher–student relationship: Influence and Proximity. As described by Wubbels et al. (2006), a number of studies conducted over nearly three decades demonstrated that successful teachers exhibit dominant (high influence) and cooperative (high proximity) behavioural patterns. The research revealed the non-verbal behaviours and strategies that facilitate this profile in teachers. These include behaviours such as continuous eye contact with students, and loud, emphatic speech. In addition, the research established the importance of accurate teacher understanding of their relationship with students, based on students' interpretations of teacher behaviour. The authors point to the risk that beginning teachers take when they try to be friendly to students (high proximity) without first establishing control (low influence). The challenge, of course, is to establish classroom control as well as exhibiting helpful, friendly and understanding behaviour.

Synthesis of classroom management approaches

An analysis of the foregoing six approaches reveals some commonality in terms of desirable classroom management strategies. An important distinction between successful and unsuccessful managers is the focus on learning rather than on a noise-free atmosphere. Good managers show personal acceptance of students, they frequently praise them, have good senses of humour and frequently offer students helpful suggestions. Further, such teachers excel in their lesson preparation and organization. In the beginning of the school year they gradually introduce procedures and routines as needed without overloading students. They model appropriate student behaviour. When it comes to disruptions they intervene early and are able to stop them before they evolve into real problems.

CLASSROOM MANAGEMENT ACROSS COUNTRIES

The catalogue of approaches to classroom management may help describe emphasis in particular practices, strategies, procedures or habits in classrooms. We will look at some examples of practices described by authors in several countries. It is important to keep in mind that usually several different approaches in countries can be found and therefore what follows describes the practices of a particular author, not necessarily the predominant approach in a country.

Ben-Peretz, Eilam and Yankelevitch (2006) report two practices in classroom management in Israeli elementary education – individualistic and systemic. Usually these are found to be combined in practice. The individual practice focuses on single students as targets of the teacher's actions. Because careful observation of an individual student's misbehaviour is the basis for deliberate teacher choice of action we can interpret this as a behavioural approach. Israel is a multicultural and multiethnic country and classrooms can be characterized by clashes of cultures. Israeli society is in need of citizens who are socialized in their new home country. Therefore a second practice, the systemic, is important. This practice focuses on the group as target of the teacher's actions. Based on the assumption that the individual is shaped by the social context, it seeks to establish group norms and relations in order to create a productive learning environment. The systemic practice clearly has its roots in the internal and ecological approach to classroom management.

Materials used in German and Swiss teacher education programmes were sampled to see what pre-service teachers are exposed to in their training (Berliner Bildungsserver 2005; Lohman 2003; Rüedi 2002). The materials revealed that elements from all approaches are presented in the programmes, though not all of them with equal attention. In line with the shift in orientation in the USA (Weinstein 1998), not very much is said about behavioural approaches. Rather, the focus is on curricular and internal control methods with some emphasis on interpersonal issues. The materials emphasize analysis and theoretical reflection by teachers, and advise them on appropriate behaviour. These recommendations predominantly stem from the ecological and, to a lesser degree, the discourse approach.

In a Slovenian study primary students were surveyed to determine the teachers' predominant disciplinary techniques (Pšunder 2005). The study found that in Slovenia disciplinary techniques with a higher degree of teacher control and lower student autonomy predominate. This description exemplifies a conceptualization of classroom management from an interpersonal perspective. From the study it is not clear whether teachers follow other approaches, since they are not mentioned. A Jordanian study (Haroun and O'Hanlon

1997) on teachers' perceptions of causes of discipline problems raises students' interference with the teacher authority as the main topic. Again this is predominantly an interpersonal issue.

Shimahara (1998b) and Nishioka (2006) show that generally in Japan the most important task of classroom management is to socialize students to the group. This reflects the cultural emphasis on group life in Japan. Therefore classroom management practices focus on the process of building a classroom community where interpersonal relations and emotional bonding between teachers and students and among students are developed. Students do learn to control themselves through elaborate and sophisticated strategies for development of self-management. In this description mainly the internal control approach is recognized.

Granström (2006) in Sweden studied troublesome behaviour and undesired dynamics in secondary classrooms. He considers students' provocative behaviour to originate from emotions, expectations, disappointments, fears and fantasies that may be projected on to the teacher. He argues that students in class have their own (social) life and want to pursue their own projects. Thus they hinder the teacher's project, though not as an attack but as a value in its own right. Teachers have to be trained to treat provocations and projections not as personal assaults and act accordingly. This analysis shows some elements from the behavioural and ecological approach, but it adds to these by introducing psychodynamic theories in the light of the programme of action of both teachers and students. Psychodynamic theory is used in order to help teachers focus more on students' inner worlds and their own more-distant role. Lewis et al. (2005) observed that the greater the student misbehaviour, the more teachers used aggressive strategies. This is not helpful because these techniques are not often effective and may harm students. This reinforces the importance of the need to help teachers not regard student misbehaviour as a personal attack. If successful, teachers might be less inclined to respond aggressively and might use more productive strategies.

CONCLUSION

In the second half of the twentieth century across the world, a shift has been observed from behavioural to internal approaches to classroom management. Nowadays, in addition to the internal approach, the ecological and interpersonal seem to be popular. In special education the behavioural approach is still valued. No large, clear or consistent differences can be found between classroom management strategies across countries. Naturally, there are small differences in emphasis between countries or cultures, but a larger variation occurs within countries or among people with similar ethnic backgrounds. For example, differences in classroom atmosphere and orientation to management can be found in the Netherlands and Belgium, countries that have similar cultures. Dutch parents might send their children to Belgian schools because they feel that discipline there is still important. On the other hand, Belgian parents may do the reverse so that their children will receive more attention from Dutch teachers. Nonetheless, in the Netherlands schools with strict discipline can be found, while student-centred schools exist in Belgium.

Approaches to classroom management may vary from culture to culture but these methods probably depend more on local circumstances than on culture *per se*. For example, in Israel the influence of extensive immigration has created a specific need for classroom management as a tool to socialize students into Israeli society. Classroom management in a Darfur refugee camp with 80 students in a 30-square-metre tent is quite different from the management in schools in Sudan's capital city, in spite of the similar culture. It seems that governments, schools and teachers throughout the world adapt to these local circumstances by choosing classroom management practices that are best-suited to their aims.

REFERENCES

Anderson, L.W., Ryan, W. and Shapiro, B.J. (1989) *The IEA Classroom Environment Study*. Oxford: Pergamon Press.

Berliner Bildungsserver (2005) *Störungen des Unterrichts* [Disturbances in Education]. bebis. cidsnet.de/weiterbildung/sps/allgemein/bausteine/storoerunegen/index.htm (accessed 5 August 2005).

Ben-Peretz, M., Eilam, B. and Yankelevitch, E. (2006) Classroom management in Israel: multicultural classrooms in an immigrant country. In C.M. Evertson and C.S. Weinstein (eds) *Handbook of Classroom Management: Research, Practice, and Contemporary Issues*. Mahwah, NJ: Lawrence Erlbaum Associates, pp. 1121–40.

Blase, J.J. (1986) A qualitative analysis of sources of teacher stress: consequences for performance. *American Educational Research Journal*, 23: 23–40.

Brophy, J. (2006) History of research on classroom management. In C.M. Evertson and C.S. Weinstein (eds) *Handbook of Classroom Management: Research, Practice, and Contemporary Issues*. Mahwah, NJ: Lawrence Erlbaum Associates, pp. 17–43.

Cazden, C. (1986) Classroom discourse. In M.C. Wittrock (ed) *Handbook of Research on Teaching*, 3rd edition. New York: Macmillan, pp. 432–63.

Creemers, B.P.M. (1994) *The Effective Classroom*. London: Cassell.

Doyle, W. (2006) Ecological approaches to classroom management. In C.M. Evertson and C.S. Weinstein (eds) *Handbook of Classroom Management: Research, Practice, and Contemporary Issues*. Mahwah, NJ: Lawrence Erlbaum Associates, pp. 97–126.

Elias, M. and Schwab, Y. (2006) From compliance to responsibility: social and emotional learning and classroom management. In C.M. Evertson and C.S. Weinstein (eds) *Handbook of Classroom Management: Research, Practice, and Contemporary Issues*. Mahwah, NJ: Lawrence Erlbaum Associates, pp. 309–42.

Evertson, C.M. and Weinstein, C.S. (2006a) Classroom management as a field of inquiry. In C.M. Evertson and C.S. Weinstein (eds) *Handbook of Classroom Management: Research, Practice, and Contemporary Issues*. Mahwah, NJ: Lawrence Erlbaum Associates, pp. 3–16.

Evertson, C.M. and Weinstein, C.S. (eds) (2006b) *Handbook of Classroom Management: Research, Practice, and Contemporary Issues*. Mahwah, NJ: Lawrence Erlbaum Associates.

Fraser, B.J. (1998) Science learning environments: assessment, effects and determinants. In B.J. Fraser and K. Tobin (eds) *International Handbook of Science Education*. London: Kluwer Academic, pp. 527–64.

Friedman, I.A. (1995) Student behavior patterns contributing to teacher burnout. *The Journal of Educational Research*, 88: 281–9.

Granström, K. (2006) Group phenomena and classroom management in Sweden. In C.M. Evertson and

C.S. Weinstein (eds) *Handbook of Classroom Management: Research, Practice, and Contemporary Issues*. Mahwah, NJ: Lawrence Erlbaum Associates, pp. 141–60.

Gump, P.V. (1967) *The Classroom Behavior Setting: Its Nature and Relation to Student Behavior.* Washington, DC: US Office of Education.

Haroun, R. and O'Hanlon, C. (1997) Teachers' perceptions of discipline problems in a Jordanian secondary school. *Pastoral Care in Education*, 15(2): 29-36.

Hickey, D. and Schafer, N.J. (2006) Design-based, participation-centred approaches to classroom management. In C.M. Evertson and C.S. Weinstein (Eds) *Handbook of Classroom Management: Research, Practice, and Contemporary Issues*. Mahwah, NJ: Lawrence Erlbaum Associates, pp. 281–308.

Hiebert, J., Gallimore, R., Garnier, H., Givin, K.B., Hollingsworth, H., Jacobs, J., Chui, A.M.Y., Wearne, D., Smith, M., Kersting, N., Manaster, A., Tseng, E., Etterbeek, W., Manaster, C., Gonzales, P. and Stigler, J. (2003) *Teaching Mathematics in Seven Countries: Results from the TIMSS 1999 Video Study*. Washington, DC: National Center for Education Statistics.

Ingersoll, R.M. (2001) Teacher turnover and teacher shortages: an organizational analysis. *American Educational Research Journal*, 38: 499–534.

Jacobson, M.J. and Kozma, R.B. (2000) *Innovations in Science and Mathematics Education*. Mahwah, NJ: Lawrence Erlbaum Associates.

Katz, L., (1999) International perspectives on early childhood education: lessons from my travels. *Early Childhood Research and Practice*, 1(1). ecrp.uiuc.edu/v1n1/katz.html (accessed 1 December 2005.)

Klaassen, C.W.J.M. (1995) *A Problem-Posing Approach to Teaching the Topic of Radioactivity*. Utrecht: CDβ-Press.

Kounin, J.S. (1970) *Discipline and Group Management in Classrooms*. New York: Holt, Rinehart and Winston.

Landrum, T.M. and Kauffmann, J. (2006). Behavioral approaches to classroom management. In C.M. Evertson and C.S. Weinstein (eds) *Handbook of Classroom Management: Research, Practice, and Contemporary Issues*. Mahwah, NJ: Lawrence Erlbaum Associates, pp. 47–72

LeTendre, G.K., Baker, D.P., Akiba, M., Goesling, B. and Wiseman, A. (2001) Teachers' work: institutional isomorphism and cultural variation in the US, Germany, and Japan. *Educational Researcher*, 30 (6): 3–15.

Lewin, K., Lippitt, R. and White, R. (1939) Patterns of aggressive behavior in experimentally created 'social climates'. *Journal of Social Psychology*, 10: 271–99.

Lewis, R. (2001) Classroom discipline and student responsibility: the students' view. *Teaching and Teacher Education*, 17: 307–19.

Lewis, R., Romi, S., Qui, X. and Katz, J. (2005) Teachers' classroom discipline and student misbehaviour in Australia, China and Israel. *Teaching and Teacher Education*, 21: 729–41.

Lijnse, P.L. and Klaassen, C.W.J.M. (2004) Didactical structures as an outcome of research on teaching–learning sequences? *International Journal of Science Education*, 26: 537–54.

Lohmann, G. (2003) *Mit Schülern klarkommen* [Coping with Students]. Berlin: Cornelsen Verlag.

Mak, G.C.L. (1998) Classroom management in China: personalizing groupism. In N.K. Shimahara (ed.) *Politics of Classroom Life*. New York: Garland Publishing, pp. 239–60.

McCaslin, M., Bozack, A.R., Napoleon, L., Thomas, A., Vasquez, V., Wayman, V. and Zhang, J. (2006) Self-regulated learning and classroom management: theory, research and considerations for classroom practice. In C.M. Evertson and C.S. Weinstein (eds) *Handbook of Classroom Management: Research, Practice, and Contemporary Issues*. Mahwah, NJ: Lawrence Erlbaum Associates, pp. 232–52.

Mitchel, K. (2001) Education for democratic citizenship: transnationalism, multiculturalism and the limits of liberalism. *Harvard Educational Review*, 71: 51–78.

Morine-Dershimer, G. (2006) Classroom management and classroom discourse. In C.M. Evertson and C.S. Weinstein (eds) *Handbook of Classroom Management: Research, Practice, and Contemporary Issues*. Mahwah, NJ: Lawrence Erlbaum Associates, pp.127–56.

Murray-Harvey, R., Silins, H. and Saebel, J. (1999) A cross-cultural comparison of student concerns in the teaching practicum. *International Education Journal*, 1 (1). http://ehlt.flinders.edu.au/education/iej/main/mainframe.htm (accessed 12 December 2005.)

Neill, A.S. (1960) *Summerhill*. New York: Hart Publishing Company.

Nishioka, K. (2006) Classroom management in post-war Japan. In C.M. Evertson and C.S. Weinstein (eds) *Handbook of Classroom Management: Research, Practice, and Contemporary Issues*. Mahwah, NJ: Lawrence Erlbaum Associates, pp. 1215–37.

Osborn, M. and Planel, C. (1999) Comparing children's learning. In R. Alexander, P. Broadfoot and D. Phillips (eds) *Learning from Comparing*, Vol. 1. Oxford: Symposium Books, pp. 261–94.

Osborn, M., Broadfoot, P., McNess, E., Planel, C., Ravn, B. and Triggs, P. (2003) *A World of Difference: Comparing Learners across Europe*. Maidenhead: Open University Press.

Pšunder, M. (2005) How effective is school discipline in preparing students to become responsible citizens? Slovenian teachers' and students' views. *Teaching and Teacher Education*, 21: 273–86.

Rüedi, J. (2002) *Disziplin in der Schule* [Discipline in School]. Berne: Haupt Verlag.

Santagata, R. (2005) Practices and beliefs in mistake-handling activities: a video study of Italian and US mathematics lessons. *Teaching and Teacher Education*, 21: 491–508.

Shimahara, N.K. (1998a) Introduction. In N.K. Shimahara (ed.), *Politics of Classroom Life*. New York: Garland Publishing, pp. 3-10.

Shimahara, N.K. (1998b) Classroom management in Japan: building a classroom community. In N.K. Shimahara (ed.) *Politics of Classroom Life*, New York: Garland Publishing, pp. 215–38.

Stigler, J.W. and Hiebert, J. (1999) *The Teaching Gap*. New York: The Free Press.

Stough, L. (2006) Professional standards, teacher education and classroom management. In C.M. Evertson and C.S. Weinstein (eds) *Handbook of Classroom Management: Research, Practice, and Contemporary Issues*. Mahwah NJ: Lawrence Erlbaum Associates, pp. 909–24.

Stubbs, M. (1976) *Language, Schools and Classrooms*. London: Methuen.

Watson, M. and Battistich, V. (2006) Building and sustaining caring communities. In C.M. Evertson and C.S. Weinstein (eds) *Handbook of Classroom Management: Research, Practice, and Contemporary Issues*. Mahwah, NJ: Lawrence Erlbaum Associates, pp. 253–80.

Weinstein, C.S. (1998) Classroom management in the United States: a shifting paradigm. In N.K. Shimahara (ed.), *Politics of Classroom Life*. New York: Garland Publishing, pp. 49–84.

Whitman, N.C. and Lai, M.K. (1990) Similarities and differences in teachers' beliefs about effective teaching of mathematics: Japan and Hawaïi. *Educational Studies in Mathematics*, 21: 71–81.

Wubbels, T., Brekelmans, M., Brok, P. den and Tartwijk, J. van (2006) An interpersonal perspective on classroom management in secondary classrooms in the Netherlands. In C. M. Evertson and C.S. Weinstein (eds) *Handbook of Classroom Management: Research, Practice, and Contemporary Issues*, Mahwah, NJ: Lawrence Erlbaum Associates, pp. 1161–92.

PART IV

Organizing Formal Institutions for the Promotion of International Education

24

Schools Self-evaluating Their International Values: a Case Study

James Cambridge and Clive Carthew

This chapter discusses the evaluation of the implementation of a questionnaire designed by the International Schools Association for the review by schools of their international values. The original questionnaire was entitled 'Self-assessing Internationalism: an Instrument for Schools' and will be referred to as 'the Instrument', although the title has since been revised. The evaluation was conducted by the International Baccalaureate Research Unit (IBRU), based at the University of Bath, UK, for the International Schools Association in partnership with a variety of schools in different parts of the world – only a few of which could be described as 'international schools'. The chapter starts with a review of the literature on school self-evaluation. It then presents an outline history of the development of the Instrument. This is followed by a section that discusses the design of the project to evaluate the implementation of the Instrument in schools. The formative and summative outcomes of the implementation of the Instrument by schools are then considered. The chapter concludes with a review of how this meta-evaluation (that is, the evaluation of an evaluation process) has contributed to the iterative development of an improved revised version of the Instrument.

THEORETICAL FRAMEWORK

A school claiming to offer 'international education' might be expected to explain its institutional philosophy and mission by making reference to 'international values' and 'education for international-mindedness'. The mission statement of the International Baccalaureate Organization (IBO) refers to the development of 'inquiring, knowledgeable and caring young people who help to create a better and more peaceful world through intercultural understanding and respect' and who 'understand that other people, with their differences, can also be right' (IBO 2006). However, it is evident that schools aspiring to promote international values in education extend beyond the community of institutions that offer the programmes of the IBO (Cambridge and Thompson 2000). It is therefore justifiable to propose that a wide variety of schools claiming to offer international education might seek to monitor and evaluate their international values or international-mindedness. This may seem to be a facile proposition, but its implementation is fraught with conceptual difficulties. Not the least of these difficulties is to define what the terms 'international values' and 'education for international-mindedness' mean, and how they might be recognized and evaluated.

One approach may be described as an 'essentialist' concept of international values. Cambridge (1998) discusses the 'contingency model' of organization as a framework for the description and analysis of international schools and other schools in an international context. This view presents the school as an entity that is interfaced with its environment and which transforms inputs into outputs by means of a variety of processes. In this model, international values or international-mindedness can be identified as 'contingent variables' or inputs that influence the production of outputs. From this perspective, international values and international-mindedness are important ingredients in the recipe for international education (Hayden 1998: 262). They can be 'added to the mix' of a school in order to make the education it offers more 'international'. Based on this assumption, a function of school evaluation is to monitor and quality assure the recipe by checking the 'contents' against the 'label on the packaging'.

An alternative approach is to conceptualize international values as the 'friction' generated when international education is happening. This may be analogous to the heat generated when an engine is running but this thermodynamic metaphor may not withstand too much analysis. The point is that the performance of the engine cannot be evaluated adequately by concentrating on analysis of fuel consumption (inputs) or exhaust gases (outputs) in isolation. It is necessary to find ways of looking at how the engine performs whilst it is in motion. In contrast to the essentialist account described above, this approach may be identified with a view of international values and international-mindedness as decentred qualities that are emergent from a discourse of international

education. To locate international values as a cultural construct, 'one must look not in individual mind, as an accumulated body of unchanging knowledge, but in the dialogue, the embodied actions "discursively rearticu-lated" between individuals in particular socio-cultural contexts at particular moments in time' (Hall 2002: 18–19). Such an interpreta-tion is implicit in the view of international education as 'a transformative discourse which locates all fields of enquiry in a supra-national frame of reference and upholds the cause of peace' (Rawlings 2000: 365).

The implications for the practice of evalua-tion are that contrasting approaches to the specification of international values may be identified, and that this contrast may be coupled to a wider issue relating to the uses of 'etic' and 'emic' constructs in the social sciences and humanities. The terms etic and emic are discussed by James Cambridge else-where in this Handbook (see Chapter 34). In brief, etic constructs are general and external to the culture being studied, whereas emic constructs are particular and belong to the culture. The prior specification by an external body of a set of standards for evaluation of a school may be interpreted as an example of an 'imposed etic'. This is because the standards (that is, specifications for international values in the case under discussion in this chapter), although they pertain to the internal workings of a school, are concepts expressed in forms of language that are external to the school. The standards may describe general qualities that are common to all schools but they are likely to be expressed in terms specific to a particular context. On the other hand, the standards that emerge from a period of reflective self-study by a school, and which describe structures and functions of the school in its own forms of words, may be interpreted as emic constructs.

In turn, this argument is linked to a wider discourse about universalism (that the same values should prevail everywhere) relativism (that different values prevail in different places) and pluralism (that different values prevail in the same place). Is it valid to identify universal values as etic constructs? Are emic constructs statements of a relativist or pluralist position? To what extent is the proposition valid that 'international values' are universal values applicable to all contexts at all times? Or should 'international values' be interpreted as being applicable to particular contexts at particular times? For persons who adhere to the universalist perspective, this latter argument may be criticized as being a position of 'moral relativism'. They would propose that it is dangerous to argue that certain standards of human behaviour are not universally applicable. On the other hand, arguments from the relativist or pluralist position would contest *whose* values should be identified as universal values.

How might approaches to evaluation of international values be theorized? Stake (1986) offers nine approaches to educational evaluation, of which three appear to be relevant to the present study. It is evident that the International Schools Association's (ISA) self-assessment instrument itself is an example of the 'institutional self-study by staff' approach, with key elements that comprise 'committee work, standards set by staff, discussion, professionalism' and pay-offs that comprise 'increased staff awareness' and 'sense of responsibility' (Stake 1967, as discussed in Hopkins 1989: 20). The issue to be resolved is how the meta-evaluation (that is, the evaluation of the implementation of the Instrument) is to be conducted. From Stake's menu of nine approaches, two appear to have relevance – the 'transaction-observation' and 'management analysis' approaches.

The 'transaction-observation' approach has the key elements of 'educational issues, classroom observation, case studies and pluralism' with the pay-off that it produces a broad picture of a programme and helps protagonists to see conflicts in values. The key elements of the 'management analysis' approach comprise 'lists of options, estimates, feedback loops, costs, efficiency' with the pay-off of giving 'feedback for decision-making' (Hopkins 1989: 20). Given that these frameworks are designed with the aims of school improvement in mind, they may not be directly relevant for the purposes of the present study and may need to be adapted. If it is agreed that the focus of the evaluation should be to find out if the intentions

of the Instrument are translated into practice, then the 'transaction-observation' approach may offer an appropriate model. This approach may be the best way of addressing the problem of interpretation – in other words, finding out if the schools participating in the study interpret the items in the Instrument in terms that are congruent with the intentions of its authors. Furthermore, a 'managerial' dimension may also be identified that concerns the practical issues of how that self-study process is conducted. To give a pair of extremes as examples, it may be proposed that one approach could be to take key members of the school community away on a retreat with the aim of completing the self-study over a weekend of intense activity, whereas another approach could be to spend an academic year in consultation with key members of the school community. Which strategy is most effective in achieving the aims of the self-study? How would the outcomes of the two approaches to management of the self-study process compare? What are the costs and benefits of either strategy? How would these approaches influence the time lines allocated to the evaluation? Taken together, the aims of the 'transaction-observation' and 'management analysis' approaches may be identified as contributing to the rationale for the evaluation.

BACKGROUND

An important aspect of the Instrument is that it presents a framework for self-evaluation by schools. It enables schools to 'speak for themselves' (MacBeath 1999). Citing examples from a variety of national education systems, including Denmark, Israel, Canada, USA, Australia and Scotland, MacBeath (1999) argues that self-evaluation is a widely distributed and recognized approach to school evaluation. School evaluation may have a variety of purposes – for political reasons, accountability, professional development, organizational development, and improvement of teaching and learning. What combination of purposes can be identified as the motivation for schools to participate in the process specified by the ISA (2001)?

MacBeath (1999) proposes that school evaluation and development may be interpreted in three dimensions representing continuums between:

- internal and external
- support and pressure, and
- top-down and bottom-up.

The form and content of the reports produced as a result of the self-evaluation process depend on their intended audience. Should the audience for the self-evaluation report be identified as the school community itself (which may comprise school administrators and managers, teachers, students, parents, governors, employers and members of the local community) – or is the audience external to the school? There are strong arguments for identifying an external audience – as well as an internal one – for the self-evaluation process discussed here. The internal audience may well find the outcome of critical reflection on its own values and attitudes salutary. The award of a certificate by the ISA in recognition of completion of the self-evaluation by the school could be one example of the way in which the audience for the report is external to the school, but other uses for such data may also be envisaged with respect to a variety of external audiences.

Implementation by schools of the Instrument may be located at the 'support' end of MacBeath's 'support–pressure' continuum. This is because schools are not coerced or pressurized to self-evaluate their internationalism – it is a voluntary activity – and the ISA offers support to those schools that elect to do so. To contrast the present study with an example from England the internationalism self-evaluation process is not a statutory requirement for schools as is an OFSTED inspection. Does this also mean that the self-evaluation is more 'bottom-up' than 'top-down'? At the 'macropolitical' or system level, this may be true because the decision for a school to participate in the self-evaluation process is not imposed by legislation or national structures. Such an arrangement may be interpreted as being more 'bottom-up'

because the school has made a voluntary decision to participate. Nonetheless, at the 'micropolitical' or institutional level the decision to participate in the self-evaluation may be either 'top-down' or 'bottom-up'. It depends on who has made the decision to participate and how that decision is implemented. Was the decision made by the senior management team or board of governors of a school and imposed on the school, or as a popular decision by the teachers, or by the whole school community? In the latter case, what sectional interests from the school community were represented at that decision-making stage? Who can claim 'ownership' of the outcome of self-evaluation?

Saunders (1999: 419) proposes that an 'English model' of school self-evaluation 'can be characterized as instrumentalist, action-oriented, rationalistic and managerial; and there is both a "weak" and a "strong" or radical interpretation of what is missing from it'. She declares her own interest in pursuit of the strong or radical interpretation that 'ethical, affective, non-rational and democratic modes of thinking are integral to the activity of school self-evaluation'. Reference to the 'ethical' and 'affective' dimensions of evaluation may be interpreted as an identification of values and attitudes as the focus of enquiry. A valid question to ask about the Instrument is what do 'international' values and attitudes constitute – and how are they addressed by the Instrument? Such values and attitudes, that address conduct, character and manner, may be identified with the 'expressive order' (Bernstein 1977). However, reference to the 'non-rational' expresses an acknowledgement that organizational cultures are frequently (if not invariably) conflict-ridden with 'dissonance between the rational model [of the school] and the institutional reality' (Saunders 1999: 422). This presents a challenge to the validity of the outcomes generated by the ISA (2001). Does self-evaluation present a view of the school as it really is – or of how it would like itself to be seen? Reference to 'democratic' modes of thinking may be interpreted as ensuring that all members of the school community are accorded a voice in performing the self-evaluation. Might it be expected that the school performing self-evaluation should specify how it maximizes inclusion and representativeness?

Saunders (1999: 419) argues that the 'strong, radical' interpretation of self-evaluation is based on the claim that the educational process is centrally concerned with:

- critical collective reflection about social and personal values in a pluralistic society
- the practical exercise of liberal democracy
- encouragement of creativity and imagination
- development of insight and empathy
- intellectual, academic and technical development.

How might these processes be operationalized in the context of self-evaluation of internationalism by schools? Are they accepted or contested in the various contexts of international schools and other institutions that might elect to evaluate their international values? These claims about the form and function of education may be applied as a guide to asking meta-evaluative questions about the self-evaluation process. For example, how might 'critical collective reflection about social and personal values in a pluralistic society' be used to describe the self-evaluation by a school of its internationalist values? What does the term 'pluralistic values' mean in this context? It may be argued that references to universal values, as made in the Instrument, and pluralism are contradictory. Universalism assumes that the same values should prevail everywhere, whereas pluralism accepts that particular sets of values are local, autonomous and distinctive. How can values – particularly those relating to quality standards – be simultaneously universal and plural? One possible approach to the reconciliation of this dilemma is to propose that the recognition of plural value systems is in itself a statement of universal values. Such a view may be identified with the European Enlightenment concept of toleration (Zaw 1996). However, it may also be argued that this view is indicative of the 'globalist' project of international education as a branded product and the role of school accreditation in 'brand management' strategies (Cambridge 2002).

Does the Instrument assist in guiding critical reflection by a school? What evidence is required to test the validity of the proposition that such critical reflection is 'collective'? The term 'collective' in this context may be interpreted as referring to the participation of the whole school – however 'participation' and 'whole school' are defined – in the practice of critical reflection. Would the establishment of a group of committees, each with a focus on a particular self-assessment matrix, be acceptable as evidence of 'collective' critical reflection? Does the application of terms such as 'collective' and 'whole school' require the inclusion and participation of a wide variety of stakeholders in the self-evaluation process? The extent to which 'social and personal values' are to be the focus of scrutiny may be contested. 'Social' values may be defined in terms of the values expressed in the structures and processes of the school. For example, does the school have 'a management regime value-consistent with its stated institutional international values' (Thompson 1998)? Access may be gained to such values by inspection of various institutional documents that are open to public audit. The inferences derived from this practice may be contested because such sources may be subject to contrasting approaches to hermeneutic elucidation (that is, the same documents may be interpreted in different ways). However, a more difficult issue is to determine how 'personal values' are to be addressed. Such values are not open to public audit in the same way as institutional documents such as handbooks and staff salary scales. Participants in the self-evaluation process may be justified in feeling defensive about whether an audit of their personal values is to be conducted. Is it ethical to examine personal values in the context of institutional self-evaluation? It has been proposed that a feature of international education is that teachers should be 'exemplars of international-mindedness' (Thompson 1998). Another way of expressing this idea is to argue that 'it is not adequate to see teachers as "delivering the curriculum" nor even as "providing role models" for their pupils ... It is more that teachers practise daily in the classroom a vocation which has intrinsic and pervasive ethical content, regardless of what subject they teach' (Saunders 1999). Thus, it may be considered valid and ethical to enquire into the visible patterns of behaviour of members of the school community in the context of the present enquiry while at the same time recognizing and respecting their privacy.

How might self-evaluation be identified with 'the practical exercise of liberal democracy'? It was proposed above that the 'practical exercise of liberal democracy' could be interpreted as embracing issues of representation and inclusion. This concept can be expanded and developed by reference to the view that an aim of international education should be to promote peace, human rights and democracy (Phillips 2002; Thomas 1998). This may be interpreted in terms of participants in the enquiry being assured 'freedom of speech and belief and freedom from fear' (United Nations 1948) but notions of freedom of expression (Article 19) coupled with the right to privacy (Article 12) may also be identified as being relevant to this context. It may be argued that references to 'liberal democracy' are vague and ambiguous. Does the term refer to a process whereby an elected dictatorship is chosen periodically by secret ballot with universal suffrage, or is a more sustained level of engagement with 'active citizenship' more appropriate in this context? Active citizenship, with respect to children and young people, is described in the following terms:

Young people may not be able to vote before they are 18, but they can make a positive contribution to their communities. Young people should be actively involved in decision-making both in schools and in the wider community. They should be encouraged to think critically about their role in society and their potential as agents for change. (Institute for Citizenship 2003)

This argument may also be applied to the inclusion of adults in active decision-making. The point being made is that a definition of who may be included as a stakeholder in self-evaluation by a school is of critical importance to claims about the process as a 'practical exercise of liberal democracy'.

The reference to 'encouragement of creativity and imagination' challenges us to consider what constitutes valid evidence in the context of school self-evaluation. Should the self-evaluation report compiled by a school take the form of a linear text, or should other forms of documentation, such as posters, photography or video, be acceptable as evidence? Saunders (1999) discusses a contribution to self-evaluation made by school students, described by Steiner-Loffler, who were invited to participate in an activity that involved them in 'taking photographs of particular places around the school they liked and did not like, and then talking about their photos in a group' (Saunders 1999: 423).

In the context of IB World Schools (schools authorized to offer one or more of the three IB programmes), at least, 'development of insight and empathy' may be identified with the section of the IBO mission statement proposing that its programmes 'encourage students across the world to become active, compassionate and lifelong learners who understand that other people, with their differences, can also be right' (IBO 2006). It may be argued that, for students to develop such attributes, members of the whole school community should put such values into practice. This may be coupled with the proposition that self-evaluation is involved with 'intellectual, academic and technical development' of the whole school community. This approach is based on the premise that self-evaluation is a rational, technical activity that requires a variety of cognitive and affective skills, and that its practice will have an improving effect in other areas of the life of the school. Meuret and Morlaix (2003: 68) identify the 'conditions of deemed success of a self-evaluation' in terms of 'its impact on knowledge and on the effectiveness of the school' and its 'impact on the school ability to improve'. They argue that the former is facilitated by 'assessment of outcomes' and 'improvement of the management of the school'. The latter is facilitated by 'a participating Steering Group, able to motivate the stakeholders' and the self-evaluation process 'completed through thorough discussions involving most stakeholders and improving relations between them'. Davies and Rudd (2001: 40) identify the following cultural changes 'in a broad range of areas of school life' as positive outcomes of school self-evaluation:

- improvement in data analysis and interpretation
- teachers' professional development
- further opportunities for the evaluation of teaching and learning styles
- opportunities to review and update teaching and learning policies
- opportunities for consideration of management issues
- increased involvement of pupils, parents, governors and non-teaching staff.

These outcomes portray self-evaluation as a practical activity leading to institutional improvement and capacity development. This interpretation is supported by reference to the Instrument in its recommendation that the self-evaluation should lead to the development and implementation of action plans for the development and improvement of practice in a variety of contexts, specified by the self-assessment matrices. Davies and Rudd (2001) is an important source in the context of the present study because it reports the outcomes of a school-based meta-evaluation project. There are contrasts between Davies and Rudd (2001) and the present study, in that the former discusses the relationship between Local Education Authorities (LEAs) and schools in the maintained sector in England and Wales. However, notwithstanding such differences, it may be argued that the relationship explored by Davies and Rudd (2001) between self-evaluating schools and external agencies acting as 'critical friends' is one that may be applied with validity to the relationship between participating schools and the ISA and IBRU respectively.

Swaffield and MacBeath (2005) argue that external inspection and honest disclosure by schools are unlikely bedfellows, no matter the political or cultural context in which they operate. They point out that this is especially acute in England, where the OFSTED regime 'has left a legacy of distrust and inspection remains a high stakes activity' (2005: 242).

The term 'critical friend' itself may be difficult to translate into other languages and cultural contexts. Swaffield and MacBeath (2005: 243) argue that:

> the *double entendre* in English does not always render itself to other languages and the ambiguity of the 'critical' often remains to engender confusion or raise anxiety. While in some countries the notion of critical friendship has a history, in others it comes as a new and unfamiliar concept and needs to be accompanied by an explication of what it pretends, and does not pretend, to be.

It is evident that the role of the ISA as a 'critical friend' to schools undergoing self-evaluation requires further exploration. Alvik (1996) proposes three contrasting models relating self-evaluation to external evaluation, comprising:

- parallel: in which the two systems run side by side, each with its own criteria and protocols
- sequential: in which external bodies follow on from a school's own evaluation and use that as the focus of their quality assurance system
- cooperative: in which external agencies cooperate with schools to develop a common approach to evaluation.

How might the role of the ISA as a critical friend for self-evaluation be interpreted in terms of Alvik's typology? Two issues appear to be salient with respect to this question:

- the nature of the intended audience for the self-evaluation
- the degree of agency allowed for the self-evaluating institution to modify the interpretation and implementation of the Instrument.

The parallel model in particular uncouples the internal and external audiences for self-evaluation from each other. An institution may be free to conduct self-evaluation, but such activity will contribute little to evaluation specified for an external audience. The internal and external audiences for self-evaluation may be coupled to each other more closely for sequential model evaluation but only in so far as the aims of self-evaluation are congruent with those of the evaluation specified for the external audience. Such an approach offers little scope for flexibility to adapt and change the Instrument to suit local conditions and needs. The role of the critical friend in this context is to assure compliance in the implementation of the Instrument. Under these circumstances there would be little to distinguish between the parallel and sequential models other than their respective timing. An advantage of the cooperative model is that it would enable negotiation to take place between the self-evaluating institution and the critical friend that may lead to the adaptation and modification of the Instrument. However, this depends on assumptions about the nature of the Instrument being shared by the members of the partnership about whether the Instrument represents a specification for evaluation that cannot be changed, or whether the Instrument is negotiable and adaptable. The form and content of the Instrument as an inventory of guiding questions suggest that the Instrument is not negotiable, and that the role of the ISA as a critical friend is to assure its Implementation. However, as will be seen in the concluding section of this chapter, this is a view that is subject to revision.

DEVELOPMENT OF THE INTERNATIONALISM SELF-ASSESSMENT INSTRUMENT

The International Schools Association is the most senior organization in the world of international education. Founded in 1951, the ISA was the first educational non-governmental organization to be granted consultative status at UNESCO. The ISA has an important historical relationship with the International Baccalaureate Organization (IBO), having initiated both the International Schools Examination Syndicate, which was the forerunner of the IBO, and the International Schools Association Curriculum, which became the IB Middle Years Programme.

A major objective of the ISA is the promotion of international education in all its aspects. It argues that the true measure of a school is not in its name but in the manner in which it lives its philosophy on a daily basis.

Consequently, the ISA developed a self-evaluation tool for schools to evaluate the extent of their 'internationalist values' and use it to improve their own curriculum, as needed. The origins of the Instrument can be found more than ten years ago, when Anne-Marie Pierce – at that time the Head of Washington International School and a senior member of the ISA Board – devised a questionnaire for schools which was designed to provide some idea of the extent of their internationalism. In 2000, the ISA Board began the development process which has resulted in the current Instrument. The SEK International University of Chile was commissioned to reflect upon and redefine the questionnaire in order to elaborate a more researched and comprehensive document. The earliest versions of the Instrument were originally produced in Spanish at that university. The first translation into English was carried out in Chile and then refined by native English speakers in the USA and in the UK. This version comprised an Introduction, Definition of Terms, a list of the areas covered and sets of questions for each area. The Instrument can be accessed via the ISA website (ISA 2006).

It can be seen that in the main the questions are informational. Many are 'yes/no' closed questions and some deal with process. The minority are open-ended requiring a qualitative or explicative response. As the concept of the self-assessment Instrument developed and matured so did the framework within which the questions were asked. During a number of iterations of the Instrument the format became one in which Dimensions, Indicators, Evidence and Evaluation provided the structure for responses. For example Sub Area 2, 'School and Values' was as shown in Figure 24.1.

Finally, the following structure became established as the one now included in the 'Self-Study Guide'. It has three headings: Domain, Guiding Questions and Examples of Evidence. Thus for the same Sub-Area 2, 'School and Values' as above the final format is as appears in Figure 24.2.

A small initial print run allowed ISA Board members and friends to look at the Instrument

Dimensions	Indicators	Evidence	Evaluation
2.1. Values and internationalism	2.1.1 Level of relationship between defined values and internationalism	• Supporting documents • documents establish a relationship	

Figure 24.1   Sub-Area 2: School and Values: early version

Domain	Guiding Questions	Examples of Evidence
1.1. Values and statement of internationalism	(a) What relationship exists between the values of the school and internationalism? (b) How do the values of internationalism coexist with other values held by the school?	Policy Manual Code of Conduct As above

Figure 24.2   Sub-Area 2: School and Values: final format

and to apply it – sometimes in part or as the whole document – in their schools. Early feedback seemed to indicate that it might have both real value and general applicability. The concept and nature of the Instrument were introduced to a wider audience at the conference in Geneva in September 2002 on 'Interpreting International Education', jointly organized by the IBO and the Centre for the study of Education in an International Context (CEIC) at the University of Bath, UK. It led to the beginnings of conversations between the ISA and the IBO about the latter's possible interest in the Instrument.

At this stage the Instrument in its original form comprised 23 pages, the first eight of which included an introduction to the ISA, to the underlying philosophy of the Association and guidelines on how the Instrument should be used. The remaining 15 pages formed the Instrument itself – a questionnaire on each of the four main areas with each area divided into a number of sub-areas. An example of the 'Curriculum and Teaching Practices' Area appears on the ISA website (ISA 2006).

DESIGN OF EVALUATION PROJECT

Following exploratory talks, the ISA invited the IBRU to join a collaborative project to evaluate the implementation of the 'Internationalism Self-Assessment Instrument'. The evaluation study, which ran between August 2003 and November 2004, was in three stages comprising the development of evaluation instruments and implementation of data collection in a range of schools, followed by a supplementary data collection and validation phase. An important component of the meta-evaluation was a desk review of the Instrument. It was subjected to close critical reading and an attempt was made to place it in the context of other contributions to the literature of school self-evaluation.

The Instrument identifies four stages in the self-evaluation process:

Stage 1: Collection and analysis of the information
Stage 2: Preparation of self-assessment reports
Stage 3: Preparation of action plans
Stage 4: Preparation of progress reports

It also identifies four self-assessment 'Matrices', divided into sub-areas, as contexts for asking evaluative questions. These matrices and sub-areas comprise:

Matrix 1:   School Philosophy and Values
Sub-Area 1: Statement of Philosophy
Sub-Area 2: School and Values

Matrix 2:   Curriculum and Teaching Practices
Sub-Area 3: Curriculum

Sub-Area 4: Teaching Practices
Sub-Area 5: Curricular Materials

Matrix 3:   The School Community
Sub-Area 6: School and Community
Sub-Area 7: School and Students
Sub-Area 8: School and Family
Sub-Area 9: School and Teachers

Matrix 4:   School Governance, Management and
Administration
Sub-Area 10: Governance
Sub-Area 11: Management,
Administrative Personnel, Secretarial
and Support Staff
Sub-Area 12: Admission Processes
Sub-Area 13: Public Relations
Sub-Area 14: Facilities

Arranged orthogonally, the two dimensions comprising the four stages in the self-assessment process and the four self-assessment matrices yield 16 cells that form foci for evaluation (Figure 24.3).

A number of 'guiding questions' are given in the self-assessment matrices. The project team was interested in finding out how these guiding questions were interpreted by different schools. It is important to emphasize here that schools were advised that there would be no 'right' or 'wrong' responses to the guiding questions. The aim of the project was to evaluate the Instrument in a variety of school contexts, so it might be developed and improved.

The brief presented by the ISA to the IB Research Unit was based on the assumptions that the Instrument was holistic and that schools should conduct the evaluation in all four matrices simultaneously. In practice, given the timescale within which the project was able to operate, the schools were only able to address the first two stages (Collection and Analysis of the Information, and Preparation of Self-assessment Reports) with respect to each matrix. Thus, the evaluation of the Instrument reported here is limited to data collected from schools about these stages. However, it may be argued that the decision to manage the evaluation in this way had an impact on the attrition rate of

schools dropping out of the project. This will be discussed later.

Schools were invited by the ISA to participate in the project. Selection of participating schools was made according to a number of criteria including a wide spread of geographical location, programmes of study offered and affiliation with membership organizations such as the ISA and the Council of International Schools (CIS) with an involvement in international education (Cambridge and Thompson 2000). The project team considered it important that the participating schools should not be members of the ISA exclusively, nor should they all be institutions that offered the programmes of the IBO. Many of the schools participating in this project would have undergone some form of evaluation before, perhaps as inspection by an external body in the context of a national education system or as an accreditation process with an international body such as the CIS, one of the North American accreditation bodies or the ISA itself.

Figure 24.4 presents a summary of some of the criteria by which participating schools were selected. This typology may be interpreted as a pragmatic solution to the problem of classification. It represents one possible approach to sorting the sample, and other frameworks using different combinations of criteria, including school location, school size, language of instruction and whether they offer residential facilities for students, are possible. It shows the intersections of four sets comprising member institutions of the ISA, members of CIS, schools and colleges accredited by CIS, and IB World Schools. Subsets in the sample included schools and colleges that are:

- ISA members only (subset A)
- IB World Schools that are ISA members (subset B)
- IB World Schools that are ISA and CIS members (subset C)
- IB World Schools that are ISA and CIS members that are also accredited by CIS (subset D)
- IB World Schools only (subset E).

A sixth subset, subset F, comprised one participating institution, which was neither an ISA nor CIS member and not an IB World School;

Self-assessment matrices	Stages in self-assessment process			
	Collection and analysis of information	Preparation of self-assessment reports	Preparation of action plans	Preparation of progress reports
School Philosophy and Values				
Curriculum and Teaching Practices				
The School Community				
School Governance, Management and Administration				

Figure 24.3　Foci for evaluation

it was a secondary school in the state sector in England, designated as a specialist language college. The practical value of this typology was that it enabled the project team to construct a sample that comprised a variety of different kinds of school – and did not all conform to a stereotypical idea of an 'international school'.

Twelve schools in eight countries accepted the invitation to participate in the data collection and analysis phase of this project by conducting self-evaluation of their own international values using the Instrument. They formed a varied group of institutions, embracing both independent schools and those in national systems of education. The aim of this project was to find out how the Instrument worked in practice in a variety of different school contexts. The project team was interested not only in *outcomes* of self-evaluation, such as reports, but also the decision-making *processes* leading to the generation of those outcomes. Because the participating schools were dispersed over a wide geographical area, including the Middle East, Europe and the Americas, the project team communicated with key respondents at various stages by telephone, e-mail or fax to discuss issues relating to the evaluation of the Instrument.

RESULTS OF EVALUATION

Analysis of qualitative data collected from participating schools yielded a number of arguments about the validity of the Instrument that may be presented in four main categories:

- comments on its nature
- assumptions
- 'emic' and 'etic' constructs
- explanations for attrition of schools participating in the project.

Respondents' formative comments to the project team, often communicated by email, were particularly revealing about the nature of the Instrument. For example, one comment was that 'to rate these questions effectively, an extensive survey would need to be done and the questions would have to be more clearly formulated'. Another was that 'the questions did not lead to interesting reflection of the topic, at least for students of 13 years of age'. A third comment was that 'the major theme of internationalism – and celebrating it among students in the middle school – proved interesting to discuss, apart from the questions listed'. Such statements are revealing about the reception given by

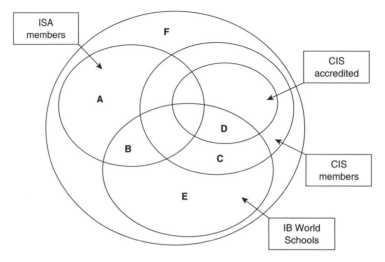

Figure 24.4   Venn diagram of participating schools. The sets comprise all schools in the sample, schools that are members of the ISA, members of CIS, schools accredited by CIS, and schools authorised to offer the programmes of the IBO. (Note that the letters represent subsets describing schools, and not the schools themselves.)

schools to the Instrument and the ways in which it was implemented. From the examples given here, it appears that the school involved had adopted a democratic and inclusive approach to self-evaluation that invited participation by students. However, as the third comment quoted here suggests, the wording of the Instrument was perceived as more of a hindrance than a help in the process. Problems were reported with the implementation of a 'rating scale' placed by the side of each item in the Instrument: 'We found it impossible to grade some boxes'. The abstracted nature of internationalism and international values expressed in the Instrument was criticized: 'The notion of internationalism is very esoteric'.

The Instrument made a number of implicit assumptions about the schools that might use it. The project team drew inferences from the ways in which schools responded to items in the Instrument, particularly how they commented on items that they thought they could not answer. Thus, it appears that the Instrument assumed that the schools using it would be independent of the local system of education, would be culturally remote from local community, and that interactions between a school and its local community would be 'cross-cultural'. While such assumptions might be true in contexts involving schools catering for expatriates located in some countries, it was not valid to make similar assumptions about the whole sample of participating schools. Schools in national systems may also have aspirations towards practising international values. The existence of school fees and scholarships was assumed, but many participating schools were free at the point of use and could report that they had no scholarship system. High turnover, transience of students, 'nomadism' and the participation of international expatriates were assumed by the Instrument, yet one school could respond that 'there are no international transitory students because our school has a strong national character'. The classification of teachers and students in terms of nationality, ethnicity or religion was assumed by the Instrument to be uncontentious, whereas in practice it may have been considered deeply embarrassing or oppressive to discriminate between individuals using such criteria.

An overarching problem associated with the Instrument may be that it constitutes an 'imposed etic' on schools attempting to implement it. A challenge associated with the development of an Instrument to be implemented in a wide range of schools is that it inevitably makes the items etic constructs. It is a 'one size fits all' strategy, which leads to the loss of the meaningful emic aspects of specific school cultures.

Attrition of schools from the sample was a problem in the enquiry. Schools that had agreed to participate in the project dropped out before its conclusion. Of the 13 schools invited to join the project, only eight completed the agreed tasks. A sufficiently wide variety of schools remaining in the project assured its validity, but the reasons offered by schools to account for non-completion constitute valuable data in their own right. Schools explained in justification that they could not complete evaluation tasks within the negotiated timescale of the project, the workload imposed by evaluation or accreditation exercises in connection with other agencies made completion of the project difficult, and some schools' own development planning followed a different timescale to that specified by the project team.

The project team offered the ISA advice on redrafting the Instrument. It was proposed that concepts such as 'internationalism', 'international-mindedness' and 'international values and attitudes' required interpretation and clarification. The work involved in implementing the Instrument had proved to be very considerable for schools, and perhaps excessive. Did the 'holism' of the Instrument really mean that schools should conduct self-evaluation with respect to all matrices at the same time? Or could they be allowed to select more narrowly defined areas for concentrated study? How might such a strategy fit with the institutional development plans of schools? It was also suggested that some terminology used in the Guiding Questions was inappropriate; particularly references to 'nationality', 'religion', 'ethnic' and 'ethnicity'. Furthermore, was there a means of communicating concepts in ways

that avoided the 'imposed etic' and enabled schools to express concepts emically in their own terms? It was also proposed that the Instrument presented a stereotypical view of a particular type of 'international' school and therefore was not relevant to all types of school.

DISCUSSION AND RECOMMENDATIONS

Following receipt of the final report by IBRU, the ISA was now ready to assimilate the considerable volume of information made available. It had already become clear through the interim evaluation reports by IBRU that the Instrument had the makings of an important contribution to the analysis and understanding of the quality of internationalism or international mindedness in schools. However, the final report made it equally clear that a number of improvements could be made to the Instrument. These centred upon three principal issues.

First it was decided to alter the title of the Instrument. The word 'instrument' itself came to be considered as overly utilitarian and scientific and when combined with the term 'assessment' the general perception was one of a somewhat mechanical test that led inevitably to a definitive outcome or even to a higher or lower score. This perception was exacerbated by the right-hand column of the questionnaire which asked users to grade their success on a scale of 1 to 4 on each guiding question. This evaluation category was removed. Clearly this is not what is envisaged or intended. As has been expressed above, and following the thinking of MacBeath (1999), the process is much more one of evaluation and in this particular context, of the self-evaluation of internationalism. Thus the original title 'Self-Assessing Internationalism: an Instrument for Schools' has evolved into the new title 'Internationalism in Schools – a Self-Study Guide'. This may serve a number of purposes, the first of which is to entitle and focus the document clearly upon the issue of 'Internationalism'. The change to 'Self-Study' also avoids the numerous connotations of activities such as 'assessment', 'review' and 'evaluation' and aims to place the document outside any concept of measurement or judgement. It is a 'guide' aimed at steering rather than directing, at suggesting rather than instructing the user.

Second, there was a need to respond to a view that the ISA 'notion of internationalism is very esoteric'. A discussion considered the advantages and disadvantages of asking users to create their own definition of the term 'internationalism'. Inevitably the arguments ranged over the possibility of simplistic definitions that might reflect no more than a geographical or numerical interpretation of the adjective 'international' to those that might invest the term with overtly political meanings. To avoid such extremes it was decided to add a constraint, but one which it is hoped will resonate acceptably with the vast majority of users. This constraint is to ask users to define their understanding of the term 'internationalism' within the framework of the United Nations Declaration of Human Rights.

In this way 'the Guide' avoids prescription and definitivism and recognizes both the diversity and pluralism of schools that will use the Guide and the wide variety of interpretations of internationalism they will present. The UN Declaration was thus introduced into the Guide both as a way of anchoring any definition of internationalism within a universalist statement and, perhaps paradoxically, as a way of constraining, guiding and benevolently prejudicing the kind of statement that schools might make as their own steer. There will be, consequently, those who can accuse the authors of the Guide of a cultural bias. So be it; the ISA is trying to offer schools a 'Guide' and not a set of commandments! To put it another way, the relativism might be seen to appear in and amongst the wide variety of contexts in which the Guide will be used as each school undertakes the self-study.

The third development which arises from the IBRU evaluation report relates to the way

that a school may use the Guide. To help to accommodate the constant demands upon time and resources that all schools experience, the Guide has been made as flexible and accessible a possible. What is to be studied, over what period of time and in what degree of detail are determined by each school. In this way the Guide speaks to and for each school. Additionally the Guide has been evolved both as a freestanding study and as the starting point for other school activities, such as curriculum development or in preparation for external accreditation.

For example, a school may choose to study only Area 3, 'The School Community' but within that area to look closely at each of the four sub-areas. Such an approach may be subject to the criticism of attempting to isolate one particular aspect of the school and thus to be decontextualizing this aspect. However, such a school may feel that this is a significantly weak area of its internationalism and one that needs to be developed and strengthened in order that it can contribute more fully and evenly to the good ongoing work of the other three areas.

A further example may be to use all or some of the areas of the guide to begin to think about internationalism for the first time. This may be the case of new schools or of existing so-called international schools, or also of national schools, who wish to develop their view of internationalism from the '4 Fs' (Flags, Food and Festivals and because it is Fashionable) into a more profound approach that will engage international-mindedness and international values. Many international schools – particularly those that offer the IB Diploma Programme – may argue for a view of international values as 'contingent variables'. However, if asked to explain the make-up of such variables, they often deconstruct the Diploma Programme and describe the contributions made by the number of nationalities represented in the school, by the Theory of Knowledge course and by their CAS activities. The Self-Study Guide does not look at the admixture of elements or variables. Rather, the areas are distinct and almost linear. It is possible, and perhaps desirable, that schools who complete the Guide may see the possibility of relating the areas and sub-areas and come to realize that they may capture an element or 'output' of holism within their study.

The argument that international values can be conceptualized as the 'friction generated when international education is happening' may be expressed as a different metaphor, contrasting the difference between a video record of an event and a photographic one. The Guide may be more related to the latter view, by analogy to a family photograph album showing the growth and development of a family. To self-evaluate is the beginning; to reflect, to identify the need for change and to prioritize the components for that change are the real purposes.

ACKNOWLEDGEMENT

The contribution of Zhen Yao, of the International Baccalaureate Research Unit, to the work leading to the preparation of this report is gratefully acknowledged by the authors.

REFERENCES

Alvik, T. (1996) *School Self-evaluation: A Whole School Approach.* Dundee: CIDREE.

Bernstein, B. (1977) *Class, Codes and Control,* vol. 3, 2nd edition. London: Routledge and Kegan Paul.

Cambridge, J.C. (1998) Investigating national and organisational cultures in the context of the international school. In M.C. Hayden and J.J. Thompson (eds) *International Education: Principles and Practice.* London: Kogan Page, pp. 197–211.

Cambridge, J.C. (2002) Global product branding and international education. *Journal of Research in International Education,* 1(2): 227–43.

Cambridge, J.C. and Thompson, J.J. (2000) Towards a framework for the description and classification of schools in an international context. *CORE (Collected Original Resources in Education)* 24(1): Fiche 3 C09.

Davies, D. and Rudd, P. (2001) *Evaluating School Self-evaluation.* Slough: National Foundation for Educational Research.

Hall, J.K. (2002) *Teaching and Researching Language and Culture.* London: Pearson Education.

Hayden, M.C. (1998) International education: A study of student and teacher perspectives, Unpublished PhD thesis, University of Bath, UK.

Hopkins, D. (1989) *Evaluation for School Development.* Milton Keynes: Open University Press.

IBO (International Baccalaureate Organization) (2006) www.ibo.org/ (accessed 6 January 2006).

Institute for Citizenship (2003) www.citizen.org.uk/ (accessed 6 November 2003).

ISA (International Schools Association) (2001) *Self-Assessment of Internationalism: an Instrument for schools.* www.isaschools.org (accessed 2006).

ISA (International Schools Association) (2006) *Internationalism in Schools – a Self-Study Guide. www.isaschools.org.*

MacBeath, J. (1999) *Schools Must Speak for Themselves: The Case for School Self-Evaluation.* London: Routledge.

Meuret, D. and Morlaix, S. (2003) Conditions of success of a school's self-evaluation: some lessons of a European experience. *School Effectiveness and School Improvement,* 14 (1): 53–71.

Phillips, J. (2002) The Third Way: lessons from international education. *Journal of Research in International Education,* 1(2): 159–81.

Rawlings, F. (2000) Abstract of doctoral thesis: globalisation, curriculum and international communities: a case study of the United World College of the Atlantic. *International Journal of Educational Development,* 20(4): 365–6.

Saunders, L. (1999) Who or what is school 'self-evaluation' for? *School Effectiveness and School Improvement,* 10(4): 414–29.

Stake, R. (1967) The countenance of educational evaluation. *Teachers College Record,* 68(7): 523–40. Abridged version reprinted in Hamilton, D., Jenkins, D., King, C., MacDonald, B. and Parlett, M. (1977) *Beyond the Numbers Game: A Reader in Educational Evaluation.* Basingstoke: Macmillan Education.

Stake, R. (1986) Evaluating educational programmes. In D. Hopkins (ed.) *Inservice Training and Educational Development.* Lewes: Falmer Press.

Swaffield, S. and MacBeath, J. (2005) School self-evaluation and the role of a critical friend. *Cambridge Journal of Education,* 35 (2): 239–52.

Thomas, P. (1998) Education for peace: the cornerstone of international education. In M.C. Hayden and J.J. Thompson (eds) *International Education: Principles and Practice.* London: Kogan Page, pp. 103–18.

Thompson, J.J. (1998) Towards a model for international education. In M.C. Hayden and J.J. Thompson (eds)

International Education: Principles and Practice. London: Kogan Page, pp. 276–90.

United Nations (1948) *Universal Declaration of Human Rights.* www.un.org/overview/rights.html (accessed 18 August 2003).

Zaw, S.K. (1996) Locke and multiculturalism: toleration, relativism and reason. In R.K. Fullinwider (ed.) *Public Education in a Multicultural Society.* Cambridge: Cambridge University Press, pp. 121–55.

25

Developing Learning-Focused International Schools: a Case Study of Two Schools

William Gerritz and Kevin Bartlett

The limited literature on the systematic improvement of international schools provides few models to guide practice or further research. Over the past several years, two established international schools have collaborated with the aim of identifying elements of a transferable improvement model. This chapter reports on this work and offers examples of approaches and practices that can be used in international schools more widely. Three questions guide the presentation:

1 In the literature on school improvement, what principles can be identified that are particularly germane to international schools?
2 Over the past 5 years, how have two international schools employed a few of these principles to improve learning?
3 To what extent have these schools improved by applying the principles?

The chapter is organized around six principles identified in the literature. After briefly describing a principle and identifying some of the related literature, its application in two international schools is described. The chapter ends with a discussion of how each school has changed – emphasizing improvements in learning. Of course, the literature describes many school improvement guidelines and suggestions. The six principles discussed here were selected because they seemed to have the most relevance and potential as the improvement efforts in each school were launched.

Research offers a wonderful variety of definitions for school improvement and of associated indicators. This chapter focuses on learning as both the definition and primary indicator for improving schools. Gains in learning quality for students and faculty represent both the primary goal and major indicator for school improvement.

Two types of measures are used to judge school improvement. Primary measures emphasize external assessments of student performance. Examples of these include scores from the International School Assessment (ISA:

developed by the Australian Council for Educational Research to assess reading, writing and mathematics literacy at 8, 10, 12 and 15 years), scores from the Iowa Test of Basic Skills (a norm-referenced assessment of reading, mathematics, language, social studies and science that can be given every year starting with 6-year-olds), International Baccalaureate (IB) results and so on. Other primary measures include internal, common assessments such as the one taken thrice yearly by students at the International School Bangkok (one of the two case study schools). Secondary measures are ones in which a positive change would be expected if learning quality was improving. For example, surveys of students and parents if tracked over time can indicate that improved learning may be occurring. Similarly, participation rates in challenging academic programmes such as those of the IB may indicate learning improvements.

The International Schools of Brussels and Bangkok (the two case study schools), at which the authors are respective Heads, have many similarities. Each enrols between 1,400 and 1,900 students and was founded in the early 1950s. Both schools have roots in the American education tradition but over time have developed an international ethos welcoming students, staff and ideas from many nations. Student backgrounds are similar in both schools. Children of expatriate families temporarily residing in Belgium or Thailand make up about 80 per cent of the enrolment in each school. Each year children from more than 50 countries will be enrolled.

In essence, this chapter is about the efforts of these two international schools to systematically improve learning opportunities for their students. The stories are complicated and the improvement paths taken at the schools offer multiple opportunities to compare and contrast. The paths have been as different as they have been similar. The differences have naturally been influenced by context. At the outset of this five-year drive for improvement, IS Brussels had no consistent documentation of intended learning, no common curriculum. Much of the focus, therefore, has been on the development of a coherent learning framework,

from kindergarten through Grade Twelve. At IS Bangkok far more had been achieved in terms of curriculum documentation and the focus shifted more rapidly to the analysis of results.

Equally influential in determining paths has been the 'natural' leadership style of the authors. After 15 years of deeply enjoyable collaboration we would caricature ourselves as 'the philosopher and the engineer', one more given to intuitive and conceptual approaches, the other to the more structured and scientific. Interestingly, diverse natural tendencies led us to the shared understanding that 'it's all about learning'. Most significantly for us, years of open sharing and 'critical friending' have enabled us to support each other's weaknesses and learn from each other's strengths.

As we addressed the six principles below, we chose to address the first three predominantly with examples from Brussels, the latter three with examples from Bangkok, in the hope that readers would take something of value from the stories of each school, and would synthesize these into a broader understanding of what it means to focus on learning.

PRINCIPLE 1: ALL SCHOOL PROCESSES SHOULD ALIGN AROUND A *CENTRAL VISION OF LEARNING* GROUNDED IN MORAL PURPOSE: THE BIG AIMS ARE IMPROVED LEARNING AND COHERENCE

Five years ago, IS Brussels was a well-established international school with 50 years of history. Successive accreditation reports had, however, stressed the need to develop a common curriculum and to bring coherence of purpose and direction to the four school divisions. A recent effort to develop a new strategic plan, with the support of an external consultant, had left an able, ambitious board of trustees somewhat frustrated, since it had failed to result in a clear sense of direction for a new millennium. The need then was for coherence, curriculum, common purpose.

These different but related needs came together in the formulation of a new mission that expressed the school's purpose and vision, and became the driver for an extended school-wide effort that brought coherence through the collaborative development and implementation of a common curriculum.

The story of the development of a central vision provides a good example of what Fullan calls a 'remarkable convergence' between business and education. He talks of 'schools with minds' and 'businesses with souls' (Fullan 2001). The board of trustees at IS Brussels has 20 members, carefully selected from the school's largely corporate community. From the board, a well-established trustee with a background in human resources was chosen to work with the new Head on the development of a mission and plan that would give the school a renewed sense of direction and inspiration. Other than the need to capture the school's true beliefs and values, this team was guided by another principle:

> Have a clear simple purpose that gives rise to complex, intelligent behaviours, not complicated rules and regulations that give rise to stupid, simplistic behaviours.

The collaboration between business and education, with simplicity of expression as a principle, led to the development of a mission statement that, in ten words (Figure 25.1), expressed the school's purpose and central beliefs and values, providing a central vision of learning that subsequently radically reshaped the school's culture towards a 'culture of learning'.

The mission commits the school to two overarching outcomes: International Citizen, Independent Learner. Critically, these outcomes were defined in terms of *learning*: International Citizen in terms of emerging empathy, perspective and self-knowledge, together taken as evidence of evolving 'human understanding'; Independent Learner in terms of the ability to explain, interpret and apply acquired knowledge and skills, taken as evidence of evolving 'intellectual understanding'. These defining 'facets of understanding' were borrowed directly from the work of the

Figure 25.1   International School of Brussels mission statement

Understanding by Design programme, led by Grant Wiggins and Jay McTighe (2000). Since the essence of their work lay in effective assessment, and in working backwards from assessable outcomes, IS Brussels had placed itself in the powerful position of being able to assess directly to its own mission statement.

The twin outcomes resonated with educators as worthy goals towards which to strive, and with corporate board members as both worthy goals and the 'products' of the school's business, in which learning is the added value. Using the mission as a driving force, the school went on to develop a comprehensive and coherent curriculum, using the 'language of understanding' to develop standards and benchmarks in all learning areas. These standards were embedded in an international knowledge base representing the common ground of human experience.

The values that sit at the heart of the mission have been equally powerful in transforming the school. By committing to 'Everyone Included, Everyone Challenged, Everyone Successful', the entire community committed to embracing diversity, differentiated practice and opportunities for success for all. These values, simple yet complex, are now deeply embedded at all levels of IS Brussels. They have shaped the central goal of a new

LEARNING-FOCUSED GOAL	IMPACT on LEARNING	INDICATORS	STRATEGIES	SUPPORT
What are we setting out to achieve?	What difference will it make?	How will we see the difference?	What actions will we take?	What assistance may we need?

Figure 25.2

long-range plan – 'Everyone will improve performance every year' – which in turn has led to the development of a basket of assessment measures selected as indicators of success, including internal assessments against the new curriculum standards and the implementation and analysis of International Schools Assessment scores. The learning vision has brought together a leadership team dedicated to improving learning, and a board that 'gets it' in terms of learning as the product of schools, devoted to allocating appropriate resources to achieve the mission.

Significantly, 'everyone included, challenged, successful' has become a mantra in the community; part of the common language, known by all, a measure of the power of a simple, compelling message in driving change and building culture.

PRINCIPLE 2: A LEADERSHIP FOR LEARNING FOCUS FOR HEADS, PRINCIPALS, AND TEACHER LEADERS PROPELS SYSTEMATIC IMPROVEMENT

A clear, shared approach to leadership for learning has been defined and continually refined by the Educational Leadership Team at IS Brussels. While there have been numerous theoretical influences, the most significant has been the work of Michael Fullan (2001), who defined the essential competencies of leadership as: moral purpose, relationship-building, knowledge creation and sharing, understanding change and coherence-making. The leadership team found this view of leadership so compelling that all job descriptions for leaders were reframed around Fullan's competencies.

Shared moral purpose was self-evident: the compelling drive to improve learning for all, in accordance with the school's mission. Planning at all levels, from individual through team to whole school, was reshaped around a

simple learning-driven template as shown in Figure 25.2.

The automatic response to project proposals thus became 'What will this do to improve student learning?'

In terms of relationship-building, a great deal of work went into understanding the range of people, aptitudes and attitudes that make up a diverse and talented faculty, and the relationships among those people. It was quickly recognized that the leadership team, operating in isolation, would never achieve the desired shift towards a culture of learning. To be successful, we needed to create new teams, and a team mentality, at all levels of the school; new roles for teacher-leaders; new training programmes for those leaders, and a more focused directing of the talents, knowledge and experience of the faculty towards the new vision. This process, along with other initiatives, has created a network of relationships among individuals with a commitment to improving learning.

IS Brussels has evolved from a school in which faculty meetings were rare, and often focused on logistical issues, to one in which faculty discussion is constant and the focus is largely on learning. While much has been invested in professional development, on and off site, probably the most effective way of creating and sharing new knowledge at the school has been the development of multiple opportunities for faculty members to come together to talk to each other using a common language and in the context of a common vision.

Interestingly, while Fullan has much to offer on the subject of change management, the IS Brussels experience bears closer resemblance to the examples of evolutionary change described by Collins in *Good to Great* (2001), where companies achieving greatness experienced no moments of radical, instant change. Rather, they experienced an extended period of relentless commitment to one simple idea. In the case of IS Brussels the idea was indeed simple to express: improving learning. This

Newmann et al.	Dufour and Eaker
• Focus on student learning • Shared norms and values • Reflective dialogue • Deprivatization of practice • Collaboration	• Shared mission and values • Collective enquiry • Collaborative teams • Action and experimentation • Continuous improvement • Results orientation

Figure 25.3

consistent, single-minded commitment has resulted in steady change, without concerted resistance, perhaps because committed professional educators will find little to argue with in this message, and these professionals were always given time to change. Successful change has been valued more highly than rapid change.

Fullan (2001) talks compellingly about chaos and complexity, about creating additional complexity by challenging the status quo, and then finding and consolidating new patterns that align with a new vision. The IS Brussels experience provides multiple examples of these new patterns. A somewhat random selection of extracurricular activities dismantled and transformed into a rich, challenging co-curricular programme shaped by the same thematic framework as the new curriculum. A new structure of teacher-leadership focused on improving learning. A haphazard 'buddy system' for new teachers transformed into a year-long, structured mentoring programme that pairs experienced talent with new talent, and focuses both on learning. This process of new coherence and new alignment has increased in pace in the later stages of this five-year transformation, as 'the flywheel gains momentum' (Collins 2001).

PRINCIPLE 3: LEARNING IMPROVES MORE RAPIDLY IN SCHOOLS WITH STRONG LEARNING COMMUNITIES

The intuitive sense of the leadership team in Brussels was that we were becoming a different kind of school. In attempting to describe both what we were becoming and what we wanted to become, we found the greatest

resonance in two sources: Newmann et al. (1996) and Dufour and Eaker (1998). Both sources refer to 'professional learning communities' as the types of school that have most positive impact on learning. Their descriptions of such communities can be summarized as shown in Figure 25.3.

In understanding these characteristics the team was better able to understand the transformation that was taking place, and better able to plan and shape that transformation. The thinking became, 'If that is what good schools look like, how do we lead the school into looking like this?'. The response to this question led to a radical transformation of a number of systems, perhaps most significantly the whole approach to professional appraisal and development, now referred to at IS Brussels as 'professional learning'. The story is as follows, mapped out in a set of rational steps (each asking an Essential Question, EQ) that lead from a learning-focused mission to the evolution of a professional learning community.

Step One: Defining professional learning communities (EQ: What do great schools look like?)

Broadly speaking, we committed to becoming the kind of school described by Newmann et al. and Dufour and Eaker.

Step Two: Defining learning (EQ: What is learning?)

We recognized that we could not progress as a learning community unless we shared a common definition of learning. In our case, it was provided by the facets of understanding embedded in our mission.

Step Three: Describing successful learners (EQ: What are the dispositions of successful learners?)

We felt it critical to turn more abstract definitions into more observable outcomes, in the form of the kinds of learners we aspired to developing. The dispositions of these learners were developed and incorporated into the curriculum as standards. For example:

> Learners demonstrate a 'can do' attitude when faced with challenges. They see a crisis as an opportunity and have confidence in their ability to solve problems. Learners respond to changing circumstances confidently and calmly. They are intrigued, rather than perturbed, by the unfamiliar, and modify their behaviour and thinking to reflect new situations.

Step Four: Describing learning environments (EQ: What does learning look like?)

We have been working with Pam Harper of Fieldwork on developing a process called 'Looking for Learning', designed to improve our practice in classroom observation. As one precursor to so doing, we brainstormed a list of 'what learning looks like' in the classroom. We then decided to take this basic idea in new directions. We held a meeting of the whole faculty in which, in small groups, we brainstormed key words that described learning in effective classrooms. The tone and approach of this workshop were deliberately 'intuitive' rather than 'rational/technical'. The thinking was that too much work in improving schools becomes overly technical and laborious, to the extent that many rationally designed systems are never implemented. We wanted to design a system that was simple, intuitive, 'common sense', so that it had some chance to provide the 'shared norms and values' of the professional learning communities of Newmann et al. We deliberately chose the simple, intuitive language of 'A sense of ...' to frame the descriptors. We then linked these to the descriptors of successful learners, building the stages of a sequence of thinking, as in the example below in relation to developing positive learners:

A SENSE OF SUCCESS

> Learning is clearly informed by the belief that all learners can and will succeed. Sustained support and encouragement are provided, resulting in a sense of confidence, pride and fulfilment. Learning is regularly demonstrated and celebrated.

Step Five: Describing professional practice (EQ: How does our work best support learning?)

We then took this thinking to the next level, asking 'If this is what learning looks like, how does our practice support it?'. In effect, this meant aligning a previous product of faculty work, a document entitled 'Professional Practices for Skilful Teaching'. This work, designed to identify best practice, was given a new context by aligning it more specifically with learning, as follows:

In relation to developing a Sense of Success we need to:

- Model a positive, can-do attitude
- Provide examples of 'what good looks like' and engage students in the analysis of these models
- Create a learning culture in which learners' efforts and achievements are valued, recognized, celebrated
- Set expectations for each learner that are challenging but achievable
- Design assessments and reporting methods that recognize 'the distance travelled'
- Focus on learners' successes, not failures.

Step Six: Designing learning-focused professional appraisal (EQ: How can we learn about our own practice?)

Again, in providing new approaches to professional appraisal, we wanted to bring coherence with our learning vision, alignment with other school-wide approaches to learning, and a simplicity of language and implementation. IS Brussels has been deeply

I SAW	I HEARD	I WONDERED	I SUGGEST

Figure 25.4

LEARNING-FOCUSED GOAL	IMPACT on LEARNING	INDICATORS	STRATEGIES	SUPPORT
What are we setting out to achieve?	What difference will it make?	How will we see the difference?	What actions will we take?	What assistance may we need?

Figure 25.5

Successful learning environments EQ: What does learning look like?	Professional learning institutes
A sense of inclusion A sense of challenge A sense of success	Differentiated learning ESL in the mainstream

Figure 25.6

involved with two Harvard-based projects: Project Zero and Making Thinking Visible. Drawing mainly from the latter we developed a simple feedback protocol to be used by professional learning partners (members of the educational leadership team, team leaders, peers) in providing constructive feedback, as shown in Figure 25.4.

This feedback is given in the context of the shared norms and values captured in our descriptors of learning environments and practice, and in the spirit of constructive collaboration in pursuit of a shared vision.

Step Seven: Designing learning-focused improvement plans (EQ: How do we plan to improve learning?)

In response to constructive feedback and personal reflection, individuals and teams begin to formulate improvement plans. Again, the template is simple and learning-focused, as shown in Figure 25.5.

Step Eight: Designing learning-focused professional development (EQ: How can we improve our professional practice?)

In response to our developing understanding of the importance of contextual learning, IS Brussels has placed increasing emphasis on extended professional development opportunities that take place on-site. Typically, for example, teams of teachers will take part in a Summer Seminar on Making Thinking Visible, and will then meet regularly throughout the year in different configurations to discuss their experiences in implementing new thinking protocols, share successes and disappointments, and reflect on implications for practice and professional learning.

Based on this premise, we set up a series of Professional Learning Institutes that offer this type of experience. These Institutes are fully aligned with the thinking outlined above, so that we are actively supporting the kind of learning to which we have all 'signed up', as shown in Figure 25.6.

The Institutes take place during the summer vacation and are followed by a year of reflective practice incorporating regular discussions with peers.

This begins to support the school in its desired development. The faculty and leadership have shared norms and values expressed through the mission and descriptors of learning. We are engaging in reflective dialogue focused on student learning. We are collaborating on practice, sharing, 'deprivatizing'. As we begin to work together on analysing student work, we are focusing on the results of new practices. In short, IS Brussels is slowly evolving into the professional learning community we set out to become.

As shared understanding develops, we find ourselves closing the circle by returning to the mission, refining our thinking and finding new ways to implement the 'simple yet complex' vision of inclusion, challenge and success for everyone.

PRINCIPLE 4: FOCUSING ON RESULTS MORE THAN PROCESSES TO SHAPE DECISION-MAKING IMPROVES LEARNING AT CLASSROOM, DIVISION AND WHOLE SCHOOL LEVELS

Empirical studies have consistently revealed that teachers and administrators usually focus on process far more than on goals and results. Typically they think about how well a lesson seemed to progress and how engaged the students were. Far less frequently do they discuss measurable progress of individuals or groups of students toward designated learning goals.

Many educational researchers have written about the power of results to propel and focus school improvement efforts. Rosenholtz (1989) provides an excellent sample of the arguments behind focusing on results. In her longitudinal study of 63 elementary schools, she found 13 where student learning had increased year by year. She labelled these 'moving' schools. The others she labelled 'stuck' schools. Each of the moving schools had specific, results-based, goal-setting

processes. Rosenholtz summarized the value of emphasizing goals when she wrote:

- Specific goals provide a basis for rational decision making, for ways to organize and execute their instruction.
- Specific goals enable teachers to gain their success.
- Specific goals promote professional dialogue.

Fullan (1999) wrote that gathering data is crucial to school improvement. He explains that implementation success is highly dependent on the establishment of effective ways of getting information on how well or poorly change is going on in the school or classroom. The key is getting the right people together with the right information.

Schmoker (1999) provides an analysis of how an increased focus on learning targets and observable learning outcomes in a wide variety of schools seemed to provoke dramatic increases in student achievement. He summarizes the importance of using data when he asks the question, 'How long will we continue to avoid using an invaluable tool, capable of telling us how we are doing, what is and is not working, and how to adjust efforts toward improvement?' (1999: 25).

IS Bangkok, in particular, has become data-rich: collecting, analysing and making sense of both primary and secondary learning results. Table 25.1 displays examples of the data sources used at IS Bangkok specifically to assess academic learning. Primary and external measures such as the International School Assessment (ISA) allow learning leaders to make judgements about the performance of IS Bangkok students compared to those in other international schools and 40 nations. Primary and internal assessments such as the writing assessment given thrice yearly to all students provide insight into individual and group progress. Secondary measures serve as proxy variables. For example, if student, parent and teacher surveys indicate an increasing level of academic challenge and learning, one can hope that learning has increased.

Of course, data alone have little value. At least three other processes had to be in place.

Table 25.1   Examples of learning data sources: International School Bangkok

Primary Sources	Secondary Sources
• Common assessments	• Student, parent, leaver and teacher surveys
• International school assessment	• Looking for learning
• Iowa Test of Basic Skills	• Participation rates
• IB/AP/SAT	• Outside evaluators
• Reading and writing continuum	• College acceptances
• Torch assessment of MS reading	

First, to contribute to improved learning, teams of teachers and administrators needed to make sense of the data, looking for trends and triangulating from multiple sources. They needed to make connections between the stories the data offered and their own concerns for students' welfare. Second, the data needed to be used to establish learning targets that had meaning to teachers and that encouraged them to adjust their own thinking and actions. Finally, teams not individuals needed to engage in target-setting and the work to achieve those targets.

At IS Bangkok, a wide range of approaches to organizing these three processes emerged over four years. In the most common one, a team of teachers, for example 6th Grade language arts, reviews available data late in the school year. With the assistance of curriculum support staff and the principal, they identify areas of worry and then prioritize them. For example, the evidence from teacher observation, reading assessments and the International School Assessment indicated that about 8 per cent of 6th graders were making inadequate progress in reading comprehension. This pattern showed up for the two previous years as well. The team then set targets for these students in terms of August to May gains on reading assessment. With a clear, meaningful target identified, the team then developed an action plan for achieving it. The plan involved professional development, collaborative work, ongoing monitoring of progress and additional instructional materials.

Another approach involved the governing board and management team in setting broad school improvement targets. Again, this work takes place in May. For example, quantitative and qualitative data on parent surveys over three years indicated that too many high school parents were dissatisfied with the quality and frequency of communication with their children's teachers. Reducing the number of parent complaints on the open-ended portion by 50 per cent of the survey, and increasing the number of satisfied responses on the quantitative portion by 5 per cent became the targets. The high school leadership team then developed interventions aimed at increasing the quality of communication among high school students, teachers and parents. The interventions included closer monitoring by administrators, training and the implementation of a Web-based communication system.

An emphasis on measurable targets based on multiple lines of evidence offers another benefit in the fragile governance world common in international schools. Many international schools, like Brussels and Bangkok, confront difficulties unknown in national schools. These include high turnover of students, faculty and boards, diverse community cultures with conflicting expectations, and diverse host country issues. Having measurable goals that are developed through collaboration and that are highly visible offers international schools resilient, compelling targets. They make it less likely that school administrators and trustees will be diverted and more likely that they will be able to stay with a fruitful process of school improvement.

At IS Bangkok, a Learning Matrix has been developed based in part on the data sources listed in Table 25.1. In the current jargon of the corporate world, the Learning Matrix serves as a 'dashboard' that allows board members to focus on results and avoid the

	Reading			Narrative Writing			Math	
	02–04	Target		02–04	Target		02–04	Target
3rd Grade	365–419	≥400		353–367	≥375		340–378	≥380

Figure 25.7   Excerpt from the Learning Matrix: International School Bangkok

micromanagement into which boards all too often fall. Figure 25.7 displays a portion of the Learning Matrix. It allows the board to hold management accountable. For example, in the ISA section of the Learning Matrix, the board has agreed upon a range of acceptable performance. If performance falls below this expectation, administration is expected to offer a remedial action plan. However, as long as performance stays within the boundaries, the board can be confident the educational programme is meeting its aims.

PRINCIPLE 5: PLANNING IN SCHOOLS NEEDS TO BE BOTH EVOLUTIONARY AND STRATEGIC

Strategic planning, long range planning, action planning, forward planning – these and other similar terms pervade international schools. For years, experts have exhorted school administrators and board trustees to follow in the paths of corporations and governments by developing and implementing comprehensive planning efforts. The experts promise that, well executed, such plans will propel improvement efforts, assure congruence between customer needs and school programmes, more efficiently allocate resources and so on. By now, the experts have succeeded and many international schools have some form of strategic planning.

Reviewing a random sample of such plans or analysing the small number of empirical studies on school planning quickly reveals several problems. Even in relatively stable government schools, the problems can be significant. In fragile, transient international schools, the problems demand alternative approaches to planning. What are these problems? As described earlier, international schools' teachers and leaders focus their efforts

overwhelmingly on inputs and processes rather than outcomes and results. School administrators usually concern themselves far more with teaching, timetables and budgets than with learning, standards and student progress. Given this priority is it any surprise that strategic plans in international schools typically have chapters on facilities, human resources, communication, finance and IT? If a plan does have a chapter on learning, it will be the final, shortest one.

After reviewing planning efforts in a number of secondary schools, Seashore Louis and Miles wrote, 'There is no single right way to plan, but there are many ways to go wrong' (1990: 190–8). She found that strategic planning with its emphasis on exhaustive searches for alternative ways of meeting goals, and careful as well as time-consuming reflection on implementation paths for the chosen alternatives, seldom works in the resource-limited, busy world of schools. Too often, planners resorted to 'shared endarkenment', relying on the knowledge of the planners rather than reaching out to the empirical literature or actively seeking best practices.

Seashore Louis and Miles argue that two major forces compel school planning to adjust the conventional strategic planning models. First, unpredictable and uncontrollable changes often impact schools. For example, national and state policies can shift abruptly. Governing boards and administrators change. Unforeseen teaching and learning approaches can emerge, especially in IT. Second, the loose coupling between targets and actions that characterizes school improvement work makes efforts to create detailed plans with multiple activities scheduled over 3–7 years an exercise of smoke and mirrors.

Instead, schools need to be seen as learning organizations in which change is really the sum

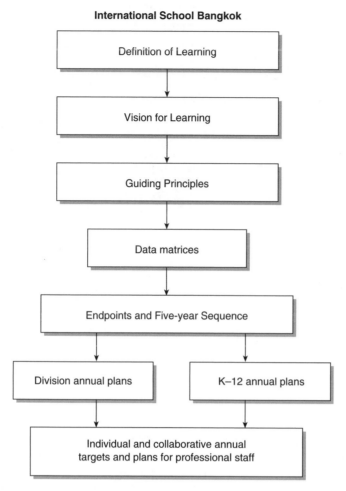

Figure 25.8   Evolutionary and strategic planning

of the knowledge and skills acquired by individual staff members as well as their increasing capacity to learn together. As the organization learns incrementally and collaboratively about which approaches are effective and which are not, the actions need to adjust as the organizational capacity and understanding grow. Seashore Louis and Miles describes this as evolutionary planning:

The approach is evolutionary in the sense that, although the mission and image of the organization's ideal future may be based on a top-level analysis of the environment and its demands, strategies for achieving the mission are frequently reviewed and refined based on internal scanning for opportunities and successes ... There is a general destination, but many twists and turns as unexpected events occur along the way. (1990: 190–8)

IS Bangkok planners endeavoured to use an approach that was both strategic and evolutionary. After six months of work, 15 drafts and the involvement of students, staff and parents, the board adopted a Vision for Learning and associated Guiding Principles. The Vision for Learning provides a brief description of the five 'transportable gifts' ISB offers its students. The Guiding Principles elaborate

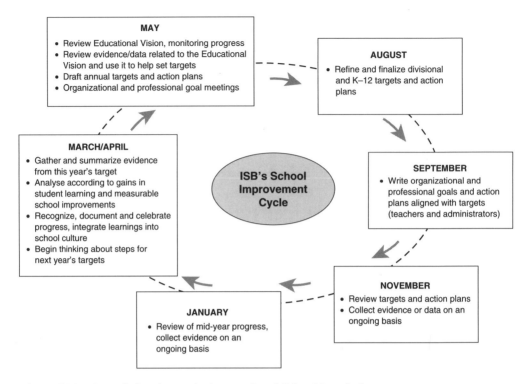

Figure 25.9   Annual planning cycle, International School Bangkok

each gift in sufficient detail to provide a rich description of what IS Bangkok can and should be. Figure 25.8 displays the names of key planning documents as well as the planning sequence.

Although the Guiding Principles document is about ten pages in length, it does not describe what measures can be used to assess progress toward the Vision. Given the school commitment to Principle 4, a one-page data matrix was created for each of the five gifts. Each matrix restates the gift and, for each of the major ideas in the related guiding principle, specifies sources of evidence and indicators.

The final document in the strategic portion of the planning model consists of the End points and Five-year Sequence. About every two years, the endpoints are reviewed and revised in accordance with organizational learning both in terms of events in the school and opportunities outside the school.

Systematic evolutionary planning occurs each year. Figure 25.9 exhibits the steps in the process. The annual planning process generates plans for elementary, middle and high school divisions as well as for the school as a whole. These plans include measurable targets, actions, responsible individuals and timelines.

However, in the spirit of evolutionary thinking, powerful ideas that emerge after the annual plans have been drafted are implemented if they promise important learning gains. For example, the 2004–5 annual plan included nothing about 'Smart Boards', IT devices that allow teachers to control Power Point presentations from the front of a classroom. However pilot tests with two boards in September quickly revealed their value. By March, the school had 40 boards in routine use.

In the final step, each teacher, counsellor and administrator drafts individual or collaborative plans. In the early stages of this work, many plans were individual. The norm now has shifted almost entirely to collaborative plans among groups with similar responsibilities. For example, the six 3rd Grade teachers have a common plan, as do the high school science teachers.

PRINCIPLE 6: SCHOOL IMPROVEMENT IS MORE LIKELY TO BE SUCCESSFUL WHEN CRITICAL FRIENDS ROUTINELY PARTICIPATE

In his autobiography, novelist Neville Shute recounts his work as an aeronautical engineer during the construction of dirigibles R-100 and R-101 during the late 1920s. The airships were built to similar specifications and costs. Because of major design flaws, R-100 crashed and burned on its maiden flight killing 53 people. In contrast, the R-101 successfully crossed the Atlantic and flew flawlessly for many years. According to Shute, the only difference between the two dirigibles was that on R-101 every engineering drawing and every piece of hardware was inspected by an external team of experts or 'critical friends'. Their job was to find mistakes and, more importantly, to identify better engineering approaches, designs and materials. Shute argues that R-100 would have been a fine ship if the work of its designers and builders had been critically friended (2000).

Of course, international schools seldom crash and burn. But Shute's lesson on the value of critical friends has been documented by a number of educational researchers. Doherty and MacBeath (2001) and Fullan (1999) have offered the most convincing empirical evidence. For example, Doherty and MacBeath (2001) describe how each of the 24 schools in their Improving School Effectiveness Project (ISEP) was assigned two critical friends who worked alongside teachers and administrators. Their results indicated that critical friends enabled the school to be more able to:

- Understand itself
- Understand the process of change
- Become more open to critique
- Engage in genuine dialogue

- Become more effective at managing change
- Be more effective at self-evaluation and self-monitoring
- Be more thoughtful in defining and prioritizing targets
- Develop greater self-confidence at self-management and self-improvement. (2001: 138–51)

In his work with schools in Ontario, Manitoba and Alberta, Fullan (1999) has documented the significance of having routine contact with external experts who can visit schools at least several times a year to review progress, provide technical assistance, coach learning leaders and ask important questions. He found that in schools with critical friends, planned improvements were significantly more likely to be successful and the pace of implementation seemed to accelerate.

As IS Bangkok embarked on its school improvement work in 2000, the educational consulting firm of Fieldwork was contracted to provide critical friend services. Four times a year, a team of two consultants visited the school for one to two weeks. They worked with teachers, administrators and the governing board. They attended meetings, asked questions, provided training, worked with teaching teams, visited classes and so on.

By the end of the first year, they had developed trusting relationships with all teachers and administrators that enabled them to observe closely and intervene appropriately. When the accreditation team from the Western Association of Schools and Colleges visited IS Bangkok in 2003, their report said that more progress had been made in the preceding two years than typical schools would achieve over five years. The team members as well as the school's administration team observed that the Fieldwork critical friends' efforts played an essential role in this rapid pace of change.

The analysis, training and guidance offered by Fieldwork contributed significantly to learning improvement at IS Bangkok. For example, Fieldwork identified the need for a data-guided annual planning process and provided associated training to administrators and team leaders. Fieldwork recognized that

Table 25.2   Mean two-year student ITBS* gain scores 4th Grade to 6th Grade: International School Bangkok

	00–02	01–03	02–03
Reading vocabulary	–6	–2	11
Reading comprehension	–3	–5	5
Spelling	–5	3	4
Punctuation	–5	5	13
Language usage	11	5	15
Mathematical concepts	4	8	18
Mathematical problem-solving	3	3	13
Average over all 7 sub-tests	–0.1	2.4	11.3

*Iowa Test of Basic Skills.

middle managers were underutilized and supported efforts to develop a year-long training programme as well as the initiation of a project called Collaboration for Learning. This effort reorganized the work of teacher teams to focus more on learning through activities such as analysing student work, sharing best practices and rewriting common assessments. During each of their visits, critical friends from Fieldwork assess progress at all levels in the school. Administrators and teacher leaders have found repeatedly that these judgements spotlight both unrecognized problems and unseen gains.

HAS LEARNING IMPROVED AT THE TWO SCHOOLS?

At IS Bangkok, several lines of evidence suggest that learning itself has improved. These lines emerge from both primary and secondary data sources. For example, Table 25.2 displays mean student gain scores on the Iowa Test of Basic Skills (ITBS) between 4th and 6th Grade. At both schools, about 20 per cent of students turn over each year. Such high levels of transience mean that conventional achievement analysis, which compares mean scores for student cohorts, is seriously flawed. Instead only the scores of 6th graders who had been enrolled as 4th graders were used in this analysis. For example, on the reading vocabulary sub-test, the national percentile ranking (NPR) on the 4th Grade test taken two years previously was subtracted from the similar 6th Grade score. These individual student gain scores were then averaged. This computation

offers a simple measure of the value-added by studying at IS Bangkok for two years.

The mean gain score for 6th graders in 2002 was –6. In other words, on average a student's NPR score in reading vocabulary had declined by 6 points. A student who scored at the 75th percentile as a 4th grader in 2000 would score at the 69th percentile in 2002. If a student progressed at the mean rate for the norm group, one would expect a gain score of zero.

The bottom row of Table 25.2 displays the average over all seven sub-tests. These average gain scores increased from –0.1 to 2.4 to 11.3 over the three years displayed in the Table. Assuming that all three cohorts have similar learning capacities, these figures indicate a substantial improvement in the value-added. On average, students in the 6th Grade in 2002 made two years of progress according to ITBS norms. In contrast, 6th Grade students in 2004 have seen their percentile scores increase by 11 per cent. A 4th Grade student at the 75th percentile in 4th Grade would on average be at the 86th percentile in 6th Grade.

The story offered by the data in Table 25.2, evidence of increased learning rates is paralleled by similar analyses between 6th and 8th Grade using ITBS scores and 3rd to 5th Grade and 5th to 7th Grade comparisons for International School Assessment results.

If the primary learning data listed in Table 25.2 seem to show increased learning, what about the secondary data? Table 25.3 offers one view. Each year every parent at IS Bangkok is asked to complete a Web-based survey organized around the five gifts of the Vision for Learning. Since about 50 per cent of parents respond to the survey each year

Table 25.3   Selected results from parent surveys at the International School Bangkok (ISB), 2003–2005

		2003	2004	2005
1	My child is being academically challenged	76	83	87
6	My child is making progress at ISB to the fullest of his/her abilities	63	64	70
3	I am confident that my child will be well prepared for his/her next school	69	71	79
19	ISB provides enough variety of activities outside the classroom (e.g. sports, clubs, ...)	84	85	84
22	ISB expects my child to work hard and to achieve his or her best	79	81	83
24	ISB provides a challenging curriculum for my child	69	74	78

The figures are percentages of parents who strongly agreed or agreed with each statement.

(750–850 completed questionnaires), the information has substantial validity.

Parents respond on a Likert Scale to 45 statements – strongly agree, agree, neutral, disagree and strongly disagree. Table 25.3 displays the results from six statements related to the first gift in the vision: *All students will achieve their academic, recognizable potential.* Three years of survey results reveal a number of interesting patterns. Most reassuring has been the stability of the numbers over time. Statements related to school programmes with no intended or accidental changes in quality vary only 1 or 2 percentage points. For example, Statement 19 regarding co-curricular programmes had 84, 85 and 84 per cent of parents indicating that they strongly agreed or agreed with the statement. During the period 2003 to 2005, these programmes were not systematically improved across the whole school and observation data suggest that overall programme quality did not change.

In contrast the other five statements, all relating to learning, indicate steadily increasing levels of parent approval. For example, the percentage of parents reporting that their children were being academically challenged increased by 11 points from 76 to 87. Of course, one could argue that learning has not improved: the school simply did a better job of communicating with parents. However, another set of results in the survey confounds this argument.

Parents respond to five open-ended questions about each of these children. More than 90 per cent of respondents answered these questions. These written responses are analysed by first identifying themes that seem to appear frequently and then counting how many parents comment on each theme. In 2003, the ratio of parents who were concerned about academic standards and challenges being too low to those who thought they were too high was about 3 to 1. On the 2005 survey, the ratio had reversed to about 1 to 2.

One would expect that when multiple sources of both primary and secondary data suggest that learning has improved, the schools' reputations would improve and they would become more attractive to new parents and teachers. In both schools, evidence from marketing and recruiting suggests that parents and teachers considering a move to a new school rely most heavily on word-of-mouth reports on school quality. One would predict that parents moving to Brussels or Bangkok who hear about the improving learning quality from their friends and colleagues whose children already attend these schools would be more likely to choose them. Apparently these communication processes are working. Enrolment at both schools has been steadily increasing and, more importantly, the market share of parents moving to Brussels or Bangkok has increased. Similarly, recruiting of excellent new teachers has become easier because of the word-of-mouth lore about the schools within the international school community.

In summary, the quality of the learning at both schools seems to have increased. The schools have a more coherent focus on learning. These changes have led to increased enrolment and greater financial stability. However, a fundamental question remains unanswered: have these improvements occurred because of the schools' emphasis on the six principles, or were they caused by other factors? The answers to this question are entirely anecdotal. When board members and administrators at both schools talk about the changes, one often hears positive observations related to one or more of the principles. Visiting accreditation teams have commented on the influence of the six principles. Critical friends at both schools have reported that the six principles have had a substantial impact. Finally, both authors believe that the six principles work. They would implement them again if they moved on to head other schools.

Unfortunately, scientifically valid answers remain elusive – to what degree has learning improved because of the six principles? At least one other question deserves consideration: what other principles can be identified in the empirical literature of school improvement that might have equal or greater merit in improving learning? Clearly these questions deserve further investigation.

CAN THESE PRINCIPLES BE USEFULLY APPLIED AT OTHER INTERNATIONAL SCHOOLS?

The six principles originated in the literature of school improvement. All six have been supported in multiple empirical studies across a variety of national schools. This chapter argues that the six principles have supported significant learning improvements at two international schools. However, among the more than 1,000 international schools around the world, the two case study schools in Brussels and Bangkok are unusually large and well-resourced. Would the use of these principles have been as effective in a school of 400 students with less money to spend on school improvement? Both authors have been heads of such schools and because of their consulting and accreditation work are familiar with them.

Focus on learning, learning leadership, strong professional communities, emphasis on results, evolutionary planning, critical friends – implementing these six principles does not require expensive programmes. Rather attitudes and priorities must change. Key leaders in a school need to be familiar with the principles

and have access to examples of how these have been implemented in other schools. Building strong professional communities should be easier in smaller schools where communication paths are less complex. All schools are data-rich if leaders know where to look. In smaller schools, planning should be accomplished more quickly. In both the schools featured in this chapter, critical friending involved expensive, external consultants. In less well resourced schools, these could be colleagues at other schools who act as reciprocal critical friends. Overall, implementation may be easier in younger and smaller schools. In our view, the same principles – though implemented in different ways – can apply across the international school sector, and many such schools could benefit from considering how they might work in their context.

REFERENCES

Collins, J. (2001) *Good to Great.* New York: Harper–Collins.

Doherty J. and MacBeath, J. (2001) Do schools need critical friends? In J. MacBeath and P. Mortimore (eds) *Improving School Effectiveness.* Buckingham: Open University Press, pp. 138–51.

Dufour, D. and Eaker, E.E. (1998) *Professional Learning Communities at Work: Best Practices for Enhancing Student Achievement.* Bloomington, IN: Solution Tree, pp. 19–46.

Fullan, M. (1999) Presentation at the European Council of International Schools conference in Paris, April 1999.

Fullan, M. (2001) *Leading in a Culture of Change.* San Francisco, CA: Jossey-Bass, pp. 1–29.

Newmann, Fred M. & Associates (1996) *Authentic Achievement: Restructuring Schools for Intellectual Quality.* San Francisco, CA: Jossey-Bass, pp. 209–27.

Rosenholtz, S.J. (1989) Workplace conditions that affect teacher quality and commitment. *Elementary School Journal,* 89(4): 421–39.

Schmoker, M. (1999) *Results: the Key to Continuous School Improvement.* Alexandria: ASCD, pp. 22–55.

Seashore Louis, K. and Miles, M.B. (1990) *Improving the Urban High School: What Works and Why.* New York: Teachers College Press, pp. 190–8.

Shute, N. (2000) *Slide Rule.* North Yorkshire: House of Stratus.

Wiggins, G.P. and McTighe, J. (2000) *Understanding by Design.* Alexandria: ASCD.

26

The Promotion of International Education in Formal Institutions: Potential for Conflict?

Wilf Stout

Institutions, no matter what role they actually play in society, are in danger of losing their influence as well as their effectiveness when they lose their social legitimacy. (Ghoshal 2005)

Great institutions such as the monarchy and aristocracy in nineteenth-century Europe, and the Church and state in the twentieth century, have suffered, and continue to suffer, from accusations of a lack of contemporary social relevance. In the past few years we have seen the collapse of economic colossuses such as Enron and Arthur Andersen on a tide of suspicion and mistrust.

Humans, by nature, are suspicious: a vestige, perhaps, of our cave-dwelling ancestry, predicated upon the belief that we can take man out of the Stone Age, but cannot take the Stone Age out of man. Current debate in management circles centres on the premise that management as a corps is intrinsically evil and, if left to itself, will exploit the managed. Society, on the other hand, believes that its corporate responsibility is to prevent, in true Marxist tradition, the exploitation of the proletariat by the bourgeoisie.

Corporate institutions are not inherently evil or harmful (although there are many heads around the world who may wish, as a result of their experiences, to challenge this statement), but the degree to which this is true depends crucially on quality of leadership and governance.

IS A FORMAL STRUCTURE A PREREQUISITE FOR THE SUCCESSFUL RUNNING OF AN EDUCATIONAL INSTITUTION?

A school is effectively a corporate institution, having a purpose (mission), vision, values and objectives modelled on traditional company lines, and having, as stakeholders, employer, employees and clients it must also guard against losing its social legitimacy. As institutions, schools require, first, strong leadership, provided by a headteacher, and secondly, a means of ensuring long-term viability and accountability by a governing body, or board, to whom the headteacher reports. Thirdly, they need staff that provide services to parents as clients, in respect of the education of their children. The mutual interaction between leadership and governance constitutes a corporate relationship and therefore there is a need for corporate accountability and good governance in fulfilling the mission of the school. In turn, the head and staff provide services on behalf of the board to parents. The success of schools, and indeed all institutions, is built on the unification of people around values (Greenfield 1991), and nowhere is this more evident than in school situations where the board has a custodial role in ensuring that all stakeholders respect and adhere to the values of the school. Schools are institutions in which all stakeholders have high aspirations and unfulfilled expectations. Nowhere is this exemplified more than in international schools.

Whether the school recognizes it or not, it must function as a business. It has inputs and outputs just as would any other business, but in the case of a school these are infinitely more valuable than purely monetary considerations. The inputs are children and the output is their education. There the analogy and its development ends, for schools represent perhaps, one of the most contentious arenas for conflict, second only to parliaments and churches.

WHAT SORTS OF STRUCTURES ARE IN PLACE?

The ownership and management of international schools falls into one of three major categories: 'proprietary', 'not for profit' and 'for profit'. Likewise, the structure of governing boards tends to conform to one of three main types.

The *self-perpetuating board* is a form of self-perpetuating oligarchy which chooses its membership largely to conform to the expectations and personalities of the existing membership. Consequently, these boards tend to maintain the status quo with respect to the way in which the school safeguards its values, its traditions and the educational standards for which it is known and usually respected. This structure is the most stable form of governance and has the major advantage to the school of conferring stability and long-term 'institutional memory'. It leads to the best long-term decisions and has the long-term welfare of the school very much to the fore. Conversely, it can be criticized since it has the propensity to lead to stagnation and a failure to innovate. Also these boards are seen by critics to be distanced from the opinions of parents and alumni and have too much power concentrated in the hands of a few people who may be perceived as having no vigour, no immediate interest, or current knowledge of their schools.

With this type of board, the skills and wisdom of an outstanding head and staff are paramount to ensure that the school remains *au fait* with current educational innovations and continues to deliver the standard of education traditionally associated with such a school. Many of the older independent schools in the UK which have enjoyed enviable reputations for centuries, the Etons and Winchesters, have just this type of board structure – which it may be argued is the very reason for their success. A number of longer-established international schools, such as Aiglon College and Dubai College, are similarly constituted. Littleford (1999) reports, however, that over the past 20 years the swing away from such a structure has been 'strong and severe'.

The *elected board* is typically constituted annually from a general meeting of the parent body. This structure is typified by the transient nature of its membership and the likelihood of picking up 'rogue' members. A transient board has no institutional memory (a requirement for good governance), which is seen by many to be a *sine qua non* for a successful school. If the tenure of board membership is one year it is likely, in extreme cases, for an entire board to be replaced every year. In practice this is not the case, as such boards usually have longer-term membership and a gradual turnover. Elected boards have positive and negative aspects: while exhibiting a high level of democracy and representation of all stakeholders, they usually manifest extremes of behaviour by the membership due to a failure to have unity of purpose. Ideally, members should be united by the desire to serve the best needs of the school, but too often members are keen to generate their own agenda or to ensure that some 'pet' idea or interest is promoted. Heads of schools with a board elected in this fashion report that experience for them is akin to 'Russian roulette'. Boards constituted in this manner are often, and unfortunately, increasingly the source of considerable conflict and distress in the working relationship between governance and management.

A more pragmatic variation upon the elected board is one where the board itself nominates, screens, recruits and presents individuals to the parent assembly ahead of time for election at the annual general meeting. This technique works well. It ensures that the 'person' nominated to join has at least the right credentials and profile to support the work of the board and has a greater chance of ensuring unity of purpose by the membership of the board. From the head's perspective, it also allows him or her to express an opinion and have the opportunity to veto anyone who, from past experience, is unlikely to have the overall interests of the school at heart.

The third form of board is one *appointed* by outsider interest groups. Depending upon the nature of the ownership these may be appointed by the founding group, be it an embassy (e.g. British School of Moscow), an NGO (e.g. UN International School of New York), a private company (SABIS schools), a property developer (Dubai International Academy in the UAE), a group of parents (International School of Cape Town in South Africa), a private individual (Dwight School in New York), an educational management provider (e.g. GEMS), or increasingly, an investment group (e.g. PHORMS Schools in Berlin). In such cases, the board is usually appointed by the interest group to serve its needs. These boards are usually typified by a stability which increases directly with increasing level of investment. The most stable boards are those appointed by a single owner

and which answer only to the owner. Even then there is a chance that a conflict of interests could result!

In addition, there are a variety of other board models which are hybrids of the three structures described above, each having unique characteristics. People are generally motivated to join school boards because they want to make a difference; occasionally that difference either relates to a personal agenda rather than the good of the community, or they join because of the perceived prestige that it brings (Tangye 2005). Too often, those keen and eager to join the board do so out of a desire for self-aggrandisement, or in the belief that this will bring them status in the eyes of fellow parents or in the mistaken belief that by serving on the board they will 'get the best for my kid' (Stout 2005). The best board members are usually those that have to be persuaded to join the board because they do not regard themselves as 'Committee folk' or they believe themselves to be too busy!

A board survey carried out by the Council of International Schools (CIS) in 2004 showed 23 per cent of boards were self-perpetuating; 23 per cent fully elected; 13 per cent fully appointed and 41 per cent a combination of elected and appointed. There is, however, a material difference between the average tenure of a member on a self-perpetuating board at 7.5 years and that of a member of a combination board at 2.8 years (CIS 2005, quoted in Hodgson and Chuck 2005).

The board needs to strike a balance between providing long-term stability with respect to policy, while being seen to be responsive and accountable to the changing needs of the community it serves. Wholly *appointed* boards run the risk of being divorced from the community and perceived as being old fashioned, reactionary and out of touch. Wholly *elected* boards run the risk of constantly effecting changes in policy in response to personal agendas, which is detrimental to the school.

The CIS Annual Board Governance Survey for 2004 goes on to reflect that

boards vary in frequency of meetings from those that meet three times each year, to those that hold twenty meetings, with the average being eight sessions/year with length of meetings from thirty minutes to three days, with the average being 2.45 hours. There is no norm, but one can safely say that any meeting as important as a school board that lasts a mere thirty minutes is frivolous, while one that last for six hours has probably delved too deep into the operational management of the school. (Tangye 2005)

Ideally, a board that meets twice per term for a meeting of two to two and a half hours following a standard agenda, and is well chaired, is likely to achieve all that is necessary to manage a successful school.

WHAT IS THE FUNCTION OF A BOARD?

Governance deals with the legitimate distribution of authority throughout a system, whether in an organization or a country. Governance is a collective endeavour which, through a planned and ordered process, takes actions that advance a shared purpose consistent with the organization's mission. In good governance an individual board member has no authority independent of the board.

The basic assumption of governance is that the board is the guardian of the school's mission. It ensures that the mission remains relevant to the needs of the school community it serves, and it monitors the success of the school in fulfilling this mission. It is often stated that boards have three roles only: the development of strategic policy; the exercise of fiduciary trusteeship; and the appointment of the head. The head's role is to carry out board policy at the operational level of the school. The chair of the board's role is to ensure that the board and the head fulfil their respective roles efficiently and effectively. Board members are bound by fiduciary duties (that is, duties of loyalty and stewardship of funds) and duties of care and skill in their development of strategic policy and the appointment of the head. A school therefore has only two leaders: the chair who manages the board and the head who manages the school. Each must respect the role of

the other, and board members should respect the positions and roles of both. The chair should act as the head's 'best friend' and the strength of their working relationship, built upon trust and mutual respect, is vital for the health of any school.

A key concept of governance is that a board must be in a position to 'lead, control and monitor' the business of an organization. A board has 'a collective responsibility to provide effective corporate governance' (King 2001).

A board should 'not be dominated by an individual or individuals, so as to ensure that an objective and intellectually honest collective mind is brought to bear on decisions' (King 2001).

The board is responsible for determining the aims and overall conduct of a school. In serving as the keepers of a school's mission and as its fiduciaries, the board should:

1   direct the school in terms of purpose, values, strategy and structure
2   establish policies and plans consistent with the school's purpose
3   ensure that the executive management implements the strategy as established and in a manner befitting the espoused values of the school
4   ensure that the school operates ethically in all its dealings and practices
5   ensure that the school has adequate systems for internal and external control, both operational and financial
6   monitor and evaluate the activities of the executive management
7   appoint the head, ensure succession and give guidance on the appointment of senior executives
8   maintain effective two-way communication with all stakeholders through appropriate channels
9   provide accountability and transparency with reference to information on the activities of the school to those legitimately entitled to it
10 provide for the succession of the chair and board members.

(Based upon a Report, 'Code of Corporate Practices and Conduct', commissioned by the Institute of Directors in Southern Africa and chaired by Judge Mervyn E. King SC, 2001).

Good governance has eight major characteristics. It is participatory, consensus oriented, accountable, transparent, responsive, effective and efficient, equitable and inclusive, and follows the rule of law. It assures that corruption is minimized, that the views of minorities are taken into account and that the voices of the most vulnerable in society are heard in decision-making. It is also responsive to the present and future needs of society. Without proper training in the principles of good governance, board members may be lacking the necessary skills to accomplish key outcomes.

HOW EFFECTIVE ARE THE BOARDS?

Bad governance is increasingly regarded as one of the root causes of evil within the organizations, institutions and businesses of present day societies. Schools, as stated earlier, are not immune in this respect. Boards of international schools, in particular, have a notorious reputation for bad governance. Adele Hodgson (2005) summed up the situation which many heads have discovered to their bitter cost, that 'truly efficeint and effective boards are rare'. John Carver (1990) put the effectiveness of boards under suspicion, when he wrote that 'Boards tend to be, in fact, incompetent groups of competent people'.

Chuck (2005) brought the role of boards sharply into focus in writing:

> The board's role (should be) focused very clearly on satisfying itself, and thereby the person, body or community that it represents, that two criteria are being met: firstly, that the school is doing what it is supposed to do ('delivering its Mission'), and secondly, that it is doing so according to its stated behavioural values and educational principles. It is both implicit and explicit that the board does not itself carry out the delivery of the Mission. So given these very distinct and logical roles, why can there be such confusion and friction? (Chuck 2005)

It is, consequently, no coincidence that in the course of the past ten years independent national schools, and most international school associations, have developed guidelines on good governance and organize regular training workshops for heads and governors. Effective governance is the cornerstone of the healthy independent and international school, yet all too often it is the proximal factor (source), as opposed to the distal factor (root cause), that is of major conflict in schools.

WHAT, THEN, IS THE PROBLEM?

Schools are not democracies and those schools that attempt to ensure that they function as such are often the least healthy in terms of governance practices, morale and good repute. More importantly, it is both prudent and essential that *parents* should see schools for what they are, which is as custodians of attitudes and values and purveyors of knowledge, concepts and skills, established and functioning for the express purpose of ensuring that their child becomes a useful addition to society. For this reason parents would be well advised to leave the leadership, management and organization of the school to those professionally qualified to be entrusted with such an important task. This does not, of course, absolve parents from their roles in the nurture and development of their own children. And parents should never forget that a child in a typical school spends no more than 15 per cent of his or her time, between the ages of 5 and 18, in school. Where, therefore, do the formative influences in a child's development take place?

We can be assured that there are very few businesses in the world that can post, report on or effect such a level of capital appreciation, in terms of human potential, as can an 'effective school'. Twenty years ago many school heads and board members of international schools served without time limits and heads and chairs of boards may have served for two decades or more. These were the halcyon days of the establishment of new schools throughout the world. Now it seems that a different climate prevails. Preliminary research undertaken at the University of Bath (Stout 2005) has supported the earlier findings of Littleford (1999), Schoppert (2001) and Hawley (1994, 1995) that there is a seemingly disproportionate number of heads who are fired, or replaced with varying degrees of unacceptable procedure, following a period of intense and bitter conflict within a school. These incidents of governance/management conflict have not abated and almost monthly one hears of yet another bout of conflict in an international school resulting in the premature departure of another 'good' head. Littleford's startling statistic in 1999, that 80 per cent of heads are fired, whilst based on North American independent schools, certainly has relevance to the situation in international schools, the majority of whom are members of the European Council of International Schools and the Council of International Schools.

The premature replacement of a head *may* be well-founded. Inappropriate behaviour and practice may leave a board with no alternative but to replace the head. If this is done in a just and fair manner and in terms of due process, no one could take issue. Current research taking place with the University of Bath is attempting to establish the extent to which heads leave schools against their wishes without due process following a period of governance/management dispute, and to discern causes and effects, both personal and institutional. Preliminary case history investigations carried out as part of the research indicate an unacceptable number of heads forced out of schools without evidence of any form of what would be described as unprofessional behaviour or misconduct. Such an event can have a detrimental effect not only on the morale, reputation and subsequent career of the head but also on the reputation of the school with negative impacts upon marketing, student and staff recruitment and financial viability.

As has been established in earlier sections of this chapter, all schools must have some form of accountability for the head who, in turn, is accountable for the staff. This is the role of the board of governors presided over by a chair. Irrespective of the phylogeny of the board structure, whether self-perpetuating, elected, appointed or any combination of these, the structure must have a constitution or some form of documentation which details the roles and responsibilities of chair, board members and head and which recognizes the boundaries of their respective jurisdictions. It is on the basis of such constitutional documentation that the rights and wrongs of management depend, and through which procedures are in place for the resolution of contentious issues that arise from the mutual interaction of board and head. Again preliminary research indicates in the majority of cases that no such policy or procedural documentation exists.

The board must retain a clear focus that their objective at all times must be to improve the learning environment for students. Organizational or administrative conflict or petty politics have no role in good governance or in effective school leadership and management. Here we come full circle; unless the activities of the board *have* demonstrably contributed to an improved learning environment, they have wasted their time, done a disservice to the students, their parents and the school community, and the board should make way for others who will hold to this noble objective.

WHAT IS THE NATURE OF THE CONFLICT?

Conflict is part of the daily order of life, be it within the family, business, church or school. It is particularly evident in situations where expectations run high. Schools, as has been previously stated, are institutions in which all stakeholders – parents, staff and students – have high aspirations and unfilled expectations. Conflict, sadly, seems to be becoming almost a way of life in many international schools. Such schools are communities characterized by a richness of ethnic, cultural, professional and experiential diversity. This very richness – desirable though it may be for cultural reasons – *may* provide a potential breeding ground for conflict if unregulated in the hands of a weak chair or head.

Conflict is a natural concomitant of social interaction and has been so since the days of Eve and her apple. It has positive as well as negative effects depending upon the way in which it is managed. Coser (1956) states that 'no group can be entirely harmonious, for then it would be devoid of process and structure'.

Social groups require a certain degree of dissonance in order to achieve progress. Disharmony as well as harmony, dissociation as well as association, need not be viewed as disruptive factors. Well-managed cognitive dissonance should result in collegiate resonance (Suchley and Stout 2005).

Unfortunately governance/management conflict too often leads to educational dysfunction, a lowering of standards, both academic and behavioural; it may destroy the reputation of the school and individual staff and is most likely to have a negative impact on marketing, student and staff recruitment and financial viability. Anstey (1999) defines social conflict as 'existing in a relationship when parties believe that their aspirations cannot be achieved simultaneously, or perceive a divergence in their values, needs or interests (latent conflict)'.

Kriesberg (1973) simplifies the definition to 'Social conflict is a relationship between two or more parties who believe that they have incompatible goals!' (p. 17).

These definitions, which are broad in the sense of their applicability to all organizations, centre on conflict having a relational perspective and an ideological perspective. For the purposes of this chapter, 'conflict' is defined as 'a situation arising in the governance and management of an international school where the parties appear to have different aims, understandings, or interests, which, if left unresolved, is likely to result in organizational dysfunction, damage to the reputation of the institution and personal and material disadvantage for at least one of the parties' (Stout 2006).

Stalemate can be reached if both parties dig in on issues of principle, past performance and tactics and use these for mutual attack rather than in searching for a sustainable solution.

One of the foremost exponents on conflict and its resolution, Deutsch, notes that as conflict escalates so there is a shift away from problem-solving, persuasion and conciliation, toward an increased reliance on strategies of power and the utilization of tactics of coercion, threat and deception. A belief emerges that the solution to the conflict is only attainable via superior force or trickery (Deutsch 1973: 39).

WHAT ARE THE SOURCES OF THE CONFLICT?

In seeking to grasp the sources of any conflict it is important to remember the beliefs and perceptions of the actors involved. Do they perceive the problem to be rooted in differing goals, structural imbalances, differing values, ambiguity, lack of coordination, lack of information, or some other cause(s)? Are *their* understandings of the situation the same or different – are they operating out of the same frame of reference? Regrettably, research to date indicates that *one* of the major causes of conflict can be traced back to some form of personality clash where an ego has been bruised or destroyed.

Experience would suggest that school boards and school leaders need to recognize and exercise a strong measure of humility, of compassion and understanding for others, and a strong desire to prevent any incident, however minor, from blowing up into full-scale destructive conflict that will jeopardize the integrity of the school. If the school executive is unable to set a standard and example in terms of the implementation of the school's values, what hope is there for the staff and students?

The trick is to avoid destructive affective conflict which can produce long-term animosity, lower staff morale and disrupt productivity while at the same time encouraging cognitive conflict where individuals critically discuss and debate ideas and issues but not personalities. (Powell 2002)

Initial investigation, conducted as part of my own research, has indicated a number of factors that appear to work singly or together to promote or prevent conflict, as follows:

(a) Conflict may manifest itself in *one* of the following ways:

- seeking support for one's own view
- seeking supporters for one's own view
- conspiracy
- breakdown in confidentiality
- overt anger
- meetings (overt and covert)
- ignoring each other
- distortion of facts
- telephone calls, e-mails, letters
- collusion
- gossiping
- loss of confidence
- bitterness and hatred
- lack of trust
- lying, exaggeration, half-truths
- closed minds

(b) Common triggers for conflict may stem from:

- the perception that head/board mismanaged a crisis
- a termination or resignation of a staff member
- policy change/issue/unpopular decision poorly, or not, communicated
- comment from leader
- one individual with agenda

(c) The course of the conflict may then see the following effects:

- support for the 'cause' is elicited and a group of dissidents is created
- an atmosphere of uncertainty is created
- management becomes distracted and board is 'troubled'
- 'management paralysis' sets in
- suspicion and uncertainty for the future prevail
- school leadership and management dysfunction sets in
- key players leave
- school's reputation suffers
- enrolment is threatened
- financial pressures set in

(d) Conversely, there are a number of ways in which conflict may be prevented/overcome:

- respect for relative roles
- open flow of information
- mutual respect for positions and roles
- desire to cooperate
- accepted hierarchy
- common goals
- shared values
- agreed agenda/plan
- adherence to common mission and purpose

HOW CAN CONFLICT BE PREVENTED?

It is postulated that schools, with the help of their professional organizations, can set about improving a major conflict in two very straightforward ways. The first is to *recognize* that a conflict between governance and management *could* conceivably arise and to *plan* ahead for such an event by having an orderly and structured procedure in place to deal with any conflict situation that may arise. Secondly, it is vital to *recognize*, and to *acknowledge*, that when a dispute cannot immediately be resolved in-house the school should seek help before the conflict escalates into a destructive mode and spirals into a lose–lose situation for all parties. It would be unusual for any school to avoid completely situations of dispute. Unresolved daily challenges and concerns, if not addressed appropriately, will become disputes. Unresolved disputes will, in turn, lead to serious ongoing conflict. In the majority of cases, dispute and conflict situations are resolved by the head. It is only when the head needs additional support that matters should be directed through the chair to the board.

Even the most efficient of boards whose schools are running like clockwork need to set aside time each year for a 'board retreat'. This provides an opportunity for new members to be oriented into the 'ways' of the board and time is taken for meeting together with the head in a social surrounding. A clear agenda will ensure that time is used wisely and that the strategy for the year ahead is articulated. Part of the 'retreat' should be devoted to a review of chair/head/board relationships, communication and clear understanding of their respective roles and duties during the coming year.

Every two years or so, time should be taken for an outside facilitator to take the board through a refresher course on good governance. Such an exercise can be cathartic in cleansing the board of its 'sins' of micromanagement, if not in *deed,* then in *heart,* and in recommitting themselves as a board to upholding good practice in the governance and trusteeship of the school.

Current research being undertaken at the University of Bath is not concerned so much with conflict arising because of what one would consider 'normal' operational school matters, but with conflict arising from within the very corridors of power in a school, the board membership. This is often the most insidious form of conflict and the one which has the likelihood of causing most damage to the lives and reputations of individuals and schools. The Bath research methodology seeks to quantify the present extent of conflict which arises at the level of governance and management and to determine both quantitatively and qualitatively the causes and effects of the conflict on heads, boards and schools. Furthermore, and more importantly, it seeks to apply techniques and protocols for conflict resolution drawn from this rapidly developing field of social science.

As with situations of alcohol, solvent and drug addiction, it is vital that boards and heads recognize the early signs that all is not well, and admit that a conflict exists and formally declare a conflict situation. This in itself signifies a mutual recognition of the problem, calls for a cessation of 'hostilities', prevents further escalation of the conflict and allows for a cooling-off period during which time the parties can negotiate in-house, preferably chaired by a neutral third party acting as a mediator. In the event that such action fails to resolve the issue, it is recommended that the chair and head jointly inform their professional membership organization of the situation and seek advice as to the way forward.

CONFLICT RESOLUTION THROUGH EFFECTIVE MEDIATION

Currently, the professional membership organizations to which international schools and international staff belong do not have a formal procedure for dealing with such situations. It is known that past Executive Secretaries of the European Council of International Schools have often called upon their own board members to help informally as well as offering assistance personally. Sometimes this has helped, but on many occasions the organization was not informed sufficiently ahead of time so what support could be given came too late. By which time, in many cases, another head had fallen.

It is disturbing to note the number of accredited schools that continue to lose heads because of unresolved governance/management issues, seemingly without any intervention or censure from the accrediting body. Moreover, it is more alarming to note how many of these schools seem to make a practice of hiring and firing heads. These heads are removed, not because of incompetence, mismanagement or impropriety, but because of an internecine issue arising within the board which the head, acting in isolation, was not able to resolve. Whilst such schools may have disciplinary and grievance procedures, these are clearly inappropriate and/or ineffective in handling governance/management conflict.

It is extremely encouraging to note that the current edition (7th) of the CIS/NEASC Standards for Accreditation (2003) acknowledges the need for good governance to be a prerequisite for accreditation. In particular, Section C: Governance and Management: Standards One, Two and Three, calls for 'The governing body (to) be so constituted, with regard to membership and organization, as to provide the school with sound direction, continuity and effective support'.

> There shall be a co-operative and effective working relationship between the governing body and the Head of the School.

The head, although accountable to a higher authority, is always the responsible leader of the school. *One* of the keys to a successful and effective school is governance by a board made up of individuals who have a selfless heart for the school and what it stands for. It is not for those who come with personal agendas, grudges and a desire for self-aggrandisement or a need for recognition. It is, however, for those with a servant-heart, those who wish to add value to the school by their contributions of time, effort and personal resources given freely, unconditionally and often sacrificially.

Their work will be remembered and cherished for the value that was added to the school during their tenure.

A board that is rich in talent may consist of several role players offering many viewpoints in a given society. The process of good governance requires the channeling and focusing of those talents, through genuine discussion mediated by a skillful chair, to reach a broad consensus based on what is in the best interests of the whole school community and the means by which this can be achieved. It also requires a broad and long-term perspective on what is needed for sustainable development and how to achieve the goals of such development. This can only result from an understanding of the historical, cultural and social contexts of the society or community served by the school, its purpose, vision and values. Accountability – who is accountable to whom – varies, depending on whether decisions or actions taken are internal or external to an organization or institution. In general an organization or an institution is accountable to those who will be affected by its decisions or actions. Accountability cannot be enforced without transparency and the rule of law.

From the above discussion it should be clear that good governance is an ideal that is difficult to achieve. Very few countries, societies, organizations or institutions have come close to achieving good governance in its totality, but there are schools where this has been the norm, in some cases for hundreds, or at least scores, of years.

However, to ensure sustainable school development, actions must be taken to work towards this ideal with the aim of making it a reality. It is the author's strong conviction that a professional education association which espouses an ethical basis for membership needs to have conflict resolution policies in place to offer as a service to members, in order to alleviate the problems arising from conflict at the level of governance and management.

In conclusion, the strong message is for boards to aim for stability in membership and balance in their decision-making. Effective chairs need to stay on longer, act with firmness and impartiality, encouraging heads to take on change thoughtfully and at a reasonable pace. Chairs should counsel continuity of leadership by supporting the head publicly and consistently when change periodically leads to an expected or unexpected reaction, be it student-, staff- or parent-initiated. And finally, to recognize the frailty of human nature and the impact of 'Eve's apple'.

We all need to recognize the times when we, or others, are acting in a manner that is selfish and unsustainable and then to exercise wisdom, tact and diplomacy in preventing an escalation in conflict, thereby effecting a satisfactory rational, emotional and professional outcome for all parties, contributing to the welfare and good report of the school.

REFERENCES

Anstey, M. (1991, 2nd ed, 1999) *Managing Conflict.* Cape Town: Juta.

Carver, J. (1990) *Boards that Make a Difference: A New Design for Leadership in Nonprofit and Public Organizations* (2nd edition, 1997). San Francisco, CA: Jossey-Bass.

Chuck, M. (2005) The Board and its operations. In *Governance in International Schools*, A. Hodgson and M. Chuck (eds) ECIS and CIS. Great Glemham: Peridot Press, p.21.

CIS (Council of International Schools) (2005) Quoted in A. Hodgson and M. Chuck (eds) *Governance in International Schools*. Effective International Schools Series. Great Glemham: Peridot Press.

CIS/NEASC (2003) *Guide to School Evaluation and Accreditation*, CIS/NEASC (7th edition).

Coser, L. (1956) *The Functions of Social Conflict.* New York: Free Press.

Deutsch, M. (1973) The resolution of conflict: constructive and destructive processes. In *The Resolution of Conflict Humanity and Society*, 13: 187–94.

Ghoshal, S. (2005) Towards a good Theory of Management: A force for good. In J. Birkinshaw and G. Piramal (eds). London: Pearson Education, p. 2.

Greenfield, W. (1991) Toward a theory of school leadership. ERA paper, Chicago, 3–7 April.

Hawley, D.B. (1994) How long do international school heads survive? Part I. *International Schools Journal*, XIV (I): 8–21.

Hawley, D.B. (1995) How long do international school heads survive? Part 2. *International Schools Journal*, XIV (II): 23–36.

Hodgson, A. (2005) Introduction to the world of governance. In *Governance in International Schools*, A. Hodgson and M. Chuck (eds) Effective International Schools Series: ECIS and CIS. Great Glemham: Peridot Press, pp. 7–11.

King, M.E. (2001) Code of Corporate Practices and Conduct. Quoted in ISASA Guidelines on School Governance.

Kriesberg, L. (1973) *The Sociology of Social Conflicts*. Englewood Cliffs, NJ: Prentice Hall.

Littleford, J.C. (1999) *The Governance Game*. CIS conference: Littleford and Associates.

Powell, W. (2002) In School Board Governance and Training (2001). In W. Powell, N. Bowley and G. Schoppert (eds) *Effective Schools Series*: ECIS and CIS: Great Glemham: Peridot Press.

Schoppert, G. (2001) What exactly is a school board? In *School Board Governance Training: A Sourcebook of Case Studies*. Great Glemham: John Catt Educational.

Stout, G.W. (2005) Conflict and its resolution in the governance and management of international schools. *International Schools Journal*, XXV (1): 15–21.

Stout, G.W. (2006) Unpublished paper.

Suchley, P.C. and Stout, G.W. (2005) The significance of cognitive dissonance in the process of action planning in the management of schools. (Operational document, GEMS Occasional Paper).

Tangye, R. (2005) The board and best practice. In A. Hodgson and M. Chuck (eds) *Governance in International Schools*. ECIS and CIS. Great Glemham: Peridot Press, pp. 12–16.

Vinge, D. (2005) The board and the school head. In A. Hodgson and M. Chuck (eds) *Governance in International Schools*. Effective International Schools Series. Great Glemham: Peridot Press, pp. 30–6.

27

Organizational Cultures in Schools: a Case Study from Peru

José Agustín Ortiz Elías

In many societies, educational organizations have for many years been among the last institutions to give an impression of stability, whilst around them was a delirious excitement generated by changes in economics, employment, politics and daily life. Teaching institutions often created a feeling of security, protection and permanence: hard market competition seemed not to have penetrated the walls that surrounded schools, colleges and universities. How valid is that impression today? In schools, teachers, tutors, directors and managers are conscious of the pressure for change and efficiency involving individuals, groups and entire organizations. They know that their students will face a highly competitive reality, and will need to be properly trained to face that challenge. At the same time, they may fear that this adaptation process to external demands will damage the characteristic moral values of their institutions and, ultimately, that the educational process itself will become a mere interchange of services.

Times are surely changing. Peter Drucker, patriarch of business management, says 'we are in one of those great historical periods that occur every 200 or 300 years, when people don't understand the world anymore, and the past is not sufficient to explain the future' (cited in Childress and Senn 1995). In terms of the complexity of everyday life, the distance between students in basic education today and their grandparents is probably many times greater than that which existed between Bronze Age men and those who lived at the beginning of the Christian Age, two thousand years later. Many educators feel that the current challenge is how to manage transition of educational institutions in totally different and diverse societies, given that they still carry responsibility for moral leadership and for the promotion of moral values.

This kind of challenge may lead us to question whether or not we need to change the culture of our organizations. Studies in commercial companies during the 1990s clearly conclude that organizations that are able to maintain sustained success are not those that are principally affected by market forces, resources or competitive positions, but those that are concerned with the beliefs, values, visions and satisfaction of their members (Cameron and Quinn 1999: 4). Systemic thinker Peter Senge, meditating about education, explains that we do not teach people any more with the same objectives as previously:

Even if these multiple symptoms of deep change are not considered, the fact is that the labour world is not looking any more for industrial workers. Future employers will place more value on listening and communication skills, on the ability to cooperate with others, and on the skill of critical and systemic thinking, because the world is more interdependent and dynamic. (Senge et al. 2002: 64; personal translation)

Societies need desperately to discover what will help them to understand that the external forces of change will not necessarily determine their nature, but that it will be the dreams and values of those within societies that will count. Undoubtedly, schools represent one sector of society that will need to address this issue. As Peter Drucker states:

What we call the information revolution is truly a knowledge revolution. What has made possible the standardisation of processes is not the machinery; the computer has only been the detonator. The software is the reorganization of the traditional work, based on centuries of experience, with the application of knowledge and, especially, logical and systematic analysis. Electronics is not the key: the key is cognitive science. This means that the emerging key words to retain leadership in economics and technology are probably the social status of the professionals that work with the knowledge and the acceptance of their values. (Drucker 2002: 21–2; personal translation)

THREE MODELS OF CULTURE AND THEIR IMPLICATIONS FOR EDUCATIONAL ORGANIZATIONS

Recently, the concept of organizational culture has received close attention in most kinds of organization. It is clear that cultural issues have great relevance for schools and universities: the usual content and methods within such institutions allow people to discuss deeply important issues for organizational development and conflict management. What follows is a discussion of three models of culture that are, currently, the most theoretically developed and widely utilized for practical purposes: the Competing Values Framework, Schein's Corporative Culture model and Hofstede's models. They have the most promising and catalytic effects for

meaningful change at school level. The theoretical components of the models will be linked in discussion with the results of a field study undertaken in June 2005 at 30 secondary schools in Lima, Peru.

THE COMPETING VALUES FRAMEWORK

Kim S. Cameron and Robert E. Quinn presented the Competing Values Framework (Cameron and Ettington 1988; Cameron and Freeman 1991; Cameron and Quinn 1999; Quinn and Spreitzer 1991) as a model to diagnose organizational culture during the consulting process and to enable companies to make positive changes. Organizational culture is assessed, in Cameron and Quinn's model, by the Organizational Culture Assessment Instrument (OCAI), an ipsative test comprising six items. For each of the items, the evaluators must distribute a total of one hundred points amongst four alternatives. Each item represents a key factor (dimension) for understanding of the organizational culture, and the four alternatives represent each of the four cultural configurations in Cameron and Quinn's typology. In each case, the evaluators first assign points to characterize the current culture of their organizations, and then score the items again, thinking about what will be the most desirable situation in five years' time. The six key dimensions of organizational culture (Cameron and Quinn 1999) are: the *dominant characteristics* of the organization (how dynamic and personal, or outcomes-oriented or controlled is the workplace); the *organizational leadership* style (oriented to mentorship, or entrepreneurial traits, achievement or management efficiency); the *management of employees* style (oriented to teamwork, risk-taking, competition or security); the *organizational glue* (the extent of cohesion, based on loyalty, mutual trust, innovativeness, goal achievement or formalization of rules and procedures); the *strategic emphasis* (supported through personnel development, creativity, the market or the operational control); and finally, the *criteria of success* inside the organization (in terms of compromise with people, the possession of unique registered products, success in the market or the permanent reduction of production times and costs).

The four configurations are an outcome of the authors' studies on the defining characteristics of the efficiency of most companies. Organizations engage consistently in the use of these strategies or orientations towards efficiency, especially those which are more adaptable or comfortable in the reality that they face and for the work style of their managers, employees and teams. Each configuration will be explained briefly, as follows:

- The *Hierarchy culture* focuses on the efficient production of goods and services with a low cost. This style owes its characteristics to Max Weber who defined 'bureaucracies': rules, specialization, meritocracy, hierarchy, impersonality, accountability and separate property. This kind of organization concentrates on schedules, efficiency and control. Their leaders are good monitors and coordinators.
- The *Market culture* defines a results-oriented company, an organization managed as a market: its teams and divisions look more outside than inside; the general goal is to do business with others (especially foreigners) and to show results in terms of income-production, competition and productivity. The main concern of the people in these companies is to fulfil the required market share, reach the expected goals and defeat the competition. The leaders of these companies tend to have great charisma and to be great competitors.
- The companies that show a *Clan culture* are very similar to a family, in which cohesiveness is based on respect for tradition, the existence of strong shared values and an orientation to care for each other. Their main systems of social control are interactions within groups and collaboration among employees. These cultures judge themselves to be successful when they achieve high morale and promote the wellbeing of their members. Participation and communication are the glue of the groups and their leaders are considered mentors or parents.
- The fourth kind of organizational culture is called *Adhocracy*. This type of organization in based on the continued creation of new ideas, services and fresh products to engage with maximum efficiency in reacting to the changeable preferences

of its clients. They function through ad-hoc multifunctional teams whose goal is to develop new competitive ideas. This is the most common configuration among companies in radical-innovativeness industries. Their leaders tend to be great visionaries and flexibly minded.

Data from the Peruvian study were obtained from the self-assessment of the organizational culture of 32 secondary schools undertaken in June 2005 by the directors and academic coordinators of private schools in Lima, Peru. A locally adapted version of the OCAI was used (Fischman 2004). Twenty-five cases were taken for analysis, making use of SPSS software version 13 (SPSS 2003), in accordance with the methodology advocated by Cameron and Quinn (1999). In every case exact non-parametric tests were applied because of the high number of cells with few cases.

Dimensions of the organizational culture

For the analysis of the dimensions of organizational culture, the configuration that the directors considered characteristic of their schools now was scored in each case. Scores for the present configurations were then compared with those judged to be most desirable in five years' time. Table 27.1 shows the scores of the characteristics perceived as dominant in the present versus the preferred ones in five more years. It can be seen that in 11 cases there is a coincidence between the current and the preferred configuration (seven in Clan, two in Adhocracy, one in Market and one in three different choices), while in 14 cases there is a switch of preferences. Among the current characteristics we can note particularly the Clan culture (12 cases), while among the future preferences the Clan takes approximately one-third of the sample (8/25), followed by Adhocracy (five cases), three different choices (four) and the Market culture (three).

Table 27.2 shows the scores on the appreciation of the current organizational leadership versus the one preferred in five years' time. The information shows that eight schools

Table 27.1 Dominant characteristics in the present versus characteristics preferred in five years' time

		Dominant characteristic preference							
		Clan	Adhocracy	Market	Hierarchy	Two choices	Three choices	Four choices	Total
	Clan	7	1	0	1	1	2	0	12
	Adhocracy	0	2	0	0	0	0	0	2
Dominant	Market	0	2	1	0	0	1	0	4
characteristics	Hierarchy	1	0	0	0	1	0	0	2
now	Two choices	0	0	2	0	0	0	1	3
	Three choices	0	0	0	0	1	1	0	2
Total		8	5	3	1	3	4	1	25

Note: Dominant characteristics now * Dominant characteristic preference crosstabulation

Table 27. 2 Organizational leadership now versus preferred type in five years' time

		Organizational leadership preference						
		Clan	Adhocracy	Market	Hierarchy	Two choices	Three choices	Total
	Clan	1	0	0	0	1	0	2
	Adhocracy	0	1	1	0	0	0	2
Organizational	Market	2	1	0	3	0	0	6
leadership now	Hierarchy	1	2	0	5	1	1	10
	Two choices	1	2	0	1	0	0	4
	Three choices	0	0	0	0	0	1	1
Total		5	6	1	9	2	2	25

Note: Organizational leadership now * Organizational leadership preference crosstabulation

coincide in their current and future preferred style, while 17 do not. However, unlike in the previous outcomes, here we can notice the coincidences around the Hierarchical culture (five cases), while the Clan-based leadership only has one coincidence, the same as the Adhocracy and the three different choices option. In the assessment of current leadership style, the most common is the Hierarchy (ten cases), followed by the Market orientation (six cases). That means that there is a strong contrast between this table and the previous table, strongly oriented to the Clan culture. Among the preferred leadership styles in the next five years the most preferred is the Hierarchy (nine cases), but this time followed very closely by Adhocracy (six cases) and the Clan (five cases). The Market-based leadership style has practically no followers (one).

Table 27.3 compares current cultural configurations on management of employees with the preferred ones in five years. There are 15

cases of coincidence between the current and desired styles, and practically all of them correspond to the Clan culture (13 cases). Almost every school that manages employees with a Clan orientation expresses satisfaction and wishes to maintain this style (13 out of 14). In the case of the other management styles, almost everyone wishes to change towards a Clan culture. Such a culture is considered as the most valuable for employees' management in 21 out of 25 cases. Moreover, it should be pointed out that the Clan culture was included among the most preferable in the two cases with more than one selection.

Table 27.4 shows the configurations of the present organizational glue versus the preferred ones. In only nine cases out of 25 do the present and future coincide, and seven of these correspond to the Clan culture. Regarding the current organizational glue, there are two preferred options, each of them with seven votes: the Market and the Clan (in

Table 27.3   Employees' management now versus that preferred in five years' time

		Employees' management preference					
		Clan	Adhocracy	Market	Two choices	Three choices	Total
Employees' management now	Clan	13	0	0	0	1	14
	Adhocracy	1	1	0	0	0	2
	Market	3	0	0	1	0	4
	Hierarchy	4	0	1	0	0	5
Total		21	1	1	1	1	25

Note: Employees' management now * Employees' management preference crosstabulation

Table 27.4   Organization glue at schools now versus that preferred in five years' time

		Organizational glue preference				
		Clan	Adhocracy	Two choices	Three choices	Total
Organizational glue now	Clan	7	0	0	0	7
	Adhocracy	0	1	0	0	1
	Market	6	0	1	0	7
	Hierarchy	3	0	1	0	4
	Two choices	5	0	0	1	6
Total		21	1	2	1	25

Note: Organizational glue now * Organizational glue preference crosstabulation

Table 27.5   Strategic emphasis at schools now versus that preferred in five years' time

		Strategic emphasis preference						
		Clan	Adhocracy	Hierarchy	Two choices	Three choices	Four choices	Total
Strategic emphasis now	Clan	5	0	0	1	1	0	7
	Adhocracy	2	1	0	1	0	0	4
	Market	2	0	1	0	0	0	3
	Hierarchy	3	0	0	0	0	0	3
	Two choices	3	1	0	1	1	1	7
	Three choices	1	0	0	0	0	0	1
Total		16	2	1	3	2	1	25

Note: Strategic emphasis now * Strategic emphasis preference crosstabulation

the case of two choices they include at least one of them). Likewise, in four cases Hierarchy is considered the current glue in the organization. These data strongly contrast with preferred configurations for the future: 21 of them correspond to the Clan culture, three to more than one style (all of which includes the Clan) and only one wishes to be based on Adhocracy (keeping the current style).

Table 27.5 compares the strategic emphasis now with the preferred emphasis in five years. There is a coincidence in eight cases between the current style and the preferred; five of them correspond to the Clan culture. Among the current configurations, there are seven votes for the Clan and the other seven include two selections (distributed among the Clan, the Market and the Adhocracy). These results show a strong difference from those of the best possible profile in five years, because in 16 of 25 cases the Clan is selected as the best culture.

Table 27.6 shows a comparison of the criteria of success that organizations' employees

Table 27.6 Criteria of success now versus those preferred in five years' time

		Criteria of success preference					
		Clan	Adhocracy	Two choices	Three choices	Four choices	Total
	Clan	7	1	1	3	0	12
	Adhocracy	1	1	1	0	0	3
Criteria of	Market	2	0	0	0	0	2
success now	Hierarchy	3	0	1	0	0	4
	Two choices	1	0	0	0	0	1
	Three choices	1	1	0	0	1	3
Total		15	3	3	3	1	25

Note: Criteria of success now * Criteria of success preference crosstabulation

should follow now versus the most preferable in five years. It should be noted that, even though there are only nine coincidences between the present and the future, both final configurations are very similar. In almost half of the cases (12) the participants think that currently internal success is obtained through the strategies of the Clan culture. Only one of these 12 cases switches its selection towards the future (to Adhocracy); in four cases, the Clan is selected with another option. Regarding future configurations, the Clan is clearly preferred (15 times) and is mentioned in all cases with more than one selection (seven times), while Adhocracy is selected as a future option in three cases.

Analysis

The first observation from this analysis is that, in most schools in the study, there is a strong expectation that the six dimensions of organizational culture will change over the next few years. On the issue of currently perceived cultural dimensions, the most frequently identified is the Clan culture, especially in the dimensions of dominant characteristics, management of employees and criteria of success. The Hierarchical culture is perceived as the most common style of leadership in schools now. In the case of the organizational glue dimension, the Market culture tied for first place with the Clan culture. Finally, in the strategic emphasis dimension there is a diversified selection. These outcomes are important in terms of the theory, because they show the most critical issues for school cultures in

contemporary times. For example, the descriptor oriented to Hierarchy in organizational leadership says: 'The leadership in the organization is generally considered to exemplify coordinating, organizing, or smooth-running efficiency'. On the other side, the Market-oriented descriptor in organizational glue says: 'The glue that holds the organization together is the emphasis on achievement and goal accomplishment. Aggressiveness and winning are common themes'. As can be appreciated, these are two key points for the dilemmas highlighted in the first part of the chapter: school directors and teaching staff clearly feel the pressure for outcomes and profitability. Meanwhile, the leadership seems to get pushed by circumstances towards isolation in an exclusively formally based power, a hierarchical position, the power that French and Raven call 'legitimate' (French and Raven 1959; Fischman 2005).

On the issue of the configuration preferred in the future, the variables cluster in two profiles: first, there is a Clan culture-oriented factor that unites the following dimensions: management of employees (21 selections), organizational glue (21), strategic emphasis (16) and criteria of success (15). The second group of factors is heterogeneous: the dominant preferred cultural characteristic is the Clan (eight selections), very closely followed by Adhocracy (five), and then the Market (three). In this cluster, the preferred leadership style is again the Hierarchy (nine), followed by Adhocracy (six) and the Clan (five). It seems that the leadership style at schools still follows the authority and command principle; although it is interesting to note the considerable proportion of schools that wish to implement an Adhocracy leadership style, based on self-directed teams – and even more interesting when we bear in mind that at present this style is perceived to be almost non-existent. The general conclusion seems to be that schools aim to conform to a culture that, in external directions, balances the criteria of stability, profitability and efficiency (dominant characteristic dimension), and for the interior of the organization keeps a strong sense of subjection to authority, but to function as personnel-oriented organizations, where strong cooperative links are established among all members. The Clan culture seems to be the most preferred culture configuration for educators.

Configurations of the organizational culture

Twenty-eight valid cases were obtained for this analysis. In summary the results show strong expectations related to the need for a cultural change in schools, towards the consolidation of a Clan culture in the future. Likewise, there seem to be two clusters of configurations: on the one hand, the Clan and Adhocracy cultures are viewed in a very positive fashion, while on the other hand, Market and Hierarchy had a negative appreciation for the future. The schools seem to consider that the features of a Clan culture are the best answer to current challenges. That implies a strong emphasis on the construction of cohesive teams, a clear sense of a vision, frequent meetings, keeping everyone informed about relevant issues, assignment of clear roles, concern for close personal relationships, carefully prepared feedback to colleagues, frequent expression of esteem, celebrations, awards, accessibility of managers and clear goals relating to people's career and personal development.

SCHEIN'S CORPORATIVE CULTURE MODEL

Edgar H. Schein is considered one of the founders of Organizational Psychology

(Schein 1992). He began his career in the 1960s, with the study of persuasion (Schein 1961) and the psychology of organizations; he then focused on the process of socialization in the workplace (Schein 1964) and the process of career development (Schein 1978). It was then that he began to study the impact of the organization's founder's ideas and behaviours on the company's culture (Schein 1983), while at the same time he developed new theoretical views on the consulting process (Schein 1988) and on the use of the clinical perspective in fieldwork (Schein 1987). This brief and incomplete summary of the works of Professor Schein is presented in order to show that his ideas about organizational culture (Schein 1992, 1999) are the result of a longstanding career searching for solutions to the practical needs of people working in organizations.

Schein's organizational cultural model has a broadly different focus from that of Cameron and Quinn. First, Schein disdains the use of tests as a means of assessing organizational culture, and proposes the use of an anthropological methodology: the clinical interview. According to this idea, organizational culture itself is a grounded theory of the company about its nature and purpose, sustained by the organization's members, and manifested at the level of their everyday conversations. Organizational culture should rise from the depth of the company's spirit; it should not be forced to fit a predetermined typology, at the cost of a critical losing of analytical information and of flexibility to manage change.

In Schein's view, the subject of cultural studies is not separate from the goal of the research and his method cannot be neutral, but is necessarily self-critical. It is not possible to understand culture as an abstract phenomenon; it needs to be seen rather as the result of a series of practical needs (Schein 1992: xii–xiii): the need to understand the dynamics of communication and cooperation between groups inside the company (subcultures analysis), to understand the way people relate to their technological needs and options, and how technology impacts on the internal dynamics of the organizations; the way to conduct people beyond national and ethnic boundaries; and the way to make longstanding changes with real possibilities of being successful and overcome the resistance of groups and individuals, and to obtain compromise and cooperation from them in order to sustain results over time and enhance people's satisfaction and well-being.

According to Schein, the shaping of an organizational culture is based on the lived experience and the shared learning: the culture is built on those assumptions that had brought success to the organization in the past and on the practices and symbols derived from them. That is why Schein defines culture as:

> a pattern of shared basic assumptions that the group learned as it solved its problems of external adaptation and internal integration, that has worked well enough to be considered valid and, therefore, to be taught to new members as the correct way to perceive, think, and feel in relation to those problems. (Schein 1992: 12)

This definition allows us to get a glimpse of the fact that the culture can be analysed at several levels with the purpose of intervening, changing or consolidating it. Such cultural 'strata' go from the most visible and manifest traits (especially for external visitors, but for group members too), to the deepest and hardly understandable features, for which it is possible to use the term 'unconscious' because they reside in the cognitive frameworks of people inside the organization (Axel 2002). A brief explanation of these strata, from most visible to least visible, is given as follows.

Artefacts of the culture

Artefacts are placed at the most visible cultural level, on the surface. They are symbols that characterize the organization and have an immediate impact upon visitors. However, as Schein points out (1992: 17), they are easy to perceive but hard to decipher, because they are metaphors of the deepest levels of the culture. The observer's risk of misunderstanding the artefacts when using his or her own conceptual categories is considerable, so that any conclusions will then be strongly biased. In order to make a completely correct interpretation, it is necessary for the observer to be involved in the dynamics of the group that produced the artefacts.

Some typical artefacts categories in organizations are: leaders' ritual behaviours (gestures, style of giving instructions, etc.), rituals of initiation (for new members), rituals of communication (coordination), rituals of rewarding (merit), rituals of integration, meetings, decision-taking, ways of sharing information, relationships with families, architecture, symbols in the physical environment, the products made by the company, the language, office design, etc.

In the Peruvian research, participants identified some characteristic types of cultural artefacts: the buildings (an artefact mentioned by almost everybody) seem to be a very important feature, transmitting seriousness, tradition, serenity and energy. In some cases, it was stated that the architecture characterizes the contrast between traditions and more recent tendencies inside the school. The physical environment is represented by artefacts whose objective seems to be to give security to the families, and to guarantee a safe place for their children. The physical environment is likewise the receptor of a series of artefacts designed to communicate the philosophy or lifestyle of the school, such as wallpaper or information bulletins. Participants pointed out that those artefacts have the goal of communicating values, to indicate the level of formality, and the degree of closeness among people. Regular standardized information is communicated by these means too. The fact that among the artefacts of the physical environment there exists some 'intangible' stuff stands out, as in the 'luminosity' that, in the view of the participants, shows 'amplitude, openness and clarity' about the school's culture. The multilingual nature of the school seemed to be a very important feature (where applicable), but language is also an instrument of respect for authority and provides an element of separation between subcultures (for example, the vocabulary of the students and the vocabulary of the teachers). All the symbolic artefacts contribute to a strong sense of identity and exert some pressure to conform with the organizational beliefs. Among such symbols are the school logo, the anthem, the school crest or coat-of-arms, graduation ceremonies, religious icons, portraits of historical personalities and declarations of principles, all of them with a powerful capacity to unite the organization's members around them. Clothing and uniforms also play a very important role in the definition of corporate identity, especially with respect to the seriousness expected by the school of its students. Curiously, the rituals are commonly oriented not to the students but to their parents or teachers: meetings with parents, sports activities for them, formal meetings and, on the other hand, teachers' awards (for long service for example), farewells and religious activities (where relevant) for the families. Student-oriented rituals seem to be more flexible or not clearly defined (something that should constitute another typical cultural trait). As for meetings, decision-taking and communication of important information, there seems to prevail a strong sense of affirmation of the internal hierarchies and the clear definition of authority.

Espoused values

Values are cognitive guidelines that underlie the artefacts and behaviours of the organization, the way to solve conflicts and to face challenges. At the beginning of the history of each group, such guidelines do not exist clearly and they are proposed by the founders or those who assume a role of leadership. As time goes by, their contents are validated by experience (for example, through reducing uncertainty) or, eventually, are refuted. In some cases, organizations insist on holding on to refuted values due to the strong influence the founders still have, which can begin to shape a powerful expectation for change. Espoused values can predict what individuals inside teams will say or think, but not necessarily what they will do in specific situations (Argyris and Schön 1978, cited by Schein 1992: 21). This implies the existence of congruent and non-congruent values with the basic beliefs shared inside the organization.

In the Peruvian research, a list of 30 organizational values was put to each of the school directors, who were asked to determine if those

were espoused values at their organizations, if they were proposed by the founders or leaders, if they were observed and if they would be required to be implemented in the future (in cases where they are not observed). With respect to the role of the leaders or founders, there appear to be two school profiles: those where the number of values proposed by the leader is high (greater than 20) and those where the number is low (less than 10). The first group is, to a large extent, made up of schools run by religious orders; the second, of non-religious schools. The congruency among espoused values and practised (observed) values seems to be considerable; there is a high demand for values such as teamwork, humour, empowerment, happiness and humility, almost all of them referring to the well-being and autonomy of the organization's members. Finally, asked about the values to be implemented in the future, participants addressed a number of specific values: humour, humility, empowerment, profitability, efficacy, loyalty, simplicity, openness to diversity, concern for people, responsibility, team work and innovation. This profile of urged-to-develop values seems to be highly congruent with the results obtained in Cameron and Quinn's model, given that they express the wish for a family or Clan culture at the schools, with important elements of innovation and highly qualified and self-directed teamwork to face new challenges (Adhocracy).

The basic assumptions

The way in which we consider the nature of things seems so natural to us that we may well be surprised to realize how much they are learned, biased, unilateral and subject to the influence of members of our groups. In Schein's words:

> When a solution to a problem works repeatedly, it comes to be taken for granted. What was once a hypothesis, supported only by a hunch or a value, comes gradually to be treated as a reality. We come to believe that nature really works this way. (1992: 21)

Among the most critical basic assumptions for the quality of life and survival in the present world there are those concerning the social dynamics of trust and cooperation: those societies that succeed in transmitting to their members a positive expectation regarding other people and what one can expect from them, those communities where people 'naturally' tend to trust in each other and attribute to their fellows a concern for the general well-being, are more likely to have a high quality of life and mental health (Axelrod 2004; Singer 2002).

Basic assumptions are very stable heuristics for social thinking, and they tend to be defended against all critics or debate. Changing such cultural assumptions is tremendously difficult, however, and there is no possibility of a true change in the dynamic of groups or organizations if they remain untouched. That is maybe the reason for the failure of many consulting processes: they touch only the surface level (artefacts), or try to force the organization to fit into a theoretical model of culture.

Schein proposes that the basic assumptions give people heuristics or thinking schemas to survive and to adapt to external challenges, defining the mission statement and the strategy of the company, its goals, the valid or appropriate means to reach them, the way to measure the indicators of results and the correct means to introduce changes in the system. They offer, too, the instructions to reach the internal commitment: creating common languages, shared nouns, defining boundaries and criteria for inclusion and exclusion, distributing power and status, developing norms of intimacy, friendship and love, assigning rewards and punishments and giving answers to the unexplainable (ideology). Basic assumptions state, too, what is the nature of the reality, the true, the human activity, the time, the space and the commitment among people in the organizations. Some assumptions could contribute to achieving the objectives of the organization.

In the Peruvian research, the assumptions are mainly related to the educational activity (a high-quality education), the internal processes and the authority, the application of punishments, the savings, and the possibility

of reaching any goal, the need for continuous assessment, to solve problems quickly and a low drop-out rate as a criterion of success. Most of these values are appreciated as positives, contributing to the success of the organization. Among those negatively assessed are the expectation of unconditional loyalty to authority and the organization, a negative attitude towards the open expression of emotions, the huge number of norms, the pressure for conformity, a permanent sense of urgency, the absence of rituals for students and the lack of effort to ensure high-level training for teachers. These last assumptions would seem to reveal a high-expectation for an Adhocracy culture, which changes the rigid norms with openness in information management, the hierarchical structures with opportunities for self-leadership and self-directed teams, and creates autonomy in decision-making (Blanchard et al. 1997).

HOFSTEDE'S MODELS: SOFTWARE OF THE MIND AND ORGANIZATIONAL CULTURE

The third exposition about organizational culture was not empirically measured in the Peruvian research; however, it is explained here because of its considerable influence on cultural studies for the past 20 years and its specific importance for international education studies and for understanding among national cultures. They are actually two closely related models, both coming from the work of the Dutch author Geert Hofstede (Hofstede 1980, 1999), who focuses on the functional level of culture and defines it, by analogy, as 'software of the mind' or mental software; a model for thinking, feeling and behaviour. Mental software partially determines the behaviour of individuals and groups, pointing to which reactions are understandable and expectable given their personal past (Hofstede 1999: 3). Culture is considered a symbolic learned process strongly deterministic over the behaviour of groups and individuals, and the other cultural strata. It has as its main role differentiating one group from another. In congruence with Schein's model, there exist here cultural strata of symbolic levels; the most superficial is the 'symbols stratum', followed by the 'heroes stratum', the 'rituals stratum', and at the deepest level, the 'values stratum'. In contact with all these levels, there is a cross-stratum, called the 'cultural practices stratum'. However, in contrast with Schein, Hofstede does not reject the use of tests as a tool for diagnosing culture; he built his own questionnaires for that purpose.

In Hofstede's view, there are three major consequences of culture: it defines the way of associating with authority, defines the concept of 'self', and defines the way of managing conflicts and expressing feelings (1999: 46). He proposes four cultural dimensions of mental software:

- *Power distance* is the measure of inequality in the relationship with authority (for example, the fear of expressing disagreement with the bosses), and the degree to which a high hierarchical distance is considered the norm. According to Hofstede's studies (1999: 64), among the countries with the most hierarchical cultures are Malaysia, Guatemala, Panama, the Philippines and Mexico; among the most 'horizontal' we find Austria, Israel, Denmark, New Zealand and Ireland.
- The *individualism–collectivism* dimension is the degree of balance between individual and collective needs. In individualistic cultures, the bonds among people tend to be relatively weak, while in collectivist cultures groups are very strong and influential, constantly protecting and supervizing individuals. The most individualistic countries (Hofstede 1999: 105) are the United States, Australia, Great Britain, Canada and the Low Countries, while the most collectivist are Guatemala, Ecuador, Panama, Venezuela and Colombia.
- *Masculinity–femininity:* according to this dimension, in 'masculine' cultures indicators of success (for men and women) are achieving a good salary, promotion, and rewards and challenges, while in the 'feminine' culture they include having a good relationship with authority, working in a cooperative workplace, living in a pleasant environment and obtaining job security. In feminine societies, men's and women's social roles are very similar, while in masculine cultures they are quite different. According to Hofstede (1999: 151) the most 'masculine' cultures are to be found in Japan, Austria, Venezuela, Italy and Switzerland, while the most 'feminine' are Sweden, Norway, the Low Countries and Denmark.

- *Uncertainty avoidance* is the typical degree of tolerance to ambiguity or unclear situations to be found in a culture, and the level of tolerance for aggressiveness and emotional expression. This dimension is closely related to the belief that differences are intrinsically dangerous for the group. The less low-ambiguity-tolerant cultures (Hofstede 1999: 194) are Greece, Portugal, Guatemala and Uruguay, and the most tolerant are Singapore, Jamaica, Denmark, Sweden and Hong Kong.

It is interesting to imagine the effect of Hofstede's cultural dimensions on the process of managing an educational organization. For example, discussing the way to create a culture based on Adhocracy and Empowerment, Randolph and Sashkin (2002) state that Adhocracy could have positive effects in low-hierarchical cultures, while in the high-hierarchical cultures it could be counterproductive.

Hofstede claims that a culture model is needed that is specifically oriented to the functional needs of organizations, and suggests six dimensions with that purpose (1999: 308): process-orientation versus outcome-orientation, employee concern versus work concern, cooperativism versus professionalism, open system versus closed system, low control versus strict control, and normativism versus pragmatism.

Again in the Peruvian study, school directors stated that they would prefer to establish a Clan culture for the future with some aspects of Adhocracy, as opposed to the present culture (Clan with strong components of hierarchy). This seems, in terms of Hofstede's model, to emphasize orientation to process over outcomes, and at the same time, employee concern, cooperation, closed systems, low control and normativism. In terms of the mental software model, it seems to be important to strengthen low power distance, corporativism, femininity and low tolerance to ambiguity.

A CONSIDERATION FOR SCHOOLS WORLD-WIDE

In this chapter so far we have analysed the expectations of the school directors who took part in our study; at the same time, we have explained the main theoretical options with the purpose of building a cultural strategy for educational organizations. However, until this point we have not asked two important questions: first, is the preference for Clan culture what educators desire world-wide? Do the feelings of these 30 Peruvian directors represent the needs and expectations of their colleagues in other countries? A second, and even more important question, is: Are their expectations right? Is it good that schools wish to develop a strong Clan culture?

For the moment we only can invite the reader to search for answers in the other chapters of this Handbook, where can be found the ideas of many scholars and practitioners on the nature and future of international education. In any case, we can always remember what was stated at the beginning: the world looks for stability within institutions, and it is, without doubt, the case that educational organizations are among those social institutions; such a role is clearly related to, and congruent with, the familiar spirit of a Clan culture.

It is very difficult to answer the second question, given the present tendencies in the world so far as politics and economics are concerned. On the one hand there is tremendous pressure for efficiency and profitability, but on the other there exists pressure for the construction of a spirit of cooperation and mutual compromise. We believe that Clan culture is actually the best option for schools, and it is also the best we as educators can do for the politics of the world. However, good intentions are not enough: we need to make it happen, and for that reason we need to think about how to implement our ideas. We need to understand that we are in the middle of a great spiritual controversy concerning what the future of the world may be, and Clan culture offers us the best chance in approaching this formidable task and in taking the necessary decisions. We have believed for many years that the direction in which to go is best achieved by making a contribution to the building of a better society, but we do so from a realization that what we have is not a mission *for* the members of society, but *with* them.

ACKNOWLEDGEMENTS

The author wishes to thank school directors and managers for their participation and authorization to use their self-reports on the organizational culture of their schools, and wishes to thank the organizers of the workshop 'Leading the Organizational Culture', at the Universidad Peruana de Ciencias Aplicadas (UPC).

A locally adapted variation of Edgar Schein's methodology was applied, which was proposed by Professor David Fischman (Fischman 2004), at the Universidad Peruana de Ciencias Aplicadas (UPC). The author wish to thank Professor Fischman for the authorization to use his work.

REFERENCES

Argyris, C. and Schön, D.A. (1978) *Organizational Learning.* Reading, MA: Addison–Wesley.

Axel, E. (2002) Una línea de desarrollo en las teorías europeas de la actividad. In M. Cole, Y. Engeström, and O. Vásquez (eds) *Mente, cultura y actividad.* Mexico: Oxford University Press, pp. 105–19. (Originally published as *Mind, Culture and Activity*, Cambridge University Press, 1997).

Axelrod, R. (2004) *La complejidad de la cooperación.* Mexico: Fondo de Cultura Económica. (Originally published as *The Complexity of Cooperation.* Princeton, NJ: Princeton University Press, 1997).

Blanchard, K., Carlos, J.P. and Randolph, W.A. (1997) *Empowerment. Tres claves para lograr que el proceso de facultar a los empleados funcione en su empresa.* Bogotá: Norma (Originally published as *Empowerment Takes More Than a Minute.* San Francisco, CA: Berrett–Koehler Publishers).

Cameron, K.S. and Ettington, D.R. (1988) The conceptual foundations of organizational culture. *Higher Education: Handbook of Theory and Research.* New York, NY: Agathon, pp. 356–96.

Cameron, K.S. and Freeman, S. (1991) Cultural congruence, strength, and type: relationships to effectiveness. *Research in Organizational Change and Development*, 5: 23–8.

Cameron, K.S. and Quinn, R.E. (1999) *Diagnosing and Changing Organizational Culture Based on the Competing Values Framework.* Reading, MA: Addison–Wesley.

Childress, J.R. and Senn, L.E. (1995) *In the Eye of the Storm.* Los Angeles, CA: The Leadership Press.

Drucker, P. (2002) *Managing in the Next Society*. New York: St Martin's Press.

Fischman, D. (2004) *Liderando la Cultura Organizacional*. Lima: Universidad Peruana de Ciencias Aplicadas (UPC).

Fischman, D. (2005). *El Líder Transformador*, 2 vols. Lima: Universidad Peruana de Ciencias Aplicadas (UPC).

French, J.R.P. and Raven, B. (1959) The bases of social power. In D. Cartwright (ed.), *Studies in Social Power*. Ann Arbor, MI: University of Michigan Institute for Social Research, pp. 150–67.

Hofstede, G. (1980) *Culture's Consequences: International Differences in Work-Related Values*. Beverly Hills, CA: Sage.

Hofstede, G. (1999) *Culturas Organizacionales: El Software Mental*. Madrid: Alianza Editorial. (Originally published as *Cultures and Organizations: Software of the Mind*. New York: McGraw Hill, 1996).

Quinn, R.E. and Spreitzer, G.M. (1991) The psychometrics of the competing values culture instrument and an analysis of the impact of organizational culture on quality of life. *Research and Organizational Change and Development*, vol. 5. Greenwich, CT: JAI Press, pp. 115–42.

Randolph, W.A. and Sashkin, M. (2002) Can Organizational Empowerment Work in Multinational Settings. *Academy of Management Executive*, 16(1), 102–15.

Schein, E.H. (1961) *Coercitive Persuasion*. New York: W.W. Norton.

Schein, E.H. (1964) Personal change through interpersonal relationships. In W.G. Bennis, E.H. Schein, D. E. Berlew and F.I. Steele (eds) *Interpersonal Dynamics*. Belmont, CA: Dorsey Press, pp. 357–94.

Schein, E.H. (1978) *Career Dynamics: Matching Individual and Organizational Needs*. Reading, MA: Addison–Wesley.

Schein, E.H. (1983) The role of the founder in creating organizational culture. *Organizational Dynamics*, Summer: pp. 13–28.

Schein, E.H. (1987) *The Clinical Perspective in Fieldwork*. Newbury Park, CA: Sage.

Schein, E.H. (1988) *Process Consultation*. vol. 1: *Its Role in Organization Development*, 2nd edn. Reading, MA: Addison–Wesley.

Schein, E.H. (1992) *Organizational Culture and Leadership*, (2nd edn). San Francisco, CA: Jossey–Bass.

Schein, E.H. (1999) *The Corporate Culture Survival Guide*. San Francisco, CA: Jossey–Bass.

Senge, P., Cambron McCabe, N., Lucas, T., Kleiner, A., Dutton, J. and Smith, B. *(2002), Escuelas que aprenden. Un manual de la Quinta Disciplina para educadores, padres de familia y todos los que se interesen en la educación*. Bogotá: Norma.

Singer, P. (2002) *One World: The Ethics of Globalization*. New Haven; CT: Yale University Press.

SPSS (2003) *Survey Analysis Using SPSS*. Chicago, IL: SPSS Inc.

28

Fragmentation in International Schools: a Micropolitical Discourse of Management, Culture and Postmodern Society

Richard Caffyn

Schools are fascinating constructs that are facing complex and challenging upheaval due to changing social times (Hargreaves 1994). International schools as unique phenomena have their own set of challenges with which to contend. The emergent paradoxes of postmodern society (Hargreaves 1995, 1997, 2000), especially the binaries of internationalism and tribalism, are part of this discourse. So too is the postmodern critique of the modernist hierarchical meta-narrative of schools as educational social norms. Schools can be viewed as positivist systems held together by authoritarian control, now becoming increasingly unravelled by greater individualism, the 'end of society' and hybrid meta-culture.

Do schools fragment into subcultures, departments and interest groups when the corporate culture is weak, imposed and if the people involved have diverse reasons for being there? Does a school fragment further into individual interests and small-scale

alliances built up on the basis of interest, goals, subcultures and power structures? Investigated beneath the glossy veneer of brochures and baccalaureate, international schools can be regarded as reactionary corporate monocultures. However, it could be that the power systems that legitimated these regimes have become more exposed and that the rationality of their existence is now being questioned. Organizations and social systems are fragmenting because what held them together, the social normalization and monocultural Western welfare state systems, has become eroded. Is it therefore not dialogue but fragmentation and the erosion of legitimation and authority that has been revealed through the lens of postmodernist organizational discourse (Falzon 1998)?

Divergent views and voices (Foucault 1977, 1986) are often marginalized and even normalized in the push for a globalized and centrally controlled system (Cambridge 2002,

2003; Cambridge and Thompson 2004). Fragmentation concerns itself with issues and situations that work against a centralized or monocultural view of an organization. It is firmly locked in the postmodernist paradigmatic perspective, which considers all aspects of the organization as having a voice. Fragmentation looks at opening the discourse as to who has control over education and brings in the historical, locational and sociological perspective when deconstructing schools and what they stand for. The relevance and application to international schools is that they are exposed to a number of powerful forces that shape society and education today (Ball 2003).

Is fragmentation necessarily a bad thing? Does it mean what is suggested, a break-up of a whole? To both of these questions the answer is no. Fragmentation can take many forms and does not necessarily mean the end of the structure. It could be a means of organic change, growth or reform. Some edifices are too large and therefore fragmentation can enable them to split and grow as separate structures. Within an institution fragmentation can exist at the departmental, interpersonal and structural levels. The larger the institution in size and populace the greater the potential for extensive fragmentation. All human organizations are fluid, dynamic and unique. They are neither predictable nor static. As with any social structure, its history, location, purpose and actors affect an organization and are interrelated to it and to each other:

> The space in which we live, which draws us out of ourselves, in which the erosion of our lives, our time and our history occurs, the space that claws at us, is also, in itself, a heterogeneous space. In other words, we do not live in a kind of void, inside of which we could place individuals and things. We do not live inside a void that could be coloured with diverse shades of light, we live inside a set of relations that delineates sites which are irreducible to one another and absolutely not superimposable on one another. (Foucault 1967: 3)

Fragmentation is a product of these fast changing times and can be regarded as part of the postmodern impact on organizations. Globalization, the increase in technology, the greater impact of individualism and different cultures suggest a propensity for considerable organizational pressure and micropolitical interplay. Micropolitics is found within any organization (Baldridge 1989; Ball 1987; Blase 1991; Bush 1995; Hoyle 1986, 1989), but fragmentation is given a greater dynamic through it. In using a Foucauldian view of power as active and accessible (Foucault 1986), micropolitical power can be seen as the subversive interplay between individuals, groups and cultures, used for fragmented individualized goals. In suggesting that all systems splinter to varying degrees, micropolitical behaviour gives power to fragmented groups and exposes hierarchical and centred control as reactionary and limited (Rizvi 1989).

In deconstructing international schools as organizations it is important to create a conceptual framework. By using a postmodernist lens enabling engagement with diverse views and interpretations, a school's structural belief system and culture can be exposed and challenged (Atkinson 2000, 2002). Four levels will be used here as a focus to illustrate the concept of fragmentation and to show how it pervades different levels of organizations. These come out of the extensive work of Ball (1987, 1990), Hoyle (1986, 1999) and Hargreaves (1994, 1995, 1997, 2000) in considering schools as affected both by the macro events of society and the micro events within themselves. These four different levels are:

1 Macro level (society)
2 Institutional level (organization)
3 Group level (substructure and subculture)
4 Micro level (individual and decentred subject).

It will also serve to theorize fragmentation as a phenomenon that pervades all aspects and levels of social structures and illustrate how it impacts on international schools, in terms of both their management and micropolitics.

INTERNATIONAL SCHOOLS

'The assault on professionalism is also a product of a gathering sense of uncertainty in the postmodern age' (Hargreaves 2000: 168).

Fragmentation of professional cultures through the deskilling and subjugation of professionals (Ball 2000; Gewirtz 2000) is an important part of the seizure of control being undertaken by neo-liberalism in contemporary society. This deskilling has placed educationalists in a position where they are centrally controlled and treated as deprofessionalized subjects, to be shaped and organized as tools to create products. 'Teachers, like many workers in the commercial sector, are now judged by the extent to which what they produce conforms to externally-specified standards, their efficiency in producing it and the extent of their loyalty to "the firm". Autonomy, reflectivity, creativity and fulfilment for teachers are only valued, if at all, where they are seen to contribute to productivity' (Gewirtz 2000: 362).

The supposed decline of professional control in education over the past 15 years, especially in Western countries, has meant that educationists as well as education have become fair game for control, surveillance and manipulation:

Management, effectiveness and appraisal, for example, as I have suggested, work together to locate individuals in space, in a hierarchical and efficiently visible organization ... It is thus that *governmentability* is achieved through minute mechanisms of everyday life and the application of 'progressive' and efficient technical solutions to designated problems. (Ball 2000: 1530–1 original emphasis)

Deskilling and managerialist control have caused professionals not only to lose their power base but also to fragment. Organizational cultures that are located in international settings have pressures on them from their location, the multinational and multicultural groups within and the cross-cultural underpinnings of their organization. Ferner and Quintanilla (1998) address the issue of multinational businesses where national modes create tensions within human resource management. The micropolitical problem that they highlight through the tension caused between Anglo-Saxon (i.e. American and British) and German human resource management priorities suggests domains of control, lack of communication and normalization, as well as linguistic cultural imperialism (Pennycook 1994, 1998).

One aspect of this is the emphasis of social responsibility and partnership towards employees in German firms. 'High investment in training, a characteristic feature of the German "model", also appears to be a continuing feature of German MNCs [multinational corporations] abroad despite Anglo-Saxonization' (Ferner and Quintanilla 1998: 726).

The cultural variants, which are subtle and layered in their impact, rather than generalized as indicators of national trait, are powerful factors that can pull apart multinational organizations. Strongly felt cultural views and norms, as well as the more unconscious traits that national cultures and subcultures have, impact significantly on the interrelationships in organizations that cross cultural boundaries. Dialogue between cultures is not static but shifting and dynamic. It is something that can synergize but in the same degree fragment. Synergistic and corporate views are powerful propaganda tools often used in multinational institutions that try to create hybrid pseudocultures to keep disparate groups together. It is vital to realize that this masks the dynamic of culture, one that argues for creation as much as fragmentation. International schools are conceptually difficult to define and any definitions are problematic in that they normalize the discourse. However the focus here is on the international school that is private, English-speaking and has a student body comprising foreign nationals and upwardly mobile local nationals. It would have an international, Anglo-American or Western European curriculum and its staff would be any mix of long-term, transient or local staff. 'International' is a problematic term in itself as it is open to many interpretations. For example, in investigating student and teacher perceptions Hayden, Rancic and Thompson problematize 'international' especially with regards to tolerance of others (2000: 117).

International schools exist in these powerful and complex situations, at the crossroads of cultural dialogue and globalizing forces (Cambridge 2002). They are so difficult a group to classify that it is better to see each as intrinsically different to the other, a product of situational and historical forces creating a cognitive schema (Hambrick et al. 1998) that can be vastly different from others. Some schools have similarities, yet if each were deconstructed using a sociohistorical paradigm, then minute details would reveal subtle differences that would affect totally the present face of the school. In other words, international schools cannot be regarded through some normalized formula or model of behavioural identification. Such schools are very closely affected by their location, topographically, culturally and socially. This influence pulls on the groups and individuals in differing ways depending on their time in the location, reasons for being there and background. These are very personal relationships with complex and often powerful forces, suggesting diverse reactions. The human element creates a dynamic dimension in the intrinsic being of the school, one that interplays with the cultures in and around it and its locational, sociological and historical background. This complex changing force creates an unpredictable situation. The changes evident in contemporary society and the pressures caused by economic recession, globalization and aggressive neo-liberal market place economics inject this already culturally diverse system with further potential for fragmentation. International schools are held together through positioned power centres generally for the good of the dominant force (Allan 2002). Their discourse is rarely about fragmented cultures but about collective corporate growth and almost evangelistic idealism. Is this a mask to prevent any deconstruction of the school in order to open up the reality?

CONCEPTUAL FRAMEWORK

Ball (2003) suggests that schools are middle-class domains of control concerned with economic positioning and advantage. He argues that education is access to cultural capital, thus underlying the class nature of society and the struggle for social improvement, betterment and self-interest (2003: 177). Although Ball is talking primarily about UK schools, his analysis can be applied to international schools. By employing a Foucauldian lens,

Ball highlights the use of technologies of control such as surveillance and fragmentary binaries of classification to create systems of accountability and discipline (Ball 1997, 2000). This friction of control causes conflict and resistance. Conflict is inevitable where there are diverse epistemological, economic and cultural backgrounds and it is within the power-knowledge dimension (Foucault 1977) that this conflict is often acted out. The postmodernist focus on economic positioning among individuals and groups is part of the discourse of conflict (Ball 2003).

As Hargreaves (1995, 1998) points out, schools are under considerable external pressure within contemporary society. There is not just market place control from governments and policy control from neo-liberalists, but economic constraints, social positioning and class struggles. All these come out of an increasingly complex and unstable global society. Schools are social microcosms and must absorb this kind of pressure. However, these pressures must have a cause-effect on the school and its community. With continued class struggle and control over education and other aspects of society (Ball 2000, 2003), teachers and education are caught up as pawns in a power game. The struggles in society are reflected in schools. In international schools the domain is possibly more controlled and less contested. Staff members are often transient and those who are more permanent can be reliant on the school as sole employer in a foreign environment. This gives a great deal of control to those who own and run schools. They can also have greater power-knowledge due to a closer understanding of local politics and the school's relationship to its social environment. Yet in the Foucauldian dynamic power is contested and therefore such power-knowledge is available to any connected with the school that have knowledge of local systems and choose to use it. However, the tensions that must exist between the staff, management, governors and school clientele and their goals and needs are more likely to play out in the arena of micropolitics, where power is dependent on how it is used (Ball 1987; Blase and Anderson 1995; West 1999).

Isolation and fragmentation have important links with each other. International schools are invariably isolated systems, particularly in their situation within a host country and culture. This situational or external isolation can be viewed in relation to a number of variables:

- physical location
- curriculum
- language
- clientele
- history
- organization
- structure and rules
- staff.

These isolation variables put the school at a distance from its immediate cultural sociological surroundings. Individuals and groups within the schools are also isolated in an isolating structure through further organizational or internal variables:

- experience
- background
- culture
- nationality or citizenship (for a fuller discussion of state and citizenship see Chapter 34 in this Handbook, by James Cambridge)
- institutional history
- informal group membership (such as place in expatriate and local societies)
- position in the school
- aims, goals and objectives
- educational views.

Neither of these lists is exhaustive, and each variable can be problematized and invites more detailed discussion. What each set of variables does, however, is underline both the complexity of international schools as structures and the need to look at a model that does not normalize interpretations of what they are, who populates them or how they are constructed.

Isolation creates cultural polarities, exaggerates cultural perspectives and encourages the development of new cultures and subcultures within schools. This results in positioning and exaggerated cultural differences, thus fragmenting school cultures into splinter cultures where survivalist strategies and cultural isolation deepen differences. Power groups and strong-minded individuals thrive where there is limited external monitoring and isolation. How then do isolated schools and individuals affect or cause fragmentation? Fragmentation can be pivotal in causing isolated groups and people to resort to power politics and conflict-orientated relationships in order to survive and promote their own goals. Isolated groups can also implode where their over-emphasis on a single focal point can create tension and conflict. This is caused through monocultural etic policies (Allen 2002; Ferner and Quintanilla 1998), where hierarchical control is reinforced with the creation of pseudo-cultures. These systems aim at grouping all staff and stakeholders in a corporate hegemonic vision where outcomes are controlled and normalized (Zsebik 2000). This re-identification with the modernist paradigm disregards the tensions and complex diversity within international schools and creates resistance and transformational systems. International schools fragment views so that there is no commonality, only the one forced by a normalized hierarchy through technologies of control (Foucault 1977). Zsebik, discussing loss of identity, suggests that 'international schools may also be suffering from this culture of silence, not because of an inability to read … but from an inability to decipher the conflicting messages found within the school and its adjoining community' (2000: 64).

For example, the host nation culture has a huge impact on labour laws within a school. What are the views of the management, staff, governors and other stakeholders as to the treatment of staff, and what are their own cultural, personal and experiential views and experiences regarding this? Individuals who have an understanding of host country rules will have different knowledge from, say, transient staff, management and parents. This power-knowledge (Foucault 1977, 1986) creates a dynamic where fragmentation of views, experiences and needs underpins dialogue. As Ferner and Quintanilla argue, German social-orientated management is at odds with dominant Anglo-American models, which emphasize other values:

A second Germanic trait that distinguishes German MNCs from their British or US counterparts is the strong continuing emphasis on the responsibilities of the company towards its employees ... Typically, German MNCs, even in the throes of restructuring, speak explicitly of the social 'responsibilities' towards their employees ... New tensions can be expected as Anglo-Saxonization collides with persistently German styles of implementation. (1998: 725)

Yet even Ferner and Quintanilla's focus on terms such as German and Anglo-Saxon creates fragmented groups, and underlines the modernist problems of terminology and using nationality as the main descriptor of culture.

How then can common ground be achieved? Is it through normalizing subjects and creating hybrid corporate visions? How does that work in locations where there is resistance to this? Managing multicultural groups is complex and problematic (Caffyn and Cambridge 2006; Shaw 2001).

THE FOUR LEVELS OF FRAGMENTATION

1 Macro level

Fragmentation is also evident in society and part of the postmodernist discussion of the contemporary industrial world, where social organizations are 'a multiplicity of separate, conflicting identities, all subject to conflicting pressures and constraints, and all subject to change' (Atkinson 2000: 92). It is this tension from social structures and postmodernist society that puts added pressure on an already complex organization such as the school. Postmodernism critiques the assumed understanding of contemporary systems as stable and predictable, and argues that the reality is far from certain. In fact it is insecure, complex and fast-changing, suggestive of a low-trust workplace system. 'Distrust is evident in the low-trust management styles in western societies (particularly the UK and the US). The presence of conflict and a lack of mutual loyalty and responsibility between workers and bosses are features of low-trust workplaces' (Troman 2000: 338).

This paradigm underpins the whole concept of fragmentation as a synchronous phenomenon. Fragmentation is the byproduct, the result of insecurity. It does not suggest that society breaks apart because of these pressures. In fact it will often find commonality. Yet this is more out of survivalism than any creative structural design or common purpose. Falzon (1998) suggests that fragmentation is not the end result of contemporary society and, in assessing Foucault, puts forward diametrically the theory of dialogue as a social product of postmodernism. This argument can be countered by suggesting that dialogue implies a genuine desire on each side for discussion and collaboration. However, this is a decidedly utopian view of humanity, society or organizational structures. More in keeping with insecurity is a fragmentary society that protects its own interests and localizes these with whatever alliances are deemed economic enough. Organizations like schools where many stakeholders can lay claims to control are at the very centre of this contemporary issue. It is the reverberation, the echoes of this insecure social phenomenon that impact the school. International schools, often isolated from support systems, are especially vulnerable and can feel the full force of this modern problem.

Hargreaves (1995) considers five paradoxes of postmodernism in society:

1   Divulgence of parent responsibility
2   Economic tightening
3   Rise of globalization
4   Greater diversity
5   Rise of nostalgia and fundamentalism.

These paradoxes underline the fragile and polarized nature of contemporary society, suggesting it is being pulled in differing ways, and it is this friction that can cause cracks to appear in social structures. With a definite shift away from state socialism towards a global capitalist climate, schools will have to think more like businesses to survive. Will international schools be ruled as businesses and all aspects of the organization, including human resources, be seen as commodities?

Survivalism and the politics of self-protection and group membership aspects could develop from contemporary economic climates.

An international school can be regarded as a loose grouping of fragmented cultures using education for economic advantage, all-too-often fragmented from its own location and cultural environment (Garton 2002). The tensions, particularly in achieving consensus over school philosophy and standards (Hayden and Thompson 1995, 1996), underline the deep and complex diversity within international schools and their stakeholder societies (Hayden and Thompson 2000; MacKenzie et al. 2001). Contemporary Western society encourages individualism, economic power and the rule of neo-liberalist market principles. It could be argued that international school systems mirror these. All these factors break apart social democratic structures, forcing individuals and groups to look to their own needs thus defining their boundaries with other groups. As the world becomes more global there is greater likelihood that certain aspects of society will become more withdrawn, parochial and less collaborative. In an international school setting is there a possibility of reactionary monocultural groups when individuals are distanced from their own environment and faced with cultural diversity in both the school and the local environment? In an international school there are greater possibilities for the changes of postmodernism to impact significantly. Here are numerous agencies acting to bring influence in a school. Within such a school is a huge melting pot of ideas, ideologies, experiences, frustrations, aspirations and fears.

2 Institutional level

This is where fragmentation impacts on an institution. In the modernist setting an institution such as a school is seen as a self-contained unit where there is a set purpose and few problematic issues. A postmodernism perspective would see a greater propensity for organizations to be less centred, and if they are reactionary, then it is to the many voices and claims for control. 'Hence, the representation

of all social relations as relations of exchange is the central feature of neo-liberalism. In relation to education, it has been able to effect its changes through various other new *techniques of government*' (Olssen 2003: 200). Institutions are artificial structures. Schools are held together by societal rules and ideas. However, these have been illusionary and with this macro fragmentation the problem is reflected in the organization. Are schools artificial creations of modernist society and therefore liable to the same kind of collapse as other modernist edifices?

That is not to suggest that collapse is a dramatic immediate occurrence: more that it can be gradual, limited and complex. Organizations such as schools are complex structures, best understood in qualitative terms (Stables 2003) and changes in them can be difficult to monitor. Schools will reflect the society they are located within (Rizvi, 1986), and therefore if the society is liable to fragment, so can the school. Regarding international schools, this possibility is more pronounced owing to the insecure foundations of its staff structure, its isolation and the paradoxical clientele and locational pressures. International schools, as a phenomenon, are unusual edifices in that they are usually isolated microcosms. This seclusion for staff can have powerful repercussions in terms of interrelationships and visions of reality. As Morgan (1997) suggests, people who have been in one place long term can see a distorted reality, an individual constructed prison: 'organizations are ultimately created and sustained by conscious and unconscious processes, with the notion that people can actually become imprisoned in or confined by the images, ideas, thoughts, and actions to which these processes give rise' (1997: 215). Although this has more to do with the micro level of fragmentation, it does put into focus that people see their organization in diverse, intrinsically complex and dynamic ways. An isolated structure can turn in on itself, with no local reference point and consequently the potential for fragmentary views and distortion increase. The history or genealogy of any organization is a crucial lens by which to view and reflect. Foucault suggests that to marginalize the sociohistorical perspective is to negate the reality of the organizational and social life (Foucault 1977).

3 Group level

Formal sub-structural level

Fragmentation between school divisions, year groups and departments is where school organizations break apart across formal structures. It is different from informal structures, in that its formal lines of delineation are organizational impositions, rather than personal or subcultural. It would also suggest that these are more stable, non-negotiable and fixed. Yet departments can fragment the organization depending on several concerns:

- central control
- department goals
- individual/personal goals
- communication.

The latter is particularly interesting in that it is often the interrelationships and links between such formal groups, juxtaposed to the centrality of power and corporate objectives, that determine the possibility of the interdepartmental fragmentation.

Informal subcultural level

Beyond the formal divisions within a school are the informal subcultural groupings based on such variables as culture, nationality, goals, experience, friendship, time or historical links with a school or locality, interest or even more fluid variables such as short-term goals or subcultures generated in reaction to and for single events or critical incidents. Any discussion of school culture needs to understand that culture is complex, changing and organic (Cambridge 2003; Pearce 2003). The neo-liberalist expressive view fails to acknowledge the reality of organizational culture and resistance to dominant cultures (Foucault 1986), especially in an international setting where these variables are often very pronounced.

Two theories unlock this discourse within a micropolitical paradigm: baronial politics (Ball 1987) and balkanization (Hargreaves 1994). Ball argues, using a late medieval analogy, that schools fragment into competing departments or fiefdoms, vying for scarce resources and control (Ball 1987). Micropolitical behaviour is therefore associated with gaining power and suggests active and synergistic relationships between groups and individuals. 'The structure of social relations in the school is the outcome of ongoing tensions and rivalries, conflicts and realignments which are played out in and through both formal and informal types of context' (Ball 1987: 213). Hargreaves extends this concept, transferring it to subcultures as well as departments, suggesting that contemporary society is marked by globalization and economic pressure has created an increase in isolationism and individualism in teacher cultures manifest as balkanization (Hargreaves 1995). Hargreaves (1994) sees four distinct features of balkanized institutions:

1 Low permeability: teachers usually associate with one group, and knowledge and beliefs differ between these groups.
2 High permanence: such groups are stable and have long-term group membership.
3 Personal identification: groups build from common backgrounds, such as training, education and school socialization.
4 Political complexion: through the group's subculture there is political competition and interplay for self-interest, resources, promotion and enhanced status (1994: 215). With this comes the sociopolitical dialogue of greed, of winning, of jealousy.

As Hargreaves states, 'Whether they are manifest or muted, the dynamics of power and self-interest with such cultures are major determinants of how teachers behave as a community' (1994: 215).

Such a model of the politics of group dynamics supports Ball's baronial politics theory and the importance of considering departmental groups when looking at power within an organization. Hargreaves considers this further, looking at the more informal subcultures that can occur within the school. These are not easily defined, although Hargreaves tries to suggest common features.

However, it is important to consider that each school can have distinct and indistinct subcultures and that these groups can have occasional as well as common membership. Contrived collegiality and balkanization exist particularly in isolated and rival dominated institutions (Nias 1999). 'Both individualism and balkanization fragment professional relationships, making it hard for teachers to build on one another's expertise. They also stifle the moral support necessary for risk-taking and experimentation' (Hargreaves 1995: 2). Both Hargreaves and Ball emphasize the dangers of fragmentation on departments and individual relationships. Weak or transient management systems and volatile staff situations help create balkanization and fragment professionality. A feature of postmodern and changing times, where there is increased volatility, is the fragmentation caused by deskilling, managerialism and aggressive neo-liberalist market place economics in education (Ball 2000, 2004).

4 Micro level

This is where formal and informal groups or the organization as a whole break apart. It does not suggest that this is a constant state; more, that it does occur and can affect the stability of the organization. It is worth considering a number of areas where this occurs. Variables such as these impact on individuals' complexities and interrelationships in the organization as well as the expatriate societies that are often part of the school society:

- nationality
- background
- gender
- goals
- subcultural membership
- hierarchical/position in the organization
- personal relationship to the locality
- length of time in school and locality
- behaviour and traits.

The micro level is composed of a set of variables suggesting a 'web-like' complexity where a myriad of realities and situations occur. Each school is made up of complex groups, subgroups and individuals; a whole

fragmented. Yet will fragmentation occur because economic pressures mean that ultimately people need money and therefore will work and sacrifice a lot to keep the organization together? In these complex times the impact of economic constraint could bring organizations and individuals together more out of necessity and negotiation than epistemological grounds (Allen 2002). Is it also possible that the international school is an intense inward-looking island in a cultural sea and that it is a microcosm, a self structured world with its own inner cultural diversity and laws?

How then do international schools bring a multidimensional, quasi-national and transient staff together as one? This is the essential paradox of such a school. Can it do this effectively and, if it tries, at what cost? Ultimately international schools are not collaborative organizations. They are artificial structures placed in complex environments with a diverse populace. They cannot create consensus because their human element is transient and too diverse. Although Hardman suggests models of teacher classification for purposes of recruitment and retention which are theoretically problematic, he does state that 'teachers are people as well, they have families and different needs, all of which produce a unique collaboration of factors that influence them when deciding to take up, or remain in, any one teaching position' (Hardman 2001: 134–5).

The idea of creating a school culture and meaning is at odds with international schools that are about cultures and diversity. Therefore it must be a structure that is imposed, no matter how beneficent, and this gives rise to the strong possibility of power struggles, conflict and political manoeuvring. Often cultures are controlled and mandated, a top-down hegemonic method centred on who controls. It is built on a lack of trust and on an inability to share power (Hargreaves, 1994): 'In contrived collegiality, collaboration among teachers was compulsory, not voluntary; bounded and fixed in time and space; implementation rather than development-orientated; and meant to be predictable rather than unpredictable in its outcome' (1994: 208).

CONCLUSION

How does situation affect conflict, power and the use and manifestation of micropolitics? The breaking apart of social systems in postmodernist times and cultural/goal differences within international schools influencing and causing the creation of subgroups and departmental differences, as well as the complex individual relationships based on power, political control and diverse goals, cause micropolitical fragmentation. The economic differences between teachers and clientele is a particular issue and one that can be used to unlock and illustrate the concept of fragmentation and how it relates to organizational micropolitics. These are significant when assessing the kinds of behaviours and interrelationships in international schools. How much control does the clientele have? What is the historical background to the school; in other words, whom was it created for and how has its history established any control or power system? The historical context of any school will reveal how it has achieved its present state. Within the international community in a locale what are the expatriate and local cultures that impact on the school through the clientele? What are the differences in goals and educational views between clientele, school staff, management and administration?

Although based on limited research into one case study Robertson suggests the control of international schools and staff accountability is in the interest of powerful external players with economic objectives:

> It is clear that, with this trend towards further economic globalisation and a stronger hegemony, corporate influence at international schools such as ISX will become more pervasive and the MNCs (multinational companies) may find their interests better served by accountability measures counter to the interests of teachers. (Robertson 2003: 298)

These diverse, dynamic and complex interrelationships produce friction, conflict and synergy. Yet all too often schools create corporate cultures to bring all within them to one defining set of goals. This usually stimulates more subversive resistances and counter-subcultures that become manifest through micropolitical behaviours. The differences between these economic groups are significant. Teachers can be regarded in a local society in very different ways. Likewise the expatriate cultures that exist in a certain location will view teachers and education in different ways and various variables can play a large part in this, such as economic status, reasons for being in the location and educational background. Often parents who place their children in international schools (Ball 2003) come from economically advantaged backgrounds or have access to them. Teachers are part of the system to further this and are usually at the lower end of the expatriate class system. It is this difference between clientele and school staff and how the latter is used that creates a fragmented community. It is fragmented both economically as well as on the use of education. Have teachers and schools become vehicles for economic advantage and how marginalized has international education become?

Hargreaves argues against the idea of trying to create consensus. He sees the importance of conflict and the critic as a necessary part of change. In trying to build one must acknowledge differences: 'We must recognise, however, that people cannot be given a purpose; purposes come from within' (1995: 2). In an increasingly individualized Western world, society is fragmenting as social systems become depressed and subgroups create their own exclusive support systems. How much are expatriate cultures a polarization of these individual cultures? International schools are a loose grouping of fragmented cultures using education for economic advantage. Contemporary Western society encourages individualism, economic power and the rule of neo-liberalist market principles. International school systems could be argued to mirror these. All the factors break apart social democratic structures, forcing individuals and groups to look to their own needs thus defining their boundaries with other groups more definitely. It could be that the power systems that legitimated these regimes have become more exposed and the rationality of their existence is now being questioned. Therefore it is not necessarily a development but a revealed reality of what knowledge has empirically existed throughout.

Organizations and social systems are fragmenting because what held them together, the social normalization and monocultural Western welfare state systems, has become eroded. Is it therefore not dialogue but fragmentation and the erosion of legitimation and authority that have been revealed through the lens of postmodernist organizational discourse (Falzon 1998)? All have different reasons to be in the school, different ideologies and goals. These can be the same, similar or opposed. Are we looking at a more chaotic system of school structure hidden in a hybrid and artificial entity? Whatever the situation, collaboration is a short-term goal and the models of balkanization, baronial politics and contrived collegiality are more in keeping with the reality of fragmented and economically defined international school structures.

REFERENCES

Allan, M. (2002) Cultural Borderlands: cultural dissonance in the international school. *International Schools Journal*, 21: 2.

Allen, K. (2002) Atolls, seas of culture and global nets. In M.C. Hayden, J.J. Thompson and G.R.Walker (eds) *International Education in Practice*. London: Kogan Page.

Atkinson, E. (2000) The promise of uncertainty: education, postmodernism and the politics of possibility. *International Studies in Sociology of Education*, 10:1.

Atkinson, E. (2002) The responsible anarchist: postmodernism and social change. *British Journal of Sociology of Education*, 23:1.

Baldridge, J.V. (1989) Building the political model. In T. Bush (ed.) *Managing Education: Theory and Practice*. Milton Keynes: Open University Press.

Ball, S.J. (1987) *The Micropolitics of the School*. London: Routledge.

Ball, S.J. (1990) *Politics and Policy Making in Education*. London: Routledge.

Ball, S.J. (1997) Good school, bad school: paradox and fabrication. *British Journal of Sociology of Education*, 18: 3.

Ball, S.J. (2000) Educational studies, policy entrepreneurship and social theory. In S.J. Ball (ed.) *Sociology of Education, Vol. 3: Institutions and Processes*. London: Routledge Falmer.

Ball, S.J. (2003) *Class Strategies and the Education Market: The Middle Classes and Social Advantage*. London: Routledge Falmer.

Ball, S.J. (2004) The sociology of education: a disputational account. In S.J. Ball (ed.) *The Routledge Falmer Reader in Sociology of Education*. London: Routledge Falmer.

Blase, J. (1991) The micro-political perspective. In J. Blase (ed.) *The Politics of Life in Schools*. London: Sage.

Blase, J. and Anderson, G. (1995) *The Micropolitics of Educational Leadership*. London: Cassell.

Bush, T. (1995) *Theories of Educational Management*. London: PCP.

Caffyn, R. and Cambridge, J. (2006) Critical approaches to researching cross-cultural management in international schools. *International Schools Journal*, XXV: 2.

Cambridge, J. (2002) Recruitment and development of staff: a dimension of international school organisation. In M.C. Hayden, J.J. Thompson, and G.R.Walker (eds) *International Education in Practice*. London: Kogan Page.

Cambridge, J. (2003) Identifying the globalist and internationalist missions in international schools. *International School Journal*, XX: 2.

Cambridge, J. and Thompson, J.J. (2004) Internationalism and globalisation as contexts for international education. *Compare*, 34:2.

Falzon, C. (1998) *Foucault and Social Dialogue: Beyond Fragmentation*. London: Routledge.

Ferner, A. and Quintanilla, J. (1998) Multinationals, national business systems and HRM: the enduring influence of national identity or a process of 'Anglo-Saxonisation'. *International Journal of Human Resource Management*, 9: 4.

Foucault, M. (1967) Des éspaces autres. *Architecture, Mouvement et Continuité*, October.

Foucault, M. (1977) *Discipline and Punish: The Birth of the Prison*. London: Allen Lane.

Foucault, M. (1986) Disciplinary power and subjection. In S. Lukes (ed.) *Power*. New York: New York University Press.

Garton, B. (2002) International schools and their wider community: the location factor. In M.C. Hayden, J.J. Thompson and G.R. Walker (eds) *International Education in Practice*. London: Kogan Page.

Gewirtz, S. (2000) Bringing the politics back in: a critical analysis of quality discourses in education. *British Journal of Educational Studies*, 48: 4.

Hambrick, D., Davison, C., Snell, S.A. and Snow, C.C. (1998) When groups consist of multiple nationalities: towards a new understanding of the implications. *Organisational Studies*, 19: 2.

Hardman, J. (2001) Improving recruitment and retention of quality overseas teachers. In S. Blandford and

M. Shaw (eds) *Managing International Schools.* London: Routledge Falmer.

Hargreaves, A. (1994) *Changing Times, Changing Teachers.* Toronto: OISE Press.

Hargreaves, A. (1995) Renewal in the Age of Paradox. *Educational Leadership*, 52: 7.

Hargreaves, A. (1997) Reconstructing restructuring: postmodernity and the prospects for educational change. In A.H. Halsey, H. Lauder, P. Brown and S. Wells (eds) *Education: Culture, Economy and Society.* Oxford: Oxford University Press.

Hargreaves, A. (1998) Pushing the boundaries of educational change. In A. Hargreaves et al. (eds) *International Handbook of Educational Change.* London: Kluwer.

Hargreaves, A. (2000) Four ages of professionalism and professional learning. *Teachers and Teaching: History and Practice*, 6: 2.

Hayden, M.C. and Thompson, J.J (1995) International schools and international education: a relationship reviewed. *Oxford Review of Education*, 21: 3.

Hayden, M.C. and Thompson, J.J (1996) Potential difference: the driving force for international education. *International Schools Journal*, 16: 1.

Hayden, M.C. and Thompson, J.J. (2000) International education: flying flags or raising standards? *International Schools Journal*, 19: 2.

Hayden, M.C., Rancic, B.A. and Thompson, J.J. (2000) Being international: student and teacher perceptions from international schools. *Oxford Review of Education*, 26: 1.

Hoyle, E. (1986) *The Politics of School Management.* London: Hodder and Stoughton.

Hoyle, E. (1989) The micropolitics of schools. In T. Bush (ed.) *Managing Education: Theory and Practice.* Milton Keynes: Open University Press.

Hoyle, E. (1999) The two faces of micropolitics. *School Leadership and Management*, 19: 2.

MacKenzie, P., Hayden, M.C. and Thompson, J.J. (2001) The Third Constituency: parents in international schools. *International Schools Journal*, 20: 2.

Morgan, G. (1997) *Images of Organization.* London: Sage.

Nias, J. (1999) Primary teaching as a culture of care. In J. Prosser (ed.) *School Culture.* London: PCP.

Olssen, M. (2003) Structuralism, post-structuralism, neo-liberalism: assessing Foucault's legacy. *Journal of Education Policy*, 18: 2.

Pearce, R. (2003) Cultural values for international schools. *International Schools Journal*, 22: 2.

Pennycook, A. (1994) *The Cultural Politics of English as an International Language.* Harlow: Pearson Education.

Pennycook, A. (1998) *English and the Discourses of Colonialism.* London: Routledge.

Rizvi, F. (1986) *Administrative Leadership and the Democratic Community as a Social Ideal.* Burwood: Deakin University Press.

Rizvi, F. (1989) In defense of organisational democracy. In J. Smith (ed.) *Critical Perspectives on Educational Leadership.* London: Falmer.

Robertson, J.E. (2003) Teachers' perceptions of accountability at an international school. *Journal of Research in International Education*, 2: 3.

Shaw, M. (2001) Managing mixed-culture teams in international schools. In S. Blandford and M. Shaw (eds) *Managing International Schools.* London: Routledge Falmer.

Stables, A. (2003) Schools as imagined community in discursive space: a perspective on the school effectiveness debate. *British Educational Research Journal*, 29: 6.

Troman, G. (2000) Teacher stress in the low-trust society. *British Journal of Sociology of Education*, 21: 3.

West, M. (1999) Micropolitics, leadership and all that: the need to increase the micro-political awareness and skills of school leaders. *School Leadership and Management*, 19: 2.

Zsebik, P. (2000) The politics of international education. In M.C. Hayden and J.J. Thompson (eds) *International Schools and International Education.* London: Kogan Page.

29

Leadership and Redefining the Three Rs

William Powell

By what criteria should schools be evaluated? Politicians are increasingly looking towards standardized test scores, the so-called objective data. Parents use anecdotal evidence about the school's reputation or its track record in university admissions. Accreditation agencies establish a more comprehensive array of success indicators. Yet one of the most startling and predictive barometers of school quality is contained in Roland Barth's (1990) classic work *Improving Schools from Within*. Barth suggests that the quality of a school is often reflected with remarkable precision in the quality of the adult-to-adult relationships within the school house. He observes that the manner in which adults speak to each other, share ideas, form work partnerships and even manage conflicts is often a profoundly accurate predictor of the quality of learning within the classroom.

But what have adult-to-adult relationships to do with student learning? For the past four decades, school people have been exhorted to be 'child-centred'. What has happened to the child in Barth's barometer? Western

educational research is finding 'the child' in the vital connections between high quality adult relationships and high quality student learning (Bryk and Schneider 2002; Garmston and Wellman 1999; Seashore Louis et al. 1996). We have known this intuitively for some time. But what is it specifically that links quality adult relationships to student learning? Both the 'hard' data and the increasingly important 'soft' data that are emerging from schools suggest that principals, department chairs and grade-level coordinators can and do have a powerful influence on school climate and that this influence nourishes powerful learning relationships and reflective craft practice (Deal and Peterson 1999; Lightfoot 1983; Marzano et al. 2005). It is within these learning relationships and reflective practice that we will find the seeds of school renaissance.

One of the limitations of this chapter is that most of the research and examples cited come from Western sources or international schools that have their philosophical roots in the American or British educational traditions.

However, there is growing evidence that the movement towards reflective professional practice and the emphasis on developing high quality adult-to-adult relationships are not limited to simply Western-style schools. In discussions with the senior leadership at the Aga Khan Educational Foundation in Paris several years ago, I became aware that one of the central planks in their forward-looking strategic plan for their schools in Africa and Central Asia was the nurturing of a culture of reflective practice. In similar conversations with the Ministry of Education in Malaysia, it has also become evident that there is an increasing awareness of the critical relationship between professional reflection and improved student learning. Perhaps more than any other non-Western country, Singapore has recognized the link between reflection and creative/critical thinking. Later in this chapter, I will focus on some of the issues that non-Western educational traditions face when they attempt to embrace cultures of reflective practice.

LEADERSHIP, BRAMBLES AND BORDER COLLIES

The search for a metaphor for school leadership followed me to the foothills of the French Pyrenees, where a number of years ago my wife and I purchased a tumble-down farmhouse surrounded by acres of alpine meadowland. Amid my ruminations on school climate and leadership, I was forced to enter in to the annual battle with the blackberry brambles. According to local sources, the European bramble is one of the fastest growing entities in the world. It was been clocked at an incredible eleven inches in a 24 hour period! And so when we return to the Pyrenees each summer our once bucolic meadows are hideously overgrown in a jungle maze of tenacious brambles, and our rustic farmhouse resembles the castle Prince Charming discovers on his quest for Sleeping Beauty. All this explains why I became a shepherd. I invested in a small flock of sheep – four to be exact. I had been reliably told that sheep would eat the spring bramble

shoots and so keep the meadows open. So with a vanguard of four ravenous sheep, I launched my pre-emptive strike against the brambles. It was not, however, the sheep that provided the germ of a school leadership metaphor. It was instead the mid-summer televised European sheep dog trials.

If you have never seen a sheep dog trial, a brief word of introduction is in order. These are timed competitions, which pit sheep farmers and their incredibly well-trained dogs against each other in the speed and efficiency with which they can move and organize a flock of sheep. The trials begin with a farmer standing on a wooden platform at one end of a huge field. The field is surrounded by spectators. On the field a hundred or so sheep are scattered. These are sheep that neither shepherd nor dog has seen before. The shepherd then calls out a series of commands to his border collie. The dog proceeds to dash off to round up the flock, and then herd the hundred or so sheep from one end of the field to a relatively small circle marked on the grass at the other end. Once the sheep are within the circle, the sheep farmer calls out another specific instruction to the collie. The dog then locates one of the sheep that has been distinctively marked, cuts that sheep out of the flock, keeping the rest within the circle, and brings the individual sheep to his master's feet. To say I was impressed would be an understatement.

During this same time, I was co-authoring a new graduate-level course entitled 'The Effective Principal: From Theory to Practice'. I was asking myself a series of probing questions about the role of the school principal. What was the ultimate purpose of school leadership? Can that purpose be achieved simply by way of mastery of a collection of capacities and the practice of an assortment of strategies? A good deal of research seemed to point in the direction of a checklist of leadership capacities. Was school leadership simply the acquisition of a toolbox of skills – a paint-by-number, mix-and-match of situations and appropriate responses? I asked myself if the truly dynamic school leaders that I have worked with had shared common attributes. And amid these musings ran flocks of sheep, skilfully chased by energetic border collies. Finally, a troubling question burst in upon my planning. If educational leadership could be reduced to a checklist of behavioural strategies, was it not analogous to the movement of sheep from one field to another?

I found the question troubling because at least some of the research I had been reading seemed to tacitly adopt this 'toolbox' model. The more I thought about it, the more distressing the question became. A principal assigns children and teachers to classes, organizes a master schedule of classes, arranges for the inventory of teaching supplies and sets attainable curricular targets. Within the classroom, the teacher sets behavioural expectations, determines learning objectives, budgets instructional time and then takes his or her students through the stages of expanding literacy and numeracy. These are necessary tasks. There is nothing inherently wrong with management and organization. Why was the shepherd analogy troubling? Going all the way back to biblical times, the conscientious shepherd has a long and noble history as a diligent and caring figure. The answer is that the metaphor is hollow and superficial because it does not address the purpose of leadership. Drawing on the work of Linda Lambert (1998), Richard Elmore (2000), James Spillane (Spillane and Sherer, 2004; Spillane et al. 2001, 2003) and others, I would like to suggest that the ultimate purpose of school leadership, whether it is practised by principals, team leaders or teachers, is to build leadership capacity in others. It is building leadership capacity in others that changes the hearts and minds of all who inhabit the school house. When sheep are moved from one field to another they remain intrinsically unchanged. In some schools the same is true for students. As young people are taken (in an orderly and efficient fashion) from the meadows of Ancient Civilizations to the fields of the Renaissance, from the pastures of Dickens and the Brontë sisters to the plains of Hemingway and Fitzgerald, these students too may remain unchanged. The fields may change, but like

skillfully herded sheep, the students remain largely unaltered by the experience. Unconnected and irrelevant information has been poured into young vessels, but the vessel itself is in much the same shape as it was before the so-called learning experience. This is both the tragedy and travesty of education.

When the purpose of leadership is to build leadership capacity in others, school people are actually transformed by the experience of working and learning together. Our hearts and minds are affected. We are not the same creatures that once grazed on the other side of the fence. When we build leadership capacity in others we create the school climate where learning relationships can flourish. The transformation of school climate that accompanies the pervasive development of leadership capacity in others provides a compelling vision of what Arthur Koestler referred to as the journey towards 'holonomy'.

HOLONOMY AND FIVE STATES OF MIND

Koestler (1972) coined the term 'holonomy' to refer to the balance between individual autonomy (self-direction and self-fulfillment) and the integration of the individual into the purpose, vision and work of a community. The movement towards holonomy, like the movement towards building leadership capacity in others, involves the resolution of seemingly opposing forces: the personal desire for power, authority and autonomy and our profound psychological and spiritual need for ego-integration (Erikson 1977) and a sense of belonging to something larger and more significant than self. Costa and Garmston (2002) suggest that there are five states of mind that, when cultivated by the individual or by an organization (Garmston and Wellman 1999), can serve as pathways to holonomy: efficacy, flexibility, consciousness, craftsmanship and interdependence. These states of mind are also, not surprisingly, pathways to building leadership capacity in others.

Efficacy

In the 1980s a landmark study by the Rand Corporation (Costa and Garmston 2002) identified teacher efficacy as the single most important variable in affecting successful school change. Neither the curriculum nor the instructional methodology mattered nearly as much as the teachers' belief in themselves. Efficacy is that 'can do' attitude that reflects personal empowerment. It is predicated on an internal locus of responsibility: the belief that I can personally make a difference. It is the hallmark of optimism and hope. In the process of building leadership capacity in others, there is arguably nothing more important than engendering efficacy in both colleagues and students.

Flexibility

Flexibility is the ability to perceive situations from multiple perspectives. It is both the capacity for empathy and the ability to disengage and take the 'balcony' view. Recent work in differentiated instruction (Kusuma-Powell and Powell, in preparation; Tomlinson and Allan 2000) is pointing to a strong correlation between effective instruction and the ability that teachers have to come to know their students as learners. When we write about 'knowing our students' we are not referring to simply superficial social knowledge: family background, friendship groups or outside interests. Of course, such information is important. However, the deep knowledge that we are referring to involves the arduous work of coming to know students' learning profiles, their intelligence preferences, their readiness for specific challenges, their cultural backgrounds and the wiles and whims of their often mercurial emotional landscapes. Flexibility of thought and perception promotes deep knowledge of others.

Consciousness

In addition to knowing our students, research (Goleman et al. 2002; Kusuma-Powell and Powell, in preparation) also suggests that a prime component of effective leadership and teaching comes from penetrating self-knowledge. Consciousness, as defined by Costa and Garmston (2002), is awareness of self and others. This involves being aware of how we select and construct our perceptions, being cognizant of the personal and cultural baggage we carry into situations, explicitly exploring how congruent our values and our behaviors are and 'mining' our experiential insights.

Craftsmanship

As leaders and learners, one of our explicit professional responsibilities is to nurture craftsmanship in self and others. Craftsmanship can be seen in the classroom as the execution of a masterful unit plan of learning. It can be seen in the larger organization in the implementation of a targeted programme of professional development. Craftsmanship is both a goal and an energy source. It comes centre stage when we seek to improve our pedagogical craft as teachers or when we assist a middle school student to improve his or her expository writing skills.

Interdependence

Interdependence is the state of mind most directly allied to holonomy. It is the process through which we cultivate in ourselves and others the confluence of individual autonomy and the constructive growth of a learning community. It is the subtle and yet critically important work of building learning relationships that simultaneously celebrates the work of the individual and the connectedness we have to common purpose.

Our conscious attention to these states of mind provides the conditions necessary for developing leadership capacity in others. There is a significant paradigm shift in accepting that the purpose of educational leadership is to develop leadership capacity in others. Leadership ceases to be a noun and becomes a verb (Lambert 1998). Leadership in schools ceases to be the exclusive and exulted position of the few and becomes a basic human right. Everyone has the potential and the right to work as a leader (1998). The psychological and emotional shift from traditional perceptions of leadership is nothing less than quantum. Leadership is no longer a personality trait. Leaders and leadership are not synonymous. Leadership becomes the communal process of learning that leads to constructive change. This shift has the potential to transform schools and the people who inhabit them. As we explore the shift in leadership, we need to unlearn some of our traditional and perhaps even unconscious perceptions about power and authority. We need to rethink the nature of our professional relationships and our various roles within the school house. What does it really mean to be a principal? To be a teacher? What are the responsibilities involved in being a good colleague? What are our shared purposes? What does trust look like when it comes to permeate the culture and climate of a school? In short, we need to re-examine the congruence between our habitual perceptions and our deeply held values.

LEARNING RELATIONSHIPS AND LEADERSHIP CAPACITY

In a seminar hosted by the Academy of International School Heads (AISH), Michael Fullan began a provocative workshop by stating that 'any school improvement initiative that does not also improve relationships is bound to be ineffective'. Increasingly, Western educational research is revealing the vital connections between high quality adult relationships and high quality student learning (Bryk and Schneider 2002; Garmston and Wellman 1999; Seashore Louis et al. 1996). By high quality adult-to-adult relationships, Roland Barth is not writing about mere civility, passive cooperation or conviviality. In fact, Garmston and Wellman (1999) see conviviality as a potential hindrance to the development of thoughtful and reflective work groups. Barth is referring to adult learning relationships that reflect hard-earned collegiality and produce thoughtful, reflective and highly productive teams. In education we have known intuitively about the connection between high quality adult relationships and accelerated student learning for some time, and many international schools have actually written mission and philosophy statements that enshrine the importance of 'team work', 'collaboration' or 'collegiality'.

Even in the hard-nosed, unsentimental world of business, a recent barrage of leadership books is touting the power of quality professional relationships. Lewin and Regine (2000), authors of *The Soul at Work*, relate the commercial world to the new science of complexity theory. According to the authors, we are no longer living in the linear world that produced Henry Ford assembly lines and time and motion efficiency experts. In the old Newtonian world, things and people may exist independent of each other, and when they do interact they do so in simple, predictable ways. However, in a post-Newtonian, non-linear, dynamic world – such as the one we are increasingly seeing ourselves as heirs to – everything exists only in relationship to everything else. And these interactions often lead to complex and unpredictable outcomes (Garmston and Wellman 1995; Wheatley 1992). Anyone who has worked in a school will be familiar with the attributes of a post-Newtonian existence. In this brave new world, relationships are the prime organizing principle.

Education has known about the importance of relationships for a long time. Even in the first quarter of the twentieth century, the great Russian cognitive psychologist Lev Vygotsky was writing about how learning occurs in a social context (1986). Teachers and students have known intuitively for years that constructive relationships within the classroom are an essential condition for learning (see, for example, Chapter 20 by den Brok and Koopman in this Handbook for a review of research on teacher–student relationships). When we think back on a particularly influential teacher from our own past experience, we tend to focus on the power of that learning relationship rather than the content that was mastered. Michael Fullan (2001) identifies five characteristics of effective leadership for school change, one of which is strong relationships. Lashway (2001) further links the development of learning relationships to the school improvement process. He writes that 'deep changes require deep learning, and leaders must build teacher learning into the everyday fabric of school life' (p. 7). Fullan characterizes learning relationships as 'knowledge building, knowledge sharing, knowledge creation and knowledge management' (p. 77).

Marzano et al. (2005), in their meta-analysis of leadership research, identify 11 factors that contribute to schools focusing on doing what he refers to as the 'right work'. One of these factors is Collegiality and Professionalism. He cites research by Brookover et al. (1978) that attests to the connection between learning relationships and school climate. 'We believe that the differences in school climate explain much of the difference in academic achievement between schools that is normally attributed to composition' (p. 303). Marzano et al. go on to write:

> In operation, collegiality and professionalism are a function of implicit or explicit norms of behavior among staff members. These norms serve to create relationships that are professional in nature while being cordial and friendly. This factor also includes structures that allow teachers to be an integral aspect of the important decisions in a school. Finally, this factor involves professional development that is focused, skill-oriented, and cohesive from session to session and year to year. (p. 89)

There is, however, an undeniable social and emotional dimension to learning relationships. Whenever we talk to principals and teachers about learning relationships we hear the words and phrases 'trust', 'risk-taking' and 'respect'. Learning relationships rarely happen spontaneously or naturally. They are not the result of some mystical interpersonal 'chemistry'. On the contrary, such relationships are painstakingly constructed by leaders, ascribed and emergent, who strive to build leadership capacity in others through humility, active listening, mediating the deep thinking of colleagues and viewing others as trusted resources in a common endeavour. Collins (2005), in his description of Level Five Leadership, the leadership that permeates the transition of good companies to great organizations, identifies the companion attributes of Level Five Leaders as humility and intense personal will.

What is it then that truly distinguishes learning relationships from other social relationships and what is it that makes these learning relationships the cornerstone of high quality schools?

REFLECTION AND SCHOOL CLIMATE

In a single phrase, I would like to suggest that the single most distinguishing characteristic of learning relationships is professional reflection. From Socrates to Solzhenitsyn, writers and philosophers have bemoaned humankind's inability to learn from raw experience. History, we are told, repeats itself because we are congenitally unable to learn from experience. We can, however, learn from *reflection on experience*. This is also true when it comes to our craft knowledge as teachers and as school leaders. We learn not from our experience in the classroom, but from our reflection on our teaching and student learning. One year's reflection is immensely more valuable than 20 years' experience. So relationships in and of themselves are not enough. Strong teacher communities can be effective or not, depending on whether teachers make breakthroughs in learning or whether they reinforce methods that do not achieve results. Fullan (2001) makes the distinction that:

> weak collaboration is always ineffective, but strong teaching communities can make things worse if, in their collaboration, teachers (however unwittingly) reinforce each other's bad or ineffective practices. This is why close relationships are not ends in themselves. Collaborative cultures, which by definition have close relationships, are indeed powerful, but unless they are focusing on the right things, they may end up being powerfully wrong. (p. 67)

Several years ago, I co-presented a weekend workshop on differentiated instruction at a large international school. Within minutes of the opening of the workshop, both presenters sensed resistance from some of the participants. Their verbal and non-verbal behaviour suggested a degree of apathy, passive resistance and in some cases overt irritation. During the first coffee break, we set out to learn more about the attitudes and dispositions that the participants had brought with them to the workshop. The first thing we learned was that the administration had declared that attendance at the Saturday and Sunday workshop would be mandatory (something the presenters had not been informed about in advance). 'We need to create', the principal informed me, 'more of a culture of professional development.' This edict had understandably had the opposite effect and had engendered no small degree of resentment. However, more interesting in terms of our exploration of professional relationships and reflection were the participants' perceptions of their school. During the weekend we heard many comments that this school was one of the finest, if not *the* finest, international school in the world. It had outstanding public examination results, highly selective admissions and exemplary university admissions. Many of the participants saw no earthly need for differentiated instruction or, for that matter, professional development. We also heard repeatedly that the school had an amazingly talented teaching staff. So far so good. But as we listened to teachers talk about their school, we also heard about a school climate that was characterized by a high degree of aggressive interpersonal and interdepartmental competition. We heard that rumour and gossip were rife, new ideas and innovations were routinely dismissed and that public ridicule was a common feature of faculty meetings. We heard that risk-taking was almost non-existent, professional development was widely scorned and that teacher turnover among younger teachers was particularly high. In the words of one teacher: 'It is a close knit teaching staff that has managed to petrify the status quo and fossilize our collective intellect.'

Fullan's words (2001) return to us: 'Collaborative cultures … are indeed powerful, but unless they are focused on the right things they may end up being powerfully wrong' (p. 67). What helps teaching faculties focus on the 'right things' is the act of reflection. While it is certainly possible to engage in solitary professional reflection (for example, keeping a professional journal), we have found that when teaching partners, groups, grade-level teams or departments engage in reflection as a collective activity the results are often extraordinarily beneficial and enriching (Langer and Colton 2005; Powell and Napoliello 2005). The fertile exchange of collegial reflection often produces powerful insights and 'ah hah!' moments that can serve as potent influences on instructional improvement. Most of the teachers that we have encountered agree that not enough time is spent on professional reflection. Kaagan and Markle (1993) write:

> Discussing educational issues is something that the diverse actors in the education drama rarely get to do. Merely providing time and resources to support team development around these issues seems to have a marked pay off. By making overtly collective and open reflections that up to now have remained singular and closed, there emerges a strong will and capacity to innovate. (p.11)

In this fast-paced, frenetic world of ours, reflection is almost a counter-intuitive activity. However, there is strong evidence – even from the business world – that 'Slow Knowing' (Claxton 1997) may actually help us distinguish between fashionable but shallow ideas that promise more than they can deliver and initiatives that are more worthy of our time and energy. The word reflection conjures up different connotations for different people and at least some of these associations may be obstacles to practice. Reflection for some teachers connotes a formal process that they may feel they lack the skills to engage in. For others it presents a time-consuming activity that detracts from their 'real' work. For yet others there are quasi-mystical associations that render images of sitting in silence in a moonlit garden in a painful yoga-like posture.

The most frequent question that emerges in conversations with teachers and school leaders about professional reflection is 'Where does the time come from?' With increasing work demands, pressures from a variety of external sources, including demanding parents and results-oriented boards of directors, teachers are despairing of having yet another professional expectation added to their already overflowing plates. If reflection were another such curricular add-on, we might agree. However, reflective practice is not something extra, a nicety to be entertained when the urgencies of our daily duties are complete. Reflection represents the critical difference between moving sheep from one meadow to another and creating a truly transformational school climate. Time is not the issue, priority and leadership expectations are. Reflection is, however, often correctly associated with the discomfort that many of us feel when we are confronted with ambiguity and cognitive dissonance. The British poet John Keats wrote in a letter to his brother about 'negative capability' – by this he meant cultivating the capacity to wait, to remain attentive even in the face of incomprehension. Keats penned the letter just after he had spent an evening with a friend who 'could not feel he had a personal identity unless he had made up his mind about everything'. As Fullan (2001) points out, this attentive waiting in the face of incomprehension requires a degree of inner security, the 'confidence that one may lose clarity and control without losing one's self' (p. 123).

There are three compelling reasons why schools should embed reflection in the fabric of their school climate and culture. First of all, the example of such collective professional reflection sets an explicit norm that within *this* school all adults are learners and that we have much to learn from each other. Within this simple statement lies profound humility and the foundations of mutual respect. Colleagues are perceived as valued educational resources. Second, when teachers and principals engage in reflective practice their knowledge of both their craft and student learning increases dramatically (Langer and Colton 2005). For example, we know that effective differentiated instruction is predicated upon the teacher having a deep knowledge of his or her students as learners and a profound knowledge of the curriculum to be taught. While some teachers may be able to achieve this level of understanding in solitude, most of us benefit enormously from the support, perspective and feedback of our colleagues. Third, collective professional reflection supports a climate of trust and shared accountability. When we share our experiences in the classroom, our triumphs and

our failures, we place in public view fragile pieces of ourselves. We take a risk and fulfill one of the little written-about expectations of our profession – courage. Too often lack of a trusting environment is cited as a reason for the absence of reflection. If we are honest with ourselves, the culprit is not the absence of trust but the absence of courage.

When we reflect with colleagues on our professional experiences, we come to share both goals and responsibility. We cease to be solitary shepherds. We begin to take professional accountability back to where it rightly belongs – away from the politicians and media – and placed in the hands of responsible and responsive classroom practitioners. In this complicated time of multiple and often conflicting demands on our profession, the implication of learning relationships and collective reflection is clear: *no teacher or principal needs to go it alone.* Collegial support and encouragement are crucial when one is engaged in the risky business of professional improvement.

REFLECTION AND COLLABORATION IN NON-WESTERN SCHOOLS

From my work with teachers coming from non-Western cultural traditions, it is evident to me that the customary hierarchical structures of the local communities may have a profound impact on the adult-to-adult relationships within schools and may serve as barriers to creating what we in the West have come to think of as 'professional learning communities'. Marilyn Friend and Lynne Cook (2003) defined collaboration as responsibility and accountability that are shared between 'co-equal' work partners irrespective of their assigned and ascribed roles. This Western egalitarianism may at times be at odds with non-Western cultural traditions. This 'clash of cultures' is not limited to the world of education and was vividly illustrated in articles in the *Asian Wall Street Journal* (Ingersoll 1999) and on the BBC (Woods 1999) that focused on the poor safety record of Korean Airlines. The articles concluded that one of the reasons for this poor safety record was the fact that while the cockpits of the Korean Airline planes (built by the Western aeronautical firm Boeing) were designed for Western-style crew collaboration, the pilots, co-pilots and other crew members were predominantly recruited from the Korean military and brought with them a hierarchical and authoritarian culture which precluded, for example, the navigator questioning the judgement of the pilot. The cockpit architecture was literally in opposition to the crew culture.

In some cases, relatively recent historical events can have a profound influence on the adult-to-adult relationships within an organization. A school administrator in China commented to me that all of his efforts to get his Chinese staff members to form effective work teams had been frustrated. He simply was unable to get them collectively to share accountability. He attributed at least part of the reluctance of the Chinese staff to share responsibility to the legacy of fear generated by the Cultural Revolution. Non-Western educators frequently comment on how the perceived 'professional egalitarianism' of the West may be seen as disrespectful by non-Western teachers and administrators. In Asia, the strength of the Confucian tradition with its emphasis on familial piety and age-graded hierarchical respect can have the effect of impeding collective reflection and organizational creativity. Singapore, in particular, has recognized this phenomenon and has launched a number of initiatives to confront it. Brown and Isaacs (2005) in their book, *The World Café: Shaping Our Futures through Conversations that Matter,* write about large-scale café-style conversations organized by the Singapore government in order to foster reflection and creative thinking. The Singapore Ministry of Defense hosted a café-style conversation to explore the question: 'How can we expand our purpose from deterrence to nation building?' In another such café-style conversation scores of Singaporean teachers were invited to reflect on the question: 'Given the changing needs of our country, what does it mean to teach?' In yet another case, a large group of Singaporean police officers were brought together in a café conversation and asked to reflect on: 'What does it mean to care? (p. 200).

The research of Richard Nisbett (2003) suggests that students and teachers coming out of an Asian tradition may actually think differently to their Western counterparts. He writes that Asian traditions of thought make Chinese and Korean students generally more sensitive to background circumstances, more likely to see shades of grey, and perhaps even more tolerant of ambiguity than their Western peers. Asian students and their teachers are less likely to be driven by strict linear logic and more likely to seek the 'middle ground'. Given this sensitivity to context and relationships, it may well be that a non-Western professional learning community will appear quite different from its Western counterpart. This may be a fruitful area for further research.

RENAISSANCE: THE WAY FORWARD

This brings me to the third 'R': renaissance. I draw much of my thoughts about renaissance schools from the work of Arthur Costa and Robert Garmston. In their remarkably insightful book *Cognitive Coaching: A Foundation for Renaissance Schools* (2002), they write about the principles that guide renaissance work in schools. The three most frequently asked questions in renaissance schools are deceptively simple and yet provocatively reflective: 'Who are we? Why are we doing this? And, why are we doing it this way?' (p. 360). These simple questions compel us to explore our professional identity, our personal and collective mission, our values and, perhaps most uncomfortable of all, how effective we are as educators and leaders. In a renaissance environment we build leadership capacity in others by framing these questions in the context of clear norms and values, frequent reflective dialogue about instructional practice, professional collaboration and shared responsibility for student learning. In the words of Garmston and Powell (2006), we no longer hear teachers talking about 'your' students and 'my' students. We hear colleagues discussing 'our' students. In a renaissance school the vast majority of norms are voluntary. Because the norms and values are clear and the locus of responsibility is internal, there is no need for a great many externally imposed rules and regulations to control behaviour. Renaissance schools have the twin goals of developing the individual and developing the organization. These are schools that are on the road to becoming holonomous. Leadership is distributed. Colleagues are strong role models for one another; they coach and consult.

This chapter opened with the troubling metaphor of the shepherd and his dog herding sheep. I will close it with a different metaphor, hopefully more apt to the work of leadership in schools. There is always a risk in employing a biblical metaphor – the possibility of offending believers or alienating non-believers. But in some respects, this chapter is all about taking risks, so here goes ... the metaphor comes from the Gospel of Matthew. As some readers may recall, when Jesus learned of the beheading of John the Baptist he withdrew in grief to a lonely place by the side of a large lake. But his fame preceded him, and a large crowd gathered on the shores of the lake. They wanted Jesus to heal their sick. They wanted to hear him preach. When evening came, Jesus noticed that the multitude had become tired and hungry, and he instructed his disciples to take the meagre five loaves of bread and two fish offered by one small boy and divide them amongst the five thousand. The disciples were understandably incredulous. How could five loaves and two small fish possibly feed such a large crowd? However, in the act of sharing, the loaves and fish miraculously multiplied and the great crowd ate and they were satisfied.

So I believe we can foster a similar miracle in our schools. Leadership is not a finite substance that needs to be guarded and controlled. Too many cooks do not spoil the broth. Leadership is not something to be rationed to the select few. When we develop leadership capacity in others, like the loaves and fish in the biblical story, there is always enough to go around. When we think of leading as a genuinely shared endeavour, we transcend power and authority relationships, territoriality, the need to control and our temptation towards scarcity mentality. When we perceive that the purpose of leadership is to develop it in others, there is neither shortage nor abundance. There is process, an energy source, a shared goal. In short, we are able to redefine the traditional foundations of schooling – the three Rs – and we create renaissance school climates in which learning relationships and reflective practice prosper and flourish.

REFERENCES

Barth, R. (1990) *Improving Schools from Within*. San Francisco, CA: Jossey–Bass.

Brookover, W.B., Schweitzer, J.G., Schneider, J.M., Beady, C.H., Flood, P.K. and Wisenbaker, J.M. (1978) Elementary school climate and school achievement. *American Educational Research Journal*, 15: 301–18.

Brookover, W.B., Beady, C., Flood, P., Schweitzer, J. and Wisenbaker, J. (1979) *School Social Systems and Student Achievement: Schools Can Make a Difference*. New York: Praeger.

Brown, J. and Isaacs, D. (2005) *The World Café: Shaping Our Futures through Conversations that Matter*. San Francisco, CA: Berrett–Koehler.

Bryk, M. and Schneider, B. (2002) *Trust in Schools: A Core Resource for Improvement*. New York: The Russell Sage Foundation.

Claxton, G. (1997) *Hare Brain, Tortoise Mind*. London: Fourth Estate.

Collins, J. (2005) Level five leadership: the triumph of humility and fierce resolve, *Harvard Business Review*, 83 (7/8): 136–46.

Costa, A. and Garmston, R. (2002) *Cognitive Coaching: A Foundation for Renaissance Schools*. Norwood, MA: Christopher Gordon.

Deal, T. and Peterson, K.D. (1999) *Shaping School Culture: The Heart of Leadership*. San Francisco, CA: Jossey–Bass.

Elmore, R.F. (2000) *Building a New Structure for School Leadership*. New York: Albert Shanker Institute.

Erikson, E. (1977) *Childhood and Society*. London: Paladin Books, Collins Publishing Group.

Friend, M. and Cook, L. (2003) *Interactions: Collaboration Skills for School Professionals*. Needham, MA: Allyn and Bacon.

Fullan, M. (2001) *Leading in a Culture of Change*, San Francisco, CA: Jossey–Bass.

Garmston, R. and Powell, W. (2006) Making reflection a cornerstone of school culture. *NESA News*, 8 (2): 6–8.

Garmston, R. and Wellman, B. (1995) Adaptive schools in a quantum universe. *Educational Leadership,* 52 (7): 6–12.

Garmston, R. and Wellman, B. (1999) *The Adaptive School: A Sourcebook for Developing Collaborative Groups.* Norwood, MA: Christopher-Gordon.

Goleman, D., Boyatzis, R. and McKee, A. (2002) *Primal Leadership: Realizing the Power of Emotional Intelligence.* Boston, MA: Harvard Business School Press.

Ingersoll, B. (1999) Pilot error is cited in Korea air crash. *Asian Wall Street Journal,* 3 November.

Kaagan, S.S. and Markle, B.W. (1993) Leaderdship for learning. *Perspective,* 5 (1): 1–16.

Koestler, A. (1972) *The Roots of Coincidence.* New York: Vintage Press.

Kusuma-Powell, O. and Powell, W. (in preparation) *Making a Difference: Differentiated Instruction in International Schools.* A/OS, US Department of State, Washington, DC.

Lambert, L. (1998) *Building Leadership Capacity in Schools.* Alexandria, VA: Association for Supervision and Curriculum Development.

Langer, G. and Colton, A. (2005) Looking at student work. *Educational Leadership,* February (Association for Curriculum Development and Supervision).

Lashway, L. (2001) Leadership for accountability. *Research Roundup,* 17 (3): 1–14 (Clearinghouse on Education Policy and Management).

Lightfoot, S.L. (1983) *The Good High School: Portraits of Character and Culture.* New York: Basic Books.

Lewin, R. and Regine, B. (2000) *The Soul at Work.* New York: Simon and Schuster.

Marzano, R. Waters, T. and McNulty, B. (2005) *Leadership that Works.* Alexandria, VA: Association for Curriculum Development and Supervision.

Nisbett, R.E. (2003) *The Geography of Thought: How Asians and Westerners Think Differently – and Why.* London: Nicholas Brealey Publishing.

Powell, W. and Napoliello, S. (2005) Using observation to improve instruction. *Educational Leadership,* February, 52–5. (Association for Curriculum Development and Supervision).

Seashore Louis, K., Marks, H. and Kruse, S. (1996) Teacher's professional community and restructuring schools. *American Educational Research Journal.*

Spillane, J.P. and Sherer, J.Z. (2004) *A Distributed Perspective on School Leadership: Leadership Practices as Stretched over People and Place.* The Distributed Leadership Study: Northwestern University.

Spillane, J.P., Halverson, R. and Diamond, J.B. (2001) Investigating school leadership practice: a distributed perspective. *Educational Researcher,* 30 (3): 23–8.

Spillane, J.P., Halverson, R. and Diamond, J.B. (2003) *Distributed Leadership: Towards a Theory of School Leadership Practice.* The Distributed Leadership Study: Northwestern University.

Tomlinson, C. and Allan, S. (2000) *Leadership for Differentiating Schools and Classrooms.* Alexandria, VA: Association for Supervision and Curriculum Development.

Vygotsky, L. (1986) *Thought and Language* (ed. A. Kozulin). Cambridge, MA: The MIT Press.

Wheatley, M. (1992). *Leadership and the New Science.* San Francisco, CA: Berrett–Koehler.

Wood, A. (1999) Korean Air spends on safety. BBC News Asia-Pacific, 26 December 1999. http://news.bbc.co.uk/1/hi/world/asia-pacific/578630.stm (accessed 27 February 2006).

PART V

Current Issues and Future Challenges

30

Critical Perspectives on Language in International Education

Trevor Grimshaw

The twenty-first century is already turning out to be an unsettling time for many people, not least those of us involved in international education. In the current era of globalization long–established notions are being challenged; familiar categories are being broken and their elements recombined in unexpected ways. Language lies at the heart of these processes. It is the means by which we identify ourselves and the means by which we create our representations of others. Whilst it can be a unifying factor, it can also serve as the medium through which people engage in conflict. These struggles take place both '*in* language' and '*over* language' (Fairclough 1989: 88; Pennycook 1994a: 324–5).

In this chapter I will examine a range of literature that offers critical perspectives on the role of language in international education. I will focus mainly on English, since this is both the pre-eminent world language and the primary medium of instruction and administration in many areas of international education. However, the issues discussed here may to some extent also apply to other major languages of international education, such as Spanish and French (Calvet 1987; La Pierre 1988; Mar-Molinero 2000).

I will begin by offering definitions of two key terms which are essential for our understanding of how language operates in its social context and which provide the theoretical framework for the subsequent discussion. I will go on to examine the important field of debate which has in recent years developed around the notion of 'linguistic imperialism'. I will then focus on two related aspects of professional practice: 'the dominant discourse of language in international education', and 'native-speakerism'. I will conclude by stressing the importance of a critical awareness of language in international education.

CRITICAL PERSPECTIVES ON LANGUAGE AND DISCOURSE

In recent years an increasing body of research has examined how language can be manipulated to shape ideology and maintain power relations within society. This literature challenges the more 'traditional' paradigm which assumes that language can operate as a neutral conduit that has no influence on the content of what is said or written. It warns us that 'we should guard against the (common-sense) assumption that language is nothing more than a clear, pure medium through which our thoughts and feelings can be made available to others' (Burr 1995: 34). In one way or another, the authors cited in this chapter all take *critical* perspectives on language.

I believe it is safe to say that, at the time of writing, *critical* is something of a buzz word. Yet the term is subject to various interpretations. Besides the common layman's usage, Pennycook (2001: 1–23) identifies three broad 'approaches to critical work'. The first is associated with mainstream 'Western' liberal-humanist education. Although precise definitions vary between disciplines and even textbooks (Ramanathan 2002: 116), this approach is generally associated with 'questioning skills' and the desire to encourage analytical abilities in students.

However, recent literature has been more concerned with the second and third 'approaches to critical work'. The second approach is associated with the neo-Marxist tradition of Critical Theory, which seeks to encourage social emancipation by interrogating the ideological forces that shape our political and economic environment (Pennycook 2001: 4–7; Young 1991). The third approach has been termed the '*post* position'. This draws upon postmodern, post-structuralist and postcolonial theory and explores the relationship between knowledge and power (Pennycook 2001: 42, citing Foucault 1980). This approach views all knowledge as political and denies that it can truly be either 'objective' or 'scientific'. According to this perspective, language is 'inherently political', playing a crucial role in the 'politics of knowledge'(Pennycook 2001: 42). Although as an educator I do not wish to undervalue the mainstream 'approach to critical work', I believe that to attain a fuller awareness of how language operates in its social environment it is also necessary to engage with the more politicized versions. The literature I discuss later in this chapter is informed primarily by theseversions, with a particular emphasis on postcolonial critique.

In recent years critical paradigms have influenced various academic fields concerned with language and culture, including applied linguistics (Canagarajah 1999; Kubota 1991; Pennycook 2001; Tollefson 2001), literacy (Street, 1995; Morgan 1997), bilingualism (Walsh 1991: 127), cultural awareness (Guilherme 2002), multiculturalism (Kubota 2004), social psychology (Ibanez and Iniguez 1997) and ethnography (Carspecken 1996). Researchers explore the links between linguistic practices, the construction of identities and the representation of social groups. They argue that language is *never* neutral; that it is *never* value-free; that it is *always* the product of some culture, whether this is institutional, professional, national, and so on. Language is always written or spoken from a particular ideological perspective, regardless of whether the writers or speakers are aware of their biases (Caldas-Coulthard and Coulthard 1996; Fairclough 1989; Gee 1996; Howarth 2000; Pennycook 1994a; Wodak and Meyer 2001).

With regard to practical applications, the findings of research have led to the development of critical language pedagogies (Benesch 2001; Brutt-Griffler and Samimy 1999; Norton and Toohey 2004; Pennycook 1994a). To some extent these relate to the broader tradition of critical pedagogy, which challenges dominant ideologies by promoting radical modes of education (Freire 1984; Giroux 1992).

Another important characteristic of recent literature is the increasing use of the term *discourse*. While definitions of this also vary, the following encapsulates some of the key features:

> A discourse refers to a set of meanings, metaphors, representations, images, stories, statements and so on that in some way together produce a particular creation of events. It refers to a particular picture that is painted of an event (or person or class of persons), a particular way of representing it or them in a certain light (Burr 1995: 48).

According to this view, social life is characterized by competing discourses, with individuals and groups making representations and seeking acceptance for their constructions of the world. Some examples are 'the discourses of democracy, law, capitalism, socialism, education, linguistics, applied linguistics and so on' (Pennycook 1994b: 128).

Discourses classify and organize knowledge. They influence our ways of thinking by controlling the meanings available to us. They define the criteria by which we make judgements (for example, what is considered right or wrong, rational or irrational). Fairclough provides one illustration which is particularly relevant to this chapter:

> Institutions construct their ideological and discoursal subjects ... For instance, to become a teacher one must master the discursive and ideological norms which the school attaches to that subject position – one must learn to talk like a teacher and 'see things' (i.e. things such as learning and teaching) like a teacher. (Fairclough, 1995: 39)

Thus, it could be said that an international educator is 'inscribed' by a number of prevailing discourses which constitute the accepted patterns of thought and behaviour within his/her discourse community.

Furthermore, in all walks of life it is possible to discern a *dominant discourse*: a way of perceiving the world which tends to be accepted as 'common sense' by most people within a discourse community. So, for example, it is possible to argue that there exists a 'dominant discourse of language in international education' which constitutes the majority view, but which is open to critique by informed practitioners.

As with the 'approaches to critical work', it is possible to identify three main approaches to the study of discourse. The first, which may be termed 'mainstream discourse analysis', is a well-established field of study concerned with 'language use above the level of the sentence' (i.e. paragraphs, conversations, etc.) and 'language use in context' (Brown and Yule 1983; Cook 1989). The second approach, Critical Discourse Analysis (CDA), operates within the neo-Marxist tradition and focuses on the social inequalities produced through language (Fairclough 1989, 1995, 2003; Chouliaraki and Fairclough 1999). It purports that: 'There is constant endeavour on the part of those who have power to try to impose an ideological common sense which holds for everyone' (Fairclough 1989: 86).

The third approach is associated with the '*post* position'. This views discourses as configurations of power-knowledge. Researchers operating within this paradigm seek to identify and deconstruct the discourses that define meanings and shape our perceptions of the social world. Again, the third approach is of most relevance to this chapter, especially regarding the contribution from postcolonial theory (Canagarajah 1999; Pennycook 1998, 2001; Said 1978).

Nowadays researchers in many areas of the social sciences are viewing familiar situations and practices in a *critical* manner and analysing the associated *discourses*. In the next section I examine a specific *critical discourse* which has had a widespread impact on the professional-academic community of international language educators.

THE DISCOURSE OF LINGUISTIC IMPERIALISM

When we talk of language in international education it is clear that certain languages enjoy particular status as the media of instruction and administration. English, Spanish and French have come to occupy privileged positions as a result of both 'geographical-historical' and 'socio-cultural' factors (Crystal 1997: 24). In the current era of globalization these languages continue to play an important role in the social and economic activities of numerous territories, facilitating many forms of commercial, cultural and educational exchange (McArthur 1998).

Yet not all observers regard this role as entirely benign. One of these is Phillipson, whose landmark publication *Linguistic Imperialism* (1992) raises important questions about the globalization of language education. Phillipson defines 'linguistic imperialism' as a process in which 'the dominance of English is asserted and maintained by the establishment and continuous reconstitution of structural and cultural inequalities between English and other languages' (1992: 47). Although he writes of other colonial languages, Phillipson singles out English for particular attention. This is not only because English is the pre-eminent world language but also because he sees it as 'the key medium' for the processes of 'Americanization' and 'Westernization', and therefore the means by which the industrialized world is able to exercise dominance over other regions (p. 59). Once the language of administration of the British Empire, English is now the language of its successor, the American Empire, and of the transnational corporations whose influence now rivals that of many nation-states. Furthermore, Phillipson argues that the English language teaching profession is 'unquestionably neo-colonialist' in that it supports these activities (p. 152).

Within the discourse of linguistic imperialism, the English language is seen as a force that damages the role and status of indigenous languages, infringing human rights and contributing to 'linguistic genocide' (Skutnabb-Kangas 2000). Linguistic imperialism, we are told, operates in much the same way as racism in that it produces hierarchical binary oppositions by assigning positive attributes to English and negative attributes to other languages (Skuttnab-Kangas and Phillipson, 1995). Thus English is glorified as an 'international language' or a 'language of wider communication', while, by implication, other languages come to be regarded as 'localized', 'of narrower communication' and so on (Phillipson 1997). Linguistic imperialism operates through the language policies of educational institutions, reinforcing social and economic inequities. It creates linguistic élites and restricts social mobility by acting as a 'gatekeeper' to higher education and to certain professions (Phillipson 1992).

Linguistic imperialism is closely related to cultural imperialism. Here, too, the nations of the politically and economically powerful 'Centre' are seen to subjugate and exploit those of the colonized 'Periphery'. Several theorists cite educational dependency as a key element of the colonial inheritance (e.g. Hardt and Negri 2000; Said 1993; Sreberny-Mohammadi 1997), while others point out that English language education continues to be promoted as an element of the 'civilizing mission' and as a means of facilitating the assimilation of 'Western' ideologies (Canagarajah 1999; Edge 2003, 2004; Pennycook 1994a, 1998;

Pennycook and Coutand-Martin 2003; Pennycook and Makoni 2005).

According to this perspective, not only is the English language culturally imperialistic, the manner in which it is taught could also be described as such. Pennycook (1994a: 159) argues that 'the export of applied linguistic theory and of Western-trained language teachers constantly promotes inappropriate teaching approaches to diverse settings'. An increasing body of research has questioned the suitability of language teaching methodologies developed in the core English-speaking countries when these are transferred to other cultural contexts (Holliday 1992a, 1992b, 1994, 2005; Kennedy, 1998; Markee 1997). Commercial interests play a major part in this process, with publishers, curriculum and assessment organizations and the providers of teacher education programmes all profiting from the dissemination of language teaching materials and methods. Several writers have highlighted the consumerist impetus which drives the promotion of the latest Western-style methodologies (e.g. Kumaravadivelu 1994; Pennycook 1994a; Richards and Rodgers 2001).

Depending on the researcher, evidence of linguistic imperialism can be found in many areas of international education. For example, in a critique of the role of language in international education, Quist (2005: 6) notes that 'the language of the former colonisers is still … the primary medium of instruction in the educational systems of the majority of former colonies'. However, it is not only in the 'former colonies' that one may witness this phenomenon. In recent decades the growth in English language teaching has been particularly notable in the 'expanding circle' of countries not formerly subject to anglophone colonization, such as Greater China and the former Eastern Bloc (Kachru 1992; Graddol 1997).

On a global scale English is the most popular choice of medium at all levels of international education. Indeed, many parents '[equate] an English-language education with an international education' (MacKenzie 2003: 75). Writing about the international schools sector Murphy, an experienced educator in this context, notes that the majority of these are monolingual schools in which the 'sole language of instruction is English' (2003b: 26; see also De Mejia 2004; Horsley 1991; Sears 1995; Tosi 1991). Meanwhile, Carder (2003: 242) laments that the term 'international curriculum' is often interpreted as one which in reality '[serves] only the dominant linguistic and cultural group, the Western, English-speaking world', and which therefore disadvantages students from other backgrounds.

In a broader discussion of the purposes of international education, Cambridge and Thompson (2004, citing Sklair 1991) describe how aspiring members of the 'transnational capitalist class' seek to maintain their competitive edge in the labour market by obtaining globally tradable qualifications. Academic literacy in an international language is a key element of such an education. Indeed, proficiency in English is a requirement for entry into tertiary education not only in the anglophone 'West' but also in many other parts of the world. All of this would appear to confirm the linguistic imperialism thesis.

RESPONSES TO THE 'LINGUISTIC IMPERIALISM' THESIS

Not surprisingly, representatives of the so-called 'Centre' have responded vigorously to the charge of linguistic imperialism. For example, Seaton (1997: 82), a former Director of English Language Teaching at the British Council, insists that international organizations such as IATEFL and TESOL guard against this by promoting the belief 'that language education can humanise us all in the best sense, and connect us internationally through understanding and choice rather than by control and coercion'. Similarly, the British Council (1996) quotes numerous 'voices from the new democracies' of central and eastern Europe who praise the role of English in facilitating access to the wider world, while Davies (1996) suggests that English as a *lingua franca* has aided the development of pan-Africanism.

Some question the assumed causal link between the spread of English and linguistic extinction. Whilst acknowledging the overall global decline in linguistic diversity, Graddol argues that in fact 'English is rarely the main, or direct, cause of this language loss' (1997: 39) and that the real threat to minority languages is caused by a general shift from local to nationally or regionally dominant languages. Others cite cases as widespread as Nigeria, Singapore and Sri Lanka, which suggest that the learning of an 'international auxiliary language' leads to additive rather than subtractive bilingualism (Bisong 1995; Chew 1999; Canagarajah 1999). This very notion underpins the European Schools curriculum, which is sometimes cited as a model for promoting multilingualism while giving equal status to national and international languages (e.g. MacKenzie 2003; Tosi 1991). International schools literature also indicates that at least some educators in this sector recognize the importance of supporting mother tongues while providing content-based instruction through the medium of English (Carder 1991; Sears 1995; several papers in Murphy 2003a).

Another major criticism of the linguistic imperialism thesis is that it underestimates pragmatic instrumentalism as a factor in the adoption of English. For instance, Bowers observes that English is chosen by 'simple decisions based on practical communication needs and guided by personal life intentions' (1997: 3). Chew (1999: 37) illustrates this with the example of Singapore, where a 'conscious decision' was made to choose English as a national language. This was simply 'the most realistic option', since English offered access to the technical and intellectual resources for modernization. Chew (1999: 40, citing Bourdieu and Passeron 1977) states that individual Singaporeans regard English as a form of 'linguistic capital' which is 'easily convertible into other forms of capital, such as educational qualifications and higher incomes'. Consequently, the notion that the English language is disseminated as part of a neo-colonial conspiracy seems 'quite alien' to Singaporeans (Chew 1999: 43).

A critical awareness of discourse is useful in helping us to understand the dynamics of linguistic politics in the postcolonial era. Whereas the linguistic imperialism thesis may be criticized on account of its determinism, postcolonial analyses place greater emphasis on the agency of language users and the identification of insurgent discourses. Canagarajah (1999) describes an approach whereby he and his fellow 'Periphery-English' users neither accept the dominant language totally nor reject it outright. Instead, they develop a 'third way', which involves the 'appropriation of the discourses, codes and grammar of English in terms of their own traditions and needs' (1999: 174). It is worth noting that this process of mediation is by no means a recent development, nor even a result of the colonial era. It is a fundamental part of cultural interaction in all contexts.

Resistance to cultural imperialism is an important part of the postcolonial picture. Having taken ownership of the international language, 'Periphery-English' users sometimes use it as a medium through which to oppose the cultural impositions of the dominant bloc, a strategy which in postcolonial literary studies has been described as 'writing back against the empire'. For Canagarajah, 'resistance' to the dominant discourses of language and culture does not imply rejection but mastery. Consequently, 'It is wrong to assume that the cultures of the subordinate groups are always passive and accommodative. They have a long history of struggle and resistance against the dominant cultures and members of these communities can tap the resources in their cultures to oppose the thrusts of alien ideologies' (Canagarajah 1999: 25).

My own research concerning the impact of English and its associated discourses on Chinese academic cultures suggests that, far from being disempowered victims of 'imperialist aggression', members of these cultures consciously and strategically assimilate elements of foreign discourses in order to protect and promote their own political, economic and cultural interests. English as an International Language thus becomes a means with which to project the Chinese national identity onto the world stage and to present counter-discourses against 'Western' imperialism (Grimshaw 2002a, 2002b).

All of the above suggests that the linguistic imperialism thesis is based on what nowadays appears to be an outmoded, ethnocentric view of the world. Whilst it cannot be denied that the major languages of international education are among the most obvious aspects of the colonial legacy, it must also be recognized that many non-Western nations have already entered a phase of development in which they no longer pay heed to the imperialist 'Centre'. Indeed, some of the most severe criticisms of Phillipson concern his 'condescending and patronising attitude' (Berns et al. 1998: 276). Several authors also highlight the irony of Phillipson's position: that in his efforts to challenge the imperialist paradigm he fails to realize that the people of the 'Periphery' do not need champions from the 'Centre' to fight their battles for them (Bisong 1995; Bowers 1997; Holliday 1997).

Yet, regardless of how dismissive we may be of its more alarmist elements, it must be recognized that the debate surrounding linguistic imperialism does raise some serious questions concerning the role of language in international education. These include the issues of linguistic elitism and exclusion, for it is clear that while mastery of an international language grants access to a few, it also denies access to the many. Another major issue is the potential loss of mother tongues and the related threat to cultural diversity, underlining the need to maintain those languages that connect students to their primary discourse communities. Perhaps most importantly, the linguistic imperialism debate prompts us to reassess some of the dominant beliefs underpinning our professional practice as international educators.

THE DOMINANT DISCOURSE OF LANGUAGE IN INTERNATIONAL EDUCATION

Quite understandably, international educators may resent being labelled 'agents of imperialism'. It is therefore important that we examine the arguments relating to our participation as individuals in the processes described above.

Theorists working within the neo-Marxist tradition tend to explain the situation in terms of 'false consciousness'. That is to say, international educators are blinded by a dominant ideology which presents the pre-eminent position of colonial languages as 'a "common sense" social fact' and international language education as a politically neutral endeavour (Phillipson, 1992: 76). International educators are thus unaware that their work helps to sustain the system of unequal global power relations. The 'myth' of international language education as an apolitical activity is reinforced by humanistic ideologies ('international-mindedness', 'global citizenship', etc.). Consequently, 'individuals with possibly the most altruistic motives for their work may nevertheless function in an imperialist structure' (1992: 46).

However, this interpretation is somewhat patronizing, for whereas the theorists construct international educators as naive and ideologically uninformed, they credit themselves with a privileged status in that they are able to see the 'true' nature of things. In contrast, the '*post* position', with its more flexible view of discourse and the 'politics of knowledge', allows for a more sophisticated understanding of the relationship between us and the forces that shape our professional activities. The Foucauldian perspective (cf. Pennycook 1994b; Canagarajah 1999 and others) does not assume any superordinate position existing beyond language or ideology. Instead, it sees social activity in terms of a multiplicity of competing discourses. Amongst these is a dominant discourse, which constitutes the established standards of behaviour and attitude within an institution and which causes rival discourses to be devalued. Although we are always speaking or writing from inside one discourse or another, it is possible for us as individuals to continue operating within an institution while holding views that run contrary to the dominant discourse.

The concept of a dominant discourse is highly relevant to the discussion of language in international education, since it helps to explain the hegemony of certain discourses of language and pedagogy. Amongst the most powerful are those discourses that serve to rationalize the active promotion of dominant languages while at the same time appearing

to render them harmless. One of these is the 'discourse of English as an International Language' (Pennycook 1994a). By portraying the dissemination of English as 'natural, neutral and beneficial', this deflects attention from the cultural politics of language and reinforces the notion that a teacher's job is 'just to teach the language' (1994a: 257). Similarly, the discourse of English as a 'tool' emphasizes the functional aspect of language (Phillipson 1992: 87). It implies that the instrument can be ideologically disconnected from the culture whence it originated: an assumption that, as we have seen, is contradicted by current theory and practice. Yet another discourse constructs languages as 'windows on the world' (Phillipson 1992: 61). This, too, is contested by theorists of media imperialism who point out that the flow of information tends to be in one direction (i.e. from the culture of the 'Centre' to the 'Periphery') and that the message is often filtered or distorted in order to fit with dominant 'Western' perceptions of the world (Golding and Harris, 1997; Sreberny-Mohammadi 1997; Tomlinson 1991).

As regards pedagogy, an expanding research base has examined the internal dynamics of the language teaching profession of the Anglophone West (Block and Cameron 2002; Hall and Eggington 2000; Holliday 1994, 1998, 2005; Pennycook 1994a, 1998, 2001; Ramanathan 2002). This literature sees the profession as a culture that generates sophisticated and persuasive discourses of practice. These inscribe us with ethnocentric modes of thought and behaviour. Thus, Pennycook explains:

> It is not that as English teachers we are necessarily either overt messiahs or duped messengers, but rather that the constant advocacy of certain teaching practices that have become bound up with the English language necessarily represents a constant advocacy for a particular way of life, a particular understanding of the world. (Pennycook 1994a: 178)

This interpretation is consonant with literature from the sociology of knowledge (e.g. Berger and Luckmann 1975) and also research dealing with teachers' beliefs and frames of reference (Borg 2001; Calderhead 1995; Johnson 1995: 16–35). As social actors and as educators we tend to perceive and construct the world in particular ways according to the socialization that we have received. It is only when this world-view is challenged by a new context or a rival world-view that we are forced to reassess our own perspective. This kind of experience is familiar to those of us who cross national or ethnic borders in our professional or personal lives. However, it is useful to think of intercultural communication not only as something that happens between national, ethnic or regional cultures. It has the potential to occur when all types of culture come into contact with one another, including institutional and professional-academic cultures (Holliday et al. 2004).

An important reason for the relative lack of critical self-awareness within the language teaching profession is the discursive construction of the discipline itself. As a relatively young discipline, applied linguistics has sought to improve its status by defining itself as a 'science' and aligning itself with the principles of scientific positivism. However, advocates of critical language pedagogy complain that the positivist paradigm encourages teachers to concentrate primarily on the technical aspects of their work, such as the pursuit of more efficient teaching methods, while failing to develop a critical understanding of social and cultural matters (Canagarajah 1999; Pennycook 1994a). Consequently, mainstream language education has tended to take relatively little advantage of knowledge from areas such as development studies, cultural theory or the sociology of education. Phillipson refers to this as the 'political disconnection' of language education (1992: 252).

So, in short, international educators are neither naive evangelists nor cynical manipulators. However, the issues discussed above suggest that there is a need for a more critical awareness of the dominant discourse of language in international education.

NATIVE-SPEAKERISM IN INTERNATIONAL EDUCATION

Recently the critique of linguistic imperialism has been to a large extent superseded by that of native-speakerism, an issue which deserves particular attention in the context of international education. Native-speakerism may be defined as an ideology which creates a dichotomy between native-English-speaking and non-native-English-speaking teachers (NESTs and NNESTs), leading to discrimination against the latter (Holliday 2005: 6).

The key issue is the 'native speaker fallacy'; that is, the belief that 'the ideal teacher of English is a native speaker' (Phillipson 1992: 217). The separation and labelling of educators as 'native' and 'non-native' speakers constitutes one of the most significant hierarchies of the profession. At its heart is the unspoken assumption that the 'non-native speaker' is in some way 'culturally deficient' (Holliday 2005:1). Native-speakerism creates 'a negatively reduced image of the foreign Other': one who is seen to lack certain desirable characteristics in relation to the dominant discourse of the anglophone Western language teaching profession. For example, within this discourse East Asian teachers and students are often constructed as lacking in the capacity for autonomous or critical thought (Grimshaw 2002b; Holliday 2005; Kubota 2001).

The postcolonial critique again provides us with insights into the nature of these processes. Central to the literature are 'the cultural constructs of colonialism', a series of dichotomies that enable the West to see itself in self-flattering opposition to the non-Western Other (Pennycook 1998; Said 1978). These stereotypes continue to be recycled in domains such as travel writing and the media. They feed into the dominant discourse of international education, influencing the ways in which 'native-speaker' practitioners discursively label and position their 'non-native' students and colleagues. This phenomenon is evident in the dominant discourse of language pedagogy, where teachers from the English-speaking West have a tendency to portray themselves as modern, progressive, scientific and masters of a technologically superior methodology. By implication, teachers and students who follow more 'traditional' forms of pedagogy tend to be constructed as conservative, backward, unscientific and technologically inferior (Holliday 2005; Pennycook 1994a).

At this point it should be stressed that the native-speakerist attitudes and practices of 'Western' educators should not be taken as evidence of deliberate cultural racism. The legacy of history and the continuing uneven distribution of resources have a profound influence on the value systems of all parties. The colonial experience shaped the colonizers as much as it did the colonized, not only in material terms but also with regard to self-image (Hall 1997; Pennycook 1998).

One consequence is that educators who have been socialized within the Western tradition have a tendency to seek to 'improve' other cultures (Holliday 2005: 13). The discourse of native-speakerism compels them to want to change the beliefs and practices of 'non-native-speaker' teachers and students in a manner that is resonant of the civilizing mission of the colonial era. Yet, as we have seen, the promotion of culturally alien pedagogies is often resented by host cultures.

A further consequence of native-speakerism is that the voice of the 'non-native' Other tends to be marginalized. Quist (2005: 4) describes the 'current discourse [of] international education' as one that 'is primarily informed and driven by the concerns and interests of the dominant, and essentially dispossessing, culture'. It is:

> A discourse characterised in the main by the western (developed) world talking to itself and demonstrating an unwillingness or inability to fully engage with the relevant perspectives and demands of colonial/post-colonial discourse. The end result is a conversation in which the much larger majority world (described variously as under-developed or developing or the 3rd world) is, at worst, largely absent or, at best, managing rather perilously on the periphery. (Quist 2005: 3–4)

Native-speakerism has other negative impacts. It is the basis of hiring policy in many institutions, where 'non-native-speaker' practitioners are often positioned in auxiliary or subordinate roles (Braine 1999; Canagarajah 1999; MacKenzie 2003; Maum 2002; Rampton 1990). In many contexts it is linked with pay scales, leading to NNESTs

sometimes being paid far less than their NEST colleagues, regardless of qualifications or experience (Braine 2005). It has also been cited as a determinant of access to teacher development programmes or opportunities to publish in international journals (Braine 2005; Jenkins 2000: 9).

However, an increasing number of people within the English language teaching profession are challenging these divisive practices. Challenges have been presented by 'native' and 'non-native' speakers from a variety of backgrounds (Kubota 1999, 2001, 2002; Kumaravadivelu 2003; Littlewood 2000; Phan 2004; Spack 1997). One of these argues that:

> Applied linguistics scholarship needs to … examine critically how racism sustains itself in various constructs such as cultural dichotomies, Othering and invisible superiority of the dominant race and civilization. We as applied linguists need to recognize that racism is woven into the very fabric of our institutions, the threads that we must work to make visible and unravel. (Kubota 2002: 90)

One collection of papers (Kubota and Lin, in press) aims to problematize 'whiteness, [the] native speaker myth, and the teaching of language and culture'. Meanwhile, an organization known as the NNEST Caucus has been formed with the aim of combating native-speakerist discrimination in the language teaching profession.

For some time critics have taken issue with the assumption that 'non-native speakers' make less effective language teachers than 'native speakers', arguing instead for a more balanced recognition of the respective strengths of both (Rampton 1990; Medgyes 1992, 1995; Brutt-Griffler and Samimy 1999; Lee 2000; Tajino and Tajino 2000). For example, they point out that NNESTs often have more understanding of the language-learning needs and strategies of their students than do 'native speakers', enabling them to serve as 'imitable models of the successful language learner of English' (Medgyes 1992: 39).

Perhaps the greatest challenge to the ideology of native-speakerism is the problematization of the 'native speaker' construct itself. Within international education there is a widespread and long-standing belief in the 'native speaker' as the yardstick against which all other speakers are measured. Parents frequently prefer their children to be taught by 'native speakers' on the assumption that they 'know' the target language better. However, it is by no means easy to produce a clear definition of who is and who is not a 'native-speaker'. After considering evidence from various perspectives, Davies (2003) concludes that the 'native speaker' is as much myth as reality. Similarly, Kramsch (1993: 49) states that in this era of increasing plurilingualism 'the notion of a generic native speaker ... has lost its meaning'. Indeed, in the globalized context of international education it is particularly common to encounter people who do not appear to have a 'native language' in the traditional sense, although they may speak several with varying degrees of proficiency and code-switch comfortably between them. This phenomenon is consonant with Appadurai's (1996) concept of 'transcultural flows'.

The dominant role of international educators from the Anglophone West is likely to be further challenged by the changing ownership of the English language. In the past, people from this background have been able to claim authority as the custodians of the language. But the globalization of English suggests that these users may have lost the prerogative to judge what constitutes a 'standard' variety of the language. Already more people around the world use English as an additional language than as mother tongue, with the result that most interactions that take place in English take place between 'non-native' speakers (Crystal 1997; Seidlhofer 2005a). Meanwhile, a substantial literature has documented the indigenization of English in numerous parts of the world (Brock and Walters 1993; Brutt-Griffler 2002; Crystal 1997; Jenkins 2003; Kachru 1992; McArthur 1998; McKay 2002; Melchers and Shaw 2003). Consequently, Graddol (1997: 3) predicts a shift in the 'centre of gravity', leading to a situation in which 'native speakers' become 'minority stakeholders in the global resource'. Of course, cultural politics play an important part in maintaining the semantic distinction

between 'native' and 'non-native speakers' (Rampton 1990). In a provocative study, Jenkins (2000) suggests that the current terminology should be abandoned altogether and that a new categorization should be adopted: one based on the distinction between monolingual and bilingual users. Jenkins is one of several researchers currently arguing for the 'democratization' of English as an International Language through the promotion of a '*lingua franca* core': a new variety that does not model itself upon the norms of 'native speaker' usage (Jenkins 2000; Jenkins et al. 2001; Seidlhofer 2005a, 2005b).

Future developments in the use of language in international education are unpredictable. The dual functions of English as a medium of international communication and as a means of developing cultural identities create simultaneous contradictory trends, towards both standardization and diversification (Graddol 1997; Widdowson 1997). So, whilst it seems likely that English will continue to be the pre-eminent language of international education, it remains to be seen whether the dominant variety will be one that is currently regarded as 'standard'. It is also important to recognize that there is nothing inherently superior about the English language that makes it more suitable than any other to function as a medium of international education, diplomacy, trade and so on. Other languages (e.g. French, Spanish) currently serve the same functions, albeit on a lesser scale, while yet others (e.g. Mandarin Chinese) continue to extend their influence (Graddol 1997).

From the above it can be seen that pressure is building for a radical reassessment of one of the most fundamental dichotomies of international education. Medgyes (1992: 31) reminds us that 'international-mindedness ... entails the rejection of discrimination, whether on grounds of race, sex, religion, education, intelligence, or mother tongue'. As members of a profession that places so much emphasis on the need for intercultural awareness, it is all the more important that international educators take the lead in achieving these ideals.

CONCLUSION

In this chapter I have reviewed a body of research that contributes to our understanding of the role of language in international education. From this it is clear that international languages represent different things to different people. To some they are a means for developing intercultural understanding and achieving conflict resolution; to others they are tools for social and economic advancement; to yet others they are a remnant of imperialism and a threat to local cultural identities. More specifically, within international education itself, language has been identified as the source of culturally divisive practices which have a damaging effect upon our profession.

So, what can be done to ensure that language plays a beneficial rather than a detrimental role in our professional activities? Quist (2005) points the way forward. He writes of the need to 'detect' and 'interrogate' the 'assumptions and contradictions' within the discourse of international education. He calls for 'a radical approach' to resolving 'the problems that divide our world'. He stresses the need for 'reading against the grain'. All of these ideas can be summed up in a single word: *critical*. But if 'critical international education' is to be more than simply another item of fashionable terminology, we must be willing to engage critically with the language that embodies the ideology of our profession. We must be prepared to question the dominant discourse.

In the opening chapter of a recent publication concerning the teaching of English as an international language, Holliday (2005) writes of 'the struggle for new relationships'. As we have seen throughout this chapter, the struggle is already ongoing. If we are to play a positive part in it, one of the most important ways is through the development of critical perspectives on language in international education.

REFERENCES

Appadurai, A. (1996) *Modernity at Large: Cultural Dimensions of Globalization.* Minneapolis MN: University of Minneapolis Press.

Benesch, S. (2001) *Critical English for Academic Purposes: Theory, Politics and Practice.* London: Lawrence Erlbaum Associates.

Berger, A. and Luckmann, H. (1975) *The Social Construction of Reality.* Harmondsworth: Penguin.

Berns, M., Barrett, J., Chan, C., et al. (1998) Review Essay: (Re)experiencing hegemony: the linguistic imperialism of Robert Phillipson, *International Journal of Applied Linguistics,* 8(2): 271–82.

Bisong, J. (1995) Language choice and cultural imperialism: a Nigerian perspective. *ELT Journal,* 49: 2.

Block, D. and Cameron, D. (eds) (2002) *Globalization and Language Teaching.* London: Routledge.

Borg, M. (2001) Teachers' beliefs. *ELT Journal,* 55(2): 186–7.

Bourdieu, P. and Passeron, J. (1977) *Reproduction in Education, Society and Culture.* London: Sage.

Bowers, R. (1997) ELT and development: projects and power (1991). In G. Abbott and M. Beaumont (eds) *The Development of ELT: The Dunford Seminars, 1978–1993.* Hemel Hempstead: Prentice Hall Europe in association with The British Council, (pp. 170–8).

Braine, G. (ed.) (1999) *Non-native Educators in English Language Teaching.* Mahwah, NJ: Lawrence Erlbaum.

Braine, G. (2005) NNS and invisible barriers in ELT. <http://nnest.moussu.net/history.html> (accessed 2 December 2005).

British Council (1996) *Voices from the New Democracies: The Impact of British English Language Teaching in Central and Eastern Europe.* British Council: printed in Britain by Crown Press.

Brock, M.N. and Walters, L. (eds) (1993) *Teaching Composition around the Pacific Rim: Politics and Pedagogy.* Clevedon, UK: Multilingual Matters.

Brown, G. and Yule, G. (1983) *Discourse Analysis.* Cambridge: Cambridge University Press.

Brutt-Griffler, J. (2002) *World English: A Study of Its Development.* Clevedon, UK: Multilingual Matters.

Brutt-Griffler, J. and Samimy, K.K. (1999) Revisiting the colonial in the postcolonial: critical praxis for non-native-English-speaking teachers in a TESOL program. *TESOL Quarterly,* 33(3): 413–29.

Burr, V. (1995) *An Introduction to Social Constructionism.* London: Routledge.

Caldas-Coulthard, C.R. and Coulthard, M. (eds) (1996) *Texts and Practices: Readings in Critical Discourse Analysis.* London: Routledge.

Calderhead, J. (1995) Teachers beliefs and knowledge. In D.C. Berliner and R.C. Calfee (eds) *Handbook of Educational Psychology.* New York: Macmillan.

Calvet, L-J. (1987) *La guerre de langues et politiques linguistiques.* Paris: Payot.

Cambridge, J. and Thompson, J. (2004) Internationalism and globalization as contexts for international education. *Compare*, 34(2): 161–75.

Canagarajah, A.S. (1999) *Resisting Linguistic Imperialism in English Teaching*. Oxford: Oxford University Press.

Carder, M. (1991) The role and development of ESL programmes in international schools. In P.L. Jonietz and N.D.C. Harris (eds) *World Handbook of Education 1991: International Schools and International Education*. London: Kogan Page, pp. 108–24.

Carder, M. (2003) Intercultural awareness, bilingualism and ESL in the International Baccalaureate, with particular reference to the MYP. In E. Murphy (ed.) *ESL: Educating Non-native Speakers of English in an English-medium International School. The International Schools Journal Compendium, Vol. 1*. Great Glemham: John Catt Educational, (pp. 236–42).

Carspecken, P.F. (1996) *Critical Ethnography in Educational Research: A Theoretical and Practical Guide*. London: Routledge.

Chew, P. Ghim-Lian (1999) Linguistic imperialism, globalism and the English language. *AILA Review*, 13: 37–47.

Chouliaraki, L. and Fairclough, N. (1999) *Discourse in Late Modernity: Rethinking Critical Discourse Analysis*. Edinburgh: Edinburgh University Press.

Cook, G. (1989) *Discourse*. Oxford: Oxford University Press.

Crystal, D. (1997) *English as a Global Language*. Cambridge: Cambridge University Press.

De Mejia, A-M. (2004) *Power, Prestige and Bilingualism: International Perspectives on Elite Bilingual Education*. Clevedon, UK: Multilingual Matters.

Davies, A. (1996) Review Article: Ironising the myth of linguicism. *Journal of Multilingual and Multicultural Development*, 17(6): 485–96.

Davies, A. (2003) *The Native Speaker: Myth and Reality*. Clevedon, UK: Multilingual Matters.

Edge, J. (2003) TEFL and international politics: a personal narrative. *IATEFL Issues*, Oct–Nov, Issue 175. www.developingteachers.com/articles_tchtraining/intlpoliticspf_julian.htm (accessed 25 September 2004).

Edge, J. (2004) English in a new age of empire. *The Guardian*, Thursday 15 April 2004. http://education.guardian.co.uk/tefl/story/0,5500,1191122,00.html (accessed 25 September 2004).

Fairclough. N. (1989) *Language and Power*. London: Longman.

Fairclough, N. (1995) *Critical Discourse Analysis: The Critical Study of Language*. Harlow: Longman.

Fairclough, N. (2003) *Analysing Discourse: Textual Analysis for Social Research*. London: Routledge.

Foucault, M. (ed. C. Gordon) (1980) *Power/Knowledge: Selected Interviews and Other Writings, 1972–1977*. Brighton: Harvester Press.

Freire, P. (1984) *The Politics of Education: Culture, Power and Liberation*. Basingstoke: Macmillan.

Gee, J. (1996) *Social Linguistics and Literacies: Ideology in Discourses*. London: Taylor and Francis.

Giroux, H.A. (1992) *Border Crossings: Cultural Workers and the Politics of Education*. London: Routledge.

Golding, P. and Harris, P. (eds) (1997) *Beyond Cultural Imperialism: Globalisation, Communication and the New International Order*. London: Sage.

Graddol, D. (1997) *The Future of English*. London: The British Council.

Grimshaw, T.A. (2002a) Discursive struggle in Chinese universities: English linguistic imperialism, resistance and appropriation. PhD Thesis, University of Kent at Canterbury.

Grimshaw, T.A. (2002b) Cultures of learning: critical perspectives on the teaching of English as an international language. Unpublished paper, School of Arts & Social Sciences, Northumbria University.

Guilherme, M. (2002) *Critical Citizens for an Intercultural World: Foreign Language Education as Cultural Politics*. Clevedon, UK: Multilingual Matters.

Hall, S. (ed.) (1997) *Representation: Cultural Representation and Signifying Practice*. London: Sage.

Hall, J.K. and Eggington, W.G. (eds) (2000) *The Sociopolitics of English Language Teaching*. Clevedon, UK: Multilingual Matters.

Hardt, M. and Negri, A. (2000) *Empire*. Cambridge, MA: Harvard University Press.

Holliday, A.R. (1992a) Intercompetence: sources of conflict between local and expatriate ELT personnel. *System*, 20(2): 223–34.

Holliday, A.R. (1992b) Tissue rejection and informal orders in ELT projects: collecting the right information. *Applied Linguistics*, 13(4): 404–24.

Holliday, A.R. (1994) *Appropriate Methodology and Social Context*. Cambridge: Cambridge University Press.

Holliday, A.R. (1997) Six lessons: cultural continuity in communicative language teaching, *Language Teaching Research*, 1(3): 212–41.

Holliday, A.R. (1998) Evaluating the discourse: the role of applied linguistics in the management of evaluation and innovation. In K. Germaine and P. Rea-Dickens, (eds) *Managing Evaluation and Innovation in English Language Teaching: Building Bridges*. London: Addison Wesley Longman, pp. 195–219.

Holliday, A.R. (2005) *The Struggle to Teach English as an International Language*. Oxford: Oxford University Press.

Holliday, A., Hyde, M. and Kullman, J. (2004) *Intercultural Communication: An Advanced Resource Book*. London: Routledge.

Horsley, A. (1991) Bilingual education in the international school – dream or reality?. In: P.L. Jonietz and N.D.C. Harris (eds) *World Yearbook of Education 1991: International Schools and International Education*. London: Kogan Page, pp. 100–7.

Howarth, D. (2000) *Discourse*. Buckingham: Open University Press.

Ibanez, T. and Iniguez L. (eds) (1997) *Critical Social Psychology*. London: Sage.

Jenkins, J. (2000) *The Phonology of English as an International Language*. Oxford Applied Linguistics Series. Oxford: Oxford University Press.

Jenkins, J. (2003) *World Englishes: A Resource Book for Students*. London: Routledge.

Jenkins, J., Modiano, M. and Seidlhofer, B. (2001) Euro-English: perspectives on an emerging variety on the mainland of Europe, from commentators in Sweden, Austria and England. *English Today*, 68 (17/4): 13–19.

Johnson, K.E. (1995) *Understanding Communication in Second Language Classrooms*. Cambridge: Cambridge University Press.

Kachru, B.B. (ed.) (1992) *The Other Tongue: English Across Cultures*, 2nd edition. Oxford: Pergamon Press.

Kennedy, C. (1988) Evaluation of the management of change in ELT projects. *Applied Linguistics*, 9(4): 329–42.

Kramsch, C. (1993) *Context and Culture in Language Teaching*. Oxford: Oxford University Press.

Kubota, R. (1999) Japanese culture constructed by discourses: implications for applied linguistics. *TESOL Quarterly*, 33(1): 9–35.

Kubota, R. (2001) Discursive construction of the images of US classrooms. *TESOL Quarterly*, 35(1): 9–38.

Kubota, R. (2002) The Author Responds: (Un)ravelling racism in a nice field like TESOL. *TESOL Quarterly*, 36(1): 84–92.

Kubota, R. (2004) Critical multiculturalism and second language education. In B. Norton and K. Toohey (eds) *Critical Pedagogies and Language Learning*. Cambridge: Cambridge University Press, pp. 30–52.

Kubota, R. and Lin, A. (eds) (in press) *Race and TESOL: Special Edition of TESOL Quarterly*.

Kumaravadivelu, B. (1994) The postmethod condition: (e)merging strategies for second/foreign language teaching. *TESOL Quarterly*, 28(1): 27–48.

Kumaravadivelu, B. (2003) Problematizing cultural stereotypes in TESOL. The Forum. *TESOL Quarterly*, 37(4): 709–19.

La Pierre, J-W. (1988) *Le pouvoir politique et les langues: Babel et Leviathan*. Paris: Presses Universitaires de France.

Lee, I. (2000) Can a nonnative English speaker be a good English teacher?, *TESOL Matters*, 10(1). www.tesol.org/s tesol/sec_document.asp?CID=195 &DID=842 (accessed 21 July 2006).

Littlewood, W. (2000) Do Asian students really want to listen and obey?. *ELT Journal*, 54(1): 31–5.

MacKenzie, P. (2003) Bilingual education: Who wants it? Who needs it? In E. Murphy (ed.) *ESL: Educating Non-native Speakers of English in an English-medium International School. The International Schools Journal Compendium, Vol. 1.* Great Glemham: John Catt Educational, (pp. 71–7).

McArthur, T. (1998) *The English Languages*. Cambridge: Cambridge University Press.

Mar-Molinero, C. (2000) *The Politics of Language in the Spanish-Speaking World: From Colonisation to Globalisation*. London: Routledge.

Markee, N. (1997) *Managing Curricular Innovation*. Cambridge: Cambridge University Press.

Maum, R. (2002) Nonnative-English-speaking teachers in the English teaching profession. www.cal.org/resources/digest/0209maum.html (accessed 2 December 2005).

McKay, S. (2002) *Teaching English as an International Language*. Oxford: Oxford University Press.

Medgyes, P. (1992) Native or non-native: who's worth more? *ELT Journal*, 46(4): 340–9.

Melchers, G. and Shaw, P. (2003) *World Englishes*. London: Edward Arnold.

Morgan, W. (1997) *Critical Literacy in the Classroom: the Art of the Possible*. London: Routledge.

Murphy, E. (ed.) (2003a) *ESL: Educating Non-native Speakers of English in an English-medium International School. The International Schools Journal Compendium, Vol. 1*, Great Glemham: John Catt Educational.

Murphy, E. (2003b) Monolingual international schools and the young non-English-speaking child. *Journal of Research in International Education*, 2(1): 25–45.

NNEST Caucus (2006) <http://nnest.moussu.net/purpose.html> (accessed 12 March 2006).

Norton, B. and Toohey, K. (eds) (2004) *Critical Pedagogies and Language Learning*. Cambridge: Cambridge University Press.

Pennycook, A. (1994a) *The Cultural Politics of English as an International Language*. Harlow: Longman.

Pennycook, A. (1994b) Incommensurable discourses? *Applied Linguistics*, 15(2): 117–36.

Pennycook, A. (1998) *English and the Discourses of Colonialism*. London: Routledge.

Pennycook, A. (2001) *Critical Applied Linguistics: A Critical Introduction*. London: Lawrence Erlbaum Associates.

Pennycook, A. and Coutand-Martin, S. (2003) Teaching English as a missionary language (TEML). *Discourse: Studies in the Cultural Politics of Education*, 24(3): 337–53.

Pennycook, A. and Makoni, S. (2005) The modern mission: the language effects of christianity. *Journal of Language, Identity & Education*, 4(2): 137–55.

Phan Le Ha (2004) University classrooms in Vietnam: contesting the stereotypes. *ELT Journal*, 58(1): 50–7.

Phillipson, R. (1992) *Linguistic Imperialism*. Oxford: Oxford University Press.

Phillipson, R. (1997) Realities and myths of linguistic imperialism. *Journal of Multilingual and Multicultural Development*, 18(3): 238–48.

Quist, I. (2005) The language of international education: a critique. *IB Research Notes*, 5(1): 2–8.

Ramanathan, V. (2002) *The Politics of TESOL Education: Writing, Knowledge, Critical Pedagogy*. London: Falmer Press.

Rampton, M.B.H. (1990) Displacing the 'native speaker': expertise, affiliation and inheritance. *ELT Journal*, 44: 2.

Richards, J.C. and Rodgers, T.S. (2001) *Approaches and Methods in Language Teaching: A Description and Analysis*. Cambridge: Cambridge University Press.

Said, E.W. (1978) *Orientalism*. Harmondsworth: Penguin.

Said, E.W. (1993) *Culture and Imperialism*. London: Vintage.

Sears, C. (1995) *Second Language Students in Mainstream Classrooms: A Handbook for Teachers in International Schools*. Clevedon, UK: Multilingual Matters.

Seaton, I. (1997) Comment: linguistic non-imperialism. *ELT Journal*, 51(4): 381–2.

Seidlhofer, B. (2005a) English as a lingua franca. *ELT Journal*, 59(4): 339–41.

Seidlhofer, B. (2005b) 'Native/non-native speaker variation – insights from corpus studies of Lingua Franca English', paper delivered at the British Association for Applied Linguistics (BAAL) 38th Annual Meeting: Applied Linguistics at the Interface, University of Bristol, UK, 17 September 2005.

Sklair, L. (1991) *The Sociology of the Global System*. Brighton: Harvester Wheatsheaf.

Skuttnab-Kangas, T. (2000) *Linguistic Genocide in Education – or Worldwide Diversity and Human Rights*. Mahwah, NJ: Lawerence Erlbaum.

Skuttnab-Kangas, T. and Phillipson, R. (eds) (1995) *Linguistic Human Rights: Overcoming Linguistic Discrimination*. Berlin: Mouton de Gruyter.

Spack, R. (1997) The rhetorical construction of multilingual students. *TESOL Quarterly* 31(4): 75–774.

Sreberny-Mohammadi, A. (1997) The many cultural faces of imperialism. In P. Golding and P. Harris (eds) *Beyond Cultural Imperialism: Globalisation, Communication and the New International Order*. London: Sage, (pp. 49–68).

Street, B. (1995) *Social Literacies: Critical Approaches to Literacy in Development, Ethnography and Education*. London: Longman.

Tajino, A. and Tajino, Y. (2000) Native and non-native: what can they offer? Lessons from team teaching in Japan. *ELT Journal*, 45(1): 3–10.

Tollefson J. (ed.) (2002) *Language Policies in Education: Critical Issues*. Mahwah, NJ: Lawrence Erlbaum.

Tomlinson, J. (1991) *Cultural Imperialism*. London: Pinter.

Tosi, A. (1991) Language in international education. In P.L. Jonietz and N.D.C Harris (eds) *World Yearbook of Education 1991: International Schools and International Education*. London: Kogan Page, pp. 82–99.

Walsh, C.E. (1991) *Pedagogy and the Struggle for Voice: Issues of Language, Power, and Schooling for Puerto Ricans*. Toronto: OISE Press.

Widdowson, H.G. (1997) The Forum: 'EIL, ESL, EFL: global issues and local interests'. *World Englishes*, 16(1): 135–46.

Wodak, R. and Meyer, M. (2001) *Methods of Critical Discourse Analysis*. London: Sage.

Young, R.E. (1991) *Critical Theory of Education: Habermas and Our Children's Future*. New York: Teachers College Press.

31

International-Mindedness and the Brain: the Difficulties of 'Becoming'

Martin Skelton

The three goals

The first goal is to see the thing itself
In and for itself, to see it simply and clearly
For what it is.
  No symbolism please.

The second goal is to see each individual thing
As unified, as one, with all the other
Ten thousand things.
  In this regard, a little wine helps a lot.

The third goal is to grasp the first and second goals,
To see the universal and the particular,
Simultaneously.
  Regarding this one, call me when you get it.

(Budbill 2002)

Much that is good gets taken over and used for other purposes. For instances, no sooner did Bob Geldof announce that he was to give three days a year as one member of one group advising the UK Conservative party about African poverty under its 2005 new leader, David Cameron, than sections of the Conservative-supporting press announced 'Geldof joins the Conservatives'. The same

is happening with the notion of international-mindedness, even if those who are appropriating it are doing so for nobler motives than those demonstrated by the UK press. What already is a complex enough notion in its own right now finds itself expected to carry the arguments of those in favour of globalization, those against globalization, those worried about the environment, those concerned about world peace and so on. Other chapters in this book will provide the evidence that 'international-mindedness' does indeed carry much on its shoulders.

It is not my place to argue that international-mindedness is *not* a part of all of these worthwhile themes and activities; that would be both foolish and wrong. But it is more helpful to see international-mindedness as a component of each of these themes rather than to blur the edges between them. When we do so the level of expectation is impossible to fulfil and is, in itself, quite dangerous. It allows the discussion and debate about international-mindedness to become not more complex but more confused, which is a different thing altogether; and in the confusion, our attempts to reach some sort of consensus create a version of international-mindedness that we might call *international-mindedness lite* – 'Buy it now: all of the good intentions but little that could be called taste.'

In the first part of this chapter I will take international-mindedness back to something more basic, to a position before the time when it began to have unbearable weight put on it, and to see precisely why it seems so elusive and so difficult to achieve. In the second part of the chapter, I will look at some aspects of recent research into the brain to see what insights they shed on this difficulty. In the concluding part of the chapter, I will suggest what this might mean for students, teachers, parents and schools and for all those concerned enough to want themselves and our young people to become more internationally minded.

WHAT IS INTERNATIONAL-MINDEDNESS?

The young child is totally egocentric – meaning not that he thinks selfishly only about himself but, to the contrary, that he is incapable of thinking about himself. The egocentric child is unable to differentiate himself from the rest of the world; he has not separated himself out from others or from objects. Thus he feels that others share his pain or his pleasures, that his mumblings will inevitably be understood, that his perspective is shared by all persons … The whole course of human development can be viewed as a continuing decline in egocentrism. (Gardner 1981)

International-mindedness, I will argue, is a part of the continuum that represents the development of 'self'. As Gardner suggests, the young child enters the world at a stage of pre-self, exhibiting very little distinction between herself and any other part of her world, person or object. (Those who have been parents and experienced the 'terrible twos' do not need a textbook to identify when the next stage, the first separation of self and other, begins to make itself obvious.) But these two stages are only the first of a number of stages at which a 'self' begins to emerge and develop. As we all develop from our own egocentric early sensory experiences and begin to see our embryonic 'self' initially reflected through an 'other', so we then begin to co-exist with an 'other' without too much engagement. (Just watch young children in Kindergarten playing alongside but not 'with' each other.) And then another 'self' begins to develop with the idea of independence from but interdependence with an 'other'; our first 'best friend' and then our family or tribe. Subsequently, this 'self' begins to accommodate the idea of being a member of a nation, and then a part of an inter-nation and finally independence and interdependence on a global scale.

This development of self, by the way, is remarkably consistent. The classical differences between West and East – 'The collective or interdependent nature of Asian society' and 'The individualistic or independent nature of Western society' (Nisbett 2003: xvii) are the difference in our inter-cultural response to the 'other', but not our denial of it. Rolf-E Breuer says that:

Reality in the global village is determined by the diversity of cultures, religions, opinions and lifestyles – in short: identities. Only when we have clearly defined our own person and identity are we able to understand other identities. The aim of this process of understanding is our mutual acknowledgement that the citizens of the global village all have equal standing and equal rights – and acknowledgement of the differences. (Breuer 2002: 15)

Note Breuer's point that 'only when we have clearly defined our own person' … can we move to … 'the aim of this process' which, in my definition, is the development of international-mindedness. As Gardner says, we are engaged on a continuum of human development that is 'a continuing decline in egocentrism'. And the place of international-mindedness on that continuum is very much to one end of it. International-mindedness represents the most complex development of the relationship between 'self' and 'other' but it is not, of itself, about the environment, peace, globalization or future work. International-mindedness is a vital (the vital?) component of each of these and many other contemporary themes but it is not the same as them.

There have been numerous attempts to plot the development of international-mindedness, all of which implicitly or explicitly take into account the progress of the development of self. Many of these attempts describe end-points with which few of us would disagree. Mark Heyward's matrix of intercultural literacy, for example, suggests that the final stage of development is one characterized by 'bicultural or transcultural identity. "Species" or "global" identity may emerge. Ability to consciously shift between multiple cultural identities' (Heyward 2002).

Bennett's (1993) model of intercultural sensitivity defines the most developed stage of *integration* as:

> The construction of reality as increasingly capable of accommodating cultural differences that constitute development … [and] … Sensitivity to the importance of cultural differences and to the point of view of other people. The recognition that 'cultures differ fundamentally from one another in the way they maintain patterns of differentiation, or worldviews', and as a person's capacity to 'differentiate phenomena in different ways'. (Bennett 1993: 4)

Other more anecdotal approaches suggest the same qualities of diminished or non-existent egocentrism. In discussing his life as a world traveller, the journalist Pico Iyer says that 'the most important thing about traveling is to leave one's assumptions at home, and to empty oneself out as much as possible … to try to see the world through the eyes of people very different from oneself' (Iyer 2002: 42).

All this is good stuff, very beneficial and an admirable goal. Nor is it necessarily unachievable. But the downside of these views is that they encourage the belief that our development through to this final stage is less problematic than it actually is. This would be worrying enough if we were talking only about adults, at a stage of development when we might hope that the combination of our life experiences and opportunity for reflection gets us close to this final throwing off of much of our egocentricity. But when we apply these goals to the development of young children and students, we create expectations that *are* unachievable,

cause teachers and students to engage in inappropriate activities and cause many of us in the profession to look for and sometimes identify 'success' where we shouldn't. What seems to be the case is that whilst a definition (or different definitions) of the characteristics of fully realized international-mindedness is possible, its actualization is another matter altogether.

In late 2005 I took part in an exercise using Bennett's 'Developmental Model of Intercultural Sensitivity' with a group of teachers working in an established and prestigious international school. This model proposes a number of positions relative to the development of intercultural sensitivity. The first three – denial, defence and minimization – Bennett describes as the 'Ethnocentric' stages. The second three – acceptance, adaptation and integration – Bennett describes as the 'Ethnorelative' stages. These teachers had selected themselves to attend a course I had been asked to deliver on the development of international-mindedness; in other words, all of us were already interested in self-reflection about these ideas. Our life experiences were interesting, too, with an average experience of more than ten years of living in a culture other than the one in which we grew up. Yet when we were shown the interpretation of our response to the inventory, none of our self-selected internationally experienced educators were described as 'integrated'; nor were any of us described as fully developed in either of the other two ethnorelative positions. Quite simply, we all have some way to go before we reach the 'integration' position.

Others who reflect on their own internationally minded lives report similar confusions and complexity. Writing about her experiences as a writer who works in a language that is not her first language, Isabelle de Courtivron says:

> What is it like to write in a language that is not the language in which you were raised? To speak and write in a language other than the one that you once believed held the seamless connection between things? Despite the fashionable postmodern emphasis on displacement and dislocation;

despite the celebration of diversity and 'more-than-oneness'; despite the intellectual persuasion that trying to find wholeness in our lives is a somewhat obsolete ideal, the anxiety about fragmentation and the search for existential coherence remain primordial human responses. The lifelong struggle to reconcile the different pieces of the identity puzzle (or at least to acknowledge that they cannot be reconciled) continues to be a painful and constantly renegotiated process. (de Courtivron 2003:1)

We often think of cultures as distinguished from each other by the content of their beliefs and practices and the way in which the internal relationship between them forms a coherent whole. However, cultures are not only distinguishable from each other but also are different internally. Single cultures have a diffuse and complex nature and cannot be summed up neatly. Individuals relate to their 'own' culture differently, from a deep commitment and involvement in the beliefs and practices of that culture to an eclectic selectivity. As a result, not even single cultures remain static and stable; the beliefs and practices that constitute the culture are always being individually and collectively reinterpreted in the light of new situations and unexpected circumstances. This complexity within single cultures is, of course, intensified and magnified as cultures brush up against and interact with each other.

Daniel Goeudevert has said that 'my experience has also taught me that diversity alone has no intrinsic value. In fact, it can even lead to the opposite of tolerance if it is not coached and guided' (Goeudevert 2002: 49). These experiential descriptions of the insecurity and complexity of our development of self along the continuum to international-mindedness are much more realistic than some of the codified descriptors that seem to be more expressions of hope than anything grounded in people's actual lives. The development of the self and our declining egocentrism is based on the messiness of our own life experiences from our earliest years, the impact those experiences have on us and the way in which that impact manifests itself in our awareness and behaviours. The truth is that our move towards international-mindedness might not be as 'natural' or 'developmental' as we wish it to be, but yet another example of the 'ambiguity, uncertainty and imperfection' (Pascale and Athos 1982) that is the progress of all of our lives.

Developmental matrices wittingly or unwittingly risk encouraging us to see each stage as progressing straightforwardly from the preceding one. Unfortunately, there is a world of difference between a description of each stage and the real-life experiences that cause or inhibit our ability to move from one to the other. And that world of difference should cause us to see the relationship between the stages of the development of self differently.

Rather than exhibiting a smooth progression along a hierarchical series of staging posts, we do not leave our previous stage of development behind but incorporate it into the succeeding stage. These stages *transcend but include* each other (Wilber 2000). What happens in a previous stage is intricately bound up with what happens in later stages. If our life experiences have enabled us to develop a secure version of self at a particular stage, then the next stage of our development may be a positive one. But if our current sense of self is insecure, then it will impact on our future development. As Wilber says:

each stage of development brings not only new capacities but the possibility of new disasters; not just novel potentials but novel pathologies; new strengths, new diseases. Annoyingly, there is a price to be paid for each increase in consciousness, and this 'dialectic of progress' (good news, bad news) needs always to be remembered. (Wilber 2000: 11)

The development of international-mindedness, then, is anything but straightforward. Few of us seem capable of achieving the descriptors at the end of the continuum and those fellow humans that do are feted precisely because they are special in this regard. Existing in the ferment that is our developing self and – as the most highly developed form of our self – dependent on all that has gone before, we need to see international-mindedness as essentially problematic rather than straightforward. Which does not mean that it is not worthwhile, of course.

If what I am saying is true of adults, then it is especially true of children and students. If parents, teachers and others are to be a part of the process through which children and students come to develop international-mindedness, then we need to develop a more sophisticated view of what is going on as learning to be internationally minded takes place and as we devise the experiences that are most helpful to the young people about whom we are concerned. Fortuitously, this is a good time for us to do this as the growing evidence from research into the brain is beginning to help us both refine our awareness of how young people learn and also, interestingly, explain why our decline in egocentrism is so problematic.

EVIDENCE FROM RECENT RESEARCH INTO THE BRAIN

I began this chapter writing about the misappropriation of many good things. Over the past 15 years brain research has suffered similar injustices. Recent growth in brain research has been exponential but the fact is that it is still in its infancy, with far more unknown than known. This, of course, has not stopped writers (including some brain researchers) from building methodologies about teaching, learning and self-growth that are unsupported by evidence from the research. So, in this section, I will limit myself to just a few results from brain research about which there is either common agreement or legitimate discussion and debate.

I will focus on just four results from research into the brain, relate them to the development of international-mindedness and try to put them in the context of children and students. They are (a) the importance of the brain as an efficient organism, (b) the impact of emotions on learning, (c) arguments about multiple intelligences and (d) evidence about the function and development of the pre-frontal cortex.

The brain as an efficient organism

The number of neurons in the brain and the number of possible connections between them

is so well documented that such information is now a staple feature of popular magazines. Images abound of the complexity involved. (Here is a particularly popular one: the number of possible connections between neurons is probably bigger than the number of atoms in the universe [Ornstein and Thompson 1984]). Such metaphors provide images of the brain as something of almost unbounded possibility and capability. But they conceal the fact that the brain is a hugely efficient organism that seeks to find the most efficient ways to work, rather than the most complex.

Two examples of this are important to recount. First, the more we develop connections in the brain and the more we re-visit these connections, the more the brain chooses to replicate them rather than any of the other possibilities available (Ratey 2001). It is just more efficient that way. When we see a stranger in the street with some of the characteristics of a friend, we are more likely initially to see the stranger as the friend rather than as a stranger. Our brain is looking for similarities that it can replicate rather than differences with which it has to deal anew. Although we have the possibility of innumerable connections the brain is learning from our responses which connections to strengthen and which to leave alone. Second, the brain does as much pruning of its connections as it does making them (Greenfield 1997). Recent evidence seems to suggest that in childhood there are two periods when pruning is most active: around the ages of 3 and 14, but neuronal and synaptic pruning continues throughout our lives.

Pruning is another example of the brain's drive for efficiency. If connections exist but are unused for long periods of time then the brain prunes them as unnecessary. (For example, the brain's capacity to learn the sounds of many different languages is wired-in from birth, but around the ages of 3 or 4 the brain prunes that capacity to focus on those sounds most often heard and used since birth.) This efficient functioning of the brain helps to explain why it is much harder to unlearn than learn and why inappropriate learning stays with us. If, for instance, you taught yourself to play the piano and did not *accidentally* come across the most efficient fingering, it will be much harder to learn that fingering when you finally have lessons. For the brain, efficient learning has already taken place.

How does this relate to the development of international-mindedness? International-mindedness, through the process of the development of self and declining egocentrism, is learned and is dependent on a series of previous learnings. What has been learned at different periods in our development of self will determine whether we create Wilber's 'novel potentials' or 'novel pathologies'.

The brain is not a moral organ; it is an efficient one. If our early development of the relationship between our 'self' and an 'other' is a confrontational one (if we observe disagreements in our families continually resulting not in discussion and resolution but in conflict and dissension; if our experiences of other cultural groups who live near us are mediated through a 'culture of division rather than a culture of connection' [Slater 2003]) then our brain will do its work as efficiently as possible, cementing this learning in place, creating the conditions under which the development of international-mindedness is already more problematic. Brain research has helped us to see why psychologist Mihaly Csikszentmihalyi observes that:

> once there is a self – even if it is little used – it begins to make its claims like any other organism. It wants to keep its shape, to reproduce itself ... A person with a self will want to keep and spread the information in his or her consciousness as well. A self identified with material possessions will drive its owner to accumulate more and more property, regardless of consequences for anyone else. The self of Stalin, built around the need for power, did not rest until everyone who might challenge his absolute rule was dead. (Csikszentmihalyi 1993: 23)

It's just more efficient that way.

How emotions affect learning

We have learned much about the role of emotions in and the effect of emotions on learning. On the one hand, positive emotions – motivation, interest and excitement – help the learning process take place. On the other hand, negative emotions – fear, uncertainty, lack of confidence – play havoc with successful learning; except, that is, from successfully helping the brain learn that learning is an unpleasant experience.

A part of the brain called the amygdala plays a large part in how emotions affect learning (Robertson 1999). Evolutionarily designed to process dangerous information fast and invoke the 'flight or fight' response, the amygdala continues to respond to more refined twenty-first-century definitions of alarm in the same way as it once responded to more immediate dangers. In sensing danger, the amygdala sends out chemical signals to the body to protect the vital organs. It is the reason why we 'go cold' when we are frightened and why we 'almost lose our minds' at moments of high tension. Quite literally, under stressful conditions, the thinking brain stops working and we find ourselves 'on automatic'. As Goleman says:

> In many or most of these moments ... our ... minds are exquisitely coordinated; feelings are essential to thought, thought to feeling. But when passions surge the balance tips: it is the emotional mind that captures the upper hand, swamping the rational mind. (Goleman 1995: 9)

Learning, by definition, is stressful. It takes place on the edge of what we know and with which we are comfortable, and asks us to jump off into the abyss of the unknown. Mark Heyward (2002) speaks with insight about the 'crisis of engagement' that ignites our hopeful leaps through the stages of development towards international-mindedness. Many of us have experienced a crisis of engagement in our responses to and engagement with other cultures. But 'crisis of engagement' seems to me to be an appropriate description of the moment of stress that all learning brings, whether to a young child realizing that they cannot remember letter sounds when others can, or to the scientist who sees a lifetime's work challenged and put at risk by the discoveries of others. It is just that the crises of engagement that lead to developments in our international-mindedness, each shock of having to move from egocentrism through to emptying 'oneself as much as possible', are so much more visceral.

How we learn to deal emotionally with these crises of engagement as we develop will have a profound effect on our capability to become internationally minded and on whether our engagement with others brings new rewards or new diseases, precisely because the continual process of becoming internationally minded is always a crisis of engagement. So our emotional development, the way in which we learn to balance the attempts of the amygdala to shut down our rational capability in order to help us fight or flee, is crucial to our response to one of the most profound crises of engagement, the intercultural. But it also has a profound effect on our development as learners, our willingness to be open and our energy to explore what is uncomfortably new rather than rest with what already exists. The psychologist Guy Claxton (1999) calls this 'learning power'. He says that:

> The feelings of being unsure of what is going on, and being set to take note of any information that may help to clarify a situation – in other words, to learn – constitute a family of emotions we might call interest/anxiety/excitement. The tentative readiness to engage and experiment, to take the risk of staying close that learning requires, generates a range of feelings from interest and absorption at one end to an apprehension that borders on fear, anger, distress, disgust, sadness or shock at the other ... So the feelings of learning are special in that they often occupy an intermediate, ambiguous position between attraction and repulsion.
>
> But as the world becomes more complex and shifting, so either reflex timidity or reflex aggression begin to carry risks, for neither of them allows the kind of engagement – and therefore the kind of increased knowledge and know-how – that learning might deliver. (1999: 40)

Which helps to explain why Wilber argues that any situation contains the possibility of good news or bad news and why Goeudevert can argue that diversity alone has no intrinsic value and can lead to the opposite of tolerance if it is not coached and guided. Diversity is a challenge to self; diversity is a crisis of engagement. Perhaps we should not be surprised that so many of us go on holiday only to surround ourselves with all that is common from where we have just left. It is either a response to our emotional incapacity to deal with what might be shockingly new or it is the way we deal with a self that has learned not to have the learning power that is developed through our emotional intelligence.

Multiple intelligences

Howard Gardner was by no means the first to propose the idea that different brains process experiences differently and nor is he the first to be at the centre of controversy about this idea. What has caused his ideas to become more established is that he has developed them with reference to evidence gathered against stringent criteria. It is also true that many teachers recognize their implicit classroom experiences in his explicit descriptions. (Continuing a minor theme of this chapter, Gardner's work has been adopted, kidnapped and misrepresented too, often in books purporting to help teachers implement it in the classroom.)

In essence, multiple intelligence theory posits that there are eight distinct ways in which the brain processes experience and creates a variety of products useful to particular cultures: mathematical-logical, linguistic, musical, kinesthetic, visual-spatial, interpersonal, intrapersonal and naturalist. The theory argues that the processing power of each of these intelligences is rigorous rather than simplistic, being concerned with the essential concepts of each. (Singing songs while learning multiplication tables may be fun but it is not using musical intelligence. It's just fun – and that's fine. Using core concepts such as rhythm, pitch and tone to compose a piece of music that reflects your experience of the market-place you visited is, on the other hand, an example of musical intelligence at work.) Each intelligence has its own characteristics and its own core ideas. Central to the notion of *interpersonal* intelligence, for example, is the core idea of the 'other'. Those people who are interpersonally intelligent are able to take on the perspective of the other, creating empathic understandings and working with them, integrating them with their own thoughts and feelings. Gardner defines another intelligence, intrapersonal, as:

> knowledge of the internal aspects of a person: access to one's own feeling life, one's range of emotions, the capacity to effect discrimination amongst those emotions and eventually to label them and to draw upon them as a means of understanding and guiding one's own behaviour. A person with good intrapersonal intelligence has a viable and effective model of himself or herself. (Gardner 1993: 23)

What we see in these two intelligences is a description of the key elements of the development of international-mindedness. First, a growing and increasingly secure development of self through intrapersonal intelligence; second, the contribution of that secure self in relationship to the other through interpersonal intelligence. There are two pieces of good news here, especially for people like me who argue that the development of international-mindedness is inherently complex and more difficult than descriptions of it indicate. The first piece of good news is that we can see that children, students and adults with developed intrapersonal and interpersonal intelligences are those people most likely to become internationally minded. The second is that we now have a signpost to what we need to do in schools to help children develop international-mindedness so that we meet Goeudevert's (2002) requirement that it needs to be 'coached and guided'.

But we need to add a couple of cautionary notes, too. First, we are still learning what it is to coach and guide children, students and adults to interpersonal and intrapersonal intelligences; in other words, we are still learning how to develop two of the key elements in international-mindedness. Second, we are still stumbling towards knowing how we can utilize the other intelligences developed in children and students who are not interpersonally or intrapersonally intelligent so that they can contribute to the development of international-mindedness. What is it, for example, about the core ideas of mathematical-logical intelligence or kinesthetic intelligence that can be used to develop linked ideas about the self and the other? And if the answer is that there is very little, does this mean that only the interpersonally and intrapersonally intelligent children and adults are capable of even engaging in a messy development towards international-mindedness?

The development of the pre-frontal cortex

Probably the most recently accepted results of brain research that have implications for learning are two discoveries about the pre-frontal cortex. First, we know now that the pre-frontal cortex has a crucial role to play in handling our most complex thinking. 'Complex' thinking is important in our attempts to come to terms with what international-mindedness is. All concepts and ideas are a mix of knowledge, skills and understanding but the most complex are those that involve significant understanding. Unfortunately, educators have created a problem by minimizing the complexity of understanding and defining it too narrowly. It is only too common to see lesson plans that confidently state that at the conclusion of this six week unit (or less) students will understand x or y. Yet when the concert pianist Andreas Schiff was asked why he had chosen to record Bach's Goldberg Variations again after a period of 20 years he replied 'Because I think I understand it a little better now.' And when the Dalai Lama was asked what he thought of the Chinese invasion of Tibet 40 years after the event, he replied 'It's too soon to tell.' Just as some of us have created international-mindedness *lite* so we are in danger of creating a classroom version of understanding *lite*, a superficial demonstration that represents little of the complexity with which understanding is rightly associated and because of which so many of us are unable to explain what we really understand.

Just in case anyone thinks I am splitting hairs, here is a not-often-enough-read quote from the gurus of teaching for understanding:

All teachers talk about wanting to get beyond coverage to ensure that students really understand what they learn. Although we talk this way, readers may find that what they thought was effective teaching for understanding really wasn't. In fact, we predict that readers will be somewhat disturbed by how hard it is to specify what understanding looks like and how easily educators can lose sight of understanding even as they try to teach for it. (Wiggins and McTighe 1998: 5)

Even for Wiggins and McTighe, understanding is actually more elusive than their work has been portrayed to suggest.

But here is the second and more thought-provoking finding from recent brain research. The pre-frontal cortex – this place that handles our most complex thinking and which has much to do with the development of international-mindedness at the far end of the continuum of declining egocentrism – is the last part of the brain to mature, most often not until between the ages of 18 and 23. This finding has done much to explain what we have previously seen only as typical teenage behaviour. Physically and sexually mature, how is it that so many teenagers just don't seem to get it? Well:

Select any of the difficulties associated with adolescence (impulsiveness, erratic mood swings, rebellion against authority, poor judgement et cetera) and you'll find that these difficulties are the result of immaturity in the pre-frontal cortex. Adulthood is the culmination of human brain development, the goal that nature was striving for. In adolescence, teens are expected to take on at least some of the pre-frontal lobe functions once handled by parents and teachers. But the pre-frontal lobes are still immature – and must also keep up with the hormonal tumult occurring within the body and the brain. (Restak 2001: 76)

Howard Gardner has expressed concern that:

Thanks to hundreds of studies during the past few decades by cognitively oriented psychologists and educators, we now know one truth about understanding: Most students in most schools – indeed, many of the best students in the best schools – cannot exhibit appreciable understanding of important ideas. (Gardner 2001: 162)

But perhaps we should not be so surprised. It is more likely that the reason that students cannot exhibit appreciable understanding of important ideas – presumably also about international-mindedness – is that their brains are still maturing to the point at which they will be able to do so. Of course, some students will display such understandings, but brain research is helping us to see that these students are the exceptions rather than the rule.

THE IMPLICATIONS FOR THE DEVELOPMENT OF INTERNATIONAL-MINDEDNESS IN SCHOOLS

In the first part of this chapter I argued that the development of international-mindedness is more complex and messy, more personal and emotional, than many seem to believe or want to admit. It is dependent upon a continually successful series of developments of the self that transcend and include each other. In the second part of this chapter, I argued that brain research is helping us to see why this is: the complex development of the relationship between self and other taking place from birth to adulthood involves the laying down of neuronal constellations about successful or unsuccessful relationships between self and other which the brain, for better or worse, is hardwired to replicate and which are difficult to unlearn. This laying down is mediated through our ability to deal with the stress of personal emotions which causes more or less helpful learning to happen and, in turn, affects our willingness to take on the necessary crises of engagement that represent the raw material of the development of international-mindedness. All of this is conducted through the processing power of our particular portfolio of neuronal constellations, which Gardner calls intelligences, some of which contribute more obviously to the development of international-mindedness and some of which less so. Finally, much of this needs to take place in a part of the brain that does not reach maturity until most students have left school.

In the light of this apparently downbeat reality, what should schools be doing to foster the development of international-mindedness? To conclude the chapter I offer a few suggestions.

First, we need to see international-mindedness *lite* for what it is. Typified in many ways by the often quoted focus on the 4Fs of Food, Festivals, Fashion and Flags, the student experiences that result are often too superficial to enable children and students to develop a sense of the other from them. In fact, there is a real danger that they become opportunities for children and students to find the features of other cultures exotic but not as having deep meaning; a real example of the danger of diversity alone 'having no intrinsic value' (Goeudevert, 2002). This will no longer do. As Suarez-Orozco and Qin-Hilliard write:

> Negotiating differences requires energy – the kind of energy that can be recycled and harnessed to bolster a cornerstone of human intelligence: the ability to consider multiple perspectives. Education's challenge will be to shape the cognitive skills, interpersonal sensibilities and cultural sophistication of children and youth whose lives will be both engaged in local contexts and responsive to larger transnational processes. We claim that two domains in particular will present the greatest challenge to schooling worldwide: the domain of 'difference' and the domain of 'complexity.' (2004: 5)

Second, to answer that challenge, we need to continue the current emphasis on the development of curricula that are deeper, more challenging and more related to the continuum of which international-mindedness is a part. These curricula, by the very nature of what they are trying to achieve, will be experimental for some time. Nevertheless, we need to offer them our support and be willing to use our schools as the testing grounds for them, engaging with students, parents, teachers and others in action research of their successes and failures. Jeffrey Abramson suggests that notions of tolerance should be replaced by notions of respect and that:

> Respect argues for a curriculum of civic education in democratic societies, a course of education sufficient to replace the distant, indifferent feeling of mere tolerance with a more intimate, knowledgable and sincere appreciation of other traditions. (Abramson 2002: 101)

Third, within those curriculum experiments we need to create learning outcomes and learning targets for children and students that are based on what we know of their capabilities at the different ages and stages of their development, rather than our definitions of end-of-the-line descriptions of international-mindedness. Whatever the majority of student skills in and understanding of international-mindedness may be – even by the end of their secondary education – it will not get close to some of the statements currently being offered to define international-mindedness at its most developed state. The fact that a few students may reach these heady levels of development is the exception that proves the rule and not the rule itself.

Fourth, we need to think carefully about the precise 'crises of engagement' we create that enable children and students to experience the shock of the other, and what we do with them. For a 6-year-old child, their first sleepover at another family's home may be just such a crisis; a crisis of different rules and systems, of different experiences at the hands of different adults and so on. It may be the first time outside the normality of their own family that they have experienced such a shock. How we discuss this with them and how we help children relate to it will help to determine whether the experience becomes worthwhile or not. Similarly, we need to think about the experiences we can offer to 14-year-olds (and others, of course) that can take real rather than superficial advantage of the opportunities their development affords.

Finally, we need to do all of this within an overall school culture where the 'other' is of profound importance. This means being open and willing to discuss difference in every aspect of school life; to value those whose growing sense of the 'other' and its relationship to their own self is important; to create structures and systems within which respect for others is a fundamental part of the school ethos, including the way teachers work with students, each other and parents; and, most importantly, to model in our own moment by moment mindfulness that which we hold of value.

REFERENCES

Abramson, J. (2002) Ideals of democratic justice. In M. Ali, N. Barley, I. Baruma, S. Dunn, H. Küng, W. Soyinka et al. (eds) *The End of Tolerance?* London: Nicholas Brealey.

Bennett, M.J. (1993) Towards ethnorelativism: a developmental model of intercultural literacy. In R.M. Paige (ed.) *Education for the Intercultural Experience*. Yarmouth, ME: Intercultural Press.

Breuer, R-E. (2002) Freedom's twin. In M. Ali, N. Barley, I. Baruma, L. Coffey, S. Dunn, H. Küng, W. Soyinka et al. (eds) *The End of Tolerance?* London: Nicholas Brealey.

Budbill, D. (2002) The Three Goals. In G. Keillar (ed.) *Good Poems*. New York: Penguin.

Claxton, G. (1999) *Wise-Up: The Challenge of Life-Long Learning*. London: Bloomsbury.

Csikszentmihalyi, M. (1993) *The Evolving Self: A Psychology for the Third Millenium*. New York: HarperCollins.

de Courtivron, I. (ed.) (2003) *Lives in Translation: Bilingual Writers on Identity and Creativity*. New York: Palgrave Macmillan.

Gardner, H. (1981) *The Quest for Mind*. Chicago: University of Chicago Press.

Gardner, H. (1993) *Multiple Intelligences – The Theory in Practice: A Reader*. New York: Basic Books.

Gardner, H. (2001) *Intelligence Reframed. Multiple Intelligences for the 21st Century*. New York: Basic Books.

Goeudevert, D. (2002) Nothing from nothing. In M. Ali, N. Barley, I. Baruma, L. Coffey S. Dunn, H. Küng, W. Soyinka et al. (eds) *The End of Tolerance?* London: Nicholas Brealey.

Goleman, D. (1995) *Emotional Intelligence: Why It can Matter More than IQ*. New York: Bantam.

Greenfield, S. (1997) *The Human Brain–A Guided Tour*. London: Phoenix.

Heyward, M. (2002) From international to intercultural: redefining the international school for a globalized world. *Journal of Research in International Education*, 1(1): 9–32.

Iyer, P. (2002) Global imagination, *Ascent* magazine, Issue 15 (Fall). (Ascent Publishing, Quebec, Canada.)

Nisbett, R.E. (2003) *The Geography of Thought: How Asians and Westerners Think Differently ... and Why*. New York: Free Press.

Ornstein, R. and Thompson, R. (1984) *The Amazing Brain*. New York: Houghton Mifflin.

Pascale, R.T. and Athos, G.A. (1982) *The Art of Japanese Management*. New York: Warner Books.

Ratey, J.J. (2001) *A User's Guide to the Brain*. New York: Pantheon.

Restak, R. (2001) *The Secret Life of the Brain*. Washington, DC: The Dana Press and The Joseph Henry Press.

Robertson, I. (1999) *Mind Sculpture*. London: Bantam Press.

Slater, P. (2003) Connected we stand. *Utne Magazine* (March/April). (Lens Publishing, Minneapolis.)

Suarez-Orozco, M.M. and Qin-Hilliard, S.B. (eds) (2004) *Globalization, Culture and Education in the New Millenium*. Berkeley, CA: University of California Press.

Wiggins, G. and McTighe, J. (1998) *Understanding by Design*. Alexandria: ASCD.

Wilber, K. (2000) *A Theory of Everything*. Boston, MA: Shambhala Publications.

32

Internationalization of Curriculum: a Critical Perspective

Fazal Rizvi

The idea of 'internationalization of curriculum' has become something of a slogan within the modern corporatized universities. One does not have to look far to find it in the mission statements of most leading universities, from Austria to Australia, from the United States to the United Arab Emirates. It is not enough, suggests a university in the United Kingdom, to expand the number of international students, it is now necessary to renovate the curriculum, making it more responsive to the compelling requirements of globalization. A global university, trumpets a *Universitas 21* document, must now be characterized by its international content, its engagement with the global circuits of knowledge and communication. A university in the United States suggests that for it to be recognized for its global character, it must rethink its reach, its networks and its role and functions as well as its curriculum. In the global knowledge economy, it insists, both curricular aims and the operational structures to implement them need to be rethought and rearticulated.

It is not only the universities that preach the internationalization of curriculum, governments and intergovernmental organizations do so as well. In search of a new paradigm, an Australian government report (Beazley 1994) asserts, for example, 'international education is an increasingly important part of Australia's international relations. It uniquely spans the cultural, economic and interpersonal dimensions of international relations'. As a matter of policy, the report encourages 'cultural understanding of all parties', and 'an international outlook' among students and academics alike. It demands a new approach to curriculum development, which is more responsive to 'the diverse and sophisticated nature of the global environment'. Internationalized curriculum, it maintains, must be based on the values of innovation, flexibility, client-centredness and enterprise culture on the one hand and intercultural understanding and sensitivity on the other. Similar sentiments may be found elsewhere. For the Swedish government, for example, the idea of the internationalization of the curriculum does not simply imply student mobility but also efforts to give all students – mobile and immobile – learning experiences that develop their international and intercultural competence.

Regional and intergovernmental organizations, such as UNESCO, the OECD and the European Union, too, highlight the importance of curriculum reform, in line with their attempts to support student mobility and cooperation between member states. The European Union, for example, has long highlighted measures to support student mobility and cooperation between member states and others. The Union's ERASMUS, SOCRATES and LEONARDO programmes are based on the principles of internationalization, as a way not only of supporting structural cooperation but also of promoting curriculum development and the creation of networks and credit transfer arrangements. The Lisbon Declaration codified some of these principles, with specific performance indicators. In order to internationalize its curriculum, suggests UNESCO (2002), the university must 'express in its knowledge work in a new and changed environment. If the university is to serve well both scholarship and national needs, if it is to prepare graduates for this new era, the university is obligated to modernize and to contribute to the global exchange of knowledge through the movement of people, information, and ideas'.

The appeal of the idea of internationalization of the curriculum appears ubiquitous and worldwide. But beyond its symbolic language and some general measures to facilitate student mobility, it is not always clear what it means, and how it might represent a more radical and systematic concept around which to prioritize and organize learning. In this chapter I want to examine some of the ways in which the idea of the internationalization of curriculum has been operationalized, based largely on an analysis provided by the Organization of Economic Co-operation and Development (OECD). I want to argue that the OECD's suggestions for curriculum reform are located, in a largely celebratory fashion, within a neo-liberal imaginary of global processes, and do not adequately engage with their complex dynamics and uneven and unequal consequences. I want to propose a more critical concept of internationalization, which seeks to develop in students a range of 'epistemic virtues', with which to critically interpret, reflect upon and engage with the contemporary processes of globalization that are now reshaping all our identities and communities.

POPULAR CONSTRUCTIONS

While the idea of the internationalization of curriculum remains largely symbolic, most of its popular constructions appear to rest on a definition suggested by the OECD in 1996. Not only can it be found in the policy statements of universities and systems of higher education around the world, it is also used by activist networks, such as Internationalization at Home (Nillson 2000), to develop their own distinctive understanding. The OECD (1996) defines the internationalization of curriculum as an attempt to introduce an 'international orientation in content, aimed at preparing students for performing (professionally/socially) in an international and multicultural context, and designed for domestic students as well as foreign students'. Such an international orientation to the curriculum, the OECD argues, is necessary partly because of the requirements of the global labour market but also because of the social and cultural developments that are heading towards 'a multicultural and globally minded society'. Here the OECD's economic instrumentalism converges with its support for a corporatist view of multiculturalism. Its rhetoric of internationalization synthesizes two discourses: of economic necessity and of cultural exchange and intercultural understanding. It thus enjoins an ethical impulse to what it views as the imperatives of the global economy.

At a conceptual level, the main problem with the OECD's definition is its lack of specificity. It encourages the introduction of an international orientation in curriculum content, but provides no clear indication of how such an introduction should be enacted in pedagogy and in curricular arrangements; nor does it specify how the notion of an 'international orientation' might be interpreted. It provides no criteria for judging the efficacy and relevance of international content, as it might relate to particular instances of disciplinary knowledge. Furthermore, the OECD's focus on content largely eschews issues of pedagogy and of the development of intercultural skills and competencies. It also ignores issues of values and attitudes in an area in which affective dimensions are arguably more important than those relating to knowledge. And finally, the OECD describes its approach as process-orientated, but as Wachter (2000: 5) points out, this approach does not 'inform us in any explicit way what the process consists of, that is, what are the means by which teaching, research and service functions are to be made international'.

If the OECD's definition of internationalization is too abstract then perhaps an inventory of the actual practices by which universities are seeking to internationalize their curriculum might help. To develop such an inventory, the OECD, through its Centre for Educational Research and Innovation (CERI), conducted in 1996 a survey of six OECD countries (Australia, Denmark, France, Germany, Japan and The Netherlands). The survey proposed a typology of initiatives that included efforts to: introduce new fields of study with international content, such as international relations and European law; broaden an existing subject area by adopting a comparative approach; introduce curricula that prepare students for international professions; stress the importance of learning foreign languages in order to develop skills of cross-cultural communication; develop interdisciplinary programmes such as area and regional studies; restructure curricula to meet the requirements of internationally recognized professional qualifications; introduce curricula leading to joint or double degrees; promote study abroad programmes; and develop courses designed specifically for international students.

Ten years later, the popular constructions of the internationalization of curriculum around the world remain embedded within this typology. So beyond the specific measures designed to support international students, most initiatives of curriculum reform fall under three interrelated categories: facilitating study abroad and educational exchange to broaden and enrich students' cultural experiences; learning about other languages and cultures as a way of developing their skills of intercultural communication; and preparing them to work in the global knowledge economy. Each of these measures is supposed to contribute to the

realization of the others. In this way, considerable scope is left to universities to develop their own distinctive range of activities.

Study abroad programmes are generally defined as involving those learning experiences that students have outside their own country, for which credit is given at the home university. Permutations of study abroad programmes are many, and include such arrangements as international exchange between two or more universities, undertaken on a reciprocal basis with tuition fees mutually waived, international industry or clinical placements or internships, international study tours taken specifically for credit, joint degree or diploma programmes, research at an overseas university for an award at home, and other similar collaborations. Administratively, study abroad programmes represent a pragmatic, quick and achievable way of internationalizing curriculum. They do not require any significant structural changes to the existing curriculum, and can always be 'added on' as options provided to students within an existing programme. Because of their high visibility moreover universities can claim success, even if the benefits of study abroad programmes cannot be easily demonstrated.

A second way universities have sought to internationalize curriculum is by encouraging the teaching of languages and cultures other than one's own. The contention here is that learning about other cultures broadens students' experiences, and is also a means through which intercultural exchange and understanding can be promoted. If the global movement of people has made most communities around the world 'multicultural' and if the global flow of ideas and media has made cultural insularity and isolation impossible, then, it is suggested, a university curriculum cannot afford to ignore these cultural realities. These arguments for internationalization are broadly similar to those that are used to support various notions of multiculturalism within the national arena. Both underscore the need for recognition of and respect for cultural diversity. Both highlight the values of openness, recognition and tolerance, regarding cultural diversity not only as a resource for the potential enrichment of individuals but also a community value that can contribute to social cohesion and economic advancement.

The link between intercultural competence and economic advancement is assumed in many attempts to internationalize curriculum, especially in professional disciplines such as Economics and Business Studies. This link is based on a particular interpretation of the requirements of the global economy, which is increasingly regarded as knowledge-based and service-orientated. In the knowledge economy, it is argued, knowing about facts and theories is less important than an understanding of the world of cultural and social relations and the networks through which knowledge is converted into innovation and commercially viable products. This has led to an emphasis on developing in students a 'global competence' that enables them to become globally mobile and work in a range of different cultural contexts. This also underscores the need to develop qualifications less geared towards the demands of the national labour market and more towards international requirements. It suggests curricular frameworks that are globally networked and fully utilize the possibilities of new information and communication technologies.

PERSISTENT LIMITATIONS

Initiatives around study abroad, intercultural exchange and understanding and global competence clearly hold out considerable potential for internationalizing curriculum, even if they are difficult to implement in a coherent and systematic institution-wide fashion. They represent attempts to prepare students for a world in which the nature of work and labour processes and of cultural exchange is constantly changing as a result not only of shifts in the global knowledge economy and social relations but also of rapid advances in information technologies. Preparing students to negotiate change has itself become an important ingredient in the processes of curriculum reform. However, promising though these initiatives are, their potential cannot be fully realized

without conceptual thinking that is more systematic, addressing a range of issues, both practical and theoretical, about the broader curriculum architecture within which the ideas of study abroad, cultural exchange and global competence might be located.

The proposition that study abroad programmes promote a more cosmopolitan outlook among students, leading them to become culturally sensitive is, for example, often asserted but seldom demonstrated. The research on the outcomes of study abroad programmes is at best limited. Much of it relates to the questions of access to these programmes and to the administrative arrangements involved in their implementation. Very little of it examines the assumptions underlying study abroad programmes. Much of it assumes that they are intrinsically good, and that global mobility will necessarily, and by itself, produce a cosmopolitan outlook in everyone alike, regardless of their gender, race and socioeconomic background, or their prior learning. There is very little examination of study abroad experiences as a curriculum issue. Nor is there any assessment of the conditions necessary for ensuring their curricular success, beyond their value as educational tourism.

Of course, many students who go on study abroad programmes often derive a great deal of personal enjoyment and benefit from them. This is hardly surprising since many of them come from affluent families who have travelled extensively and are already predisposed towards cosmopolitan experiences, especially when it is presented to them as a consumable commodity, consistent with the desire for cultural voyeurism. The students are led to believe that international experience is advantageous to them in the global labour market, which increasingly celebrates the value of what the human resource management literature refers to as 'intercultural competence'. More positively, many students feel that the insights developed during the study abroad programme enable them to acquire a deeper interest in the country they visit, and to become more adaptable, confident, open and tolerant, qualities considered essential for international business.

Yet, other students come back from study abroad programmes disillusioned. Some even have their cultural stereotypes and prejudices confirmed, perhaps even extended. Clearly, the outcomes of study abroad programmes are as varied as the students themselves. One of the persistent problems with study abroad programmes is a lack of any systematic curriculum thinking in their design and evaluation. As a result, students are often poorly prepared for educational experiences abroad and most universities have not yet developed ways of fully accommodating into the curriculum the intercultural insights and questions the students bring back home. Not surprisingly many students complain that while they are encouraged to go abroad, their experiences are accorded little pedagogic value upon their return. Many believe that their teachers have simply not considered ways in which study abroad programmes could be pedagogically productive. The programmes are often viewed as 'add-on' experiences, treated as if they were 'extra-curricular'.

Beyond these legitimate student concerns, however, there are more serious issues surrounding study abroad programmes. They relate to questions not only of access and educational experience but also about the development of transnational networks and the global politics of cultural knowledge and communication. Here the questions of which students go on study abroad programmes, and where, are crucial. Evidence suggests that much of the study abroad traffic is within the developed world (Clyne and Rizvi 1999), and that the universities in the First World generally fail to develop effective sustainable exchange arrangements with universities in the Third World. Students too, it seems, prefer to remain in their cultural 'comfort zone', and the universities in turn do little to challenge them into exploring broader issues of global inequalities. Despite much talk about global interconnectivity and interdependence, international contact remains within globally differentiated cultural communities – the West versus the Rest. In so far as transnational mobility is considered a major characteristic of the current phase of globalization, the circulation of students through study abroad programmes appears to reproduce asymmetrical power relations within the world community.

It is within the context of these power relations that the objectives of learning about other cultures and developing intercultural communication skills are located. These objectives are based on the recognition that under contemporary conditions of mass migration and other forms of mobility, both of people and ideas, all communities are exposed to the growing flows of cultural meanings and knowledge emanating from other societies. Advances in information and communication technologies have made it almost impossible for people to remain isolated, and we 'now have the means to access rapidly far greater quantities of cultural meanings of every kind than ever before and from a multiplicity of sources' (Cohen and Kennedy 2000: 27). We live in a world in which our consumerist tastes converge, and our cultural traditions come into contact with others, but in ways that are not always easy to reconcile. This demands an approach to curriculum that helps students to develop skills of intercultural communication, dialogue and negotiation, through learning about other cultures.

Now while this goal is indeed important, the conceptual framework within which it is located is at best limited, if not flawed. To begin with, it interprets the need to learn about other cultures largely in instrumental economic terms. Cultural meanings are thus reduced to the benefits that students are able to accrue within the global market place. In the process, it converts students into economic units, with the implication that only those aspects of other cultures that are commercially productive are worthy of attention. As I have already noted, this approach is commonplace in business schools around the world, which sustain a particular approach to cultural learning. But the consequences of this approach are that only the superficial aspects of a cultural tradition are learnt, making much learning appear patronizing, especially to marginalized groups and nations.

Another problem with this approach is that it risks reifying cultures, viewing them as somehow static. Far too often it embraces a notion of culture that is inherently naturalistic and anthropological, conceptualized as a 'way of life', reduced to cultural forms made visible in language, habits, customs and objects. This reduction both appeals to, and lends itself to, cultural essentialism, and thus ignores and obscures the historical and political construction of cultural traditions. This essentialism implies that all societies are fundamentally constituted by an uninterrupted accord between the various interests that exist within those societies. However, as a number of critics (for example, Hall 1996) have pointed out, this view of society ignores the workings of power and privilege. It presupposes harmony and agreement as natural states within which differences can co-exist without disturbing the prevailing structural norms.

The presumption of cultural homogeneity is thus fundamentally misguided, especially in the era of global mobility of people. It contradicts the fact that cultural meanings and practices are forged in histories and that in the global era they are established within symmetrical and incommensurate cultural spaces defined by cross-border mobility of ideas, images and ideologies as well as of people. This mobility has led to increased cultural interaction, mixture and fusion, as most societies have become multicultural and hybridized. In a world increasingly constituted by flows of finance, technology and people, through tourism, education and migration, hybridization has become a defining characteristic of social existence, as cultures have become deterritorialized (Tomlinson 2000: 34). If this is so then national cultures cannot be easily defined, since they represent dynamic processes imbricated in broader global relations. As Tomlinson maintains, these processes are leading to 'the gradual and constant alterations in the cognitive maps of people, in their loyalties and in their frames of social and cultural reference' (p. 34).

This perspective on culture has major implications for the way we might think about the notion of 'global competence' that is believed to be necessary for living and working in a global economy and society. If knowledge of and ability to interact productively with people from quite different cultural backgrounds, both within our own society and across the globe, is what is meant by the notion of 'global competence' then cultural traditions need to be viewed as dynamic and creative, and cultural relations as always contingent and historically specific. The focus must be learning not so much about cultural traditions but about the modalities of cultural interactions, how these are produced across differing political and economic interests, and how these have differential consequences for different individuals and communities. The notion of 'the requirements of the global economy' itself needs to be deconstructed, as do the ideological assumptions about the nature of individuals and societies that are implied by the idea of 'global competence'. Crucially important here are the questions of competence: 'for what ends', 'to do what', 'in whose interests' and 'with what consequences'?

NEO-LIBERAL IMAGINARY

These questions are seldom taken seriously in most accounts of the internationalization of curriculum. In my view, this is so because contemporary discourses of internationalization of education have become trapped within a neo-liberal social imaginary that privileges economic considerations over other concerns equally important in education. Of course, the idea of international education itself is not new. There has always been international mobility of students and researchers in search of new knowledge, and training where this is not available within the nation. And there has always been an interest in intercultural knowledge, and in programmes in foreign languages and studies as a way of enhancing international understanding and cooperation. In the past, the more 'developed' nations sponsored international students with a view to developing their skills, attitudes and knowledge so that, upon their return, they could make a robust contribution to national development, in the image of their sponsors.

The neo-liberal imaginary has transformed these sentiments into a new economic discourse of trade, which seeks to redefine the ways in which educational institutions must engage with the emerging 'imperatives' of globalization (Rizvi 2005). This discourse points to the commercial opportunities offered by the increasing movement of people, capital and ideas. It encourages a new kind of knowledge about international relations based on a particular interpretation of the changing nature of the global economy, which is assumed to be knowledge-based and requires an increased level of intercultural communication. International cooperation and the value of knowledge networks are couched almost exclusively in economic terms, as education itself is commodified and converted into a commercial product for sale. It is not surprising then that debates about curriculum are now refracted through this social imaginary.

The philosopher Charles Taylor (2004) has recently provided a very helpful account of how social imaginaries involve a complex, unstructured and contingent mix of the empirical and the affective; not a 'fully articulated understanding of our whole situation within which particular features of our world become evident' (p. 21). A social imaginary is a way of thinking shared in a society by ordinary people, the common understandings that make everyday practices possible, giving them sense and legitimacy. It is both implicit and normative: it is embedded in ideas and practices and events, and carries within it deeper normative notions and images, constitutive of a society. It involves 'something much broader and deeper than the intellectual schemes people may entertain when they think about social reality in a disengaged mode' (p. 24). It is carried in images, myths, parables, stories, legends and other narratives and, most significantly, in the contemporary era, in the mass media.

In the global era, we live amid a multiplicity of intersecting social imaginaries, with different and competing ways of interpreting the contemporary realities of global interconnectivity and interdependence, and of deriving educational implications from them. But these imaginaries do not exist in a neutral space, but in a context in which a particular formation

has become dominant. It is in terms of this formation that most recent accounts of education, promoted by governments and intergovernmental organizations (IGOs) and transnational corporations alike, appear to be couched. Indeed, IGOs, such as the OECD, have become major sites for the organization of knowledge about education, creating an influential and cajoling discourse around the 'imperatives of the global economy' for education. Recognizing that developments in communication and information technologies have enabled increased circulation of ideas, images and ideologies across national spaces, IGOs have created a space within which educational ideas are now explored, exchanged, promoted and steered, leaving few nations entirely free to choose their own educational priorities.

Many of these educational ideas are based on a particular way of imagining the processes of globalization described by a range of scholars (for example, Apple 2004) as 'neo-liberal'. The neo-liberal imaginary consists of a range of images, precepts and generalizations about how the world is becoming increasingly interconnected and interdependent, giving rise to a set of social processes that imply 'inexorable integration of markets, nation-states and technologies to a degree never witnessed before – in a way that is enabling individuals, corporations and nation-states to reach round the world farther, faster, deeper and cheaper than ever before' (Friedman 2000: 14). Such integration is of course variously described and is far from entirely complete or coherent. As Larner has pointed out, the neo-liberal imaginary of globalization can be interpreted as policy, ideology or governmentality – 'a system of meaning that constitutes institutions, practices and identities in contradictory and disjunctive ways' (2000: 12).

The neo-liberal imaginary accords a major role for education because it regards the emerging global economy to be a knowledge economy that requires people with the capacity to operate in an ill-defined and ever-changing labour market, with expanding geographical and time horizons. Neo-liberalism demands a system-wide understanding of the global processes that are assumed to flow from technological developments in transport, communication and data processing. These developments, it is assumed, have transformed the nature of economic activity, changing both modes of production and of consumption. They have also altered the nature of politics and cultural relations, propelling an enormous increase in the movement of people and ideas, leading to the hybridization of cultural practices. Such a context demands the development of a range of cross-cultural skills and what is referred to as the 'global competence'.

More fundamental to the neo-liberal imaginary, however, is a human capital theory (Becker 1964), which views education as an investment. In the global economy, this investment is considered essential for individuals, corporations and nations if they wish to secure competitive advantage. In its popular form, neo-liberalism imagines all human behaviour to be based on the economic self-interest of individuals operating within free competitive markets. It assumes economic growth and competitive advantage to be a direct outcome of the levels of investment in developing human capital. It suggests that in a global economy, performance is increasingly linked to people's knowledge stock, skills level, learning capabilities and cultural adaptability. It therefore demands policy frameworks that enhance labour flexibility not only through the deregulation of the market but also through reform to systems of education and training, better aligned to the changing nature of economic activity.

In its more radical form the human capital theory demands a fundamental reconceptualization of the very purposes of education. The OECD (2004) has suggested, for example, that the advances in information and communication technologies have so transformed the nature of knowledge production and utilization, the organization of work and labour relations, modes of consumption and trade, and patterns of cultural exchange that education now needs to produce different kinds of subjectivities who are better able to work creatively with knowledge; who are flexible, adaptable and mobile; who are globally

minded and interculturally confident; and who are life-long learners. What this view implies is that learning for learning's sake is no longer sufficient, and that education does not have any intrinsic ends as such, but must always be linked to the instrumental purposes of human capital development and economic self-maximization. This does not mean that ethical and cultural issues are no longer relevant to education; but that they should be interpreted within the broader framework of education's economic ends. In this way, neo-liberalism rests on what George Soros (1998) has called 'economic fundamentalism', a kind of conceptual prism through which even such moral notions as diversity and equity are re-articulated in economic terms.

The idea of the internationalization of curriculum is closely associated with these assumptions. It is linked to the notion of a knowledge economy that demands a new approach to education, grounded not so much in the amount of schooling individuals have but in the learning attributes they are able to develop, with which to deal effectively and creatively with diverse, unfamiliar and constantly changing conditions of work. The idea of lifelong learning similarly suggests that learning must be continuous, and not restricted to formal schooling, and must involve continuous upgrading of work and life skills throughout life. The renewed emphasis on the teaching of Science and Mathematics displays a similar logic. The teaching of these subjects is encouraged not for its own sake or for better understanding of the natural world around us but as a way of better engaging with the knowledge economy. The same applies to the learning of English, which is widely regarded as the language of global trade, providing job opportunities, access to higher education and a broader flow of information, as well as facilitating diplomatic discussions and business negotiations.

CRITICAL ALTERNATIVES

Now in themselves the notions of knowledge economy, lifelong learning and teaching of Science and Technology and English are eminently sensible. But framed within the neo-liberal imaginary they have the effect of narrowing the scope of curriculum reform. In its wake, education is viewed as a private good, providing benefits to the individual consumer. This should be a matter of concern for those of us who see in education the potential to benefit the entire community, as a public good. It is important to note, however, that it is not the conditions of globalization *per se* that have increasingly linked education to the logic of the market, but a particular neo-liberal imaginary of global processes which redefines the way in which education's role in society should be conceptualized. As a private good, education is viewed as a commodity that can provide an individual with advantage over other individuals, thus creating a system in which people are differentiated in terms of their economic value. As a public good, on the other hand, all can share education. In this sense, education can be viewed as expanding the general welfare of society, even if it does not bring any direct benefits to the individual.

David Labaree (2003) has observed that education has traditionally been thought to have three distinct, but sometimes competing, purposes: democratic equality, social mobility and social efficiency. In the past, these three purposes were held in a balance, which neo-liberalism has largely altered. Education is now closely tied to the requirements of social efficiency. It is required to play a more instrumental role in developing workers able to contribute to the economic productivity of nations and corporations alike. Its focus is not so much on the needs and development of individuals as on the efficiency with which the educational systems operate. The emphasis in on the system's capacity to make an adequate return on investment, assessed in terms of its contribution in producing workers with knowledge, skills and attitudes relevant to increasing productivity within the knowledge economy. Of course, the concerns of democratic equity and social mobility have not been entirely

overlooked but are now incorporated within the broader discourse of social efficiency. For example, it has become possible for the OECD (2004) to assert that a focus on efficiency can in fact lead to greater equality and opportunities for social mobility.

However, this shift in policy discourse, sourced in a neo-liberal reading of globalization, has major implications for many individuals and communities. It has greatly benefited some countries and groups of people, while it has had disastrous consequences for others. It has given rise to a range of contradictions that can no longer be ignored. For example, the promotion of devolved systems of governance has left many educators and educational systems feeling disenfranchised, especially when they are expected to conform to unrealistic accountability regimes, and deliver outcomes for which they have not been adequately funded or resourced. Their professionalism has been sapped of any real meaning, as they are now required to become efficient and effective in contexts that are culturally, economically and politically complex. At the same time, the policy shift towards privatization has compromised the goals of access and equality and has widened inequalities not only across nations but also within the same communities. It has made the goals of gender and racial equity more difficult to realize. The exclusive emphasis on social efficiency, embodied in the regimes of new public administration of education, has resulted in greater focus on the operational requirements of the systems rather than upon the lives of human beings and their communities.

There is, however, nothing inevitable or necessary about locating the requirements of neither education nor globalization within the neo-liberal imaginary. It is indeed possible to understand the facts of global interconnectivity and interdependence in a radically different way, with implications for rethinking the internationalization of a curriculum that do not simply call for a return to some romanticized past, but require us to engage with the transformations brought about by recent developments in information and communication technology, in ways that do not privilege the economic over all other human concerns. It must be possible to imagine and work with an alternative form of globalization, rooted much more in democratic traditions; a form that does not rely entirely on the logic of the market, and is able to tame its excesses. Such a view of globalization demands not ready-made technocratic solutions to problems of education but a focus instead on open dialogue across cultures and nations. It requires thinking and acting both locally and globally, simultaneously. It demands an education that teaches students to see our problems as inextricably linked to the problems of others. It demands the development of critical skills and attitudes that enable students to imagine our collective futures, for humanity as a whole.

Such a critical alternative to neo-liberalism must recognize that, as Appadurai (2000: 14) has pointed out, imagination as a collective social fact in the era of globalization has a split character. 'On the one hand, it is in and through imagination that modern citizens are disciplined and controlled, by states, markets and other powerful interests. On the other hand, it is also the faculty through which collective patterns of dissent and new designs for collective life emerge.' This suggests that there is a constant political struggle over our imaginary. As an imaginary, neo-liberalism steers us towards a particular formation of subjective or phenomenological awareness by people. It encourages not only a particular interpretation of recent changes in global economy and culture but also a set of values attached to that interpretation. As Cohen and Kennedy (2000) suggest, it is designed to develop a set of subjectively internalized 'changes associated with globalization so that they are now incorporated into our emotions and our ways of thinking about everyday life' (Cohen and Kennedy 2000: 34).

It does this by portraying globalization as 'a pre-given thing, existing outside of thought' (Smith 2001: 21) with its own developmental logic. It thus conceives of various aspects of globalization as historically inevitable, representing a juggernaut, with which people and nations simply have to come to terms, and

negotiate them as best as they can. This view is based on a politics of meaning that seeks to accommodate people and nations to a certain taken-for-grantedness about the ways the global economy operates and the manner in which culture, crises, resources and power formations are filtered through its universal logic. It 'ontologizes' the global market logic creating global subjects whose options become restricted by neo-liberalism's conceptual prism. A critical alternative to this must involve developing a different imaginary in students, a different sense of global interconnectivity and interdependence, paying particular attention to the discursive and material practices by which people create the regularized patterns that enable and constrain them. It must treat people as agents of their collective destinies, and not simply as expressions of the deeper logic of economic imperatives. It must come to terms with their 'situatedness' in the world.

EPISTEMIC VIRTUES

A view of internationalization of the curriculum aligned to a more critical understanding of global interconnectivity and interdependence curriculum reform must involve attempts to help students come to terms with their situatedness in the world – situatedness of their knowledge and of their cultural practices as well as their unique positionality in relation to social networks, political institutions and social relations that are no longer limited to particular communities, but span the globe. This understanding is of course best achieved collectively in transcultural collaborations, in seeking to understand local problems comparatively, and in relation to global processes. While such collective learning might not always be possible, an examination of the hegemonic manner in which neo-liberalism holds us captive of its presuppositions can nevertheless be interrogated. Such interrogation is clearly necessary to develop a different imaginary with which to think about our lives and life options in the materiality of our collective and interlinked circumstances, and also to imagine how things could be otherwise. This requires a different kind of learning about the world around us, in all its cultural diversity and complexity.

It is now possible to do this pedagogic work through networked learning, both formal and informal, bringing together people from different cultural backgrounds. Such learning must necessarily encourage students to think outside their own parochial boundaries and cultural assumptions, to consider how global processes affect communities differentially and to examine the sources of these differentiations and inequalities. Instead of learning about cultures in an abstract manner, a critical approach must help students to explore the criss-crossing of transnational circuits of communication, the flows of global capital and the cross-cutting of local, translocal and transnational social practices, and their differential consequences for different people and communities. Such learning must involve students considering the contested politics of place-making, the social constructions of power differentials and the dynamic processes relating to the formation of individual, group, national and transnational identities, and their corresponding fields of difference.

This criticality should not only be viewed as a way of contesting the neo-liberal imaginary but also as a way of imagining a more global society that is more just, democratic and humane. The current attempts at the internationalization of curriculum highlight the importance of intercultural experiences, through such programmes as study abroad, but they do not seriously address the issues of how such experiences might produce effective learning about the new global configurations of economic and cultural exchange. The critical approach, in contrast, should encourage students to examine the cultural meaning of intercultural experiences, seeking to locate it within transnational networks that have become so much a part of the contemporary era of globalization. Appadurai (1996) has argued that 'globalization is not simply the name of a new epoch in the history of capital or in the biography of the nation-state. It marks a new role for imagination of social life'. If this is so then one of the major goals of internationalization of curriculum should be the development of a critical global imagination, based on a recognition that we all have 'elaborate interests and capabilities in constructing world pictures whose very interaction affects global processes'. Internationalization should demand the deparochialization of the processes of learning and teaching, highlighting the importance of 'grassroots' global networks capable of interrogating dominant neo-liberal narratives.

In this sense, internationalization should be mainly concerned with the development of attitudes and skills for understanding not other cultural traditions *per se* but the ways by which global processes are creating conditions of economic and cultural exchange that are transforming our identities and communities; and that reflexively we are contributing to the production and reproduction of those conditions, through our uncritical acceptance of the neo-liberal imaginary. It is indeed in our collective power to develop an alternative imaginary with which to interpret global interconnectivity and interdependence, one that is not informed by the universalizing logic of the market but by our determination to develop a sense of global collectivity based on a critical cosmopolitanism that views all of the diverse people and communities as belonging to the same moral universe. It requires the development of a sense of moral responsibility among students directed not only towards their families and nations, but also towards humanity as a whole.

Such an approach to the internationalization of curriculum demands a new approach to learning about other cultures and intercultural exchange, based on a set of 'epistemic virtues'. Indeed, the development of these virtues – an approach to the ways in which we develop knowledge about others and how to engage with them – should be viewed as fundamental to the project of internationalization. I use the phrase 'epistemic virtues' to highlight both the cognitive and ethical dimensions of intercultural learning, and to suggest that learning about others requires learning about ourselves. It implies a dialectical mode of thinking, which conceives cultural differences as neither absolute nor necessarily antagonistic, but deeply interconnected, so much so that they reveal how the tensions between cultures indeed can be comprehended and transcended. In a dialectical approach, we understand others both in *their* terms as well as *ours*, as a way of comprehending how both our representations are socially constituted.

This suggests the importance of understanding intercultural exchange historically, as a matter of an epistemic virtue that highlights the fact that cultural traditions cannot be understood without reference to the historical interactions that produced them. We live in a world that is characterized by various social networks of money, technologies, people and ideas and of their articulations with real spaces at different scales. But these networks have histories, without an understanding of which we cannot fully comprehend how people's sense of their collectivity, as solidarity in its positive manifestation and as marginalization in its negative, has been forged. The past is thus linked to the present, and plays an important role in our imagining the future. It is only through this realization that we recognize that our identities are forged in the history of contact between groups of people, where knowledge and resources are traded, borrowed, improved upon, fought over and passed on to others. The notion of a pure culture located within its own territory is a myth, because all cultures result from encounters with others.

If this is so, then relationality must also be an epistemic virtue that must be incorporated in any attempt to internationalize curriculum. If we cannot learn about cultures in their pristine and authentic form then our focus must shift to the ways in which cultural practices become separated from their 'homes' and are converted into new forms in their new contexts, and on how this changes both the places that people leave and the places they come to inhabit. In a world in which flows of information, media symbols and images and political and cultural ideas are constant and relentless,

new cultural formations are inevitable, and are relationally defined. This focus on relationality must therefore replace approaches that treat 'other' cultures as entirely separable from our own. Other cultures can only be understood in relation to each other, historically formed and globally interconnected through cultural mobility, exchange and hybridization.

A relational understanding of global interconnectivity and cultural exchange also points to the importance of another epistemic virtue: reflexivity. Reflexivity requires people to be self-conscious and knowledgeable about their own cultural traditions and how they are subject to transformation as a result of their engagement with other cultural traditions (Beck 1994). Reflexive individuals are able to challenge the taken-for-granted assumptions that are often found in official and popular discourse alike. Such reflexivity cannot be achieved, however, without a critical recognition of our own cultural and political presuppositions, and the epistemic position from which we speak and negotiate cultural differences. This must involve a realization that knowledge about cultures is never neutral and that our efforts to learn about and engage with other cultures take place within asymmetrical configurations of power. But these need not prevent us from continuing to explore, engage and learn from other cultural traditions in an effort to transform our own.

CONCLUSION

In this chapter, I have argued that most popular constructions of the notion of the internationalization of the curriculum, especially those articulated by the intergovernmental organizations such as the OECD, are located within and promote a neo-liberal imaginary of the ways in which economic and cultural exchange are now globally interconnected and interdependent; and that this imaginary has led to curricular reforms that are narrow in scope and do not adequately prepare students to engage critically with the cultural politics of globalization. These reforms highlight the importance of intercultural understanding and communication in the era of globalization but rest on assumptions about cultures and cultural learning that are mistaken. They treat cultures as entirely enclosed and coherent entities, and pay insufficient attention to the fact that cultures are always forged historically through constant processes of interaction and exchange.

In the contemporary era, the volume and speed of intercultural exchange have increased at an unprecedented rate, creating greater possibilities of trade, transfers of technology, cultural cooperation and skirmishes, and even war, than ever before. Never before therefore has there been a greater need of intercultural understanding and communication, predicated not on essentialist conceptions of cultures, but based on a need to explore the dynamics of cultural interactions. New ways of thinking about economic and cultural exchange are necessary involving conceptions of others and ourselves that are defined relationally, as complex and inherently dynamic products of a range of historical processes and the contemporary cultural economies of global interconnectivity. Epistemologically, all cultural understanding is comparative because no understanding of others is possible without self-understanding. If this is so, then not only is it important to develop in students epistemic virtues of historicity, criticality and relationality but also of reflexivity in all our attempts at intercultural learning.

A critical approach to the internationalization of curriculum thus involves both a view of global interconnectivity and interdependence different from neo-liberal imaginary, and an ethic recommending a certain attitude and response to the intercultural exchange. It conceives of the relation between self and others dialectically, denies that our cultures are fixed and essentially distinct, and suggests the possibilities of continuous self-examination, learning and transformation. It underscores an ethic that urges people to engage differences and explore possibilities of learning as a basis for imagining forms of

globality designed to ensure the survival and moral growth of the human species.

REFERENCES

Appadurai, A. (1996) *Modernity at Large: Cultural Dimensions of Globalization.* Minneapolis: University of Minnesota Press.

Appadurai, A. (ed.) (2000) *Globalization.* Durham, NC: Duke University Press.

Apple, M. (2004) *Educating the Right Way.* London and New York: Routledge.

Becker, G. (1964) *Human Capital: A Theoretical and Empirical Analysis, with Special Reference to Education.* New York: Columbia University Press.

Beazley, K. (1994) *International Education in Australia through the 1990s,* Ministerial Statement, Canberra: Australian Government Printing Service.

Beck, U. (2000) *What is Globalization?* Cambridge: Polity Press.

Clyne, F. and Rizvi, F. (1999) Outcomes of Student Exchange, in D. Davis and A. Olsen (eds) *Outcomes of International Education: Research Findings.* A set of commissioned research papers presented at the 12th Australian International Education Conference, Canberra, 1998. Canberra: IPD Education Australia.

Cohen, R. and Kennedy, P. (2000) *Global Sociology.* New York: New York University Press.

Friedman, T. (2000) *The Lexus and the Olive Tree.* New York: First Anchor Press.

Hall, S. (1996) *Stuart Hall: Critical Dialogues in Cultural Studies.* London: Routledge.

Held, D. and McGrew, A. (eds) (2000) *The Global Transformation Reader: An Introduction to the Globalization Debate.* Cambridge: Polity Press.

Labaree, D. (1997) *How to Succeed in School Without Really Learning.* New Haven, CT: Yale University Press.

Larner, W. (2000) Neo-liberalism: policy, ideology and governmentality. *Studies in Political Economy,* 63: 5–25.

Nillson, B. (2000) Internationalizing the curriculum. In P. Crowther et al. *Internationalization at Home: A Position Paper.* Amsterdam: European Association for International Education.

OECD (1996) *Internationalizing the Curriculum in Higher Education.* Paris: OECD.

OECD (2004) *Innovation in the Knowledge Economy: Implications for Education and Learning.* Paris: OECD (produced by CERI).

Rizvi, F. (2005) Globalization and the dilemmas of internationalization in Australian higher education.

Access: Critical Perspectives on Communication, Cultural and Policy Studies, 24(1): 86–101.

Smith, M.P. (2001) *Transnational Urbanism: Locating Globalization.* Oxford: Blackwell.

Soros, G. (1998) *The Crisis of Global Capitalism.* Boston, MA: Little, Brown.

Taylor, C. (2004) *Modern Social Imaginaries.* Durham, NC: Duke University Press.

Tomlinson, J. (2000) *Globalization and Culture.* Cambridge: Polity Press.

UNESCO (2002) Education for the New Era. http://portal.unesco.org/education/en/ev.php-URL_ID=7687&URL_DO=DO_TOPIC&URL_SECTION=201.html (accessed January 2006).

Wachter, B. (2000) Internationalization at home – the context. In P. Crowther et al. (eds) *Internationalization at Home: A Position Paper.* Amsterdam: European Association for International Education.

Challenges from a New World

George Walker

INTERNATIONAL EDUCATION: RESPONSE TO A PREVIOUS WORLD

International education put down its first enduring roots in 1924 with the opening of the International School of Geneva (École Internationale de Genève). Ecolint, as it became known, fulfilled the practical need of providing an education for the multinational children of the new breed of international civil servants working at the League of Nations. But its founders had more complex ambitions, namely to instil into these young people the same values of international understanding and tolerance that were enshrined in the League's own Covenant. In this way, perhaps, there would be no repetition of the carnage of the First World War. International education could help the process of nation speaking to nation.

The school's style of education was far ahead of its time and a radical suggestion, made by the chairman of its governing board in 1925, proposing an international school-leaving certificate, fell on deaf ears. But the most telling blow to its visionary ambitions came with the outbreak of the Second World

War. Nonetheless, it survived and when the war was over Ecolint helped to found a sister school with similar aspirations in New York, the United Nations International School (UNIS). This postwar period saw a rapid growth of international schools, matching the expansion of world trade, the associated support of diplomatic missions and the steady growth of international agencies, many of them linked to the United Nations. Some of these so-called 'international schools' maintained an unashamedly national (particularly American and British) education set down in the midst of foreign, sometimes even hostile, countries far from home. But others were inspired by the example of Ecolint and UNIS to develop something new, something more visionary, something that would perhaps ensure the world would never again see horrors such as those of the Second World War. International education could help to foster a new spirit of international tolerance.

These mushrooming international schools were soon given practical support in their mission by their own organization, the International Schools Association (ISA), established in 1951 in close association with the recently founded United Nations Educational, Scientific and Cultural Organization (UNESCO) by parents who were international civil servants working in Geneva, New York and Paris. Predictably, the ISA reinforced the visionary aspect of international education and the first aim in its current mission statement remains 'To further world peace and international understanding through education' (ISA 2006).

Ten years later another event had a profound effect on the developing international school movement: the opening in 1962 of Atlantic College in Wales. By now memories of the Second World War were fading, but only to be replaced by the superpower tensions of the Cold War, with its ever-present threat of wholesale nuclear destruction. Surely, it was argued, a residential experience, founded on the experiential philosophy of Kurt Hahn – 'an enterprising curiosity, an undefeatable spirit, tenacity in pursuit, readiness for sensible self denial, and above all, compassion' (Hahn 2006) – an experience that offered the world's brightest and best teenagers the opportunity to live and study for two years amongst a complete mix of different cultures and backgrounds and to make lifelong friendships across sometimes forbidden national frontiers, surely this would somehow reduce the chances of another world war. Thus, with the creation of the first United World College, the visionary dimension of international education that had been promoted 40 years earlier in Geneva was further reinforced. Schools, and the young people in them, could transcend the barriers of even the Cold War's frontiers.

INTERNATIONAL EDUCATION IN A CHANGING SOCIAL ENVIRONMENT

To be a realistic alternative to national, or state education, international education must coexist with existing social, economic and political structures. It must fulfil a practical need, institutions offering it must become established and attract suitable staff; governments must at least accept, if not welcome it and its curriculum and qualifications must be widely recognized. All these conditions were satisfied during the rapid development of international education taking place in the last century. Moreover, international education went further, seeming to offer at least a response, if not a solution, to some of the most pressing moral challenges of a century ravaged by war.

However, at the beginning of the twenty-first century the social environment of education is changing in response to the accelerating processes of globalization and to the ever-widening participation of new educational stakeholders. Hitherto, international education has been largely concerned with the relationships between groups contained within different geographical boundaries; indeed, as we have seen, its origins lay in the initiatives taken by international schools to encourage mutual understanding between different nation-states. However, as immigration between nations has increased, making the classrooms of national schools more and more culturally diverse, and as the conflicts *between* nations give way to culturally-based conflicts *within* nations, national and international education are beginning to merge, weakening the earlier link between international education and international schools and making international education more of a national responsibility.

A society's formal system of learning – the education that it provides for its citizens – looks both within the society and, at the same time, outside it. On the one hand, it is the means to maintain, develop and transmit to the next generation elements of the distinctive culture that provides the group's particular source of identification and belonging. On the other hand, education is also the means to an understanding of the culture of others and to building a bridge between the two, between 'them' and 'us'.

It is a rare group that has no contact with the outside world, though there are closed orders of different religious persuasions that seek such a condition, promoting an education for their students that avoids distraction or adulteration, and therefore sometimes encouraging forms of extremism. It is also a rare group that puts a concern for the whole world before a more selfish interest, though the United World Colleges might offer such an example. If these define the two limits of an axis, then most systems of education fall somewhere in between, seeking to strike an appropriate point of balance between what might be described as the internal and the external.

There have been many different reasons for a group of people of one culture wanting to associate with, and therefore better to understand, those of a different culture. Trade and the desire to minimize harmful conflict are two obvious examples; less obvious, but no less important, is the need to refresh the culture through immigration and interbreeding. Education has always provided the instruments and the experiences to enable that association to take place. Do they speak my language? Do we have a common history? Are their gods also our gods? There has always been an international, a 'them', element to education.

Nonetheless, education policy has hitherto been primarily perceived as a national priority and has remained rather firmly contained within national frontiers, even today seeming to resist the pressures of globalization that have reshaped so many other areas of national life. Although there is international interest in the educational performance of other countries, and in tracking down the magic ingredients of other nations' successes, there is little evidence of a globally shared framework for school-based education, still less a globally acknowledged curriculum, that would allow students to transfer with minimal disruption between different countries. State education has been guarded jealously as one of the few remaining levers of national social policy and in recent years the governments of several countries with previously widely devolved education systems – for example, Australia, the United Kingdom and the USA – have all intervened to impose national policy above local.

We need to bear in mind, however, that government-funded education is itself a rather recent phenomenon, historically trailing far behind the provision for schooling made by philanthropic individuals, charitable institutions and religious groups. The intervention of the state represented a significant shift along the internal–external axis, moving education away from the more limited self-interests of particular groups in society (seeking, for example, a better standard of religious instruction) to the priorities of the nation as a whole: national heroes and myths, an articulate electorate, an administrative elite and, most recently, a competitive workforce. During the past century, although particular educational initiatives may have had more exotic origins, their lasting development, their incorporation into an enduring education system, has taken place through state education. To choose a very recent example, the United Nations millennium goal of universal elementary education by the year 2015 had its origins in UNESCO but it will only be achieved, if it is to be achieved at all, through the cooperation of individual national governments.

Nonetheless, at the start of the new century a number of influences are beginning to erode the monolithic position of state education, in some countries even encouraged by the governments themselves. Legislation in China and India has permitted the development of private education, while charter schools in the USA and city academies and trust schools in the UK have engaged new stakeholders. The reasons behind this widening base of engagement are several: huge government administrative superstructures have clogged up the existing system, stifling any chance of reform; the rapid increase in the middle-class demand for education in many developing countries is too great to fund through a single route of direct taxation; the capacities of more sophisticated technologies have stimulated the search for new partners both to fund and to influence the nature of education.

We are therefore witnessing a discernible move from 'state education' to a more widely based 'public education' that engages the active participation of different stakeholders in society. This development is once more shifting the position of education along the internal–external axis as groups (for example the business community) that have stronger international sympathies and experience, assume a degree of responsibility for the provision of education.

Internal education is merging with external education and all this is taking place against the trends of increasing migration and ease of communication. This, in turn, implies that an education to understand different cultures living in other countries will, in future, have to be modified to take into account different cultures living just down the road or using new technology in ways that make it unimportant where they are living.

THE NEW GLOBAL CHALLENGES

International education aimed to bring about the meeting of nations: rubbing shoulders, building tolerance and lifting the barriers of national frontiers. All this has a twentieth-century ring to it, but it is less relevant in the twenty-first century where nations already rub shoulders daily in a thousand different ways, international forums (albeit far from perfect) exist to resolve disputes causing international tension and very few countries remain off-limits to the committed traveller. The challenge of the new century is not to bring people of different cultures together, but to address some of the issues that arise when this happens on a daily, hourly, minute-by-minute basis, thanks to the impact of globalization.

What are the particular global challenges for the century that lies ahead and how can international education help to meet them? Suárez-Orozco suggests that working with difference and complexity will be particularly important keys to understanding the future. On the former, he emphasizes not just meeting together, but living together, often in the closest proximity:

Children growing up today are more likely than in any previous generation to face a life of working, networking, loving, and living with others from different national, linguistic, religious and racial backgrounds ... The friction that meaningful cultural contact and incommensurable difference generate can be a threat if mismanaged – as intergroup violence and anomie in multicultural cities suggest. But friction can also generate constructive energy ... When intercultural difference interrupts 'thinking as usual' – the taken-for-granted understandings and world views that shape cognitive and metacognitive styles and practices – it can do most for youths growing up today. (Suárez-Orozco 2005: 211)

On complexity, Suárez-Orozco writes:

Globalization engenders complexity. It is generating more intricate demographics, economies, politics, environmental choices, scientific realities, technology and media, cultural facts and artefacts, and identities ... An intellectually curious, cognitively autonomous, socially responsible, democratically engaged, productive, and globally conscious member of the human family in the 21st century cannot be educated in the 20th-century factory model of education. (Suárez-Orozco 2005: 211)

Gardner expresses similar sentiments and reflects on the implications for the school curriculum:

Many – perhaps most – of the most vexing issues facing the world today (including the issue of globalization!) do not respect disciplinary boundaries. AIDS, large-scale immigration, and global warming are examples of problems in need of interdisciplinary thinking. How best to begin to introduce rigorous multiperspective thinking into our classrooms is a challenge that we have only begun to confront. (Gardner 2004: 254)

and his first priority for the future is an understanding of the new realities of the global system itself:

The trends of globalization – the unprecedented and unpredictable movement of human beings, capital, information, and cultural life forms – need to be understood by the young persons who are and will always inhabit a global community. Some of the system will become manifest through the media; but many other facets – for example, the operation of worldwide markets – will need to be taught in a more formal manner. (Gardner 2004: 253)

Friedman (2005) makes a similar point in his analysis of the forces that have 'flattened' the worlds of business, commerce and education. His conclusions make equally uncomfortable reading for the Old World and the New World as he predicts the steady erosion of their current competitive advantages as countries like India, China and Russia seize the new opportunities offered by what he calls a triple convergence: the power of the Internet, changes in practices that reflect new and more efficient ways of doing business and the consequent addition of some 3 billion new people to competitive markets. For Friedman the reconciliation of widening capitalism with the fate of its seemingly inevitable victims, lies in a form of 'compassionate flatism' in which education will play an essential part.

Friedman's argument that the balance of global power is shifting away from the West (as he points out, to be 'one in a million' in China is to be part of a group numbering 1,300) is derived from an essentially economic perspective: 'The jobs are going to go where the best educated workforce is with the most competitive infrastructure and environment for creativity and supportive government. It is inevitable' (Friedman 2005: 323).

Jacques agrees:

> We are moving into a world in which the West will no longer be able to call the tune as it once did. China and India will becomes major global players alongside the US, the EU and Japan. For the first time in modern history the West will no longer be overwhelmingly dominant. (2006)

but he adds a moral dimension to the argument:

> it is no longer possible for Europe to ignore the sensibilities of peoples with very different values, cultures and religions. First, Western Europe now has sizeable minorities whose origins are very different from the host population and who are connected with their former homelands in diverse ways. If European societies want to live in some kind of domestic peace and harmony ... then they must find ways of integrating these minorities on rather more equal terms than, for the most part, they have so far achieved. (Jacques 2006)

The shock generated by the London bombings in July 2005 and the destructive rioting in the suburbs of many French cities that occurred later in the year was due not only to their happening but also to the uncomfortable fact that they were caused by national citizens rather than malevolent outsiders.

Rischard (2002) lists no fewer than 20 global issues that, in his opinion, must be resolved in the next 20 years. They are grouped into three categories: those that have to do with sharing the global living space (e.g. global warming), social and economic issues (e.g. world poverty), whose solution requires 'a critical mass that only global coalitions can achieve', and legal and regulatory issues (e.g. intellectual property rights) that demand a common rule book. Rischard argues that the world lacks effective mechanisms for dealing with these issues and, indeed, his main thesis is that current institutions have not kept pace with either world demographic or world economic changes.

In summary, then, these are what experts perceive to be the new challenges of the twenty-first century:

- Living and working with difference – kinship, gender, language, race, ethnicity and inequality; therefore interrupting the process of 'thinking as usual'.
- Enjoying the challenge of complexity which means assessing problems from a variety of different perspectives and accepting the absence of a single solution.
- Acquiring a better understanding of the driving forces behind globalization and its impact on different groups; understanding, for example, the interconnectivity of buying habits.
- Recognizing that the balance of economic power in the world is shifting to different parts of the world and that increasingly education will be the determinant of economic success.
- Coping with cultural differences, not as a visitor or expatriate in another country, but on a daily, and sometimes potentially confrontational, basis at one's own back door.
- Seeking new styles of working that do not depend upon outdated and inefficient institutions that were designed for a previous era.

To what extent, then, does international education, as currently practised, prepare young people for these new challenges?

INTERNATIONAL EDUCATION IN PRACTICE: THE INTERNATIONAL BACCALAUREATE

The curriculum and the associated values of international education were formalized, institutionalized and made available world-wide with the creation of the International Baccalaureate Organization (IBO) in 1968. This initiative, which was supervised by the ISA and funded by UNESCO and a number of American foundations, was largely driven by teachers in schools like Ecolint, UNIS and Atlantic College, working together to solve that frustrating problem anticipated some 40 years earlier – the creation of an international pre-university programme that could be studied anywhere in the world and providing access to any of the world's best universities. The result was the IB Diploma Programme, a values-inspired response to a practical problem (Peterson, 1987).

Nearly two generations later that programme has achieved its early, ambitious goal to a remarkable degree yet still retains much of the overall shape with which it was launched (IBO, 2006). Three influences largely determined its design: the idealism represented by ISA and UNESCO, the classroom experience of subject specialist teachers and the requirements of university admissions tutors. The result was a compromise: an intellectually demanding liberal arts programme with a strong international dimension, an emphasis on critical thinking skills, the encouragement of foreign languages and an insistence on community service. Several of its constituent parts, notably the Theory of Knowledge course, the compulsory element of Creativity, Action, Service (CAS) and the extended essay, continue to attract widespread interest, but it is the diploma's overall shape, carefully designed to be more than just the sum of those constituent parts, that remains so distinctive, even today.

For more than a generation, its Diploma Programme maintained the IBO in a small but increasingly influential niche position, winning recognition by offering a welcomed passport to the world's most sought-after universities. Surprisingly, and for some international purists, somewhat annoyingly, the greatest rate of growth was in the USA, where public schools, not especially interested in its international nature, were attracted to a high-quality programme with internationally

benchmarked assessment. But the capacity to infiltrate state systems has been crucial to its development and many different governments have taken an interest in the IB Diploma Programme, incorporating elements of it within their own national programmes (Hill 2007).

During the 1990s, in the most significant developments since its founding, the IBO added a Middle Years Programme and then a Primary Years Programme, thereby greatly widening the organization's role and responsibilities. From that moment the IBO has made the running in the development of international education: indeed, it has been suggested (Cambridge 2002) that the IB programmes might even be regarded as the educational global equivalent of Nike or Coca-Cola. In practice, for many schools across the world, participation in international education has meant authorization to offer one or more of the International Baccalaureate programmes – for them international education has become synonymous with the IB. It is therefore not unreasonable to rephrase the earlier question so as to ask how relevant the IB programmes will be in preparing young people for the globalized world of the twenty-first century.

According to Suárez-Orozco and Qin-Hilliard: 'Education systems tied to the formation of nation-state citizens and consumers bonded to local systems to the neglect of larger global forces are likely to become obsolete, while those that proactively engage globalization's new challenges are likely to survive' (Suárez-Orozco and Qin-Hilliard 2004: 23). Clearly, the IBO was itself a direct response to a global force – increasing international trade – and the programmes' different international dimensions, including the study of modern languages and world literature as well as its international teams of curriculum developers and examiners, mean that it is not bonded to any local system. However, to what extent do the programmes 'proactively engage globalization's new challenges?'

Gardner specifically commends the Theory of Knowledge course as an appropriate basis for an introduction to interdisciplinary work, and the so-called 'areas of interaction', which form an important interdisciplinary focus in the IB Middle Years Programme, offer a similar opportunity to examine a particular issue from a variety of disciplinary standpoints. Developing cultural understanding also plays an essential part in all three IB programmes but this is usually in an international context where engagement is often temporary and optional, rather than the local context of an immigrant group that constitutes a growing minority on the other side of the same city. IB students in the Midlands or North of England are more likely to choose French, Spanish or *ab initio* Japanese as their foreign language than Urdu or Gujarati.

One of the strengths of the twentieth-century model of the IB has been its close association with schools. Teachers and administrators have contributed to every aspect and at every level of the organization: developing the curriculum, training new teachers, lobbying governments, examining students and participating in its governance. In the future, however, this strength could become a serious weakness if IB programmes remain exclusively bound to particular institutions. The successful spread of educational opportunity to match the new distribution of economic wealth does not imply the death of schools, but it does mean that they will become just one part of a much wider and varied network of education providers, all making use of the latest technology.

Acquiring responsibility for three programmes of international education – Kindergarten to grade 12 – has encouraged the IBO to engage in an extensive study of the key factors that underpin them in a search for a more generic description of what the IB represents: what are the common threads that are progressively developed from elementary schooling through to pre-university graduation, the essential ingredients of this version of an international education? They have been expressed in the so-called 'IB learner profile' (IBO 2006), which, perhaps unsurprisingly, restates many of the qualities that were in the minds of the early pioneers: for example, critical thinking, communication,

caring and reflecting. The list of ten chosen qualities divides roughly into two categories which could be said to reflect the nature of the IB experience itself and thus of much of the current practice of international education: a critical mind linked to a compassionate heart.

Perhaps this is the description of the social entrepreneur; indeed Friedman himself writes: 'I have come to know several social entrepreneurs in recent years and most combine a business school brain with a social worker's heart' (Friedman 2005: 363).

Bornstein (2004), noting that during the 1990s the number of registered international citizen organizations (not-for-profit organizations with a global influence) increased from 6,000 to 26,000, suggests that several factors are encouraging the world-wide mobilization of citizens: the replacement of many authoritarian governments, surplus wealth in many economies (albeit very unevenly distributed), greater longevity and better education, more extensive participation of women and new forms of technology.

It seems likely that the IB graduates will have a particular contribution to make to what could become a really significant movement of the new century: 'Across the world, social entrepreneurs are demonstrating new approaches to many social ills and new models to create wealth, promote social well-being, and restore the environment. The citizen sector is conspicuously leading the push to reform the free market and political systems' (Bornstein 2004: 9), because unarguably there is deep disillusion concerning the capacity of governments to address and solve the growing list of serious global problems and private enterprise is widely perceived as making a bad situation worse.

However, a final word of caution is needed because 'business school brains' and 'social worker hearts' are both very Western phrases. They describe concepts that fit comfortably with the IB and its model of international education, which is founded upon a Western humanist philosophy that encourages freedom of speech, challenges authority and rewards individual initiative: 'the configuration of learning presumed in international academic curricula is a Western configuration based on conceptual learning as the dominant form of learning' (van Oord 2005: 187). Those from different cultural backgrounds may reason differently and attach different priorities to what they value in their society. Unable to match business school brains to social worker hearts, and fearing social and economic marginalization as the global economy further reinforces the power of Western capitalism, their difference is being expressed with increasing emphasis, sometimes with increasing violence, around the world.

The final sentence of the IBO's mission statement insists that:

> These [IB] programmes encourage students across the world to become active, compassionate and lifelong learners who understand that other people, with their differences, can also be right. (IBO 2006)

Just how right 'other people, with their differences' will be allowed to be, and just how right these other people will insist on being, are issues that will surely pose the biggest future challenge to international education. If international education is really preparing young people to face the new rather than the past century, then it will start by recognizing that in the West '[t]oo many young people have a sense of entitlement, are complacent and even condescending towards the rest of the world and this could be our downfall' (Seefried 2005: 4).

REFERENCES

Bornstein, D. (2004) *How to Change the World.* Oxford: Oxford University Press.

Cambridge, J. (2002) Global product branding and international education. *Journal of Research in International Education,* 1(2): 227–43.

Friedman, T. (2005) *The World Is Flat.* London: Allen Lane.

Gardner, H. (2004) How education changes: considerations of history, science and values. In M.M. Suárez-Orozco and D.B. Qin-Hilliard (eds) *Globalization: Culture and Education in the New Millennium.* Berkeley, CA: University of California Press.

Hahn, K. (2006) www.KurtHahn.org (accessed 20 March 2006).

Hill, I. (2007) International Baccalaureate programmes and educational reform. In P. Hughes (ed.) *Secondary Education at the Crossroads.* Dordrecht: Springer (in press).

International Schools Association (2006) www.isaschools.org (accessed 20 July 2006).

Jacques, M. (2006) Europe's contempt for other cultures can't be sustained. *Guardian,* 17 February.

International Baccalaureate Organization (2006) www.ibo.org (accessed 18 March 2006).

Peterson, A.D.C. (1987) *Schools Across Frontiers.* La Salle: Open Court.

Rischard, J.F. (2002) *High Noon.* New York: Basic Books.

Seefried, M. (2005) Speech to South Carolina IB Association. www.ibo.org (accessed 20 July 2006).

Suárez-Orozco, M.M. (2005) Rethinking education in the global era. *Phi Delta Kappan,* 87(3): 209–12.

Suárez-Orozco, M.M. and Qin-Hilliard, D.B. (eds) (2004) *Globalization: Culture and Education in the New Millennium.* Berkeley, CA: University of California Press.

Van Oord, L. (2005) Culture as a configuration of learning: hypotheses in the context of international education. *Journal of Research in International Education,* 4(2): 173–91.

34

Realism and Antirealism in International Education Research

James Cambridge

In this chapter, I propose to critique the application of research methodologies involving questionnaire-based surveys, with reference to a case study involving an inventory of items derived from Hofstede (1986). My metatheoretical position will be to discuss the selected research methodologies from realist (that is, positivist and postpositivist) and antirealist perspectives. My antirealist critique will be informed mainly by the philosophy of early Foucault, but also with reference to post-Foucauldian theorists such as Edward Said. It may be argued that cross-cultural enquiry forms an important strand of research in international education. However, the ways in which 'culture' may be conceptualized are contested.

From a realist perspective, culture may be seen in essentialist terms, as a set of 'programs' carried in the minds of individuals that influence their behaviour. However, although the outcomes of certain types of behaviour may be observed in concrete form (that is, artefacts), the values underlying those products are not directly observable. The task of the researcher is to operationalize those values

in ways that elicit observable behaviours that may lead to the formation of inferences about the values of the individual. Such a perspective is a product of the ideology of scientism. A problem with this style of research is how it addresses the problem of interpretation – the 'double hermeneutic'.

Antirealist perspectives argue that 'facts … do not exist, only interpretations' (Nietzsche 1888; in Kaufmann 1976: 458). From this perspective, the subject is decentred; culture does not reside in the mind of the individual but is a process that arises from the social interactions between individuals in groups. Culture is a construct of language and discourse. Foucault argues that there is an intimate relationship between power and knowledge. Not only does knowledge confer power on the knower, but power relations determine what is accepted as and passes for knowledge. From this perspective, it may be argued that a survey instrument such as that developed from Hofstede (1986) is a means of surveillance and discipline, casting a normalizing gaze over the subjects of enquiry through the construction of binary hierarchies and coercive assignment. The content of items in such instruments has the effect of 'orientalizing' other cultures by seizing control over discourse and the terms in which other cultures are represented.

PROBLEMATIZING RESEARCH METHODOLOGIES IN INTERNATIONAL EDUCATION STUDIES

A distinction may be drawn between research methods and methodology. The latter term is 'frequently misused by those who wish to impress as a synonym for method but one which should be confined to its proper meaning, which refers to questions about the ontological and epistemological status of our research procedures, questions of philosophical justification' (Byrne 2002: 14). It has been proposed that 'the aim of methodology is to help us to understand, in the broadest possible terms, not the products of scientific enquiry but the process itself' (Cohen and Manion 1989: 42). Whereas research methods may be identified with the technologies of data collection and analysis, research methodology discusses the concepts and theories that underlie the creation of propositional knowledge through research. The aim of this chapter is to discuss methodological issues as they apply to enquiry in the context of international education studies, and to critique the technical issues relating to data collection methods.

At least five paradigms for the conduct of enquiry in the human sciences (comprising positivism, postpositivism, critical theory, constructivism and participatory paradigms) may be identified (Lincoln and Guba 2000). The assumptions of these paradigms may be contrasted in terms of their approaches to ontology, epistemology and methodology. Ontologically and epistemologically, there appears to be a division between paradigms that assume the existence of an external social reality that can be known objectively (positivism and postpositivism), and paradigms that assume that that knowledge of the social

is subjective and constructed (critical, constructivist and participatory paradigms). Positivist verification and postpositivist falsification of hypotheses involve the assumption that the conduct of scientific enquiry can be objective and 'value-free'. Methodological positions that adopt a subjectivist epistemology contest this view by arguing that enquiry cannot be value-free and that, on the contrary, enquiry is loaded with assumptions and values. This is the influence of ideology. Wallace and Poulson (2003: 14) argue that the term ideology:

> implies a system of beliefs, attitudes and opinions about some aspect of the social world based on particular assumptions. An ideology guides action to realise particular interests or goals. The 'educational philosophy' espoused by many teachers and lecturers is an ideology comprising their system of beliefs, attitudes and opinions about education … it will be intrinsically value-laden, because any view of the purposes, content and methods of education, and of the ideal balance of control between the different groups involved, entails considerations about what should and should not be done that reach beyond facts.

It may be argued that research enquiries in international education are frequently comparative studies because they either compare the outcomes of contrasting programmes of study (e.g. Cambridge 2002a; Hinrichs 2002, 2003; Reimers 2004; Caffyn and Cambridge 2005) or make comparisons between classes of subjects assigned to contrasting categories (e.g. Humphreys 1996; Lam 2002; Popper and Sleman 2001; Slater et al. 2002). Studies such as these may be identified with the positivist 'agricultural botanical' paradigm (Hopkins 1989) because they address differences between two populations that are assumed to be matched save for the treatment that the experimental group has received and to which the control group has not been exposed, or else they are quasi-experiments that assume different historical experiences between the contrasting groups. In other words, they make assumptions about social reality (ontology) and the ways in which knowledge claims can be made about it (epistemology). These assumptions are criticized by Scott (1996) in terms of whether:

- a valid account of social interactions can be obtained, and the agenda for the investigation set, without reference being made to the way participants in the research understand and interpret their world
- a research method can be decided upon without reference to the emerging data and preceding fieldwork, that is to say the formative contribution of data emerging from the study to the development of hypothesis formation, and prior studies conducted by the researcher
- the presence of the researcher in the research setting affects the data collected
- data are 'atheoretical' in the sense that settings can be described and analysed without reference to any theoretical framework or a priori way of understanding
- correlational studies can prove causality.

Comparative studies in the positivist paradigm often use surveys and questionnaires for data collection. The data are disaggregated according to criteria that are identified as explanatory variables (for example, age cohort, nationality, exposure to a particular programme of study), and comparisons made between the disaggregated groups. These comparisons may take the form of statistical measures of similarity and difference. Technical arguments may be deployed about the nature of the variables. Four types of variables, each with particular properties, may be found in quantitative educational studies (Bryman 2004: 226–5). They comprise:

- interval or ratio variables, with the distance between the categories being identical across the range
- ordinal variables, whose categories can be rank ordered but where the distances between the categories are not equal across the range
- nominal or categorical variables, whose categories cannot be rank ordered
- dichotomous variables, containing data with only two categories.

An unresolved methodological issue is whether the numerical outputs of responses

to Likert-type items constitute ratio, ordinal or nominal variables. The validity of the application of statistical tests (for example, parametric or nonparametric) to data analysis depends on whether the data conform to certain criteria (Field 2000). A robust solution is to assume that the outputs of such methods yield parametric data that show normal distribution around one central tendency and may be treated as ratio or equal interval variables, but it may be argued that there is little justification for making such assumptions. Furthermore, there are other profound issues to be addressed about the assumptions underlying the application of these methods of data collection and analysis to educational research.

One issue is the problem of how responses to a data collection instrument such as a questionnaire are to be interpreted. The validity of the assumption that respondents interpret an item in the same way that the researcher interprets it may be contested. This is known as 'the double hermeneutic' (Scott and Usher 1996: 20) and it has been argued that it represents a fundamental problem associated with survey research based on inventories of attitude statements.

> The social sciences operate with a double hermeneutic involving two way ties with the actions and institutions of those they study. Sociological observers depend upon lay concepts to generate accurate descriptions of social processes; and agents regularly appropriate themes and concepts of social science within their behaviour, thus potentially changing its character. This ... inevitably takes it some distance from the 'cumulative and uncontested' model that naturalistically-inclined sociologists have in mind.
> (Giddens 1984: 31)

A researcher cannot know directly what the respondent knows. The best that can be achieved is that the researcher causes the respondent to perform some type of behaviour that is then interpreted by the researcher. However, it cannot be assumed that the respondent and researcher interpret the same event, such as a response to the stimulus of a questionnaire item, in the same way. A solution to this problem is to triangulate observations made using contrasting data collection methods to elicit responses that converge in their descriptions of the same phenomenon (Cohen and Manion 1989). However, this solution makes the ontological assumption that there exists an independent version of social reality that may be observed using contrasting methods. What if the observer's view of reality is dependent on the method used to observe it, such that different perspectives yield different observations? For example, Cambridge (2002a) critiques a comparative study of the development of international understanding among students enrolled on the International Baccalaureate Diploma Programme and another programme of study that claims that participation in the Diploma Programme is a causal variable that 'may be effective in promoting international understanding' (Hinrichs 2002: 8).

> It may be argued that it is equally valid to assume that a positive attitude to international understanding might predispose American high school students to enrol in the IB Diploma Programme. That is to say, international-mindedness is the cause not the effect, which is the opposite of the relationship proposed by this author. What research has been carried out to describe and analyse what decisions have been made by these students and their parents to enrol in the IB Diploma Programme in preference to a College Board Advanced Placement programme, or any other programme? What reasons might the respondents give that account for their choice in senior high school programmes? What prior knowledge might they have had of the nature and values of the IB Diploma Programme? (Cambridge, 2002a: 11)

Application of a survey instrument and quantitative data analysis in the positivist paradigm might lead to a conclusion that could be falsified were data of a more context-related and 'sociological' nature, in a different (critical, constructivist or participatory) paradigm, also collected and analysed. Depending on the observer's view of social reality, participation in a given programme of study could change from being identified as a cause to being interpreted as an effect.

Another methodological problem associated with survey-based enquiry relates to the 'etic–emic' distinction. This refers to the issue of whether concepts from one culture can be used to describe another culture with validity and reliability. The terms 'etic' and 'emic' are derived from linguistic terminology. 'Phonetic notation is meant to be a general system which can describe all sounds in all languages, while phonemic is meant to describe sounds that are meaningful in a given culture' (Brislin et al. 1973: 24). Transposed to the context of cross-cultural psychological research, 'the problem for psychologists is that by administering cross-culturally a test standardised in one country (usually their own), they may be imposing an artificial etic and losing the emic or meaningful aspect of the other culture as practised by their members' (Brislin et al. 1973: 24). This may be interpreted in terms of contesting the ownership of the research agenda. It may be argued that the use of an inventory of questionnaire items, for example describing a set of educational values derived from a cross-cultural management theorist such as Hofstede (1986), constitutes an 'imposed etic' which may be criticized on the grounds that the statements of educational values have been derived from a published source beyond the international schools community and not from that community itself. The practical implications of the 'etic–emic' distinction may be demonstrated by reference to the wording of questionnaire items. It is necessary for researchers to express concepts in terms that will be recognizable by the respondents. To use a relatively trivial example, what terminology should be adopted when referring to the leading member of staff of a school? Should the gender-specific terms 'Headmaster' or 'Headmistress' be used? Or should the gender-neutral terms 'Head', 'Headteacher' or 'Principal' be used instead? Some schools may use titles such as 'Rector' or 'Dean' that have an educational resonance. Other institutions may use titles with a more managerial resonance such as 'School Manager', 'Director', 'Superintendent', 'Chief Executive Officer' or 'President'. This latter use of terminology may be culturally specific and be used more in schools with a strong USA-based management culture. Thus, a dozen or more terms may be used that refer to the (apparently) relatively simple concept of the person who is in charge at a school. Nomenclature may indicate whether an educational leader or a business manager occupies the post, or a combination of the two, or it may give away no clues about the nature of the position and how it is viewed by a particular institution. Each use of terminology may be interpreted as an emic feature of a particular school culture. From an anthropological perspective, schools are rich sources of emic constructs about concepts ranging from titles for managers and teachers to site-specific words and expressions for lessons, breaks between lessons, homework, toilets and items of clothing, to more abstract concepts. Such emic constructs may be recognized as a rich local argot replete with slang expressions. The danger of using an imposed etic concept in a questionnaire, by using one general form of nomenclature when a variety of different forms are practised at specific locations, is that the respondents may fail to interpret it in the way intended by the researcher and translate it into their own cultural context. Unfortunately, in the interests of standardization and the pressure of drawing 'valid' comparisons between different cohorts of respondents, questionnaires are often designed according to a 'one size fits all' approach. It is therefore important to take advice from as wide a range of respondents as possible at the piloting stage of the development of the data collection instrument. It is advisable that these respondents should come from a wide variety of cultures that replicates the mix of cultures in the intended target audience of the survey.

The disaggregation of data in terms of explanatory variables presents a variety of methodological problems. An assumption made by many statistical tests is that 'each element is a member of one and only one class' (Engen 1978). For example, a researcher may wish to disaggregate data about respondents ('elements') in terms of their nationality ('class'). The problem arises because the task of disaggregation may be more complicated in practice than the idealized view presented here. Respondents may be assigned to more than one class by having dual nationality, they

may have changed nationality or they may be stateless. This problem may be regarded as a technical issue, but there are also critical methodological issues concerning the relationship between concepts of ethnicity, nation, state, society and culture. Walby (2003: 531) argues that:

> it is inappropriate to treat nation-states as the main type of society for four reasons:
>
> - There are more nations than states;
> - Several key examples of supposed nation-states at their most developed moments were actually empires;
> - There are diverse and significant polities in addition to states, including the European Union (EU) and some organized religions, as well as the emergence of multi-lateral and global forms of governance; and
> - Polities overlap, notwithstanding the popular myth of nation-state sovereignty over a given territory. This means that the economic, political and cultural domains are not neatly overlapping in discrete bounded units.

Numerous identity markers may be recognized at different times in different contexts by the same individuals. As Grant (1997: 13–14) argues:

> Peoples' ways of defining themselves vary in time and place. We are all composites; it is perfectly feasible to be simultaneously (say) a Lewisman, a Gael, Scottish, British, European, a Free Presbyterian, a Nationalist, a primary school teacher, an ornithologist and any other role definition, as well as the partner, relation, friend and neighbour of identifiable individuals. Such a list could be prolonged almost indefinitely for any one of us, embracing all our group identifications, class and occupational memberships, all the things that define who we are, whether we have chosen them or not. The particular ones that we emphasise (or which others emphasise for us, correctly or not) may change according to circumstance.

This passage demonstrates how the concept of 'national identity' may be problematized. However, McCrone and Kiely (2000: 22) argue that 'nation, state and society belong to different orders of understanding – the cultural, political and social, respectively'. Nationality and citizenship belong to different spheres of activity and meaning. Nationality is 'a cultural concept which binds people on the basis of shared identity' whereas 'citizenship is a political concept deriving from people's relationship to the state' (p. 25). What are the criteria for identification of an individual with a particular nation or state? Such criteria are by no means universal, having evolved in a 'highly implicit manner' since states first appeared. McCrone and Kiely use the examples of Germany, France and the USA as case studies to illustrate their arguments about the application of the contrasting concepts of *ius sanguinus* (the law of blood) and *ius soli* (the law of territory) as routes to nationality and citizenship. They argue that 'while Germany was a nation which became a state, France was a state which transformed itself into a nation' (p. 28).

> The late unification of Germany in 1871 did not create Germans; they already existed in ethnic terms, and were governed by other states – Austria, Prussia, Russia and so on. Hence, anyone with German blood could claim to be German whether or not they lived on German soil. France, however, was a state before it was a nation, created as it was as a dynastic state by a succession of monarchs who claimed territorial jurisdiction on the basis of who happened to live there. Such a state had then to create French people. (p. 27)

While it is evident that the USA is in many respects an example of 'territorial' nationhood, like France, it has not been untouched by definitions of nationhood based on ethnocentric criteria. The USA:

> went about inventing citizens in a spectacularly successful fashion. It had to. This was the state which became a nation *par excellence*. Its founding myths of the 'melting point' and its successful mobilising of mechanisms of 'banal' nationalism – most obviously the daily pledge of allegiance in American schools – helped to forge a national identity of robust and lasting form. (p. 28)

However, the 'optimistic and liberal' view of the United States as an example of 'a state which forged a succession of immigrant people into citizens with a fierce pride in their nationality, regardless of their diverse origins and ethnicity' is challenged on the grounds that in the 'classical territorial state, some ethnicities were more equal than others. White Anglo-Saxon Protestants (WASPs) were not only more favoured in economic and social

terms, but occupied a central part of the American foundation myth' (p. 29).

McCrone and Kiely (2000) argue that 'the view of the world populated by autonomous societies-nations-states which we have inherited since the Enlightenment is one which is growing redundant. We live increasingly in a political world beyond the sovereign state in which absolutism whether it is of the ethnic-nationalist or the civic-state variety is no longer operative' (p. 30). Concepts of nationality and citizenship as categories for classifying respondents in social research appear to be unstable because the premises upon which they are founded are varied and unclear. What constitutes a valid criterion for assigning a person to a category is not universal and fixed, but particular and subject to revision, according to individual and local circumstances. This may be further complicated in cases in which the identity of an individual person may be assigned to more than one category. 'Multiple identity is common and appears to be getting commoner. This is a rather different position from cultural indeterminacy. Individuals, even whole groups, may operate in more than one culture, without moving totally from one to the other' (Grant 1997: 20). Sarup (1996: 142) argues that 'we should be thinking in terms beyond the nation-state. Internationalism is inadequate because it assumes the existence of the nation-state'.

Arguing from the point of view of comparative and international education, Crossley and Watson (2003) propose that the context of their field has been transformed by the spread of globalization. Whereas in the past it might have been possible to conduct research using the nation-state as the unit of comparison, the processes of globalization create a context in which researchers must now take into account approaches that make supra-national, regional and sub-national comparisons. Furthermore, they must also take into account comparisons made between deterritorialized units of study, including categories based on social and economic criteria, class, gender, ethnicity and religion. Issues such as social inclusion, social mobility, cultural capital, access to the World Wide Web, access to clean drinking water,

HIV/AIDS, migration and urbanization – to name but a few – are identified as the legitimate focus of study. They argue that the scope of such enquiry is limited only by the imagination of the researcher as the technological-rationalist approach to evaluation of educational development projects – a classical focus of study – is superseded by more qualitative and critical approaches that demand the development of new paradigms for the proposition and testing of knowledge claims. Take the concept, derived from radical geography, of 'counter-topography' as a potential approach to spatial analysis applied to educational enquiry.

> Countertopographies involve precise analyses of particular processes that not only connect disparate places, but also in doing so enable us to begin to infer connections in unexamined places in between. In topographic maps … it is the measurement of elevation at selected sites that enables contour lines to be drawn without measuring every inch of the terrain. The connections reflect precise analytic relationships, not homogenizations. Not every place affected by globalizing capitalist production or consumption is altered in the same way, and the issues that arise from place to place can vary and play out differently depending upon the constellation of social relations encountered in various locations. (Katz 2001: 722)

One can speculate that the sorts of deterritorialized categories suggested here give structure to the imaginative approaches that could supersede the nation-state as the unit of analysis, as Crossley and Watson (2003) propose.

Commenting on the internationalization of education in Europe, Coulby and Jones (1995: 56) argue that 'the terms "Europe" and "European" are conventionally used in a rather similar way to the use of the term "race"', and that, in the European context, there is a movement 'from an ethnocentric racism to a Eurocentric racism, from the different racisms of the different member states to a common market racism'. In other words, the concepts of 'Europe' and 'European' may be defined in a variety of geographical, political, economic, linguistic, cultural and ethnocentric terms. Coulby and Jones (1995: 56) propose that 'it should be incumbent on people to explain not just *what*

they mean by Europe and European but *why* they wish to use those classificatory terms. Although on the surface, they seem helpful, they should be examined constantly to see if their use is descriptive or political' (emphasis in original).

INTERNATIONAL EDUCATION STUDIES AS DISCOURSE

Lather (1991: 166) uses the term discourse 'in the Foucauldian sense of a conceptual grid with its own exclusions and erasures, its own rules and decisions, limits, inner logic, parameters and blind alleys. A discourse is that which is beneath the writer's awareness in terms of rules governing the formation and transformation of ideas into a dispersal of the historical agent, the knowing subject'. Discourse 'generally refers to a type of language associated with an institution, and includes the ideas and statements which express an institution's values. In Foucault's writings, it is used to describe individuals' acts of language, or "language in action" – the ideas and statements that allow us to make sense of and "see" things' (Danaher et al. 2000: x). The important point about discourse is that it embraces not only what is included but also what is excluded. In other words, discourse is political because it involves the exercise of power to include or exclude knowledge. Foucault proposes that truth is what the discourse makes it to be, a view that is in contrast to the 'scientific' view that truth exists 'out there', independent of the enquirer. On the contrary, truth is 'produced' by discourse. 'Foucault's power/knowledge thesis argues that power relations and scientific discourses mutually constitute one another' (Simons 1995: 27). That is to say, power and knowledge directly imply one another because 'there is no power relation without the correlative constitution of a field of knowledge, nor any knowledge that does not presuppose and constitute at the same time power relations' (Foucault 1977: 27). This is because Foucault argues that not only is power produced by the acquisition of knowledge, but it is also exerted in legitimizing what constitutes knowledge. Thus, 'truth' is to be understood 'as a system of ordered procedures for the production, regulation, distribution, circulation and operation of statements' (Foucault 1980: 133).

Using the model of Bentham's 'panopticon', or central lookout tower, a product of rational Enlightenment thought for making discipline and punishment more humane but no less arduous compared to premodern times, Foucault (1977) introduces the idea of how societies exert power over discourses through techniques of surveillance. Foucault argues that if the subject of surveillance knows that he or she is being watched or thinks that there is the possibility that he or she might be watched, then their behaviour will be changed in response to that knowledge and discipline is institutionalized. The point of this is that in modern societies, unlike premodern societies in which discipline was imposed in public view by cruel and exemplary physical punishments, subjects discipline themselves. 'He who is subjected to a field of visibility, and who knows it, assumes responsibility for the constraints of power; he makes them play spontaneously upon himself; he inscribes in himself the power relation in which he simultaneously plays both roles; he becomes the principle of his own subjection' (Foucault 1977: 203).

Foucault identifies the implementation of 'dividing practices' as one of the processes producing discourse. These practices comprise the construction of binary hierarchical oppositions that privilege one category over another, and the coercive assignment of subjects to these categories. These practices are explained in terms of examples that include definitions of madness and sanity (Foucault 1971) and the normalization of sexuality (Foucault 1981). 'Authorities exercising individual control function according to a double mode; that of *binary division* and branding (mad/sane; dangerous/harmless; normal/abnormal); and that of *coercive assignment*, of differential distribution (who he is; where he must be; how he is to be characterized; how a constant surveillance is to be exercised over him in an individual way)' (Foucault 1977: 199, original emphases). Dividing practices are commonly employed in educational contexts e.g. differentiating between students in terms of academic performance, social class, 'race', language, gender, sexuality and/or disability (Borg and Mayo 2001; Choi 2003; Copeland 1997, 1999; Graham and Neu 2004; Kazmi 1997; Pillow 2003; Selden 2000; Slaughter 1997). Foucault's approach demonstrates

> how language has been used to construct binaries, hierarchies, categories, tables, grids and complex classification schemes that are said to reflect an innate, intrinsic order in the world. In humanism, deep structures, myriad layers of orderly schemes, provide foundations that ameliorate and support the day-to-day confusion and random nature of living. As these structures are 'discovered', they are named and slotted into existing and ever-increasing classificatory schemes. (St Pierre 2000: 481)

Coulby and Jones (1995: 84–5) list numerous ways in which minorities and education systems can be differentiated. They argue that 'the nature of the defining process lies at the heart of one of the key debates of postmodernity, namely the construction and representation of identities. If dominant groups define minorities, they are likely to compile a different list from one compiled by members of the groups so defined' (p. 82).

According to Lather (2004: 23–4), 'Policy is to regulate behaviour and render populations productive via a "biopolitics" that entails state intervention in and regulation of the everyday lives of citizens in a "liberal" enough manner to minimize resistance and maximize wealth stimulation. Naming, classifying, and analyzing: all work toward disciplining through normalizing.' For Foucault:

> The power of normalization imposes homogeneity; but it individualizes by making it possible to measure gaps, to determine levels, to fix specialities and to render the differences useful by fitting them one to another. It is easy to understand how the power of the norm functions within a system of formal equality, since within a homogeneity that

is the rule, the norm introduces, as a useful imperative and as a result of measurement, all the shading of individual difference. (1977: 184)

By normalization Foucault means 'the establishment of measurements, hierarchy, and regulations around the idea of a distributionary statistical norm within a given population – the idea of judgment based on what is normal and thus what is abnormal' (Ball 1990: 2).

Normalising judgement and hierarchical surveillance are particularly conspicuous in examinations. Exams lie at the heart of discipline, as one of its most ritualized procedures, precisely because in them the need to observe and supervise and the right to punish are deeply intertwined with one another. Nowhere does the super-imposition of power and knowledge assume such perfect visibility. (Merquior 1985: 94)

The concept of 'naturalization' is important in this context. It indicates that behaviour and attitudes are not 'natural' conditions but constructed through discursive disciplinary practices. 'Once a discourse becomes "normal" and "natural", it is difficult to think and act outside it. Within the rules of a discourse, it makes sense only to say certain things. Other statements and other ways of thinking remain unintelligible, outside the realm of possibility' (St Pierre 2000: 485). In a discussion of what constitutes a 'proper' teacher, McWilliam (2004: 146) concludes that:

good teachers conduct themselves according to prescriptions of good teaching that are available to be thought – and felt. To speak of proper feelings is to draw attention to the fact that probities around our desires and our pleasures are not natural but trained. This fact is rendered invisible by the very appearance of good pedagogy as 'natural' ... It is easy to forget ... that 'naturalness' itself is a modern construct, a means of organizing language in such a way that certain ideas about what is proper come to be thinkable.

Modern society 'has not been progressing toward a freer, more enlightened state, but, instead, has become increasingly colonised by disciplinary power that proliferates and is diffused into every aspect of human life' (St Pierre 2000: 492). Techniques of educational management such as target-setting and appraisal may be interpreted in terms of the implementation of disciplinary regimes that control discourse (Ball 1990, 1994). Selwyn (2000) examines the impact of the Internet on the distribution of power/knowledge in education, with reference to the panopticon metaphor. Reid (2000) identifies the development of a culture of surveillance in teacher education in England that incorporates a high level of centralization not only in the control of the curriculum but also in terms of how teaching and learning should proceed. It is from this perspective that Wain (1998: 166) argues that the human and social sciences 'are part and parcel of the disciplinary technologies or instruments of government and policing of the modern state. They are, therefore, to be regarded with suspicion rather than hope'.

ORIENTALISM AND INTERNATIONAL EDUCATION STUDIES

Influenced by Foucault, Edward Said argues that the construction of knowledge of the 'Other' must be seen as a crucial site for the operation of colonial governance: 'without examining Orientalism as a discourse one cannot possibly understand the enormously systematic discipline by which European culture was able to manage – and even produce – the Orient politically, sociologically, militarily, ideologically, scientifically, and imaginatively during the post-Enlightenment period' (Said 1979: 3). Orientalism is 'a style of thought based upon an ontological and epistemological distinction made between "the Orient" and (most of the time) "the Occident"' (p. 2). It is 'the corporate institution for dealing with the Orient – dealing with it by making statements about it, authorizing views of it, describing it, by teaching it, settling it, ruling over it: in short, Orientalism as a Western style for dominating, restructuring, and having authority over the Orient' (p. 3).

Orientalism ... is not just an airy European fantasy about the Orient but a created body of theory and practice in which, for many generations, there has been considerable material investment. Continued investment made Orientalism, as a system of knowledge about the Orient, an accepted grid for filtering through the Orient into Western consciousness. (Said 1979: 6)

According to this perspective, Western academic scholarship about other cultures may be interpreted as a travesty that distorts not only the way Western societies see other cultures but also how the other cultures see themselves. Such distortions aid and abet imperialism and colonialism, because imperialism colonizes not only other countries materially but also the minds of the inhabitants of those countries (Pennycook 1998). Normalizing judgements are inscribed in the power relationships between the colonist and the colonized. Said argues how much scholarship about the archaeology, anthropology and other disciplines relating to countries of the Middle East and Far East is written in European languages, and published in books and journals that originate in the developed world, and are not indigenous to the countries being studied.

Four 'principal dogmas of Orientalism' are identified (Said 1979: 300–1) which comprise a set of dichotomies contrasting the way 'Western' scholarship sees itself in relation to the Orient:

1   Absolute and systematic difference between the West (rational, developed, humane, superior) and the Orient (aberrant, undeveloped, inferior).
2   Abstractions about the Orient, particularly those based on texts representing a 'classical' Oriental civilization, are always preferable to direct evidence drawn from modern Oriental realities.
3   The Orient is eternal, uniform, incapable of defining itself, therefore … a highly generalized and systematic vocabulary for describing the Orient from a Western standpoint is inevitable and even scientifically 'objective'.
4   The Orient is at bottom something either to be feared or to be controlled (i.e. by pacification, research and development, outright occupation).

Pennycook (1994: 60) recognizes that 'in order to avoid reinscribing people within a new academic discourse, it is crucial to seek to avoid essentializing representations of the "Other" (the Arabs, the Chinese, and so on) and for the "Other" to find ways of achieving representation outside these discourses'.

However, he also seeks clarification about what he interprets as

> Said's ambivalence about whether he is discussing Orientalism as a misrepresentation of "reality" (i.e. Orientalism fails to describe accurately the reality of the Orient) or whether he is dealing only with Orientalism as system of representation (i.e. the Orient is a construct of the discourse of Orientalism and thus there cannot be a question of misrepresentation) … In the one view … there is a reality that is misrepresented and therefore a possibility that proper representation could indeed reveal the truth. In the other view, there is no reality outside the discourses that construct our realities, only the possibility of critically analysing the truth effects of these discourses. (p. 164)

Lave (2003) presents a case study of the role of a British 'international' school in Portugal that highlights its 'practices of exclusion' in the production of an expatriate national identity. Lave (2003: 499) draws attention to 'an unusual facility on the part of the British to continue reproducing their position as arbiters of class culture in the transnational ambience'. Reference is made in a case study of an expatriate British community in Portugal to 'palpable fears of pollution' experienced by long-term expatriates 'through contaminating contact with Portuguese people of all kinds and a variety of differently but robustly British others' (Lave 2003: 506).

> Attempts to keep Portuguese children out of [the school] and their parents from intimate participation in the governance of school, church, and club, the dangers of speaking Portuguese too well, the avoidance and second-ranking of Portuguese club members and teachers at the school – all of these express, create, and sustain fear of contamination, or, ultimately, mistaken identity. In this transnational imaginary to be taken for Portuguese would amount to being taken for a native, an inferior. (Lave 2003: 507)

This example of the use of nationality to define 'otherness' in relation to the dominant group in a school context reinforces the point made above that it should be examined to see if its use is 'descriptive or political'. The assumption is contested that the nationality construct might be used in a benign way to categorize people. The classification of respondents according to 'nationality' may be identified as a potential focus of economic and intercultural conflict. Underlying this categorization is the issue of economic and social stratification, and the differential distribution of access to power. A variety of critical questions may be developed from this perspective. For example, does a school recruit 'professional' staff such as teachers and managers from the expatriate community, and 'support' staff from the local community? Are there salary differentials between expatriates and locally recruited employees (Knapp 2001)? Does the pattern of employment of staff contracts resemble a model such as Charles Handy's 'shamrock organization' with its administrative core of managers, professional fringe of expatriate teachers employed on short fixed-term contracts and a locally hired 'flexible labour force' of support staff, for example secretaries, clerks, cooks, cleaners and gardeners (Cambridge 2002b)? It is evident that a more developed understanding of the sociology of international education is a necessary prerequisite for addressing such issues.

CONCLUSION

It is proposed that survey-based data collection methodologies using questionnaires, with responses disaggregated according to presumed explanatory variables, should be approached with caution. This is because the ontological and epistemological assumptions are not warranted that there exists an external social reality that may be known through the application of such methods. The items in the data collection instrument may be interpreted in different ways by the researcher and the respondent (the double hermeneutic). The content of such instruments may be interpreted as constituting 'imposed etic' constructs that coerce the respondent into commenting on the world in the researcher's terms, while such a world-view may bear scant resemblance to the respondent's own viewpoint. The description of the social reality of the respondent expressed in the researcher's terms may be identified with the project of

'orientalism'. Furthermore, the essentialist view of 'values' and 'culture' being located in the mind of the individual is contested by alternative approaches that conceptualize culture as a discourse. According to this view, culture and values are decentred because they arise out of the processes of communication between various members of the population. Survey instruments constitute a disciplinary system that exerts power over subjects by coercively assigning them to categories by making normalizing judgements about them.

How might research enquiries in international education be designed in ways that mitigate the problems identified here? A few critical questions are identified below that may be used to evaluate research design. It is important that the language used in the data collection phase is understood clearly by the target audience. This may involve not only translation into other languages if the language of the researcher is not that of the respondents but also the use of language that is emic to the respondents. That is to say, concepts should be expressed in terms that are interpreted unambiguously by the target population, particularly in cases in which generalized etic constructs may be open to misinterpretation. Careful piloting and revision of the language of a data collection instrument should be designed to address the issue of emic and etic constructs, and their interpretation. Do the items present a normalizing view of a particular set of respondent attributes, such that 'if you are not in "category x" then you must be in "category y"'? This is particularly apparent in data collection instruments that operationalize constructs in terms of binary oppositions identified with the extreme ends of a linear dimension, for example, 'Masculinity/Femininity' (Hofstede 1986).

Assumptions about the nature of variables should be made explicit. For example, is it justified that the outputs of data collection are assumed to be equal interval or ratio variables, showing a normal distribution? Is the application of parametric statistical testing warranted, based on such assumptions? How are numerical data to be disaggregated? To what extent are the respondents aware of the categories into which they are placed? Are respondents 'coercively assigned' to such categories by the researcher or do they have the opportunity to criticize and influence the method of disaggregation themselves? Disaggregation of data by nationality of respondents is particularly problematic, because issues of ethnicity, nationality, citizenship and the state are complex and frequently – if not invariably – politically motivated and exclusionary. To what extent is the researcher aware of the implications of such disaggregation practices for respondents whose identification is with a persecuted minority nation within a state, who have dual passport nationality, who have changed passport nationality, or who are stateless and have no recognized passport nationality?

Furlong and Oancea (2005) propose a framework for the evaluation of quality in applied and practice-based educational research that embraces dimensions of 'scientific' and 'social and economic robustness'. In the context of mission-led schools with explicit international values, it is important that the research methodology employed should demonstrate an ethical 'value for people'.

REFERENCES

Ball, S. (1990) *Foucault and Education: Disciplines and Knowledge.* London: Routledge.

Ball, S. (1994) *Education Reform: A Critical and Post-Structural Approach.* Buckingham: Open University Press.

Borg, C. and Mayo, P. (2001) Social difference, cultural arbitrary and identity: an analysis of a new national curriculum document in a non-secular environment. *International Studies in Sociology of Education,* 11 (1): 63–84.

Brislin, R.W., Lonner, W.J. and Thorndike, R.M. (1973) *Cross-Cultural Research Methods.* London: John Wiley.

Bryman, A. (2004) *Social Research Methods.* Oxford: Oxford University Press.

Byrne, D. (2002) *Interpreting Quantitative Data.* London: Sage.

Caffyn, R. and Cambridge, J. (2005) From Middle Years Programme to Diploma Programme: a critical response to Candice Reimers. *IB Research Notes,*

5 (2): 2–9. Available online at //www.ibo.org/ibo/index.cfm?contentid=77ED3DF6–A375–2558–481 83B45AC555912&method=display&language=EN (accessed 1 November 2005).

Cambridge, J. (2002a) Response to Judy Hinrichs article. *IB Research Notes,* 2 (1): 11. Available online: at //www.ibo.org/ibo/index.cfm?contentid=000DA004 -A069-1C98-8A4D80C12645FE68&method= display&language=EN (accessed 1 November 2005).

Cambridge, J. (2002b) Recruitment and deployment of staff: a dimension of international school organization. In M.C. Hayden, J.J. Thompson and G. Walker (eds) *International Education in Practice.* London: Kogan Page, pp. 158–69.

Choi, P.K. (2003) The best students will learn English: ultra-utilitarian and linguistic imperialism in post-1997 Hong Kong. *Journal of Education Policy,* 18 (6): 673–94.

Cohen, L. and Manion, L. (1989) *Research Methods in Education.* London: Routledge.

Copeland, I.C. (1997) Pseudo-science and dividing practices: a genealogy of the first educational provision for pupils with learning difficulties. *Disability and Society,* 12 (5): 709–22.

Copeland, I.C. (1999) Normalisation: an analysis of aspects of special needs education. *Educational Studies,* 25 (1): 99–111.

Coulby, D. and Jones, C. (1995) *Postmodernity and European Education Systems.* Stoke-on-Trent: Trentham Books.

Crossley, M. and Watson, K. (2003) *Comparative and International Research in Education: Globalisation, Context and Difference.* London: RoutledgeFalmer.

Danaher, G., Schirato, T. and Webb, J. (2000) *Understanding Foucault.* London: Sage.

Engen, S. (1978) *Stochastic Abundance Models, with Emphasis on Biological Communities and Species Diversity.* London: Chapman and Hall.

Field, A. (2000) *Discovering Statistics using SPSS for Windows.* London: Sage.

Foucault, M. (1971) *Madness and Civilisation: A History of Insanity in the Age of Reason.* London: Tavistock Press.

Foucault, M. (1977) *Discipline and Punish: The Birth of the Prison.* London: Allen Lane.

Foucault, M. (1980) The eye of power. In C. Gordon (ed.) *Power/Knowledge: Selected Interviews and Other Writings, 1972–1977.* Brighton: Harvester Press, pp. 146–82.

Foucault, M. (1981) *The History of Sexuality,* Volume 1. London: Penguin.

Furlong, J. and Oancea, A. (2005) *Assessing Quality in Applied and Practice-based Educational Research: A Framework for Discussion.* Oxford University: Department of Educational Studies. Available online at www.bera.ac.uk/pdfs/Qualitycriteria.pdf (accessed 1 November 2005).

Giddens, A. (1984) *The Constitution of Society.* Cambridge: Polity Press.

Graham, C. and Neu, D. (2004) Standardized testing and the construction of governable persons. *Journal of Curriculum Studies,* 36 (3): 295–319.

Grant, N. (1997) Some problems of identity and education: a comparative examination of multicultural education. *Comparative Education,* 33 (1): 9–28.

Hinrichs, J. (2002) The effect of the International Baccalaureate Diploma Programme on international understanding. *IB Research Notes,* 2 (1): 3–9. Available online at www.ibo.org/ibo/index.cfm?contentid=000DA004-A069-1C98-8A4D80C126 45FE68&method=display&language=EN (accessed 1 November 2005).

Hinrichs, J. (2003) A comparison of levels of international understanding among students of the International Baccalaureate Diploma and Advanced Placement programs in the USA. *Journal of Research in International Education,* 3 (2): 331–48.

Hofstede, G. (1986) Cultural differences in teaching and learning. *International Journal of Intercultural Relations,* 10 (3): 301–20.

Hopkins, D. (1989) *Evaluation for School Development.* Milton Keynes: Open University Press.

Humphreys, M. (1996) Cultural difference and its effect on the management of technical education. *Leadership and Organization Development Journal,* 17 (2): 34–41.

Katz, C. (2001) Vagabond capitalism and the necessity of social reproduction. *Antipode,* 33 (4): 709–28.

Kaufmann, W. (1976) *The Portable Nietzsche.* London: Penguin.

Kazmi, Y. (1997) Foucault's genealogy and teaching multiculturalism as a subversive activity. *Studies in Philosophy and Education,* 16: 331–45.

Knapp, R. (2001) The implications of a two-tier salary scale on teacher relations: a case study. *International Schools Journal,* XXI (1): 57–68.

Lam, Y.L. (2002) Defining the effects of transformational leadership on organisational learning: a cross-cultural comparison. *School Leadership and Management,* 22 (4): 439–52.

Lather, P. (1991) *Getting Smart: Feminist Research and Pedagogy with/in the Postmodern.* London: Routledge.

Lather, P. (2004) This IS your father's paradigm: government intrusion and the case of qualitative research in education. *Qualitative Inquiry,* 10 (1): 15–34.

Lave, J. (2003) Producing the future: getting to be British. *Antipode,* 35 (3): 492–511.

Lincoln, Y.S. and Guba, E.G. (2000) Paradigmatic controversies, contradictions, and emerging confluences. In N.K. Denzin and Y.S. Lincoln (eds) *Handbook of Qualitative Research,* 2nd edition. London: Sage, pp. 163–88.

McCrone, D. and Kiely, R. (2000) Nationalism and citizenship. *Sociology,* 34 (1): 19–34.

McWilliam, E. (2004) What does it mean to feel like teaching? In B.M. Baker and K.E. Heyning (eds) *Dangerous Coagulations? The Uses of Foucault in the Study of Education.* New York: Peter Lang, pp. 135–50.

Merquior, J.G. (1985) *Foucault.* London: Fontana.

Pennycook, A. (1994) *The Cultural Politics of English as an International Language.* London: Longman.

Pennycook, A. (1998) *English and the Discourses of Colonialism.* London: Routledge.

Pillow, W. (2003) 'Bodies are dangerous': using feminist genealogy as policy studies methodology. *Journal of Education Policy,* 18 (2): 145–59.

Popper, M. and Sleman, K. (2001) Intercultural differences and leadership perceptions of Jewish and Druze school principals. *Journal of Educational Administration,* 39 (3): 221–32.

Reid, I. (2000) Accountability, control and freedom in teacher education in England: towards a panopticon. *International Studies in Sociology of Education,* 10 (3): 213–25.

Reimers, C. (2004) From MYP to Diploma: an investigation into the impact of the International Baccalaureate Middle Years Programme on International Baccalaureate Diploma candidates. *International Schools Journal,* XXIV (2): 11–8.

Said, E. (1979) *Orientalism.* London: Penguin.

Sarup, M. (1996) *Identity, Culture and the Postmodern World.* Edinburgh: Edinburgh University Press.

Scott, D. (1996) Methods and data in educational research. In: D. Scott and R. Usher (eds) *Understanding Educational Research.* London: Routledge, pp. 52–73.

Scott, D. and Usher, R. (1996) *Understanding Educational Research.* London: Routledge.

Selden, S. (2000) Eugenics and the social construction of merit, race and disability. *Journal of Curriculum Studies,* 32 (2): 235–52.

Selwyn, N. (2000) The National Grid for Learning: panacea or Panopticon? *British Journal of Sociology of Education,* 21 (2): 243–55.

Simons, J. (1995) *Foucault and the Political.* London: Routledge.

Slater, C.L., Boone, M., Price, L. and Martinez, D., Alvarez, I., Topete, C. and Olea, E. (2002) A cross-cultural investigation of leadership in the United States and Mexico. *School Leadership and Management,* 22 (2): 197–207.

Slaughter, S. (1997) Class, race and gender and the construction of post-secondary curricula in the United States: social movement, professionalization and political economic theories of curricular change, *Journal of Curriculum Studies,* 29 (1): 1–30.

St Pierre, E.A. (2000) Poststructural feminism in education: an overview. *Qualitative Studies in Education,* 13 (5): 477–515.

Wain, K. (1998) Review article. *Studies in Philosophy and Education,* 17: 163–76.

Walby, S. (2003) The myth of the nation-state: theorizing society and polities in a global era. *Sociology,* 37 (3): 529–46.

Wallace, M. and Poulson, L. (2003) *Learning to Read Critically in Educational Leadership and Management.* London: Sage.

35

Voices from Abroad: a Contextual Approach to Educational Research and Cultural Diversity

Michael Allan

The cultural diversity of an international school poses many methodological problems for researchers. A lack of cross-cultural validity, for instance, precludes many of the methods commonly used in national educational research from being applied. Part of the problem is undoubtedly due to the fact that international schools, with their mobile, culturally and linguistically diverse student body, are not homogeneous. The use of structural models as a way of understanding schools is thus limited by the absence of uniformity in the identification and measurement of inputs and outcomes. Scientific methodology is also prohibited by a lack of generalizability and the scale of comparative models is usually too large to be considered by most researchers.

This chapter examines ways in which the cultural complexity of school and classroom can be penetrated by interpretive methodology, enabling crucial process factors to be identified and described within the context of the international school. This enables such issues as classroom interaction, cognitive development, international pedagogy and the effect of culturally specific discourses and cross-cultural interaction on learning and cultural identity to be investigated. It explores how researchers can endeavour to provide these situated understandings by examining more critically the theoretical constructs that currently underlie the educational treatment of linguistically and culturally diverse students and the routine practice of international schools.

In this chapter, the importance of context both in the determination of states of affairs and in their interpretation is examined initially. Various types of ethnomethodology from within the interpretive paradigm are assessed as a means of understanding the complex nature of international schools, particularly those approaches derived from cultural studies, applied linguistics and discourse analysis. An example of one such methodology, the ethnographic case study, is then described in more detail and finally a syncretic research model using a combination of theoretical and

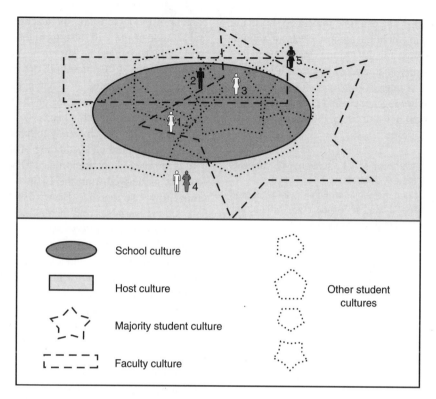

Figure 35.1 Cultural borderlands – areas of cultural interaction (Allan 2002: 78)

methodological tools is suggested for use in the international school context.

THE IMPORTANCE OF CONTEXT

> The primary objective of school, success for all, … is rarely achieved because … institutions do not consider the cross-cultural context in which teaching and learning occur. (Cushner 1990: 98)

Culture does not make people do things, it is the things people do that make culture. Migrant children will have been socialized by this reciprocal interaction with the cultural norms in their society which they continue to encounter daily in their home environment. However, much of the reinforcement process, which is part of the daily interactions between an individual and his/her own culture, will have been replaced by interactions with the new host and school culture and children from

other societies. The differences may cause a culture clash between home and school, as encounters may not validate the sense of identity and the cultural norms with which children from many cultural backgrounds will have been socialized and which may also be in conflict with the expectations of the school.

How can research help us to understand the interactive process and the effect on identity and learning? Allan used the analogy of 'cultural borderlands', where the child's experience of the school takes place. Each school culture has individual and specific characteristics. Into this cultural space will come students of differing backgrounds and histories, bringing with them certain experiences, attitudes, expectations and preconceptions which constitute their own individual cultural characteristics (Allan 2002).

A simple model (Figure 35.1), of the nature of a Venn diagram, may illustrate this process figuratively. The example illustrated shows the overlapping cultural environments of school, host country, faculty culture, majority student culture, and other student cultures. It is apparent that an international school experience is far from homogeneous, and a student can find him/herself in a number of different situations, for example:

1   in an in-school social situation with students from different cultures
2   in a class, perhaps an English as a Second Language or Mother Tongue class, without any students from the majority culture
3   in a normal class where the majority student culture might predominate
4   in a social situation outside school with a friend from a different culture
5   at home in their own culture (which may also be bi-cultural).

Each one of these situations will involve one or more cultural frontiers, and crossing these frontiers daily is bound to engender cultural dissonance, if not conflict, in the myriad cross-cultural interactions which take place. A student's daily experience of an international school is therefore by no means homogeneous, and, as Cushner reminds us, 'Research suggests that there are preferred learning styles and particular patterns of behavior among many cultural and ethnic groups that may be in conflict with the traditional school setting' (Cushner 1990: 108). Any study which hopes to present an understanding of the experience of different groups must be able to incorporate the school effect.

The context of the school culture not only forms the frame that will define the situation and the students' experiences, it is also a determinant factor in the process of cross-cultural interaction; students will interact with the school culture as much as with each other (Allan 2003). This school culture is manifest in many ways and on many levels. Language issues, including the status of languages other than English, and their accompanying cultures, are fundamental, but the cultural values of the predominant student nationalities, as well as the cultural rules (behaviour and discipline) of the school, the cultural style and

content of the lessons and the teaching styles and attitude of the staff, also form the 'framework' which defines the situation. As Robin Alexander puts it: 'Culture both drives and is everywhere manifested in what goes on in classrooms, from what you see on the walls to what goes on in children's heads' (Alexander 2000: 266). Thus for any study to have meaning and validity, an understanding of the context is of paramount importance. The word 'context' is derived from the Latin root *contexere*: to weave together (Brown 1993: 493). The actions, variables and factors involved in school culture are interwoven in constant reciprocal interaction; a dialectic in which the subjects both influence and are influenced by the context in which their actions take place.

Traditional quantitative techniques are inadequate here, since they rely on the concept of testing empirically a hypothesis generated from theory on a sample, and generalizing from the sample to a larger population: 'the systematic, controlled empirical and critical investigation of hypothetical positions' (Kerlinger 1969: 4). The cultural diversity of international schools prohibits this. Quantitative tradition also reflects an underlying tendency to look for causal factors explaining individual behaviour, where causality is denoted by the use of dependent and independent variables, and relies on other factors being controlled. In a complex, dynamic process of cross-cultural interaction, variables cannot be controlled.

Qualitative research can, on the other hand, investigate by comparing cases to each other rather than using a predetermined formula: 'In this method the different elements or dimensions of the phenomenon being studied are thought of as causal factors, that is independent variables, linked to each other by (possibly complex) mutual causal relations' (Alasuutari 1995: 16). In studying international schools the methodology must permit the researcher to step outside culture-specific ideas of education and examine the process of interaction, or dialectic, of the various actors and the context which frames this. When we are trying to study a situation, such as classroom interaction in a science lesson, or an attitude such as intercultural awareness in an institution, or the implications of both external and internal school policy, we cannot isolate one from the other.

A poststructuralist view in the broad sense also recognizes the reflexive nature of the effects of these contexts and the dialectics involved, which, in a cross-cultural situation more than any other, may vary along a consonant/dissonant dimension. Ethnomethodology can provide the means of penetrating the complexity of the context of school culture and of understanding the relations and processes that govern the outcomes of education, a proposition that will be considered in the next section.

ETHNOMETHODOLOGY

People are constantly trying to understand what is going on in any situation and using these understandings to produce appropriate behaviour of their own. Ethnomethodology is the study of the methods ordinary people use for producing and making sense of everyday social life. Artefacts and text for analysis do not have any independent objective meaning or nature; they have only the interpretations that the various actors place upon them. It is these interpretations that ethnomethodology tries to discover and the task of the researcher is to provide the rich, thick description that shares insights with the readers of research and also enables them to gauge its plausibility and transferability. In this section the ethnographic approaches of cultural, sociolinguistic and discourse analysis are examined.

Cultural studies, or a phenomenological approach

Schools and classrooms are complex social environments. They consist of different groups of people interacting with each other in various ways. The most obvious area where this can be observed is in the pupil–teacher and pupil–pupil interaction and communication patterns (Stables 2003). Much research in recent years has focused on the verbal interchanges

between teachers and pupils, including issues such as the style of teacher talk and learning (Edwards and Westgate 1994; Ripich and Creaghead 1994; Cazden 2001). Other research has focused upon the ways a child's culture shapes communication and interaction in the classroom (Mercer 1992; Wells and Chang-Wells 1992). The common denominator in all of this research is that what teachers and pupils actually say and do becomes the major focus for attention. However, classrooms and lessons have a history, and meanings must be 'situated' (Gee, 1999), that is, interpreted within the wider school context; in international schools, they must also be interpreted within the respective cultures of the students and teachers. Teachers and students make constant references to the social contexts of the lessons and the identities of the students. It is impossible to appreciate fully what is happening without paying attention to these contexts.

Alasuutari (1995) asserts that this idea aligns with the discourse-analytical or ethnomethodological approach to what Goffman (1975) describes as the concept of frame, the sets of rules that constitute activities of a certain type. When in everyday life we form some kind of picture of 'what is going on', we have located a frame that makes the situation (at least partially) understandable. Rather than being a framework for interpretation, as in symbolic interactionism, or a means of regulating meaning within the cultural context, as in structuralism, here it is asserted that in situations that are always 'framed' in one way or another, it is not so much that the situation is interpreted within this framework, rather that the framework defines the situation.

Wieder (1974) identified a particular institutional context through the 'code', or 'insider talk' peculiar to a situation, group or institution, which is used in, and at the same time delineates, the frame of the situation. He showed how the 'code' is derived, and the rules of the 'code' are picked out, in the course of conversations with the subjects, but then abstracted from those conversations into claims and categories to serve as explanatory resources for the researcher. Narrative analysis in cultural studies takes this code as the topic of study, and asks how it is used, thus shifting from talk as an explanatory resource to talk as a topic in its own right. It takes subjects' explanations as the object of study rather than as a validation of their own interpretations. Why has this version been produced? What does the talk do and what does it achieve? It produces a version of what is going on in the immediate circumstances – it establishes the interaction in one way rather than in another (Potter and Wetherell 1987). Ethnomethodology has this characteristic of using talk to reproduce role relations and not just a pre-written script – 'the nature of interaction does not arrive pre-packaged and pre-ordained but is reproduced on each occasion. To put it another way, the participants do not passively respond to what is going on but actively produce it' (Potter and Wetherell 1987: 21). This type of approach in anthropology and cross-cultural psychology is an emic approach (Patton 1987), as the stories are situated within the subject's own discourse.

> According to this view, cultural behaviour should always be studied and categorized in terms of the inside view – the actor's definition – of human events. That is, the units of conceptualization in anthropological theories should be 'discovered' by analyzing the cognitive processes of the people studied, rather than 'imposed' from cross-cultural (hence, ethnocentric) classifications of behaviour. (Pelto and Pelto 1978: 54)

A phenomenological approach to the use of discourse analysis in ethnography tries to avoid semiosis, the interpretation of meanings, and concentrates on studying observable clues, such as practices or modes of speech used, in making interpretations about the discourses or structures of meaning. The identification of such discourses as 'methods of common understanding' (Garfinkel 1984: 31), however, enables the phenomenon to be understood. Polyani (1979) believes that oral narratives of personal experience illustrate core concepts of culture and are sources of insights into those concepts. The point of the narrative must be 'culturally salient material generally agreed upon by members of the producer's culture to be self-evidently and importantly true' (1979: 207). Narratives

are cultural texts available for analysis, and narrative analysis becomes 'a methodology for identifying and investigating beliefs about the world held by members of a particular culture' (p. 213). An example of this type of ethnographic case study is discussed in further detail below.

Sociolinguistic approaches

There are a number of important points of contact between sociolinguistic and ethnographic research in educational settings. Both are ethnomethodological in that they are concerned with what participants are doing in making sense of each others' utterances, and both look at patterns and irregularities in classroom talk. Sociolinguistic analyses focus upon the way in which talk is oriented towards particular parties. Ethnographic approaches widen the focus of interest to include a much broader range of factors that may influence what goes on between the teacher and pupils in the classroom.

There are several policy areas relevant to international schools where sociolinguistic research has made an impact. For example, the question of bilingualism and bilingual schools, mother tongue teaching, teaching standard English to speakers of non-standard English, the organization of classroom talk and, in particular, teacher talk itself, have all been examined using a sociolinguistic perspective.

Talk in the classroom displays some important individual characteristics – it is typically organized around the completion of tasks and activities, and perhaps the most important characteristic is the way one speaker, the teacher, attempts to control and direct the talk (Cazden 2001). Sociolinguistic analysis can highlight how teachers' utterances or questions are heard by pupils as demonstrated in the contextual features of the transcripts, for example, and conversely how teachers hear and respond to pupils' contribution to the lesson. Following Garfinkel (1984), ethnomethodologists refer to phenomena of this kind as reflexive features of talk. As Potter and Wetherell point out, 'Talk is not just about actions, events and situations, it is a potent and constitutive part of those actions, events and situations' (1987: 21). An utterance is not just a description of a rule; it also formulates the nature of the action and the situation and has a number of practical consequences within that situation.

Culture can also be seen in Riessman's way of looking at the pragmatics of the language being used in asking why stories are told in a certain way: 'The methodological approach examines story and analyses how it is put together, the linguistic and cultural references that it draws on' (Riessman 1993: 2). Riessman's methodology for analysing narratives in texts, an extension of the Labov–Mishler model (Labov 1992; Mishler 1986) also incorporates context: 'The story metaphor emphasizes that we create order, construct texts in particular contexts' (Riessman 1993: 2). In her method, narrative analysis limits itself to investigation of story – first person accounts by respondents of experience: 'The purpose is to see how respondents in interviews impose order on the flow of experience to make sense of events and notions in their lives' (Riessman 1993: 2). This approach gives the opportunity to recognize wider cultural influences on the construction of a respondent's narrative, as well as those of the individual situation, and to understand how the subject experiences the situation, rationalizes it and how this determines action and interaction with other parties. However, if we also consider voice, the individual subject position of the actor, we can also achieve an understanding of how power relationships are perceived by each actor, using grammatical syntax as a metaphor to understand how they create their narrative. Cortazzi (1993) describes the manifestation of Goffman's 'multiple selves' in narratives in this way, as well as his ideas of 'frames' (Kintsch and van Dijk 1983), 'ritual and face' and 'performance' (Goffman 1967). This means that we do not need to be limited to individual narratives; conversation such as classroom discourse can also be transcribed and analysed in this way. According to Cortazzi (1993), conversation analysis has shown that long stretches of apparently casual conversation are in fact highly structured and demonstrate the social knowledge needed to tell a narrative in conversation. Conversation analysis has been widely applied to study classroom talk by Hymes (1985), Edwards and Westgate (1994) and Cazden (2001), *inter alia*.

Discourse analysis

As was outlined in the introduction, culture does not determine people's behaviour, as was thought in structuralism; it *is* people's behaviour. While structuralism takes the view that culture contains deep structures that determine meaning, in poststructuralist discourse theory, the 'deep structures' of culture only exist as people act and behave in accordance with those structures, or make use of them in their activities.

> To say that two people belong to the same culture is to say that they interpret the world in roughly the same ways and can express themselves, their thoughts and feelings about the world, in ways which will be understood by each other. Thus culture depends on its participants interpreting meaningfully what is happening around them, and 'making sense' of the world, in broadly similar ways. (Hall 1997: 2)

On the other hand, it is stressed that the meaning structures commonly used constitute the culture of that society, and it is precisely this dual nature of meaning systems that the poststructuralist concept of discourse seeks to understand; the juxtaposition between reality and constructions of reality.

Meaning structures do not use people; people use meaning structures to understand the world and their place in it, and the chief concern in an ethnomethodological approach is to look at how the individual makes sense of the world and tries to interpret it. Geetz (1973) argues that to understand the meanings others have placed on experience is a cultural approach to the study of communication. Critical theorists take this view further, stating that traditional ethnographers' concern with describing a social setting "as it really is" assumes an objective, "common-sense" reality where none exists. Rather this reality should be seen for what it is – a social and cultural construction, linked to wider power relations, which privileges some and disadvantages other participants' (May 1997: 199).

It is the reflexivity, or dialectic, inherent in the poststructuralist approach to discourse, incorporating such theorists as Fairclough (1995) and Edwards (1997) *inter alia*, that makes it so suitable for exploring a culturally diverse institution. No societal or institutional situation is static, neither are personal attitudes and characteristics. Poststructuralist discourse theory allows both for the influence of the current state of affairs on the group, or individual, discourse; action and relations between them; and the way in which these discourses are acting to change the situation. In this dynamic, cross-cultural interaction in terms of relations of power between discourses of different actors, or voices, is also taken into account. Changes in power structures in society such as cultural hegemony, or micro-politics in institutions such as the influence of a predominant cultural group or within groups like class or peer groups, can also be incorporated and explained.

Critical theory

The importance of context in poststructuralist discourse theory is also paramount in the theory, propounded most notably in the writings of Michel Foucault, of the conjunction of power and knowledge (Foucault 1972). From Foucault comes the idea of discourse as a regulated way of speaking that defines and produces objects of knowledge, thereby governing the way topics are talked about and practices conducted. For Foucault 'truth' did not mean objective or intrinsic facts about the nature of people; rather he argued that in constructing ideas that are ascribed the status of 'truths', they become 'normalizing' in the way they shape and constitute people's lives. He asserts the inseparability of power and knowledge in showing how the 'truths' of traditional notions of knowledge positioned one form of knowledge in ascendancy over another. Discourse thus embodies meaning and social relationships and itself serves to empower its users and marginalize others from the debate by determining the frame of reference within

which their standpoint may be judged. The discourses then not only form the objects of discussion but become them: 'Discourses ... do not identify objects, they constitute them and in the practice of doing so conceal their own invention' (Foucault 1971). In this paradigm, knowledge does not reflect the power relations between different groups of society, but embodies them. Power and knowledge are inseparable and mutually reinforcing, and are made manifest in discourse. 'Discourses are therefore about what is said and thought, but also who can speak, when and with what authority ... The possibilities for meaning and interpretation are pre-empted through the social and institutional position from which a discourse comes' (Ball 1990: 17).

This understanding has led to a body of thought in recent postmodern educational work which generally falls under the title of critical theory. Although this was originally a post-Marxist view of knowledge expressed by the 'Frankfurt school' (Adorno, Horkheimer) and later associated with Gramsci and Habermas, critical theorists in education have come to be more concerned with combining this view of epistemology with Foucauldian ideas of discourse and power, Vygotskian perspectives on learning and the critical pedagogy of Paulo Freire, in examining the position of discourses of underprivileged groups in schools (Giroux 1992; McLaren 1997; Corson 1998; Cummins 2000). This standpoint became apparent in feminist studies but more especially in the examination of treatment and performance of cultural minorities in Western education systems, which are characterized as consisting of modernist discourses where 'the dualistic way of seeing reinforced a rationalistic, patriarchal, expansionist, social and political order, welded to the desire of power and conquest' (Kincheloe and Steinberg 1997: 36). Critical multiculturalism attacks the privilege and bias afforded by Eurocentric (white, middle-class and patriarchal) discourses in schools and deconstructs learning, enabling the power structure implicit in the relative positions of different discourses to be exposed and attacked (McLaren 1997). As these discourses are not always congruent, dissonance among them must result, though not necessarily to the extent that they can be described as conflict. A school may not be 'a cultural arena where ideological, discursive and social forces collide in an ever-unfolding drama of dominance and resistance' (Kumaravadivelu 1999: 475), but critical discourse analysis can be seen as a way of exposing the dynamics of interaction among culturally different groups as well as situating them within a wider context.

Critical theory pays much attention to the socioeconomic and political nature of cultural injustice which may not be applicable in international schools, although we might only have to substitute 'international' for 'regular' to agree with Corson that parents 'want the best of both worlds for their children's education: they certainly want admission to the mainstream and high-status culture of literacy that is the chief output of regular education, but they also want schools to recognise "their own things" – their own cultural values, language varieties, traditions, and interests' (Corson 1998: 203).

THE ETHNOGRAPHIC CASE STUDY

Ethnography has long been used, and was indeed developed, in cultural research and has since been appropriated and adapted for use in educational contexts. The traditional ethnographic case study approach strives for cultural validity by locating the study within the culture being studied and modern versions acknowledge cultural bias in the form of interaction and interpretation by the researcher (Hammersley 1990, 1997; Thomas 1992; Alasuutari 1995). In an ethnographic case study, contingency variables, etic in the cultural sense, are constant across the population, although their effects may differ. The whole population then becomes the sample for analysis, and generalizations are not made to a greater population. This does not stop us drawing conclusions from the study, however; in such a case we can generalize to a hypothetical universe:

It is the universe of all possible samples (which may be limited universes) which could have been produced under similar conditions of time, place, culture and other relevant factors. (Hagood 1970: 66)

Theory can then emerge from the particular situation and thus be grounded in the data generated by the research (Glaser and Strauss 1967). Allan adopted this approach by using narrative analysis to ascertain which cross-cultural process factors were involved in an international school education. The whole school population was taken as a sample, and students were asked to write a story describing their experiences when they first arrived at the school. These narratives were then analysed in the context of cultural dissonance, defined as 'a disharmony in cultural interactions, in the dimensions of communication, behaviour, expectations and experience, due to divergence of cultural characteristics' (Allan 2002: 104). Several process factors in terms of interaction within the school culture were identified as being significant in intercultural and academic learning. The case study involved 171 students aged 11–18 years, and used a phenomenological approach to narrative analysis which categorizes phenomena occurring in narrative by examining their cultural interpretations of states of affairs. Students were asked to write a story of the experiences of a pupil starting at the school; they were told that the stories did not have to be autobiographical, but the subject should be someone of their own age, sex, language, national and cultural background and similar personal history. This is an emic approach, incorporating a student's own interpretation of events, and situated in their own discourse and culture. Students expressed their feelings historically and contemporaneously, giving their own interpretation of causality and consequence, the learning process and insights into personal development (Allan 2002). In cultural studies, narratives as retrospective accounts of a personal past are seen as documents reflecting the storytellers' current, situation-bound theories and construction of selves (Alasuutari 1995).

This case study presented both a comparative and dynamic version of the intercultural process of change, in differing perspectives among students from different cultural backgrounds and after different lengths of time at the school, and in retrospective accounts of their changing ideas. In telling stories about past events, 'respondents narrativise particular incidents in their lives, often when there has been a breach between ideal and real, self and society' (Riessman 1993: 3). Stories are organized around consequential events. Analysing narratives involves looking for these accounts of consequential events or critical incidents; coding and classification of these phenomena then enable us to construct theory. This process is characterized by Thomas (1992: 5) as follows: 'The essence of the interpretive stance is a temporal cycle working backward from the present to help the construction of a defined, refined, corrected and coherent past'. In this case analysis involves looking for the cultural perspectives involved in students' creation of their version of events.

Coding, classification and theory generation

According to Strauss and Corbin (1998: 57), traditional narrative analysis begins with micro-analysis: 'The detailed line-by-line analysis [is] necessary at the beginning of a study to generate initial categories (with their properties and dimensions) and to suggest relationships among categories; a combination of open and axial coding'. In doing this by hand, the researcher uses an index system of numbered cards containing biographical details of each student, where critical or significant incidents in the data or 'phenomena' are recorded as their narratives are read. A digital, and much less laborious, method of recording and sorting is reported in Allan and Brown (2002). Although at this first stage the data are approached with no classification system in mind, during this process the incidence and similarity of certain events begin to suggest categories and labels. Differences or anomalies inevitably draw attention to themselves as general concepts begin to emerge, and further investigation leads us to look at the cultural characteristics of the individual student as seen in their biographical details, or relating to instances

in the literature or personal experience in seeking explanations. Thus the process of theory-forming starts even in the first stage of analysis. But, as Strauss and Corbin (1998: 58) explain, 'analysis is not a structured, static or rigid process. Rather it is a free-flowing and creative one in which analysts move quickly back and forward between different types of coding, using analytic techniques and procedures freely and in response to the analytic task before analysts'. These suggestions and observations can be recorded as memos, to be used in later stages of coding and classification. In this type of analysis it is important to remember that homogeneity among story content is not required, as the researcher is not looking for aggregate totals of incidents in specific categories. The purpose of research is to find out what is going on, and one detailed story can provide us with as much insight as several more superficial or less specific accounts. However care must be taken that any conclusions or theory derived from the data must be inclusive and applicable to all the data. To appropriate an aphorism: when we are looking in the horse's mouth, we are not interested in the number of teeth the horse has, but rather what its teeth tell us about its health relative to other horses (Allan and Brown, 2002). By comparing phenomena in the same domain we can see the workings of the process involved in the formation of cultural attitudes and identity in the setting of an international school. Analysis thus enables a model of the process of intercultural learning to emerge in the form of grounded theory (Glaser and Strauss 1967). This can be generalized in terms of process to other situations where enough similarity exists for researchers to be able to say reliably that the same process is operating (Hagood 1970), even though contingency variables in terms of, for example, size, or nationalities among student groups, or host country, may vary.

The relationships between the phenomena in the narratives and their implications are complex, and derived-etic generalizations in this respect (Berry 1969) cannot be fully understood without reference to cross-cultural psychology and other acculturation studies.

The situating of the conclusions in the context of other research forms part of the process of this type of discourse analysis in which theory is formed in the interpretation of data by comparing phenomena to each other, the experience of the researcher and also to the literature (Alasuutari 1995; Strauss and Corbin 1998).

Although there are many methods of data collection associated with this methodology (such as interviews, observation and discourse analysis), one common element is that the primary data are the interpretations of the observer: 'the observer is the instrument' (Robson 1993: 195). This element of the methodology enables the teacher to use his or her most valuable asset as a researcher – his or her experience: 'Experience and knowledge are what sensitize the researcher to significant problems and issues in the data and allows him to see alternative explanations and to recognize properties and dimensions of emergent concepts' (Strauss and Corbin 1998: 59). Any extensive experience of international schools that teachers may have will also enhance the cultural sensitivity of researchers that Alasuutari (1995) claims is essential if confidence in their interpretation of cross-cultural situations is to be generated.

There is a danger that, in carrying out research in a familiar situation where the researcher is known, he or she is open to factors such as respondent bias, personal reactivity, observational bias, selective encoding, personal expectations or hasty judgement (Hammersley 1990). According to Alasuutari (1995), the general strategy is 'to seek to recognize and discount all biases' by including them in the realm of competence of the researcher, and by being open about them with the subjects (and the subsequent readers) of the research. Most importantly, ethnographic research needs to describe its methodology clearly and in detail so that, as fellow researchers, we can determine its trustworthiness.

A COMBINED OR 'LAYERED' APPROACH

This chapter has examined the disciplines of cultural studies, sociolinguistics and critical discourse analysis and their respective merits in ethnographic understanding. However, these disciplines are not mutually exclusive, even though their adherents might like to claim paradigmatic differences. Each has its own specific merit in illuminating our understanding of different dimensions of interaction within school culture. Language in the anthropological ethnographic tradition of cultural studies can give insight into the social, cultural and interpersonal aspects which influence the interaction of teachers and pupils in school and classroom contexts. The ethnography of communication in sociolinguistic analysis aims to 'examine the situations and uses, the patterns and functions of speaking as an activity in its own right' (Frake 1962: 101). Critical discourse analysis draws attention to 'how texts selectively draw upon *orders of discourse*' (Fairclough 1995: 188). But as Corson says, 'A major task of critical realist researchers is to untangle the ways in which wider structures and processes filter into educational institutions and then into classrooms' (Corson 1998: 208). A syncretic approach opens up a wide range of possibilities, especially in terms of the relationship between language, culture and classroom behaviour, but will entail a combined use of the methodological approaches of cultural and linguistic (formalist, poststructural and critical) discourse analysis.

This is illustrated in Figure 35.2, and its nature described in Table 35.1, showing how the 'nested contexts' (Cazden 2001) of the discursive interaction in the school which forms the process of education can be investigated.

The three contexts or layers of discourse are those of 'discourse', 'narrative' and 'voice'. In the cognitive dimension, the three contexts can be said to parallel Cazden's ideas of nested contexts: in the mind (students), in learning communities (schools and classrooms) and communities (local educational policy-makers) (Cazden 2001). In terms of cognitive developmental processes, they are sometimes concentric, sometimes overlapping, rather than the cycle of Haste's (1987) 'intra-individual, interpersonal and sociohistorical' (p. 175, Figure 9.1), and the dialectic,

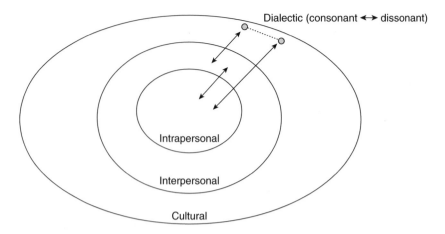

Figure 35.2   Nested contexts

Table 35.1   Summary of layers or contexts of discourse

Layer	Sociopsychological level	Physical concept	Methodological
Discourse(s)	Cultural	School (or societal as manifest therein)	Critical discourse analysis
Narrative(s)	Interpersonal	School and classroom	Sociolinguistic analysis
Voice(s)	Intrapersonal	School, classroom and individual	Phenomenological, narrative analysis

or 'negotiation of meaning' (p. 175) among them, which she describes as interpersonal processes, is seen as a discursive dialectic.

In the three-dimensional framework of critical discourse analysis, 'the link between sociocultural practices and the other two dimensions involves the integration of "macro" and "micro" analysis of discursive events, where the former includes analysis of discourse technologization process' (Fairclough 1995: 97) (cf. Foucault's hegemony, 1979). The 'discursive events' can be seen in the 'phenomena' of the cultural studies approach and also their manifestations via the semiotics of 'visual sociology' (Kress and van Leeuwen 1996; Prosser and Warburton 1999). In a multilingual/cultural setting, not only the 'ideology' of the discourse, but also the pragmatics of the language itself become the 'technology' which asserts power. This, therefore, must be explored using more traditional sociolinguistics, helping us understand the effects of the predominance of English in international schools, for example. Narrative analysis gives insight into the connection between discourse and cognition, which may tell us whether this will also result in a culturally specific transference of 'knowledge' from teacher to student or whether, in their internal 'intrapsychological' narratives, students are able to construct their own 'culture-critical' version of knowledge.

These perspectives are represented in Table 35.1 and Figure 35.2, which attempt to link the 'layers' of discursive practice: *discourse*, *narrative* and *voice* as defined earlier, with theoretical and methodological perspectives. It can be seen that in the more physical dimension they also correspond to Haste's and Cazden's views of schools and classrooms respectively, and their interdependence is echoed in Alexander's stricture that 'separating the cultural, educational and social into three apparently independent free-wheeling "systems", which can then be translated into a collection of factors for the purposes of statistical correlation, is conceptually untenable' (Alexander 2000: 29). As these are 'nested contexts' there is interplay or dialectic conversation between each level, which is reflexive and will manifest itself in each layer.

Fairclough describes the critical approach to discourse analysis as follows: 'The method of discourse analysis includes linguistic *description* of the language text, *interpretation* of the relationship between the (productive and interpretative) discursive processes and the text, and *explanation* of the relationship between the discursive processes and the social processes' (1995: 97; emphasis in original).

The model suggested as appropriate for international schools tries to discover the effects on learning of cross-cultural aspects of the nature of discourse rather than the nature of discourse itself. It corresponds to critical discourse analysis in that the generation of discourse is seen to be reflexive, productive and multidimensional, but differs in the following ways. First, it is hard to differentiate among the techniques of description, interpretation and explanation; they all seem to be interpretive and what varies is the means of interpretation. The idea that 'description' can be objective seems to ignore the subjective position of the researcher. Description using sociolinguistic narrative analysis is also interpretive, insofar as the researcher is trying to give the subject's interpretation rather than a formalist, grammatologist interpretation. If 'explanation' refers to some overarching sociohistorical framework then it seems to be at odds with other references to Foucault's ideas of discourse being self-generative or self-reinforcing in practice: 'the link between sociocultural practice and text is mediated by discourse *practice* ... and how they (orders of discourse) are articulated together depends upon the nature of the sociocultural *practice* which the discourse is a part of' (Fairclough 1995: 97; emphasis added), and it is here that discursive and cultural practices in the form of sociolinguistic pragmatics (for example, classroom discourse) can be observed and that cultural hegemony is also active. The dialectic between 'macro phenomena' and discursive 'practice' can be seen in the 'phenomena' of the cultural studies approach and 'control over the discursive practices' (1995: 88) in the sociolinguistic realm. The most fundamental difference is the adding of another level, the intrapsychological or 'voice', and the incorporation of the sociohistorical into the culture of the institution, where there may be more than one version operating.

Phillips (1972) is an early example of a combined anthropological and sociolinguistic approach, which found that where there is a 'congruence' between the sociolinguistic styles and social relationships of both the school and the home culture then the children tended to perform better and develop greater levels of verbal interactional participation. The application of narrative analysis in discursive psychology links to the intrapersonal, as well as the cognitive. 'The reflective condition of the inner dialogue also deserves, therefore, to be valued for its contribution to learning, and the oscillation of inner and outer speech can be promoted and utilised in a variety of ways that have not yet been clearly documented or evaluated' (Stables 2003: 21). Gee (1999), especially, demonstrates the use of an integrated approach to discourse analysis of spoken and written language as it is used to enact social and cultural perspectives and identities.

This research model is intended to be exploratory rather than confirmatory, but by focusing on an area of interaction that has been identified by analysis of literature and previous research on the subject, a well-defined focus to the study can be maintained without sacrificing 'looseness' in interpretation. Discourse theory can incorporate the various contexts and further analyse the relative effects of each on the particular situation. This also has benefits in terms of transferability. If phenomena in a case study are situated within various wider discourses, then it is easier for other researchers to transfer conclusions to a different situation, as the effect of macro-discourses will have been incorporated, and other researchers can situate their case relatively within the same discourses. Most importantly the context of the research is investigated holistically as an integral component in all interaction.

CONCLUSION

Interpretive analysis of qualitative data has sometimes been described as an art as much as a science, but although creativity must play a part it is not artistic in the sense of free-form jazz or abstract painting. It is governed by logic, which is scientific in its use of rules and categories, relationships and conclusions. Although the more radical of interpretive theorists may prefer 'ad hoc fumbling around' to the 'systematic thematic analysis' suggested by Glaser and Strauss (1967), theory does not simply emerge or come into being. It is the researcher who conceptualizes from data, although this is a process that does require certain attitudes and qualities of creativity (Woods 1985). Some conclusions or interpretations may be arrived at 'intuitively' but this intuition is the product of the expertise and experience of the observer, who is constantly reflecting on and analysing experience in order to form an explanation of what is going on, in the desire to improve practice.

In the last resort, research and theory construction will only be as good as the people doing it. Hammersley (1990), assessing the value of interpretive research and its usefulness to other researchers, asserts that plausibility and transferability are more important than generalizability. Here teachers are not only able to use their detailed knowledge and insider experience in providing the deep, detailed description by which fellow practitioners can judge, but they can also bring their insight and intuition to bear on the interpretation of data and generation of theory with the authority of those who have spent their working life 'in the field'.

Apart from research involving English as a second language, little attention has been paid to what goes on in international school classrooms. Is it different from what goes on in national school classrooms? If so, how? And how can we make international schools more effective and improve the teaching of culturally diverse student bodies? Although there is much to be learned from research that can locate educational problems in their larger social context, educators also need research methodologies and theoretical frames that provide the possibility of more local explanations for the dilemmas and problems facing international education. Situated understandings of education provide insights into the cognitive and social consequences of school policies and pedagogical practices. The significance of developing a deep understanding of schools and their social organizations is that only by doing so can research reliably inform the policies and practices of international education.

REFERENCES

Alasuutari, P. (1995) *Researching Culture: Qualitative Method and Cultural Studies.* London: Sage.

Alexander, R. (2000) *Culture and Pedagogy.* Malden, MA: Blackwell.

Allan, M.J. (2002) Cultural borderlands: a case study of cultural dissonance in an international school. *Journal of Research in International Education,* 1 (1): 63–90.

Allan, M.J. (2003) Frontier crossings: cultural dissonance, intercultural learning and the multicultural personality. *Journal of Research in International Education,* 2 (1): 83–110.

Allan, M.J. and Brown, R. (2002) The observer is the instrument: using technology to support research. *IB Research Notes,* 2 (4): 3–11.

Ball, S.J. (1990) *Politics and Policy-making in Education.* London: Routledge.

Berry, J. (1969) On cross-cultural comparability. *International Journal of Psychology,* 34: 363–400.

Brown, L. (1993) *The New Shorter Oxford English Dictionary.* Oxford: Clarendon Press.

Cazden, C.B. (2001) *Classroom Discourse: The Language of Teaching and Learning.* Portsmouth, NH: Heinemann.

Corson, D. (1998) *Changing Education for Diversity.* Buckingham: Open University Press.

Cortazzi, M. (1993) *Narrative Analysis.* London: Falmer Press.

Cummins, J. (2000) *Language, Power and Pedagogy: Bilingual Children in the Crossfire.* Clevedon, UK: Multilingual Matters.

Cushner, K. (1990) Cross-cultural psychology and the formal classroom. In R.W. Brislin (ed.) *Applied Cross-Cultural Psychology.* Newbury Park, CA: Sage.

Edwards, A.D. and Westgate, D.P.G. (1994) *Investigating Classroom Talk.* London and Washington, DC: Routledge.

Edwards, D. (1997) *Discourse and Cognition.* London: Sage.

Fairclough, N. (1995) *Critical Discourse Analysis: The Critical Study of Language.* Harlow: Longman.

Foucault, M. (1971) Orders of discourse. *Social Science Information,* 10: 7–30.

Foucault, M. (1972) *The Archaeology of Knowledge.* London: Tavistock.

Foucault, M. (1979) *Discipline and Punish: The Birth of the Prison.* New York: Vintage Books.

Frake, C.O. (1962) The ethnographic study of cognitive systems. In T. Gladwin and W.C. Sturtevant (eds) *Anthropology and Human Behaviour.* Washington, DC: Anthropological Society of Washington.

Garfinkel, H. (1984) *Studies in Ethnomethodology.* Cambridge: Polity Press.

Gee, J.P. (1999) *An Introduction to Discourse Analysis: Theory and Method.* New York: Routledge.

Geetz, C. (1973) *The Interpretation of Cultures.* New York: Basic Books.

Giroux, H.A. (1992) *Border Crossings: Cultural Workers and the Politics of Education.* New York: Routledge.

Goffman, E. (1967) *Interaction Ritual: Essays on Face-to-face Behaviour.* New York: Doubleday.

Goffman, E. (1975) *Frame Analysis.* London: Penguin.

Glaser, B. and Strauss, A. (1967) *The Discovery of Grounded Theory: Strategies for Qualitative Research.* Chicago: Aldine.

Hagood, M.J. (1970) The notion of a hypothetical universe. In D.E. Morrison and R.E. Henkel (eds) *The Significance Test Controversy: A Reader.* Chicago: Aldine.

Hall, S. (ed.) (1997) *Representation: Cultural Representation and Signifying Practices.* London: Sage.

Hammersley, M. (1990) *Reading Ethnographic Research: A Critical Guide.* New York: Longman.

Hammersley, M. (1997) On the foundations of critical discourse analysis. *Language and Communication,* 17 (3): 237–48.

Haste, H. (1987) Growing into rules. In J.P. Bruner and H. Haste (eds), *Making Sense of Language: The Child's Construction of the World.* pp. 163–95.

Hymes, D. (1985) Introduction. In C. Cazden, V.P. John and D. Hymes (eds) *Functions of Language in the Classroom.* Prospect Heights, IL: Waveland Press, pp. xi–xvii.

Kerlinger, F.N. (1969) *Foundations of Behavioural Research.* New York: Holt, Rinehart and Wilson.

Kincheloe, J.L. and Steinberg, S.R. (1997) *Changing Multiculturalism.* Buckingham: Open University Press.

Kintsch, W. and van Dijk, T.A. (1983) *Strategies of Discourse Comprehension.* London: Academic Press.

Kress, G. and van Leeuwen, T. (1996) *Reading Images: The Grammar of Visual Design.* London: Routledge.

Kumaravadivelu, B. (1999). Critical classroom discourse analysis. *TESOL Quarterly,* 33 (3): 453–84.

Labov, W. (1992) Speech actions and reactions in personal narrative. In D. Tannen (ed.) *Analysing Discourse: Text and Talk.* Washington, DC: Georgetown University Press, pp. 219–47.

May, S. (1997) Critical ethnography. In N. Hornberger and D. Corson (eds) *Research Methods in Language and Education.* Boston, MA: Kluwer.

McLaren, P.J. (1997) Introduction. In J.L. Kincheloe and S.R Steinberg (eds) *Changing Multiculturalism.* Buckingham: Open University Press.

Mercer, N. (1992) Culture, context and the construction of knowledge in the classroom. In P. Light and G. Butterworth (eds) *Context and Cognition.* Hemel Hempstead: Harvester Wheatsheaf.

Mishler, E.G. (1986) *Researching Interviewing: Context and Narrative.* Cambridge, MA: Harvard University Press.

Patton, M.Q. (1987) *How to Use Qualitative Methods in Evaluation.* Newbury Park, CA: Sage.

Pelto, P.J. and Pelto, G.H. (1978) *Anthropological Research: The Structure of Enquiry.* Cambridge: Cambridge University Press.

Phillips, S.U. (1972) Participant structures and communicative competence: War Springs children in community and classroom. In C. Cazden, D.H. Hymes and V.P. John (eds) *Functions of Language in the Classroom.* New York: Teachers College Press.

Polyani, L. (1979) So what's the point? *Semiotica,* 25 (3/4): 207–41.

Potter, J. and Wetherell, M. (1987) *Discourse and Social Psychology.* London: Sage.

Prosser, J. and Warburton, T. (1999) Visual sociology and school culture. In J. Prosser (ed.) *School Culture.* London: Paul Chapman, pp. 82–97.

Riessman, C.K. (1993) *Narrative Analysis.* Newbury Park, CA: Sage.

Ripich, D.N. and Creaghead, N.A. (1994) *School Discourse Problems.* San Diego, CA: Singular Publishing Group.

Robson, C. (1993) *Real World Research: A Resource for Social Scientists and Practitioner Researchers.* Oxford: Blackwell.

Stables, A. (2003) School as imagined community in discursive space: a perspective on the school effectiveness debate. *Journal of Educational Enquiry,* 4 (1): 1–18.

Strauss, A. and Corbin, J.M. (1998) *Basics of Qualitative Research: Techniques and Procedures for Developing Grounded Theory.* Thousand Oaks, CA: Sage.

Thomas, D. (1992) Putting Nature to the Rack: Narrative Studies as Research. Paper presented at the Teachers' Stories of Life and Work Conference, Liverpool, UK. 9–11 April.

Wells, G. and Chang-Wells, G.L. (1992) *Constructing Knowledge Together: Classrooms as Centers of Inquiry and Literacy.* Portsmouth, NH: Heinemann.

Wieder, L. (1974) Telling the code. In R. Turner (ed.) *Ethnomethodology.* Harmondsworth: Penguin.

Woods, P. (1985) Ethnography and theory construction. In R.G. Burgess (ed.) *Field Methods in the Study of Education.* London: The Falmer Press, pp. 51–78.

36

International Schools, Education and Globalization: Towards a Research Agenda

Hugh Lauder

International schools are growing in popularity for several reasons. For those that study for the International Baccalaureate (IB) qualifications, they provide a broad and sophisticated education, and, quite rightly, the IB is increasingly being seen as the 'gold standard' qualifications framework across many countries. But arguably the idealism that initially motivated the IB is being overtaken by the economic and social class interests that have been structured by globalization. This chapter explores the role of international schools under what may be considered the new global capitalism. It argues that there are grounds for seeing international schools as providing a fast track to the top universities for global and indigenous elites and that they may constitute one element in the construction of a transnational ruling class.

It could be argued that there is little new in such propositions, that international schools, of the kind defined below, have always catered for an elite that have graduated to prestigious universities. However, this view does not take into account that changing nature of the new global capitalism and in particular the role of

education within it. There are several points to make here. The first concerns the question of size. The international school system (ISS) is growing rapidly to keep pace with the growing numbers of global workers. This in turn raises the question of whether we are seeing the education of a small elite or of a considerable number of students with the potential for far more widespread influence than hitherto. At the same time the demand for global workers is also increasing because of the growth of multinational corporations (MNCs) and nongovernmental organizations (NGOs). Moreover, the *nature* of the demand for the kind of workers these organizations require is also changing, as we shall see. Equally, the links between the ISS and an emerging global league table of universities means that there may be a tightening bond between 'gold standard' qualifications like the IB and access to the top universities. If this is the case then students who do not have the appropriate international education may be excluded. This brings me to the final point. The ISS may attract national professional and managerial elites away from national education systems for precisely this reason, thereby impoverishing the latter because a middle-class 'voice' will no longer be heard in the demand for rising standards and resources.

It should be stressed that in many ways the international school system is in its infancy, and having established grounds for the above two related propositions the chapter concludes by setting out a research agenda to test them.

While there has been a major debate about the definition of what counts as an international school, this chapter focuses (i) on those that cater for an expatriate elite: the sons and daughters of MNC managers and executives, NGO workers and diplomats: these constitute a growing cadre of global workers and account for some of the growth in international schools; (ii) on schools that cater for aspirant indigenous elites who seek an international qualification to enable their children to access leading universities across the globe; and (iii) on schools that offer internationally recognized gold standard qualifications to enable such access.

However, part of the complexity of the international school system is that amongst those recruiting from international or indigenous elites or classes there are at least two systems of education: one is British-inspired and is focused around the International Baccalaureate; it sees the related qualifications as providing entrance to the most prestigious universities around the world. The other emanates from the USA and is primarily focused on the American secondary school curriculum and entrance to elite higher education in the United States.

These two systems provide different types of education which, in turn, may lead to different understandings of the problems confronting globalization as well as different routes and mechanisms into the global labour market. It is important therefore not to anticipate that the international school system is uniform in the creation of factors relating to elite or class formation, nor that students from the two systems will share common views regarding social, political and economic factors as a result of their school experience.

In order to explore the issues raised above there are three kinds of theory that can be drawn upon: Reich's (1991) theory about the nature of global labour markets, global positional competition theory and theories abut the emergence of a global ruling class.

REICH'S THEORY OF GLOBAL LABOUR MARKETS

One of the features of the current round of globalization is that MNCs are generating international labour markets. There is a debate about the nature, power and global reach of multinational corporations and hence their impact on capitalist societies (Doremus et al. 1998; Hirst and Thompson 1996; Rugman and Verbeke 2004). However, it can be argued that there is now in place a *global auction* (Brown and Lauder 2001) for foreign direct investment and for the supply of skills. In both cases it is a Dutch auction in which MNCs are seeking the lowest costs given an equality of infrastructure and skills. The most high profile example of this process is that of offshoring: the relocation of semi-skilled and skilled work from Western economies to the cheaper cost centres of India, China and South East Asia (Brown et al. 2001).

However, by generating international labour markets through the processes of the global auction, of which offshoring is the clearest example, it can be argued that MNCs may also have a profound effect on national education and welfare regimes. Reich's (1991) *The Work of Nations* has developed a prognosis that is worth considering, if only because it can be used to compare future findings. Reich argues that global economic technologies and practices are generating a class of symbolic analysts: those that are skilled in manipulating and marketing abstract symbol systems such as those relating to IT, languages and maths, which he sees as the core, most highly rewarded work in the emerging 'knowledge-based economy'. These symbolic analysts constitute a core group in the sense that they are appropriating an increasing percentage of the costs of goods and services created. This core group has access to a global labour market, which means that they travel the world for their work. In doing so, he argues that they will secede from national educational and welfare systems. (This has led some neo-Marxist theorists to argue that we are witnessing the rise of a transnational ruling class: see Sklair (2001) and Robinson (2004) and the following discussion.) There may be many consequences arising, if such a prognosis was proved to be correct. Many welfare regime theorists would argue that the secession from national education and welfare commitments would serve to impoverish both systems, because not only revenue might be lost (symbolic analysts might not believe they should pay taxes since they don't avail themselves of a country's services) but also the professional middle-class 'voice' in improving state funded services.

THE POSITIONAL COMPETITION FOR CREDENTIALS

In terms of international schools, there are two consequences that arise from Reich's prognosis. The first concerns the positional competition for credentials. A defining characteristic of a positional good is that it is scarce in a socially imposed sense (Hirsch 1977) and that accordingly allocation proceeds through the 'auction of a restricted set of objects to the highest bidder' (pp. 28–9). This then leads to two effects when applied to educational credentials. First, as individuals see that a first degree is necessary to gain access to a good job, so there is an excess demand for such degrees leading to credential inflation. In turn, this initially creates a degree of scarcity for the next credential up in the hierarchy until such times as this too becomes common currency. But this process also has an impact in equality of opportunity because it is only those that have the time and resources that can then move to the next step on the credential ladder. It is worth noting that positional competition undermines the view that there is a direct link between education, selection for a job, income and productivity because credential inflation may lead to overqualification for any given set of jobs.

How then can this theory be applied to globalization and especially the role of international schools? Here there are several observations that can be made. The first is that international schools and the IB in particular are beyond the powers of any nation-state, once the decision has been made to admit international schools. This is not to say there may not be close co-operation between states and schools but that in key issues of admissions and qualifications they are by and large independent. In turn this raises a question about what may be called the democratic deficit (Brown 2000). In the past, positional competition has been regulated within nation-states through the democratic process. To give an example, Turner (1961) has described two kinds of system mobility based on educational selection – sponsored and contest – which he argued were implicated in the construction of social classes. Looking at the English tripartite system, selection to the elite grammar schools was undertaken at the age of 11. This he saw as the ideal-typical form of sponsored mobility.

According to Turner, under sponsored mobility, elite recruits are chosen by an elite and elite status is *given* on the basis of some criterion of supposed merit and cannot be taken by any amount of effort or strategy. Upward mobility is like entry into a private club (1961: 122). In contrast, under contest mobility 'elite status is the prize in an open contest and is taken by the aspirants' own efforts' (p. 122). Here the ideal-typical example of a contest system was the comprehensive or common school system found at that time in the USA. For Turner these systems of organizing upward mobility are at root concerned with legitimization and social control. The most conspicuous control problem, he argues, is that of ensuring loyalty in the disadvantaged classes toward a system in which they receive less than a proportional share of society's goods. Under a sponsored system this is achieved by training the masses to see themselves as relatively incompetent to manage society and by restricting their access to the skills and manners of the elite. Nevertheless, some access to the disadvantaged classes is required in order for legitimacy to be sustained. Under the contest system everyone is encouraged to think they can achieve elite status and to have the future-oriented attitudes and aspirations to keep the dream of success alive. In this system, in contrast to sponsored mobility, it is possible to be a late developer.

For Turner, these mobility systems are ideal types and he acknowledges that there may be competing and conflicting views as to the most appropriate system of upward mobility; nor do they map on to what he calls the 'complex interplay' (p.122) of social, economic and ideological conditions. In the British case, the system of selection was largely changed from one of sponsored mobility to that of contest mobility through the creation of comprehensive schools. These changes were the result of democratic debate and they came about because it had been shown that selection to grammar school at the age of 11 was arbitrary for those who had IQ scores in the range of approximately 114–120 (Floud and Halsey 1961) and that many working-class students at grammar school did not progress to university (Floud et al. 1956). However, in the case of the international schools, there is no possibility of national democratic debate about their impact in terms of selection and the inequalities that might arise. At the same time, selection to many of them is based on the wealth and wishes of parents (Brown 1997). In itself this is likely to produce considerable inequalities that are not based on concepts of merit. However, these inequalities only take on a more systematic form when considered against global changes in the ranking and status of universities.

INTERNATIONAL SCHOOLS AND THE EMERGING GLOBAL RANKING OF UNIVERSITIES

This brings us to the second point. What are the inequalities that might arise? Here we need to consider the rise of international schools within the context of the globalization of higher education. Higher education systems are becoming increasingly global, coalescing in a hierarchy based on reputation and starting to form a winner-takes-all global market (Wolfe 2002). In such a market, the best students are attracted to the universities with the highest reputations that in turn attract the best academics because they can pay for them. Since so much of the research basis for the 'knowledge economy' has come from the

USA and, to a lesser extent, the UK, it is not surprising that it is the leading universities in these countries that have been attracting students from overseas.

However, it is important not to overemphasize these trends. Room (2000) has, for example, noted that the market for overseas students is segmented: 'International flows of students follow well-defined routes which in many cases are underpinned by traditional linguistic and cultural links between the former imperial powers and their colonial territories' (p. 111). At the same time, many former colonial nations are developing their own high standard higher education systems. Malaysia, for example, as part of its 20/20 vision has the goal of becoming a centre of excellence for higher education, taking a larger market share away from Western universities. It is significant that when Singapore decided to raise its research profile it invited MIT and INSEAD (Paris) to set up in the city-state.

That said, the global market in higher education is such that the elite American and European universities are likely to provide the benchmark for performance, creating the pressure, as Room (2000: 110) notes, for others to abandon national practices and to follow perceived international best practice. This tension will be exacerbated by GATS which will effectively open up higher education to private providers on a global scale, which has been provided for by the Education White Paper. The tension between the pull of globalization and the national demands for equity is currently being exposed. Attempts to introduce positive discrimination in favour of, say, working-class or ethnic minority students can be seen as running counter to the need for the 'best' universities to attract the 'best students'. Yet the stakes are high. It is only those universities that follow such practices that will enable students into the competition for elite jobs. We know already that these leading universities largely recruit from high-earning families. The richer their background, the more likely students will attend the 'Harvards' and 'Oxfords' of the higher education system (Wolfe 2002). Any attempt at positive discrimination in favour of the less well off is likely to be controversial.

Against this background it is important to note what has become a dominant ideology amongst MNCs. That is the 'war for talent' which intensifies the competition for places at elite universities.

THE WAR FOR TALENT

The war for talent is a central focus of the human resources literature. It is about the selection procedures that identify those that are likely to be the leaders of the next generation of corporate senior managers. The search for this talent assumes that rather like the Bell Curve in the distribution of IQ, only a few individuals are likely to be really outstanding and that the failure to identify them will be costly, hence the metaphor of a 'war' because upon it depends the fate of corporations (Woodruffe 1999).

Michaels et al. (2001) identify two reasons as to why this 'war for talent' has become so pressing. 'The shift to the Information Age is far from over. As the economy becomes more knowledge-based, the differential value of highly talented people continues to mount' (2001: 3).

Secondly, globalization also has a role to play as the demand for high-calibre managerial talent is growing because the job has become 'more challenging as globalization, deregulation and rapid advances in technology change the game in most industries' (2001: 4). Consequently, 'Companies today need managers who can respond to these challenges. They need risk takers, global entrepreneurs, and techno-savvy managers. They need leaders who can re-conceive their business and inspire their people' (p. 4). Cohen (2001) elaborates upon this point:

> Traditional markets are being redefined, new economies are rapidly developing, and technology and new trade agreements are levelling the playing field globally. In this context, the need for skilled and competitive labor is ongoing. The talent of top performers has become the critical difference between those companies that grow and innovate and those that falter or merely survive.

The reason why selection is now so pressing is because companies no longer support long-term careers where 'talent' can be identified and sponsored upward over time, selection of an elite of the talented effectively short-circuits this process (Brown and Hesketh 2004; Tulgan 2001). The ideology of the 'war for talent' is consistent with the view that much knowledge work is or will become routinized and devalued. For it suggests that the creative and innovative will be the chosen few of 'talent' distinct from other knowledge workers.

It will be clear that those who have a strong multilingual (including English) and cultural background will have a head start in this war for talent, which is why an education at an elite international school may provide a head start not only to access the top universities but also for subsequent entry to the fast-track management systems of the MNCs.

It is important to stress that in the short term these trends do not substantially alter the national character of credential competition, where the vast majority of students remain firmly locked into national systems of assessment. Their academic performance will reflect the quality of local schools, colleges and universities within a framework of national education (including the investment in school buildings; teacher expertise; staff to student ratio; and pedagogy). But, as noted by Brown (personal communication 2006), there are questions to be asked about the stability of national competitions for credentials if the professional and managerial classes in different countries see their children in direct competition for the same jobs in the global labour market.

It is these elites, who have the ability to mobilize their material and cultural resources in the acquisition of credentials, who are likely to benefit most from qualifications like the IB in a global competition for high-skilled jobs (Lowe 1999). And here it is important to note that access to international schools is typically through the 'wealth and wishes of parents' (Brown 1997) rather than through ability and motivation such as in sponsored systems or the open system of access that are characteristic of comprehensive schools. Competition systems based on meritocratic rules may extol the virtues of equality of opportunity in the domestic competition for a livelihood, but social elites (or those aspiring in that direction) may feel that they are being held back in the global competition, when compared to students in a global market system, such as that of the international schools.

Consequently, the professional middle classes from countries with a traditional commitment to state systems of education such as Germany, France and Sweden, may press for greater market freedom to maintain a level playing field beyond their national boundaries. The alternative is to 'exit' into the international school system or into those schools that offer its credentials, since one of the key factors distinguishing elites in countries where English is not the major language is their access through education to English (Lai and Byram 2003). This has now become a major point of distinction because English has become the *lingua franca* of globalization. Many international schools teach in the medium of English and this is an added attraction for national elites.

The kind of prognosis that has been developed above now needs to be placed in the context of the idea that we are witnessing the formation of a global ruling class. Clearly one condition for the creation of such a class is that the positional competition favours one group of students (that is, international school students) over others. And here we have seen how the paths for such a possibility are now being laid. But there are further issues that need to be considered from this perspective.

INTERNATIONAL SCHOOLS AND THE CREATION OF A GLOBAL RULING CLASS?

The construction of a global or transnational ruling class is derived form neo-Marxist theories (Robinson 2004; Sassen 2005; Sklair 2001). However, before considering this approach in relation to international schools, it should be emphasized that these three commentators have different theories as to what constitutes a transnational or global ruling class and in many ways they reproduce the debates within the Marxist tradition as to how the lines between classes are to be drawn. Hence, this approach is not unproblematic, as we shall see, especially so when we consider some of the issues in relation to international schools below. However, they have in common an understanding of how globalization is eroding national boundaries and bringing together networks of powerful elites that speak to each other across the globe. In the past networks have been seen in national terms and perhaps, a century ago, this was epitomized by the various clubs in which informal business and views could be exchanged. However, the advent of electronic communications and long-distance air travel have made networks across the globe possible.

It has long been understood that networks constitute a key social dimension to the structuring of elites and classes (Scott 1991) and they have been identified as of particular significance to current globalization processes (Castells 2000). Networks can be understood as having a vertical dimension which would link new recruits such as university graduates to senior power holders and a horizontal dimension which relates to the reach of their networks, geographically and across different types of organization. The character of these networks is also important in the sense that those forming the network have a common view as to (i) political, social and economic issues, (ii) the degree to which membership is viewed as having rights, obligations and common interests and (iii) the degree to which they can be mobilized to exert influence or pressure on other power holders. Understanding the nature of these networks may help to determine whether what we are witnessing is the formation of global elites or a transnational class or indeed some looser weaving of elites at a global level. The question is whether they may coalesce into a class in the Marxian sense in which there are both common economic and political interests and a common understanding (consciousness) of how the economic, social and natural worlds are constructed and changing.

Why is this approach to globalization important? Because it raises issues of who controls the global economy and consequently key elements of the distribution of power and resources. Insofar as a global ruling class is emerging then it follows that national democracies, embraced so warmly by President Bush and Prime Minister Blair, are either weakened or merely act as a rubber stamp for decisions made by executives elsewhere. There is no doubt that neo-liberal theory is widespread across the multilateral agencies as well as deeply ingrained in the dominant loci of power in the United States through the Washington–Wall Street axis (Stiglitz 2002). And this may be seen as the unifying ideology of a global ruling class. Equally, the sense of decisions being made far removed from their point of impact has led to a sense of helplessness and lack of agency on the part of ordinary people across the globe. However, the idea of a global ruling class runs into both conceptual difficulties and empirical difficulties.

CONCEPTUAL PROBLEMS WITH THE NOTION OF A GLOBAL RULING CLASS

The fundamental criticism that can be made of this neo-Marxist theory is one that will be familiar to all those that have debated the merits of Marxist theory. It threatens to founder on the one aspect of economic change that Marxist theoreticians have had difficulty with: nationalism. The key issue here is the extent to which ruling class interests override national interests in the construction of a global economic system (Lauder et al. 2006). It may well be that there is a common neo-liberal ideology, as Stiglitz (2002) suggests, amongst key global elites but that does not mean that they view national interests as subordinate to class interests. Equally, it is not clear that the interests of NGOs are the same as those of nation-states or MNCs. Many MNCs are still rooted in national cultures and interests and it is often difficult to divorce national interest in the creation of global champions from transnational interests (Brown et al. 2001): although, even here that may now be changing. Current work by Brown, Lauder and Ashton (2006) suggests that there are quite rapid changes in this direction.

INTERNATIONAL SCHOOLS AND THE CONSTRUCTION OF A GLOBAL RULING CLASS

Neo-Marxist theorists will have an interest in education because it is one means for the reproduction of privilege and enables closer bonding and a shared world-view to be sustained through the common experience of a privileged background and elite schooling. Here, the key question may turn on the issue of how international students conceptualize their rights and obligations as global citizens and how they approach the fundamental global questions of the age: inequalities between and within nations, environmental sustainability and the control of technology (Lauder et al. 2006).

However, while it might be argued that the educational conditions for the emergence of such a class are being made possible by the international schools and a globalizing market for higher education, there are grounds for being sceptical. The idea that a common form of schooling will give rise to a common perspective or consciousness assumes that the students from these schools see themselves as global citizens rather than having a commitment to the welfare of their country of origin or heritage. In so far as they may be influenced by their family background, it should be noted that their parent(s) comprise a heterogeneous community ranging from multinational and diplomatic employees to those working for non-governmental organizations. It would be surprising if the children from such a mixed community emerged with the same dominant view of globalization and its implications for solving fundamental problems. That said, this is an area that is greatly under-researched and more needs to be understood about how these emerging global factors, the labour market and education systems, are combining to reproduce inequalities and possibly ideologies.

CONCLUSION: TOWARDS A RESEARCH AGENDA

There are, then, three dimensions that relate the theoretical issues concerning global elite or class formation and positional competition to international schools. The first concerns the nature of the networks that international students are members of. The second relates to the formation of their views concerning key economic, social and political issues concerning globalization and their own role as global citizens. The third raises the question of the mechanisms of recruitment into the international school system and the international labour market – the underlying issues of positional competition. The three dimensions can throw light on the theoretical questions as follows: the degree to which the students have vertical and horizontal networks can inform our understanding of the reach of their associations. If they are geographically circumscribed but vertically extensive then this suggests the likelihood of the presence of an elite. Were their networks to be broad in terms of geography and organizations then this would be indicative of the formation of a class. However, it is likely that this evidence could at best be only indicative, given the early stages of their careers.

With respect to their views as global citizens, of the issues and problems confronting globalization and how they may be addressed, it would need to be acknowledged that these may be subject to change and indeed could be subject to a process of incorporation, once in the global labour market. Finally, the investigation of mechanisms and processes of recruitment should illuminate the degree to which class closure is evident.

In all these cases, the evidence collected is more likely to address directly the question of *potential* for elite or class formation in students' orientations and skills in relation to networking and their views as to their roles as global citizens. The issue of recruitment should give direct evidence of closure or openness, in relation to entry to the global labour market. Here the major question to be addressed is: do international school students who have been to elite universities have an advantage over those who perhaps have only attended national state schools?

This issue is further complicated by the nature of the social background of international school students. If we are to understand the relative weight of influences for the political,

social and economic views of students we need to also understand something of their specific social background and life experiences. Here, three concepts may be important as initial theoretical resources in seeking to explain the similarities and differences in the views of international school students. The first concerns the distinction between those that are genuinely multicultural and those that are multilingual. The former denotes those students who have an in-depth understanding and empathy with at least two cultures, while the latter refers to an instrumental orientation towards acquiring more than one language. In part, these orientations to language may be seen as a function of how students relate to their passport country. Many 'third culture' or global nomad students (Langford 1997; Useem 1993) may have moved around so much that they do not have a country that they identify as 'home'. These students may therefore have quite different views about the issues facing globalization than those who strongly identify with a country as 'home'. Equally, for indigenous students attending international schools, the experience of living in one country may provide a very clear focus in the way they conceptualize the nature of globalization and the problems it presents. However, their views may be modulated or changed by attending an international school.

Clearly, the type of international school attended and the type of background students bring to the school may have an influence on their views regarding globalization. In turn this raises a further question concerning citizenship. In terms of this research, the key question here is how students conceptualize their own rights, obligations and political, economic and social practices as citizens when considering the key problems confronting globalization.

This chapter has sought to raise key questions about the political economy of the type of international schools that conform to the criteria outlined. It is important to stress that we are only at the start of the present round of globalization and that what the chapter is focusing on is a set of emerging educational, social and economic conditions. Nevertheless, it is hoped that the theoretical resources brought to bear on these conditions will raise fruitful questions for further research.

REFERENCES

Brown, P. (1997) The Third Wave: education and the ideology of parentocracy. In A.H. Halsey, H Lauder, P. Brown, and A. Stuart Wells, (eds) *Education: Culture, Economy and Society.* Oxford: Oxford University Press.

Brown, P. (2000) The globalization of positional competition? *Sociology*, 34 (4): 633–53.

Brown, P. and Hesketh, A. (2004) *The Mismanagement of Talent: Employability and Jobs in the Knowledge Economy.* Oxford: Oxford University Press.

Brown, P. and Lauder, H. (2001) *Capitalism and Social Progress: The Future of Society in a Global Economy.* Basingstoke: Palgrave.

Brown, P., Green, A. and Lauder, H. (2001) *High Skills: Globalization, Competitiveness and Skill Formation.* Oxford: Oxford University Press.

Brown P., Lauder H. and Ashton, D. (2006) ESRC Project: The Global Skill Strategies of MNCs (work in progress).

Brown, P., Lauder, H., Ashton, D. and Tholen, G. (2005) *Towards a High Skills, Low Waged Economy? A Review of Global Trends in Education, Employment and the Labour Market.* Cardiff University: School of Social Sciences.

Castells, M. (2000) *The Rise of the Network Society*, 2nd edition. Oxford: Blackwell.

Cohen, D. (2001) *The Talent Edge.* Toronto: John Wiley.

Doremus, P., Keller, W., Pauly, L. and Reich, S. (1998) *The Myth of the Global Corporation.* Princeton, NJ: Princeton University Press.

Floud, J., Halsey, A.H. and Martin, F.M., (1957) *Social Class and Educational Opportunity.* London, Heinemann.

Floud, J. and Halsey, A.H. (1961) Introduction to A.H. Halsey, J. Floud, and C. Anderson (eds.) *Education, Economy and Society.* New York: The Free Press.

Hirsh, F. (1977) *The Social Limits to Growth.* London: Routledge and Kegan Paul.

Hirst, P. and Thompson, G. (1996) *Globalization in Question*, 2nd edition. Cambridge: Polity Press.

Lai, P. and Byram, M. (2003) The politics of bilingualism: a reproduction analysis of the policy of mother tongue education in Hong Kong after 1997. *Compare*, 33(3): 315–34.

Langford, M. (1997) *Internationally Mobile Pupils in Transition: The Role of the International School.* Unpublished MA in Education dissertation, University of Bath, UK.

Lauder, H., Brown, P., Dillabough, J. and Halsey, A.H. (2006) Introduction: The Prospects for Education: Individualization, Globalization and Social Change. In H. Lauder, P. Brown, J. Dillabough, and A.H. Halsey (eds) *Education, Globalization and Social Change:* Oxford, Oxford University Press.

Lowe, J. (1999) International examinations, national systems and the global market. *Compare*, 29, (3): 363–77.

Michaels, E., Handfield-Jones, H. and Axelrod, B. (2001) *The War for Talent.* Boston, MA: Harvard Business School Press.

Phillip, P., Lauder, H., Ashton, D. and Tholen, G. (2006) *Towards a high-skilled, low-waged economy? A review of global trends in education, employment and the labour market.* London: Sector Skills Development Agency.

Reich, R. (1991) *The Work of Nations.* New York: Simon and Schuster.

Robinson, W. (2004) *A Theory of Global Capitalism.* Baltimore, MA: Johns Hopkins University Press.

Room, G. (2000) Globalisation, social policy and international standard setting: the case of higher education credentials. *International Journal of Social Welfare*, 9: 103–119.

Rugman, A. and Verbeke, A. (2002) (2004) The regional multinationals: the location-bound drivers of global strategy. Paper presented to a symposium for John Stopford, London Business School, June 2002.

Rugman, A and Verbeke, A, (2004) 'A Perspective on Regional and Global Strategies of Multinational Enterprises'. *Journal of International Business Studies*, 35(l):3–8.

Sassen, S. (2005) New Global Classes: Implications for Politics. In A. Giddens and P. Diamond (eds) *The New Egalitarianism.* Cambridge: Polity Press.

Scott, J. (1991) *Who Rules Britain? Social Network Analysis* (2nd edition 2000). Cambridge: Polity Press.

Sklair, L. (2001) *The Transnational Capitalist Class.* Oxford: Blackwell.

Stiglitz, J. (2002) *Globalization and Its Discontents.* Harmondsworth: Penguin.

Tulgan, B. (2001) *Winning the Talent Wars.* London: Nicholas Brealey.

Turner, R. (1961) Modes of social ascent through education: sponsored and contest mobility. In A.H. Halsey, J. Floud and C. Anderson (eds) *Education, Economy and Society.* New York: The Free Press.

Useem, M., (1976) Third Culture Kids, *Today's Education*, 65(3): 103–5.

Useem, R. (1993) Third culture kids: focus of major study. *Newslinks,* XII (3): 1–27.

Wolfe, A. (2002) *Does Education Matter? Myths about Education and Economic Growth.* London: Penguin.

Woodruffe, C. (1999) *Winning the War for Talent.* Chichester: John Wiley.

37

Investigating Educational Policy Transfer

David Phillips

There was a time – in the 1970s and 1980s – when it became the fashion in comparative education to talk of 'convergence theory'. Education systems in the Western world were said to be moving closer together in terms of form and content. The most obvious manifestation of the trend was the move towards the common secondary school, towards a 'comprehensive' system of secondary schooling which was replacing traditionally differentiated forms in many countries, but there were many other dimensions to the phenomenon. There was much discussion too of 'equivalences', of ways in which syllabuses and curricula could be compared so that qualifications might be recognized from one country to another, the assumption being that there were increasingly identifiable commonalities between systems. These were the years before the developing concept of 'globalization' introduced ways of looking at world-wide tendencies towards a common approach to a wide range of political and social issues, education among them. What some of the early convergence theorists and the globalization and present 'world system theory' proponents have in common is a fascination with the notion of the cross-national transfer of ideas, of influence, of policy and practice.

An interest in the transfer of educational ideas from one country to another is at the very heart of comparative enquiry in education and it has been a topic addressed frequently and to varying degrees in the literature – in particular at impressive length and detail in studies by Zymek (1975) and Gonon (1998) and more recently in a series of doctoral theses and related texts (Beech 2005, 2006; Ochs 2005; Tanaka 2003) and in edited collections (Phillips and Ochs 2004b; Schriewer 2000; Schriewer and Caruso 2005; Steiner-Khamsi 2004). While the notion of policy 'borrowing' had often been seen as a naive effort by early travellers to achieve what is in most cases impossible, that is, simply to transplant ideas and practices from one context to another, recent serious attention to what it was that many of these early investigators were trying to do has revealed that many of them had a much deeper understanding of the problems involved in educational transfer than had been assumed.

As Almut Sprigade (2005) has demonstrated, even in the early decades of the nineteenth century there were sophisticated attempts to observe educational phenomena 'elsewhere' and to discuss the implications of such practice for the 'home' situation. The evidence produced could be used both to criticize the current situation in the observer's own country, or to defend it. The foreign example could therefore be used both negatively and positively – as Gita Steiner-Khamsi habitually puts it, to 'scandalize' or to 'glorify'.

There was much fascination with the statistics of education as the nineteenth century progressed and as techniques of data collection and analysis improved. Impressive levels of educational provision in other countries could then be shown to exist through the figures on national enrolment and attendance. Considerable attention was paid, for example, to the detailed statistics on education produced by the Prussian government and made widely known through Victor Cousin's important work *Rapport sur l'état de l'instruction publique dans quelques pays de l'Allemagne, et particulièrement en Prusse* (1833) (an English translation of which, by Sarah Austin, was published in 1834.) But the many commentators on Cousin, while they generally admired the thoroughness of his investigations, were not all convinced that the case was proven for the superiority of 'German' education on the basis of the statistics on provision alone. Here is a warning from Frederic Hill (1803–96), a member of the famous Hill family of educationists, which shows an early concern for the kinds of issues that are very much on the education agenda today:

> It is not enough to inform us that so many children are at school, and that such and such subjects are laid down in the course of instruction; – nay, it is not enough to do what Mons. Cousin has done (and in this his report is very superior to sweeping statements and vague generalities which are so frequently put forth), to point out the machinery provided for carrying the regulations into effect. The first question that presents itself – that about which all must be most anxious – that which alone can attract the earnest attention of the many to the examination of the general system – is, *What*

> *are the results produced?* (Hill 1836: Vol. II, pp. 71–2; original emphasis)

'I hope with time to convince people', Matthew Arnold was to write in a letter of April 1868, 'that I do not care the least for importing this or that foreign machinery, whether it be French or German, but only for getting certain English deficiencies supplied' (Murray 1997: 240). The foreign example might serve to put these deficiencies right, but only if the results observed elsewhere justified any new means to be introduced in the home context.

The notion of 'learning lessons' from experience in other countries, of seeking to 'borrow', has been a constant in the policy-making discourse since the early 1800s. Analysis of the great reform commissions of the nineteenth century in Britain shows that on many occasions very thorough investigations of education in a remarkable range of countries were undertaken – for the Newcastle (1861), Clarendon (1864) and Cross (1888) Commissions, for example. Matthew Arnold (who counts as a significant early comparativist) wrote reports of considerable detail on education in Germany and France particularly, and his work for official commissions went on to receive much wider attention when published separately (Arnold 1861, 1868, 1874, 1892 (1864)). It was with the establishment of the London Office of Special Inquiries and Reports under the directorship of Michael Sadler in 1895 that a period of remarkable analysis of all aspects of education in other countries began, and Sadler soon established himself as a significant contributor to the development of comparative education, determining some of its principal characteristics as a field of academic enquiry. Sadler's speech in Guildford of 1900 ('How Far Can We Learn anything of Practical Value From the Study of Foreign Systems of Education?') is today frequently quoted for its warnings about simplistic attitudes towards policy borrowing, without due regard to the context in which educational phenomena are essentially embedded (Higginson 1979; Phillips 2006). Over a hundred years later comparativists are still pointing out that no aspect of educational provision elsewhere which is perceived to be successful should be seen in isolation from the particular context that has created it and which to a large degree accounts for its success.

And so when we consider the many accounts of educational provision in Japan, for example, we should remember that that system's achievements have been to a great extent the result of cultural phenomena unique to the country (the importance of the group, the role of the *juku*, the special support given by mothers to their children's education, etc.). When we admire features of the German system of vocational education and training, we must recall that it is the result of a unique and long-standing compact between the state and the employers which has created conditions that are simply not to be found anywhere else. When we note that Finland has performed exceptionally well in the OECD's PISA surveys (2001, 2004), our principal question should be: 'What special – or unique – sociopolitical imperatives in Finland create the conditions for such success?' In short, we should remember that other countries are not Finland.

APPROACHES TO THE ANALYSIS OF POLICY BORROWING PROCESSES

In Oxford Kimberly Ochs and I have developed various models for the analysis of educational transfer and 'borrowing'; these are reproduced as Figures 37.1–37.4 in the Appendix to this chapter, and all of our publications on the subject are listed in the references. Here I shall summarize the main points. We see 'borrowing' as one part of a spectrum of educational transfer (Figure 37.1) which ranges from policy that is 'imposed' (as under totalitarian/authoritarian rule of various kinds), through that which is 'required under constraint' (as in defeated or occupied countries), 'negotiated under constraint' (required by multilateral or bilateral aid agreements) and 'borrowed purposefully' (intentional imitation of policy observed elsewhere), to 'introduced through influence' (the general international

spread of educational ideas and practices – through the work of such significant figures as John Dewey or Jean Piaget, for example, and in the nineteenth century through the dissemination of the ideas of Pestalozzi or Froebel). We define 'policy borrowing' as the 'conscious adoption in one context of policy observed in another', and as a 'deliberate, purposive phenomenon' (Phillips and Ochs 2004a).

There are many possible impulses for policy borrowing, among them (see Figure 37.3):

- internal dissatisfaction (public concern about provision)
- systemic collapse (as in the post-communist countries)
- negative external evaluation (following IEA reports, PISA surveys, etc.)
- economic change/competition (need for a better trained workforce to combat economic decline)
- political and other imperatives (manifestos for change and development)
- novel configurations (new political and economic alignments, as with the EU)
- knowledge/skills innovation (exploitation of new technologies)
- political change (change of direction following national or regional elections).

And such impulses can be associated with motives that range from worthy to ignoble in character:

- serious scientific/academic investigation of the situation in a foreign environment
- popular conceptions of the superiority of other approaches to educational questions
- politically motivated endeavours to seek reform of provision by identifying clear contrasts with the situation elsewhere
- distortion (exaggeration), whether or not deliberate, of evidence from abroad to highlight perceived deficiencies at home (Phillips 2000b).

These impulses can result in the identification of a number of foci of attraction, ranging from a general 'guiding philosophy' ('education for all', 'equality of opportunity', etc.) through what we list as 'ambitions/goals' (free nursery education, wider access to higher education), 'strategies' (administrative, managerial, financial), 'enabling structures' (new institutions) and 'processes' (curricular change, new examinations, qualifications), to 'techniques' (teaching styles). These policy foci in terms of the attractiveness of foreign models are seen against a detailed contextual background (political, economic, cultural, religious, geographical, etc.), as illustrated in Figure 37.2 (Ochs and Phillips 2002a, 2002b).

We depict the impulses for borrowing, and the foci of attraction that result from them, as the first stage ('cross-national attraction') in a four-stage process, the other three stages being 'decision', 'implementation' and 'internalization/indigenization' (see Figure 37.3).

During each of these successive stages the observed policy or practice can undergo change or can be blocked by 'significant actors' with the power to do so. In any case the original policy (termed 'practice$_1$' in Figure 37.4) will inevitably be somewhat different once it is implemented, having passed through various 'filters' in the 'home' situation that modify it ('practice$_2$' in Figure 37.4).

We have principally used the example of British interest in education in Germany over the past two hundred years or so to illustrate the four stages of policy borrowing as we define them. But the models in Figures 37.1–37.4 can be used to analyse and explain policy transfer in other contexts, as some of the authors in *Educational Policy Borrowing: Historical Perspectives* (Phillips and Ochs 2004b) have attempted to show.

POLICY BORROWING: HISTORICAL EXAMPLES

A few historical examples can serve to illustrate some of the aspects of policy transfer raised so far.

England: The Newcastle Commission

Towards the end of the 1850s in England there was serious concern that elementary education would have to be put on a firmer footing. Various attempts over many years to legislate for improvement had failed, principally as a result of denominational controversies. In 1858 a Royal Commission was appointed 'to inquire into the state of Popular Education in England, and to report what Measures, if any, are required for the extension of sound and cheap elementary instruction to all classes of people'. The 'Newcastle' Commission reported in 1861 and included accounts of education in France, French Switzerland and Holland, written by Matthew Arnold, and a paper on Germany, written by Mark Pattison, later to be Rector of Lincoln College, Oxford.

The Newcastle Commission used the German example to argue *against* compulsion, because compulsion, whatever its practical advantages, could only succeed with the will of the people:

> Any universal compulsory system appears to us neither attainable nor desirable. In Prussia, indeed, and in many parts of Germany, the attendance can scarcely be termed compulsory. Though the attendance is required by law, it is a law which entirely expresses the convictions and wishes of the people. Such a state of feeling renders the working of a system of compulsion, among a people living under a strict government, comparatively easy. Our own condition [...] is in many respects essentially different. But we also found that the results of this system, as seen in Prussia, do not appear to be so much superior to those which have been already attained amongst ourselves by voluntary efforts, as to make us desire an alteration which would be opposed to the feelings, and, in some respects, to the principles of this country.
>
> An attempt to replace an independent system of education by a compulsory system, managed by the Government, would be met by objections, both religious and political, of a far graver character in this country than any with which it has had to contend in Prussia, and we have seen that, even in Prussia, it gives rise to difficulties which are not insignificant. And therefore, on the grounds of a long-established difference between our own position and that of the countries where a compulsory system is worked successfully; on the grounds of the feelings, both political, social and religious, to which it would be opposed; and also on the ground that our education is advancing successfully without it, we have not thought that a scheme for compulsory education to be universally applied in this country can be entertained as a practical possibility. (Newcastle Report 1861: 300).

Pattison's contribution on Germany contains caveats on the usefulness of foreign models:

The same difficulties with which we have to contend have to be met in the several countries of Germany, only under conditions so altered and infinitely varied, as to afford a most instructive lesson. Their experience has been longer than ours, and has in some points passed through stages we are only approaching. It is, indeed, true that the legislation in any country is always determined by its own necessities, and is not influenced by the knowledge of what is being done in another. In this country we are little likely to err on the side of a hasty imitation of foreign modes, or to adopt a usage from a neighbouring country, forgetful that its being successful, there is no guarantee that it will thrive when transplanted to our climate. But when debating how we shall legislate, we cannot afford to ignore the vast storehouse of experience which the history of the last fifty years of primary instruction in Germany offers. Much rather is every one who has any information on foreign systems to give, called upon to come forward with it, not as precedent to be followed, but as material for deliberation. (Pattison 1860: 168)

Pattison mentions one of the questions he was asked to address. He was to 'attempt to form general opinions as to whether the general character of the people appears to have been distinctly altered by an advance or decline of education' (1860: 241). His response to this was, 'I must confess that I cannot find any one of the national characteristics of any part of the German populations which I can on reliable grounds trace to the methods or the matters taught in the schools' (p. 241). His report is in the finest tradition of scholarly analysis and argument. It embraces some one hundred pages of text and remains a valuable source on the outsider view of education in Germany in the middle decades of the century.

This particular example illustrates the desire to explore the possible outcomes of a putative policy decision by means of analysis of foreign models where the policy in question was in place. In this case the example of Germany helped to dissuade the commissioners from recommending free and compulsory state-controlled education.

Japan: the Iwakura Mission

A dozen or so years later Japan took an extraordinary initiative to learn from foreign examples. The Japanese government had sent missions abroad in the 1860s in various attempts to benefit from Western learning. The 'embassy' convened in 1871, however, went far beyond all previous efforts. Iwakura Tomoni led a group that sailed to Europe and the USA and spent in all a year and nine months away from Japan. It had 107 members and included half the government. Its aims were to present credentials to countries with which treaties had been concluded; to begin treaty revisions; and to observe and investigate advanced societies in order to determine what features of those societies might assist with the modernization of Japan. The embassy visited the United States of America, Britain, France, Belgium, The Netherlands, Germany, Russia, Denmark, Sweden, Italy, Austria and Switzerland. It included several inspectors and other officials from the Ministry of Education, and a detailed report on its travels and findings was put together by the Confucian scholar Kume Kunitake (Kume 2002). The report includes records of the mission's investigation of educational provision in the countries visited. Here, for example, is an extract from an account of education in the USA:

The federal government does not interfere much with the methods of education, and such matters are left to the state or territory. Each state government regards education as its major administrative responsibility and expense. Every year the state governments set the education taxes and discuss how to increase the funds raised from taxes. Building schools, managing schools, encouraging school attendance, and staffing are all done at the initiative of each state, and the states compete among themselves. There is no single, nation-wide, unified system of education. (Kume Vol. I: 55)

There was similar reporting on the provision observed in Prussia, and it was Prussia that was to provide a model for the future structure of the Japanese education system:

The standard of education in Prussia ranks among the highest in Europe, and it is an area of particular concern for the government. The construction of elementary schools is always paid for with taxes from the residents in each town and district. Their maintenance is a mandatory responsibility of local officials, and it is compulsory for parents to send their children to school. Every year 2 per cent of government revenue is spent on sending children from poor backgrounds to school to receive an education at public expense. (Kume Vol. III: 277)

The Iwakura Mission constituted one of the most thorough attempts on the part of a government to learn directly from the foreign example, and the Prussian imprint on Japan's education system (still observable in the Prussian-style uniforms of Japanese schoolchildren) was to be clearly identifiable in the years to come. Japan, of course, underwent another period of susceptibility to influence from abroad following the Second World War, when US schooling patterns were introduced.

The Mission's intentions fall within our definition of borrowing as a deliberate, purposive phenomenon, and since its members were figures of considerable influence they became the 'significant actors' who could ensure that policy decisions were followed through.

England: Joseph Payne, Michael Sadler

To return to British interest in Germany, we might take the account by the first Professor of Education in England, Joseph Payne (1808–76), as an outstanding illustration of serious academic study of a foreign example in order to provide impulses for a rethinking of approaches to education in England. Payne set himself the task of examining Kindergarten education in Germany and visited schools in Hamburg, Berlin and elsewhere during 1874, a time when compulsory elementary education in England was in its infancy. Payne was a very well informed specialist with impressive knowledge of the work of German educationists and policy-makers, and he was anxious in his use of the German example to point out the difference between education and instruction:

The question ... whether we shall educate with a view to instruction as in Germany, or instruct with a view to education as in England ... is answered by the facts. No sane person will challenge a comparison between the average results of German primary education and ours. (Payne 1892: iv)

Payne calls Germany 'the land of scientific pedagogy' and describes some of the practices he observed in considerable detail, with an eye especially on the pedagogical lessons to be learned in England from the patent evidence of German practice. His work exemplifies our identification of 'strategies' and 'techniques' among the foci of attraction observable in the early stages of processes of policy borrowing.

We have noted above that Michael Sadler presided over a period of detailed investigation of educational provision in other countries during the eight years from 1895 when he was Director of the Office of Special Inquiries and Reports. Eleven volumes of 'Special Reports on Educational Subjects' were produced which 'made available for English readers a large amount of useful information otherwise difficult to get at, but served an even more valuable purpose in the way of suggestion and inspiration' (Selby-Bigge 1927: 214). The coverage in these reports was vast and constituted a bank of authoritative briefings designed precisely to 'suggest' and 'inspire' in the policy-making process. Sadler's precipitate departure from the Office of Special Inquiries and Reports was in part the result of his insisting on the neutrality of his work – he objected to any notion of its serving political decision-making to order.

USA: Reports on Japan and Germany; Austria: reports on comprehensive schools

From Sadler we might jump to more recent examples of governments – through various agencies – seeking to collect evidence from other countries germane to internal policy discussion and development. Often such activity is spurred by an external event of the kind listed under 'impulses' in Stage 1 of our four-stage model of policy borrowing (Figure 37.3). Following the 'Sputnik' shock of the 1950s, for example, it was natural for policy-makers in the United States to examine the Soviet education system. Trace's book of 1961, *What Ivan Knows That Johnny Doesn't*, exemplifies the approach. And following the appearance of the critical US government report *A Nation at Risk* (National Commission on Excellence in Education, 1983), it was not surprising that a study of Japanese education was commissioned (US Department of Education 1987). Later a similar study was undertaken of education in Germany (US Department of Education 1999).

In the early 1970s, following widely publicized reports on the problems of education in its neighbour Germany, the Ministry of Education in Austria commissioned studies of education in the USA, the Soviet Union, England, France and Italy. As Gruber relates, however, with a change in the political climate of Austria the resulting reports did not produce the hoped-for enlightenment in the comprehensive school debate (Gruber 2004: 142).

The experiences of the USA and Austria in these instances illustrate our notion of internal dissatisfaction or negative evaluation or political change as triggers for forms of cross-national attraction.

England: 'Aspects of Education' series, 1980s and 1990s

In England the mid-1980s saw the first of a remarkable series of reports from the Inspectorate on aspects of education in other countries. Their publication coincided with various government initiatives that were to lead to the Education Reform Act of 1988, and they clearly formed part of the agenda for change. It was not surprising that the first report was on education in Germany, with a focus on assessment and the curriculum, two themes that were to be prominent in the 1988 legislation (Department of Education and Science 1986). There followed in quick succession further reports on Germany, on Japan and on the United States, together with others on France, Italy, Denmark and elsewhere. The purpose of these reports (some 30 in all, continuing into the new century) was clearly to stimulate debate around matters of key interest to policy-making in England at the time: apart from the curriculum and assessment, major topics included vocational education

and training (Germany, France, USA, Taiwan, Malaysia), teacher education (France, Germany, USA), and primary education (France, Japan, The Netherlands, Italy). This particular series is important not only for the dissemination of information on aspects of education in other countries but also for the insights it provides into what was exercising the minds of policy-makers at various times. The many reports are replete with ideas which have 'externalising potential'.

CONCLUSIONS

From these selective examples it can be seen that policy transfer manifests itself in a variety of ways, chief among them the attempts on the part of policy-makers in one location in very particular circumstances to take on board ideas from another. Sometimes these ideas will eventually be rejected, but might help to confirm the *status quo*. Sometimes they will be amended to suit the situation 'at home'. Sometimes they will be accepted without significant change (as in the case of 'borrowed' pedagogical techniques).

But in every instance the foreign example has been sought out and used within a process of change and development in education. This provides a valuable dimension in educational policy-making that enriches the discussion, even when 'foreign' examples are not adopted. In our Figure 37.4 we illustrate how an observed practice can pass through various processes of modification before it is eventually implemented in another context.

In terms of the huge variety of issues comprehended within 'international education' the models described above could help to understand and explain the various influences that serve to shape policy, from the highest levels of decision-making to the pragmatic application of teaching techniques in classrooms. The models need to be tested in a variety of national contexts and then further developed. In particular it will be important to consider the extent to which less developed countries – often the receivers of policy 'lent' by outside agencies – fit into the explanatory schemata we have proposed.

Educational policy transfer remains one of the central points of interest in the field of comparative and international education. As Steiner-Khamsi puts it:

> There is no doubt that the study of transfer has helped to legitimize and sustain our field. It is important to recall, however, that in addition to a long history of research on educational transfer, we also look back on a strong tradition of skepticism. Numerous warnings have been articulated about borrowing, whether wholesale, selective, or eclectic. (2000: 155–6)

The warnings, *pace* Sadler, are obvious enough and do not need reiterating (except in the case of disingenuous politicians); what analysts like Gita Steiner-Khamsi, Jürgen Schriewer, Kimberly Ochs and the present author have been attempting to do is to provide explanatory tools for the investigation of the many processes involved in borrowing, in order to illustrate its complexity and its significance at a time of increasing cross-national influence in education and to provide a stimulus for others to investigate educational transfer in a range of different contexts.

REFERENCES

Arnold, Matthew (1861) *The Popular Education of France*. London: Longman, Green, etc.

Arnold, Matthew (1868): *Schools and Universities on the Continent*. London: Macmillan.

Arnold, Matthew (1874): *Higher Schools and Universities in Germany*. London: Macmillan.

Arnold, Matthew (1892 [1864]): *A French Eton*. London: Macmillan.

Beech, Jason (2005): International agencies, educational discourse, and the reform of teacher education in Argentina and Brazil (1985–2002): a comparative analysis. Unpublished PhD thesis, University of London.

Beech, Jason (2006): The theme of educational transfer in comparative education: a view over time. *Research in Comparative and International Education*, 1 (1): 2–13 (www.wwwords.co.uk/RCIE).

Cousin, Victor (1833): *Rapport sur l'état de l'instruction publique dans quelques pays de l'Allemagne, et particulièrement en Prusse*. Paris: Levrault.

Cousin, Victor (1834): *Report on the State of Public Instruction in Prussia*, translated by Sarah Austin. London: Effingham Wilson.

Department of Education and Science (1986): *Education in the Federal Republic of Germany: Aspects of Curriculum and Assessment*. London: HMSO.

Gonon, Philipp (1998): *Das Internationale Argument in der Bildungsreform*. Berne, etc.: Peter Lang.

Gruber, Karl Heinz (2004): The rise and fall of Austrian interest in English education. In David Phillips and Kimberly Ochs (eds) *Educational Policy Borrowing: Historical Perspectives*. Didcot (Symposium), pp. 185–97.

Higginson, J.H. (ed.) (1979): *Selections from Michael Sadler. Studies in World Citizenship*. Liverpool: Dejall & Meyorre.

Hill, Frederic (1836): *National Education: Its Present State and Prospects*. London: Charles Knight.

Kume Kunitake (2002): *The Iwakura Embassy, 1871–73: A True Account of the Ambassador Extraordinary & Plenipotentiary's Journey of Observation Through the United States of America and Europe*, compiled by Kume Kunitake. Editors-in-Chief: Graham Healey and Chushichi Tsuzuki. The Japan Documents, 2002, 5 volumes.

Murray, Nicholas (1996 [1997]) *A Life of Matthew Arnold*. London: Sceptre.

National Commission on Excellence in Education (1983): *A Nation at Risk*. Washington, DC: US Government Printing Office.

Newcastle Report (1861): *Report of the Commissioners appointed to inquire into the State of Popular Education in England*. London: HMSO.

Ochs, Kimberly and Phillips, David (2002a): *Towards a Structural Typology of Cross-national Attraction in Education*. Lisbon: Educa.

Ochs, Kimberly and Phillips, David (2002b) Comparative studies and 'cross-national attraction' in education: a typology for the analysis of English interest in educational policy and provision in Germany. *Educational Studies*, 28 (4): 325–39.

Ochs, Kimberly (2005): Educational policy borrowing and its implications for reform and innovation: a study with specific reference to the London Borough of Barking and Dagenham. Unpublished DPhil. thesis, University of Oxford.

OECD (2001): *Knowledge and Skills for Life: First Results from PISA 2000*. Paris: OECD.

OECD (2004): *Learning for Tomorrow's World: First Results from PISA 2003*. Paris: OECD.

Pattison, Mark (1860): Report of Assistant Commissioner the Rev. Mark Pattison, B.D., Fellow of Lincoln College, Oxford, on the State of Elementary Education in Germany. Newcastle Report, Vol. IV.

Payne, Joseph (1892): *Lectures on the History of Education, with a Visit to German Schools*. London: Longmans, Green, and Co.

Phillips, David (1989): Neither a borrower nor a lender be? The problems of cross-national attraction in education. *Comparative Education*, 25 (3): 267–74.

Phillips, David (1993): Borrowing educational policy. In D. Finegold, L. McFarland and W. Richardson (eds) *Something Borrowed, Something Learned? The Transatlantic Market in Education and Training Reform*. Washington, DC (The Brookings Institution), pp. 13–19.

Phillips, David (1997): Prolegomena to a history of British interest in education in Germany. In: Christoph Kodron et al. (eds) *Vergleichende Erziehungswissenschaft: Herausforderung – Vermittlung – Praxis*. Cologne: Böhlau, pp. 673–87.

Phillips, David (2000a): Beyond travellers' tales: some nineteenth-century British commentators on education in Germany. *Oxford Review of Education*, 26 (1): 49–62.

Phillips, David (2000b): Learning from elsewhere in education: some perennial problems revisited with reference to British interest in Germany. *Comparative Education*, 36 (3): 297–307.

Phillips, D. (2002): *Reflections on British Interest in Education in Germany in the Nineteenth Century (A Progress Report)*. Lisbon: Educa.

Phillips, David (2004): Toward a theory of policy attraction in education. In G. Steiner-Khamsi (ed.) *Lessons from Elsewhere: The Politics of Educational Borrowing and Lending*. New York: Teachers College Press, pp. 54–67.

Phillips, David (2005): Policy borrowing in education: frameworks for analysis. In Joseph Zajda (ed.) *International Handbook on Globalisation, Education and Policy Research*. Dordrecht: Springer, pp. 23–34.

Phillips, David (2006): Michael Sadler and comparative education. *Oxford Review of Education*, 32(1): 39–54.

Phillips, David and Ochs, Kimberly (2003a): Processes of policy borrowing in education: some analytical and explanatory devices. *Comparative Education*, 39 (41): 451–61.

Phillips, David and Ochs, Kimberly (2003b): Educational policy borrowing: some questions for small states. In Stephen Matlin (ed.) *Commonwealth Education Partnerships 2004*. London: Commonwealth Secretariat, The Stationery Office, pp. 131–6.

Phillips, David and Ochs, Kimberly (2004a): Researching policy borrowing: some methodological challenges in comparative education. *British Educational Research Journal*, 30 (6): 773–84.

Phillips, David and Ochs, Kimberly (eds) (2004b) *Educational Policy Borrowing: Historical Perspectives*. Didcot (Symposium).

Schriewer, Jürgen (ed.) (2000): *Discourse Formation in Comparative Education*. Frankfurt am Main: Peter Lang.

Schriewer, Jürgen and Caruso, Marcelo (eds) (2005): *Nationalerziehung und Universalmethode – frühe Formen schulorganisatorischer Globalisserung*. Leipzig: Leipziger Universitätsverlag.

Selby-Bigge, Sir Lewis Amherst (1927): *The Board of Education*. London: G.P. Putnam's Sons.

Sprigade, Almut (2005): Where there is reform there is comparison: English interest in education abroad, 1800–1839. Unpublished DPhil. thesis, University of Oxford.

Steiner-Khamsi, Gita (2000): Transferring education, displacing reforms. In Jürgen Schriewer (ed.) *Discourse Formation in Comparative Education*. Frankfurt am Main: Peter Lang, pp. 155–87.

Steiner-Khamsi, Gita (ed.) (2004): *Lessons from Elsewhere: The Politics of Educational Borrowing and Lending*. New York: Teachers College Press.

Tanaka, Masahiro (2003): The transfer of university concepts and practices between Germany, the United States, and Japan: a comparative perspective. Unpublished PhD thesis, University of London.

Trace, Arther S. (1961) *What Ivan Knows That Johnny Doesn't*. New York: Random House.

US Department of Education (1987): *Japanese Education Today*. Washington, DC: Department of Education.

US Department of Education (1999): *The Educational System in Germany: Case Study Findings*. Washington, DC: Department of Education.

Zymek, Bernd (1975): *Das Ausland als Argument in der Pädagogischen Reformdiskussion*. Ratingen: Aloys Henn Verlag.

APPENDIX

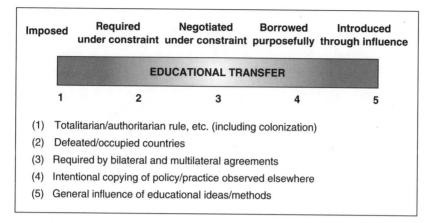

Figure 37.1   **Spectrum of educational transfer (Phillips and Ochs 2004b)**

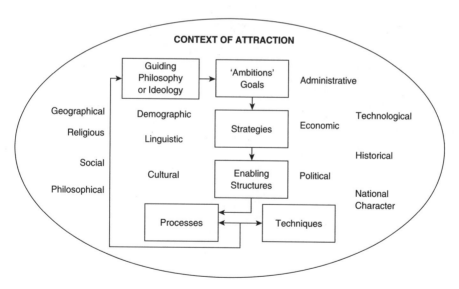

Figure 37.2   **Foci of cross-national attraction (Ochs and Phillips 2002a, 2002b)**

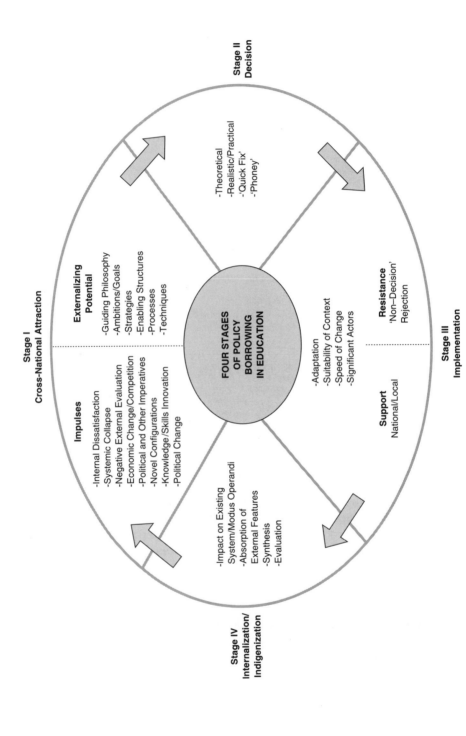

Figure 37.3   Four stages of educational borrowing (Phillips and Ochs 2003a, 2003b, 2004a, 2004b)

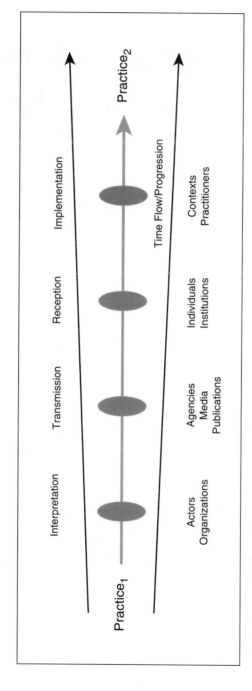

Figure 37.4   Filters in the policy borrowing process (Phillips and Ochs 2004b)

38

The Internationalization of Education Policy in Latin America

Silvina Gvirtz and Jason Beech

This chapter analyses the latest reforms in Latin American educational systems, suggesting that although education policies in the region have always been shaped by international influences, in the 1980s and 1990s the internationalization of education policy in Latin America has been intensified, making education policy in Latin American countries more similar at the level of official rhetoric. However, it will also be suggested that these similarities in the principles that guide education reform in the region do not necessarily imply that actual policies are the same in different countries, since the process of policy formulation is affected by different political and institutional cultures.

The chapter is divided into three sections. The first examines the principles that guided educational reforms in Latin America in the 1980s and 1990s. The second section uses the Argentine case to illustrate the relation between educational policies as a construction of the state and the effects of these policies in practice. In the concluding section some ideas

are opened up to reflect upon the growing internationalization of education policy in Latin America and its consequences for the region.

EDUCATION POLICY IN LATIN AMERICA IN THE 1980S AND 1990S

The development of educational systems in Latin America has always been shaped by international influence. The first institutions of formal education in what is currently known as Latin America were founded by the Spanish Jesuits, who based their education philosophy on the ideas of the counter-reform that they brought from Southern Europe (Cano 1985). Later, with the independence movements, the Lancaster method attracted the attention of some of the political leaders of the time, and schools of that type were founded in Mexico, Venezuela, Argentina, Brazil and many other countries. Modern educational systems were created in the late nineteenth and early twentieth century following European models and ideas, especially the French educational system and positivism.

Nevertheless, even though educational systems in Latin America had similar international influences, there were also significant differences in the ways in which these influences were translated into educational policies, resulting in educational systems that responded to the cultural, political and economic specificities of each country. For example, the first university in what is currently the Dominican Republic was founded in 1538, while Brazil did not have a university until the 1920s. Multilingual education is a significant issue in countries like Guatemala, Peru, Bolivia and in Southern Mexico, where strong and lively indigenous cultures coexist with the Westernized cultures that were born with European colonization. However, multilingual instruction is not such a big concern for education policy in Argentina, Uruguay or the south of Brazil, where most indigenous cultures were eliminated or incorporated into the hegemonic Europeanized cultures. Educational statistics also indicate the enormous differences between Latin American educational systems. For example, in 1990 the enrolment ratio in secondary education was 81 per cent in Uruguay, but it reached only 35 per cent in Venezuela. In that same year 40 per cent of students in primary education went to a private school in Chile, while only 10 per cent were enrolled in private institutions in Bolivia. The rate of adult literacy was only 40 per cent in Haiti and 61 per cent in Guatemala, while it reached 90 per cent in Paraguay and about 96 per cent in Argentina, Cuba and Uruguay (UNESCO 2006).

From the early twentieth century, educational systems in Latin America had very similar structures, divided into primary, secondary and higher education, with primary education being compulsory and free of charge for students with a curriculum based on the teaching of Spanish or Portuguese, mathematics, some basic notions of the natural and social sciences, and citizenship. However, within these common structures educational systems were quite diverse, resulting in different educational

experiences for the children who went to schools in each country. In addition, the examples presented in the previous paragraph suggest that educational systems in Latin America faced different and specific problems in the 1990s.

In the late 1980s and the 1990s a wave of educational reform struck Latin America. Ecuador passed its *Ley de Educación* in 1983. In Uruguay the *Ley de Educación* was sanctioned in 1985. In Chile the *Ley Orgánica Constitucional de Enseñanza* (Organic Constitutional Law of Teaching) was approved in 1990. In that same year an educational law was passed in El Salvador. In 1992 a Ten-Year Educational Plan was established in the Dominican Republic. In 1993 the *Ley Federal de Educación* was passed in Argentina and a new educational law was sanctioned in Mexico. Bolivia approved its *Ley de Reforma Educativa* in 1994 and in that same year the Colombian *Ley General de Educación* was passed. In 1996 the *Lei de Diretrizes e Bases da Educação* (Law of Guidelines and Foundations of Education) was approved in Brazil (Braslavsky and Gvirtz 2000; OEI 2004).

Thus, in a 13-year period, many countries in Latin America established new laws that regulate their educational systems. Furthermore, the reforms initiated with these laws were based on similar principles: decentralization, school autonomy, the professionalization of teachers, a curriculum based on competencies and the setting up of central evaluation systems (Braslavsky and Gvirtz 2000; Martinez Boom 2000).

For example, in an eight-year period central evaluation systems were established in 11 Latin American countries. In 1986 the *Programa de Pruebas Nacionales del Ministerio de Educación Pública* was set up in Costa Rica. In 1988 the *Sistema de Medición de la Calidad de la Educación* was established in Chile. In Brazil, the *Sistema Nacional de Avaliação Básica* was founded in 1990, and in that same year a National Evaluation System was created in Colombia. In 1992 similar systems were established in Paraguay and Mexico. The *Sistema Nacional de Evaluación de la Calidad* in Argentina was set up in 1993. Uruguay and Bolivia started their own National Evaluation Systems in 1994. Similar centralized systems were established in Ecuador in 1995 and in Peru in 1996 (Gvirtz and Larripa 2002).

In most cases these reforms implied significant ruptures with previous education policy in these countries. For example, the traditional encyclopaedic culture that dominated curricular regulation – emphasizing contents related to the provision of information and facts – was replaced by a curriculum based on the fostering of competencies.

In addition, another characteristic of these reforms is that they were 'global reforms', in the sense that these policies were not aimed at changing only some aspects of these educational systems. Rather, these reforms proposed a complete revision of the Latin American educational systems to adapt them to the twenty-first century. The comprehensiveness of these policies can be illustrated with the Brazilian and the Argentine case.

In Brazil, a new *Lei de Diretrizes e Bases da Educação* (Law of Guidelines and Foundations of Education) was passed in 1996 (Brazil 2002). In addition, the reformist view that dominated Brazil at that time resulted in a great number of regulations, projects and programmes: Education for All; Ten-Year Educational Plan; National Curricular Parameters and National Curricular Guidelines for basic education, for higher education, for pre-school education, for adult education, for professional and technological education and for teacher education; a National Evaluation System for Basic Education (SAEB); a scheme called National Examination of Courses that evaluates different university courses through an examination for graduates; a National Examination for Middle School graduates; the decentralization of primary education to municipalities; the Fund for the Maintenance and Development of Primary Education and Teacher Enhancement (FUNDEF); and the Law of Autonomy for Universities.

Similarly, in Argentina, the Law of the Transfer of Educational Services was passed in 1992 and one year later the 're-foundation' of

the Argentine educational system was launched by the *Ley Federal de Educación* (LFE) (Argentina, 1993a). For the first time in Argentine history a law of education regulated all the levels and modalities of the educational system as an integrated unit (Braslavsky and Gvirtz 2000; Van Gelderen 1996). There was also a Higher Education Law (Argentina 1995); the Federal Council of Education was re-instituted (Argentina 1993b); a Federal Educational Pact was signed; and the whole structure of the Argentine educational system – traditionally divided into seven years of primary education and five years of secondary education – was changed (Argentina 1993a). In addition, several programmes were established, such as the National System of Evaluation of Education (SINEC) (Argentina 2002), the National Commission for the Evaluation of Universities (CONEAU) (Argentina 1993c), a Social Educational Plan (Argentina 1993b), a Federal Net for Continuous Teacher Training (Argentina 1994) and Curricular Reforms for Pre-school Education, General Basic Education, *Polimodal* (secondary education) (Argentina 1996a) and for Teacher Education (Argentina 1996b).

The justification for these all-embracing reforms was found in the need to adapt to 'external pressures'. In other words, the logic was that there was a series of changes taking place at the 'world level' (globalization, information age, knowledge economies) and, since these changes could not be controlled by the Latin American national states, the aim of education policies should be to reform the educational systems that had been created in the late nineteenth and early twentieth century to adapt them to the new social conditions.

These assumptions led to the series of reforms mentioned above. The simultaneity and similarity in the principles that guided these reforms can be explained by the influence that international agencies had on educational policies in the region through the universal model of education for the information age that they promoted during the late 1980s and 1990s (Beech 2005).

A recent study (Beech 2005) has shown that UNESCO, the World Bank and OECD consider that one of their main roles is to disseminate 'cutting-edge' knowledge about education. Each of these agencies has different proposals for education. Furthermore, these agencies have conflicting views on some educational issues and they even engage in explicit controversy (as when UNESCO criticizes the World Bank for making teachers the 'villains' of the difficulties faced by countries to reduce educational costs) (Carnoy 1999; Mayor and Tanguiane 1996).

However, although the proposals of UNESCO, the World Bank and OECD differ, there are a series of underlying assumptions that were common to the proposals of these organizations, revealing a general system of thought that made these simultaneous and apparently contradictory opinions possible.

An analysis of the assumptions about the future embedded in the work of these three agencies revealed a striking similarity in the way that these agencies read the future as 'the information age'. The proposals of these agencies were based on the assumption that the future will present a 'forever rapidly changing world' influenced by the rhythm of technological 'progress'. Of course, it follows that if the world will be ceaselessly changing in the future this will have consequential effects for education. Thus, the self-proclaimed task of these organizations was not only to look for solutions to existing educational problems, but also to identify – or rather predict – the problems that will arise in the future. In this way, OECD, UNESCO and the World Bank positioned themselves not only as the 'scientific experts' that can predict the future, but also as those that can design universal educational solutions that adapt to this (imagined) future. Furthermore, these agencies not only have a similar reading of the future, but they also promote very similar educational principles that should be used to adapt most educational systems to the information age. Thus, within the educational proposals of these agencies a single universal model of education for the 'information age' can be identified, rather than three different models.

The universal model of education for the information age promoted by these agencies was based on:

- decentralization/school autonomy
- lifelong learning
- centralized curriculum based on competencies:
  - communication skills
  - creativity
  - flexibility
  - learning to learn
  - ability to work in groups
  - problem-solving
- central evaluation system(s)
- professionalization of teachers.

This model is offered as an ideal for most educational contexts. It should be used to judge most educational systems and, then, once the faults have been identified, as a model for reform. The similarity between the principles that guided the latest educational reforms in many Latin American countries and the model described above suggest that the influence of international agencies can at least partly explain the simultaneity and similarity in educational reforms in the region (and probably in many other parts of the world).

In a context in which the nation-states have lost much of their legitimacy (Carnoy and Castells 2001), and they are described as being 'too small for the big problems of life and too big for the small problems of life' (Bell cited in Giddens 1990), international agencies have become a significant source of authority (or financial resources in the case of the World Bank) that can legitimize a policy agenda. However, international agencies do not just *legitimize* a pre-existing policy agenda. As international agencies promote their abstract universal model of education as an ideal to adapt an existing system to 'the information age', they are *defining and promoting* an education policy agenda.

Thus, the increasing importance of international agencies as promoters of educational reform is one of the ways in which education policy is becoming increasingly internationalized, but not the only one. The flow of people and ideas through social, academic and political networks as a result of the technological revolution and the shrinking of space and time allows for more contact between academics, political leaders and technocrats that define and implement education policy in different countries. This facilitates and accelerates the possibilities of transferring policy 'solutions' from one context to another, especially when there is a generalized feeling that as a result of the processes of economic and cultural global-ization most countries in the world share a set of similar challenges. Also, there are new (or increasingly more powerful) players in the global educational field, like international agencies, development agencies, foundations and 'policy entrepreneurs', charismatic acade-mics that sell their 'solutions' in the academic and political markets (Ball 1998). In times of uncertainty, these global magical solutions become extremely attractive for some govern-ments because of their simplicity (Ball 1998).

So, given these and other processes, edu-cational systems in Latin America and in many other parts of the world are becoming increasingly similar, at least at the level of official rhetoric, promoting similar types of educational principles.

However, even though at the level of offi-cial discourse education policy is becoming more homogeneous in different countries, and the specificities of each context seem to be less influential in defining the principles that guide education reform, it is important to keep in mind that a gap could exist between the postulates that are used to justify a reform and the actual formulation and implementation of policies. In order to explore this gap, the next section will analyse some of the effects of the global educational reform that was imple-mented in Argentina.

THE FORMULATION AND IMPLEMENTATION OF EDUCATION POLICY IN ARGENTINA IN THE 1990S

This section analyses the formulation and implementation of education policy in the 1990s in Argentina by identifying seven principles that guided the reform and how each of these prin-ciples was translated into actual policy. It is suggested that most of the postulates used to justify the reform were not accomplished

due to the centralizing and hyper-regulatory practices of the national state.

As counterpoint to this analysis, we will reflect upon what we consider to be one of the most problematic characteristics of the Argentine educational system in the past four decades: the tendency that shows that, since the 1960s, the most advantaged sectors of society are moving from the public to the private sys-tem. It will be suggested that this tendency has not been brought to an end partly because of the internationalization of policies, which results in an emphasis on tackling global challenges which gives less importance to specific national or local problems. Thus, before moving into an analysis of the principles that guided the reform, an overview of the privatization of edu-cational space in Argentina is offered.

As can be seen from Figure 38.1, some pub-lications have presented empirical evidence showing a significant growth in private enrol-ments in Argentina since the late 1950s – for example at the primary level, where 1941 repre-sented the lowest percentage of private enrol-ments. Since that year, a period of sustained expansion started in which the annual growth rate of private enrolments was almost three times higher than the annual growth rate of the public system for the same period (1.6 per cent). The number of students in the private sector increased considerably from fewer than 289,000 pupils in 1967 to almost 717,000 in the mid-1990s – 40.3 per cent growth in absolute terms.

It is important to point out that the expan-sion of the private sector in school education in Argentina ceased in 1994. In that year the private sector represented 21.34 per cent of total enrolments at primary level and 25 per cent when all levels are considered, with some significant peaks of more than 50 per cent and up to 65 per cent in urban districts with a high middle-class population, such as Vicente López and San Isidro. In that same year, in Buenos Aires City, 50 per cent of the students went to private institutions. However, if only teacher training institutions are taken into account, enrolments in the private sector were even higher.

In addition, it is interesting to point out that there is a direct (and very strong) relation

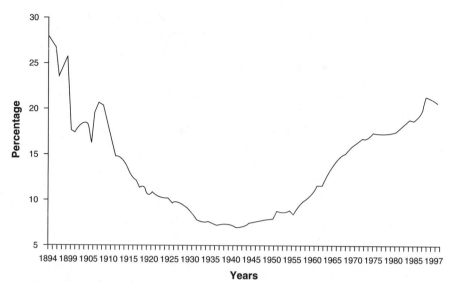

Figure 38.1   Private sector participation in total enrolments, primary level (Morduchowicz et al. 1999)

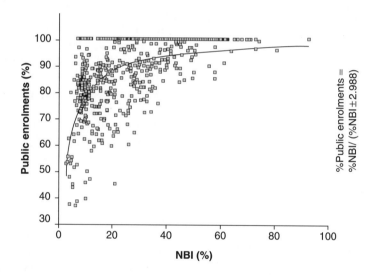

Figure 38.2   Public Enrolments vs. NBI (unsatisfied basic needs): real and estimated (non-linear OLS estimation) values (Narodowski and Nores 2000)

between public enrolments and percentage of the population with 'unsatisfied basic needs' (Narodowski and Nores 2000). This means that public schools in Argentina mainly cater for the most economically disadvantaged sectors of the population (see Figure 38.2).

The data also show that private enrolments are concentrated within the families with the highest incomes. Thus, according to official data, the following conclusion can be drawn: for every ten students that study in private institutions, nine belong to the most economically advanced sectors. This situation especially affects the big urban centres, where the increase in private schools has had the most significant impact.

Finally, another notable feature of the process of privatization that has occurred in Argentine education is that the state subsidises private schools in two ways. In the first place, some schools receive direct subsidies from the state that permit, at least in theory, a reduction of the fees paid by students. In some cases, like in many *escuelas parroquiales* (Church schools located in economically disadvantaged areas), fees are dropped to an insignificant figure or sometimes even eliminated, offering education at no cost for students' families. On the other hand, the state gives 'indirect subsidies', when it does not charge any (or some) taxes to private schools.

The process of privatization that took place during the past 40 years of the twentieth century has not been external to the state. Rather, the state continued to finance an important portion of private education through subsidies, which were not awarded by competitions or bids, nor were they subject to evaluation. The sums that are awarded are not small: for example, in 2001, 19 per cent of the total economic resources that were destined for education in Buenos Aires City were directly transferred to the private sector without using any public mechanisms to decide which schools should benefit from the scheme.

Since the 1980s, strong criticism has appeared in the press and in public opinion towards the increasing privatization of education and towards the deterioration of the public school system. It was quite clear that the state was having serious difficulties in sustaining an efficient provision of educational services. The sense of educational crisis and a call for educational reform were rapidly increasing. It was only in the 1990s, however, that educational problems were given a central position in the political agenda and a reform of the system was initiated, as in most countries in Latin America.

Argentine educational policy in the 1990s has been based on seven principles (Gvirtz 2005):

- An increase in public investment in education.
- The decentralization of macro-political decisions in education from the national state to each one of the 24 provinces.
- The reform of the structure of the system.

- The strengthening of educational institutions.
- The design of common basic contents.
- The promotion of in-service training for teachers.
- The creation of a national system of evaluation.

Each of these will be addressed in turn.

Public investment

Even though research has suggested that increasing investment in an educational system does not imply its improvement, the problem of educational investment has been permanently present in the governmental agendas of the 1990s, especially in Argentina. The *Ley Federal de Educación* in 1993 established that total public investment in education should be doubled in five years, at a minimum rate of 20 per cent per year starting in 1993. In addition, this should guarantee an increase in enrolments at the primary and secondary levels.

As can be seen in Table 38.1, through the 1990s investments in education grew both at the basic and higher education levels (except for higher education in 1991). However, the growth in investments in higher education is greater than in basic education. The accumulated annual rate is almost double for higher education. Thus, it can be said that at the governmental level there is a greater interest in higher education.

Comparing investments in the different jurisdictions during the same period shows that, by 1991, the provinces had increased their investments in education. However, since 1992, provincial expenditures have gradually started to decline while, at the same time, they have increased at the national level (Table 38.2).

Decentralization

Since the 1960s the national state has started to withdraw from the provincial jurisdictions. Two laws were passed – the last one in 1991 – transferring all schools administered by the national state to the provinces. These laws were designed to redistribute the roles and responsibilities for education between the

Table 38.1   Total public investment in million pesos in education, culture, and Science and Technology, 1980–1999

Year	Basic education	Higher education (including universities)
1980	5,425	1,214
1991	5,618	1,192
1992	6,222	1,546
1993	7,051	1,837
1994	7,525	1,949
1995	7,252	2,185
1996	7,365	2,240
1997	8,214	2,272
1998	8,445	2,465
1999	9,136	2,641
Var.% 99/80	68.4%	117.5%
Var.% 99/91	62.6%	121.6%
Accumulated annual rate 99/91	7.8%	15.2%

Source: Analysis of alternatives for financing basic education through federal fiscal institutions. Universidad Torcuato Di Tella-Ministerio de Cultura y Educación de la Nación. Juan Pablo Nicolini, Pablo Sanguinetti, y Juan Sanguinetti. Final Report. August, 2000

Table 38.2   Public investment in education, culture, and science and technology (as a percentage of total expenditures) by governmental level, 1980–1999

Year	National	Provincial	Municipal
1980	48.3	49.6	2.0
1991	36.0	61.9	2.1
1992	21.9	76.1	2.0
1993	22.5	75.5	2.0
1994	22.8	74.9	2.3
1995	23.1	74.3	2.5
1996	23.4	73.2	3.4
1997	23.4	73.6	2.9
1998	22.8	74.2	3.0
1999	23.0	74.0	3.0

Source: Analysis of alternatives for financing basic education through Federal fiscal institutions. Universidad Torcuato Di Tella-Ministerio de Cultura y Educación de la Nación. Juan Pablo Nicolini, Pablo Sanguinetti, y Juan Sanguinetti. Final Report. August, 2000

nation and the provinces and to organize a federal educational system. The *Ley Federal de Educación* (Argentina 1993) also aimed at the federalization of the system. However, by 2004 some jurisdictions had yet to pass their own laws of education.

'Decentralization' can be defined as the delegation of the capacity to operate and of real power for decision-making. Meanwhile, 'de-concentration' is the delegation of certain functions to organizations that are not autonomous, but rather kept under direct control of the central power (Hervia 1991). Thus, the changes that occurred in Argentine education

in the 1990s are closer to a 'de-concentration' of certain functions than to a decentralization. Some researchers (Llach et al. 1999) refer to this process as the '*provincialization* of education', which intensified the problems related to the financing of public education. This was partly due to an increase in expenditure in intermediate bureaucracies.

Meanwhile, other processes were taking place in the private sector. The *Ley Federal de Educación* placed public and private schools at the same level: both were defined as 'public schools', but with different 'types of administration'. However, these schools not only have different types of administration, but they are also subject to different rules. Private schools that do not receive subsidies from the state are not subject to restrictions imposed by provincial authorities (for example, they do not have to comply with the official school calendar). Private schools were included within the transfer of educational services from the nation to the provinces. However, while the public schools had to adapt to the modalities, plans and structures of the provinces, private schools only had to adapt their structures, since the provinces were forced to accept the different characteristics (extracurricular subjects, optional services, school uniforms, etc.) of the institutions that they received. Finally, the provinces were required to maintain the subsidies to private schools that were benefiting from this scheme at the national level. The provinces were not allowed to reconsider each specific case according to their particular educational needs.

Reform of the structure

One of the most significant changes introduced by the *Ley Federal de Educación* was the design of a new structure for the Argentine educational system. The new configuration extended compulsory education from seven to ten years. Initial Education has been made compulsory in its last year, and the seven years of primary education have been replaced by General Basic Education (EGB), which consists of nine years of compulsory instruction divided into three-year cycles. Finally, *Polimodal*, a post-compulsory level that lasts three years, has replaced a five-year secondary education.

These changes have resulted in operational difficulties in public schools, since most of these institutions were either primary or secondary schools. Even in the case of schools that catered for both the primary and secondary levels, these were generally offered in separate buildings. These buildings needed to be refurbished, and in many cases classrooms had to be added in parts of the buildings that were unsuitable for this kind of room. The extension of compulsory education implied an increase in enrolments and, thus, the need for larger facilities.

On the contrary, the new structure of the educational system did not cause many problems for private institutions. Since most private schools already offered primary and secondary education (and in some cases also initial education), the adaptation to the new structure implied a new format that did not have an effect on the fundamental nature of institutions. Furthermore, private schools were not affected by the expansion of enrolments, since the middle and higher sectors of society normally continued in the educational system until they finished secondary education.

The new structure was implemented differently in different provinces. Therefore, various ways of organizing educational trajectories coexisted in the 24 Argentine provinces that used to have the same educational structure. In the first place, some jurisdictions still maintain the traditional division into a seven years primary school and a five or six years secondary school (Buenos Aires City). Others divide educational routes into two sets of two cycles each, annexing the third cycle of EGB to secondary education. Finally, a third position, in compliance with the *Ley Federal de Educación*, establishes three cycles of General Basic Education and a three-year *Polimodal* (Province of Buenos Aires).

Strengthening of educational institutions

Another of the central proposals in the educational reform of the 1990s was the strengthening of educational institutions. Until the 1990s, every strategy for educational change in Argentina had concentrated on changing the curricula and on reforming teacher education. Schools were considered to be a group of teachers that had to execute the directives of the national or provincial states. The system was hierarchical, rigid and organized in a clearly vertical structure. Supervisors received the orders from the central organizations, which held the monopoly for decision-making. Then, the supervisors would transmit these orders to school principals. These would then instruct the teachers, who had to execute the orders. The supervisor and principal of each school not only transmitted orders, but they also had to control the execution of these mandates. They observed lessons, they read students' notebooks and inspected teachers' plans. They were the guarantors of the compliance to the orders of the central powers.

The reforms of the 1990s were aimed at changing this hierarchical and vertical structure of the educational system. These reforms proposed a certain degree of autonomy for schools, so that some decisions, like selecting some of the contents of instruction, could be made at the institutional level. In return, schools were required to present to the authorities their own 'Institutional Project'. The 'Institutional Projects' were proposals for change designed in each school. All of the actors involved in an institution were required to participate in the design of the Project. They were divided in groups and had to decide on such aspects as the management of the school, the administration of resources, the assessment of students, the relations with the community, etc. They were encouraged to base their decisions on the priorities and problems of each particular school, but they had to respect the general guidelines established by the national state.

Consequently, the sequence and organization of curricular contents and the rhythm and method of teaching varied from one school to another according to their institutional differences. In this sense, the existence of these Projects implies a depoliticization of school practices: principals and teachers are no longer seen as members of the state apparatus, subject to political control. Instead, they are seen as professionals, subject to local and communitarian control.

However, the legal framework has not been changed (for example, teachers are not chosen at the school level – by the principal; they are appointed at the central level and imposed on the school). Supervisors and principals were not assigned new roles, and an information system that would allow schools that perform well to be distinguished from schools that do not perform so well has not been established.

In addition, current literature has shown that even though the design of Institutional Projects has been made compulsory for schools, this has not been followed by processes that encouraged real autonomy in schools – which were accustomed to a vertical structure (Andrada 2002). In this context, Institutional Projects became yet another set of bureaucratic documents that the central administration required from schools. Far from fostering the participation of teachers and teamwork, Projects were in most cases written by principals with the sole objective of presenting the documents to their superiors.

Both the national state and the provinces invested great amounts of money in publishing a number of documents (some consisting of four volumes of more than 1,000 pages each) that were meant to teach the principals how to design an Institutional Project. However, since the overall legal frame was not altered, schools did not gain much real autonomy. The traditional model of administration overpowered the principle of school autonomy, and with it, the Institutional Projects.

Common basic contents

Argentine educational policy in the 1990s included the implementation of a new curricular reform. This reform has its particularities when compared to past curricular changes. As has been mentioned above, until the 1990s programmes and curricula for different educational levels were designed with great detail by national or provincial states. Teachers had to restrict their lessons strictly to the contents included within these documents and they also had to follow the sequence that was established. Some curricular documents even defined the activities that the teacher should perform in the classroom in order to transmit the contents. The curricular design of Buenos Aires City in 1981 was one of the clearest cases of 'curricular hyper-prescription' (De Titto 2002).

The curricular reform of the 1990s not only changed the contents that had to be taught, it was also aimed at redesigning the relation between the national state, the provincial states, teachers and contents. The general proposal of the curricular reform, following the *provincialization* of educational services, was to leave in the hands of the provinces the responsibility for curricular design. On the other hand, in order to guarantee minimal common contents for all Argentine students, common basic contents (CBC) were designed. These were to be used as guidelines for the design of provincial curricula.

The National Ministry of Education produced these contents, which were then approved by the *Consejo Federal de Educación* (formed by the ministers of education of each of the Argentine provinces). Common basic contents were designed for Initial Education, General Basic Education, *Polimodal* and for Teacher Education.

Even though these contents were supposed to act as guidelines for the design of the actual curricula in the provinces and then in the institutions, in practice, they became the new curricular design used by schools. A number of reasons can explain this situation:

- The contents were not defined for each year, but for three-year cycles. As far as different readings of 'minimum' contents could be done, they could be seen as being quite flexible. However, so many contents were considered to be 'basic', that it became almost impossible for schools to teach anything other than the basic contents.
- Once the basic common contents were approved, they were not sent to the provincial educational authorities. Instead, the CBC were distributed directly to all schools in the country.
- At the same time, some provinces did not modify their curricular designs because they thought that they already complied with the CBC, whilst those that did change their curricula took several years to do so.
- When public school teachers received the CBC in their schools, they followed the traditional logic of the Argentine educational system, considering this document to be the curriculum that they had to follow.
- Publishing companies could not adapt to each of the provincial markets. Consequently, they published the same textbooks – based on the CBC – for every province.
- Due to the harsh criticisms that were being made of the traditional educational system, the private schools wanted to lead the reform, so they appropriated the CBC as the contents that they should transmit.

In summary, the CBC were taken as the new curricula in Argentine schools. As a result of the slowness in defining the details of the curricula in the provinces and in schools, the new textbooks performed, in some ways, this function and became a guide for teachers when planning their lessons (Gvirtz and Beech 2004).

In-service training for teachers

In-service training for teachers was another of the strategies used in the reforms of the 1990s for attaining real change in the educational system. New contents, a new structure and new roles for the schools required teachers with new capacities. A massive scheme of in-service training was planned to include all of the 650,000 teachers in the system. The scheme was coordinated by the *Red Federal de Formación Docente Continua* (Federal Net for Continuous Teacher Training), which had been created by the National Ministry of Education (Argentina 1994).

The massive scheme was based on a credit system. The number of credits that each course would award participants depended on the length (in time) of the course, and not on what the teachers actually learned. In order for a course to be part of the credit system, it had to be authorized by the *Red*, but the authorization system was far from being clear and transparent. Consequently, the courses that were offered to teachers were not related to the needs of the reform. Instead, it was the lobbying capacity of the teachers who attended the courses, or of the institutions that offered them, that determined the inclusion of a given course within the scheme.

Since the public schools never became the 'agents of change', teachers attended courses to improve their individual careers, not considering the needs of the school in which they worked. The School of Teacher Training of Buenos Aires City offered courses such as tango, folklore and handicrafts for teachers of any discipline, and awarded many credits to those who attended. The criteria for selecting the lecturers who taught in this school were not transparent, even though many of these lecturers were respected professionals. It can be said that teacher training has been one of the weakest aspects of the reform.

Creation of an evaluation system

One more principle that was central to the political agenda of the 1990s was the creation of an evaluation system. Before the reform – and for more than 100 years – the state had tried to guarantee the performance of the Argentine educational system by regulating teaching methods through a unified curriculum and through the daily control of principals and supervisors over teachers' work. After the reform, the state intended to guarantee the performance by evaluating what pupils had learned. The National System of Evaluation (SINEC) was created within the National Ministry of Education (see Argentina 2002). Consequently, evaluation programmes are periodically conducted to assess the learning that takes place in schools, municipalities, or provinces. This, of course, allows for comparisons to be made.

Differently from what happens in other countries – such as Chile for example – in Argentina no rankings of schools are published. Thus, the evaluation system did not introduce a competitive element in the Argentine educational system. Paradoxically, even though the tests were conducted on samples of students, the National Ministry awarded prizes to those schools that had obtained the best results, saying they were the best schools in the system. However, it was quite clear that the Ministry could not know that these were the best schools in the system, since not all students nor all schools had been evaluated. At the same time, some schools that had obtained good results became sites for internships or technical assistance for other schools, which in some cases had not been evaluated.

The culture of evaluation, which was initially resisted by teacher unions, has been established in Argentine education. However,

it has never been very clear, from the state policies, what kind of use should be made of the results of these evaluations, and this resulted in technical problems in the evaluation system.

On the other hand, the National Ministry of Education has retained the responsibility for conducting the evaluations. This has implied that the usual defects of the state bureaucratic administration, such as lack of transparency and limited federal participation, have been transferred to the evaluation system (Llach et al. 1999; Narodowski et al. 2001).

CONCLUSION

The Argentine case is just one example of the ways in which the local reformulates the global, where institutional and political cultures affect proposals put forward by international agencies. The diversity of public policies which resulted from a similar group of proposals in Latin America in the 1990s provides evidence of the need to identify a precise diagnosis of each situation and study the global–local relation in its complexity.

International agencies and other actors in the academic and political world set discursive limits and define certain issues in the political agenda which act as boundaries to reflect upon current problems. Yet, the ways in which these subjects are captured in each country and each region vary significantly from one to another.

Thus, countries like Chile and Nicaragua have implemented demand subsidy systems, whereas other Latin American countries differ greatly from these financing mechanisms. Regarding the centralization–decentralization issue, Chile has introduced a dual system in which the economic and financial matters have been decentralized and pedagogical decisions remain relatively concentrated at the central level. In this same topic, Argentina has 'provincialized' both the economic and pedagogical spheres, as opposed to Peru, where this problem has only recently reached the political agenda. The case of Colombia adds a different feature to the situation, where –

despite its intention to decentralize towards subnational levels of government – only 10 per cent of the Colombian territory is operating with the new system. Brazil, on the other hand, has policies that vary greatly from state to state, as can be seen in the cases of Porto Alegre and Minas Gerais.

What is certainly clear from this situation is that the government institutional designs corresponding to each educational system have a strong influence on the international proposals. The alterations in local policies produced by these influences have resulted in different scenarios which vary from situations where policies have been adapted to the 'global model', to others where there has been an overlaying of policies, and cases in which these proposals have been co-opted by traditional policy features. Ignoring the specificity of these processes suggests ignoring the fact that there are two sides to this growing internationalization process.

REFERENCES

Andrada, M. (2002) Autogestión y autonomía de la institución escolar moderna. *Finalidades, estrategias y regulaciones en el sistema educativo de la Provincia de Buenos Aires (1993–2000)* [Purposes, strategies and regulations in the educational system of the Province of Buenos Aires]. Masters in Sociology thesis Facultad Latinoamericana de Ciencias Sociales, Buenos Aires.

Argentina (1993a) *Ley Federal de Educación* [Federal Law of Education]. No. 24, 195.

Argentina (1993b) Ministerio de Educación de la Nación and Consejo Federal de Cultura y Educación, Argentina. *Resolución N. 31/93 C.F.C.Y E.*

Argentina (1993c) Comisión Nacional de Evaluación Universitaria [National Commission for the Evaluation of Universities] (accessed July 2006).

Argentina (1994) *Red Federal de Formación Docente Continua* [Federal Net for Continuous Teacher Training]. Ministerio de Educación y Cultura de la Nación.

Argentina (1995) *Ley de Educación Superior* [Higher Education Law]. No. 24, 521.

Argentina (1996a) Ministerio de Educación, Argentina, *Contenidos Básicos Comunes Para La Educación Polimodal* [General Basic Contents for Polimodal Education]. Available from www.me.gov.ar/consejo/

documentos/cbc/polimodal/cbcep/ (accessed July 2006).

Argentina (1996b) Ministerio de Educación, Argentina, *Contenidos Básicos Comunes Para La Formación Docente* [Common Basic Contents for Teacher Training] www.me.gov.ar/consejo/documentos/cbc/formación_docente/cbctodonivell.pdf (accessed July 2006)

Argentina (2002) Instituto Nacional de la Administración Pública *Evaluación En La Gestión Pública: Caso Del Sistema Nacional De Evaluación Educativa [Evaluation in Public Administration: The Case of the National System of Evaluation of Education]* www.inap.gov.ar/publicaciones/publ_activ_elect/publ_estudios/evalua~2.pdf (accessed July 2006).

Ball, S. (1998) Big policies/small world: an introduction to international perspectives in education policy. *Comparative Education*, 34 (2): 119–29.

Beech, J. (2005) International agencies, educational discourse, and the reform of teacher education in Argentina and Brazil (1985–2002): a comparative analysis. Unpublished PhD thesis, Institute of Education, University of London.

Braslavsky, C. and Gvirtz, S. (2002) Nuevos desafíos y dispositivos en la política educacional Latinoamericana de fin de siglo [New challenges and devices in Latin American educational policy at the end of the century]. In *Cuadernos de la OEI: Educación Comparada*. Madrid: Organización de Estados Iberoamericanos para la Educación, la Ciencia y la Cultura (OEI).

Brazil (1996) *Lei De Diretrizes E Bases Da Educação* [Law of Guidelines and Foundations of Education]. Available from www.presidencia.gov.br/ccivil_03/Leis/L9394.htm (accessed July 2006).

Cano, D. (1985) *La Educación Superior en la Argentina* [Higher Education in Argentina]. Buenos Aires: Facultad Latinoamericana de Ciencias Sociales.

Carnoy, M. (1999) Globalization and educational reform: what planners need to know. In *Fundamentals of Educational Planning*. París: UNESCO–International Institute for Educational Planning.

Carnoy, M. and Castells, M. (2001) Globalization, the knowledge society, and the network state: poulantzas at the millennium, *Global Networks* 1 (1): 1–18.

De Titto, Raúl (2002) *Las políticas curriculares y la práctica docente. La Ciudad de Buenos Aires entre 1960 y 1990.* [Curricular policies and teaching practices. The City of Buenos Aires between 1960 and 1990]. Thesis for Masters in Education, University of San Andrés, Argentina.

Giddens, A. (1990) *The Consequences of Modernity.* Cambridge: Polity Press, p. 65.

Gvirtz, S. (2005) *De la tragedia a la esperenza. Hacia un sistera educavito justo*, democrátito y de calidad [from tragedy to a just and democratic education system]. Buenos Aires: Academia Nacional de Educacion.

Gvirtz, S. and Beech, J. (2004) From the intended to the implemented curriculum in Argentina: exploring the relation between regulation and practice. *Prospects,* 34 (3).

Gvirtz, S. and Larripa, S. (2002) Reforming school curricula in Latin America: a focus on Argentina. In S. Tawil (ed.) *Curriculum Change and Social Inclusion: Perspectives from the Baltic and Scandinavian Countries.* Geneva: IBE–UNESCO.

Hervia, R. (1991) *Política de descentralización en la educación básica y media en América Latina.* Santiago: UNESCO/REDUC.

Llach, J., Montoya, S. and Roldan, F. (1999) *Educación para todos* [Education for All]. Buenos Aires: Ieral.

Martinez Boom, A. (2000) Políticas educativas en Iberoamérica [Education Policies in Iberoamerica]. In *Cuadernos de la OEI: Educación Comparada.* Madrid: Organización de Estados Iberoamericanos para la Educación, la Ciencia y la Cultura (OEI).

Mayor F. and Tanguiane S. (1994) *UNESCO – an Ideal in Action: The Continuing Relevance of a Visionary Text.* Paris: UNESCO, p. 84.

Morduchowicz, A., Marcón, A., Iglesias, G., Andrada, M., Pérez, J., Victoria, A. and Duro, L. (1999) *La Educación Privada en la Argentina: Historia, Regulaciones, y Asignación de Recursos Públicos* [Private Education in Argentina: History, Regulations and the Allocation of Public Resources]. Serie Documentos de Trabajo, No. 38. (Buenos Aires, Fundación Gobierno y Sociedad).

Narodowski, M. and Nores, M. (2000) *Quiénes quedan y quienes salen? Características socioeconómicas en las escuelas públicas y privadas de la Argentina* [Who remains and who exits? Socioeconomic features of public and private schools in Argentina]. Buenos Aires: Fundación Gobierno y Sociedad.

Narodowski, M., Nores, M. and Andrada, M. (2001) *Nuevas Tendencias en Políticas Educativas* [New Tendencies in Educational Policies]. Buenos Aires: Granica.

Nicolinil, J.P., Sanguinetti, P. and Sanguinetti, J. (2000) *Análisis de alternativas de financiamiento de la educación básica en Argentina en el marco de las instituciones fiscales federales* [An analysis of alternatives in the financing of education within fiscal federal institutions]. Buenos Aires: Ministerio de Educación.

OEI (Organización de Estados Iberoamericanos para la Educación, la Ciencia y la Cultura) (2004) *Observatorio Para La Educación Iberoamericana.* Available from www.oei.es/observatorio/leyes.htm (accessed July 2006).

UNESCO (2006) Institute for Statistics. Available from www.uis.unesco.org (accessed 2006).

Van Gelderen, A. (1996) *La Ley Federal de Educación de la República Argentina* [Federal Law of Education of the Argentine Republic]. Buenos Aires: Academia Nacional de Educación. pp. 2, 55.

39

The Impact of Globalization on Higher Education

Daphne Hobson

Globalization has had a profound effect on both the mission and the goals of higher education throughout the world. The accelerated developments of instantaneous communication, multinational organizations and worldwide travel have significantly influenced the ideologies, curricula, enrolment, outreach and economic viability of universities. This chapter attempts to summarize these trends and to offer thoughts on the changing identity of the tertiary university.

THE CHALLENGE

The enormous and unprecedented, international, economic expansion that followed the Second World War transformed higher education from a luxury into a critical prerequisite for advanced nation-building. In the postwar environment, governments expected, and indeed required, universities to contribute to economic progress, equality, democratization and the social betterment of the nation-state. The Cold War made it impossible for countries to ignore international awareness as a higher educational priority. More recently, the collapse of the Soviet Union and the onset of the international Information Age have forced tertiary institutions to reinvent themselves.

Today's globalized world is not only interconnected, but also highly competitive. The global contest is at once economic, political and social, as organizations and governments vie for market share not only of products and services, but also of ideas and values. The contest on the ground is most directly played out among fully multinational global enterprises. The nation-state – itself an old-fashioned notion and by definition not multinational – and its university system must struggle to find ways to cope by both collaborating and competing (Friedman 2000). Indeed, one of the basic questions facing universities today is whether to form partnerships or to go it alone. Higher education is confronting a series of conflicting challenges that offer an opportunity for the sector to reexamine its mission and purpose. Nearly 200 international educators from nine nations listed the following global trends through to 2025 (Parker et al. 1999):

- The economic gap among countries and between people within countries will widen significantly.

- Information technologies will significantly reduce the privacy of individuals.
- Inequalities between those with access to information technologies and those without it will increase dramatically.
- Conflicts of interest between developing and developed nations will increase as a result of environmental deterioration. The costs of obtaining necessary supplies of water will rise dramatically as a result of population growth and environmental deterioration.
- In developing countries, population growth will result in a dramatic increase in the percentage of people, especially children, living in poverty. Individuals, families and communities will lose political influence due to increased levels of regulation and control by governments.
- It will be increasingly difficult to develop a shared belief of what constitutes the common good. Drug-related crime will increasingly dominate social life in urban areas. People's sense of community and social responsibility will decline significantly. Consumerism will increasingly dominate social life. Genetic engineering will create more complex ethical questions.

A number of studies have tried to predict future educational needs. The Organization for Economic Co-operation and Development (OECD) identified five strategic challenges facing the world's education system (Zajda 2005: 23):

1 A reconceptualization of teaching.
2 Creating high performance.
3 Building capacity and managing knowledge.
4 Establishing new partnerships.
5 Reinventing the role of government.

Higher education has responded to these educational, economic and informational challenges in a number of ways. These include rethinking and restating mission and goals, initiating new programmes, reforming curricula and adopting a more entrepreneurial approach to the delivery of knowledge. These approaches are discussed below.

MISSION AND GOALS

Clearly, the competitive atmosphere spawned by globalization has created the need for better-educated students and graduates. As articulated by US Secretary of Education Margaret Spellings in spring 2005, the message is simple: 'In today's global economy, the best jobs go to the most skilled and most motivated workers. Over 80 per cent of the fastest-growing jobs require at least some postsecondary education. That means a college education is more important than ever.' (Spellings 2005). According to Stanford University professor Sven Groennings, an 'outside–inside' tradition has divided international studies at the higher educational level into two distinct domains. On the one hand, cultural diplomacy and nation-building involved the university in world affairs. In this loose sense, the university and the nation-state shared an overlapping domain. In addition, a second domain sought to promote awareness of international issues through specific curricular offerings within certain academic disciplines such as political science, economics and history, or on an interdisciplinary basis, notably through area studies (Groennings 1989: 10).

This traditional split can either encumber or enhance the redefinition of mission and terms. Today, to take full advantage of the latest globalizing trend, institutions may have to redefine, depart from or even abandon this traditional model for a unified strategy touching all aspects of the educational enterprise. Educators of all stripes – scholars, researchers and administrators – are struggling with the questions of what students need, not only to perform successfully in the fast-changing world economy, but also to become fully realized and responsible global citizens. Universities are looking at ways to reframe what they do, integrating traditional liberal arts and professional training with global preparedness. According to Lyn Carter, 'It is the responsibility of education to explore the way globalization constructs contemporary education' (Carter 2005: 742). Below is a sampling of how major universities have emphasized the importance of internationalism and globalism. Some institutions have reexamined, modified or changed their missions and goals since the events of September 11, 2001, a defining global moment that, among other things, unleashed a torrent of international discussion about Samuel Huntington's famous 'Clash of Civilizations'.

In the USA, Columbia University has a long international tradition, having been a leader in transcultural and international education since the days of John Dewey. Columbia's mission statement reads as follows:

> Columbia University is one of the world's most important centers of research and at the same time a distinctive and distinguished learning environment for undergraduates and graduate students in many scholarly and professional fields … It seeks to attract a diverse and international faculty and student body, to support research and teaching on global issues, and to create academic relationships with many countries and regions … and to convey the products of its efforts to the world. (*About Columbia* 2006)

The University of Edinburgh in Scotland is one of the oldest universities in the UK. Its mission statement focuses on bringing international standards to a national mandate:

> The University's mission is the advancement and dissemination of knowledge and understanding. As a leading international centre of academic excellence, the University has as its core mission: to sustain and develop its position as a research and teaching institution of the highest international quality and to benchmark its performance against world-class standards … As a great civic university, Edinburgh especially values its intellectual and economic relationship with the Scottish community that forms its base and provides the foundation from which it will continue to look to the widest international horizons, enriching both itself and Scotland. (University of Edinburgh 2006)

Korea University, located in Seoul, South Korea, is well aware of the need to globalize students to meet the demands of this century. Its statement emphasizes global citizenry and the importance of the international information highway:

> Educational boundaries between disciplines and traditional major areas of study are merging to meet the multidisciplinary and multicultural needs of life in a global society. And global information networks are gradually tearing down technological boundaries that once separated the rich nations from the poor … Korea University embraces the challenges of the 21st Century by building new

bridges across old boundaries. These bridges include new educational programs that stress … new international relationships that bring Korea University students together with students, faculty and programs of other leading universities around the world. Aggressive investments in new research facilities, information systems and infrastructure give these bridges the strength and flexibility to extend far into the next century. (Korea University 2006)

PROGRAMMES AND INITIATIVES

Backed by effective leadership within the institution, such mission statements can give both definition and impetus to wholesale policy choices centred on globalizing the learning community. Some universities are adding and changing undergraduate requirements. In some cases, academic departments are receiving financial incentives to infuse their curricula with coverage of the key transborder issues of our time – terrorism, trade, pandemics, global warming, environmental degradation, etc. Federal government money, from such programmes as the Abraham Lincoln Study Abroad Fellowship Program and the Ron Brown Fellowship Program, provides financial assistance for many new initiatives. Below are examples of specific innovations implemented by US universities in their efforts to define new academic agendas for the twenty-first century.

Lehigh University, a medium-sized private institution in the northeast United States, has promulgated seven goals, five of which mention the importance of international perspectives and relationships. The school's first goal states: 'First and foremost, Lehigh must strive to be a true university and not simply a research institute … The Lehigh community should be inclusive and both welcoming and supportive to those of differing races, cultures and backgrounds. It also should strive to be international in its people, programmes and outlook …' (*Seven Goals for Lehigh* 2006). In the four colleges at Lehigh (Liberal Arts, Business, Education and Engineering), international relationships and opportunities have been established. The Global Council, the Global Citizens Programme, the Global Union, International Programmes and Exchange and Study Abroad are just a few of the initiatives connecting students to the world beyond Lehigh's campus and national borders.

Other colleges and universities are also broadening international opportunities in creative ways. Duke University, for example, has taken giant steps to internationalize its school community. An administrative team has been created to oversee the university's globalization push and to allocate the financial resources necessary to help it succeed. Duke says it is now possible for all its undergraduates to study abroad 'regardless of economic circumstances' (*Securing America's Future* 2003). The SOCRATES and ERASMUS initiatives are fully funded European Union programmes to support students studying in Europe (Europa 2002). Many major EU universities are in the process of establishing a common curriculum and degree requirement structure to encourage students to study in countries other than their own. Some Far East governments, such as those of Singapore and Thailand, are seriously funding higher education, and large companies, such as Petronas, a major oil company in the Far East, are supporting tuition costs for undergraduate students in order to create a better-educated workforce. Universities, especially Western ones, are clearly shifting their agendas. Despite pressures to cap escalating costs, capital has begun to flow to global initiatives from federal governments, international organizations and private donors.

CURRICULAR REFORM

The function of higher education has shifted from a critical function to a more pragmatic role in providing qualified manpower and the production of knowledge. (Gibbons 1998:1)

Internally, many universities are looking at ways to reframe their curricula, integrating traditional liberal arts and professional training with global preparedness. In a 1994 global

survey of the field, Arnove and Torres identified 81 university programmes and centres in 21 countries on all continents that had at least one full-time equivalent staff member and taught at least four graduate courses in comparative and international education (1999: 12). It is important to note that this study was conducted more than 12 years ago, well before the dramatic post-9/11 shift in the geopolitical climate. Similarly, Altbach and Davis wrote in 1999, 'A comparative and global approach to thinking about higher education benefits everyone – the experience of one country may not directly be relevant to another, but issues and solutions touch many nations' (1999). Jane Knight (1991) provided a template for universities to integrate an international, intercultural and comparative dimension to their academic programmes. The model is divided into four areas: academic programmes; research and scholarly collaboration; external relations; and services and extracurricular activities. The model was developed for institutions to examine and assess their own international activities and as a guide for campuses worldwide to advance their globalization initiatives in a reasonably uniform manner. Knight's academic programmes include strategies relating to student exchange, foreign language study, international curricula, area and thematic studies, international students and joint and double degree programmes. Research and scholarly collaborations include international research agreements, international conferences and seminars, area and theme centres and international research partners in academic and other sectors. External relations and services include partnerships and projects involving multicultural and intercultural components. This section of the template also includes organizing off-shore sites and distance education. The last category – extracurricular activities – includes international and intercultural campus events and clubs as well as social, cultural and academic support systems (Knight and de Witt 1999: 24).

As early as 1981, Eurich identified five common curricular changes occurring in higher education throughout the world:

- the importance of teaching
- the practical experience and career orientation
- multidisciplinary approaches
- fewer study periods
- new communication media.

These changes continue to challenge colleges and universities in the twenty-first century. The first focuses on the importance of teaching, where many countries have problems. There is a shortage of qualified teachers at all levels in virtually all national systems. Much attention is being given to providing institutions with qualified teachers, what Eurich calls 'the knowledge holders' (1989: 121). Mexico, for example, is burdened with too many part-time teaching faculty, and is trying to solve this problem. In the Middle East, many countries struggle with a lack of qualified professionals and a dependence on foreign faculty. Thailand has tried to train its own teachers, so far without success. Knowledge providers are increasingly becoming a premium commodity. A second shift in curriculum involves providing practical experience and career orientation. Many institutions are establishing certificate and short credit programmes to emphasize lifelong learning. Internships and practice periods, traditionally associated with teaching and medical training, are spreading into many other professions.

Programmes in multidisciplinary studies have also become quite popular. These programmes have changed the way higher education is delivering and altering content. Centres are common on today's campuses, with Global Citizenship Centres particularly in vogue. In some countries, centres have been created to study national issues. For example, Thailand established institutes designed to examine social problems and concerns such as population control. Saudi Arabia has developed a network of institute training centres to address employment needs – a trend that is spreading to other Arab states as well. Five prominent Australian universities have broken down the traditional barriers between disciplines and created more integrated programmes. Clearly, higher education institutions are creating new programmes of

study both to examine international issues and to educate students about global concerns.

The fourth common curricular change is the amount of time needed to offer and complete courses and prepare professionals. Universities are offering intensive week-long courses, mini weekend courses, travel credit courses, etc. An undergraduate can complete a degree in less than four years if he or she is willing to engage in these time-efficient learning modules. Germany, for instance, has so many students awaiting entrance that they have tried to shorten periods of learning in order to accommodate the massive numbers of incoming students. Learners are eager to complete their studies and move on, and universities and colleges are evolving to respond to these demands.

The last common curricular trend, new communication media such as Internet education, should come as no surprise. Britain's Open University (OU), which provides such education throughout the world, was one of the first institutions to offer online degrees. Other countries have followed suit. Japan's University of the Air offers a Bachelor's degree. In the USA, the University of Phoenix has followed the Open University and now has campuses throughout the globe in addition to its online offerings. It is expensive, however, and subject to rapid change. Nonetheless, technology is central to information storage and retrieval. Obviously, the use of technology is at its early stages but does have the greatest potential for transformational change in education, especially at the tertiary level (Altbach and Davis 1999).

These five major curricular changes are challenging higher education by posing questions about the dissemination of information and about what knowledge should be taught. Change, innovation, global concerns and needs, and technological advances will continue the paradigm curricula shift in higher education. The traditional institution, offering learning for learning's sake, is disappearing.

ENTREPRENEURSHIP

Public expenditure on higher education is shrinking, and universities are looking at ways to bring in additional revenue (Tilak 2005). Importing students and exporting learning services have become clear revenue streams, as universities become increasingly entrepreneurial. They employ staff specifically to recruit foreign students and oversee international initiatives. They are forming partnerships and alliances to deliver offshore degree programmes. Higher education is taking advantage of new technology to reach a wider audience. In particular, universities are offering an increasing array of e-learning and distance learning options for students. (For more information on distance learning, see Chapter 16 by Dabbagh and Benson in this Handbook.) They are moving off campus as well, trying to meet their audience wherever they work and live. In Internet cafes, for example, people casually avail themselves of high-tech connectivity and the commoditization of knowledge, and can access a variety of online degrees at reasonable rates. Merrill Lynch has valued the global market for higher education at $15 billion (Rosen 2000). It is no wonder that international advisory boards and global task forces have sprouted like mushrooms at higher educational institutions. With a clear economic imperative to expand into the international arena, universities are pushing ahead, and the education race is on. Private entrepreneurs have begun competing with universities for revenue. In Scotland, education is the second biggest national industry after tourism. This has piqued the interest of businesspeople as they capitalize on Scottish educational products: courses, professors and course materials (Rosen 2000). For example, the Scottish Knowledge Company of Edinburgh markets knowledge-holders – people who have knowledge, have made contributions to a particular field and who happen to be Scottish – whether they live in Scotland or abroad. In Australia, Advanced Manufacturing Technologies Center (AMTC) of Perth is doing the same with Australian academics by combining university knowledge with commercial principles to create a learning commodity (Rosen 2000).

The information age has spawned new ways of marketing higher education, through both importing foreign students and exporting knowledge. Perhaps more than ever, knowledge is a bankable global commodity. It is not irrational, therefore, to imagine the eventual creation of a knowledge futures market. According to the Open Doors 2004 report on International Educational Exchange, international students injected $13.3 billion dollars into the US economy in 2004–05 through tuition, living expenses and other related costs (Davis and Chin 2004). The US Department of Commerce estimates that higher education is one of the five largest service sectors in terms of exports. The Open Doors 2004/2005 data reveal that 72 per cent of this funding comes from personal and family sources. Colleges and universities with large populations of foreign students – many if not most of whom are full-paying clients – generate additional revenue for their communities in the form of payment for supplies, transportation, health care and other support for themselves and accompanying family members (Davis and Chin 2004). The survey also indicates, however, that enrolment of international students declined 2.4 per cent in the USA since 9/11. The reasons vary, but relatively high tuition costs, difficulty in obtaining student visas and international competition, including a rise in the number of high-quality educational alternatives in students' home countries, are all contributing factors (Open Doors 2005). Restrictive US student visa policies in the wake of 9/11 prompted vociferous complaints from American university presidents. Thwarted international students turned to British Commonwealth countries, Europe and overseas-based American universities as an alternative (Altbach 2004: 24). The competition for these students remains fierce.

Because of the global race for higher education market share, an increasing number of universities have upgraded their overseas recruiting and have begun offering support services such as English instruction, counselling, technological support and international campus-wide events (Altbach 2004: 24). Partnerships between universities and governments, corporations, non-governmental organizations (NGOs) and other schools have transformed the role and responsibility of higher education. In the future, the most successful universities will likely be those that exhibit the greatest international activism and connectivity.

OFFSHORE INSTITUTIONS

Developing countries are turning to the West and Australia for assistance in creating competitive higher educational institutions. Australia is the world leader in exporting degree-granting programmes internationally (Symonds 2004). The world also has aggressive new knowledge importers. Their economies flush with cash, the United Arab Emirates, Kuwait and Qatar are all establishing university cities in partnership with established outside institutions in order to provide an ultra-modern, high-tech setting for the delivery of highest-quality knowledge in an integrated learning environment. In Qatar's Education City, Cornell University has opened a medical school, Georgetown University has replicated its own School of Foreign Service and a number of other US institutions also have presences. George Mason University, among others, will soon open a centre in the United Arab Emirates. INSEAD, a top graduate school of business long based outside Paris, France, opened a sister campus in Singapore aimed at capturing Far Eastern market share. Sylvan, a for-profit US company, bought control of Universidad de las Americas in Santiago five years ago and is now Chile's largest operator of private universities. Clearly, whether they negotiate with governments to provide knowledge services or whether they take the risk to go it alone, universities are crossing borders.

INTERNET AND E-LEARNING

As alluded to above, modernized, technology-based distance learning has also become big business. The Internet offers a knowledge highway available to anyone with access, and

eventual universal access may be taken as a given. David Gelernter predicted in *Forbes* magazine (2005) that when college-level courses are standardized and delivered electronically, '[t]he world of online teaching will blow wide open'. The result, according to Gelernter, will be a true free market in higher education. Of course, many institutions have already capitalized on this exploding market; among the biggest players are the Open University and the University of Phoenix. According to an article in the *US News and World Report* (Shea and Boser 2001), 90 per cent of American colleges and universities offer at least one course online.

Research shows that online learning is effective. Thomas Russell of North Carolina State University researched all types of distance learning and concluded that there was 'no significant difference between education inside and outside the conventional classroom'.

Gelernter emphasizes the ability of entrepreneurial educators to patch courses together with an assortment of virtual contributors. Locale is irrelevant; finding the best and the brightest to participate is not. The best scholars and teachers will be able to 'peddle knowledge around the world'. Students will be free to shop for an online education from an assortment of suppliers as emerging degree-granting organizations offer and issue credentials worthy of global recognition – and to an evolving international standard of excellence (Gelernter 2005).

STUDY ABROAD AND EXCHANGES

International education exchange is the most significant current project designed to continue the process of humanizing mankind to the point, we would hope, that nations can learn to live in peace (J. William Fulbright, in *About Fulbright* 2006)

We support transnational academic mobility for students, faculty and scholars, including the unfettered freedom of cross-border exchanges of people and ideas. International education is an integral part of higher education. (Halkidiki Declaration, UNESCO 2002)

Governments throughout the world have long encouraged university-bound students to venture abroad in pursuit of deep and lasting knowledge that will contribute to the national agenda. In response, an array of traditional and non-traditional exchange and study abroad programmes has been established over the years for both undergraduate and graduate students. The field is rich and varied. Traditional programmes engage students experientially while allowing them to progress academically. These programmes can be for a semester, a year or even short-term classes or events occurring during inter-sessions (breaks) or summers. In addition, there are internship programmes, academic international global majors and minors in a variety of disciplines. Finally, universities have taken advantage of technological advances and greatly enhanced their distance education offerings. These programs adroitly cross borders to include international students. According to the National Association of Foreign Student Affairs (NAFSA), education abroad improves returned-student classroom performance, positively assists students' development and helps students become contributing and empathetic global citizens (Hoffa and Pearson 1997).

The value of these educational goals should not be underestimated. In addition to one-way study abroad, student and faculty exchanges have increased dramatically with globalization. The movement was successfully bolstered by such initiatives as the Fulbright and Rhodes scholarship programmes in the USA and UK and by the US Peace Corps (Hoffa and Pearson 1997). Faculties at various universities regularly collaborate on small projects with international colleagues and institutions. A number of government agencies, such as the US Agency for International Development (USAID) and various NGOs, sponsor projects that encourage international exchange. Aggressive university pursuit of international students both at home and abroad has been fuelled by an increase in global mobility. Global demand for higher education is forecast to increase from 97 million in 2000 to 263 million in 2025 (Davis

2003). This increase in growth will come from countries such as China, India, Turkey, Morocco, Kazakhstan, Russia and others.

In its Atlas Project, UNESCO estimated that over 1.7 million students are pursuing higher education in countries other than their own. And the IDP Education Australia report predicted that by 2025 almost eight million students will be educated transnationally (Davis 2003: 4). By 2025, China and India are predicted to have 50 per cent of the global demand for international education (Davis, 2003: 56). This report also indicates that increasing numbers of students are studying intra-regionally, rather than the more traditional pattern of movement from the developing world to Western Europe and the United States. Even so, the tradition is still highly significant. Today the United States is the largest host nation for international students studying at the tertiary level, followed by the United Kingdom, Germany, France and Australia. These five nations host 75 per cent of students studying in countries other than their own. This mobility occurs from, within and across socioeconomically developed nations (Davis, 2003: 11). The Group of Eight (G-8) highly industrialized countries has set a goal to increase exchanges during this decade. It can be assumed that Europe and North America will continue to dominate the field for some time, with China, Japan, Korea, Taiwan and India making significant advances.

An increase in study abroad and exchange activity can only occur with a focused political effort. In the United States, NAFSA and other organizations have been encouraging an increase in study abroad and exchanges. They believe that study abroad needs to become an integral part of every college student's education. Supporters have lobbied federal, state and local governments in the USA to articulate policies on international education that would include strong support for study abroad. They would also like to see funding to support disadvantaged students and to look for creative ways to use existing grants and loans. They are also encouraging colleges and universities to integrate study abroad into various degree programmes, to involve faculty in designing and teaching in study abroad courses and to effect change through adjustments to the curriculum. International education advocates also support new programmes for non-traditional students and believe that those who study abroad should be allowed to do so without losing credit towards graduation.

According to the Commission on the Abraham Lincoln Study Abroad Fellowship Programme (2006), Harvard University has made a study abroad component mandatory for fulfilling graduation requirements. San Francisco State University plans to double the number of students studying abroad by the year 2010. Goucher College made national news in the USA in September 2005 by announcing that study abroad would become a degree requirement; the college backed up this institutional mandate with a $1,200 travel voucher for every student. Yale University is focusing on redefining its international goals in what Yale President Richard C. Levin calls 'The globalization of the University' (Levin 2006).

CONCLUSION

Globalization has created an ever-widening and deepening process of increasing interdependence of peoples and states. It has turned the world upside down. Globalization puts the world at risk, yet opens new and exciting opportunities for vast and unprecedented improvements in the lives of populations everywhere. Higher education plays an important role in providing these opportunities by creating innovations and inventions and developing new knowledge through research and instruction. Yet the interplay between globalization and dissemination of knowledge is complex. This chapter offered an overview of the numerous roads higher education is travelling to meet international demand for change. Despite a primarily Western focus, the chapter attempted to demonstrate how colleges and universities throughout the world are examining and experimenting with delivery systems of knowledge. Entrepreneurialism, exchange

and study abroad programmes and new curricula are all meeting the challenges of this knowledge explosion.

The most significant change will come about through e-learning. Technology may eventually provide the answer to transmitting knowledge in an equitable and efficient way to all students of all ages throughout the world. Currently, this is not technologically possible. Bandwidth limitations and the lack of 3–D displays in many virtual learning environments prevent e-learning from competing with on-site education. According to Ray Kurzweil, however, this will change within the next 20 years with the development of visual auditory virtual reality environments. He predicts that most colleges and universities will follow MIT's lead and that students will increasingly attend classes virtually. 'Classes will be available for all grade levels and all languages', Kurzweil writes. 'Accessibility will be worldwide and at any time and from any place'. He believes that the nature of education will change even more dramatically when human intelligence merges with non-biological intelligence (2005: 337). Future forecasting cannot be proven, of course, but it can encourage us to think about the possibilities of transferring and sharing knowledge and information.

For the present, as Altbach (2004: 22) puts it, 'We are at the beginning of the era of transnational higher education in which academic institutions from one country operate in another, academic programmes are jointly offered by universities from different countries and higher education is delivered through distance technologies'.

REFERENCES

About Columbia (2006) Mission statement. Available from www.columbia.edu/about_columbia/mission.html (accessed 21 February 2006).

About Fulbright (2006) Council for International Exchange of Scholars, Washington, DC. Available from www.cies.org/about_fulb.htm (accessed 22 February 2006).

Altbach, P.G. (2004) Higher education crosses borders. *Change*, 36: 2.

Altbach, P.G. and Davis, T.M. (1999) *Global Challenge and National Response: Notes for an International Dialogue on Higher Education.* Center for International Higher Education at Boston College. Available from www.bc.edu/bc_org/avp/soe/cihe/newsletter/News14/text1.html (accessed 22 February 2006).

Arnove, R.F. and Torres, C.A. (eds) (1999) *Comparative Education: The Dialectic of the Global and the Local.* New York: Rowman and Littlefield.

Carter, L. (2005) Globalization and policy reforms: science education research. *International Handbook on Globalization, Education, and Policy Research.* Dordrecht: Springer, pp. 733–44.

Commission on the Abraham Lincoln Study Abroad Fellowship (2006) *Global Competence and National Needs.* Available from www.lincolncommission.org/report.html (accessed 15 January 2006).

Davis, T.M. (2003) *Atlas of Student Mobility.* New York: Institute of International Education.

Davis, T.M. and Chin, H. (ed.) (2004) *Open Doors 2004: Report on International Educational Exchange.* New York: Institute of International Education.

Eurich, N.P. (1981) *Systems of Higher Education in Twelve Countries: A Comparative View.* Westport, CT: Praeger.

Europa (2002) *SOCRATES: European Community Action Programme in the Field of Education 2000–06.* Luxembourg: Office for Official Publication of the European Communities. Available from http://europa.eu/education/programmes/socrates/socrates_enhtml (accessed 22 August 2005).

Friedman, T.L. (2000). *The Lexus and the Olive Tree: Understanding Globalization.* New York: First Anchor Books.

Gelernter, D. (2005) Who needs a college campus? *Forbes Magazine,* 28 November.

Gibbons, M. (1998) Higher education relevance in the twenty-first century. *UNESCO World Conference on Higher Education.* Paris: UNESCO.

Groennings, S. (1989) American higher education's comparative advantage in our global economy. Keynote address presented at the Annual Meeting of the Association for the Study of Higher Education, Atlanta, GA.

Hoffa, W. and Pearson, J. (eds) (1997) *NAFSA's Guide to Education Abroad for Advisers and Administrators,* 2nd edition. New York: NAFSA Association of International Educators.

Knight, J. and de Witt, H. (1999) Internationalization in higher education. In *Quality and Internationalization in Higher Education,* Paris: OECD pp. 13–28.

Korea University (2006) Power of Korea University spirit: the pride of Korea at the centre of the world. Available from www.korea.edu/ (accessed 21 February 2006).

Kurzweil, R. (2005). *The Singularity is Near: When Humans Transcend Biology.* New York: Viking/Penguin Group.

Levin, R.C. (2006) Yale and the world. Available from *world.yale.edu/* (accessed 9 February 2006).

Open Doors international student and total student enrollment data (2005) Available from http://opendoors.iienetwork.org/?p=69692 (accessed 21 February 2006).

Parker, W.C., Ninomiya, A. and Cogan, J. (1999) Educating world citizens: toward multinational curriculum development. *American Educational Research Journal,* 36 (2): 117–45.

Rosen, M. (2000) You've got the brains, let's make lots of money. *The Sunday Herald,* 1 October.

Securing America's Future: Global Education for a Global Age (2003) Report of the Strategic Task Force on Education. New York: NAFSA.

Seven Goals for Lehigh (2006) Available from www.lehigh.edu/~inhro/forms/SevenGoals.html (accessed 21 February 2006).

Shea, R.H. and Boser, U. (2001) So where's the beef? *US News and World Report,* 15 October.

Spellings, M. (2005) *A National Dialogue: Commission on the Future of Higher Education.* Speech presented at University of North Carolina, Charlotte, NC, 19 September 2005.

Symonds, W.C., Roberts, D. and Franklin, J. (2004) Colleges: the newest export. *Business Week,* 9 February. Available from www.businessweek.com/magazine/content/04_06/b3869156.htm (accessed 2006).

Tilak, J.B.G. (2005) Global trends in funding higher education. *IAU Horizons* (International Association of Universities), March 2005.

UNESCO (2002) World Declaration on Higher Education for the Twenty-First Century: Vision and Action. Symposium on the Challenges of Internationalizing Higher Education in South Eastern Europe. Halkidiki, Greece.

University of Edinburgh (2006) *Our mission.* Available from www.planning.ed.ac.uk/Profile/MissionStatement.htm (accessed 21 February 2006).

Zajda, J. (ed.) (2005) *International Handbook on Globalisation, Education and Policy Research: Global Pedagogies and Policies.* Dordrecht: Springer.

Author Index

Subject Index